Theory of International Law

Theory of International Law

G. I. Tunkin

Translated,
with an Introduction,
by William E. Butler

Harvard University Press
Cambridge, Massachusetts
1974

Acknowledgments

The image of a translator working in seclusion with his typewriter and dictionary, warding off his family with diverse manifestations of ill humor, is only partially accurate in this case. In the course of consulting the extraordinary range of source materials utilized by the author, I have accumulated a very great debt to the staffs of a number of institutions that I would like to acknowledge: the Lenin Library, the Social Science Library of the USSR Academy of Sciences, the Gorky Library of Moscow State University, the various libraries of the University of London, the British Library, the Squire Law Library at Cambridge University, the University of Graz Library, the Harvard Law School Library, and the Library of Congress.

For the opportunity to spend a semester as a guest senior scholar at the Department of International Law, Faculty of Law, Moscow State University in 1971-1972, where a draft of this translation was discussed with its author, I am indebted to the International Research and Exchanges Board and to University College London. The Rockefeller Foundation, through the incomparable hospitality of the Villa Serbelloni, made it possible to review a number of important questions with colleagues at an extended conference on socialist legal systems in August 1972.

Several typists have labored strenuously on various portions of the manuscript, but the major burden has been capably borne by Miss Sylvia New. I also should like to record my gratitude to Miss Gillian Hoxley who at the most impossible moments was able to provide additional typing assistance.

London   W.E.B.

v

Contents

Contents

Contents

Introduction
William E. Butler

Whether we speak of "international law in a divided world" or of an "international law of peaceful coexistence and cooperation," there are ample and compelling reasons for lawyers and specialists in international affairs to study closely the doctrinal writings of international lawyers in the socialist countries. Legal science—even the term itself still rings oddly in the Anglo-American lawyer's ear—is not a universal body of knowledge whose concepts and basic principles comprise a single "language" comprehensible to jurists everywhere. Not even international or transnational law has yet attained this level of sophistication, although momentous strides have been made. The Anglo-American international lawyer receives his professional training in the common law; in these enlightened times he more often than not will pursue graduate law studies overseas and expose himself in a rudimentary way to continental schools of thought. And many of his continental counterparts, trained in the civil law tradition, will likewise endeavor to broaden their horizons.

But Soviet, or for that matter prerevolutionary Russian, doctrines and practices have for linguistic reasons remained largely beyond the pale for the common lawyer. There is to be sure a not insubstantial body of secondary material in the English language about Soviet views on international law, and increasing attention is being given to evidence of Soviet state practice. Soviet jurists too are contributing more frequently to English-language media, and from time to time Moscow publishing houses issue books on international law in western tongues. The principal contributions of Soviet jurists to international legal science, however, the specialized treatises on substantive problems of the law of nations, are essentially an internal literature unknown abroad.[1]

1. One must hasten to add that Anglo-American lawyers may well conclude after reading this book that their own literature is "internal" insofar as a Soviet readership is concerned, a problem which Soviet jurists themselves are coming to recognize. In calling for unceasing struggle against bourgeois legal ideology at the annual meeting of the Soviet Association of International Law in January 1972, Tunkin also criticized some Soviet legal writing for being too general in its criticism of bourgeois views, for failing to differentiate among diverse trends of thought, for being content with mere rejections of views in place of reasoned argumentation, or for showing merely the political harmfulness of a particular view: "Frequently, there is inadequate knowledge

For continental jurists the situation is rather more favorable. Though uncompromisingly Marxist-Leninist, Soviet international legal doctrine is heavily indebted, just as prerevolutionary Russian writings, to continental legal thought for its categories of law and its concept of international legal science. Soviet international lawyers are rule-oriented, are prone to lengthy discourse about abstract definitions and propositions of law, and, although disposed to scrutinize the class essence of law, are as reluctant as most of their continental colleagues to inquire into the legal process. Hence, no doubt, the proclivity of Soviet international lawyers to cite extensively and to polemicize primarily with continental jurists. European international lawyers, for their part, have translated works of and entered into dialogue with the Soviet international legal community to a greater degree than their common law brethren.

Whatever roots it may have in continental legal traditions, Soviet international legal theory possesses its own peculiar attributes equally alien to the Anglo-American approach to international law. As a Marxist-Leninist theory of international law, it is part of a larger philosophical and ideological framework with its own distinctive world outlook and language. As a Soviet theory of international law, it is a product of the same practices and constraints which govern the general exposition of academic views on foreign policy or law in the USSR. It is not "official," yet neither does it transgress prevailing party policy at the moment of its appearance. Soviet jurists are extremely sensitive to prior formulations of particular issues and frequently have recourse to terms or phrases which, though obscure or "propagandistic" to the common lawyer, are an integral part of a sophisticated mode of communication deeply rooted in the revolutionary movement, party history, ideology, relations within the socialist community of nations, attitudes toward nonsocialist powers, and international law itself. For many readers the attempt to convey in English the outlines, the atmosphere, the general approach of a Soviet jurist to international legal theory may be of greater value than an undertaking to isolate the substance of a particular point of Soviet doctrine and to rethink and reformulate it in a conventional Anglo-American manner. The present translation will indeed have achieved some purpose if the reader comes away with a little feeling for the various strands of Marxist-Leninist, continental, international, and Russian elements of the mental background in which the exposition originates.

of the material, in consequence of which the works of occasional authors are subjected to criticism, untypical quotations are given, and basic orientations and their theoreticians remain beyond the purview." G. I. Tunkin, "Zadachi nauki mezhdunarodnogo prava v svete reshenii XXIV s"ezda KPSS," *Sovetskoe gosudarstvo i pravo*, no. 7 (1972), p. 34.

Introduction

The appearance of G. I. Tunkin's *Teoriia mezhdunarodnogo prava*, published in 1970 and presented herewith, is a signal event in several respects. Within the Soviet Union, it is the first book to merit the unqualified appellation "theory of international law." In the past, Soviet jurists have produced "outlines," "basic principles," "questions of theory," "courses," "manuals," and so forth treating certain aspects of theory or written with certain presumptions about theory in mind. The writings of Korovin, Stuchka, Pashukanis, Krylov, Kozhevnikov, Levin, Minasian, Bobrov, and other names more or less well-known to Anglo-American international lawyers belong to this genre. Vyshinskii's celebrated definition of international law is another example; his formulation dominated Soviet legal thought for nearly two decades, but it was not in and of itself a theory, despite its enormous influence on Soviet writing about the nature of international law.

Tunkin's treatise can therefore be fairly described as the most profound and comprehensive study of international legal theory yet produced by a Soviet jurist. Effectively blending the author's broad experience in diplomacy and academic pursuits, it is a masterfully conceived and executed application of Marxist-Leninist concepts and principles to the advancement of Soviet interests in the era of peaceful coexistence. It is also, rather surprisingly, the first major work of a Soviet international lawyer (or, of a Tsarist jurist) to be translated into the principal language of the common law.

Regrettably, the 1970 edition of Tunkin's *Teoriia* does not contain a preface. In the prefatory remarks to his *Voprosy teorii mezhdunarodnogo prava* published in 1962, of which the 1970 version is a revised, much enlarged, and significantly retitled edition, Tunkin related his inquiry to two domestic happenings. The first was the "profound analysis of the international situation and long-term prospects for its development" reflected in the decisions of the Twenty-second Congress of the Communist Party of the Soviet Union held in 1961. The second was the rejection by the Twentieth Party Congress in 1956 of the "cult of personality of Stalin, alien to Marxism-Leninism and the bases of our social system" and the embarking on a course "to liquidate its harmful consequences" and open a "broad road for the development of the social sciences, including international law." After the Twentieth Party Congress,

> Soviet jurists carried out significant work in investigating urgent problems of contemporary international law, and in overcoming Vyshinskii's incorrect, dogmatic conceptions, particularly on the essence of international law, the role of coercion in international law,

the co-relation of international law in foreign policy, the definition of state sovereignty, and others. Much has been done to get rid of dogmatism and citation mania, the legal nihilism and unreality peculiar to the period of the cult of personality, although remnants of this still frequently make themselves felt and impede the development of international legal science.[2]

In the absence of an express statement in the 1970 edition, it falls to me to divine and describe the changes introduced by the author.[3] The 1970 version retains intact the theory of international law which runs throughout the author's earlier writings and also preserves the essential structure of the 1962 volume, itself reflective of Tunkin's approach. The author has, of course, updated the materials, especially with references to recent multilateral conventions, developments in international organizations, and doctrinal literature published since 1962. Many sections have been rewritten, deleted, or augmented. Copious references to N. S. Khrushchev in the 1962 edition have been replaced by quotations of equally suitable statements or documents authored by members of the present Soviet leadership. Of greatest importance is the addition of several new chapters treating the influence of the 1917 October Revolution on the development of international law and the legal nature of contemporary general international organizations. Substantial modifications also are introduced into the discussion of norm-formation and socialist internationalism. In all, these changes have added 180 pages to the 330 in the 1962 edition.

The principal changes in the 1970 Russian edition are as follows. In Part I the first chapter treating the international legal ideas of the October Revolution and the making of contemporary international law is a new addition. Chapter 2 on peaceful coexistence and international law and on the breakup of the colonial system has been enlarged and rewritten to take account of recent events and of comments made by western jurists on the author's earlier views. The third chapter expands the discussion of the principles of nonaggression and of peaceful settlement of disputes to include the relevant deliberations of United Nations bodies in the intervening period. The principle of self-determination of peoples is relegated from "the most important" to "one of the most important" generally recognized principles of contemporary international law. Subsection 3(A)(4) on the principle of peaceful coexistence is reworked and abbreviated, leaving the impression that this principle is a shade less

2. Tunkin, *Voprosy teorii mezhdunarodnogo prava* (Moscow: Gosiurizdat, 1962), pp. 3-4.

3. Changes made for the English translation by the author are described in the Translation Note.

important than formerly. The principles of disarmament and of human rights are new to the 1970 edition.

Parts II and III of the 1970 edition have been recast from Part II of the 1962 version. The effect is to delineate sharply the discussion of the norm-formation process from the necessarily more abstract consideration of the legal nature and essence of contemporary international law. As part of his expanded treatment of international organizations in the 1970 edition, the author has introduced into Chapter 4, subsections A(2) and (3) on treaties between states concluded within the framework of international organizations and on regulations adopted by specialized international organizations; similarly, Chapter 4(A)(4) on treaties of international organizations has been updated and expanded, reflecting the author's perception of their enhanced role in creating rules that are becoming part of the international legal system. *Opinio juris* is treated in greater detail in Chapter 4(B), as is the interrelationship between treaty and custom in 4(C). Section 4(D) on *jus cogens* is new. The materials on subsidiary processes of norm-formation are kept distinct in the 1970 edition from the role of international legal doctrine and from the problem of "general principles of law." Distinctions also are drawn clearly in the 1970 edition between United Nations General Assembly resolutions and those of other specialized international organizations; both are discussed at greater length. Chapters 5(C) and (D) and Chapter 6 contain only very minor modifications. However, the discussion of "general principles of law" in Chapter 7 has been substantially augmented.

In Part III of the 1970 version, the treatment of the legal nature of agreement in Chapter 8 has been expanded somewhat to take account of recent writings, particularly those of Professor Paul Guggenheim. Chapter 9(A) contains an enlargement of the author's previous criticism of the natural law school and of solidarism, the latter with special reference to Professor George Scelle. The remainder of Chapter 9 is substantially rewritten; some of the materials on the concept of a world state that appeared in Chapter 6(2) of the 1962 volume are transferred to a new Chapter 16 in the 1970 version. Chapter 6(3) of the 1962 volume on the "cold war and international law" appears here as Chapter 9(D), "the question of an 'intermediate status' between war and peace."

In Part IV of the 1970 edition, Chapter 10 is basically unchanged; Chapter 11 reformulates certain aspects of the influence of international law on foreign policy and diplomacy; and Chapter 12 expands upon the author's critique of Professor M. S. McDougal's views.

Part V is new; Part VI is virtually unchanged from the 1962 edition.

Part VII contains substantial changes which reflect an expanded program of economic integration within Eastern Europe and reformula-

tions of the doctrine of socialist internationalism following the Czechoslovak events of 1968.[4]

The author's long experience in day-to-day diplomacy has strongly
influenced his conception of international law, for, as he is fond of
pointing out to his students, it is at international meetings and conferences or within international organizations that one can observe most
readily the process of state wills being brought into concordance. The
range of that experience is evident in accounts of Tunkin's personal
achievements and his publications.

Grigorii Ivanovich Tunkin was born in the Arkhangel'sk Province of the
Soviet Union on October 13, 1906.[5] Of peasant stock, he graduated from
a forestry technical school in 1928 and enrolled in the Moscow Juridical
Institute in 1932. Upon completion of his undergraduate law studies in
1935, he was invited to proceed immediately to postgraduate research. His
kandidat thesis, defended in 1938, was entitled "The Parliamentary
Reform of 1832 in England." In 1938-1939 Tunkin served briefly as head
of the Department of the Theory and History of State and Law of the
All-Union Legal Academy, leaving in 1939 to enter the diplomatic service.
In the Ministry of Foreign Affairs of the USSR he served first as assistant
to the head of the legal section and then as the Soviet consul in Gorgan
(Iran).

4. Part VII of this book has been the source of some controversy among western
reviewers. In an editorial published in the *American Journal of International Law*,
J. N. Hazard observed that Tunkin's 1970 volume placed emphasis " . . . on a Socialist
international law which is more than emerging. It is here . . . In relationships between
Marxian Socialist states a new law is applicable." See Hazard, "Renewed Emphasis
upon a Socialist International Law," *American Journal of International Law*, LXV
(1971), 144. Hazard's view is given qualified support in C. Osakwe, "Socialist
International Law Revisited," *ibid.*, LXVI (1972), 596-600. The present writer found
Tunkin's formulations on this issue less conclusive, particularly in light of a subsequent
article by Tunkin signed to press nearly fourteen months after the 1970 volume. There
Tunkin refers to socialist principles of international law as "the basis of a new type of
international law, a socialist international law of the future." See Tunkin, "V. I. Lenin
i printsipy otnoshenii mezhdu sotsialisticheskimi gosudarstvami," *Sovetskii ezhegodnik
mezhdunarodnogo prava 1969* (1970), p. 28. My own views are laid down in W. E.
Butler, " 'Socialist International Law' or 'Socialist Principles of International Relations,' " *American Journal of International Law*, LXV (1971), 796-800. Professor
Tunkin modified the last clause of the fourth paragraph of Chapter 20 of this
translation to read " . . . the basis of which is . . . coming to replace . . . " instead of
"going to replace," as the 1970 Russian version read.
5. The biographical sketch of the author is based on personalia published in
Pravovedenie, no. 3 (1966), pp. 152-153; *Vestnik moskovskogo gosudarstvennogo
universiteta; pravo*, no. 5 (1966), pp. 90-91; *Sovetskii ezhegodnik mezhdunarodnogo
prava 1968* (1969), pp. 334-335; *Recueil des cours*, XCV (1958), 3; CXIX (1966), 3;
Annuaire de l'Institut de Droit International, XLVIII(II) (1959), 404-406.

From 1942 to 1944 he was posted in Canada as counselor of the Soviet Embassy. Returning to Moscow, Tunkin was appointed deputy head of the Ministry's Second European Section (1944-1945) and then head of the First Far Eastern Section (1946-1948). The latter posting evidently commenced a period, several years in duration, of sustained concentration on Asian affairs. Tunkin published extensively on Korea, editing a collection of North Korean legal documents in the Russian language and devoting considerable attention to the international legal aspects of the Korean conflict. From 1948 to 1951 he was Minister-Counselor of the Soviet Embassy in the Korean People's Democratic Republic, returning briefly in 1951-1952 again as head of the First Far Eastern Section. In 1954 he submitted and defended a massive doctoral dissertation on "The Korean Problem After the Second World War in the Light of International Law"; the degree *doktor iuridicheskikh nauk* (doctor of juridical sciences) was conferred in 1955.

In May 1952 Tunkin became head of the legal section of the Ministry of Foreign Affairs, a position he occupied until August 1965. While legal adviser, he also held adjunct academic appointments as head of the Department of International Law of the Moscow Juridical Institute (1949-1954), as docent and then professor of international law at Moscow State University, as head of the Department of Legal Disciplines of the Higher Diplomatic School of the Ministry of Foreign Affairs, and as professor at the Moscow State Institute of International Relations (1954-1963).

In his dual role of diplomat and scholar, Tunkin has played a prominent role in shaping the orientation of international law in the Soviet Union. Shortly after assuming the post of legal adviser in 1952, he registered strong disagreement with Korovin's concept of two international laws: bourgeois and socialist. Setting forth what has continued to be the dominant theme in his own conception of international law, Tunkin insisted that "*agreement* between states lies at the base of international legal norms." Such agreement, he argued, "is incompatible with the concept of two international laws . . . which is contrary to Soviet international legal theory and the diplomatic practice of the Soviet state."[6]

Tunkin elaborated his thesis in a small but highly influential supplemental text published by the Higher Party School attached to the Central Committee of the Communist Party of the Soviet Union.[7] His view has

6. See a report of a discussion organized by the Department of International Law of the Academy of Social Sciences attached to the Central Committee of the All-Russian Communist Party (bolshevik) and by the Sector of International Law of the Institute of Law of the USSR Academy of Sciences, in *Sovetskoe gosudarstvo i pravo*, no. 7 (1952), p. 69.

7. Tunkin, *Osnovy sovremennogo mezhdunarodnogo prava* (Moscow, 1956).

come to be accepted by the great majority of Soviet international lawyers and can be said without exaggeration to comprise one of the principal legal pillars on which East-West cooperation has been constructed following the Twentieth Party Congress of the Communist Party of the Soviet Union in 1956.

As a member of the United Nations International Law Commission from 1957 to 1966 (Chairman in 1961; Second Vice-Chairman in 1958 and 1964), Tunkin had ample opportunity both to expostulate his approach to international legal theory and to observe the process of international law creation. During his tenure on the Commission, he worked on draft articles relating to the law of the sea, diplomatic and consular relations, the law of treaties, and special diplomatic missions. At the 1958 and 1960 Geneva Conferences on the Law of the Sea and the 1961 Vienna Conference on Diplomatic Intercourse and Immunities, he was head of the Soviet delegation. He also has been in attendance at the conclusion of the Soviet-Polish treaty on the legal status of Soviet forces in Poland (1956), signed the 1957 Soviet-Norwegian sea frontier agreement on behalf of the USSR, was acting head of the Soviet delegation at the 1959 conference to draft the treaty on the Antarctica, served as the USSR delegate at the Sixteenth Session of the Sixth (Legal) Committee of the United Nations General Assembly in 1961, and has been a member of or adviser to other Soviet delegations at international conferences.

In autumn 1965 Tunkin assumed a full-time professorship in and chairmanship of the Department of International Law in the Law Faculty of Moscow State University.

Professor Tunkin has been President of the Soviet Association of International Law since its establishment in 1957. He was a member of the editorial board of the *Soviet Yearbook of International Law* for 1958 and editor-in-chief for the 1959-1962 issues. From 1956 to mid-1969, he served on the editorial board of the central law journal in the USSR, *Sovetskoe gosudarstvo i pravo*. In the diplomatic service he holds the career rank of Minister Extraordinary and Plenipotentiary, Second Class.

Tunkin has lectured at the Hague Academy of International Law (1958 and 1966), is an Associé of the Institute of International Law (1959) and a member of the Hague Permanent Court of Arbitration (1960), is an honorary member of the Indian Society of International Law, and in November 1972 was awarded a doctorate *honoris causa* by the University of Paris (Sorbonne). The title Honored Scientist of the RSFSR was conferred upon Professor Tunkin by Edict of the Presidium of the Supreme Soviet of the RSFSR on November 16, 1972, "for services in developing legal science and fruitful pedagogical activity."[8]

8. *Vedomosti verkhovnogo soveta RSFSR* (1972), no. 47, item 1122; *Vestnik moskovskogo gosudarstvennogo universiteta; pravo*, no. 3 (1973), p. 96.

Tunkin's Soviet colleagues have paid tribute to his immense energy, his great erudition and expertise, and his ability to link "science with practice." The majority of his more than 150 scientific writings were prepared while he was engaged in diplomatic service. His principal works on international legal theory are noteworthy in comparison with most Soviet publications in this field—and, indeed, most western treatises—for their extensive utilization of a wide variety of foreign materials. Tunkin draws extensively upon not merely the principal classical and modern writings of continental and Anglo-American jurists, but also those by Latin American, African, and Asian international lawyers.

The 1970's auspiciously promise a further reduction of tensions in relations between the great powers and perhaps the beginnings of a reconstituted Europe and Asia. International law will both affect and reflect developments of this nature. The present volume is eloquent testimony that international law in the Soviet Union, for the moment at least, is no longer among those disciplines lacking "a specific place in the system of Soviet jurisprudence."[9] Perhaps the English version of Tunkin's work will cast a flicker of illumination to aid those who seek to comprehend and come to terms with the positions of an opposite party.

9. The words are Professor Korovin's, written when he undertook to produce the first Soviet manual on international law. See E. A. Korovin, *Mezhdunarodnoe pravo perekhodnogo vremeni* (Moscow-Leningrad: Gos. izd-vo, [1924]), p. 5.

Translation Note

Translators arrogate to themselves a near insuperable task in attempting to transfer an intellectual product from one linguistic medium to another. Styles vary, equivalents of terminology or of colloquialisms may be nonexistent, expressions of great precision in one language may appear nonsensical or ambiguous in another, phrases deliberately vague in the original may be "improved" in the course of translation, and so forth. These are familiar problems, and every effort has been made to deal with them as conscientiously as possible here.

On occasions, however, the translator or publisher may take other liberties which significantly alter the final form of the work. Thus, for example, passages may be deleted or the author's "mistaken" or "unscientific" notions corrected by adding appropriate commentary. Or passages may be rendered more or less dramatically or accurately than the original.[1]

The present volume does differ in several key respects from the original Russian version that appeared in 1970. To avoid any misunderstanding, and to assist those who may wish to consult the original edition on a particular point, it seems appropriate to outline the editorial practices followed and changes introduced in preparing this English language version.

The substance of the book is identical to the 1970 Russian edition in

1. In the Soviet Union the publishing house specializing in translations of foreign literature is under a strict party injunction when publishing bourgeois literature in the fields of philosophy, history, economics, diplomacy, and law: "Books of this type should be published in a limited edition, expurgating from the text passages which are not of scholarly or practical interest, and should be prefaced by an extended foreward or note." Decree of the Central Committee of the C.P.S.U. of June 4, 1959, "O rabote izdatel'stva inostrannoi literatury," reproduced in *O partiinoi i sovetskoi pechati, radioveshchanii i televidenii. Sbornik dokumentov i materialov* (Moscow: izd-vo Mysl', 1972), pp. 460-463.

toto, except where Professor Tunkin himself has requested additions or deletions. More than 130 such modifications have been made, consisting principally of the following: (1) references to literature which came to the author's attention after the 1970 edition was in press [See Chapter 2 (notes 14, 18, 27, 33); Chapter 3 (notes 24, 36, 40); Chapter 4 (notes 35, 71, 74, 82, 116, 117, 131, 155, 156, 214, 219); Chapter 5 (notes 24, 35, 40, 62); Chapter 7 (notes 10, 22, 33, 42); Chapter 8 (note 15); Chapter 9 (notes 26, 73, 75, 82); Chapter 11 (notes 29, 30); Chapter 13 (note 41); Chapter 14 (notes 17, 46); Chapter 15 (note 36); Chapter 16 (note 7); Chapter 17 (notes 3, 4); Chapter 18 (notes 29, 64, 74, 80, 81); Chapter 19 (note 8); Chapter 20 (note 1)]; (2) an attenuation of remarks made regarding the Federal Republic of Germany [Chapters 2(A) and 3]; (3) materials relating to the Twenty-fourth Congress of the Communist Party of the Soviet Union; (4) references to the 1970 United Nations Declaration on the Principles of International Law; (5) the insertion of a subheading for Chapter 4(B) relating to international custom and other materials; (6) further observations on *jus cogens* [Chapters 4(D), 6, and 20]; (7) materials relating to recent developments in the Council of Mutual Economic Assistance [Chapter 19]; (8) recent International Law Commission reports on state responsibility [Chapters 17 and 18]; (9) remarks on the extension to third states of provisions of general multilateral treaties [Chapter 4(C)(3)]; (10) remarks appertaining to the codification of international law and peaceful coexistence [Chapter 2(A) and (B), Chapter 3(A)(4)]; disarmament [Chapter 3(A)(5)]; and human rights [Chapter 3(A)(6)]; (11) substantial additions relating to customary international law; (12) further comments on the legal nature of international organizations, their capacity to conclude treaties, and the binding nature of United Nations resolutions; (13) new materials reflecting the improvement in United States-Soviet relations; (14) an elaboration of the critique of Professor M. S. McDougal's views; and (15) recent writings concerning the nature of general international law.

The translator has reworked the footnotes completely, modifying the form of citation to correspond to general western practices and making numerous corrections; errors in spelling, pagination, volume number, and so forth have been set right. Full citations to the relevant works of Marx, Engels, and Lenin have been provided, sometimes followed by a bracketed reference to the time and place of original publication. Quotations have been checked against the original source in virtually every instance. Words or phrases deleted from material quoted in the original Russian version but not so stipulated by punctuation have been appropriately indicated here. A glossary of international legal terms has been supplied as well.

At the translator's request, Professor Tunkin has made available a list of his published writings, which has been reproduced with additional material.

The translator has benefitted immensely from several discussions with the author about problems of terminology that arose during the preparation of the English text. The considerations entering into the choice of English equivalents for several key terms may be of interest to the reader. One of the most vexsome was *zakonomernost'* or *zakon razvitiia obshchestva*, rendered herein as "law of societal development." Soviet international lawyers, as Professor Tunkin points out in the text, have themselves sometimes failed to distinguish between rules of international law and the laws of societal development; hence the importance of delineating sharply between the two concepts here. Terms such as "natural law," "natural imperative," or "law of evolution," favored by others who have translated Tunkin's works, have been discarded on the ground they were likely to mislead those to whom such expressions have meaning outside a Marxist framework.

Central to the author's concept of the norm-formation process in international law is the phrase *soglasovannye voli gosudarstv*, translated as "concordant wills of states," and *soglasovanie vol'*, expressed rather awkwardly as "bringing wills into concordance." The author's preference for this terminology is intended to stress two points. First, norm-formation in his view is a *process*, dynamic in nature and not mechanical. He wishes the reader to visualize states interacting, struggling, to bring their separate wills into agreement with respect to a particular rule of law. Second, "concordance" as a term is meant to connote something different from theories of "common" or "coincident" wills that have been advanced by other jurists. The extent to which the author succeeds in establishing his view on this point is for the reader to judge.

The term *sblizhenie* is given here with considerable misgivings as "rapprochement." It arises in connection with the "rapprochement" or, more literally, the "coming together" of peoples. It implies something more than rapprochement as that term is commonly used in international relations. Peoples are contemplated as "coming together" virtually to the point of amalgamation, and the term is especially used in connection with the various peoples inhabiting the Soviet Union.

While the author has been generous in responding to various queries I have raised and has prepared the revisions described above, he in no sense has endorsed or approved the final text; errors of omission or commission in translation and editing must rest squarely with me.

The Library of Congress transliteration system, with minor modifications, has been utilized for cyrillic language publications.

W.E.B.

Part I *The Development of International Law Since the Great October Socialist Revolution*

Chapter 1 *The International Legal Ideas of the October Revolution and the Making of Contemporary International Law*

The Great October Socialist Revolution, from which commenced the creation of a new socioeconomic entity, affected all aspects of social relations. It also initiated profound changes in international relations and international law.

The socialist state created by the revolution, fundamentally different in its class nature from all states which had existed theretofore, put forward a number of new guiding principles for relations among peoples and states. Symbolically, the first decree of the socialist state was the Decree on Peace. "In the international arena," says the Program of the Communist Party of the Soviet Union, "a state arose for the first time which advanced the slogan of peace and began to implement new principles in relations among peoples and countries. Mankind had found a dependable bulwark in its struggle against annexationist wars, for peace and the security of peoples."[1]

The political and international legal ideas and principles of the October Revolution infused a qualitatively new spirit into international relations and international law. These principles reflected the class nature of the Soviet state; the fundamental principles of the new socialist social system were linked inseparably with the basic tenets of the ideology of the working class. But inasmuch as the working class is the leading fighter for the liberation of all working people, the international legal ideas of the October Revolution reflected the basic expectations and interests of the broad masses of the people. The humanism of these ideas and principles, their internationalism, also is determined by this.[2]

1. *Programma Kommunisticheskoi partii Sovetskogo Soiuza* (Moscow: Politizdat, 1964), p. 12.
2. On the humanism of socialist ideas, see A. F. Shishkin and K. A. Shvarstman, *XX vek i moral'nye tsennosti chelovechestva* (Moscow: izd-vo Mysl', 1968).

On the level of their influence upon international law and international relations, the international legal ideas of the October Revolution can be divided into three basic, closely interconnected groups:

(a) principles of socialist internationalism in relations between socialist states;

(b) principles of equality and self-determination of nations and peoples, whose spearhead is aimed against the system of colonialism, as well as against any national oppression and inequality;

(c) principles of peaceful coexistence, aimed first and foremost at relations between states with different social systems.

These ideas and principles of the October Revolution have operated in the direction of creating new international relations and a new international law.

A. The Principles of Socialist Internationalism

The principles of socialist internationalism correspond to the new type of international relations: to relations between socialist states. The bases of these principles were formed by the theory of Marxism-Leninism and by the practice of the workers' movement. These were the principles of the international workers' movement and the principles of relations between nations and peoples.

The guiding principle of the international workers' movement was the principle of proletarian internationalism, which signified the fraternal friendship, close cooperation, and mutual assistance of the working class of various countries in the struggle for their liberation.

The principle of proletarian internationalism emerged as the principle of the workers' movement when the development of capitalism and of the workers' movement itself attained a sufficiently high level. The internationalization of the domination of capital, the intensification of ties among the workers of individual countries, the growth of the consciousness of the unity of purpose and the need for unified efforts of the proletariat of various nations in the struggle for their liberation and for the creation of a new society not knowing exploitation—these are the basic reasons for the emergence of the principle of proletarian internationalism.

In emphasizing the significance of the fraternal solidarity of workers of various countries, Marx wrote in the founding manifesto of the International Association of Workers: "The experience of the past showed that a scornful attitude toward a fraternal alliance, which must exist among the workers of various countries and impel them to stand behind each other firmly in their struggle for liberation, is punished by the general defeat of their uncoordinated efforts."[3]

V. I. Lenin pointed out that since the domination of capital is international, the struggle of workers of different countries for their liberation can be successful only if their efforts are unified. "That is why," said Lenin, "the German worker and the Polish worker and the French worker is a comrade of the Russian worker in the struggle against the capitalist class, just as the Russian, Polish, and French capitalists are his enemy."[4]

The objective laws of societal development of capitalism, the experience of the workers' movement, are reflected in the class consciousness of the proletariat; proletarian internationalism is becoming an inseparable part of working class ideology. The slogan "Proletarians of all countries, unite!" put forward in the Communist Manifesto proclaimed the international character of the struggle of the working class and since has become the immutable motto of every true proletarian movement.

Proletarian internationalism is part of the ideology of the working class. It is an ideology of the fraternity and friendship of workers of all countries and, at the same time, an ideology of the friendship of peoples. Proletarian internationalism reflects not only the interests of the working class, but also the interests of all working people. The working class, as the vanguard class of modern society waging a struggle for the overthrow of capitalism and the creation of a socialist society, acts in the interests of all working people and, together with them, as their allies.

Other principles applied both in the relations of the working class of various countries and its parties and in relations between nations or, depending upon the character of the principles, only to relations between nations, also have been molded together with the principles of proletarian internationalism in the developmental process of the workers' movement.

The principles of proletarian internationalism were embodied in the mutual relations of the Soviet republics formed on the territory of the former Russian Empire after the October Revolution. Under the leadership of the Bolshevist party, the class-conscious workers and peasants and the Soviet governments created in the individual republics strove for unification in order to build socialism together and to defend the gains of the socialist revolution together from the swoops of imperialists. Relations of the new type between the Soviet republics, crowned by the formation

3. *K. Marks, F. Engel's, V. I. Lenin o proletarskom internatsionalizme* (Moscow: Gospolitizdat, 1957), p. 41.

4. Lenin, "Proekt i ob"iasnenie programmy sotsial-demokraticheskoi partii," *ibid.*, pp. 217-218.

of the Union of Soviet Socialist Republics, were molded precisely on the basis of the principles of proletarian internationalism.[5]

The principles of socialist internationalism influenced the entire foreign policy of the proletarian state and its international legal position. In every instance the Soviet state acted in the international arena by taking into account the principles of proletarian internationalism. It always took into account its duties with regard to the working class and the oppressed peoples of other countries, at the same time relying upon their support. "In alliance with the revolutionaries of the advanced countries and with all oppressed peoples," wrote V. I. Lenin, "against any and all imperialists—this is the foreign policy of the proletariat."[6]

Revolutions occurred in a number of western European countries under the influence of the October Revolution: revolutions in Germany and in Hungary. And although the periods during which the revolutionary governments existed in these countries were very brief—these revolutions were repressed by imperialism—those principles on which the Soviet state intended to build its relations with them were manifest at once; these were the principles of proletarian internationalism.

Notification of the revolution in Germany was received at the beginning of November 1918. The Soviet government hailed the revolution, and the very next day the VTsIK adopted a decree on sending grain to revolutionary Germany despite the gravely serious grain situation in Russia itself. In the decree of the VTsIK of November 13, 1918, on the annulment of the Treaty of Brest-Litovsk, the Soviet state, pursuant to the principles of proletarian internationalism, proposed to the peoples of Germany and Austria-Hungary to establish not only peaceful relations but an " . . . alliance of the toiling masses of all nations in their struggle to create and strengthen the socialist system . . . "[7] V. I. Lenin's greeting to the Bavarian Soviet Republic, formed in April 1919, was imbued with cordiality and fraternal solidarity.[8]

A revolution took place in Hungary in 1919, and a Hungarian Soviet Republic was formed. The Eighth Congress of the Russian Communist Party of Bolsheviks, convened in March 1919, approved a warm greeting to the Hungarian Soviet Republic drawn up by V. I. Lenin with an

5. For more detail, see O. I. Chistiakov, *Vzaimootnosheniia sovetskikh respublik do obrazovaniia SSSR* (Moscow: Gosiurizdat, 1955); D. L. Zlatopol'skii, *SSSR—federativnoe gosudarstvo* (Moscow: izd-vo MGU, 1967).

6. V. I. Lenin, "Vneshniaia politika russkoi revoliutsii," *Polnoe sobranie sochinenii*, 5th ed. (Moscow: Gospolitizdat, 1962), XXXII, 337. [Published in *Pravda*, June 27(14), 1917.]

7. Ministerstvo inostrannykh del SSSR, *Dokumenty vneshnei politiki SSSR* (Moscow: Gospolitizdat, 1957–), I, 566.

8. See Lenin, "Privetstvie bavarskoi sovetskoi respubliki," *Polnoe sobranie sochinenii*, XXXVIII, 321.

assurance that the Russian working class would assist it with all its strength and together with the workers of all countries "shall not permit the imperialists to raise their hands against the new Soviet republic."[9] "In the whole world," V. I. Lenin wrote to the Hungarian workers, "everything that is upright in the working class is on your side."[10]

This support from the first proletarian state in the world met with a warm response in Hungary. The leader of the Hungarian Communist party, Bela Kun, declared on March 23, 1919: "We are pleased and proud that Hungary is the second Soviet republic . . . We express gratitude and send greetings to the Russian Soviet Republic, which unfailingly has rendered assistance to us . . . "[11] "Relations between Soviet Russia and Soviet Hungary," writes Academician I. I. Mints, "based upon friendship and mutual assistance, were a prototype of the fraternal relations which have been formed now among countries of the socialist commonwealth."[12]

Relations with Mongolia, which began several years after the October Revolution, are a shining example of relations based upon the principles of proletarian internationalism. The people's revolution triumphed in Mongolia with the fraternal assistance of the Soviet Union. The Mongolian People's Republic has achieved great economic and cultural successes and, by-passing the capitalist stage of development, has proceeded to the construction of socialism.

The principles of socialist internationalism were developed further in relations among the countries of the world socialist system. While remaining political principles, at the same time they also are becoming international legal principles, their content is being enriched, and a number of new socialist principles and norms operative in relations among socialist countries are being formed (see Part VII).

B. The Principles of Equality and of Self-Determination of Nations

The principles of equality, self-determination, and sovereignty of nations advanced by the October Revolution possessed enormous potential force. They correctly reflected one of the most important laws of

9. Lenin, "Privetstvennaia radiotelegramma ot imeni s″ezda pravitel′stva vengerskoi sovetskoi respubliki," *ibid.*, p. 186.

10. Lenin, "Privet vengerskim rabochim," *ibid.*, p. 388. [Published in *Pravda*, May 29, 1919.]

11. Bela Kun, "Vengriia—vtoraia sovetskaia respublika; rech′na soveshchanii upolnomochennykh kommunisticheskoi partii," *O Vengerskoi Sovetskoi respublike; izbrannye stat′i i rechi* (Moscow: Politizdat, 1966), p. 137.

12. V. A. Zorin and others, eds., *Istoriia diplomatii*, 2d ed. (Moscow: Politizdat, 1959-1965), III, 195.

societal development of the new epoch opened by the October Socialist Revolution: the downfall of the colonial system.

Worked out by the classics of Marxism-Leninism and by the practice of the workers' movement, these principles were not merely a revival of principles which had been advanced by bourgeois revolutions of the seventeenth and eighteenth centuries. Nor were they a reproduction of the "nationality principle," which never was generally recognized even within the framework of European international law and did not interfere with the annexationist policy pursued by European states.

On the basis of the teachings of Marxism-Leninism, the Soviet state raised the entire problem of national self-determination in a new way, in the aspect of the interests of the class struggle of the proletariat for the liberation of all working people. The principle of self-determination of nations is regarded as a "consistent expression of the struggle against any national oppression."[13]

"The right of nations to self-determination," V. I. Lenin pointed out, "means solely the right to independence in a political sense, to free political separation from the oppressor nation."[14] Thus, the principle of self-determination in its new formulation meant the right of a nation to determine its own foreign policy status, the right to decide its own affairs, the inadmissibility of coercion upon the will of the nation.

But, holding to the positions of the working class, the Bolshevist party always has accorded priority in its policy to the interests of the revolutionary struggle of the working class for the liquidation of capitalism and the construction of socialism.

A nation has the right to self-determination. But a nation in a capitalist society has been divided into antagonistic classes waging a bitter struggle among themselves. Realization of the self-determination of nations is not only an all-national, but also a class problem. Which class will stand at the head of the struggle for the self-determination of nations is of decisive significance. The content and the results of that struggle are dependent on this.

The Bolshevist party naturally strove so that the leading role in realizing self-determination of nations belonged to the working class and so that the self-determination of nations was part of the socialist revolution. And in this instance, as the experience of the self-determination of the nations that had been part of the former Russian Empire confirmed, self-determination can be realized most completely and profoundly when one finds expressed therein the interests and the will of the working people, the overwhelming majority of a nation.

13. Lenin, "Sotsialisticheskaia revoliutsiia i pravo natsii na samoopredelenie," *Polnoe sobranie sochinenii*, XXVII, 255.

14. *Ibid.*

International Legal Ideas of the October Revolution

The principles of equality and of self-determination of nations re-sounded in the Decree on Peace, which proposed "to all belligerent peoples and their governments to commence immediate negotiations for a just and democratic peace."[15] It was explained in the Decree that "by such a peace the government considers an immediate peace, without annexations (that is, without the seizure of foreign lands; without forcibly annexing foreign peoples), and without indemnities."[16]

The Decree contained the celebrated Leninist definition of annexation, which at the same time was a definition of the principle of self-deter-mination of peoples. Annexation was defined as "any addition of a small or weak people to a large or powerful state without the definitely, clearly, and voluntarily expressed consent and desire of this people irrespective of when this coerced addition occurred and also irrespective of how devel-oped or backward the nation forcibly annexed or forcibly retained within the frontiers of the state concerned. Irrespective, finally, of the fact that this nation lives in Europe or in lands far beyond the seas." The Decree went on to say: "If any nation whatsoever is retained within the boundar-ies of a given state by coercion, if despite its expressed desire it is not granted the right by a free vote, . . . with the complete withdrawal of the forces of the annexing or generally more powerful nation, to decide without the slightest coercion the question of the form of state existence of this nation, then its accession is an annexation; that is, by seizure and coercion."[17]

In the Appeal to the Toiling Masses of All Countries in the name of the All-Russian Executive Committee of Workers', Soldiers', and Peasants' Deputies, of the All-Russian Peasants' Congress, of the Petrograd Soviet of Workers' and Soldiers' Deputies, of the Headquarters of the Red Guard, and of Trade Union representatives of December 22, 1917, the workers of all countries were called upon "to struggle for a general armistice, for universal peace without annexations and indemnities on the basis of self-determination of nations."[18]

15. *Dokumenty vneshnei politiki SSSR*, I, 11.

16. *Ibid.*, p. 12.

17. *Ibid.* Bourgeois international legal doctrine frequently asserts that the principle of self-determination of nations supposedly was put forward as a universal principle of international law for the first time by President Woodrow Wilson in his well-known Fourteen Points, set forth in a Message to Congress on January 8, 1918. See, for example, A. Verdross, *Völkerrecht*, ed. S. Verosta and K. Zemanek, 5th ed. (Vienna: Springer Verlag, 1964), p. 84. The unfoundedness of this assertion already has been pointed out in the literature of the socialist countries. See, for example, Zorin and others, eds., *Istoriia diplomatii*, III, 112-115; S. Iu. Vygodskii, *U istokov sovetskoi diplomatii* (Moscow: Politizdat, 1965), pp. 14-15; R. Arzinger, *Das Selbstbestim-mungsrecht im allgemeinen Völkerrecht der Gegenwart* (Berlin: Staatsverlag der DDR, 1966), pp. 70-71.

18. *Dokumenty vneshnei politiki SSSR*, I, 59.

The Soviet state and the Communist party emphasized (and this was exceedingly important) that the principle of self-determination must be applied to all nations. Lenin said that "the proletariat must demand the freedom of political separation of colonies and nations being suppressed by 'its' nation,"[19] that is, to come out against its own imperialists. "Otherwise," Lenin said, "the internationalism of the proletariat remains empty and verbal."[20] The Appeal of the People's Commissariat of Foreign Affairs of the Russian Republic to the peoples and governments of the allied countries in December 1917 contained a call " . . . to build peace upon the basis of the complete and unconditional recognition of the principle of self-determination for all peoples . . . "[21]

The People's Commissar for Foreign Affairs, G. V. Chicherin, wrote V. I. Lenin on March 10, 1922: "Our international program must bring all oppressed colonial peoples into the international scheme. The right to separation or to home rule must be recognized for all peoples . . . The novelty of our international scheme must be in the fact that Negroes, as well as other colonial peoples, have participated on an equal footing with European peoples in conferences and committees and have had the right not to permit interference in their domestic life."[22] On this letter V. I. Lenin underlines the words "and other colonial peoples have participated on an equal footing," "not to permit interference" and on the margins makes the notation: "Right!"[23]

The Soviet state gave the world a shining example of resolving the national question on the basis of the principle of self-determination. The Soviet state made the principles of equality and self-determination its own constitutional principles. The equality and sovereignty of the peoples of Russia already had been announced in the Declaration of Rights of the Peoples of Russia of December 15, 1917: the right to self-determination up to and including separation and the formation of an independent state; the abolition of all national privileges and restrictions; freedom of national minorities to develop.[24] These principles were confirmed in the first Soviet constitution—the RSFSR Constitution of 1918.

Emphatically disassociating himself from the bourgeois understanding of the principle of self-determination as having the purpose to create "nation-states," V. I. Lenin stressed that the principle of self-determina-

19. Lenin, "Sotsialisticheskaia revoliutsiia i pravo natsii na samoopredelenie," *Polnoe sobranie sochinenii*, XXVII, 257.

20. *Ibid.*

21. *Dokumenty vneshnei politiki SSSR*, I, 69.

22. Reproduced in Lenin, "Pis'mo G. V. Chicherinu," *Polnoe sobranie sochinenii*, XLV, 36.

23. *Ibid.*

24. *Dokumenty vneshnei politiki SSSR*, I, 15.

tion is, on the contrary, a means of bringing nations together on the basis of socialism. "The purpose of socialism," he said, "is not only the destruction of those who would splinter mankind into small states and of those who would isolate nations, not only the bringing together of nations, but also of amalgamating them."[25] But Lenin emphasized that it is possible to arrive at this point "only through a transition period of complete liberation of all oppressed nations; that is, their freedom and separation."[26] Lenin said that in the event the principle of self-determination is fully realized on the basis of and within the framework of socialist social relations, national narrow-mindedness and national prejudice may be done away with and mankind will proceed along the path of bringing the nations together.

The Russian Communist party struggled for the unification of all nations of Russia because the interests of the proletarian revolution required this; struggled for unification on a voluntary basis, so that individual nations in exercising their right to self-determination have expressed themselves freely for unification with the other socialist soviet republics. The Union of Soviet Socialist Republics was created on this basis.

The Soviet state broke completely and immediately with the colonial policy of tsarism and repudiated all treaties of Tsarist Russia having a colonial, annexationist, unequal character.[27] It steadfastly has pursued the principles of equality and self-determination of nations, being a consistent fighter against colonialism and racial discrimination.

As treaty norms, these principles were fixed for the first time in treaties of the Soviet state with countries of the East. These treaties signified the establishment of new relations with such countries, which the imperialist countries had considered to be objects of their colonial expansion.

First and foremost should be mentioned the treaty with Persia of February 26, 1921, the treaty with Afghanistan of February 28, 1921, and the treaty with Turkey of March 16, 1921.

In the treaty between the RSFSR and Persia the Soviet government condemned the policy of the government of Tsarist Russia as "not only having violated the sovereignty of the states of Asia, but also as having led to organized brute violence of the European plunderers upon the living

25. Lenin, "Sotsialisticheskaia revoliutsiia i pravo natsii na samoopredelenie," *Polnoe sobranie sochinenii*, XXVII, 256.

26. *Ibid.*

27. For greater detail, see N. V. Zakharova, "Otkaz Sovetskogo gosudarstva ot dogovorov tsarskoi Rossii, narushavshikh prava narodov vostochnykh stran," *Sovetskii ezhegodnik mezhdunarodnogo prava 1962* (Moscow: izd-vo AN SSSR, 1963), pp. 126-134.

body of the peoples of the East."[28] The parties recognized in Article 4 of the treaty "the right of each people to the free and unimpeded resolution of its own political fate."[29]

The treaty between Russia and Turkey of March 16, 1921, proclaimed "the principles of the fraternity of nations and the right of peoples to self-determination," noted "the solidarity in the struggle against imperialism" existing between the RSFSR and Turkey, and declared "the contiguity between the national and liberation movement of the peoples of the East and the struggle of the working people of Russia for a new social system."[30] When the Soviet ambassador presented his credentials in July 1921, the leader of the new Turkish government, Ataturk, said in his speech: "We are highly appreciative that Soviet Russia has repudiated the former treaties and put forward the principle of self-determination."[31]

The revolutionizing influence of the great principles of equality and self-determination of nations and peoples upon international law truly was enormous. As a result of the struggle of the Soviet Union, of the working class of the capitalist countries, of the peoples of colonies and dependent countries, and of all progressive forces, these ideas took hold in international law, being transformed into international legal principles and norms and supplanting old institutions in international law that had sanctified national oppression and colonial domination.

The notion of the invalidity of unequal treaties, advanced in the Decree on Peace, played and continues to play a large role in the development of international law.[32] The Soviet state announced in this Decree that it would commence immediately to publish Russian secret treaties. "The entire content of these secret treaties," said the Decree on Peace, "insofar as it was aimed, as in the majority of instances it was, at giving advantages and privileges to Russian landowners and capitalists, at maintaining and increasing annexations of the Great Russians, the government announces their unconditional and immediate abrogation."[33]

Among the treaties published and repudiated by the Soviet state were, in particular, the 1915 Russo-Japanese agreement relating to joint coloni-

28. *Dokumenty vneshnei politiki SSSR*, III, 537.

29. *Ibid.*, p. 538.

30. *Ibid.*, pp. 597, 599.

31. See "Zarubezhnaia pechat' o revoliutsii v Rossii i sobytiiakh v Sovetskoi respublike," *Mezhdunarodnaia zhizn'*, no. 4 (1967), p. 63. [Citing *Biulleten' NKID*, no. 91 (September 10, 1921), pp. 61-62.]

32. See A. N. Talalaev and V. G. Boiarshinov, "Neravnopravnye dogovory kak forma uderzhaniia v kolonial'noi zavisimosti novykh gosudarstv Azii i Afriki," *Sovetskii ezhegodnik mezhdunarodnogo prava 1961* (Moscow: izd-vo AN SSSR, 1962), pp. 156-169.

33. *Dokumenty vneshnei politiki SSSR*, I, 13.

alist operations in China, the 1916 agreement among Russia, Great Britain, and France concerning the partition of Turkey, the 1907 Anglo-Russian secret treaty and convention relating to spheres of influence in Iran, and others.

For the first time in history, a great power voluntarily repudiated treaties granting it rights and privileges in other countries. In place of the cabalistic treaties of Tsarist Russia, the Soviet state began to conclude treaties with countries of the East on the basis of full equality and respect for sovereignty. In the treaty between the RSFSR and Persia of February 26, 1921, the Soviet government once again solemnly declared "the irrevocable repudiation by Russia of the rapacious policy, with regard to Persia, of the imperialist Russian governments overthrown by the will of its workers and peasants."[34] "In conformity therewith, and in wishing to see the Persian people independent, prosperous, and freely disposing of their own property," the treaty went on to say, "the Russian Soviet government declares all treaties, conventions, and agreements concluded by the former Tsarist government with Persia and resulting in derogation of the rights of the Persian people to be abrogated and to have lost any force."[35] The Soviet government also declared "its refusal to take part in any measures whatsoever tending to weaken or violate the sovereignty of Persia," and announced as "abrogated and having lost any force, all conventions and agreements concluded by the former government of Russia with third powers to the detriment of Persia or relating thereto."[36]

In the treaty between the RSFSR and Turkey of March 16, 1921, the contracting parties agreed to recognize "as abrogated and not having force" all treaties concluded between Russia and Turkey, as the parties had recognized that they "did not correspond to their mutual interests."[37]

Renunciation of consular jurisdiction, one of the important instruments of colonial domination, was a major element of the Soviet state's policy toward the countries of the East. Thus, the treaty with Turkey said: "The government of the Russian Socialist Federated Soviet Republic, recognizing the regime of capitulations to be incompatible with the free national development of any country, as well as with the full exercise of its sovereign rights, shall consider as having lost force and as abrogated any kind of activities or rights having any relation whatsoever to this regime."[38] The treaty with Persia, wherein the Soviet government

34. *Ibid.*, III, 536.
35. *Ibid.*, pp. 536-537.
36. *Ibid.*, p. 537.
37. *Ibid.*, p. 599.
38. *Ibid.*, pp. 599-600.

affirmed a declaration renouncing consular jurisdiction made previously, said that "Russian citizens residing in Persia, as also Persian citizens residing in Russia, from the moment the present treaty is signed shall enjoy the rights and shall be subordinate to the laws of the country of their residence equally with local citizens."[39]

In the agreement between the USSR and the Republic of China of May 31, 1924, the parties agreed to annul "all conventions, treaties, agreements, protocols, contracts, and so forth, concluded between the government of China and the Tsarist government and to replace them with new treaties, agreements, and so forth, on the basis of equality, mutuality, and justice ... "[40] The Soviet government confirmed once again in this agreement the declaration previously made abrogating all treaties and agreements concluded by Tsarist Russia with third countries which affect the "sovereign rights and interests of China."[41] The Soviet government renounced special rights and privileges relating to concessions in China acquired by the Tsarist government, as well as rights of extraterritoriality and consular jurisdiction.[42]

The idea of the invalidity of unequal treaties set forth in the Decree on Peace, the abrogation by the Soviet state of all unequal treaties contracted by Tsarist Russia, and the conclusion of treaties with all countries, large and small, on the basis of equality were an inspiring example for the dependent countries. It has become much more difficult for imperialist states to impose unequal treaties, although, taking advantage of the weakness of some states, especially the new ones, they also frequently compel them to sign such treaties at the present time.

C. The Principles of Peaceful Coexistence

The third group of ideas and principles put forward by the October Revolution was aimed at ensuring international peace and the peaceful cooperation of states with different social systems.

To the question of how relations should be built between states of opposed social systems when the first socialist state in the world comes into existence, Lenin and the Communist party, in working out the theory of the proletarian revolution, gave an answer even before October 1917. After the revolution, these propositions were developed further and were transformed into reality.

39. *Ibid.*, p. 542.
40. *Ibid.*, VII, 332.
41. *Ibid.*, p. 332.
42. *Ibid.*, p. 335.

In rejecting the "absurd leftist" trotskyist "permanent revolution," V. I. Lenin resolutely opposed the concept of extending the socialist revolution to other countries by force of arms. In an article, "Strange and Monstrous," published in *Pravda* on February 28 and March 1, 1918, V. I. Lenin wrote in appealing to the authors of a resolution adopted by the Moscow Regional Party Bureau: "Perhaps the authors suppose that the interests of the international revolution require that it be given a push, and such a push can be given only by war, never by peace, which might give the masses the impression that imperialism was being 'legitimized.' Such a 'theory' would break completely with Marxism, which always has opposed 'pushing' revolutions, which develop with the growing acuteness of the class antagonisms that give birth to revolutions."[43]

A resolution of a conference of the foreign sections of the Russian Social-Democratic Workers' party convened in Berne from February 27 to March 4, 1915, pointed out that the future state of the dictatorship of the proletariat will resort to war only "to protect the gains won in the proletariat's struggle against the bourgeoisie."[44] A resolution of the Seventh (April) All-Russian Conference of the RSDRP(b) of 1917 indicated that in the event the proletariat took power in Russia it "immediately and openly would propose a democratic peace to all peoples on the basis of a complete renunciation of any annexations or indemnities whatsoever."[45]

In conformity with these propositions the newly emergent Soviet state proposed to lay down the principle of peaceful coexistence as the basis for the peaceful regulation of future international relations. In the Decree on Peace of November 8, 1917, the socialist state declared that annexationist, aggressive wars it "considers the greatest crime against humanity . . . " and called upon all belligerent states to cease the sanguinary war and to commence immediate negotiations for a just and democratic peace.[46]

At the same time, basing his remarks on the experience of history, particularly the experience of bourgeois revolutions and especially the eighteenth century French bourgeois revolution, Lenin cautioned the party, the working class, and the working people of Russia that the ruling classes of capitalist states would not leave the newly emergent socialist state in peace, that they are using every means, including military, to attempt to destroy the new social system just emerging based upon the

43. Lenin, "Strannoe i chudovishchnoe," *Polnoe sobranie sochinenii*, XXXV, 403. [Published in *Pravda*, February 28-March 1, 1918.]

44. *KPSS v rezoliutsiiakh i resheniiakh s"ezdov, konferentsii i plenumov TsK* (Moscow: Gospolitizdat, 1954), I, 329.

45. *Ibid.*, p. 337.

46. *Dokumenty vneshnei politiki SSSR*, I, 11-12.

liquidation of private ownership of the instruments and means of production and signifying the end of domination of the capitalist class in Russia, the beginning of the end of the capitalist system in general. As early as the report on peace to the Second All-Russian Congress of Soviets on November 8, 1917, V. I. Lenin said: "The governments and the bourgeoisie are using every effort to unite themselves and to crush the workers' and peasants' revolution in blood."[47] The Seventh Congress of the Russian Communist Party (bolsheviks) in March 1918 declared in its resolution on war and peace: "Repeated military attacks of imperialist states (both from the West and from the East) against Soviet Russia historically are inevitable in the present period of the beginning era of socialist revolution."[48] Regrettably, one did not have to wait long for confirmation of this scientific prediction. The capitalist countries quickly brought down their armed forces upon the young Soviet state.

In the Report of the Central Committee to the Eighth Congress of the RKP(b) on March 18, 1919, Lenin said: "We live not only in a state, but *in a system of states*, and the existence of the Soviet Republic side by side with imperialist states for a prolonged period is inconceivable. Ultimately either one or the other shall be victorious. And when this end comes, a number of terrible conflicts between the Soviet Republic and bourgeois states are inevitable."[49]

This utterance of Lenin's, as well as a number of his other remarks on this question, are cited repeatedly by opponents of peaceful coexistence in justification of their fabrications that Lenin supposedly regarded peaceful coexistence between states of two systems as impossible and that, in Lenin's view, the new socialist state must go to war against capitalist states in order to spread socialism with the aid of arms.[50] These ravings of opponents of communism have nothing in common with reality.

Lenin pointed out that the attempts of imperialists to suppress the

47. Lenin, "Doklad o mire 26 Oktiabria (8 noiabria)," *Polnoe sobranie sochinenii*, XXXV, 17.

48. *KPSS v rezoliutsiiakh*, I, 404.

49. Lenin, "Otchet tsentral'nogo komiteta 18 marta," *Polnoe sobranie sochinenii*, XXXVIII, 139.

50. See, for example, the speech of the Uruguyan representative, Dominguez-Campora, at the 465th plenary session of the United Nations General Assembly on December 2, 1953. United Nations General Assembly (VIII), *Official Records*, p. 391; also see the speech of the French representative, Georges-Picot, at the Twelfth Session of the General Assembly. United Nations General Assembly (XII), *Official Records*, p. 273; G. Kennan, "Peaceful Coexistence: A Western View," *Foreign Affairs*, XXXVIII (1960), 173; B. Meissner, "Zwölf Gebote der Koexistenz; Moskaus neue Völkerrecht," *Der Spiegel*, XVIII (1964), no. 3, pp. 62-63.

young Soviet state could and would lead inevitably to military conflicts between states of the two systems despite the peace policy of the socialist state. Lenin spoke of the "self-defense" of the proletarian state in calling for it to create its own military organization. Lenin warned the party and the people of the need for vigilance and for strengthening the defense capability of the socialist state.

V. I. Lenin and the party did not consider the policy of peaceful coexistence of a socialist state with capitalist countries which the Soviet state pursued as a temporary policy, dictated by the then existing military-industrial supremacy of capitalism over socialism, but as the policy most responsive to the interests of the working people and to the requirements of proletarian internationalism. The Soviet state has struggled persistently for peace. A resolution of the Seventh All-Russian Congress of Soviets in December 1919 said: "The Russian Socialist Federated Soviet Republic wishes to live in peace with all peoples."[51]

The Soviet government has emphasized repeatedly that a socialist state is prepared to establish not only normal, but also friendly relations, and it is not its purpose to extend the socialist system and communist ideology by force of arms.

Thus, a note of the People's Commissar of Foreign Affairs to the German Consul General of September 18, 1918, stated: "The Workers'-Peasants' government desires with full resolve the observance of good-neighborly relations and peaceful cohabitation with Germany despite all the differences in the system of both states, and it is convinced that the German government also wishes to live together peacefully with it; while living together, it shall survive by itself, as also the German government, and it expects that the latter, as itself, will consider these differences with all of the consequences, which, however, have not obstructed the establishment now taking place between both states of good-neighborly relations corresponding to the true and deeply rooted interests of both sides."[52]

In his statement to the newspaper correspondents of the *Observer* and *Manchester Guardian* in 1922 Lenin pointed out: "We believe that completely friendly relations with both powers [having in mind France and England—*G.T.*] are wholly possible and constitute our purpose."[53]

V. I. Lenin and the party proceeded from the fact that after the failure of the armed intervention against Soviet Russia, economic competition

51. *Dokumenty vneshnei politiki SSSR*, II, 298.
52. *Ibid.*, I, 488.
53. Lenin, "Interv'iu korrespondentu "Observer" i "Manchester Guardian" M. Farbmanu," *Polnoe sobranie sochinenii*, XLV, 237.

had become the decisive sphere of struggle for the states of the two systems. In 1921 Lenin said: "Now we are exerting a major influence upon the international revolution by our economic policy ... But this field of struggle has been transferred to a world-wide scale. We solve this task—and we have won once and for all on an international scale. Therefore, questions of economic construction acquire very exceptional significance for us. On this front we must gain victory slowly, gradually— never quickly—but by a steady rise and movement forward."[54]

In a draft decree on the tasks of the Soviet delegation at the 1922 Genoa Conference, V. I. Lenin pointed out that peaceful coexistence necessarily includes mutually advantageous agreements of the Soviet state with capitalist countries not only upon economic, but also political questions.[55] Lenin derided proponents of the concept of "no compromises with capitalist states," showing the absurdity and harmfulness of this concept from the standpoint of the proletarian revolution. At the same time, Lenin stressed that the Soviet state, in making compromises, would not depart from positions of principle.

Would capitalist countries establish economic and other relations with the Soviet state? V. I. Lenin answered this question as follows: "There is a force greater than the desire, will, and decision of any of the hostile governments or classes; this force is general world-wide economic relations, which compel them to embark upon the path of intercourse with us."[56]

On a broad historical plane, Lenin understood peaceful coexistence of states of opposed social systems, socialist and capitalist, to be a form of struggle of these systems in the course of which a new system triumphs over the old; such a struggle precludes armed struggle between states of these systems and includes cooperation between them on various questions of mutual interest.

The Soviet state strove so that the principle of peaceful coexistence entered into international law and became a generally-recognized principle.

This principle received international legal expression for the first time in treaties with countries of the East: Persia, Afghanistan, and Turkey.

The leading capitalist countries refused to accept the peaceful coexist-

54. Lenin, "Rech' pri zakrytii konferentsii 28 maia," *Polnoe sobranie sochinenii*, XLIII, 341.
55. Lenin, "Proekt postanovleniia TsK RKP(b) o zadachakh sovetskoi delegatsii v genue," *ibid.*, XLIV, 407.
56. Lenin, "O vnutrennei i vneshnei politike respublike; otchet VTsIK i SNK 23 dekabria," *ibid.*, pp. 304-305.

ence of states of two systems, expecting to destroy the new system. "There is one category of people," said the herald of anticommunism, Winston Churchill, at this time, "with whom it is useless, in my view, to seek agreements. I speak of the Bolsheviks . . . "[57] The imperialists organized armed intervention, a blockade, and other aggressive actions against Soviet Russia. But life compelled capitalist states to recognize the Soviet state, to conclude treaties with it, to create an anti-Hitler coalition, as well as to accept the United Nations Charter, where this principle received wide, and then universal recognition (see Chapter 3).

On the plane of developing the principles of peaceful coexistence, the young Soviet state advanced two exceedingly important and fruitful ideas in the Decree on Peace: the ideas of the prohibition of and the criminality of aggressive war. "The government considers it the greatest crime against humanity to continue this war so that the strong and rich nations can divide among themselves the weak peoples they have seized," said the Decree.[58] The Fourth Extraordinary All-Russian Congress of Soviets condemned "all predatory wars" in the decree ratifying the Brest Peace Treaty in 1918.[59]

The principle of prohibiting aggressive war already had been laid down in a general form in the treaties of Soviet Russia with Persia, Afghanistan, and Turkey concluded at the beginning of 1921. It received more concrete expression in treaties of the USSR on nonaggression and neutrality with Turkey of December 17, 1925, and with Persia of October 1, 1927. The treaty with Turkey, for example, said that "each Contracting Party shall be bound to refrain from any attack upon each other . . . , not to participate in any hostile act by one or several third powers directed against the other Contracting Party."[60]

The idea of the criminality of aggressive war expressed in the Decree on Peace later was reflected in a number of international documents and was transformed into a prevailing principle of international law (see Chapter 3).

For the past half-century, international law has developed under the beneficial influence of the ideas of the Great October Socialist Revolution. The international legal ideas of the October Revolution injected into

57. See "Zarubezhnaia pechat' o revoliutsii v Rossii i sobytiiakh v Sovetskoi respublike," *Mezhdunarodnaia zhizn'*, no. 3 (1967), p. 86. [Citing *Biulleten' NKID*, no. 2 (March 10, 1920), p. 1.]

58. *Dokumenty vneshnei politiki SSSR*, I, 12.

59. *Ibid.*, p. 213.

60. *Ibid.*, VIII, 740.

international law as a result of the struggle of the Soviet Union and other progressive forces have led to its fundamental change.

The creative role of the international legal ideas of the October Revolution is far from exhausted. The change of the co-relation of forces to the advantage of socialism and peace ensures a further increase in the role of the international legal ideas of the October Revolution in the development of contemporary international law.

Chapter 2 *Peaceful Coexistence and General International Law. The Influence of the Breakup of the Colonial System*

The problem of the co-relation of peaceful coexistence and international law has three aspects.

The coexistence of states with different social systems means their simultaneous existence. Peaceful coexistence is a type of such coexistence. If the coexistence and struggle of two systems are a law of the transition period from capitalism to socialism, then peaceful coexistence is a necessity and a possibility which grow and to an ever greater degree are realized. But, as the experience of more than half a century of the coexistence of states with opposed social systems shows, it was not always peaceful. Academician P.N. Fedoseev is completely correct in writing: "Having proclaimed the principle of peaceful coexistence of states with different social systems, Lenin at the same time repeatedly cautioned that one must be constantly on the alert, be prepared to repulse imperialist aggression. He understood the principle of peaceful coexistence as a real necessity and possibility, but not as an already achieved result guaranteed by the immutable laws of history. He firmly explained that the entire world situation is determined by the struggle between the Soviet republics and the imperialist states standing against them."[1] Therefore, the first aspect of the problem being considered is what influence is exerted on international law by the very fact of the coexistence and struggle of the two opposed social systems.

A second and more important aspect is the influence which peaceful coexistence exerts on international law. This influence is so multifaceted that it is dealt with in many chapters of this work. In the present chapter it is considered very generally.

1. P. N. Fedoseev, "V. I. Lenin—velikii teoretik kommunizma," *Kommunist*, no. 1 (1969), p. 17.

And finally, the third aspect of the problem of the co-relation of peaceful coexistence and international law is what influence international law exerts on the peaceful coexistence of states with different social systems; that is to say, what is the role of contemporary international law in securing peace in general and the peaceful coexistence of states of opposed social systems in particular. The answer to this question can be given only after an analysis of those fundamental changes which have taken place in international law during the past half-century, and in connection with a consideration of the problem of the essence of contemporary international law (see Chapter 9).

A. The Unfoundedness of the Theory That the Development Base of International Law Is Contracting

"The contemporary epoch," says the Program of the CPSU, "whose basic content is comprised of the transition from capitalism to socialism, is the epoch of the struggle of two opposed social systems, the epoch of socialist and national liberation revolutions, the epoch of the downfall of imperialism, and the liquidation of the colonial system, and the epoch of transition to the path of socialism of all new peoples, of the triumph of socialism and communism on a world-wide scale."[2]

Is general international law, that is, a law recognized by all states and regulating relations among them, possible in a period of the existence of states of two opposed world social systems? If such a law is possible and exists, is its developmental base expanding or contracting? What significance does the breakup of the colonial system and the formation of a large number of new states have for international law?

At the present time, these questions not only are of theoretical interest, but are vital questions of international relations. Two international legal positions corresponding to two trends in international politics have emerged: one position, a component part of the policy "from a position of strength," amounts to an actual denial of the possibility of the existence of general international law and to a justification of power politics in international relations; the second position, the position of the socialist and other peaceloving states, proceeds from the fact that general international law exists and the possibilities of its progressive development are not diminishing, but are growing.

The concept that during the past fifty years the developmental base of general international law has contracted in consequence of the existence

2. *Programma Kommunisticheskoi partii Sovetskogo Soiuza* (Moscow: Politizdat, 1964), p. 5.

Peaceful Coexistence and General International Law

of states of two opposed social systems and opposed ideologies, as well as the emergence of a large number of new states whose cultural heritage is substantially different from western civilization, is widely disseminated in the bourgeois doctrine of international law. Politically, this concept reflects first and foremost the influence of the policy of anticommunism, which rejects peaceful coexistence of states with opposed social systems and the possibility of agreement between them. Bourgeois legal doctrine is its theoretical base.

By virtue of its class nature, bourgeois legal science seeks not to reveal the true essence of law but, on the contrary, to lead inquiry away from it, to seek its essence in those phenomena which would conceal the exploitative nature of bourgeois law and would permit it to be characterized as an expression of the interests of all of society. The easiest path leading in this direction is to search for the bases of law in general, and consequently, of international law, in a particular community, including a common ideology. Among the devotees of this concept, exceedingly widespread in the bourgeois theory of international law, we find writers of very different political complexions, from blatant anticommunists to actual proponents of peaceful coexistence.

Proceeding from the aforementioned idealistic concept, according to which law, including international law, is a reflection of common ideology, and stipulating that there is no such common ideology now between the states of the two systems, some bourgeois international lawyers maintain that general international law is impossible in the presence of two opposed social systems and ideologies or they believe that it only is functioning temporarily, insofar as the heritage of the past has remained with us, and gradually is breaking up into separate regional systems. Other bourgeois jurists express apprehension for the fate of general international law or assert that the developmental base of general international law has contracted with the emergence of socialist states and the new states of Asia and Africa.

Thus, a West German jurist, E. Kordt, attempts to ascribe to the Soviet state and to Soviet international legal theory the thesis that general international law is rejected in order to justify his own personal arguments that there is no place for general international law in relations between socialist and capitalist states since there is no common ideology. "Since," he writes, "the minimum community of views is absent, of course, this assumption [relating to the existence of general international law—G.T.] falls."[3]

3. E. Kordt, "Weltherrschaftsstreben und Völkerrecht," *Jahrbuch für Internationales Recht*, XI (1962), 199. [*Festschrift für Rudolf Laun zu seinam achtzigsten Geburstag.*]

Another West German jurist, Professor G. Leibholz, asserts that in order to speak of an "international legal community" there must be a "minimum community world outlook," which at present there is not.[4]

A Dutch professor, F. Asbeck, writes " . . . nations are divided by a high wall—a conflict of fundamental convictions . . . As long as the antagonism in fundamental convictions continues to divide the world, the road to an international legal order for the world as a whole lies barred . . . "[5]

An English professor, H. A. Smith, wrote in 1947 that within the last thirty years the " . . . common cultural unity upon which the law was originally founded" has been destroyed.[6] In his view, there is no basis for international law since there is "no common agreement upon a Divine or 'natural' law to which all human law and all political power, even the mightiest, is bound to conform."[7]

An American professor, J. Kunz, in his 1955 lectures at the Hague Academy entitled "La Crise et les Transformations du Droit des Gens" raises the question: "Could not global ideological conflict lead to the disintegration of the existing universality of international law?" In essence, the author answers this question affirmatively, referring to the "crisis of contemporary international law" and considering this crisis to be the result of a "moral, philosophical, and religious crisis."[8]

Doubt about the possibility of developing general international law is expressed by Q. Wright, an American professor, in whose opinion " . . . international law tends to split into opposing ideologies of western and Soviet international law."[9]

In an extensive article on "International Law and Global Ideological Conflict," an American professor, K. Wilk, reaches very pessimistic conclusions regarding the future development of general international law. He begins with the customary thesis of bourgeois legal scholars that for law to exist within any group there must be a common understanding of the values within it.[10]

4. G. Leibholz, "Zur gegenwärtigen Lage des Völkerrechts," *Archiv des Völkerrechts*, I (1948-1949), 415-423.

5. F. M. Asbeck, "Growth and Movement of International Law," *International and Comparative Law Quarterly*, XI (1962), 1071.

6. H. A. Smith, *The Crisis of the Law of Nations* (London: Stevens & Sons, 1947), p. 18.

7. *Ibid.*, p. 101.

8. J. Kunz, "La crise et les transformations du droit des gens," *Recueil des cours*, LXXXVIII (1955), 18, 25.

9. Q. Wright, "International Law and Ideologies," *American Journal of International Law*, XLVIII (1954), 617.

10. See K. Wilk, "International Law and Global Ideological Conflict," *American Journal of International Law*, XLV (1951), 657.

Peaceful Coexistence and General International Law

The acceptance of obligations necessary for the existence of international law, says Wilk, "depends upon a minimum of human relationships across national frontiers that admit of and call for international regulation, and upon a minimum of values that are understood or understandable across national frontiers and that may serve as standards for such regulations. On this assumption, the area of the dominion of international law extends as far as such relationships and commonly understood or understandable values extend."[11] In Wilk's view, the said relationships across national frontiers do exist. But he is doubtful that there exist some "shared standards," since there are differing points of view as to whether there are "legal standards" in general.

Wilk correctly notes that a common ideology is by no means necessary to the existence of international law. As evidence of this he cites the fact that "national societies live under law without achieving comprehensive or fundamental unity of belief in values, or even agreement as to what values are the fundamental ones." As regards international law, he points out that "there is no reason to consider wider or more basic agreement internationally the prerequisite of international law. To expect it of global law, international or supra-national, is utopian."[12]

Yet Wilk comes to the conclusion that the deep division between the major states on fundamentals encourages trends away from general international law, to its breaking-up, and toward the development of local agreements and the growth of regional systems of international law. He points out that the development of international law in this direction could lead to the fact that "universal agreement would no longer survive on matters that used to be governed by universal international law. Carried to its extreme, such a development could break up the universal system of international law, as it has come down to us, into regional or other partial systems, with no international legal rules to govern the actions of states across the frontiers of the various systems. This would involve, he says, "a state, if not of virtual isolation, then of extreme hostility . . . "[13]

We dwell such on Professor Wilk's article only because he set forth in greater detail than other bourgeois specialists in international affairs the concept of the breakup of general international law.

This point of view, widely propagated in the United States, is shared by many leading bourgeois international lawyers in other countries. Another more widespread and more moderate concept, tending in the same direction, is that in consequence of the emergence of the socialist

11. *Ibid.*, p. 658.
12. *Ibid.*, p. 667.
13. *Ibid.*, pp. 668-670.

countries and the new states of Africa and Asia, the developmental base of contemporary general international law has contracted.

In Professor C. de Visscher's view, the enormous and sudden expansion in international relations from the standpoint of the participation "of human communities which enter into international relations, as from the standpoint of the interests which these relations embrace . . . diminishes the homogeneity of the traditional community of law . . . "[14]

An American Professor, A. Freeman, believes that the emergence of new independent states "has impeded, not advanced, the emergence of a mature code of conduct,"[15] for example, international law as a whole.

An Indonesian writer, J. J. G. Syatauw, suggests that "the growing interdependence . . . may have a favourable influence on the development of world prescriptions, but this interdependence being principally of material rather than of ideological nature, will certainly not lead to the strengthening of the Christian principles of international law." The author calls this a "weakening development."[16]

Professor A. Verdross previously also regarded the October Revolution and the gaining of independence by colonial peoples as a manifestation of a trend toward a contracted base of general international law. He pointed out in this connection that the Soviet Union "does not recognize all previously existing international law in its entirety, but only individual customary law norms and the international treaties which it has concluded."[17]

As regards the emergence of new states in consequence of the liberation of colonies, in Verdross's view this also represents a certain danger to international law, since "new states have entered the community of states which never have belonged to Christian-European culture and which therefore represent legal attitudes that diverge from the western concept of law."[18]

14. C. de Visscher, *Théories et réalites en droit international public*, 2d ed. (Paris: Editions A. Pedone, 1955), p. 198. One can only welcome the fact that in the latest edition of this book the author refers not to a "weakening of the unity of the traditional legal community" but to a "weakening of the traditional unity of the international community." *Théories et réalites en droit international public*, 4th ed. (Paris: Editions A. Pedone, 1970), p. 178. This, of course, corresponds to reality.

15. A. V. Freeman, "Professor McDougal's *Law and Minimum World Public Order*," *American Journal of International Law*, LVIII (1964), 712.

16. J. J. G. Syatauw, *Some Newly Established Asian States and the Development of International Law* (The Hague: Martinus Nijhoff, 1961), p. 21.

17. A. Verdross, *Mezhdunarodnoe pravo*, trans. from 3d ed. by F. A. Kublitskii and R. L. Naryshkina, ed. G. I. Tunkin (Moscow: izd-vo IL, 1959), p. 67.

18. *Ibid.*; on the unfoundedness of analogous views of western jurists, see N. Singh, *India and International Law* (New Delhi, 1969).

Verdross nonetheless refrained from accepting the concept of the "breakup" and "degradation" of international law. He said that all states recognize international law and, since it "derives from universally human values in the ethical nature of man, we may hope that these values will be generally accepted in the near future."[19]

In the latest edition of his treatise on international law, Verdross still expresses no doubts and emphasizes the importance of the cooperation of all states for the progressive development of international law.[20]

The concept that the basis of law is community, particularly a common ideology, is completely unfounded. Proponents of this concept frequently point out that in the absence of a specific community between people, the existence of law in general and of international law in particular is impossible. Of course, in the absence of a specific community between people, the existence of human society, and consequently of law, is inconceivable, but it still does not follow that this community is the reason for the formation of law or is reflected in law. The history of human society shows completely the opposite: in a pre-class society, where this community between people was more significant, there was no law: only with the emergence of class contradictions, with the destruction of the tribal community, does law emerge.

Law, including international law, emerged not as a result of an increase in community among people, but as a result of the division of society into classes and the formation of new class contradictions unknown to tribal society. International law, just as municipal law, is a phenomenon peculiar to a class society.

The theoretical unfoundedness of the concept of a common ideology as a necessary condition for the existence and development of international law does not make this concept less dangerous.

Of course, as has been noted previously, among the proponents of this concept are people of various political orientations. The most reactionary of these (Dulles, Smith, Kordt, Asbeck, and others) assert that the Soviet Union and socialist ideology, whose content they distort beyond all recognition, are guilty of everything. The majority of those who accept this concept simply state the fact of a deep ideological conflict and draw, proceeding from the thesis that a common ideology is the basis of law, the corresponding theoretical, and sometimes practical, conclusions.

What are these practical conclusions?

Professor P. Jessup sees a withdrawal toward creating a "selective community," by which he means the so-called "free world," and he

19. Verdross, *Mezhdunarodnoe pravo*, pp. 67-68.
20. A. Verdross, *Völkerrecht*, 5th ed. (Vienna: Springer Verlag, 1964), pp. 83-94.

appeals for the creation and development of a regional international law of the "free world."[2] [1]

Professor J. Kunz believes that "profound ideological differences are leading to the concluding of regional alliances."[2] [2]

Professor F. Asbeck, in asserting that ideological differences preclude the creation of a common world legal order, writes: "Let us then work all the more strenuously to achieve a real regional legal order."[2] [3]

The danger of this concept consists in the fact that the practical conclusions which are derived therefrom correspond to the political credo of the most reactionary circles of the imperialist powers. In reality, even putting to one side the aspersions relating to the foreign policy of the Soviet Union disseminated by the most reactionary adherents of this concept, the conclusion itself of the impossibility of agreement between capitalist and socialist states by virtue of the ideological differences existing between them plays into the hands of advocates of the policy "from a position of strength." As is well-known, the champions of this policy attempt to justify their assertions that agreements among capitalist and socialist states are impossible, that such agreements are of little value, and that in relations with the socialist countries one supposedly can only rely upon force. The former United States Secretary of State, John Foster Dulles, declared, for example, at a news conference on October 16, 1957: "An agreement is a meeting of the minds, and so far I do not know of any agreement that the Soviet Union has made which has reflected a real meeting of the minds. We may have agreed on the same form of words, but there has not been a meeting of the minds."[2] [4]

The aforesaid by no means signifies that ideological differences have no importance for the development of international law. But everything depends upon how concretely the question of ideology is raised.

Many international lawyers approach the question formalistically of whether the emergence of socialist states, as well as of new states created in consequence of the liberation of the colonies, has led to a limitation of the developmental base of general international law. They frequently point out that the Soviet Union did not recognize all norms of general international law prevailing at the time it emerged. However, in this connection the most important fact is lost sight of—that the Soviet Union refused to accept only reactionary norms of international law.

The Soviet state collided with the international law existing at the time

21. P. Jessup, *The Use of International Law* (Ann Arbor: University of Michigan Law School, 1959), pp. 29, 153.

22. Kunz, "La crise et les transformations du droit des gens," p. 15.

23. Asbeck, "Growth and Movement of International Law," p. 1071.

24. *The Department of State Bulletin*, XXXVII (1957), 711-712.

of its formation, which, together with democratic principles and norms aimed at ensuring friendly relations among states (the principle of respect for state sovereignty, the principle of equality, the principle of noninterference, and others), contained reactionary principles and norms that reflected and strengthened the system of national oppression, colonial plundering, and imperialist robbery (colonies, protectorates, unequal treaties, spheres of influence, consular jurisdiction, and so forth).

The international legal position of the Soviet state had already been formulated by V. I. Lenin on the day after the Revolution. In concluding the Report on Peace of November 8, 1917, Lenin said: "The secret treaties must be published. The provisions concerning annexations and contributions must be abrogated. There are various provisions, comrades— why the predatory governments not only agreed about the plunderings, but amidst such agreements they also accommodated economic agreements and various other provisions concerning good-neighborly relations . . . We reject all provisions regarding plunder and coercion but all provisions where good-neighborly terms and economic agreements have been concluded we heartily welcome, we can not reject these."[2][5]

The statement of the Soviet state opposing reactionary institutes of international law commenced its being cleared of harmful weeds which "justified" oppression and inequality in international relations. At the same time, the Soviet country accepted all generally-recognized democratic provisions of the then-existing international law (and, above all, such principles as respect for state sovereignty, equality, noninterference in internal affairs) and was strictly guided by these in its relations with other states. Moreover, it promoted in every possible way the deepening and the development of the content of these principles.

It should be mentioned that previously the said principles and norms of international law were operative essentially only in relations among "civilized," or "Christian" countries. Almost all of Africa and a significant portion of Asia had colonial status. But even in relations with independent states of Asia and Africa, the colonial powers did not consider themselves bound by the principles and norms of international law, flagrantly flouting the sovereignty of these states, brazenly interfering in their internal affairs, rejecting with disdain the idea of complete equality of the eastern and western countries as subjects of international law.

The young Soviet state was then the only country which favored the complete application of the democratic principles of international law to all states, for true equality. In the Decree of the Council of People's

25. V. I. Lenin, "Zakliuchitel'noe slovo po dokladu o mire 26 oktiabria (8 noiabria)," *Polnoe sobranie sochinenii*, 5th ed. (Moscow: Gospolitizdat, 1962), XXXV, 20.

Commissars of the RSFSR of June 4, 1918, for example, it was said: "The Russian Socialist Federated Soviet Republic proceeds in its international relations from recognizing the full equality of large and small nations." It is further pointed out in the Decree that "in conformity with the basic idea of international law—as a community of equal states—to consider as identical plenipotentiary representatives all diplomatic agents of foreign states accredited to the Russian Socialist Federated Soviet Republic, irrespective of their rank."[26]

It is correct that with the emergence of the Soviet state certain norms of the then existing norms of general international law rejected by the Soviet state ceased to be norms of general international law. But it is very important to add in this connection that the contraction of general international law occurred at the expense of reactionary norms.

There is, however, another aspect to this problem, which bourgeois international lawyers usually lose sight of. The Soviet Union, and now the other socialist states as well, tirelessly struggle for the introduction of new progressive principles and norms into international law so that it becomes a more effective means of strengthening international peace and developing friendly relations among states on the basis of equality and self-determination of peoples.

Proceeding therefrom, the Soviet Union and the other socialist countries favor the progressive development of international law and its strict observance by all states.[27] At the initiative of the socialist states, for example, as well as a number of Asian and African states, despite the opposition of western powers, important resolutions defining the basic orientation of United Nations activity in the progressive development and codification of international law were adopted at sessions of the United Nations General Assembly.

It had been pointed out in a resolution of the Fifteenth Session of the United Nations General Assembly[28] that work on the codification and progressive development of international law should promote "the establishment of friendly relations and cooperation among states." A resolution of the Sixteenth Session of the United Nations General Assembly emphasized even more distinctly the "important role of codification and progressive development of international law with a view to making international law a more effective means of furthering the purposes and

26. Ministerstvo inostrannykh del SSSR, *Dokumenty vneshnei politiki SSSR* (Moscow: Gospolitizdat, 1957–), I, 345-346.

27. See A. P. Movchan, *Kodifikatsiia i progressivnoe razvitie mezhdunarodnogo prava* (Moscow: izd-vo Iuridicheskaia literatura, 1972).

28. G.A. Res. 1505 (XV), December 12, 1960.

principles set forth in Articles 1 and 2 of the Charter of the United Nations."[29] This same resolution provided that the Sixth Committee of the General Assembly be called upon to work out the fundamental principles of contemporary international law.

The position of the Soviet Union and the other socialist states on questions of the progressive development and codification of international law in the United Nations General Assembly, in the International Law Commission, the Commission on Human Rights, and at international conferences convincingly shows that the Soviet Union and the other socialist countries are striving tirelessly to perfect international law as an instrument of peace and international cooperation.

New states which have arisen in consequence of liberation of the colonies now represent a great force in developing international law. It suffices to point out that they comprise more than half the members of the United Nations and specialized agencies and the majority of participants in general diplomatic conferences concerning the codification and development of international law. It is completely natural that the international legal position of these states attracts great attention.

From the concept that the basis of law, including international law, is a common ideology, it follows that the emergence of a large number of new states in the international arena whose cultural heritage undoubtedly is distinct from "western civilization" leads to a contraction of the developmental base of contemporary general international law. This conclusion is rarely expressed openly and expressly, but it inevitably arises out of the said concept.

In this case, however, this conclusion is groundless. The attitude of new states toward international law is defined first and foremost by the fact that they did not participate directly in its creation and that the principles and norms of international law were in their time frequently a means of enslaving and exploiting peoples of these countries. Their position, which coincides a great deal with the position of the Soviet state and which consists in the fact that they do not consider themselves automatically bound by principles and norms of international law only because such principles have been accepted as generally binding by existing states, is, therefore, wholly justified and, as we have seen above, a lawful one.

As the Indian member of the International Law Commission, R. Pal, correctly stated: "International law is no longer the almost exclusive preserve of peoples of European blood, 'by whose consent it exists and for the settlement of whose differences it is applied or at least invoked.' Now

29. G.A. Res. 1686 (XVI), December 18, 1961.

that international law must be regarded as embracing other peoples, it clearly required their consent no less . . . "[30]

The new states declare that they reject all provisions relating to colonial seizures, colonial domination, and racial inequality, the doctrine of acquired rights, unequal treaties, the western doctrine of succession to international treaties, provisions concerning responsibility for harm caused to aliens, protection of foreign citizens, and others.

Since the time of its formation, the Soviet state has consistently opposed these and other reactionary provisions of the old international law. As Abi-Saab correctly notes, "one should not underestimate the impact of this position of the Soviet state upon the attitude toward international law of states which have emerged as a result of colonial liberation."[31]

Before a large group of new states had come into being, these and other reactionary principles and norms of international law had, as a result of the struggle of the Soviet Union and later of the other socialist countries, as well as of emergent new states of all progressive forces, already ceased to exist if they were principles and norms of general international law binding upon all states.

While frequently opposing the said provisions, official and unofficial representatives of the new states take them almost for norms of prevailing international law, not taking into account the fact that everything already had been done to liquidate these provisions of international law before their emergence into the international arena. The representatives of new states thereby unwittingly assume the position of western jurists, who all are still attempting to claim these provisions are prevailing international law, and weaken the position of all those who are struggling to completely purge international law of reactionary survivals.

Just as the young Soviet state, the new states do not reject international law as a whole. In noting the prudent position of the new states, the Indian author R. P. Anand correctly emphasizes: "This does not, however, mean that the 'new' Asian-African countries are not prepared to accept

30. United Nations, *Yearbook of the International Law Commission 1957* (New York: United Nations, 1958), I, 158; also see R. P. Anand, "Attitude of the Asian-African States Toward Certain Problems of International Law," *International and Comparative Law Quarterly*, XV (1966), 63; H. Bokor-Szegó, "The New States and International Law," *Questions of International Law* (Budapest: Hungarian Lawyers' Association, 1968), p. 22.

31. See G. M. Abi-Saab, "The Newly Independent States and the Rules of International Law," *Howard Law Journal*, VIII (1962), 101. [The editor is unable to locate a phrase in this publication which corresponds to that cited by Professor Tunkin. However, Abi-Saab does remark in this connection on p. 101 that: "The influence of the earlier example of the Soviet Union can not be minimized."]

the whole body of present international law. International law has in fact come to be accepted by these countries except where it is still found to support past colonial rights or is clearly inequitable by the present standards of civilization."[3][2]

In the majority of cases the new states favor, together with the socialist countries, the progressive development of international law, manifesting an interest, naturally, in the development first and foremost of those areas of international law which in their view are especially important for economic, technological, and cultural development and protecting their newly gained independence. Thus, the new states display great activity in questions of international law connected with the struggle against colonialism and neocolonialism, the elimination of racial discrimination, sovereignty over natural resources, economic development, international trade, and others.[3][3]

At the same time, they also are very active in questions of international law relating to problems of maintaining international peace and security, disarmament, the prohibition of nuclear weapons, the creation of nuclear free zones, and so forth. They resolutely supported the proposal of the socialist countries concerning the codification of the basic principles of contemporary international law, which grants to new states a highly exceptional opportunity to participate in the general work of reviewing and developing the basic provisions of contemporary general international law. Thus, for example, the 1964 Declaration of the Cairo Conference of Heads of States and Governments of Non-Aligned Countries points out that "The Conference recommends that the United Nations General Assembly adopt in connection with its twentieth anniversary, a declaration on the principles of peaceful coexistence. Such a declaration would be an important step on the path toward preparing a code of such principles."

These states, which previously not only had no opportunity to take part in creating norms of international law but with regard to whom international law was an instrument of suppression, now are making a valuable contribution to the cause of the progressive development of international law.

Thus, the emergence of the socialist states and the formation of the

32. R. P. Anand, "Role of the 'New' Asian-African Countries in the Present International Legal Order," *American Journal of International Law*, LVI (1962), 388; also see Abi-Saab, "The Newly Independent States and the Rules of International Law," p. 106; M. Sahovic, "Influence des états nouveau sur la conception du droit international," *Annuaire français de droit international*, XII (1966), 30-49; Bokor-Szegó, "The New States and International Law," pp. 7-35.

33. See M. A. D'Estefano, *Subdesarollo y derecho internacional publico* (Havana: Editorial Pueblo y Educacion, 1973).

world system of socialism and the appearance in the international arena of new Asian and African states are by no means leading either to a split of general international law or to a contraction of its developmental base. On the contrary, the growth of the forces of peace supporting international law as a means of ensuring peace signifies that the developmental base of general international law is expanding and growing in strength.

Graphic evidence of this is the immeasurably higher rate of the progressive development of international law in our day in comparison with that, for example, of the League of Nations period. Suffice it to point out that only one conference for the codification of international law (1930) was convened in the period between the First and Second World Wars, and that ended in failure. In the years following the Second World War, numerous broad international conferences, as well as international organizations, have adopted a number of international conventions which frequently embrace entire branches of international law (the 1958 Geneva Conventions on the Law of the Sea, the 1961 Vienna Convention on Diplomatic Relations, the 1963 Vienna Convention on Consular Relations, the 1967 Treaty on Principles of Activities of States in Outer Space, the 1969 Vienna Convention on the Law of Treaties, the Treaty on Non-Proliferation of Nuclear Weapons, the Treaty on the Prohibition of the Emplacement of Nuclear Weapons and Other Weapons of Mass Destruction on the Sea-Bed and the Ocean Floor and the Subsoil Thereof, the Convention on the Prohibition of the Development, Production, and Stockpiling of Bacteriological [Biological] and Toxin Weapons and Their Destruction, and others).

The Soviet doctrine of international law has proceeded and does proceed from the fact that general international law, whose norms regulate relations among all states irrespective of their social systems, exists and the possibilities of its further development are increasing with the growth of the forces of peace.

International lawyers in other countries of the socialist camp also support the development and strengthening of general international law.

The attempts of some bourgeois international lawyers to ascribe to the Soviet state or to Soviet international legal science the concept of the rejection of general international law[34] is explainable in the majority of

34. See, for example, H. Kelsen, *The Communist Theory of Law* (New York: Frederick A. Praeger, 1955), p. 156; W. W. Kulski, "Les tendances contemporaines dans le droit international soviétique," *Revue de droit international de sciences diplomatiques et politiques*, XXXI (1953), 272; A. Ulloa, *Derecho internacional publico*, 4th ed. (Madrid: Ediciones iberoamericanas, 1957), I, 18-19; W. L. Gould, *An Introduction to International Law* (New York: Harper, [1957]), p. 92.

instances by an insufficient knowledge of the facts, and sometimes by their deliberate distortion.[35]

This does not mean, of course, that there are no serious obstacles in the path of developing contemporary general international law. Such obstacles exist, but they derive not from the socialist states or other states adhering to the principles of peaceful coexistence. They are created by those states and those social forces which pursue the policy "from a position of strength," the policy of an arms race and the preparation of a new war.

B. Peaceful Coexistence of States with Different Social Systems and General International Law

The Leninist teaching on the peaceful coexistence of socialist and capitalist states has been further developed in documents of the Communist party of the Soviet Union and of the Soviet government, in the practical policy of the Soviet state. A detailed characterization of peaceful coexistence has been given in the Program of the CPSU. *"Peaceful coexistence,"* says the Program of the CPSU, "presupposes: renunciation of war as a means of deciding questions in dispute among states, settling them by negotiations; equality, mutual understanding, and trust among

35. A Canadian professor, E. McWhinney, maintains in a recent article, for example, that some time ago Soviet jurists, and especially Professor E. A. Korovin, "evidently were disposed to cast aside all norms of international law . . . which existed before 1917." The author goes on to assert that changes have occurred in the Soviet doctrine of international law since Tunkin "publicly recognizes" the "old democratic principles of international law." E. McWhinney, "Le 'nouveau' droit international et la 'nouvelle' communauté mondiale," *Revue générale de droit international public*, LXXII (1968), 326. The fact is, as I noted in 1956, the Soviet state, as well as the Soviet doctrine of international law, despite individual unfortunate utterances of some Soviet international lawyers, always has recognized the existence of general international law and the presence therein of customary norms. See G. I. Tunkin, "Mirnoe sosushchestvovanie i mezhdunarodnoe pravo," *Sovetskoe gosudarstvo i pravo*, no. 7 (1956), pp. 5-6; see also Tunkin, "Coexistence and International Law," *Recueil des cours*, XCV (1958), 59-60; Tunkin, *Ideologicheskaia bor'ba i mezhdunarodnoe pravo* (Moscow: izd-vo Mezhdunarodnye otnosheniia, 1967). In 1925-1926 E. Pashukanis defined international law in the "technical juridical" sense as the "aggregate of norms regulating relations between states." E. B. Pashukanis, "Mezhdunarodnoe pravo," *Entsiklopediia gosudarstva i prava* (Moscow: izd. Kommunisticheskoi Akademii, 1925-26), II, col. 857. With respect to sources of international law, Pashukanis wrote: "Since states have no higher authority above them which would establish norms of conduct for them, the sources of international law in the technical juridical sense of the word are custom and treaty." *Ibid.*, col. 873.

states, having regard to each other's interests; noninterference in internal affairs, recognizing for every people the right independently to decide all questions of their own country; strict respect for the sovereignty and territorial integrity of all countries; the development of economic and cultural cooperation on the basis of complete equality and mutual advantage."[36]

Peaceful coexistence is not some sort of idealistic concept, divorced from reality; it reflects the laws of relations among socialist and capitalist states.

Relations among states always have been characterized by a struggle among them. The roots of this struggle, which had a varying degree of intensity, are found in the class contradictions of society.

Earlier in history, relations took place among states with different social systems, but these always were relations among states based on private ownership and the exploitation of man by man (for example, relations among bourgeois and feudal states of the eighteenth century). With the emergence of the Soviet socialist state, and thereafter the entire system of socialist states, relations arose among states not only with different but with diametrically opposed social systems: with the old capitalist states, whose social system is characterized by the existence of private ownership of the means of production and the exploitation of man by man, and new socialist states, whose social system is based upon social ownership and the elimination of exploitation of man by man. There had never been such international relations in the history of mankind.

If earlier, when nonopposed class states existed, the struggle among them was a law of international relations, this law was all the more peculiar to our epoch, when class-opposed states exist. In the contemporary world system of international relations, relations among states with opposed economic and social systems are the most acute and dangerous for mankind.

The concept of peaceful coexistence is based on and reflects this law. "Peaceful coexistence," says the Program of the CPSU, "serves as the basis of peaceful competition between socialism and capitalism on an international scale and is a specific form of class struggle between them."

Of course, states, not classes, enter into international relations; international relations are relations among states. But the foreign policy of states is determined by the predominant classes in these states; this is class policy. Therefore the struggle of the two systems, socialist and capitalist, affects relations among socialist and capitalist states.

Thus, the specific feature of this "class struggle" consists, first and

36. *Programma Kommunisticheskoi partii Sovetskogo Soiuza*, p. 59.

foremost, in the fact that this struggle manifests itself in relations among states, and not directly between classes.

At the same time, the concept of peaceful coexistence does not allow every means of struggle among states; it precludes armed struggle and permits only peaceful competition among them. Consequently, reflecting the true inevitability of struggle among states of the two systems, the concept of peaceful coexistence includes this struggle. But struggle does not preclude cooperation. In reality, struggle and cooperation exist simultaneously in relations among states of the two systems and in international relations in general; cooperation has been permeated by struggle. The intensity of struggle and the degree of cooperation differ in relations among various and between one and the same states on various questions and at various times.

In defining the position of the CPSU on this question, the Secretary General of the Central Committee of the CPSU, L. I. Brezhnev, stated in one of his recent speeches: "The CPSU has proceeded and is proceeding from the fact that class struggle of the two systems—capitalist and socialist—in the sphere of economics, politics, and, of course, ideology will continue. It could not be otherwise, for the worldview and class objectives of socialism and capitalism are opposed and irreconcilable. But we shall strive so that this historically inevitable struggle follows a course not threatened by wars, dangerous conflicts, or an uncontrolled arms race. This will be an enormous gain for the cause of peace throughout the world and for the interests of all peoples and all states."[37]

Historical experience has shown the correctness of the Leninist thesis that economic competition is the decisive domain of struggle of states of the two systems during peaceful coexistence. In ensuring a higher tempo of economic development, a steady rise in the material prosperity of the people, the socialist states in fact are proving the correctness of Marx's theory, according to which the transformation of private ownership, the liquidation of the power of monopolies, the elimination of the exploitation of man by man, and the creation of a socialist society is dictated not only by the requirements of social justice, but also by the need to ensure the future progress of human society. At the same time, side by side with economic competition of the two systems, there occurs economic cooperation of socialist and capitalist states on the basis of mutual advantage.

The concept of peaceful coexistence includes political struggle between states of the two opposed social systems. This struggle is not only inevitable and natural, but without it the concept of peaceful coexistence

37. L. I. Brezhnev, *O piatidesiatiletii Soiuza sovetskikh sotsialisticheskikh respublik* (Moscow: Politizdat, 1973), pp. 42-43.

itself would be a wish that is out of touch with reality. A struggle of all the forces of peace against the forces of aggression and war is necessary to prevent war and to ensure peaceful coexistence in contemporary conditions. The policy of the Soviet Union and the fraternal socialist countries, therefore, is aimed at the "unity of all anti-imperialist peace-loving forces, the struggle against the forces of reaction and war."[38]

Side by side with this there is a wide field for cooperation of states of the two systems not only on economic, but also on political questions. The principal examples of such cooperation are the creation of the United Nations, the 1947 peace treaties, the 1954 Geneva agreements on Indochina, the 1962 agreement on the neutrality of Laos, the 1963 Moscow treaty on the prohibition of nuclear tests in three spheres, the 1967 treaty on the principles of activities of states in outer space, the 1968 treaty on the nonproliferation of nuclear weapons, and the numerous Soviet-American agreements concluded in 1972-1973.

A recent and very important example of peaceful coexistence in action, an example of the possibility of agreements between states with different socioeconomic systems upon important and, perhaps, at first glance seemingly insoluble international problems, are the treaties between the USSR and the Federal Republic of Germany and between the People's Republic of Poland and the Federal Republic of Germany in 1970, and the agreement between the USSR, United States, England, and France on questions relating to West Berlin of September 3, 1971.

Peaceful coexistence of socialist and capitalist states does not and can not mean cessation of the ideological struggle between them. "In the contemporary world," says a Decree of the Central Committee of the Communist Party of the Soviet Union published on August 10, 1968, "a sharp struggle of the two ideologies—socialist and capitalist—is in progress, a struggle reflecting the incompatibility of the class positions of the proletariat and bourgeoisie, of socialism and capitalism."[39] A specific feature of this form of struggle is the fact that compromises and agreements here are impossible.

Peaceful coexistence is applicable only to relations among states. It does not mean class struggle in individual countries or the struggle of colonial peoples for their independence. Class struggle within a state is an internal affair and can not be regulated by international law. As regards the national liberation movements in colonies, contemporary international law, the most important principles of which are the principles of equality

38. "Tezisy TsK KPSS '50 let Velikoi Oktiabr'skoi sotsialisticheskoi revoliutsii,' " *Pravda*, June 25, 1967, p. 4.

39. Decree of the Central Committee of the CPSU, "O podgotovke k 100-letiiu so dnia rozhdeniia Vladimira Il'icha Lenina," *Pravda*, August 10, 1968, p. 1.

and self-determination of peoples, affirms the right of these peoples to use any means, including military, in the struggle for independence which is being denied to them. The Current Report of the Central Committee of the Communist Party of the Soviet Union to the Twenty-third Congress said in this regard: "Of course, there can not be peaceful coexistence where the question is one of the internal processes of a class or national liberation struggle in capitalist countries or in colonies. The principle of peaceful coexistence is inapplicable to relations between the oppressors and the oppressed, between the colonizers and the victims of colonial oppression."[40]

The primary element of peaceful coexistence consists in the fact that, despite the very sharp struggle between states with opposed social systems, it precludes armed conflicts and ensures peace and the development of cooperation among them in the interests of strengthening world peace. The question is whether in the epoch of transition from capitalism to socialism, the greatest and, as all great upheavals, very painful upheaval underway in society will proceed without international armed conflicts (internal conflicts are inevitable).

Such an understanding of peaceful coexistence reflects objective reality and does not in the least testify to the Soviet Union's reluctance to cooperate with capitalist states. The Current Report of the Central Committee of the Communist Party of the Soviet Union to the Twenty-third Congress said: " . . . The Soviet Union, in regarding the coexistence of states with different social systems as a form of class struggle between socialism and capitalism, at the same time consistently favors the maintenance of normal, peaceful relations with capitalist countries, the decision of interstate questions in dispute by negotiations, and not by means of war."[41]

Understanding peaceful coexistence as a specific form of class struggle between socialism and capitalism reflects the immutable laws of societal development in the contemporary stage, which can not be changed or repealed by people.

Excluding armed forms of such struggle—and this is most important—is not yet a reflection of such laws. This part of peaceful coexistence is a necessity and a possibility for whose realization one must struggle. This element of the concept of peaceful coexistence also is not a mere wish or appeal, but is based on specific trends and laws of societal development.[42]

40. *Materialy XXIII s"ezda KPSS* (Moscow: izd-vo Politicheskoi literatury, 1966), p. 29.
41. *Ibid.*
42. For greater detail, see R. L. Bobrov, *Osnovnye problemy teorii mezhdunarodnogo prava* (Moscow: izd-vo Mezhdunarodnye otnosheniia, 1968), pp. 89-121.

The Program of the CPSU says on this plane: "*Peaceful coexistence* of socialist and capitalist states is an *objective necessity* for the development of human society."[43]

War no longer is a means of settling international disputes, both by its nature and because it has been prohibited by international law. The emergence of terrible means of mass destruction makes the question of the inadmissibility of a thermonuclear world war a question of the existence of human civilization.

The most important element of this objective necessity of peaceful coexistence is the internationalization of economic life. The internationalization of economic life and other aspects of contemporary society is a law of development which decisively influences the expansion and development of international cooperation in various areas, the most convincing evidence of which is the development of international organizations.

Peaceful coexistence also is a real possibility based not only on the said objective factors but also on the growth of social forces which oppose war.

The mightiest power of the modern world, the Soviet Union, is a great factor for peace and peaceful coexistence. The policy of peaceful coexistence arises out of the very essence of the socialist system and is a law thereof. "*The Soviet Union consistently has upheld and will uphold the policy of peaceful coexistence of states with different social systems,*" says the Program of the CPSU.[44] The Twenty-fourth Congress of the CPSU affirmed anew this orientation of the foreign policy of the Soviet Union. The Resolution of the Twenty-fourth Congress on the Report of the Central Committee of the CPSU says: "The Congress charges the Central Committee of the CPSU henceforth to implement consistently the principle of peaceful coexistence, to expand mutually advantageous links with capitalist countries."[45]

This law also is peculiar to the policy of other states of the socialist system which, together with the Soviet Union, favor peaceful coexistence. The absence of private ownership of the instruments and means of production and its replacement by social ownership, the elimination of exploitation of man by man, the transfer of power to the hands of the working people create the necessary basis for the peaceful policy of these states. In the socialist states there are no forces which would have an interest in war. Peoples who always have suffered from war are therefore opposed to war. The aspiration for peace is peculiar to the very nature of

43. *Programma Kommunisticheskoi partii Sovetskogo Soiuza*, p. 59.
44. *Ibid.*, p. 60.
45. *Materialy XXIV s"ezda KPSS* (Moscow: Politizdat, 1971), p. 196.

socialist states as states which reflect the interests and expectations of peoples. "The Leninist principle of peaceful coexistence and economic competition of socialist countries with capitalist countries is the firm basis of the foreign policy of the socialist countries," says the Statement of the Meeting of Representatives of Communist and Workers' Parties held in 1960.[46]

The breakup of the colonial system and the formation of independent states which, as a rule, are for peace, oppose imperialism, and uphold the policy of peaceful coexistence have the greatest significance for developing and strengthening peaceful coexistence. Relations of sincere friendship, reflecting a coincidence of the vital interests of the peoples of these two groups of states, have been formed and are developing among the socialist countries and these new states. *"The unity of effort of the peoples of countries which have been liberated and the peoples of socialist states in the struggle against the danger of war is the greatest factor for universal peace,"* says the Program of the CPSU.[47]

A broad zone of peace has been created in which, side by side with socialist states, there are a significant number of nonsocialist states which are not interested, for various reasons, in an unleashing of war.

The popular masses, whose opportunities actively to intervene in deciding international questions have grown immeasurably, are becoming an ever more powerful force of peaceful coexistence.[48] The international working class—the most consistent fighter against imperialist wars—is the great organizing force of the all-people's struggle for peace, against war. The all-people's movement for peace is the greatest factor for peaceful coexistence.[49]

Together with the unprecedented growth of the forces of peace there has occurred a sharp, comprehensive weakening of capitalism and an aggravation of its general crisis. The essence of imperialism, its aggressive nature, of course, has not changed. Therefore, while imperialism remains, the danger of aggressive wars will remain, but a world war would be the ruin of imperialism. At the same time, the possibilities of imperialism have contracted sharply, as the aggressive war of American imperialists in Vietnam testifies in particular. For several years the greatest imperialist

46. *Programmnye dokumenty bor'by za mir, demokratiiu i sotsializm* (Moscow: Gospolitizdat, 1961), p. 60.

47. *Programma Kommunisticheskoi partii Sovetskogo Soiuza*, p. 50.

48. Professor R. L. Bobrov is wholly correct in emphasizing that there exists an "interest in preserving peace unreservedly common to the working people of both socioeconomic systems . . . " Bobrov, *Osnovnye problemy teorii mezhdunarodnogo prava*, p. 166.

49. For greater detail, see V. M. Chkhikvadze, *Bor'ba za mir—neodolimoe dvizhenie sovremennosti* (Moscow: izd-vo Mysl', 1969).

power has not been in a position to subdue the opposition of the Vietnamese people fighting for their independence, whose just cause enjoys the support of the socialist countries and progressive mankind as a whole.

Proceeding from the new co-relation of forces in the world arena and the prospects for its development, the Program of the CPSU draws the following conclusion: "The unified efforts of the mighty socialist camp, of peace-loving nonsocialist states, of the international working class, and of all forces upholding the cause of peace *can avert a world war.* The growing preponderance of the forces of socialism over the forces of imperialism, the forces of peace over the forces of war, is leading to the fact that even before the complete victory of socialism on earth, while capitalism remains in part of the world, a real possibility is arising of excluding world war from the life of society. The victory of socialism throughout the entire world finally will eliminate the social and national causes of the origins of all wars. *To eliminate wars, to maintain eternal peace on earth, is the historic mission of communism.*"[50]

Peaceful coexistence of socialist and capitalist states is the only reasonable policy and state of relations between them, since it creates the greatest possibilities in contemporary conditions for guaranteeing the prevention of a world war and the best means of promoting the progress of human society. Such progress in our epoch is bound up with the transition of society to socialism and communism. This transition, dictated by the laws of societal development, is a most profound social revolution on a world scale, being formed from social upheavals in individual countries. Peaceful coexistence is directed first and foremost toward the fact that the transition from capitalism to socialism should not give rise to international armed conflicts. Communists openly declare that they do not renounce the struggle to restructure society, that peaceful coexistence, in promoting progress, promotes the victory of socialism, but they see in peaceful coexistence one of the possibilities of ensuring the most painless transition of society from capitalism to socialism. Therefore, the Program of the CPSU says: "Consistently pursuing the line of peaceful coexistence, the socialist countries are striving for the continued strengthening of the position of the world socialist system in its competition with capitalism. More favorable possibilities for the struggle of the working class of capitalist countries are created in conditions of peaceful coexistence, and the struggle of peoples of colonial and dependent countries for their liberation is facilitated. Supporting the principle of peaceful coexistence also is responsive to the interests of that part of the bourgeoisie which understands that thermonuclear war also does not spare the ruling

50. *Programma Kommunisticheskoi partii Sovetskogo Soiuza,* p. 58.

classes of capitalist society. The policy of peaceful coexistence is responsive to the basic interests of all mankind, except for the bosses of large
monopolies and the militarists."[5][1]

Opponents of peaceful coexistence are distorting the views of our
party, asserting that the doctrine of Marxism-Leninism has nothing in
common with peaceful coexistence, that the slogan "peaceful coexistence" is a temporary tactical maneuver of communists, and such. An
American senator, William Knowland, declared in the United States
Senate: "It is my belief that the Soviet Union is advancing the Trojan
horse of coexistence only for the purpose of gaining sufficient time to
accomplish . . . atomic stalemate."[5][2] The West German Chancellor, Kon-
rad Adenauer, speaking in 1956 at Yale University, declared that for the
Soviet Union peaceful coexistence is "only a new tactical phase in
weakening the bonds of the free world." The Deputy Permanent Representative of the United States at the United Nations asserted that
"communist doctrine" precludes "countries with different social systems
from living in peace with one another" and does not correspond to
peaceful coexistence.[5][3]

The opponents of peaceful coexistence most often attempt to represent
the concept of peaceful coexistence advanced by the Soviet Union as
consisting of the absence of war, as being the parallel existence of states of
two opposed social systems excluding cooperation between them.

Thus, a committee of the American Branch of the International Law
Association states that it opposes "peaceful coexistence" because this term
signifies "a struggle for power rather than cooperation."[5][4] The Chief
Legal Advisor of the English Foreign Office, F. Vallat, in his lecture at the
University of London in January 1962 declared that, according to the
Soviet point of view, " . . . peaceful coexistence is not the same as
anything expressed in the Charter of the United Nations and does not
mean friendly co-operation and mutual respect between the Soviet
Socialist and other systems of government."[5][5] Professor John Hazard, of
Columbia University, alleges that the Marxist concept of peaceful coexist-
ence presupposes only the "maintenance of peace between the two

51. *Ibid.*, pp. 59-60.

52. *United States News and World Report*, November 26, 1954, p. 74.

53. Plimpton, in the Sixth Committee, United Nations General Assembly (XVI),
Official Records, p. 161 (December 1, 1961).

54. *Proceedings and Committee Reports of the American Branch of the International Law Association 1961-1962* (New York: New York University Law Center,
1962), p. 72.

55. F. Vallat, "International Law—A Forward Look," *Yearbook of World Affairs*,
XVIII (1964), 251.

opposed systems" and therefore non-Marxists prefer the term "cooperation."[56]

Frequently there also are cases when peaceful coexistence is presented as a "balance of terror." Thus, Professor Hans Morgenthau writes in one of his recent works that taking into consideration the saturation of nuclear weapons, a conflict of the two superpowers would have catastrophic consequences. "As a result of this," he writes, "they have decided that they should avoid a direct confrontation. Herein lies the true political and military meaning of the slogan 'peaceful coexistence.' "[57]

Such an interpretation of the concept of peaceful coexistence has nothing in common with its basic idea, with that understanding of peaceful coexistence for which not only the socialist, but also all other states striving to strengthen international peace and to develop international cooperation are struggling.

As already has been pointed out, peaceful coexistence means both cooperation and struggle. The assertion that peaceful coexistence supposedly does not include the cooperation of states has nothing in common with reality. Suffice it to note that the Program of the CPSU says that peaceful coexistence presupposes "mutual understanding and trust among states" and the "development of economic and cultural cooperation on the basis of complete equality and mutual advantage."[58]

Peaceful coexistence is understood by the Soviet state as something more than peace and the absence of war, although peace and refraining from settling questions in dispute with the aid of war are the primary elements in the concept of peaceful coexistence.

In this connection one must note the completely unfounded and artificial contrast of "peaceful coexistence" and "active peaceful coexistence" which certain Yugoslav international lawyers allow. They assert that "active peaceful coexistence" should be distinguished from "peaceful coexistence," which includes cooperation between states and therefore is a higher level of "peaceful existence."

In a report on the topic "The Juridical Aspects of Active Peaceful Coexistence Among States" submitted in 1956 to a conference of the International Law Association, a Yugoslav professor, M. Bartos, asserted that two types of peaceful coexistence exist: passive coexistence and

56. J. Hazard, "Codifying Peaceful Coexistence," *American Journal of International Law*, LV (1961), 111-112; see also the speeches in the Sixth Committee of the U. N. General Assembly of the Belgian (November 8, 1963) and the Canadian (November 20, 1963) representatives.

57. H. Morgenthau, *A New Foreign Policy for the United States* (New York: Frederick A. Praeger, 1969), p. 119.

58. *Programma Kommunisticheskoi partii Sovetskogo Soiuza*, p. 59.

active coexistence.[59] In his view, "passive peaceful coexistence" is reflected in the fact that a state is bound not to violate the rights of another, not to resort to force nor to the threat of force in its relations with other states. "Such coexistence," Bartos says, "is peaceful because the use of force is prohibited; it is passive because it is reflected in refraining from actions prohibited by the U.N. Charter which could harm other states."[60]

In Bartos's opinion, "active peaceful coexistence" consists in the fact that "each state should develop its own activity in the international community, participate in the organization and improvement of this community, develop its activity with the guarantee that it will not be the object of aggression, that its activity will not give rise to obstacles, and that means which could breach the peace or create a threat to peace will not be used against it."[61]

Bartos says, in concluding, that "Coexistence is an ancient institute. Peaceful coexistence is a comparatively new institution and depends basically upon the prohibition of resort to war. Active coexistence is an institute which has emerged very recently and depends upon a democratic order in international relations, the principle of equality and of sovereign equality of states, and the right to participate in the affairs of an international organization."[62]

Another Yugoslav jurist, Professor M. Radoikovich, also expresses the same thought when in his memorandum submitted to the Committee on the Juridical Aspects of Coexistence of the International Law Association he wrote: "A very long path has been traversed from 'coexistence' to 'peaceful coexistence' and 'active peaceful coexistence'. . . "[63] In Radoikovich's view, "active peaceful coexistence" presupposes, in comparison with "peaceful coexistence," a "significantly more developed life of international society; that is to say, a significantly greater degree of economic integration of the community of states, organized from both the political and juridical point of view to realize common purposes and especially to maintain peace."[64]

Of course, as a condition of relations among states peaceful coexistence

59. M. Bartos, "Aspect juridique de la coexistence pacifique active entre états," *Report of the Forty-Seventh Conference of the International Law Association* (London, 1957), p. 33.

60. *Ibid.*

61. *Ibid.*, p. 34.

62. *Ibid.*, p. 36.

63. *Report of the Forty-Ninth Conference of the International Law Association* (London, 1961), p. 371.

64. *Ibid.*

is not something fixed once and for all. Peaceful coexistence in one period may significantly differ from peaceful coexistence in another developmental period of international relations, both from the viewpoint of the breadth and depth of cooperation and also with regard to the reliability of peaceful coexistence, and so forth. Peaceful coexistence of the two opposed social systems in our days differs significantly from peaceful coexistence before the Second World War.

Peaceful coexistence between different states also is characterized by a differing degree of cooperation which, as has just been pointed out, in its turn is dynamic.

In principle, however, it is untrue to assert that peaceful coexistence can be "passive" and that it signifies only refraining from violating the rights of another state and from using force against other states. This assertion coincides with the views of bourgeois jurists and politicians previously set forth. In reality, there never has been "passive peaceful coexistence." Peaceful coexistence as passive coexistence characterized only by refraining from actions is inconceivable.

The attempt to create a distinction between "peaceful coexistence" and "active peaceful coexistence" and to contrast one to another distorts the content of the concept "peaceful coexistence" which has been widely recognized both on the part of states and of peoples. Such a contrast brings confusion, by representing "peaceful coexistence" as supposedly inadequate and in contrasting it to the so-called "active peaceful coexistence," which in fact adds nothing new to the concept of peaceful coexistence.[65]

What is the influence of the peaceful coexistence of states of opposed social systems on international law? In considering this problem, one must keep in mind that the question is not one of "interbloc" law,[66] which is nonexistent (of course, there are norms of local international treaties concluded between individual socialist and capitalist states), but of general international law.

Norms of international law are created and are modified in the course of international relations. It is therefore natural that the state of international relations exerts a decisive influence upon the development of

65. In the report of the Committee on the Juridical Aspects of Coexistence of the International Law Association, after a lengthy discussion at the Geneva session of this committee in June 1960, the word "active" was deleted at the insistence of the author of the present work. In a note to the Committee's Report it was pointed out that some members of the committee favored the term "peaceful coexistence" and others suggested the epithet "active" be added, but "all were agreed that the concept of peaceful coexistence includes active cooperation among states." *Ibid.*, p. 365.

66. See E. McWhinney, *"Peaceful Coexistence" and Soviet-Western International Law* (Leiden: A. W. Sijthoff, 1964).

international law. The cooperation and agreement of states—above all, the states with different social systems—is required to create norms of general international law. Moreover, cooperation and agreement among states are the most important elements of the peaceful coexistence of states with different social systems.

The co-relation of international relations and of international law is characterized by the fact that, even though international law influences the development of international relations, the latter exert a basic and decisive influence on the development of international law. Therefore, the influence which peaceful coexistence exerts as a state of international relations upon the development of international law is basic and decisive in the co-relation of peaceful coexistence and international law. The more developed is peaceful coexistence of states with different social systems, the more durable and favorable are the conditions for the progressive development of international law.

Since general international law is now universal, the struggle and cooperation of states on a world-wide scale influences its development. In this world-wide system relations are a reflection of the contradictions which presently exist among economic systems, state structures, legal systems, ideologies, and so forth, of various countries. Obviously, since international relations are not the total amount of relations among states of the two opposed social systems, the contradictions which are present in international relations are not the sum total of the contradictions among socialist and capitalist states.

On the plane of world-wide international relations one often speaks of the peaceful coexistence of states "irrespective of their social system." One should always bear in mind in this connection that relations among socialist countries, united by ties of proletarian solidarity, are built upon the principles of socialist internationalism, and not upon the principles of peaceful coexistence.

The development of contemporary international law must be regarded, consequently, not only on the plane of peaceful coexistence of socialist and capitalist states, but also in the wider aspect of relations among all states. But at the same time one must stress again that peaceful coexistence of states of the two opposed social systems is determinative.

The degree of development of peaceful coexistence has significance first and foremost in the sense of improving the international climate, of promoting the progressive development of international law.

Peaceful coexistence of states with different social systems is, as already has been pointed out, that state of relations between them which is characterized by a more or less significant degree of cooperation and agreement between them on international questions. But the possibility of agreement of states, above all the possibility of agreement of states of two opposed social systems, which does not preclude struggle between them but is born in such struggle, also is the basic condition that is essential for general international law to exist, since its principles and norms are created by agreement between states (see Chapters 8 and 9). Consequently, the possibility of peaceful coexistence of states with different social systems includes the possibility of the existence of general international law. The social forces which act in pursuance of ensuring peaceful coexistence are at the same time forces which promote the development and strengthening of general international law.

The contrast of ideologies and uncompromising ideological struggle are not an insuperable obstacle to creating norms of international law. When states of the two systems reach an agreement relating to recognizing a particular rule as a norm of international law, the question is not one of agreement on ideological problems.[67] There is no need for states to have reached agreement on the nature of international law, its social essence, and so forth. It is important that they can agree with regard to specific principles and norms of international law.

For thousands of years jurists have debated about definitions of law, but notwithstanding this law has existed. States, politicians, and jurists of different countries can hold various theories relating to the nature of international law, but this difference of opinion does not create insuperable obstacles to achieving agreements relating to the acceptance of specific rules of conduct as international legal norms.

The development of international cooperation in the interest of peace, characteristic of peaceful coexistence, promotes the creation of new norms of international law, which is strengthened by the level of international cooperation achieved as well as of norms aimed at further developing and strengthening peaceful coexistence.

The history of international relations since the Great October Socialist Revolution confirms this thesis. The progressive development of international law in general has reflected the development of peaceful coexistence of states of the two opposed social systems.

67. For greater detail, see Tunkin, *Ideologicheskaia bor'ba i mezhdunarodnoe pravo.*

Chapter 3 *Modification of the Fundamental Principles of International Law During the Period of Coexistence of the Two Systems*

If one retraces the development of international law during the period of coexistence of the two opposed social systems, one can not help but note the substantive changes which have occurred in international law. Many reactionary institutes have gone out of fashion; new principles and norms having important significance for ensuring peace and the independence of peoples have emerged; and the old democratic principles and institutes of international law have been developed and strengthened.

These changes, being the result of the struggle of progressive forces against reaction, have affected all branches of international law in varying degrees. They are reflected not only in the changes in principles and norms as such, but also in the changes in the character and essence of international law (see the following chapters).

We limit ourselves in the present chapter to examining the changes in the fundamental principles of contemporary international law, without claiming to treat the question exhaustively.[1]

A. The Emergence of New Principles of International Law

(1) The principle of nonaggression. One of the most important changes in international law during the period of coexistence of the two systems was the emergence of the principle of nonaggression.

1. On the question of the concept of fundamental principles of international law see V. Outrata, "K pojmu obecných a základních zásad mezinárodniho práva," *Časopis pro mezinárodni právo*, no. 3 (1961), pp. 177-191; V. M. Chkhikvadze and others, eds., *Kurs mezhdunarodnogo prava v shesti tomakh* (Moscow: izd-vo Nauka, 1967), II, 5-15; P. A. Steiniger, ed., *Die sieben Prinzipien der friedlichen Koexistenz* (Berlin: Staatsverlag der DDR, 1964); B. Graefrath, *Zur Stellung der Prinzipien im gegen-*

Development of International Law Since the October Socialist Revolution

Before the Great October Socialist Revolution international law had recognized the right of states to go to war (*jus ad bellum*), pursuant to which one state could resort to war against another whenever it considered this advisable. Of course, a particular claim always was found against the state that was attacked in order to justify the aggression, the claims being well-grounded or unfounded.

The principle of nonaggression emerged at first as the prohibition of aggressive war, being transformed later into the principle of the prohibition of the use or threat of force.

The principle of the prohibition of aggressive war entered international law in the period between the First and Second World Wars. Immediately after its emergence, the Soviet state raised the question of prohibiting aggressive war. The Decree on Peace of October 26 (November 8), 1917—the first decree of the Soviet state—solemnly declared that an annexationist war is "the greatest crime against humanity."[2]

This idea met with a warm response in the hearts of not only the peoples of Soviet Russia, but also those far beyond its frontiers.

The consistent struggle of the Soviet Union for peace and the demand of progressive forces to have done with war, which brings enormous casualties and deprivations to peoples, were the principal reasons that led to the prohibition of aggressive war by international law.[3]

The Covenant of the League of Nations did not prohibit aggressive war, although it restricted the right of member states of the League to resort to war and provided for sanctions with regard to members who waged war in breach of the provisions of the Covenant.

In this respect, the Covenant of the League of Nations was a noteworthy step forward in comparison with the Hague conventions of 1899 and 1907 on the peaceful settlement of international disputes, which in fact merely contained an appeal "before recourse to arms" to have recourse "as far as circumstances allow" to good offices or mediation.[4]

---

wärtigen Völkerrecht (Berlin: Akad. Verlag, 1968); G. Geamanu, *Principiile fundamentale ale dreptului international contemporan* (Bucharest: Editura Didactică Si Pedagogică, 1967), pp. 7-35; R. Bierzanek, "Legal Principles of Peaceful Coexistence and Their Codification," *Polish Yearbook of International Law 1966/67*, I (1968), 17-44.

2. Ministerstvo inostrannykh del SSSR, *Dokumenty vneshnei politiki SSSR* (Moscow: Gospolitizdat, 1957—), I, 12.

3. On this question see G. Sharmazanashvili, *Printsip nenapadeniia v mezhdunarodnom prave* (Moscow: izd-vo AN SSSR, 1958); Sharmazanashvili, *Ot prava voiny k pravu mira* (Moscow: izd-vo Mezhdunarodnye otnosheniia, 1967); K. A. Baginian, *Bor'ba Sovetskogo Soiuza protiv agressii* (Moscow: Sotsekgiz, 1959); V. Romanov, *Iskliuchenie voiny iz zhizni obshchestva* (Moscow: Gosiurizdat, 1961); Chkhikvadze, *Kurs mezhdunarodnogo prava*, II, 111-145.

4. L. A. Modzhorian and V. K. Sobakin, comps., *Mezhdunarodnoe pravo v izbrannykh dokumentakh*, ed. V. N. Durdenevskii (Moscow: izd-vo IMO, 1957), II, 248.

The Period of Coexistence of the Two Systems

The draft Treaty on Mutual Assistance adopted by the League of Nations Assembly in 1923 (but which did not move farther) echoed still more distinctly the reasons for the Soviet Decree on Peace. "The High Contracting Parties," said the draft, "solemnly declare that aggressive war is an international crime and severally undertake that no one of them will be guilty of its commission."[5]

Aggressive war also was classified as an "international crime" in the Declaration on Aggressive Wars adopted by the League of Nations Assembly in 1927.

Finally, the Pact of Paris of August 27, 1928, despite certain imperfections in its provisions, contained a prohibition of aggressive war. Article 1 of the Pact provided: "The High Contracting Parties solemnly declare in the names of their respective peoples that they condemn recourse to war for the solution of international controversies, and renounce it as an instrument of national policy in their relations with one another." Article 2 of the Pact stipulated the obligation of the parties to settle their disputes by pacific means.[6]

H. Kelsen attempts to construe the provisions of the Pact of Paris in such a way that it does not prohibit a war in defense of violated rights. In referring to the provision of the Pact on renunciation of war "as an instrument of national policy," Kelsen considers it possible to interpret the Pact so that a war which is a reaction against a violation of international law—that is, a war undertaken in support of international law—also is considered to be an instrument of international policy.[7]

In criticizing Kelsen's view, Verdross correctly points out that if the matter stood as Kelsen represents it, this would mean that the Pact of Paris had introduced nothing new in comparison with the classical doctrine, according to which a state could resort to war whenever its rights had been violated by other states.[8]

If one examines the interdependence of its provisions, the 1928 Pact of Paris undoubtedly introduced a new, exceptionally important principle into international law. Renunciation of war "as an instrument of national policy," reinforced by the obligation to settle disputes only by peaceful means, signified a renunciation of aggressive war—that is, a war which a state commences first. Kelsen's construction is farfetched and unfounded.

5. League of Nations, *Official Journal*, Records of the Fourth Assembly, Plenary Meetings, Special Supplement No. 13 (Geneva, 1923), p. 403.

6. See Modzhorian and Sobakin, comps., *Mezhdunarodnoe pravo v izbrannykh dokumentakh*, III, 4.

7. H. Kelsen, *Principles of International Law*, ed. R. W. Tucker, 2d ed. (New York: Holt, Rinehart, & Winston, 1967), p. 38.

8. See A. Verdross, *Mezhdunarodnoe pravo*, trans. from 3d ed. by F. A. Kublitskii and R. L. Naryshkina, ed. G. I. Tunkin (Moscow: izd-vo IL, 1959), p. 426.

War "as an instrument of national policy" is understood in the Pact as a war which a state commences itself, in contrast to actions undertaken pursuant to the resolution of a competent international organ.

The Soviet Union did not participate in working out the said international documents. It is indisputable, however, that the Soviet state, the very fact of whose emergence caused the powerful growth of the forces of peace and progress and which put forward and steadfastly propagandized the idea of prohibiting aggressive war, played a decisive role in the birth of this principle. In acceding to the Pact, the Soviet government pointed out that, in its views, wars for the purpose of suppressing national liberation movements should be prohibited, as well as such military activities as, for example, blockade, intervention, military occupation of foreign territory, of foreign ports, and so forth.[9]

The principle of nonaggression was developed further in the charters of the Nuremberg and Tokyo international tribunals, which proceed from the fact that not only aggressive war, but also its preparation, have been prohibited by international law.[10]

The United Nations Charter was an important new stage in the development of the principle of nonaggression. The United Nations Charter does not limit itself to prohibiting aggressive war, but prohibits as well the threat or use of force "against the territorial integrity or political independence of any state, or in any other manner inconsistent with the purposes of the United Nations" (Article 2(4)). At the same time, the Charter contains an obligation to settle international disputes "by peaceful means in such a manner that international peace and security and justice are not endangered" (Article 2(3)).

According to the Charter, only the United Nations Organization has the right to use armed force against a state first (preventive measures) in accordance with Articles 39-43 of the Charter. An individual state may use armed force against another state individually or collectively with other states, but outside the framework of the United Nations, only in response to an armed attack (Article 51). Special instances of the lawful use of force against former enemy states are provided for by Articles 53 and 107.

The principle of the prohibition of the use or threat of force was included among the seven principles whose drafting was entrusted by the

9. *Izvestia*, September 1, 1928.
10. See P. S. Romashkin, *Voennye prestupleniia imperializma* (Moscow: Gosiurizdat, 1953); Romashkin, *Prestupleniia protiv mira i chelovechestva* (Moscow: izd-vo Nauka, 1967); A. N. Trainin, *Zashchita mira i bor'ba s prestupleniiami protiv chelovechestva* (Moscow: izd-vo AN SSSR, 1956); A. I. Poltorak, *Niurnbergskii protsess* (Moscow: izd-vo Nauka, 1966).

The Period of Coexistence of the Two Systems

United Nations General Assembly to a special committee created by it. The committee discussed the content of this principle at a number of its sessions and only at its last session in 1970 approved the formula which also had been included in the Declaration on Principles of International Law adopted by the United Nations General Assembly on October 24, 1970.[11] In one of its reports the special committee, having worked out the text of the declaration, emphasized that the principle of the prohibition of the use or threat of force was "the cornerstone of the contemporary international legal order and of the cooperation, friendly relations, and peaceful coexistence of States."[12]

The content of the principle of nonaggression in contemporary international law consists of two parts: the prohibition of aggressive war and the prohibition of the use or threat of force as this has been defined in the United Nations Charter. As regards the prohibition of aggressive war, which constitutes the core of the principle of nonaggression, there were no substantive disagreements in the committee unless, of course, one considers the closely related question of the definition of aggression, which is at a standstill as a result of the resistance of the western powers.[13]

In the Declaration on Principles of International Law, the prohibition and criminality of aggressive war are fixed very precisely: "A war of aggression constitutes a crime against the peace, for which there is responsibility under international law."

In the special committee, however, a significant difference emerged in the positions of states with regard to the second part of the content of the principle of nonaggression: the prohibition of the use or threat of force. Two lines emerged: the line of the imperialist powers and their allies, having the purpose to narrow the concept of the prohibition of the use of force, and the line of the socialist and developing countries, having the purpose to make the prohibition of the use of force in international relations as broad as possible.

Agreement ultimately was reached with regard to a number of questions relating to this part of the principle of the prohibition of the use or threat of force, and appropriate provisions were inserted in the Declaration on the Principles of International Law. The Declaration reproduces the content of Article 2(3) and (4) of the United Nations Charter, and

11. G.A. Res. 2625 (XXV), October 24, 1970.

12. Report of the Special Committee on Principles of International Law Concerning Friendly Relations and Co-operation among States, Doc. No. A/6799 (XXII), para. 29 [hereinafter: Report of the Special Committee on Principles of International Law].

13. For the new Soviet draft definition of aggression see Doc. No. A/AC.134/L.12 (XXIV), February 25, 1969.

thereafter follow a number of concrete instances of the prohibited use of force. In accordance with the Declaration, the content of this principle includes, in particular, the prohibition of:

(a) the use or threat of force to violate the existing international boundaries of another state or as a means of solving international disputes, including territorial disputes and problems concerning frontiers of states, or to violate international lines of demarcation, including armistice lines;

(b) acts of reprisal involving the use of force;

(c) organizing or encouraging the organization of irregular forces or armed bands, including mercenaries, for incursion into the territory of another state;

(d) organizing, instigating, assisting or participating in acts of civil strife or terrorist acts in another state or acquiescing in organized activities within its territory directed toward the commission of such acts, when the acts referred to involve a threat or use of force;

(e) the military occupation of the territory of a state resulting from the use of force in contravention of the United Nations Charter;

(f) the acquisition of the territory of another state resulting from the threat or use of force;

(g) forcible actions which deprive peoples of their rights to self-determination, freedom, and independence.

In the special committee a far from new question aroused significant discussion: whether the term "force" in Article 2(4) means only armed force, which the representatives of the western powers insisted upon, or whether it also contemplates other kinds of force (for example, economic force), which representatives of the socialist and developing states favored. Ultimately, a paragraph was inserted in the preamble of the Declaration recalling "the duty of states to refrain in their international relations from military, political, economic or any other form of coercion aimed against the political independence or territorial integrity of any State." Thus, the Declaration contains the wholly correct provision that not only the use of armed force or the threat of armed force is prohibited under contemporary international law, but also specific kinds of political and economic coercion upon a state.

The question discussed in the special committee of the right of peoples of dependent territories to use force "against colonial domination"[14] was not expressly reflected in the Declaration, since the western powers resolutely opposed the inclusion of this provision in the Declaration. However, in the section on the principle of equal rights and self-determination of peoples it was said that in their actions against forcible actions depriving them of the right to self-determination colonial peoples may seek and receive support from without. It is obvious that colonial peoples

14. Report of the Special Committee on Principles of International Law, para. 111.

may use retaliatory forcible actions by virtue of the right to self-defense in their liberation struggle against "forcible actions."

This position arises out of the United Nations Charter and has been reflected, for example, in such international documents as the 1954 Geneva agreements concerning Indochina[15] and in numerous United Nations General Assembly resolutions, particularly in the Declaration on Granting Independence to Colonial Countries and Peoples of December 14, 1960; resolution 2107 (XX) of December 21, 1965, resolution 2184 (XXI) of December 12, 1966; and resolution 2270 (XXII) of November 17, 1967.[16]

In the form in which it was defined by the provisions of the United Nations Charter, the principle of nonaggression is a principle of general international law. More than 120 states are presently members of the United Nations. Other states which have not yet been admitted repeatedly have declared in one form or another that they recognize the principles of the United Nations Charter as binding in relations among all states. Therefore, the said principles, including the principle of nonaggression, undoubtedly must be considered to be generally recognized principles of international law.

One can not agree, therefore, with those bourgeois jurists who suggest that the provisions of the United Nations Charter are only principles of a "particular international law" in contrast to general international law. Proceeding from this premise, they frequently draw the conclusion that norms prohibiting the use of force in international relations are lacking in contemporary general international law. Professor Kelsen, for example, regarding the previously cited provisions of the Charter concerning the prohibition of force as relating to the "law of the United Nations," declares that "general international law does not prohibit the use of force or war and that, consequently, any state may resort to force in conformity with general international law if it supposes that its rights were violated by other states." "General international law," Kelsen says, "authorizes the state, the individual member of the international community, to resort, in case of a violation of its rights, to reprisals or war against that state which is responsible for the violation."[17]

15. M. Lachs, *Zhenevskie soglasheniia 1954 g. ob Indo-Kitae* (Moscow: izd-vo IL, 1956), pp. 189-193.

16. Also see the Declaration of the Cairo Conference of Heads of States and Governments of October 10, 1964; the Declaration of the Conference of Jurists of the Afro-Asian Countries adopted at a Conference in Conakry, October 1962. *Revue de droit contemporain*, IX (1962), no. 2, p. 174; and M. Sahovic, "Influence des états nouveaux sur la conception du droit international," *Annuaire français de droit international*, XII (1966), 42-43.

17. H. Kelsen, "Collective Security and Collective Self-Defence Under the Charter of the United Nations," *American Journal of International Law*, XLII (1948), 783.

Kelsen maintains in another work: "If reprisals and war—typical measures of self-help—are not considered as legal sanctions because a minimum of centralization is considered to be an essential element of the law, the social order we call general international law can not be regarded as law in the true sense of the term."[18]

And so according to Kelsen, international law can not exist without war. The conclusion follows inevitably from this that if it prohibits war, it thereby undermines its own basis. One can reach this absurd conclusion only by carrying formalism to an extreme.

One also can not agree with those bourgeois writers who underestimate the significance of this most important principle of contemporary international law. Thus, although one Argentine professor, Moreno Quintana, refers in his treatise on international law to the 1928 Pact of Paris, recapitulating its provisions, not one word is said in the work about the fact that the Pact of Paris represented an important stage in the formation of a generally recognized principle of international law prohibiting aggressive war. Moreno Quintana only remarks pessimistically that "the absence of sanctions for those who violate this Pact deprived the said document of any effectiveness."[19]

One can note the same tendency in Professor de Visscher's work. He speaks of this principle among others, thereupon declaring: " . . . to bring about an effective renunciation of a prerogative so closely bound up with the individualist conception of sovereignty as is the right of war will certainly require something more than the signature of conventions, however solemn they may be, between states."[20] Of course, to prohibit the use of force still does not mean cessation of the use of force, just as to prohibit the killing of persons in municipal law does not signify the elimination of murders. But the great significance of this principle of international law is incontestable.

Contemporary international law prohibits states from resorting to war against other states. But this does not mean, of course, that with the emergence of the principle of nonaggression international law as a system of norms regulating specific social relations has become weaker. The

18. Kelsen, *Principles of International Law*, p. 31; see also P. Guggenheim, "Les principes de droit international public," *Recueil des cours*, LXXX (1952), 169; Guggenheim, *Traité de droit international public* (Geneva: Librairie de l'Université, 1954), II, 93-94; R. Quadri, *Diritto internazionale publico*, 2d ed. (Palermo: G. Priulla Editora, 1956), p. 23; R. Monaco, *Manuale di diritto internazionale publico* (Torino: Unione Tipografico-Editrice Torinese, 1960), pp. 421-425.

19. L. M. Moreno Quintana, *Tratado de derecho internacional* (Buenos Aires: Editorial Sudamericana, 1963), II, 401.

20. C. de Visscher, *Théories et réalites en droit international public*, 2d ed. (Paris: Editions A. Pedone, 1955), p. 359.

international legal prohibition of aggressive war undoubtedly was a step forward on the path of transforming international law into a more effective means of securing peace, of developing the peaceful coexistence of states. And if with the prohibition of aggressive war international law turned its face toward peace for the first time in history, then its role in securing peaceful coexistence has grown and it consequently has become more effective.

The new generally recognized principle which has emerged as a result of the activity of progressive forces, the principle of nonaggression, has enormous significance for securing peaceful coexistence, since peaceful coexistence means above all, although not only, the renunciation of war, joint existence in conditions of peace.

(2) The principle of peaceful settlement of disputes. The principle of peaceful settlement of disputes, that all states are bound to settle their disagreements solely by pacific means, is linked closely to the principle of nonaggression. Both these principles are, in a sense, two sides of the same coin. If states are prohibited from resorting to force in their relations with other states and, consequently, in settling disputes with such states, this means that only peaceful methods of settling disputes are available. On the other hand, the principle of peaceful settlement of disputes means that force can never be used to settle them.

But, as is seen from the above comparison, the principle of nonaggression is broader in the sense that it prohibits resort to war and the use of force in relations among states in all instances in accordance with Article 2(4) of the United Nations Charter. Of course, resorting to force first is prohibited, just as the use of force in response to an attack would be self-defense.

The principle of peaceful settlement of disputes developed in parallel with the principle of nonaggression. It did not exist in international law prior to the Great October Socialist Revolution. The 1899 and 1907 Hague conventions on the pacific settlement of international disputes only contain the desire, "when possible," to refrain from using force and to have recourse to peaceful means of settling disputes. "With a view to obviating as far as possible recourse to force in the relations between states," says Article 1 of the 1907 Hague Convention, "the Contracting Powers agree to use their efforts to ensure the pacific settlement of international differences."[21] Article 2 of this Convention provided an obligation "in case of serious disagreement or dispute, before an appeal to

---

21. Modzhorian and Sobakin, comps., *Mezhdunarodnoe pravo v izbrannykh doku-mentakh*, II, 247-248.

arms, . . . to have recourse as far as circumstances allow to the good offices or mediation of one or more friendly Powers."[22]

Thus, according to the Hague conventions, peaceful means of settling disputes were not even a compulsory stage in settling disputes. The obligation contained in the convention "before an appeal to arms," to have recourse to peaceful means of settling disputes in essence amounted to nothing and was transformed into a simple desire by the stipulation "as far as circumstances allow."

The Covenant of the League of Nations went significantly further in this respect. It contained specific elements of the principle of peaceful settlement of international disputes, but this principle still was not completely embodied therein.

According to the League Covenant, the use of peaceful means of settling disputes "likely to lead to a rupture" was obligatory, but the use of peaceful means did not preclude resort to force.

Article 12 of the League Covenant provided that members of the League will submit disputes arising between them "likely to lead to a rupture" either to arbitration or judicial settlement, or to enquiry by the League Council. "They further agree," it goes on to say, "in no case to resort to war until three months after the award by the arbitrators, or the judicial decision, or the report by the Council."

If a dispute between League members "likely to lead to a rupture" were not submitted to arbitration or judicial settlement, it could be submitted for consideration of the League upon the notice of one of the disputant parties. If, in considering the dispute, the Council fails to reach a unanimous decision, or if the dispute were considered by the League Assembly and the respective report were not concurred in by all League members (exclusive in each case of the representatives of the parties to the dispute), members of the League were free "to take such action as they shall consider necessary for the maintenance of right and justice" (Article 15, League Covenant).

In this instance, therefore, peaceful means expressly were transformed into the first stage of settling a dispute.

If the Council unanimously adopted a report or the Assembly adopted a report with the concurrence of representatives of all League members represented on the Council and the majority of the other members (exclusive in each case of the representatives of the parties to the dispute), the members of the League were bound "not to resort to war against any Party which conforms to the findings of the report" (Article 15, League Covenant). The latter provision also in this instance legally and in fact opened the possibility of having recourse to force and transformed the

22. *Ibid.*, p. 248.

peaceful procedure of settling disputes merely into the initial stage of settling them.

With regard to certain disputes the League Covenant seemed to provide the principle of their compulsory peaceful settlement, but again this obligation was not carried through to the end. Article 13 of the League Covenant said: "Disputes as to the interpretation of a treaty, as to any question of international law, as to the existence of any fact which if established would constitute a breach of any international obligation, or as to the extent and nature of the reparation to be made for any such breach, are declared to be among those which are generally suitable for submission to arbitration."

However, the very same article opened the way to nonpeaceful means of settling disputes. It said that League members will not resort to war against states complying with an arbitral or judicial decision and that in the event of the failure to carry out the decision, the League Council shall propose steps which should ensure its execution. Consequently, it speaks here again of the possibility of resort to war in the event of the failure to carry out an arbitral or judicial decision, and the procedure for consideration of the question by the League Council, as already has been pointed out, did not preclude this.

Thus, the complex provisions of the League Covenant concerning the settlement of disputes did not embrace all possible disagreements between states and did not preclude nonpeaceful means of settling the disputes to which they extended.

The 1928 Pact of Paris, having established the principle of nonaggression as a principle of the prohibition of aggressive war, also established the principle of peaceful settlement of disputes. Article 2 of this Pact stated: "The High Contracting Parties agree that the settlement or solution of all disputes or conflicts of whatever nature or of whatever origin they may be, which may arise among them, shall never be sought except by pacific means."[2 3]

In proclaiming that any disputes between states must be resolved by peaceful means, the Pact of Paris formulated the principle of the peaceful settlement of disputes which, just as the principle of nonaggression, gradually was transformed into a generally recognized principle of international law.

The General Act for the Pacific Settlement of International Disputes, adopted by the Assembly of the League of Nations of September 26, 1928, provided for the compulsory submission of disputes between parties to the act, which have not been settled by negotiations or a conciliation procedure, for decision of the Permanent Court of International Justice or

23. *Ibid.*, III, 4.

an arbitration tribunal; that is to say, the General Act provided for the compulsory jurisdiction of the Permanent Court of International Justice. Only twenty states ratified the General Act, and it did not play a notable role. With certain formal changes arising out of the fact of the creation of the United Nations, the liquidation of the Permanent Court of International Justice, and the formation of the International Court of Justice of the United Nations, this Act was adopted by the General Assembly on April 28, 1949, and had been ratified by six states (Belgium, Sweden, Norway, Denmark, Luxembourg, Upper Volta) on January 1, 1969.

Thus, at the time the United Nations Charter was adopted, the principle of peaceful settlement of disputes already existed in international law and remained only to be fixed in precise form. This was done in Article 2(3) of the United Nations Charter, where it said that: "All Members shall settle their international disputes by peaceful means in such a manner that international peace and security, and justice, are not endangered."

The content of the principle of peaceful settlement of disputes consists of states being bound to settle all disputed questions arising between them by peaceful means. The principle of peaceful settlement of disputes leaves the selection of such means to the discretion of the states concerned. According to Article 33 of the United Nations Charter, "parties participating in any dispute, the continuation of which could threaten the maintenance of international peace and security" must first attempt to settle the dispute by negotiation, enquiry, mediation, conciliation, arbitration, judicial settlement, recourse to regional organs or agreements, or other peaceful means of their choice. It is important that states should settle their disputes solely by peaceful means. As regards the use of a particular peaceful means, the states concerned may choose any one of them, taking into account the circumstances of the specific dispute. The right of "free choice" of peaceful means of settling international disputes by the parties is emphasized in the 1970 Declaration on the Principles of International Law. The Declaration provides: "International disputes shall be settled on the basis of the sovereign equality of States and in accordance with the principle of free choice of means." At the same time, the Declaration emphasizes that the "parties to a dispute have the duty, in the event of failure to reach a solution by any one of . . . the peaceful means, to continue to seek a settlement of the dispute by other peaceful means agreed upon by them."

(3) The principle of self-determination of peoples. One of the most important generally recognized principles of contemporary international law is the principle of self-determination, which has received recognition

as a result of the persistent struggle of the Soviet Union and other progressive forces.[24]

As is well-known, the origin of the said principle dates back to the period of the bourgeois revolutions. Under the banner of the "principle of nationality," the bourgeoisie, striving to establish its predominance, struggled in the nineteenth century for the creation of independent national states in Europe. The "principle of nationality," however, was not generally recognized even within the framework of European International Law.[25]

A new period of struggle to introduce the principle of self-determination of nations into international law began with the emergence of the Soviet state.

Having placed the right of nations to self-determination at the base of its policy on the nationality question, the Soviet government pressed for the recognition of the principle of self-determination of nations as a principle of international law. In the Decree on Peace the Soviet government had proposed the adoption of the principle of self-determination of nations as the basis of a peaceful settlement after the First World

24. For greater detail on this question, see G. B. Starushenko, *Printsip samoopredeleniia narodov i natsii vo vneshnei politike Sovetskogo gosudarstva* (Moscow: izd-vo IMO, 1960); Starushenko, *Natsiia i gosudarstvo v osvobozhdaiushchikhsia stranakh* (Moscow: izd-vo Mezhdunarodnye otnosheniia, 1967); D. I. Baratashvili, *Za svobodu i nezavisimost' narodov* (Moscow: izd-vo IMO, 1960); Baratashvili, *Novye gosudarstva Azii i Afriki i mezhdunarodnoe pravo* (Moscow: izd-vo Nauka, 1968); L. V. Speranskaia, *Printsip samoopredeleniia v mezhdunarodnom prave* (Moscow: Gosiurizdat, 1961); D. B. Levin, "Printsip samoopredeleniia natsii v mezhdunarodnom prave," *Sovetskii ezhegodnik mezhdunarodnogo prava 1962* (Moscow: izd-vo Nauka, 1963), pp. 25-45; R. A. Tuzmukhamedov, *Natsional'nyi suverenitet* (Moscow: izd-vo IMO, 1963); N. V. Chernogolovkin, *Krushenie kolonializma i mezhdunarodnoe pravo* (Moscow: Gosiurizdat, 1963); G. V. Ignatenko, *Ot kolonial'nogo rezhima k natsional'noi gosudarstvennosti* (Moscow: izd-vo Mezhdunarodnye otnosheniia, 1966); L. A. Modzhorian, *Kolonializm vchera i segodnia* (Moscow: izd-vo Mezhdunarodnye otnosheniia, 1967); V. M. Chkhikvadze and others, eds., *Kurs mezhdunarodnogo prava v shesti tomakh* (Moscow: izd-vo Nauka, 1967–), II, 202-234; L. Antonowicz, *Likwidacja kolonializmu ze stanowiska prawa miedzynarodowego* (Warsaw: Panstwowe wyd-wo naukowe, 1964); R. Arzinger, *Das Selbstbestimmungsrecht im allgemeinen Völkerrecht der Gegenwart* (Berlin: Staatsverlag der DDR, 1966); H. Bokor-Szegö, *New States and International Law* (Budapest: Akademiai kiado, 1970); Geamanu, *Principiile fundamentale ale dreptului international contemporan*, pp. 110-166; G. Dumitrescu, "Neocolonialismul—incalcare a principiilor dreptului international contemporan," *Principii de drept international public* (Bucharest: Editura Stientifica, 1968), pp. 162-190.

25. See V. Danevskii, *Sistemy politicheskogo ravnovesiia i legitimizma i nachalo natsional'nosti v ikh vzaimnoi sviazi* (St. Petersburg: Tipo. R. Golike, 1882), p. 267.

War. As already has been pointed out, on the initiative of the Soviet Union the principle of self-determination of nations was reflected in a number of bilateral treaties concluded by the USSR with eastern countries.

At the height of a difficult war against fascism, in an interallied conference at London in September 1941, the Soviet government, striving to strengthen the anti-Hitler coalition, declared its agreement with the basic principles of the Atlantic Charter. In doing so, the Soviet government contrasted the vague and diffuse formulas of the Atlantic Charter on respect for the right of all peoples "to choose the form of government under which they will live" and on the aspiration "to see sovereign rights and self-government restored to those who have been forcibly deprived of them" to a precise and clear position on the question of the right of nations to self-determination.

In a declaration at this conference, the government of the USSR stated: "The Soviet Union has implemented and is implementing in its foreign policy the high principle of respect for the sovereign rights of peoples. In its foreign policy the Soviet Union has been and is being guided by the principle of self-determination of nations . . . Being guided in all of its policies and in all of its relations with other peoples by these principles, the Soviet Union unfailingly has opposed with consistency and resolve all violations of the sovereign rights of peoples, aggression and aggressors, and all and any attempts of aggressive countries to impose their will upon peoples and to plunge them into war."[26]

Proceeding from the basic principles of the nationality policy of our state, the Soviet delegation, when the United Nations Charter was being worked out, strove to include therein appropriate provisions which would strengthen the principle of self-determination of nations as a principle of contemporary international law.

The USSR delegation proposed to supplement Article 1 of the Charter by stipulating that one of the purposes of the Organization is the development of friendly relations among nations "based on respect for the principle of equal rights and self-determination of peoples."[27] This proposal of the Soviet delegation was included among the four-power amendments which were submitted to the San Francisco Conference on May 5, 1945, and adopted by it.

During the discussion of the American draft chapter of the United

26. *Vneshniaia politika Sovetskogo Soiuza v period Otechestvennoi voiny* (Moscow: Gospolitizdat, 1944), I, 146.

27. *Documents of the United Nations Conference on International Organization* (London and New York: United Nations Information Organizations, 1945), III, 622; see also S. B. Krylov, *Istoriia sozdaniia OON*, ed. G. I. Tunkin (Moscow: izd-vo IMO, 1960), p. 94.

Nations Charter relating to international trusteeship, the Soviet delegation, coming to the defense of the rights of dependent peoples, proposed to stipulate in the Charter that an objective of trusteeship is the development of trust territories not only in the direction of self-government but also in the direction of self-determination "having the aim to expedite the achievement by them of the full national independence."[28]

The delegations of the imperialist powers—the United States, England, and France—attempted by every means to prevent the inclusion of this Soviet amendment in the Charter. Taking advantage of their majority at the conference, they succeeded in changing the Soviet amendment, striking out the words concerning the speedy achievement of full state independence. They were, however, compelled to include a reference to independence in the Charter as one of the purposes of trusteeship together with "self-government." But a reference to independence was not included in the Declaration Regarding Non-Self Governing Territories (Chapter XI of the Charter), as a result of which Article 73 of the Charter speaks only of the obligation of members of the organization within whose jurisdiction these territories are situated "to develop self-government."[29]

Notwithstanding the imperfections of the provisions contained in the Charter on this question (the formula "self-determination of peoples" was not developed), they represent an exceedingly important step in the development of contemporary international law, signifying the confirmation of the principle of self-determination of peoples as a most important principle of international law being now generally recognized.

The history of the origin of the principle of self-determination of nations is an example of the bitter struggle which frequently takes place during the formation of international legal principles. Recognition of the principle of self-determination of peoples in the United Nations Charter by no means brought an end to the struggle over this principle; it quickly became even more sharp and bitter. Representatives of the colonial powers, while recognizing the words of the principle of self-determination of peoples, in fact strove to transform it into an empty shell, to emasculate and reduce its liberation orientation to nothing, and sometimes even to deny the existence of this principle of international law.

The sharp struggle over the principle of self-determination of peoples developed in connection with the preparation of draft declarations and covenants on human rights. The proposal put forward by the Soviet delegation in the course of the discussion at the Third Session of the

28. *Documents of the United Nations Conference on International Organization*, III, 618; Krylov, *Istoriia sozdaniia OON*, p. 157.

29. Krylov, *Istoriia sozdaniia OON*, p. 161.

United Nations General Assembly in 1948 of the Universal Declaration of Human Rights to include in the draft declaration an article on the right of nations to self-determination served as the point of departure for the subsequent consideration of this question in the organs of the United Nations.

Representatives of the colonial powers prevented the inclusion of the article on the right of peoples to self-determination proposed by the Soviet Union in the draft Declaration on Human Rights. They also strove to prevent the inclusion of an analogous article in the draft covenants on human rights. Hypocritically stating that they recognize the principle of self-determination of nations, the representatives of the colonial powers pointed out the danger of applying this principle, the possibility of a "violation of the public order and of the rights and interests of other states," urged one should not be precipitous, and occupied themselves primarily with a theoretical working out of the concept of a "people" and "nation," and so forth. Frightened by the growth of the national liberation movement, they even opposed those proposals which in essence only repeated the provisions of the United Nations Charter. Thus, at the Eighth Session of the Commission on Human Rights in 1952 the United States representative voted alone against a point contained in a draft resolution proposed by the Indian delegate in which it was recommended "that Member States of the United Nations should uphold the principle of self-determination of peoples and nations and respect their independence."[30]

Some western jurists attempted and still are attempting to dispute the existence of the principle of self-determination of peoples in contemporary international law. Such attempts have been undertaken, in particular, in the Commission on Human Rights. Through an arbitrary interpretation of United Nations Charter provisions, some representatives of western powers in the Commission attempted to maintain that Articles 1 and 55 of the United Nations Charter, where it speaks of the self-determination of peoples, do not mean the right of peoples to self-determination at all, but respect for state sovereignty.[31]

Professor C. de Visscher resolutely denies the existence of the principle of self-determination of peoples. He says that this principle "in its present total lack of precision, in no way represents a principle of law."[32]

An American professor, C. Eagleton, in passing over the question of

30. Doc. No. E/CN.4/L.26, Rev. 1. (ECOSOC, 8th session, Commission on Human Rights.)

31. See the Report of the Commission on Human Rights (8th session), Doc. No. E/2256.

32. Visscher, *Théories et réalites en droit international public*, p. 166.

self-determination of peoples as a principle of international law, attempted to reduce it to a moral principle. He called the principle of self-determination of peoples a "laudable ideal," but at the same time he classified the discussion in the United Nations on extending this principle to all peoples and nations as "wild talk." Cautioning against a "rash" application of the principle of self-determination of peoples, Eagleton urged in essence that one should wait to realize this principle in practice until the United Nations works out appropriate "criteria and methods."[33]

A French professor, M. Sibert, calls the principle of self-determination of nations "hypothetical and fallacious," asserting that this principle contains within it the "embryo of struggle and destruction" of a state and nation. Sibert confines the application of the principle of self-determination of peoples within very narrow limits, requiring the observance of a number of conditions which must be stated in advance by the United Nations, in essence urging the establishment of some "permissive system" for peoples to take advantage of the right to self-determination.[34]

In a monograph devoted to the self-determination of nations, an English jurist, A. Cobban, proceeding from the concept of the international legal personality of the individual, comes to doubt even the possibility of the existence of the right of nations to self-determination.[35]

The attempts to dispute the existence of the principle of self-determination of peoples as an international legal principle are completely unfounded; they contravene sufficiently definite provisions of the United Nations Charter.

The principle of self-determination of peoples fixed in the United Nations Charter found authoritative confirmation and concretization in resolutions adopted by the United Nations General Assembly on February 5 and December 16, 1952; in the Declaration of the United Nations General Assembly on the Granting of Independence to Colonial Countries and Peoples, adopted December 14, 1960, upon the initiative of the Soviet Union (Resolution 1514 (XV) of December 14, 1960), in the Declaration on Principles of International Law of October 24, 1970, in the documents on human rights, and in many other international documents.

Eighty-nine states voted for the 1960 Declaration, the text of which was proposed by a group of forty-three Asian and African states; nine

33. C. Eagleton, "Self-Determination in the United Nations," *American Journal of International Law*, XLVII (1953), 91-93.

34. M. Sibert, *Traité de droit international public* (Paris: Librairie Dalloz, 1951), I, 304-305.

35. A. Cobban, *National Self-Determination* (Oxford: Oxford University Press, 1945), p. 47.

states abstained (the United States, England, France, Australia, Belgium, Portugal, Spain, the Union of South Africa, the Dominican Republic), and not one state voted against.

The General Assembly Declaration "solemnly proclaims the necessity of bringing to a speedy and unconditional end colonialism in all its forms and manifestations." "All peoples," the Declaration says, "have the right to self-determination; by virtue of that right they freely determine their political status and freely pursue their economic, social and cultural development." The Declaration stresses that no references to inadequate political, economic, social, or cultural preparedness may serve as a pretext for delaying the granting of independence.

The Declaration classified colonialism as an unlawful phenomenon, pointing out that the "subjection of peoples to alien subjugation, domination, and exploitation constitutes a denial of fundamental human rights, is contrary to the Charter of the United Nations and is an impediment to the promotion of world peace and cooperation." Opposition to the national liberation movement is a violation of international law, and references to the inadequacy of the development of a particular people can not be a pretext for such violations.

The provisions of the Declaration not only confirm and interpret but they also develop the respective provisions of the United Nations Charter which, as the Soviet delegation pointed out at the San Francisco Conference, did not go far enough. As a resolution of the United Nations General Assembly, the Declaration does not have direct legally binding force. Its great significance, however, both on the factual and legal planes, consists primarily in the fact that it draws specific conclusions from the general provisions of the Charter. On the basis of the experience of the struggle of peoples for the liberation of colonies and dependent countries, the Declaration formulates the basic elements of the content of the principle of self-determination of peoples, representing an authoritative expression of the position of the overwhelming majority of states, including states of different social systems. This fact has very important significance in the process of creating norms of international law by means of custom (see Chapter 4).

Finally, the covenants on human rights adopted on December 16, 1966, by the United Nations General Assembly contain a detailed formulation of the right to self-determination, which was absent in the 1948 Universal Declaration of Human Rights. Article 1 of both covenants states:

1. All peoples have the right to self-determination. By virtue of that right they freely determine their political status and freely pursue their economic, social, and cultural development.
2. All peoples may, for their own ends, freely dispose of their natural

wealth and resources without prejudice to any obligations arising out of international economic cooperation, based upon the principle of mutual benefit, and international law. In no case may a people be deprived of its own means of subsistence.

3. All States Parties to the present Covenant, including those having responsibility for the administration of Non-Self-Governing and Trust Territories, shall promote the realization of the right of self-determination, and shall respect that right, in conformity with the provisions of the Charter of the United Nations.[36]

Thus, as has been pointed out repeatedly in Soviet literature and in the literature of other socialist countries, the right of peoples to self-determination is defined in these documents not merely as the right of a people or nation to create its own state. It includes the right of a people independently to decide the question of its own economic, social, and cultural development and to dispose of its own natural wealth.[37]

The question of "the principle of equality and self-determination of peoples" was discussed at sessions of the United Nations General Assembly Special Committee on the Principles of International Law Relating to Friendly Relations and Cooperation Among States beginning in 1966. The colonial powers, having attempted in general to prevent progress on this question, especially objected to the adoption of provisions on the illegality of colonialism, the prohibition of colonial wars, and the right of colonial peoples to resort to means of armed struggle in the struggle for independence.[38] In the 1970 Declaration on the Principles of International Law it says: "By virtue of the principle of equal rights and self-determination of peoples enshrined in the Charter, all peoples have the right freely to determine, without external interference, their political status and to pursue their economic, social and cultural development, and every State has the duty to respect this right in accordance with the provisions of the Charter."

The Declaration goes on to point out that every state has the duty to promote the realization of this principle, refraining from any forcible actions which deprive peoples of their right to self-determination, and in their actions against such measures peoples struggling for independence are entitled to seek and receive support.

The principle of self-determination of nations does not predetermine

36. G.A. Res. 2200 (XXI), December 16, 1966.

37. For greater detail on the legal content of the right to self-determination, see Bokor-Szegó, *New States and International Law*, pp. 30-51.

38. See the proposal of Czechoslovakia (Doc. No. A/C.125/L.16, part VI); the proposal of Algeria, Ghana, India, Cameroon, Kenya, Madagascar, Nigeria, United Arab Republic, Syria, and Yugoslavia (Doc. No. A/AC.125/L.48).

the international legal status of a particular nation. A nation has the right freely to unite itself with another nation or nations, and depending upon the nature of the unification in this event, the corresponding national entity will or will not enter into international relations as a subject of international law (in the USSR, the union republics are subjects of international law, whereas the autonomous republics and other national entities do not act independently in international relations). A nation may elect the course of creating its own individual state which, of course, will enter into international relations as a subject of international law.

Thus, the creation of a state formation—a subject of international law—depends upon the free decision of the nation or people itself.

The opposition of a colonial power to the realization of the aspiration of a people of a colonial or dependent country for independence is a most flagrant violation of international law. A nation struggling for independence and the creation of its own state must, therefore, under contemporary international law be considered to be a subject of international law, even though as a result of the opposition of the colonizers it could not form an independent state yet but is only on the path of creating it.[39]

The principle of self-determination of nations by no means signifies, however, that a nation is obliged to want to create a state unifying the entire nation. The right of nations to self-determination is a right, not a duty. There are several historical examples where individual parts of a nation populating a defined territory have created an independent state which began to develop along several or completely different economic or political paths. As H. Meyrowitz correctly points out, "there is no norm in general international law which would prescribe or guarantee the coincidence of the nation and the State."[40]

The so-called principle of self-determination which West German militarists and revanchists juggle in striving to obstruct the conclusion of a German peace treaty has nothing in common with the real principle of

39. See, for example, V. N. Durdenevskii and S. B. Krylov, eds., *Mezhdunarodnoe pravo* (Moscow: Iurizdat Ministerstva iustitsii SSSR, 1947), p. 111; G. I. Tunkin, *Osnovy sovremennogo mezhdunarodnogo prava* (Moscow: Tipo. Vysshei partiinoi shkoly pri TsK KPSS, 1956), p. 17; E. A. Korovin, ed., *Mezhdunarodnoe pravo* (Moscow: Gosiurizdat, 1951), p. 158 (the part written by S. B. Krylov); L. A. Modzhorian, *Sub"ekty mezhdunarodnogo prava* (Moscow: Gosiurizdat, 1958), p. 14. N. A. Ushakov is of the opinion that every nation "as a bearer of the right to self-determination is a subject of international law irrespective of whether it has achieved independent statehood or not." N. A. Ushakov, "Sub"ekty sovremennogo mezhdunarodnogo prava," *Sovetskii ezhegodnik mezhdunarodnogo prava 1964-1965* (Moscow: izd-vo Nauka, 1966), p. 64.

40. H. Meyrowitz, "Les deux états allemands," *Annuaire français de droit international*, XVI (1970), 112.

self-determination of nations as a principle of contemporary international law. In proclaiming the Federal Republic of Germany to be the sole legal successor of the former German Reich and in refusing to recognize the German Democratic Republic, they, in speaking of the right to self-determination, in fact have in mind the preparation of aggression against the German Democratic Republic, the absorption of the German Democratic Republic by the West German state.

The farcical character of the references of West German leaders to the principle of self-determination of nations is exposed in a Memorandum of the Government of the USSR to the Government of the FRG of August 3, 1961, concerning a German peace treaty. "The Soviet Union consistently and steadfastly favors the true realization everywhere of the democratic right of nations to self-determination, including with regard to the German question as well," says the Memorandum. "Pursuant to this right, each nation and people themselves determine their own fate and establish that order which best corresponds to their interests. But this means that no foreign powers whatsoever, as is suggested in the Federal Government's Memorandum, but the Germans themselves should now decide their domestic questions, including the question of unification."[41] The memorandum goes on to point out: inasmuch as two states now exist in Germany, they should come to an agreement about one or another form of unification which they find suitable.

As Professor R. Arzinger correctly points out, under contemporary conditions, with the existence of two German states which are at different stages of historical development, two subjects of international law have emerged: the people of the German Democratic Republic and the people of the Federal Republic of Germany.[42] The right of reunification is an independent right of each of these subjects.[43]

The government of the Federal Republic of Germany, in speaking of the necessity of unification, at the same time for a long period excluded the single possible means of unification: the development of contacts between the two existing German states.[44]

(4) The principle of peaceful coexistence. The emergence of the principle of peaceful coexistence opens a new page in the development of international law.

The Soviet state also has played a leading role in the making of this principle of international law.

41. *Pravda*, August 5, 1961, p. 5.
42. Arzinger, *Selbstbestimmungsrecht im allgemeinen Völkerrecht*, p. 391.
43. *Ibid.*, p. 405.
44. See G. I. Tunkin, "Mezhdunarodnye-pravovye aspekty zakliucheniia germanskogo mirnogo dogovora," *Sovetskoe gosudarstvo i pravo*, no. 10 (1966), pp. 178-192.

Being guided by the interests of peoples, for whom war always entails death and deprivation, the Soviet state steadfastly has pursued a policy of peaceful coexistence, striving that the principle of peaceful coexistence be recognized by all states as a principle of international law. "We know, we know too well," V. I. Lenin said at the Ninth All-Russian Congress of Soviets, "what unprecedented hardships war brings with it for workers and peasants. We therefore must treat this question with caution and circumspection. We are making the very greatest concessions and sacrifices; we make them only to preserve the peace which we have bought at such a dear price."[45]

Having already proclaimed the idea of peaceful coexistence in the Decree on Peace, the Soviet state consolidated this principle in treaties with oriental countries contracted in the initial years of the existence of Soviet power. Although the expression "peaceful coexistence" is not used in these treaties, the idea of peaceful coexistence permeates them from beginning to end (see Chapter 1).

The leading capitalist countries at that time refused to recognize the principle of peaceful coexistence of socialist and capitalist states, believing that they would succeed in destroying the first socialist country in the world. But in the end they had to begin normalizing relations with Soviet Russia.

Recognition of the Soviet state by the major capitalist countries was an important stage in forming the principle of peaceful coexistence in contemporary international law. First, it signified official recognition of the fact that relations between capitalist states and socialist states are regulated by generally recognized norms of international law, which at that time already contained specific elements of the principle of peaceful coexistence (for example, the principle of respect for sovereignty, the principle of equality of states and of noninterference in internal affairs); second, recognition, as a constituent part of the normalization of relations between states of the two systems, facilitated the further development of these relations.

At the same time, the chief prerequisite for the emergence of the principle of peaceful coexistence in general international law was lacking at that time, the principles of nonaggression and of peaceful settlement of disputes still being in the formative stage. The emergence of the principle of the prohibition of aggressive war and of the principle of peaceful settlement of disputes, and the broader recognition of these principles by

45. V. I. Lenin, "O vnutrennei i vneshnei politike respubliki: otchet VTsIK i SNK 23 dekabria [1921]," *Polnoe sobranie sochinenii*, 5th ed. (Moscow: Gospolitizdat, 1962), XLIV, 297.

states, were an important step in the course of forming the principle of peaceful coexistence.

The tireless struggle of the Soviet Union and the struggle of all progressive forces for peace, disarmament, the prohibition of aggressive war, the liberation of peoples of colonies and dependent countries, and the organization of a collective rebuff to mounting fascist aggression have played a decisive role in forming the principle of peaceful coexistence.

From the standpoint of the process of forming the principle of peaceful coexistence, the Second World War had two aspects. On the part of the fascist aggressors, this was a war against peaceful coexistence. On the part of the anti-Hitler coalition, despite anti-soviet currents within it, objectively this as a whole was a war against aggression, for the liquidation of the consequences of aggression, and for peaceful coexistence. Cooperation of states of the anti-Hitler coalition was an important experiment in the cooperation of states of the two systems, clearly demonstrating that it might develop significantly further than perhaps both sides had previously believed.

The experience of states of the two systems and, especially, the cooperation of these states during the Second World War led to the principle of peaceful coexistence being placed at the base of the United Nations Organization, whose Charter was being drawn up even as the bloody world battle was being fought. Tens of millions of people who fought against fascism with weapon in hand, many of whom gave up their life in this struggle, demanded their governments take such measures as would be a sufficient guarantee against a rebirth of aggression and as would ensure peaceful coexistence. Such was the urgent demand of all freedom-loving peoples.

This demand of peoples was reflected in the provisions of the United Nations Charter. Although the term "peaceful coexistence" is not used in the Charter, the principle of peaceful coexistence runs throughout the Charter of this international organization. The preamble of the Charter speaks of the determination "to save succeeding generations from the scourge of war," "to establish conditions under which justice and respect for the obligations arising from treaties and other sources of international law can be maintained." States are called upon "to practice tolerance and live together in peace with one another as good neighbours." Article 1 of the United Nations Charter obliges states "to maintain international law and peace and security, and to that end: to take effective collective measures for the prevention and removal of threats to the peace, and for the suppression of acts of aggression or other breaches of the peace, and to bring about by peaceful means, and in conformity with the principles of justice and international law, the adjustment or settlement of international disputes or situations which might lead to a breach of the peace," "to develop friendly relations among nations," to take "other appropriate measures to strengthen universal peace," "to achieve international cooperation in solving international problems of an economic, social, cultural, or humanitarian character, and in promoting and encouraging respect for human rights and for fundamental freedoms for all without distinction as to race, sex, language, or religion." Finally, the United Nations Charter says that this international organization must "be a centre for harmonizing the actions of nations in the attainment of these common ends," having in view, naturally, the harmonized actions of states of different social systems.

The inclusion of the principle of peaceful coexistence in the United Nations Charter was a decisive stage in the process of transforming this principle into a generally recognized principle of international law.

However, the "cold war" against the countries of socialism slowed down the further development of the principle of peaceful coexistence for a long time. The term "peaceful coexistence" itself was interdicted in a number of capitalist states.

The auspicious development of events in the world in recent years has shown once again, though for many this was obvious long ago, that confrontation and "cold war" among states belonging to different socio-economic systems is not the only possible state of relations, as anticommunists assert. The changes which have taken place in the world have proved convincingly that another path is possible for the development of relations among states in general and among states with different socio-economic systems in particular; that the development of these relations is possible on the basis of peaceful coexistence, for which cooperation among states, peaceful competition, and the settlement of international disagreements by peaceful means are characteristic.

One of the most important indicators of this new stage in international relations was the explicit recognition by the capitalist states—the second acknowledgement, as this was first done in the United Nations Charter—of peaceful coexistence as the basis of relations among states with different social systems. This recognition was expressed in the practical policy of the development of cooperation of the western powers with the USSR and other socialist states and was fixed in the 1971 "Principles of Relations Between the USSR and France," in the 1970 treaty between the USSR and the Federal Republic of Germany which entered into force in 1972, in treaties between the People's Republic of Poland and the Federal Republic of Germany, between the German Democratic Republic and the Federal Republic of Germany, and many other documents. It is noteworthy that in the Basic Principles of Relations signed at Moscow on May 29, 1972, by L. I. Brezhnev for the USSR and by Richard Nixon for the United States of America, a state which opposed peaceful coexistence longer and more resolutely than other capitalist states, it was specially emphasized that the parties "will proceed from the common determination that in the nuclear age there is no alternative to conducting their mutual relations on the basis of peaceful coexistence."

The principle of peaceful coexistence presupposes the existence of other important principles of international law, such as nonaggression, respect for sovereignty, noninterference in internal affairs, equality of states and peoples, and others. It reflects their content in a generalized form, although it does not constitute the simple sum of these principles.

The principle of peaceful coexistence as a principle of general international law has the character of universality; it is a principle of ensuring peace and security and of the development of cooperation between states "irrespective of their social system."[46] Professor M. Virally is completely correct in calling attention to the importance of this formulation.[47] R. L. Bobrov writes that the principle of peaceful coexistence as a principle of general international law signifies "the obligatoriness of maintaining good-neighborly relations among states irrespective of their social system on the basis of the democratic principles consolidated by the United Nations Charter."[48]

At the same time, it is exceedingly important to emphasize that the peaceful coexistence of states of the two opposed social systems is the principal element in the content of this principle. Professor Bobrov is wholly correct in noting that "the decisive sociopolitical trend of the principle of peaceful coexistence of contemporary states consisted of the demand to ensure the peaceful coexistence of *states with different social systems.* This demand is the general trend of the general international legal principle of peaceful coexistence . . . "[49]

As a principle of general international law, the principle of peaceful coexistence includes the obligation of states to recognize the social systems existing in various states, not to attempt to impose its own system on another state with the aid of force, economic pressure, and so forth.

46. See Tunkin, *Osnovy sovremennogo mezhdunarodnogo prava,* p. 31.

47. M. Virally, "Jusqu'au la coexistence pacifique," *Revue de droit contemporain,* XIII (1966), no. 1, p. 19.

48. R. L. Bobrov, *Osnovnye problemy teorii mezhdunarodnogo prava* (Moscow: izd-vo IMO, 1968), p. 204. [The last two words of Bobrov's original text in the quotation above are "obshche-demokraticheskikh osnovakh," or "general democratic bases."]

49. Bobrov, *Sovremennoe mezhdunarodnoe pravo* (Leningrad: izd-vo LGU, 1962), p. 80; Bobrov, *Osnovnye problemy teorii mezhdunarodnogo prava,* p. 199.

One must agree with Professor Suzanne Bastid of the University of Paris, who says that "to effectuate peaceful coexistence means to cast aside the idea that one system must prevail over another and, if necessary, put an end to the crusade with the aid of force. This means a particular system should be considered as a different form of political organization; this means it should be recognized that political disagreements can arise between states without necessarily raising the question of the legality of one or another political, economic, or social system. One should not expect that states might live in complete harmony, without problems or disputes arising among them, but one can expect that they will not mutually dispute the legality of their political, economic, and social systems . . . "[50]

An important aspect of the principle of peaceful coexistence is the idea of the equality of the two systems side by side with the equality of states, irrespective of their social system.[51]

In international organizations and at international conferences it is finally being realized that any attempts to decide international questions on a plane unacceptable to the socialist states, who for the time being are in the minority, are harmful to the cause of peace and international cooperation, and that the single correct means of deciding such questions is agreement among the states of the two systems. In the United Nations this idea has been reflected first and foremost in the principle of unanimity of the permanent members of the Security Council (see Chapters 13 and 14), and in recent years also in the structure of a number of subsidiary organs (for example, the Committee on Disarmament and the Committee on the Peaceful Uses of Outer Space).

The principle of peaceful coexistence requires not only renouncing methods of the use or threat of force against other states, renunciation of war, but also renunciation of policies which could lead to war, and includes the obligation to pursue policies which promote the strengthening of international peace and security. The 1970 Declaration on Principles of International Law points out that all states shall "strive to adopt appropriate measures to reduce international tensions and strengthen confidence among states."

50. S. Bastid, "Les conditions juridiques de la 'coexistence,' " *Politique étrangere*, XX (1955), 10; see also M. Bartos, "Aspect juridique de la coexistence pacifique active entre états," International Law Association, *Report of the Forty-Seventh Conference of the International Law Association* (London, 1957), p. 32; C. Chaumont, "Les rôles respectifs de l'Assemblée Générale et du Conseil de Securité," *Revue de droit contemporain*, XII (1965), no. 2, pp. 24-25.

51. See R. L. Bobrov, "Printsip ravnopraviia dvukh sistem v sovremennom mezhdunarodnom prave," *Sovetskoe gosudarstvo i pravo*, no. 11 (1960), pp. 42-50; M. Lachs, "The United Nations and Peaceful Co-existence," *Polish Perspectives*, III (1960), no. 4, p. 9.

The Period of Coexistence of the Two Systems

Since in contemporary conditions peace is indivisible, the obligation to maintain international peace and security naturally also includes the duty of states to strengthen mutual understanding, trust, and cooperation with other countries in questions of maintaining and consolidating international peace. As is said in the Declaration on Principles of International Law, "States have the duty to cooperate with one another, irrespective of the differences in their political, economic and social systems, in the various spheres of international relations, in order to maintain international peace and security and to promote international economic stability and progress, the general welfare of nations and international co-operation free from discrimination based on such differences."

The principle of peaceful coexistence includes the obligation to develop economic and cultural cooperation between states on the basis of complete equality and mutual advantage irrespective of their social systems and, consequently, includes renunciation of a policy of boycott against individual states on the ground that their social system does not please the ruling circles of a given state.

The principle of peaceful coexistence is aimed at maintaining and strengthening peaceful relations between states, primarily between states of the two opposed social systems in their peaceful competition in the economic, scientific, technical, cultural, and other spheres of peaceful construction.

In reflecting and legally strengthening the practice of cooperation of states of different social systems, the principle of peaceful coexistence contains in the most general form the basic requirements of peaceful coexistence.

From the principles of peaceful coexistence and nonaggression arises the right of states to peace, which in a political sense can be called the right of peoples to peace, since ensuring the right of states to peace is, in fact, ensuring peace for peoples.

(5) The principle of disarmament. The process of forming new progressive principles and norms of international law is continuing. The formation of the principle of general and complete disarmament has special significance. "A radical means of ensuring eternal peace is general and complete disarmament under strict international control," says the Program of the CPSU.

Under the pressure of peace-loving forces, certain provisions relating to the limitation of armaments were included in the League of Nations Covenant. Article 8 of the Covenant recognized "that the preservation of peace requires limiting national armaments to the minimum obligations imposed by common action." The League Council was charged with preparing plans for the limitation of armaments to be submitted subsequently to the governments for consideration. In the same spirit, the League Assembly repeatedly adopted resolutions on questions of reducing armaments.[52]

However, the Preparatory Commission for a Disarmament Conference, which commenced its work in 1925, and the Disarmament Conference itself, which opened in 1932, distinctly showed the reluctance of imperialist circles to limit armaments. Proposals of the Soviet government concerning complete disarmament, as well as proposals concerning partial disarmament, were rejected. The capitalist monopolies saw in the arms race not merely a source of enormous profits, but also a means of ensuring their domination both within their own countries and also in the colonies.

The United Nations Charter, prepared with the active participation of the Soviet Union, reflects a different international situation, characterized by a significant growth of democratic forces. The United Nations Charter contains with regard to the disarmament question provisions which are more specific and far-reaching than those in the League of Nations Covenant. Article 11 of the Charter empowers the General Assembly "to consider the general principles of cooperation in the maintenance of international peace and security, including the principle governing disarmament and the regulation of armaments, and to make recommendations with regard to such principles to the Members or to the Security Council or to both." Article 26 entrusts to the Security Council "responsibility for formulating, with the assistance of the Military Staff Committee referred to in Article 47, plans to be submitted to the Members of the United Nations for the establishment of a system for the regulation of armaments."

A General Assembly resolution of December 14, 1946 (41/I) said that in pursuance of Article 11 of the Charter and with a view to strengthening international peace and security, the General Assembly "recognizes the necessity of an early general regulation and reduction of armaments and armed forces."

The same motives are echoed in numerous subsequent resolutions of the General Assembly. In particular, a General Assembly resolution of November 4, 1954 (808/IX) relating to the extent of disarmament measures said that an international convention on disarmament should provide for "the regulation, limitation and significant reduction of all

52. See E. A. Korovin and V. V. Egor'ev, *Razoruzhenie* (Moscow: Gosizdat, 1930); V. M. Khaitsman, *SSSR i problema razoruzheniia (mezhdu pervoi i vtoroi mirovymi voinami)* (Moscow: izd-vo AN SSSR, 1959); O. V. Bogdanov, "Razoruzhenie v svete mezhdunarodnogo prava," *Sovetskii ezhegodnik mezhdunarodnogo prava 1958* (Moscow: izd-vo AN SSSR, 1959), pp. 93-123.

armed forces and all conventional armaments," as well as "the complete prohibition of the use and manufacture of nuclear weapons and any type of weapon of mass destruction, as well as the conversion of existing stocks of nuclear weapons to peaceful purposes."

Despite some vagueness of the Charter provisions regarding disarmament questions which resulted from the positions of a number of capitalist states who did not want disarmament, important progressive principles are contained in it. The United Nations Charter opposes the arms race, stressing the need to reduce armaments in order to ensure peace. The principle of disarmament and the regulation of armaments, according to Article 11, relates to "general principles of cooperation in the maintenance of international peace and security."

The United Nations Charter imposes upon members of the Organization the obligation to cooperate for the purpose of reducing and regulating armaments.

It should be added that the arms race, inevitably leading to an aggravation of the international situation, contravenes the principle of peaceful coexistence of states which is laid down in the United Nations Charter and is a generally recognized principle of international law. Consequently, the obligation to refrain from an arms race also arises out of this principle.

However, a reduction of armaments under contemporary conditions already is inadequate. The international situation urgently requires a more cardinal statement of the disarmament question.

The General Assembly Resolution "On General and Complete Disarmament" of November 20, 1959 (1378/XIV), adopted at the initiative of the Soviet Union, emphasizes the need for general and complete disarmament under effective international control in order to be delivered from the danger of a new destructive war. The General Assembly recognized "that the question of general and complete disarmament is the most important one facing the world today."

Realization of general and complete disarmament would have decisive significance for increasing the effectiveness of international law. From the standpoint of the progressive development of international law, the Soviet proposal was linked closely with the principle of nonaggression.

The principle of nonaggression, as already has been pointed out, includes the prohibition of aggressive war and the use or threat of force in international relations against the territorial integrity and political independence of any state.

Even though establishing a legal norm which prohibits war does not mean that war is eliminated, a real diverse influence of the norm upon the conduct of subjects of international law is possible. The actual guarantees of the effectiveness of an international legal norm may be legal or nonlegal.

The next logical stage of the development of international law in this sphere should be the international legal prohibition of the means of aggression; that is to say, general and complete disarmament.

The conclusion of a treaty on general and complete disarmament and the elimination of weapons of war would create effective legal and material guarantees for the observance of the principle of nonaggression and consequently also of the principle of peaceful coexistence.

The said proposal of the Soviet Union signifies an advancement of the principle of general and complete disarmament, which is a development of the principle of disarmament established in the United Nations Charter. This position was reflected in the Declaration on Principles of International Law, where it is said: "All States shall pursue in good faith negotiations for the early conclusion of a universal treaty on general and complete disarmament under effective international control . . . "

The formation of the principle of disarmament is taking place in contemporary international law. It therefore would not be incorrect to assert that contemporary international law does not contain any state obligations with regard to disarmament. At the same time, it is doubtful whether one can assert that a generally-recognized principle of disarmament already has been completely formulated.

In order to correctly define the formative stage of this principle and its content at the present time, one must proceed from the fact that the principle of disarmament could emerge in international law and could develop and be filled with broader content only on the basis of the agreement of states. The logical conclusions from the other principles of international law may carry weight and make an impact upon the formation of the principle, but these in themselves are not sufficient to prove the existence or define the content of any principle or norm of international law.

The question is, therefore, what is the content of the already existing agreement between states relating to disarmament, which is still in the process of being negotiated? To assert, for example, that at the present time the entire matter consists of states fulfilling their obligations arising out of the principle of disarmament is to put the cart before the horse and to pretend a wish is a reality.

From what has been said it follows that the content of the principle of disarmament in contemporary international law comes down to the obligations of states to refrain from an arms race and to strive for disarmament (partial or complete) by concluding an international agreement.[53]

Thus, the principle of disarmament, although very general, already exists in contemporary international law. And at the same time, it is in the formative stage, since its content still lacks the most important element: the obligation of states to disarm or to reduce their armaments. But even in its present form the principle of disarmament is an important step forward in the development of international law. The obligation to strive for disarmament by the conclusion of an international agreement has special significance.

The conduct of states testifies to the fact that they recognize this obligation, and it has been confirmed in a number of international treaties, particularly the 1963 Moscow treaty prohibiting nuclear tests in three spheres and in the 1968 treaty on the nonproliferation of nuclear weapons. The international community attaches very great significance to this obligation and insists that it be observed, demanding the conclusion of agreements both on partial and more cardinal disarmament measures.

(6) The principle of respect for human rights. The emergence in international law of principles and norms affecting human rights was part of the process of progressive change in international law. Here the influence of the ideas of the Great October Socialist Revolution and of socialist democracy as a new, higher type of democracy has had a very distinct effect. It is sufficient to point out that if the provisions of the Covenant on Civil and Political Rights basically reflect similar legislative norms of capitalist and socialist states, the provisions of the Covenant on Social, Economic, and Cultural Rights reflect norms of Soviet legislation concerning the right to work, the right to social security, the right to education, and so forth.[54]

53. See, for example, O. V. Bogdanov, *Vseobshchee i polnoe razoruzhenie* (Moscow: izd-vo Mezhdunarodnye otnosheniia, 1964), p. 130; V. A. Zorin and G. I. Morozov, eds., *OON i aktual'nye mezhdunarodnye problemy* (Moscow: izd-vo Mezhdunarodnye otnosheniia, 1965), p. 113; S. A. Malinin, *Pravovye osnovy razoruzheniia* (Leningrad: izd-vo LGU, 1966), p. 27; see also G. Hajdu, "Co-operation and Disarmament," *Questions of International Law* (Budapest: Hungarian Lawyers' Association, 1962), p. 28; J. Schulz, *Völkerrecht und Abrüstung* (Berlin: Staatsverlag der DDR, 1967), pp. 123-124.

54. See A. P. Movchan, *Mezhdunarodnaia zashchita prav cheloveka* (Moscow: Gosiurizdat, 1958); N. V. Mironov, *Sovetskoe zakonodatel'stvo i mezhdunarodnoe pravo* (Moscow: izd-vo Mezhdunarodnye otnosheniia, 1968), pp. 119-133; Ia. A. Ostrovskii, *OON i prava cheloveka* (Moscow: izd-vo Mezhdunarodnye otnosheniia, 1968).

The most material changes in the international protection of human rights occurred after the Second World War. The upsurge of the struggle of peoples against fascism, with its appalling flouting of human rights, led to the principle of respect for the basic human rights and freedoms, although this had been fixed in a general form in the United Nations Charter. The Charter urges "to reaffirm faith in fundamental human rights, in the dignity and worth of the human person, in the equal rights of men and women of nations large and small" (Preamble). The Charter stipulates that with a view to the creation of conditions which are necessary for peaceful and friendly relations among states, the United Nations shall promote "universal respect for, and observance of, human rights and fundamental freedoms for all without distinction as to race, language, or religion" (Article 55).

While not giving a list of "fundamental human rights and freedoms," the United Nations Charter nonetheless introduced the principle of respect for basic human rights into international law, imposing corresponding obligations on states.

The bitter struggle between states of the two systems unfolded in the United Nations during the process of drafting the Universal Declaration of Human Rights in 1947-1948. The Soviet Union and the other socialist countries sought to work out a document which could be used in the struggle for the rights of the working people. They insisted upon including in the Declaration provisions concerning economic and social rights, provisions aimed against colonialism, social discrimination, fascist propaganda, social and religious enmity, and so forth. This struggle of the socialist states was not without result; it positively affected the content of the Universal Declaration of Human Rights adopted by the United Nations General Assembly on December 10, 1948. The western powers, however, taking advantage of the "mechanical majority" they then had in the United Nations General Assembly, rejected many proposals of the Soviet Union and the other socialist countries.[55] Because of this, the socialist states abstained in the voting on the Declaration.

An even more bitter and prolonged struggle between the states of the different socioeconomic systems unfolded as the covenants on human rights were being worked out.[56] The crux of this struggle remained

55. For greater detail, see Ostrovskii, *OON i prava cheloveka*, pp. 46-61; I. Szabo, "La portée juridique de la Déclaration," *Revue de droit contemporain*, XV (1968), no. 1, pp. 39-52.

56. See A. Movchan, "Sovetskii soiuz i utverzhdenie printsipa vseobshchego uvazheniia osnovnykh prav i svobod," in F. I. Kozhevnikov, ed., *Sovetskoe gosudarstvo i mezhdunarodnoe pravo* (Moscow: izd-vo Mezhdunarodnye otnosheniia, 1967), pp. 289-312; Ostrovskii, *OON i prava cheloveka*, pp. 78-122.

generally the same as in working out the Universal Declaration of Human Rights. However, the negative attitude of the capitalist states toward including obligations with regard to socioeconomic rights in an international convention was manifested even more clearly. As a result, at the insistence of the western powers the single draft covenant on human rights was divided into two covenants, one for civil and political, and another for the social, economic, and cultural rights. The covenant on economic, social, and cultural rights was so formulated that it does not impose strict obligations on its parties to grant such rights to citizens.[57]

During the preparation of the covenants on human rights which the General Assembly adopted in 1966, such important international conventions on human rights as the Convention on the Prevention of the Crime of Genocide (1948), the Convention on the Political Rights of Women (1953), the Convention on the Nationality of Married Women (1957), and the Convention on the Elimination of All Forms of Racial Discrimination (1965) also were adopted within the framework of the United Nations.

Many conventions aimed at ensuring human rights were adopted by specialized agencies, especially by the International Labor Organization and UNESCO. Nor should one forget the four 1949 Geneva conventions on the protection of victims of war.

The principle of respect for basic human rights has become one of the most important principles of international law. A new branch of international law is emerging which defines the duties of states to ensure the basic rights and freedoms to all peoples, irrespective of race, language, religion, or sex.

The content of the principle of respect for human rights as a principle of general international law is defined above all by the provisions of the Charter of the United Nations. It also is necessary to take into account in this connection other international documents concerning human rights. This content comes down roughly to the following: (a) all states have a duty to respect the fundamental rights and freedoms of all persons within their territories; (b) states have a duty not to allow discrimination by reason of sex, race, language, or religion; (c) states have a duty to promote universal respect for human rights and fundamental freedoms and to cooperate with one another in achieving this objective.

Contemporary international law proceeds from the fact, and this is exceedingly important, that a close link exists between a state's ensuring basic human rights and freedoms and the maintenance of international peace and security. This link is stressed in many international conventions

57. See Article 2 of the Covenant on Economic, Social, and Cultural Rights. G.A. Res. 2200 (XXI), December 16, 1966.

(particularly the Convention on the Elimination of All Forms of Racial Discrimination and the covenants on human rights) and in United Nations General Assembly resolutions.

International law had intruded into an area which was considered to relate to the domestic jurisdiction of states and in which specific features of the different social systems are manifested very prominently and strongly. However, this "intrusion" of the regulatory influence of international law into the domain of human rights does not mean that human rights are directly regulated by international law nor that they have ceased basically to be the domestic affair of a state.

At the same time, the emergence in international law of norms relating to human rights raises a number of theoretical problems, especially as regards the content of such norms.

The extent and character of human rights within a specific state (they do not exist outside a state) are defined in the final analysis by the nature of the state, and this nature is itself a product of the economic system of a given society.[58] And both the extent of rights and their substance are different in states with different social systems.

The differences in the content of socialist democracy and bourgeois democracy frequently raise doubts about the possibility of concluding agreements on human rights among socialist and capitalist states. Life has shown that such assertions are unfounded.

As regards the content of norms concerning the international protection of human rights, it, just as the content of international legal norms in general, is determined in each specific instance by the content of the agreement between states relating to the creation of such norms. In the present instance, two circumstances have decisive significance. The first is that, notwithstanding the completely different essence of socialist and bourgeois democracy, there is a general concept of democracy and a general democratic concept of human rights.[59]

One should bear in mind in this connection, of course, that "pure" democracy and "pure" human rights do not really exist. There are, in fact, various historical types and forms of democracy. But fascism, for example, was a negation of democracy and of human rights in general and representatives of both the capitalist and socialist states agreed to this (see, for example, the provisions of the 1945 Potsdam Agreements on Germany).

Second, it is also of great importance that international norms concerning human rights are expected to be implemented through the municipal

58. For greater detail, see V. M. Chkhikvadze, *Gosudarstvo, demokratiia, sotsializm* (Moscow: Gosiurizdat, 1967).

59. For greater detail, see G. I. Tunkin, *Ideologicheskaia bor'ba i mezhdunarodnoe pravo* (Moscow: izd-vo IMO, 1967), pp. 27-32.

law of individual states, taking into account the special features of their socioeconomic system. Conventions on human rights do not grant rights directly to individuals, but establish mutual obligations of states to grant such rights to individuals.

That which exists in contemporary international law pertaining to human rights is far from perfected, but it also is not the end of an ongoing evolution. There are many untapped possibilities for the further development of international law in this field, especially with regard to social and economic rights, as well as the improvement of methods for international control over the implementation of conventions on human rights. The further development of the international protection of human rights depends upon many circumstances, primarily upon improving the international situation, terminating the aggressive activities of imperialist powers, the arms race they have engendered, and the aggravation of international relations.

One proposition of cardinal importance should not be forgotten: securing human rights remains and will remain basically the domestic affair of states. Therefore, the principal field of struggle for human rights is the internal system of a state, and especially its socioeconomic system. The international protection of human rights, effectuated primarily by international legal means, is, although important, merely an auxiliary means of securing such rights.

(7) The prohibition of war propaganda. The principle of the prohibition of war propaganda essentially arises out of the principle of the prohibition of aggressive war. If aggressive war has been prohibited, then the preparation of such an especially dangerous criminal act also is unlawful.

The said principle also arises out of the principle of peaceful coexistence, inasmuch as war propaganda aimed at stirring up hatred among peoples, at worsening relations among states, contravenes the principle of peaceful coexistence.

The Second World War showed with full clarity how important an instrument war propaganda is for the preparation of war; fascist Germany and imperialist Japan, intending to unleash an aggressive war, extensively developed ideological preparation for war. As the Chief Prosecutor for the USSR, R. A. Rudenko, pointed out at the Nuremberg trials, the propaganda machine of fascism worked at full capacity, for the purpose of preparing an aggressive war, instilling in the German people the absurd idea of racial supremacy, stirring up savage instincts, appealing openly or covertly for the destruction of other peoples.[60]

60. See K. P. Gorshenin and others, eds., *Niurnbergskii protsess; sbornik materialov* (Moscow: Gosiurizdat, 1952), I, 248-250.

Basing itself on the principle of the prohibition of aggressive war, the International Military Tribunal, as the court for the major German war criminals, recognized that the planning and preparation of war were a crime against peace.[61] The same principles are found in the Charter of the Tokyo Military Tribunal.

Although the Charters of the International Military Tribunals as a court for the major war criminals are concerned with the responsibility of physical persons, this responsibility, especially as it relates to crimes against peace, is linked closely with state responsibility arising out of their breaches of norms of international law.

Since the ideological preparation of war and, consequently, war propaganda are recognized as an international crime in the charters and judgments of the international military tribunals, state responsibility for war propaganda and, consequently, the principle of international law as a result of whose violation such responsibility arises, also is recognized thereby.

In a resolution adopted December 11, 1946, the General Assembly affirmed the principles of international law recognized by the Charter and the judgment of the Nuremburg tribunal. In a draft Code of Offenses against the Peace and the Security of Mankind drawn up by the International Law Commission in conformity with the said United Nations General Assembly resolution, the preparation by the authorities of any state for the employment of armed force against another state is considered to be a crime against the peace and security of mankind. According to this draft, conspiracy to commit the crimes specified in the draft code, the direct complicity in their commission, also are considered to be crimes against the peace and security of mankind.[62]

Moreover, it is possible to regard the principle of war propaganda arising out of the principles of nonaggression and peaceful coexistence as having been consolidated in the said documents as an independent principle of international law.

Soon after the Second World War, however, the imperialist powers seemingly forgot about the existence of this principle. The licentious campaign against the Soviet Union in a number of capitalist countries was accompanied by an exaggerated war psychosis and an extensive propaganda war against the Soviet Union and the other socialist states. Under such conditions the Soviet Union, steadfastly aspiring to strengthen peace among peoples, brought a draft resolution concerning measures which

61. See the Statute of the International Military Tribunal, *ibid.*, p. 16; the Judgment of the Nuremberg International Military Tribunal, *ibid.*, II, pp. 452, 456.

62. See United Nations, *Yearbook of the International Law Commission 1951* (New York: United Nations, 1962), II, 135.

should be adopted against the propaganda and the instigators of a new war to the 1947 session of the General Assembly.

On the international legal plane, the purpose of this proposal was to confirm the principle of the prohibition of war propaganda and to formulate precisely the state obligations arising therefrom.[63]

As a result of this step of the Soviet Union, the session of the General Assembly adopted a resolution concerning measures which should be taken against propaganda and the inciters of war.[64] In this resolution the General Assembly condemned "all forms of propaganda in whatsoever country conducted, which is either designed or likely to provoke or encourage any threat to the peace, breach of the peace, or act of aggression." The purport of this resolution is that war propaganda is considered to be contrary to the principles of the United Nations Charter, and this also means of principles of international law in general. The resolution, therefore, confirmed and strengthened the principle of the prohibition of war propaganda. In recent years the principle of the prohibition of war propaganda has received new confirmation in Article 20 of the International Covenant on Civil and Political Rights and in the 1970 Declaration on Principles of International Law, which provides: "In accordance with the purposes and principles of the United Nations, States have the duty to refrain from propaganda for wars of aggression."

It follows from the principle of the prohibition of war propaganda that states are bound not only to prevent the conducting of war propaganda by their own agencies, but also to take measures so that war propaganda is not carried on by private persons, organizations, and so forth on their territory.[65]

The principle of the prohibition of war propaganda was confirmed in numerous resolutions of such authoritative international social organizations as the congresses of advocates of peace, the Congress of Democratic Lawyers, and others. An Appeal of the Second World Congress of the Advocates of Peace to the United Nations said: "We believe that the propaganda of a new war creates the greatest threat to the peaceful cooperation of peoples and is one of the gravest crimes against humanity."

Expressing the will of the Soviet people, the Supreme Soviet of the USSR adopted a Law on the Defense of Peace on March 12, 1951, which says:

63. Doc. No. A/BUR/86, September 18, 1947.

64. G.A. Res. 110 (II), November 3, 1947.

65. For greater detail on this question, see A. N. Trainin, *Zashchita mira i bor'ba s prestupleniiami protiv chelovechestva* (Moscow: izd-vo AN SSSR, 1956), pp. 161-177; G. I. Morozov, "K voprosu ob otvetstvennosti za propagandu voiny," *Sovetskii ezhegodnik mezhdunarodnogo prava 1959* (Moscow: izd-vo AN SSSR, 1960), pp. 312-323.

1. War propaganda shall be regarded in whatever form it is carried out as undermining the cause of peace, creating the threat of a new war, and is by virtue thereof the gravest crime against humanity.
2. Persons guilty of war propaganda shall be bound over to a court and tried as very grave criminals.

The Law of the USSR on Criminal Responsibility for Crimes against the State of December 25, 1958, provides punishment in the form of deprivation of freedom for a term of three to eight years for the conducting of war propaganda in any form.[66]

Legislative provisions providing for the prohibition of war propaganda also have been adopted in other socialist countries.[67]

Despite the fact that the principle of the prohibition of war propaganda constantly is violated in imperialist states, there is every reason to suppose that it will develop and grow stronger; it has a firm base in international law, since its principles are generally recognized and it enjoys the powerful support of the socialist states and the peoples of the world.

B. The Development and Strengthening of the Old Democratic Principles of International Law

Side by side with the formation of important new principles aimed at ensuring peace and the development of friendly relations among states, the further development and strengthening of the old democratic principles of international law, such as the principles of respect for state sovereignty, noninterference in internal affairs, equality of states, good-neighborly fulfillment of international obligations (*pacta sunt servanda*), and so forth, has taken place during the period of coexistence of the two systems.

The struggle of the Soviet Union, and later also of other socialist countries, the developing countries, and all progressive forces, to strengthen and to develop these democratic principles of international law further has produced results.[68]

66. *Vedomosti verkhovnogo soveta SSSR* (1959), no. 1, item 8.
67. See *Zakony o zashchite mira* (Moscow: Gosiurizdat, 1953); P. S. Romashkin, *Prestupleniia protiv mira i chelovechestva* (Moscow: izd-vo Nauka, 1967), pp. 40-49.
68. On this question, see E. A. Korovin, "Bor'ba SSSR za suverenitet," *Uchenye zapiski Akademii obshchestvennykh nauk pri TsK VKP(b)* (Moscow: Tipo. Vysshei partiinoi shkoly pri TsK VKP(b), 1947), I, 3-46; F. I. Kozhevnikov, *Sovetskoe gosudarstvo i mezhdunarodnoe pravo* (Moscow: Iurizdat, 1948); S. B. Krylov, "Bor'ba SSSR za osnovnye printsipy mezhdunarodnogo prava," *Uchenye zapiski Akademii*

The Period of Coexistence of the Two Systems

In the old international law these principles were obliged to get along with such institutions as spheres of influence, the regime of capitulations, consular jurisdiction, unequal treaties, intervention, and so forth, which consecrated the predatory policy of imperialism. This could not but limit the content of these democratic principles of international law.

As the reactionary institutions, principles, and norms were rooted out, the path was cleared for the fuller development of the democratic content of the said democratic principles.

The emergence of important new progressive principles has exerted great influence upon the further development of the old generally-recognized democratic principles of international law. Thus, the emergence of the principle of nonaggression in that form in which it exists in contemporary international law also affects the content of such principles as respect for sovereignty and noninterference in the internal affairs of states. Aggressive wars, armed interventions, armed reprisals, and the threat of force were the most flagrant forms of violating the sovereignty and interfering in the internal affairs of states. Their prohibition in conformity with the principle of nonaggression led, naturally, to an expanded and more profound democratic content of the principles of respect for state sovereignty and noninterference in the internal affairs of states.

In this respect the emergence of the principle of peaceful coexistence which, as the guiding principle of contemporary international law, influences the content of all its other principles and norms was of great significance.

Thus, the development of international law during the period of the existence of states of the two systems is characterized by the emergence of new and the strengthening and development of old principles aimed at ensuring the peaceful coexistence of states, irrespective of their social system, and ensuring the equality and self-determination of peoples.

---

obshchestvennykh nauk pri TsK VKP(b), III (1949), 19-32; Baginian, *Bor'ba Sovetskogo Soiuza protiv agressii*; N. A. Ushakov, *Suverenitet v sovremennom mezhdunarodnom prave* (Moscow: izd-vo IMO, 1963); L. A. Modzhorian, *Osnovnye prava i obiazannosti gosudarstv* (Moscow: Iurizdat, 1965); D. I. Fel'dman, *Priznanie gosudarstv v sovremennom mezhdunarodnom prave* (Kazan: izd. Kazanskogo universiteta, 1965); Kozhevnikov, ed., *Sovetskoe gosudarstvo i mezhdunarodnoe pravo*; Chkhikvadze and others, eds., *Kurs mezhdunarodnogo prava*, I-III.

Part II *The Process of Forming Norms of Contemporary General International Law*

In approaching the question of the essence of international law, the investigation must begin with the process of the formation of its norms.

Those social forces which determine the normative content and the essence of international law as a whole also operate in the process of norm-formation; that is, in the course of creating, of developing, and of changing norms of international law.

Norms of international law are formed in the process of relations among states. There is no organ in international relations similar to the legislative organ of a state that can promulgate legal norms binding upon states as the basic objects of international law.

One of the important peculiarities of international law is that its norms are created by the subjects of this legal system themselves. This peculiarity makes the process of norm-formation in international law much more complex in comparison with the process of norm-formation in the municipal law of individual states.

The process of forming norms of general international law includes basic processes, which include those methods of forming norms as a result of whose completion an international legal norm emerges, and also subsidiary processes, which are specific stages of the process of making an international legal norm but which, however, do not complete this process.

Chapter 4 *The Basic Processes of Forming Norms of International Law*

A. International Treaties

(1) Treaties between states. We encounter most of all in contemporary international law an enormous number of norms created by treaties between states. An interstate treaty as a method of creating norms of international law is a clearly expressed agreement between states relating to the recognition of a particular rule as a norm of international law or to the change or liquidation of existing norms of international law.

Taking into consideration that, with rare exceptions, treaties are concluded in written form, the draft articles on the law of treaties adopted by the International Law Commission in 1966 and the 1969 Vienna Convention on the Law of Treaties define a treaty as "an international agreement concluded between states in written form" (Article 2 of the Convention). Article 3 of the Convention, however, stipulates that this does not affect the legal force of agreements which were not concluded in written form, nor "the application to them of any of the rules set forth in the present Convention to which they would be subject under international law, independently of the Convention."

A conventional norm of international law is the result of an agreement expressed in a specific form, in the form of treaties between states. The name of a treaty (treaty, convention, agreement, declaration, exchange of notes, and so on), and whether a treaty consists of one or several documents, of course, has no influence upon its law-making role.

In the second half of the nineteenth century, especially in the works of C. Bergbohm and H. Triepel, the theory that only a certain group of international treaties plays a role in norm-formation was worked out. According to Bergbohm, two categories of treaty exist between states.

The Process of Forming Norms of International Law

Some treaties contain provisions which do not go beyond the possible limits already granted to states under prevailing international law; these were contractual treaties.[1] Such treaties never or very rarely are sources of international law. Treaties creating abstract norms which are recognized or established by states as norms of conduct for the future comprise another group of treaties. These are law-making treaties. In Bergbohm's view, not just treaties with a large number of parties, but also bilateral treaties, may come within the group of law-making treaties.

The difference between the said two groups of international treaties, according to Bergbohm, is defined by the difference of purpose which the contracting parties set for themselves. If the purpose of the treaty were to establish a general abstract norm, this is a law-making treaty, a source of international law. If the parties did not assume the task of establishing a norm of conduct for a long period of time, this is a contractual treaty, which is not a source of international law.

The Russian scholar N. Korkunov similarly divided international treaties into "constitutive" and "regulatory" treaties. Constitutive treaties, according to Korkunov, regulate "an individual concrete relationship"; they "do not establish a legal norm as the general rule." Regulatory treaties have the purpose of "standardizing a whole series of uniform relationships" and establish "general norms for all uniform relationships."[2] As will be shown below, however, he believed that this division was not significant from the viewpoint of the norm-forming role of treaties.

Another Russian scholar, F. Martens, divided treaties into "those formulating legal norms binding upon states which are respected in practice as principles of international law," and into contractual treaties "concerning private interests." Noting the similarity of provisions of international treaties pertaining to private questions, however, Martens says: "Considered from this viewpoint, private agreements undoubtedly must be recognized to be a substantive source of positive international law."[3]

Triepel, concurring with the division of international treaties into those which are norm-establishing and those which do not create norms of international law, believes the basis of Bergbohm's division is inadequate. He attempts to find a more profound distinction between these two categories of international treaties. In Triepel's view, there is a divergence

1. C. Bergbohm, *Staatsverträge und Gesetze als Quellen des Völkerrechts* (Dorpat: Druck von C. Mattieson, 1876), pp. 79-81.

2. N. Korkunov, *Mezhdunarodnoe pravo* (St. Petersburg: Tipo. Morskogo ministerstva, 1886), pp. 121-122.

3. F. F. Martens, *Sovremennoe mezhdunarodnoe pravo tsivilizovannykh narodov*, 2d ed. (St. Petersburg: Tipo. Ministerstva putei soobshcheniia, 1887), I, 189.

of wills of the contracting parties in a treaty which does not create norms of international law (*Vertrag*), whereas there is coincidence of wills and their amalgamation into a common will (*Gemeinwille*) in a treaty which creates norms of international law (*Vereinbarung*).[4]

Great attention has been devoted subsequently in international legal literature to the problem of dividing treaties into law-making treaties and contractual treaties. The theory of Bergbohm, Korkunov, and Triepel was adopted by the majority of scholars and jurists of the second half of the nineteenth and the beginning of the twentieth century.

Many contemporary writers also adhere to a point of view very close to the said theory. In his voluminous treatise on international law, a Peruvian jurist, A. Ulloa, expresses the view that the majority of international treaties are not a source of international law and do not influence its development. Such treaties, in Ulloa's opinion, simply arise out of prevailing international law.[5]

An Austrian, Professor A. Verdross, divides international treaties into law-making treaties (*Vereinbarungen*) and contracts (*Rechtsgeschäfte*). To the first category he relegates multilateral and bilateral treaties which establish general abstract norms, and to the second, treaties pertaining to specific questions.[6]

Rousseau expresses himself in the same spirit, asserting that since Bergbohm and Triepel only "law-making treaties" (*traités-lois*) are recognized as sources of international law.[7]

A Uruguyan, Professor Jimenez de Arechaga, believes that although both law-making and contractual treaties create legal norms, only those treaties which form general norms are a source of international law. "Consequently," he writes, "a contractual treaty establishing particular legal norms is not a source of international law, as is, on the contrary, a law-making treaty, which creates general legal norms."[8]

4. H. Triepel, *Völkerrecht und Landesrecht* (Leipzig: Verlag von C. L. Hirschfeld, 1899), pp. 26-81.

5. A. Ulloa, *Derecho internacional publico*, 4th ed. (Madrid: Ediciones iberoamericanas, 1957), I, 51-52.

6. A. Verdross, *Völkerrecht*, 5th ed. (Vienna: Springer Verlag, 1964), pp. 143-144. The Russian translation made from the third edition gives a division of treaties into law-making and bilateral transactions. A. Verdross, *Mezhdunarodnoe pravo*, trans. F. A. Kublitskii and R. L. Naryshkina, ed. G. I. Tunkin (Moscow: izd-vo IL, 1959), pp. 156-157. The issue is treated differently in the last edition.

7. C. Rousseau, *Principes généraux du droit international public* (Paris: Societé française d'imprimerie, 1944), I, 135; Rousseau, *Droit international public* (Paris: Recueil Sirey, 1953), pp. 19-20; see also G. Dahm, *Völkerrecht* (Stuttgart: Kohlhammer Verlag, 1958), I, 21.

8. E. Jimenez de Arechaga, *Curso de derecho internacional publico* (Montevideo: Centro Estudiantes de Derecho, 1959), I, 102.

The Process of Forming Norms of International Law

The elaboration of this problem, especially in the initial period, was characterized by the transference of categories of municipal law into international law, which naturally could not lead to correct conclusions.

At the present time, many bourgeois writers reject the division of international treaties into law-making and contractual treaties or recognize the conditional nature and theoretical unfoundedness of such a division. Thus, Rousseau says that the said division of international treaties is of interest only from the viewpoint of description and classification. "In effect," he continues, "a contractual treaty and a law-making treaty have the same force in positive international law and no hierarchy exists between them as exists, for example, between contract and law in municipal law."[9]

The Oppenheim-Lauterpacht treatise on international law points out that, although the division of treaties into "law-making treaties" and "contractual treaties" in a certain sense is of practical importance, it is "theoretically faulty" and "in principle, all treaties are law-making inasmuch as they lay down rules of conduct which the parties are bound to observe as law."[10]

C. de Visscher remarks that although law-making treaties and contractual treaties play an unequal role in the development of international law, both are law for the contracting parties, "creating in the relations between the parties an objective law of a local character."[11] He sees a difference between the first and the second only in that "contractual treaties" (traités-contracts) are concluded with regard to private questions, are short-term, and after being fulfilled terminate their operation, whereas "law-making treaties" (traités-lois) relate to a wider sphere of relations and are concluded for a prolonged period.

Kelsen completely rejects a similar division of treaties, since "the essential function of the treaty is to make law, that is to say, to create a legal norm, whether a general or an individual norm."[12] "The so-called law-making treaties," Kelsen says, "are treaties creating general norms, whereas the others are law-making treaties creating individual norms."[13]

Professor P. Guggenheim notes that the difference between law-making

9. Rousseau, *Principes généraux du droit international public*, I, 137.
10. L. Oppenheim, *International Law*, ed. H. Lauterpacht, 8th ed. (London: Longmans, 1955), I, 878-879.
11. C. de Visscher, "Coutume et traité en droit international public," *Revue générale de droit international public*, LIX (1955), 360; see also M. Sibert, *Traité de droit international public* (Paris: Librairie Dalloz, 1951), I, 34-35.
12. H. Kelsen, *Principles of International Law*, ed. R. W. Tucker, 2d ed. (New York: Holt, Rinehart & Winston, 1967), p. 457.
13. *Ibid.*

Basic Processes of Forming Norms of International Law

treaties and contractual treaties "has no importance." "The difference," he says, "affects only the content and, essentially, the interpretation, but not the legal nature of international conventions."[1][4]

The view has been expressed in Soviet international legal literature that any international treaty has law-making significance. Pointing to the controversial division of treaties into normative treaties (law-making treaties) and contractual treaties, F. I. Kozhevnikov wrote: "All treaties in principle have a norm-formative character in one degree or another, since they establish rules of conduct which their parties are bound to observe." In Kozhevnikov's view, treaties may be divided into those establishing rules "for the whole sphere of relations among states" and into "those devoted to a definite concrete question."[1][5] V. M. Shurshalov adheres to Kozhevnikov's view.[1][6]

In the opinion of E. A. Korovin, the division of treaties into law-making and contractual treaties is "unfounded, since any treaty, as an act originating with states-subjects of international law, has a particular law-making significance."[1][7]

A Polish professor, M. Lachs, referring to the thesis expressed by some jurists that only a multilateral treaty may be norm-formative, and a bilateral treaty, being essentially a contract, does not have such a character, writes: "In reality, however, an international treaty, either bilateral or multilateral, is a source of rights and duties, even when it regulates very commonplace questions of everyday life."[1][8]

In Lachs's view, the more correct method is to compare a new treaty with already binding treaty law principles, with norms arising out of treaties, and with other sources of law. On this basis, he proposes the following division of treaties:

14. P. Guggenheim, *Traité de droit international public*, 2d ed. (Geneva: Librairie de l'Université, 1967), I, 130; see also A. Sereni, *Diritto internazionale* (Milan: Dott. A. Giuffre, 1956), I, 136; I. Shihata, "The Treaty as a Law-Declaring and Custom-Making Instrument," *Revue Egyptienne de droit international*, XXII (1966), 56-57.

15. See F. I. Kozhevnikov, ed., *Mezhdunarodnoe pravo* (Moscow: Gosiurizdat, 1957), pp. 244-245; see also his section of V. N. Durdenevskii and S. B. Krylov, eds., *Mezhdunarodnoe pravo* (Moscow: Iurizdat, 1947), p. 396; Kozhevnikov, *Uchebnoe posobie po mezhdunarodnomu pravu* (Moscow: Iurizdat, 1947), p. 117.

16. See V. M. Shurshalov, *Osnovnye voprosy teorii mezhdunarodnogo dogovora* (Moscow: izd-vo AN SSSR, 1959), p. 118; E. Pashukanis only mentions a similar division of international treaties, but does not express a definite attitude toward this division. See E. B. Pashukanis, *Ocherki po mezhdunarodnomu pravu* (Moscow: izd-vo Sovetskoe zakonodatel'stvo, 1935), pp. 153-154.

17. E. A. Korovin, ed., *Mezhdunarodnoe pravo* (Moscow: Iurizdat, 1951), p. 16.

18. M. Lachs, *Mnogostoronnie dogovory*, trans. from the Polish by G. F. Kalinkin, ed. V. N. Durdenevskii (Moscow: izd-vo IL, 1960), p. 263.

(1) Treaties affirming or formulating certain already existing binding principles and norms of law for the purpose of greater clarity;

(2) Treaties creating new principles and norms;

(3) Treaties applying existing principles or norms of law *ad casum.*[19]

The significance of this problem, in our view, is much exaggerated in bourgeois international legal literature. It essentially never arises in practice. Even Korkunov, in referring to the division of treaties into law-making treaties and contractual treaties, wrote: "In accepting this classification, however, we must mention that its significance is exclusively theoretical. It has no practical significance, since all agreements without distinction have identical force and importance."[20]

Any valid international treaty has legally binding force for its parties and in this sense is law-making. However, the different significance in the international legal system of general treaties, in which all or nearly all states participate, of multilateral agreements with a limited number of parties, and of bilateral treaties; of treaties establishing norms of a general character, concluded for a long period, and of treaties containing provisions relating to narrow and less-important questions and of short-term validity, should be taken into account.

If, further, one approaches treaties from the viewpoint of introducing new elements into international law, then as Professor Lachs correctly suggests, one must compare their content with prevailing principles and norms of international law and appraise each treaty individually.

A treaty may reproduce and, consequently, affirm norms of prevailing international law, render them more concrete, develop them, or create new or liquidate old norms.

The United Nations Charter is an example of an international treaty which has all of these elements. It affirms the principle of sovereign equality of states (Article 2(1)) and the principle of peaceful settlement of disputes between states (Article 2(3)). The Charter affirms and develops the principle of the prohibition of aggressive war (principle of nonaggression), establishing the prohibition of the use or threat of force against the territorial integrity or political independence of any state or in any other manner inconsistent with the purposes of the United Nations (Article 2(4)). The Charter affirms the principle of self-determination of peoples, proclaimed earlier in certain local international treaties and agreements, develops it, and raises it to the level of a generally-recognized principle of international law.

The experience of the United Nations International Law Commission and of various international conferences in codifying international law

19. *Ibid.*, p. 264.
20. Korkunov, *Mezhdunarodnoe pravo*, p. 122.

also testifies that, as a rule, a new general international treaty includes both elements of a declarative order and elements of the progressive development of international law. The preamble of the 1958 Convention on the High Seas indicates specially that its provisions are generally declaratory of existing principles and norms of international law. In contrast, the 1958 Convention on the Continental Shelf contains basically new norms. The 1958 Convention on the Territorial Sea and Contiguous Zone includes provisions reproducing, often more precisely, prevailing norms of international law as well as new provisions.

The conclusion of an international treaty is a process embracing several stages: negotiations, initialing, adoption by the international conference or organ of the international organization, signature, confirmation, ratification, exchange or deposit of instruments, entry into force.

It is not obligatory that the conclusion of a specific treaty pass through all of these stages. Depending upon the arrangements of the parties, individual stages may be omitted. Until recently, signing a treaty was an obligatory stage in the process of concluding it. During recent decades, however, there have been instances when even the original partners to the treaty do not sign it. In the International Labor Organization, for example, conventions adopted by the ILO General Conference are not signed by states. These conventions are ratified by states without a signature beforehand.[21]

The process of concluding an international treaty is the process of bringing the wills of states into concordance, the result of which is an agreement that is embodied in the norms of the treaty. When does this process commence, and when does it end?

The rapporteur of the International Law Commission for the law of treaties, an English jurist, G. Fitzmaurice, a former member of the United Nations International Court, divorcing the text of a treaty from the content of agreement between states, regarded the drafting of a text of a treaty as a technical process irrelevant to the process of bringing wills into concordance and forming agreement.

In fact, however, Fitzmaurice himself was obliged tacitly to recognize the incorrectness of this judgment, since he considers the signature of a

21. See Article 19, Constitution of the International Labor Organization. Ministerstvo inostrannykh del SSSR, *Sbornik deistvuiushchikh dogovorov, soglashenii i konventsii, zakliuchennykh SSSR s inostrannymi gosudarstvami* (Moscow: Gospolitizdat, 1925–), XVI, 360-361. An Israeli professor, Rosenne, has noted that the trend toward simplifying the process of concluding treaties in the United Nations is essentially characteristic of all international organizations wherein international treaties are concluded. See S. Rosenne, "United Nations Treaty Practice," *Recueil des cours*, LXXXVI (1954), 431-432.

treaty to be the final establishment of the text and, moreover, as consent to the text. But the question is one of consent to the content of a treaty—that is, of agreement among the plenipotentiary representatives of states with respect to the treaty text. This agreement still may not be final, but is only one stage in the formation of the final agreement; it cannot be considered to be simple consent to the text, as with a collection of formulations not connected with agreement. In this instance one has in view the negotiating process among representatives of states as distinct from the preparation of a draft treaty by experts who are not plenipotentiary representatives of states. The process of concluding a treaty commences with negotiations among official state representatives irrespective of the form or level wherein these negotiations take place.

Fitzmaurice goes on to say in his reports that establishing and authenticating the text of a treaty strikes him as a formality.[22] This assertion of the author is not in accord with his basic premise, which is to consider a text from the technical legal viewpoint, in isolation from agreement; one cannot speak of the validity of a text unless one regards it as the text of a treaty and, consequently, as a text fixing agreement or a specific stage in the process of forming agreement.

The construction proposed by Fitzmaurice is artificial; it does not reflect reality because it isolates the form of a treaty from its content.[23] The International Law Commission did not follow this path.

The working out of the text of a treaty by plenipotentiary representatives of states is the process of forming agreement. The content of agreement is formed in the course of working out a treaty text during the process of negotiations between states, at international conferences, and in organs of international organizations, and is fixed in this text. The final establishment of a treaty text occurs by initialing, signature, or enactments of international conferences or international organizations. Completion of this stage of concluding a treaty signifies that the text has been established, and no participant in the negotiations or conferences can insist upon its being changed. This in principle completes the forming of the content of agreement with regard to a particular treaty norm.

There is, however, an exception to the general rule: the institution of reservations. Reservations may introduce a new element into the content of an agreement even after the stage of working out the treaty text is completed.[24]

22. United Nations, *Yearbook of the International Law Commission 1956* (New York: United Nations, 1957), II, 111.

23. For a discussion of this question, see *ibid., 1959*, I; see also A. N. Talalaev, *Iuridicheskaia priroda mezhdunarodnogo dogovora* (Moscow: izd-vo IMO, 1963), pp. 77-79.

24. On the question of reservations see S. Borisov, "Suverennoe pravo gosudarstv—uchastnikov mnogostoronnykh dogovorov zaiavliat' ogovorki," *Sovetskoe gosudarstvo*

Basic Processes of Forming Norms of International Law

Under contemporary international law any state participating in the process of concluding a treaty or acceding to a treaty has the right to make reservations unless the particular treaty contains provisions prohibiting reservations thereto. At the same time, each party to the treaty has the right to agree or not to agree with reservations put forward by other parties to the treaty. If not a single party to the treaty expresses objections against the declared reservation, it introduces changes into the content of the treaty in its application between the state which has declared the reservation and all other parties to the treaty. If some states-parties to the treaty object to the declared reservation, it is operative only between the state which has declared the reservation and those states-parties which have not objected to it. As regards states which have objected to reservations, the legal consequences depend upon the nature of the objection.[25] Objections to reservations may take the character of declarations which do not have any legal consequences in view. A state objecting to a reservation may consider itself not bound by the terms of a treaty with the state which has made the reservation.[26]

A norm of international law is, as a rule, the result of the completion of the process of concluding an international treaty. Such a concluding stage may be the exchange of instruments of ratification, depositing them,

---

i pravo, no. 4 (1952), pp. 64-69; V. N. Durdenevskii, "K voprosu ob ogovorkakh v mezhdunarodnykh dogovorakh," *Sovetskoe gosudarstvo i pravo*, no. 4 (1956), pp. 97-100; Kozhevnikov, ed., *Mezhdunarodnoe pravo*, who wrote chapter 6 treating this question; S. V. Filippov, *Ogovorki v teorii i praktike mezhdunarodnogo dogovora* (Moscow: izd-vo IMO, 1958); V. F. Gubin, "Sovetskii soiuz i ogovorki k mnogostoronnim dogovoram," *Sovetskii ezhegodnik mezhdunarodnogo prava 1959* (Moscow: izd-vo AN SSSR, 1960), pp. 126-141; Gubin, "Vozniknovenie i razvitie instituta ogovorok k mnogostoronnim dogovoram," *ibid., 1960*, pp. 232-240.

25. Article 20 of the 1969 Vienna Convention on the Law of Treaties says with regard to this question: "An objection by another contracting state to a reservation does not preclude the entry into force of the treaty as between the objecting and reserving state unless a contrary intention is definitely expressed by the objecting state." In the International Law Commission the author of the present work proposed to indicate that the nonacceptance of a reservation did not preclude the entry into force of a treaty between the respective states unless the objecting state declared a contrary intention, but this proposal was not adopted then.

26. In the Comments on the draft Single Convention on Narcotic Drugs sent by the Ministry of Foreign Affairs of the USSR to the United Nations Secretary-General in 1960, the right of states to enter reservations to the treaty was noted, and it was pointed out further: "The legal consequences of such reservations is that the treaty is operative between the state which has entered the reservation and all other parties to the treaty, with the exception of that part of the treaty to which the reservation relates. Each state may also notify the Secretary-General of the United Nations that it does not agree to consider itself bound by the Convention with the State which entered the reservation, and in this event the Convention will not be considered to be operative between this state and the state which entered the reservation."

ratification, confirmation by governments, signature—depending upon the terms of the specific treaty.

One must distinguish the entry of a treaty into force, which may not coincide with any of the aforesaid acts, from completion of the process of concluding a treaty. A treaty may provide that it enters into force at a specified time after signature, exchange of instruments of ratification, or deposit; the treaty may provide that it enters into force only when a specified number of instruments of ratification have been deposited or upon the expiry of a certain period thereafter, and so forth.[27]

The process of concluding a treaty is completed by the last act or acts of states which have been provided for in the particular treaty. If a treaty enters into force at a certain time after completion of the process of concluding it, a norm of international law emerges in this instance with the completion of the process of concluding the treaty, but during this time it still is not a prevailing norm.

Sometimes the co-relation is reversed, as when a treaty enters into force before the process of concluding it is complete; for example, from the moment of signature, but subject to later ratification.[28]

In these instances a legal norm exists and commences to operate even

27. Thus, the 1958 Geneva conventions on the law of the sea have the following article: "1. This Convention shall come into force on the thirtieth day following the date of deposit of the twenty-second instrument of ratification or accession with the Secretary General of the United Nations.

"2. For each state ratifying or acceding to the Convention after the deposit of the twenty-second instrument of ratification or accession, the Convention shall enter into force on the thirtieth day after deposit by such State of its instrument of ratification or accession." United Nations Conference on the Law of the Sea, Geneva, 1958, *Official Records* (London: United Nations, 1958), II, 132-143.

28. A provision on the entry of a treaty into force from the moment of its signature and on subsequent ratification is found, for example, in the Treaty on Friendship, Mutual Assistance, and Postwar Cooperation between the USSR and Czechoslovakia of December 12, 1943; the Treaty on Friendship, Mutual Assistance, and Postwar Cooperation between the USSR and Poland of April 21, 1945; the Treaty on Friendship, Cooperation, and Mutual Assistance between the USSR and Rumania of February 4, 1948; the Treaty on Friendship, Cooperation, and Mutual Assistance between the USSR and Bulgaria of March 18, 1948; the Agreement on Cultural Cooperation between the USSR and the Republic of Guinea of November 26, 1959. The Treaty on Trade and Navigation between the USSR and Iran of March 25, 1940, says that the Treaty is to be ratified, but it enters provisionally into effect on the day of its signature. The Trade Agreement between the USSR and Canada of February 29, 1956, says that the Agreement will be ratified and enter formally into force on the day of the exchange of instruments of ratification; however, the Agreement will enter into force provisionally on the day of its signature. An analogous formulation is found in the Agreement on Navigation between the USSR and the United Arab Republic of September 18, 1958.

before the process of concluding the treaty is completed. The operation of such a norm is provisional, however, since a refusal to ratify is possible.

Until a treaty norm of international law has entered into force, no legal obligations whatever arise for parties to the negotiations on the basis of it. This does not affect the question of obligations which may arise from the agreement itself concerning negotiations. The consent of states to enter into negotiations does not in itself impose obligations to conclude a treaty. The process of concluding a treaty may be interrupted at any stage, particularly if a state refuses to continue negotiations, or if, when agreement concerning the text is achieved, a state refuses to initial or sign the treaty, or if, after signing a treaty, a state sometimes does not ratify it. Instances also are possible when a state has ratified a treaty, but has not deposited its instruments of ratification.

Completion of the process of concluding an international treaty is completion of the process of forming a norm of international law.

Modification or liquidation of a treaty norm may occur by treaty, and in certain instances, also by means of custom. Modification of a norm by treaty occurs by concluding a supplemental or a new treaty. Inasmuch as all parties to a treaty are equal and no one party or group of parties to a treaty may modify treaty provisions without the consent of the other parties, any modification of a treaty requires the consent of all parties unless the treaty itself provides otherwise.[29]

In a number of instances, however, individual parties to a multilateral treaty may have created or create norms which are different from the norm of this treaty but which concern the same questions. Norms of such a narrow treaty bind only its parties; norms of the first treaty continue to be operative in relations between the states which concluded the narrow treaty and all other parties to the broader treaty.

Modification of international legal treaty norms sometimes may be

29. See Lachs, *Mnogostoronnie dogovory*, p. 222; Arechaga, *Curso de derecho internacional publico*, I, 175. In a Note of the USSR chargé d'affaires in France to the Minister of Foreign Affairs of September 2, 1926, in connection with a Spanish proposal to convene a conference to review the Act of Algericas of April 7, 1906, it was said in particular: "I am authorized by my Government to remind you that my country, having taken part in the Algericas Conference, has the same right as other members of this Conference to participate in the proposed revision in order to set forth its own views, based on the principles of its foreign policy, on the questions being put forward."

In a Note of the French Ministry of Foreign Affairs to the Ambassador of the USSR of July 7, 1945, in connection with a forthcoming Meeting of the Four Powers relating to a revision of the regime of Tangiers it was stated: " . . . the French Government considers that the Government of the USSR, as a signatory of the Act of Algericas, must participate in this revision in the same capacity and on the same conditions as the other parties to this Act."

accomplished by means of custom. The liquidation of an international legal treaty norm occurs, as a rule, by means of the treaty (expiry of the term of the treaty, agreement of the parties, denunciation, abrogation, and so on) and, exceptionally, by means of custom (see Section 3 of this chapter).

(2) *Treaties between states concluded within the framework of international organizations.* International intergovernmental organizations increasingly are concentrating in their hands the organizing of the conclusion of multilateral treaties among states concerning questions which relate to the domain of their activities. In this connection certain new forms of the process of concluding international treaties, in comparison with the traditional procedure, are being formed.[30]

Within the framework of the United Nations the process of concluding international treaties is, in general, close to the traditional. The text of an international treaty is adopted by the United Nations General Assembly or by a special conference convened by decision of the General Assembly. It is subject to signature by the plenipotentiary representatives of states, whereafter follows ratification and the depositing of instruments of ratification.

In contrast, in specialized international organizations the texts of international treaties are adopted in the majority of instances by organs of the international organizations. There is an obvious trend toward simplifying the procedure of concluding international treaties.

Thus, for example, according to the Constitution of the International Labor Organization a convention adopted by the General Conference of the ILO is signed by the conference chairman and the director-general of the ILO, after which certified copies of the convention are sent to the member states. Each state, having ratified a convention, notifies the director-general of the ILO about this ratification (Article 19, ILO Constitution). The said procedure does not provide, therefore, for signature of the treaty by representatives of states, nor for deposit of instruments of ratification. An analogous simplified procedure for concluding international treaties is provided for by the UNESCO Constitution (see Article 4). In addition, the UNESCO Constitution (as also the constitutions of certain other specialized agencies) provides for the possibility of convening, by decision of the General Conference of UNESCO, international conferences to discuss and adopt corresponding international conventions (see Article 4).

30. Tunkin, "Remarks on the Normative Function of Specialized Agencies," *Estudios de Derecho Internacional Homenaje a D. Antonio de Luna* (Madrid: Instituto Francisco de Vitoria, 1968), pp. 282-291.

The role of international organizations in concluding treaties among states consists of preparing and adopting the final text of an international treaty or of preparing the preliminary text of a treaty (if a special international conference is convened).

What place does such activity of international organizations occupy in the process of creating treaty norms of international law?

The process of forming both customary and treaty norms of international law has two aspects: bringing into concordance the wills of states with respect to the content of rules of conduct and with respect to recognition of this rule as a norm of international law. These two aspects may coincide chronologically, but most often they do not (see Chapter 8).

In concluding multilateral international treaties among states within the framework of international organizations, these two aspects of bringing the wills of states into concordance never coincide. The adoption of a treaty text as final by an organ of an international organization or by a conference of plenipotentiaries of states created by decision of this organization represents completion of the process of bringing into concordance the wills of states with regard to the content of the norms of an international treaty.[31] When a treaty text is adopted by an organ of an international organization, this portion of bringing the wills of states into concordance is completed within the framework of the international organization. In the event a special international conference is convened to work out and adopt a treaty text, only part of this process proceeds within the international organization itself.

There remains the second part of the whole process of norm-formation: bringing the wills of states into concordance with regard to recognition of treaty norms as norms of international law. This part is formed from the individual actions of states (signature of the treaty, ratification, deposit of instruments of ratification or notification of ratification, and so forth), without which the treaties adopted by an international organization could not become legally binding upon states.

(3) Regulations adopted by specialized international organizations. Many specialized international organizations (the Universal Postal Union, International Telecommunications Union, World Health Organization, World Meteorological Organization, International Civil Aviation Organization, and others) adopt normative regulations (having various names). The emergence of such regulations has arisen out of the increase in the quantity of primarily technical questions with which the corre-

31. The institute of reservations to multilateral treaties is an exception to this general rule.

sponding international organizations have had to occupy themselves. Since technology moves forward rapidly, norms relating to technical and organizational questions must change frequently. Making them outside the framework of the basic convention (or charter, statute, or such) permits these changes to be effectuated by way of a simplified procedure.

Regulations are adopted by plenary organs of international organizations (the International Telecommunications Union, Universal Postal Union, World Health Organization, World Meteorological Organization) or by lesser organs (for example, the Council of the International Civil Aviation Organization).

The charters of modern international organizations provide two types of procedure for the entry of a regulation into force: express or tacit adoption by states. Thus, Universal Postal Union regulations are subject to ratification, and International Telecommunications Union regulations require the approval of states.

Tacit approval of regulations by states is a comparatively new practice, but already is widely used. The procedure of tacit recognition consists of a state's not objecting or not refusing to accept a particular regulation within a prescribed period, the regulation then being regarded as accepted. Thus, for example, sanitary regulations adopted by the World Health Organization become binding upon all member states within a prescribed period (usually from three to nine months) which have not declared their refusal to recognize a particular regulation or have not notified their reservations thereto. The question of the acceptability of reservations is decided by the World Health Organization Assembly, which may reject a reservation if it contravenes the character or purpose of the corresponding regulation. In this instance the corresponding regulation does not apply to the state which made the reservation. The International Civil Aviation Organization and the World Meteorological Organization also apply tacit recognition to the entry of regulations into force.[32]

What is the legal nature of regulations promulgated by specialized United Nations agencies? Some writers suggest that such regulations are international legislation. Professor P. Guggenheim, referring to the sanitary rules adopted by the World Health Organization, says "they are an expression of a new technique of creating norms of international law which approximates the legislative and regulatory procedure of municipal law."[33]

32. On ICAO's very flexible practice, see T. Buergenthal, *Law-Making in the International Civil Aviation Organization* (Syracuse: Syracuse University Press, 1969).

33. Guggenheim, *Traité de droit international public*, I, 284; see also E. Giraud, "Modification et terminaison des traités collectifs," *Annuaire de l'Institut de droit international*, XLIX(I) (1961), 151.

Basic Processes of Forming Norms of International Law

Professor W. Friedmann, referring to those same sanitary rules, writes that "those powers, which have been exercised through the issue of nomenclature and sanitary regulations, are in effect legislative."[3][4]

Professor P. Vellas, of the University of Toulouse, writes: "Here one speaks of true legislative power: regulations promulgated by an international organization are adopted in execution of its constitution just as state laws are adopted in execution of the domestic constitutions of states."[3][5]

Professor Ingrid Detter, of the University of Stockholm, in suggesting that although regulations have nothing in common with simplified agreements, decisively repudiates the theory according to which regulations are "if not identical, yet equivalent to treaties between states." "Regulations," she continues, "are more acts of the organization than agreements between the Member-States."[3][6]

The legal adviser of UNESCO, H. Saba, pointing to the regulations, conventions, and recommendations adopted by United Nations specialized agencies, writes: "These examples show that international conventions, the character of concluding which has changed considerably, are not the sole means of creating international norms. The community of nations now has at its disposal those forms which depart more and more from the concept of a contract freely concluded by states and are coming to resemble unilateral legislative acts enacted by a parliament and having binding force."[3][7]

In order to define the legal nature of regulations correctly, they must be considered in the context of the processes of creating norms of international law.

In confirmation of the viewpoint that regulations are a form of international legislation, it is usually pointed out that they have binding force after their promulgation upon all states which have not objected.

And although such a reference is factually correct, the interpretation of this factual aspect is incorrect. Indeed, any regulation becomes binding upon member states of a respective international organization only if this

34. W. Friedmann, *The Changing Structure of International Law* (New York: Columbia University Press, 1964), p. 280.

35. P. Vellas, *Droit international public; institutions internationales* (Paris: Librairie Générale de Droit et Jurisprudence, 1967), p. 210.

36. I. Detter, *Law-Making by International Organizations* (Stockholm: P. A. Norstedt & Soners Forlag, 1965), pp. 321-322. See also K. Skubiszewski, "A New Source of the Law of Nations: Resolutions of International Organizations," *Recueil d'études de droit international en hommage à Paul Guggenheim* (Geneva: Imp. de la Tribune de Geneve, 1968), pp. 508-520.

37. H. Saba, "L'Activité quasi-législative des institutions spécialisées des Nations Unies," *Recueil des cours*, CXI (1964), 615-616.

state accepted it. In one case this "acceptance" is, as we have seen, clearly expressed; in the other case, tacitly. But when, in conformity with the charter of an organization, a regulation becomes binding unless a state objects within a prescribed period, the state has a choice—to accept the regulation or not. If the state accepts, it makes no statement at all; if it does not accept, then it declares its objections and the regulation does not become binding upon it. Consequently, when a state makes no statement whatever, it thereby expresses its will and accepts this regulation.[38]

From the viewpoint of the process of creating norms of international law, a regulation adopted by an international organization is in the same position as the text of an international treaty adopted by an international organization. The content of the norms already has been finally determined. But for the norms to become binding upon states, an expression of its will is necessary (express or tacit) to recognize such norms as international legal norms. The conclusion is that regulations are, in essence, international treaties.[39]

The process of concluding such treaties differs significantly from the ordinary. This is a new phenomenon, linked to the development of international organizations and having the purpose of accelerating and simplifying the process of concluding or modifying this kind of international treaty. But the binding force of norms of regulations is based upon agreement (that is, upon bringing the wills of states into concordance), and not upon the legislative power of international organizations.

(4) Treaties of international organizations. Treaties of international (intergovernmental) organizations between themselves and with states, which appeared essentially only after the First World War, have become exceedingly numerous since the Second World War.

The existence of such agreements is a result of the development of international organizations that are subjects of international law.

There are, at present, two categories of treaties of international organizations: treaties concluded by international organizations with each other, and treaties concluded by international organizations with states.

Virtually all treaties concluded by international organizations are bilateral, although several international organizations frequently are a party. Thus, the United Nations, International Labor Organization, United Nations Food and Agricultural Organization, UNICEF, International Civil

38. See H. Waldock, "General Course on Public International Law," *Recueil des cours*, CVI (1962), 99; H. Blix, Review of I. Detter, *Law-Making by International Organizations*, in *Cooperation and Conflict*, I (1966), no. 2, p. 111.

39. See E. A. Shibaeva, *Spetsializirovannye uchrezhdeniia OON* (Moscow: izd-vo Mezhdunarodnye otnosheniia, 1966), p. 105.

Aviation Organization, World Health Organization, International Telecommunications Union, World Meteorological Organization, International Atomic Energy Agency, Universal Postal Union, and Intergovernmental Maritime Consultative Organization participate as a party in the Standard Agreement on Mutual Assistance to Jordan.[40]

In the majority of instances the treaties of international organizations take the form of an ordinary international treaty with all of its attributes. In rare instances, just as treaties between states, they take the form of an exchange of notes. Frequently an exchange of notes constitutes the last act of concluding such treaties. There also are exceedingly rare instances of the conclusion of agreements between international organizations through the adoption of parallel resolutions.[41]

Treaties of international organizations relate, by object, to a significantly narrower sphere of relations than treaties between states. Thus, under agreements between the United Nations and specialized international organizations, the latter acquire the status of specialized agencies of the United Nations. The agreements basically provide for mutual representation at conferences and in committees, the exchange of information, granting to specialized agencies the right to request advisory opinions from the International Court, and cooperation in questions of administration and statistics.[42]

Agreements between specialized agencies provide for cooperation and consultation in questions of general interest to such organizations, mutual representation at conferences and in committees, the exchange of information and documents, cooperation in statistical questions, and so forth.[43]

Agreements of international organizations with states relate primarily

40. See the *Statement of Treaties and International Agreements Registered or Filed and Recorded with the Secretariat* (New York: United Nations, 1968), p. 5.

41. See H. Chiu, *The Capacity of International Organizations to Conclude Treaties and the Special Legal Aspects of the Treaties so Concluded* (The Hague: Martinus Nijhoff, 1966), pp. 51-63.

42. See, for example, the Agreement between the United Nations Organization and the International Labor Organization of 1946, 1 U.N.T.S. 186; the Agreement between the United Nations Organization and UNESCO of 1946, 1 U.N.T.S. 233; the Agreement between the United Nations Organization and the Universal Postal Union of 1948, 19 U.N.T.S. 219; the Agreement between the United Nations Organization and the International Telecommunications Union of 1949, 30 U.N.T.S. 316.

43. See, for example, the Agreement of the International Labor Organization with UNESCO, concluded in 1948, 18 U.N.T.S. 345; the 1948 Agreement between the ILO and FAO, 18 U.N.T.S. 335; the 1948 Agreement between the World Health Organization and FAO, 76 U.N.T.S. 171; the 1959 Agreement between the International Labor Organization and the Intergovernmental Maritime Consultative Organization, 327 U.N.T.S. 309.

to the location of the organizations and their organs, the holding of conferences and meetings, privileges and immunities, as well as the rendering of technical assistance to states by international organizations or by other states through the medium of international organizations. The latter group of treaties is very numerous. Treaties of mutual assistance usually provide for obligations of an international organization relating to the granting of assistance, the amount and types of such assistance, the procedure of granting it, cooperation with the government, as well as the obligation of the state to whom assistance is rendered to cooperate with the organization, to submit necessary data, to render other cooperation, and to grant the organization and its employees privileges and immunities on its territory.[44]

What is the legal nature of treaties concluded by international organizations? Are such treaties international treaties, and if so, how do they differ from treaties between states?

The view has been expressed in Soviet international legal literature that treaties of international organizations are treaties between states or are a special category of treaties between states. Naturally this view arose out of a denial of the legal personality of international organizations. It was expressed in general form by L. A. Modzhorian in 1948[45] and in a more definite and developed form in 1958. In Professor Modzhorian's view, agreements concluded by the United Nations "give rise to obligations and rights not for the United Nations as such, but for member states of the U.N."[46] "However," Modzhorian went on to write, "the activity of both the United Nations and of specialized agencies, strictly defined by member-states, gives rise to rights and duties only for their member-states . . . "[47]

44. See, for example, the Basic Agreement between the World Health Organization and the Government of Ghana for the Provision of Technical Advisory Assistance, concluded in 1958, 307 U.N.T.S. 3; the Basic Agreement between WHO and the Government of Indonesia of 1958 for the Provision of Technical Advisory Assistance, 307 U.N.T.S. 15; the Agreement between the United Nations, the International Labor Organization, FAO, UNESCO, the International Civil Aviation Organization, WHO, the International Telecommunications Union, and the World Meteorological Organization, on one side, and Saudi Arabia, on the other, of February 17, 1957, 271 U.N.T.S. 2. Of the treaties providing for aid by one state to other states through the medium of an international organization, one can mention the Agreement of the International Atomic Energy Agency and the Soviet Union of May 11, 1959, on the Making Available of Special Fissionable Materials to the Agency, 339 U.N.T.S. 341.

45. See L. A. Modzhorian, *O sub"ekte mezhdunarodnogo prava* (Moscow: Tipo. TASS, 1948), pp. 13-14.

46. Modzhorian, *Sub"ekty mezhdunarodnogo prava* (Moscow: Gosiurizdat, 1958), p. 33.

47. *Ibid.*, pp. 33-34.

Professor F. I. Kozhevnikov wrote rather more cautiously but in the same spirit: "States are subjects of a treaty. Treaties concluded by international organizations reflect in the final analysis a delegation of rights by the states themselves as subjects of international law."[48] He repeated this formulation in 1966 with a modification: "However, in the final analysis these treaties reflect a delegation of rights by the states themselves as the principal subjects of international law."[49]

Professor Modzhorian later also softened her position somewhat, indicating that agreements of international organizations "give rise to rights and duties in the final analysis for their member-states. . ."[50]

With the confirmation in Soviet international legal doctrine of the thesis that international organizations have legal personality, the view that treaties of international organizations are in fact "treaties of international organizations" and not simply a variant form of treaties between states also has been confirmed.[51]

In international practice the treaties of international organizations have occupied a definite place as treaties under which international organizations acquire rights or assume specific obligations. International organizations are created by states, but they are organizations distinct from states; they are brought into operation by states, but the actions of international organizations are not the same as actions of states, either in fact or in law (see Chapter 13).

It is characteristic that in discussions of the draft articles on the law of treaties in the International Law Commission, in the Sixth Committee of the General Assembly, as well as in the Vienna Conference on the Law of Treaties in 1968-1969, neither the international character of treaties of international organizations nor their distinctiveness from treaties between states were the subject of doubt.

The International Law Commission initially proposed to include trea-

48. Kozhevnikov, ed., *Mezhdunarodnoe pravo*, p. 242.

49. F. I. Kozhevnikov, ed., *Kurs mezhdunarodnogo prava* (Moscow: izd-vo Mezhdunarodnye otnosheniia, 1966), p. 327.

50. L. A. Modzhorian, *Osnovnye prava i obiazannosti gosudarstv* (Moscow: Iurizdat, 1965), p. 24.

51. See G. I. Tunkin, *Osnovy sovremennogo mezhdunarodnogo prava* (Moscow: Tipo. Vysshei partiinoi shkoly pri TsK KPSS, 1956), p. 11; Tunkin, *Voprosy teorii mezhdunarodnogo prava* (Moscow: Gosiurizdat, 1962), pp. 80-84; I. I. Lukashuk, "Mezhdunarodnaia organizatsiia kak storona v mezhdunarodnykh dogovorakh," *Sovetskii ezhegodnik mezhdunarodnogo prava 1960* (Moscow: izd-vo AN SSSR, 1961), pp. 144-154; Lukashuk, *Storony v mezhdunarodnykh dogovorakh* (Moscow: Iurizdat, 1966), pp. 133-141; Talalaev, *Iuridicheskaia priroda mezhdunarodnogo dogovora*, pp. 30-35; Shibaeva, *Spetsializirovannye uchrezhdeniia OON*, p. 109; V. M. Chkhikvadze and others, eds., *Kurs mezhdunarodnogo prava v shesti tomakh* (Moscow: izd-vo Nauka, 1967–), V, 128-129.

ties of international organizations within the scope of the draft articles on the law of treaties.

In the report of Professor J. Brierly, the first special rapporteur on the law of treaties, the article defining the operative sphere of the articles was formulated as follows: "A 'treaty' is an agreement in writing between two or more States or international organizations which establishes a relation under international law between the parties thereto."[52]

Brierly pointed out in his commentary that now "it is impossible to ignore this class of agreements, or to regard its existence as an abnormal feature of international relations."[53]

After discussing Brierly's report, the Commission recorded in its own report that "a majority of the Commission were also in favour of including in its study agreements to which international organizations are parties."[54]

At the following session in 1951, however, the Commission decided, without changing in principle its decision also to occupy itself with treaties of international organizations, that it was necessary first to work out articles having in view only treaties between states in order to study later what modifications are required to be introduced in these articles to make them applicable to treaties of international organizations. At the suggestion of the American member, Professor M. Hudson, the Commission decided "to leave aside, for the moment, the question of the capacity of international organizations to make treaties, that it should draft the articles with reference to States only and that it should examine later whether they could be applied to international organizations as they stood or whether they required modification."[55]

The Commission's second rapporteur on this question, Professor H. Lauterpacht, defined the operative sphere of the articles on the law of treaties in his report as follows: "Treaties are agreements between States, including organizations of States, intended to create legal rights and obligations of the parties."[56]

Pointing out that agreements of international organizations "have now become a prominent feature of international relations,"[57] Lauterpacht insisted that the Commission prepare draft articles on the law of treaties which also would apply to treaties of international organizations. Lauterpacht submitted in this connection that treaties of international organizations are very close to treaties between states. "An analysis of any of these

52. United Nations, *Yearbook of the International Law Commission 1950*, II, 223.
53. *Ibid.*, p. 228.
54. *Ibid.*, p. 381.
55. *Ibid., 1951*, I, 136.
56. *Ibid., 1953*, II, p. 93.
57. *Ibid.*, p. 100.

treaties," he wrote, "will show how closely they approach the traditional type of treaty."[58]

The Commission's third rapporteur on the law of treaties, G. Fitzmaurice, also proceeded from the fact that the draft articles on the law of treaties should extend to treaties of international organizations.[59]

Professor H. Waldock, the Commission's fourth rapporteur on the law of treaties, wrote in his first report: "In fact the number of international agreements concluded by international organizations in their own names, both with States and with each other, and registered as such with the Secretariat of the United Nations is now very large, so that inclusion in the general definition of 'international agreements' for the purposes of the present Articles seems really to be essential."[60]

The Commission, however, affirmed its previous decision to work out at the beginning draft articles relating only to treaties between states. At the same time, as was pointed out in the Commission's report, it "recognized that international organizations may possess a certain capacity to enter into international agreements and that these agreements fall within the scope of the law of treaties."[61]

In discussing the final draft articles on the law of treaties in 1965, the Commission excluded from the definition of a treaty, at the suggestion of the author of the present work, any mention of "other subjects of international law"[62] in order to bring this definition into conformity with the scope of the articles. The new definition stated: "The present articles relate to treaties concluded between States."[63] But in its own report the Commission again emphasized that treaties of international organizations "fall within the scope of the law of treaties."[64] The Commission's report also pointed out the following: "If a ... convention covering treaties concluded between States were concluded, then it would ... remain possible, if found desirable, to supplement it by a further convention dealing specially with treaties concluded by international organizations."[65]

Thus, the International Law Commission held consistently to the view that agreements concluded by international organizations are international treaties.

The sentiment was the same in the Sixth Committee of the United

58. *Ibid.*, p. 99.
59. *Ibid., 1956*, II, 107.
60. *Ibid., 1962*, p. 32.
61. *Ibid.*, p. 161.
62. See *ibid., 1965*, I, p. 11.
63. *Ibid.*, II, 159.
64. *Ibid.*, p. 158.
65. *Ibid.*

Nations General Assembly, where the overwhelming majority of delegates concurred with the Commission's position. At the same time, some delegates of developing countries stressed the significance of these treaties for developing countries and expressed regret that the draft submitted by the Commission does not embrace them.[66]

The international character of treaties concluded by international organizations is determined by the international legal personality of international organizations. If an international organization has been delegated the powers to conclude treaties with other subjects of international law, those treaties within the scope of the international organization *qua* subject will be international treaties.[67]

The special rapporteur of the International Law Commission on the question of treaties concluded by international organizations, Professor P. Reuter, also proceeds in his reports submitted to the Commission from the proposition that relations of international organizations *inter se* and with third states, and consequently also the respective treaties "must be subordinate to general norms which could not but be part of general international public law."[68]

However, even writers who consider treaties between subjects of international law as not necessarily being international treaties or who do not have a definite position on this question also come to the conclusion that the overwhelming majority of treaties of international organizations have an international character.[69]

66. See, for example, the observations of the representatives of Ceylon, Cyprus, Dahomey, and Liberia. United Nations Conference on the Law of Treaties, *Analytical Compilation of Comments and Observations Made in 1966 and 1967 with respect to the Final Draft Articles on the Law of Treaties: Working Paper Prepared by the Secretariat*, I, pp. 53-58. Doc. No. A/CONF.39/5.

67. In his report on the law of treaties, Lauterpacht correctly noted that "it is not the subjection of an agreement to international law which makes of it a treaty. It is its quality as a treaty which causes it to be regulated by international law." One may suppose in this connection that the international character of a treaty, in Lauterpacht's view, is determined by the fact that it was concluded by subjects of international law. United Nations, *Yearbook of the International Law Commission 1953*, II, 100.

68. Second Report on the Question of Treaties Concluded Among States and International Organizations or Among Two or More International Organizations, Doc. No. A/C.4/271, May 15, 1973, para. 20.

69. See J. Brierly, "Report on the Law of Treaties," *ibid., 1950*, II, p. 228; K. Zemanek, *Das Vertragrecht der internationalen Organisationen* (Vienna: Springer Verlag, 1957), pp. 54ff; B. Kasme, *La capacité de l'Organisation des Nations Unies de conclure des traités*, preface by P. Reuter (Paris: R. Pichon et R. Durand-Auzias, 1960), pp. 111-115; Chiu, *The Capacity of International Organizations to Conclude Treaties*, p. 209.

The validity of treaties of international organizations is determined on the basis of international law, primarily on the basis of the charters of these organizations, which are international treaties. Questions arising in connection with the operation of the said treaties do not fall within the scope of the municipal law of states unless the treaty itself provides otherwise, but are resolved in an international procedure by means of negotiations, arbitration, and so forth.

Recognizing agreements of international organizations as international treaties in no way signifies that such treaties can be equated to treaties between states. The specific feature of international organizations as subjects of international law affects the treaties which they conclude.

Norms of treaties concluded by international organizations between themselves, just as norms of treaties concluded by international organizations with states, always are of a secondary nature.[70] Their basis always is the charter of an international organization, which contains norms of a primary order. Therefore, treaties of international organizations, in contrast to treaties between states, contain, at the present time at least, only local norms.

As regards the application to agreements of international organizations of norms of the law of treaties which relate to treaties between states, it would be just as untrue to deny this as to insist upon their unconditional and complete application. The International Law Commission therefore acted completely correctly, having decided to work out at the beginning articles applicable to treaties between states in order to study later to what extent and with what changes these norms may be applied to treaties of international organizations.

Thus, the general conclusion is that treaties of international organizations may create and in fact do create norms that enter into the system of contemporary international law which are binding upon parties to such treaties.

B. International Custom

(1) Elements of a customary norm of international law. Customary norms play a significant role in international law. States constantly are referring to them in their mutual relations.

The problem of customary norms of international law is one of the

70. See Zemanek, *Das Vertragrecht der internationalen Organisationen,* pp. 60-61; I. I. Lukashuk, *Istochniki mezhdunarodnogo prava* (Kiev: Laboratoriia pechat' KGU, 1966), p. 55a.

most important and, at the same time, one of the most complex theoretical problems of international law. It is therefore natural that the question of customary norms of international law has been the object of the constant attention of specialists for a century.

Customary norms of international law are being formed in international practice, as a rule, gradually. What are the basic elements of international practice which lead to the creation of customary norms of international law?

It should be pointed out that the process of forming a customary norm of international law, just as a treaty norm, is the process of the struggle and cooperation of states. The formulation of a customary rule occurs as a result of the intercourse of states, in which each state strives to consolidate as norms of conduct those rules which would correspond to its interests.

A customary norm of international law arises in consequence of the repeated actions of states. The element of repetition is basic to the formation of a rule of conduct. In the majority of instances the repetition of specific actions in analogous situations can lead to the consolidation of such practice as a rule of conduct.

The element of repetition in individual instances also may not take place, but a rule of conduct arises as a result of only one precedent.[71] Such instances are, however, a rare exception.

Continuity, that is to say, the element of time, also usually plays an important role in the process of forming a customary norm of international law. The element of time, however, does not in itself create a presumption in favor of the existence of a customary norm of international law. There is even less basis to believe that it is legally necessary for a customary rule to be "old" or of significant antiquity.[72]

Indeed, characterizing a particular rule as "old" can have two aspects. On one hand, it could mean that a given rule observed in international practice for a long period has passed the test of time. This very characteristic at the same time raises the question: to what extent is this "old" rule responsive to contemporary circumstances?

Although time in fact plays a significant role in the process of forming a customary norm of international law, legally the element of time has in

71. See Rousseau, *Principes généraux du droit international public*, I, 825; A. Klafkowski, *Prawo miedzynarodowe publiczne* (Warsaw: Panstwowe wyd-wo naukowe, 1964), p. 33; B. Cheng, "United Nations Resolutions on Outer Space: 'Instant' International Customary Law?" *Indian Journal of International Law*, V (1965), 23-48.

72. See J. Basdevant, "Règles générales du droit de la paix," *Recueil des cours*, LVIII (1936), 513, 518; J. Kunz, "The Nature of Customary International Law," *American Journal of International Law*, XLVII (1953), 666.

and of itself no significance. Depending upon the circumstances, a customary norm may be formed over a long period or it may be formed quickly.[73] Therefore, one can agree completely with Professor R. R. Baxter, who says that "the time factor as a separate element in the proof of custom now seems irrelevant."[74]

It has been pointed out repeatedly in international legal literature that not every repetition creates a customary norm of international law. Repetition of one and the same action also may not lead to the creation of a norm of conduct, and if such a norm of conduct emerges, it is not necessarily a legal norm: it may be a usage (a custom which is not legally binding), a norm of international morality, or a norm of international comity. In international relations, especially in the area of diplomatic relations and maritime navigation, there are many norms that have existed for a long period which, however, are not norms of international law. Thus, exempting diplomats' baggage from customs inspection and a number of diplomats' privileges on the territory of third states ordinarily are granted by all states. Before the entry into force of the 1961 Vienna Convention on Diplomatic Relations, the respective norms were not regarded as international legal norms, but were considered to be norms of international comity.

Some writers express the view that only uninterrupted international practice can lead to the creation of a customary norm of international law.[75] This assertion does not correspond to reality. It would be more correct to say that very likely not a single customary norm of international law has come to light as a consequence of uninterrupted international practice.

Take, for example, the principle of noninterference, one of the generally-recognized principles of international law. This principle was advanced for the first time during the bourgeois revolutions of the eighteenth century. Its introduction into international law took a significant period of time and was far from uniform. It earned ever greater recognition, although in the formative process it sometimes retreated before the pressure of reactionary forces. After the French Revolution of the eighteenth century, when the policy of intervention was proclaimed to be the official policy of the European powers (Napoleonic wars, policy of the Holy Alliance, and so forth), the process of forming the principle of

73. See Verdross, *Mezhdunarodnoe pravo*, p. 154.

74. R. R. Baxter, "Treaties and Custom," *Recueil des cours*, CXXIX (1970), 67.

75. See, for example, A. Cavaglieri, "Règles générales du droit de la paix," *Recueil des cours*, XXVI (1929), 336-337; G. Morelli, *Nozioni di diritto internazionale*, 3d ed. (Padova: CEDAM, 1951), p. 29; Kunz, "The Nature of Customary International Law," p. 666; Sereni, *Diritto internazionale*, I, 121.

noninterference in essence ceased. But then this process began again, and gradually the principle of noninterference was transformed into a generally-recognized principle of international law.

It would at the same time be incorrect to assert that an interruption of international practice exerts no influence upon the formation of a customary norm of international law. Interruption may destroy a customary rule of conduct which is still in the formative process or may lead to no rule of conduct being formed in general; everything depends upon the character of the interruption. At the same time, and this is the main point, noninterruption, just as the element of time, does not play a decisive role in the formative process of a norm of international law.

The question of whether a customary norm of international law only arises out of positive actions or whether abstaining from actions also can lead to the formation of a customary norm of international law has produced many arguments. Professor J. Basdevant, representing France in the *Lotus* Case before the Permanent Court of International Justice in 1927, expressed an opinion on this question which still is cited frequently. He stated: "The custom observed by states to refrain from prosecuting foreign nationals accused of causing a collision of vessels on the high seas is a customary norm of international law."[76]

A contrary view was expressed by the Turkish representative and by Judges Nyholm and Altamira, who asserted that acts of abstaining from actions do not create a customary norm of international law.[77]

A customary norm of international law grows out of international practice. State practice may consist of their undertaking specific actions in certain circumstances or, on the contrary, of abstaining from taking actions. As a rule, it is much easier to ascertain the existence of a customary norm of international law when states take positive actions: however, there is no basis for rejecting the possibility of creating a customary norm by the practice of abstaining from actions. The custom not to undertake actions under specific circumstances in a number of instances undoubtedly leads to the creation of a norm of conduct which may be a legal norm.

76. Permanent Court of International Justice, Series C, Acts and Documents Relating to Judgments and Advisory Opinions Given by the Court, No. 13—II—Twelfth (Ordinary) Session (1927), Documents Relating to Judgment No. 9 (September 7th, 1927), *The "Lotus" Case* (Leyden: A. W. Sythoff, 1927), p. 69.

77. *Ibid.*, p. 112. Permanent Court of International Justice, Collection of Judgments, Series A, No. 9, *The Case of the S. S. "Lotus"* (Leyden: A. W. Sythoff, 1927), pp. 59, 96; an analogous view is expressed by G. Gianni, *La coutume en droit international* (Paris: Editions A. Pedone, 1931), p. 126; K. Strupp, "Règles générales du droit de la paix," *Recueil des cours*, XLVII (1934), 307.

Basic Processes of Forming Norms of International Law

Everything said previously with regard to the elements of repetition, time, and noninterruption also applies to the practice of abstention.

It should be noted that many principles and norms of international law contain to some extent the obligation of states to abstain from specific actions in their relations with other states. Thus, the principle of respect for sovereignty obliges states to abstain from any actions which represent interference in the internal affairs of another state. How could such customary principles of international law arise unless the practice of abstention also is regarded as leading to the creation of a customary norm of international law?

Thus, not only positive actions of states, but also the abstention from actions in specific situations, may lead to the creation of a customary norm of international law.[78]

All the aforesaid elements of a customary norm of international law in aggregate still do not create a customary norm of international law. They testify only to the existence of a usage. The term "usage" has not taken root in Soviet international legal literature and practice. The 1947 textbook of international law gave a very confused and imprecise demarcation between a usage and a custom.[79] Usage is not mentioned at all in the 1957 textbook.[80]

As we use it, the term "custom" has two meanings: in the sense of a customary rule which is not a legal norm, and in the sense of a customary norm of international law. To avoid confusing different concepts, it would be advisable in the first instance to speak of an international custom, and in the second, of an international legal custom or, better still, of a customary norm of international law.

Consequently, the statement that an international custom (or usage) exists is not the same as a statement that a customary norm of international law exists, for a custom, or a customary rule of conduct, is not necessarily a legal norm.

The establishment of a custom is a specific stage in the formative process of a customary norm of international law. This process is completed when states recognize a custom as legally binding; that is to

78. Ulloa, *Derecho internacional publico*, I, 48-49; P. Guggenheim, "Les deux éléments de la coutume en droit international," *La technique et les principes du droit public; études en l'honneur de G. Scelle* (Paris: Librairie générale de droit et de jurisprudence, 1950), I, 280; Y. Gouet, *La coutume en droit constitutionnel interne et en droit constitutionnel international* (Paris: Editions A. Pedone, 1932), p. 73; M. Sørenson, *Les sources du droit international* (Copenhagen: Einar Munksgaard, 1946), pp. 98-101.

79. See Durdenevskii and Krylov, eds., *Mezhdunarodnoe pravo*, p. 24.

80. See Korovin, ed., *Mezhdunarodnoe pravo*, p. 8.

say, recognize a customary rule of conduct as a norm of international law.

The process of forming a customary norm of international law is completed and an international custom (or usage) becomes an international legal custom or, that is to say, a customary norm of international law, only as a result of such recognition.[81]

It is in this sense, in our view, that Article 38(b) of the Statute of the International Court of Justice (the imperfection of its formulation is pointed out constantly in international legal literature), according to which "international custom, as evidence of a general practice accepted as law," is one of the sources of international law, should be understood.

A customary norm of general international law presupposes, above all, general practice, even though "general practice" does not necessarily mean the practice of all states. Frequently, individual states for various reasons could not have a practice on certain questions (for example, states having no sea coast could not have a practice on questions of the breadth of territorial waters, contiguous zones, or the shelf) or, although in principle they could have a practice, do not now have one (for example, states not taking part in Antarctic or space research have no practice on the respective issues).

The imperfection of the formulation of Article 38 of the Statute of the International Court is seen distinctly. Practice may not be general, but its recognition as a legal norm must be general. Of course, the wider the practice, the greater basis for presuming that it has been generally recognized as a norm of law.

The necessity of "recognition as an international legal norm" for a rule of conduct being formed in practice to become a norm of international law is a generally-recognized proposition.

Recognition by states of a customary rule (or usage) as a legal norm completes the process of its formation. Sometimes the first stage (formation of usage) and the second stage (recognition of usage by states as a legal norm) of the process of forming a customary norm of international law occur in practice simultaneously, as for example happened with certain norms of space law, and then it can be shown that the formation of a customary norm comes down to the single latter stage. Thus, on the basis of an analysis of the origin of norms of space law B. Cheng came to the conclusion that "International customary law requires only one single constitutive element, namely, the *opinio juris* of states."[82] One can not,

---

81. Professor de Visscher correctly points out: "In a given instance, fact precedes juridical classification; but the latter remains decisive, and uniformity and external repetition never in themselves give a basis for conclusions regarding its normative significance." Visscher, "Coutume et traité en droit international public," p. 357.

82. Cheng, "United Nations Resolutions on Outer Space: 'Instant' International Law?" p. 45.

Basic Processes of Forming Norms of International Law

however, concur with this view. Even in those instances when the first and second stage occur virtually simultaneously, they nonetheless strictly speaking do not blend and it is necessary to distinguish them. In the majority of instances these two stages are distinctly demarcated.

In Soviet international legal literature it was formulated carelessly in V. N. Durdenevskii's and S. B. Krylov's textbook, where it was said that "custom has more norm-establishing character, whereas usage contains a mixture of a legal source and a certain technical norm, and therefore has a dispositive, and not an imperative, character."[83] V. I. Lisovskii speaks only of practice repeated over a long period.[84]

In all other recent Soviet international legal literature, however, this proposition is considered to be a necessary element of a customary norm of international law.[85]

The absolute necessity of "recognition" or *opinio juris* for the creation of a customary norm of international law also is emphasized in the literature of other socialist countries.[86]

International legal doctrine of other countries, with rare exceptions, considers "recognition," or *opinio juris*, a necessary and decisive element for the creation of a customary norm of international law.[87]

83. Durdenevskii and Krylov, eds., *Mezhdunarodnoe pravo*, p. 24.

84. V. I. Lisovskii, *Mezhdunarodnoe pravo* (Moscow: izd-vo Vysshaia shkola, 1961), p. 9.

85. Korovin, ed., *Mezhdunarodnoe pravo*, p. 16; Tunkin, *Osnovy sovremennogo mezhdunarodnogo prava*, p. 13; D. B. Levin, *Osnovnye problemy sovremennogo mezhdunarodnogo prava* (Moscow: Iurizdat, 1958), p. 100; N. M. Minasian, *Istochniki sovremennogo mezhdunarodnogo prava* (Rostov: izd-vo Rostovskogo universiteta, 1960), p. 98; P. I. Lukin, *Istochniki mezhdunarodnogo prava* (Moscow: izd-vo AN SSSR, 1960), p. 80; Lukashuk, *Istochniki mezhdunarodnogo prava*, p. 58; Kozhevnikov, ed., *Kurs mezhdunarodnogo prava*, p. 40; Chkhikvadze and others, eds., *Kurs mezhdunarodnogo prava*, I, 181.

86. See, for example, M. Genovski, *Osnovi na mezhdunarodnoto pravo*, 2d ed. (Sofia: Nauka i izkustvo, 1966), p. 22; Klafkowski, *Prawo miedzynarodowe publiczne*, pp. 32-33; L. Gelberg, *Zarys prawa miedzynarodowego* (Warsaw: Panstwowe wyd-wo naukowe, 1967), p. 74; S. Nahlik, *Wstep do nauki prawa miedzynarodowego* (Warsaw: Panstwowe wyd-wo naukowe, 1967), pp. 351-371; S. Avramov, *Medjunarodno javno pravo* (Belgrade: Savremena administracija izdavacko-stamparasko preduzece, 1963), pp. 47-48; A. Magarasevic, *Osnovi medjunarodnog prava* (Novi Sad: Univerzitet u Novom Sadu, 1965), pp. 85-86. M. A. D'Estefano, a Cuban professor, believes in contrast to this that a customary norm of international law is a norm observed by states repeatedly and without interruption; a second necessary element, in M. A. D'Estefano's view, is the conformity of this norm "to the idea of justice and humanity." M. A. D'Estefano, *Derecho internacional publico* (Havana: Editoria Universitaria, 1965), p. 12.

87. See, for example, Oppenheim, *International Law*, I, 26; C. de Visscher, *Théories et réalites en droit international public*, 2d ed. (Paris: Editions A. Pedone, 1955), p. 188; Verdross, *Völkerrecht*, p. 138; Morelli, *Nozioni di diritto internzaionale*, p. 25;

Very few bourgeois international lawyers adhere to the normativist concept that the international practice of states in and of itself is a norm of international law without the necessity of its being recognized by states as a legal norm.

H. Kelsen writes: "The basis of customary law is the general principle that we ought to behave in the way our fellow men usually behave and during a certain time used to behave. If this principle assumes the character of a norm, custom becomes a law-creating fact. This is the case in the relations between states. Here custom, a long-established practice of states, creates law."[88]

At the same time, however, Kelsen says: "If the conduct of the states is not accompanied by the opinion that this conduct is obligatory or right, a so-called 'usage,' but not a law-creating custom, is established."[89] Moreover, the new edition of *Principles of International Law* prepared by R. Tucker even speaks about the consent of states. "Indeed," it says in this edition, "it is redundant to stress the importance of consent in the development of custom since it is obviously implicit in the constituent elements of custom."[90] This inconsistency is actually the result of the fact that previously Kelsen had rejected the necessity of this second element.[91]

An analogous evolution, which can only be welcomed, has taken place in Professor P. Guggenheim's works.

Previously, Guggenheim had resolutely opposed *opinio juris*. He asserted that usage (*consuetudo*) without any *opinio juris*, without any

Rousseau, *Droit international public*, p. 63; M. Sørenson, "Principes de droit international public," *Recueil des cours*, CI (1960), 47; F. Berber, *Lehrbuch des Völkerrechts* (Munich and Berlin: C. H. Beck'sche Verlagsbildhandlung, 1960), I, 43; P. Reuter, "Principes de droit international public," *Recueil des cours*, CIII (1961), 464; Arechaga, *Curso de derecho internacional publico*, I, 56; Waldock, "General Course on Public International Law," pp. 47-48; Friedmann, *The Changing Structure of International Law*, p. 121; D. O'Connell, *International Law* (London: Stevens & Sons, 1965), I, 16; A. K. Pavithran, *Substance of Public International Law Western and Eastern* (Madras: A. P. Rajendran, 1965), pp. 62-63; I. Brownlie, *Principles of Public International Law* (Oxford: Oxford University Press, 1966), pp. 6-7; Sereni, *Diritto internazionale*, I, 121; J. G. Starke, *Introduction to International Law*, 6th ed. (London: Butterworths, 1967), p. 37; G. Schwarzenberger, *A Manual of International Law*, 5th ed. (London: Stevens & Sons, 1967), p. 32; M. Virally, "The Sources of International Law," in M. Sørenson, ed., *The Manual of Public International Law* (New York: St. Martin's Press, 1968), p. 130.

88. Kelsen, *Principles of International Law*, p. 441.

89. *Ibid.*, p. 440.

90. *Ibid.*, pp. 453-454.

91. Verdross, for example, points to this, citing Kelsen's article in *Revue internationale de la théorie du droit* (1939). See A. Verdross, "Das völkerrechtliche Gewohnheitsrecht," *Japanese Annual of International Law*, VII (1963), 1.

Basic Processes of Forming Norms of International Law

"recognition by states as a legal norm," is a customary norm of international law. Acceptance of the concept of *opinio juris*, or recognition of a customary rule as a norm of international law, he wrote, makes custom superfluous as an independent source of international law. He believed it necessary to eliminate this "subjective element."[92]

Ultimately, however, Guggenheim in fact arrived at "recognition." He wrote: "The existence of custom should be considered as proved when repeated positive or negative acts become an expression of conduct which organs competent to apply the corresponding rule classify as custom."[93]

But what does "classify" mean? Classify means recognizing as norms of international law. According to Guggenheim though, recognition proceeds not from states, but from international organs. These organs, in the author's view, must be guided by defined criteria, by continuity, and by constant and effective application. In addition, breach of a rule should be linked with a sanction.[94] Guggenheim went on to say: " . . . an organ attributes the quality of a customary norm to universal acts, basing itself upon its own discretionary power. It confers upon the material element of a rule the character of a legal norm . . . "[95]

Thus, Guggenheim in fact has allowed for the necessity of recognizing a customary rule as a legal norm. But in believing that such recognition should follow from an international organ, he has led his discussion up a blind alley, since no international organ exists which would attach to its authority the legal character of customary rules of conduct.

In the second edition of his *Traité de droit international*, the first volume of which appeared in 1967, Guggenheim already specifically refers to two elements of a customary norm of international law. Citing Article 38 of the Statute of the International Court of Justice, Guggenheim writes: "Under these conditions, an organ which considers itself bound by a usage (*usage*) should be convinced not only that its repeated actions conform to an actual usage, but also that it acts in conformity with a norm of positive law . . . "[96]

Among those few writers who now reject the necessity of state recognition of a usage as a norm of international law, is, for example, an Italian professor, R. Quadri. "Custom," he wrote, "represents in social reality nothing other than a tradition, a series of uniform actions,

92. Guggenheim, "Les deux éléments de la coutume en droit international," pp. 275-280.

93. *Ibid.*, p. 280.

94. *Ibid.*, p. 281.

95. *Ibid.*, p. 284.

96. Guggenheim, *Traité de droit international public*, I, 104. [" . . . non seulement de se conformer d'une manière constante et uniforme à un usage utile et opportun . . . "]

generalized and prolonged for an indefinite period."[97] "Tradition" becomes a norm of law not because it has been recognized by a state as such, but because the "will of a social organism attaches such capacity to it."[98] The sociological explanation of this phenomenon given by Quadri is that tradition creates an "expectation" that actions will be repeated, which is important for "social equilibrium."[99]

An American professor, O. Lissitzyn, also decisively rejects the second element of a customary norm of international law, calling this construction "artificial."[100] The author, following McDougal, mixes the legal and other elements or, rather, simply casts the legal elements aside. In rejecting the need for a usage to be recognized as a norm of international law, the author inevitably comes to proclaim practice as a norm of international law. ". . . Custom, or 'general practice,' " Lissitzyn writes, "creates legally binding norms."[101]

The writers who deny the second element of an international legal norm lose sight of the specific features of legal norms. "Universal practice" creates not merely legal, but also moral international norms and norms of international comity. But of the general mass of such international norms, only those become norms of international law which acquire the said second element—recognition by states as international legal norms.

Our view also was held by the International Law Commission when the question arose of whether a particular customary norm of international law exists. Thus, in considering the question of diplomatic privileges and immunities of administrative and technical personnel, as well as of the service personnel of diplomatic representations, the Commission ascertained that certain states (the United States, Great Britain, the Soviet Union, and others) grant diplomatic privileges and immunities to administrative-technical personnel, and some even to service personnel of foreign diplomatic representations, although there are significant differences in the extent of their privileges and immunities, on the basis of reciprocity. Taking into account the absence of universal practice on this question, the Commission came to the conclusion that "in these circumstances it cannot be claimed that there is a rule of international law on the subject . . . "[102]

97. R. Quadri, *Diritto internazionale publico*, 4th ed. (Palermo: G. Priulle Editore, 1963), p. 95.

98. *Ibid.*, p. 96.

99. *Ibid.*, p. 95.

100. O. Lissitzyn, *International Law Today and Tomorrow* (New York: Oceana Publications, 1965), p. 34.

101. *Ibid.*, p. 35.

102. See the Report of the International Law Commission on the Work of Its X Session. United Nations, *Yearbook of the International Law Commission 1958*, II, 101.

Basic Processes of Forming Norms of International Law

With regard to exempting diplomats from customs duties upon articles imported for personal use, the Commission stated: "In general, customs duties are likewise not levied on articles intended for the personal use of the diplomatic agent or of members of his family belonging to his household (including articles intended for his establishment)." Thus, the Commission came to the conclusion that in this case the practice of exemption from customs duties is, in essence, universal. But it was noted at the same time that the said exemption from customs duties "... has been regarded as based on international comity," and, consequently, although universal practice does exist in the present instance, it still has not been recognized as a legal norm. On its part, the Commission proposed, inasmuch as this practice was widespread, to recognize it as a norm of international law. A corresponding provision was included in the draft Convention on Diplomatic Relations and Immunities.[103] The 1961 Vienna Conference incorporated this norm in the Convention on Diplomatic Relations (Article 36).

The unanimous or virtually unanimous recognition by representatives of different social systems and ideologies, as well as by international practice, of the position that two elements—the emergence of a rule of conduct and its recognition by states as a legal norm—are necessary for a customary norm of international law to arise is exceedingly important for the practice of international law. This does not mean that disagreements over customary norms of international law have no practical significance. But the said unanimity of opinion is sufficient for customary norms of international law, which still comprise an important part of contemporary general international law, to function and develop.

(2) A customary norm as the result and embodiment of tacit consent. The operative sphere of a customary norm. What is recognition by states of a specific rule as a norm of international law? What is the essence of such recognition? Recognition or acceptance by a state of a particular customary rule as a norm of law signifies an expression of a state's will, the consent of a state, to consider this customary rule to be a norm of international law. It must be emphasized that one is speaking of recognition "as a norm of international law" and not "as a legal norm" in general. States, for example, also recognize "as a legal norm" the norms of national legal systems of other states. Moreover, courts of states frequently apply norms of foreign law.

But the Statute of the International Court refers to recognition of a particular rule as an international legal norm or, more precisely, of a norm of general international law. The Statute speaks of "general practice,"

103. *Ibid.*, p. 26.

"accepted as law"; that is, local customary international legal norms are pushed to the side. Such norms exist, although they do not play a large role in the general system of international law.

It would be more accurate to say "recognized as an international legal norm" in Article 38(b) of the Statute instead of "accepted as law." Taking into account, however, that the words "is to decide in accordance with international law such disputes as are submitted to it" were included in the preamble of Article 38 of the Statute upon the proposal of the Chilean delegation at the San Francisco Conference,[104] the prevailing text of the Statute indicates sufficiently clearly that the question is one just of recognition "as an international legal norm."

This fact is of material importance. In recognizing a norm of international law, a state takes upon itself before other states the obligation to observe a rule of conduct as binding upon itself, from which it may not arbitrarily free itself. At the same time, it acquires the right to demand that this norm be observed by other states.

Thus, the bonds between a state accepting a customary norm of international law and the other states who already have recognized this norm are basically identical with those bonds established among states with the aid of an international treaty.[105]

Consequently, the essence of the process of creating a norm of international law by means of custom consists of agreement between states, which in this case is tacit, and not clearly expressed, as in a treaty. (On the legal nature of agreement see Chapter 8.)

If a customary norm of international law is the result of agreement between states, the operative sphere of this norm is limited to relations between states who have recognized it as a norm of international law, that is to say, to relations between those states who are parties to the corresponding tacit agreement.

The operative sphere of a principle or customary norm of international law may gradually expand, and it is by this means, as a rule, that customary norms of international law become generally recognized. There are frequent instances when the declaration of a single state is a formative moment. Many principles of international law were proclaimed, for example, by revolutionary France in the eighteenth century. Among them are the principles of respect for state sovereignty, noninterference, equality of states, and the principle that military operations must be directed only against military objects and not against the civilian population, and others. In the Decree on Peace and other state documents, the

104. See S. B. Krylov, *Istoriia sozdaniia OON*, ed. G. I. Tunkin (Moscow: izd-vo IMO, 1960), p. 228.

105. See Tunkin, *Osnovy sovremennogo mezhdunarodnogo prava*, p. 11.

Soviet state advanced the principles of the prohibition and criminality of aggressive war, the principle of self-determination of nations, the principle of peaceful coexistence, and a number of other principles of international law.

In all of the aforesaid instances the principles initially proclaimed by one state gradually were recognized by other states and were transformed partially by custom and partially by treaty into generally recognized principles of contemporary international law.

The question frequently is raised: how can the origin of a norm of international law be explained on the basis of the concept of agreement if another customary norm of international law already exists on the given question? Professor Basdevant says, for example, that the doctrine pursuant to which the essence of the process of creating a customary norm of international law consists of tacit agreement is in contradiction with the changed character of customary norms. He declares that it is impossible, without resorting to a fiction, to assert that "we have here the case of a tacit agreement consecrating this change, an agreement to which all states who previously were bound by the corresponding customary norm are participants."[106]

One should not forget, however, the specific feature of international law that subjects of international law are themselves the creators of norms of international law. The fact that states are bound by prevailing norms of international law does not preclude the possibility of their creating new norms of international law by treaty or custom that may differ from prevailing norms. With regard to norms of international law which are not of an imperative character, the question is resolved relatively simply.

A new norm deviating from a prevailing norm (and, consequently, recognized by the respective powers) will, of course, be binding only upon states which have recognized it, and this new norm replaces the respective old norm in relations among these countries. The latter, however, will be operative among states which still have not recognized the new norm, as well as in relations between these states, on one side, and the powers who already have recognized the new norm, on the other. The operative sphere of this new norm gradually may be expanded at the expense of reducing the operative sphere of the old norm, and ultimately the new norm may completely supplant the old norm.

The principle of the prohibition of aggressive war, for example, entered international law as a conventional principle of the 1928 Pact of Paris. In the relations among parties to this treaty the said principle replaced the previously prevailing principle of general international law under which

106. Basdevant, "Règles générales du droit de la paix," pp. 515-516.

each state had the right to go to war. The new principle was recognized by other states either by accession to the Pact of Paris or by custom, so that for some countries this was a conventional principle whereas for others, a customary principle of international law. By such means the principle of the prohibition of aggressive war gradually was transformed into a generally recognized principle of international law, having replaced "the right of states to go to war." This principle was developed further in the United Nations Charter.

One of the principal arguments advanced against the concept that the essence of custom as a specific method of creating a norm of international law consists of agreement between states is the assertion that this concept contradicts the situation supposedly existing wherein a customary norm legally binds states irrespective of its being "recognized" or "accepted" by these states. This kind of objection is advanced both by proponents and opponents of the concept of *opinio juris*.

H. Kelsen, calling the notion that a customary norm is a tacit agreement a fiction, asserts that "international customary law could be interpreted as created by a consent of the states only if it were possible to prove that the custom which evidences the existence of a norm of international law is constituted by the acts of all the states which are bound by the norm of customary law, or that a norm of customary law is binding upon a state only if this state by its own acts participated in establishing the custom in question."[107] In developing this thought, Kelsen points out that since customary norms of international law are binding upon all states, it would be necessary to prove that all states have agreed to the recognition of all customary norms of international law by their actual conduct, by participating in creating the respective custom which testifies to the existence of a customary norm. Such evidence, Kelsen says, is not needed under international law. Customary norms of international law, he asserts, are created not by the "common consent of members of the international community," but by the "long-established practice of a great number of states, including the states which with respect to their power, their culture, and so on, are of certain importance . . ."[108]

Kelsen maintains in addition that it supposedly should follow from the concept of agreement that all states must participate in creating each norm of international law. It is wholly obvious that this is not so. It is not obligatory in the least that a respective practice leading to the creation of a customary norm of international law be "universal."

A customary rule may be created by the practice of a limited number of states. In being recognized as a legal norm, it sometimes is initially a

107. Kelsen, *Principles of International Law*, p. 444.
108. *Ibid.*, p. 445.

Basic Processes of Forming Norms of International Law

customary norm having a limited sphere of application which, as this norm is recognized by other states, gradually expands, bringing the respective norm closer to a generally recognized norm of international law.

Expansion of the operative sphere of a customary norm is to some extent analogous to that which takes place with regard to conventional norms of international law. In reality, norms of a particular international treaty very frequently are created by only a few of the countries which become parties to this treaty. Those states which subsequently accede to the treaty have not participated in creating the norms of this treaty.

Many other writers, together with Kelsen, insist that the position—which in their view is the existing position—that customary norms of international law recognized by a large number of states become binding in virtue thereof upon all states makes the concept of the customary norm as a tacit agreement unacceptable and contrary to reality. "Tacit agreements," writes A. Sereni, "bind only states which are parties to these agreements; a customary norm, on the contrary, binds states as soon as it is formed irrespective of their consent or participation in its formation."[109]

It is difficult to avoid noticing that the argumentation of these writers pretends to have proved just what is to be proved; to wit, the binding character of customary norms upon all states which have been recognized by the majority of states.

The thesis that a customary norm of international law recognized by a significant number of states is binding upon all other countries enjoys wide support in contemporary bourgeois international legal literature.

Professor Verdross makes an interesting reservation: "Despite the fact that the formation of a general customary norm does not presuppose its application by all states, a universal customary rule may not arise which would contravene the legal convictions of any civilized people."[110] But if recognition of a new customary norm of international law as such is necessary on the part of a respective state, why should a newly-formed state be in a worse position? Why may this state not object to any customary norm of international law with which it does not agree? This was at one time the position of the Soviet state and is now the position of new states formed in consequence of the liberation of colonies.[111]

109. Sereni, *Diritto internazionale*, I, 123; see also Arechaga, *Curso de derecho internacional publico*, I, 59-60; Quadri, *Diritto internazionale publico*, p. 94; Guggenheim, *Traité de droit international public*, I, 107-108.

110. Verdross, *Mezhdunarodnoe pravo*, p. 155.

111. See G. M. Abi-Saab, "The Newly Independent States and the Rules of International Law," *Howard Law Journal*, VIII (1962), 106; R. P. Anand, "Attitude

The concept that customary norms of international law recognized as such by a significant number of states must be considered to be binding upon all states is actually based upon the presupposition that a majority of states may dictate norms of international law binding upon all other states in international relations.

This position is carried out to its logical conclusion by R. Quadri, an Italian professor. In developing his theory of a "collective or social will" (*volontà collettiva o sociale*), Quadri maintains that will, the decision of a group of states, may create legal norms in international relations binding upon all states; that is to say, create norms of general international law. According to Quadri, international law is based upon a decision of the predominant force in the international community.[112] In another work, published in the *Recueil de cours* of the Hague Academy of International Law, Quadri explains what he means by the expression "predominant force." He writes: "It is sufficient that there exist a will, decision, and action common to a specific group which is in a position, if necessary, to impose its authority."[113]

This concept is in blatant contradiction to the fundamental principles of international law, especially the principle of equality of states.

Indisputably, this principle signifies only legal equality, which does not correspond to the real inequality of states in international relations. Here there is a definite contradiction between real and legal relations. There is no doubt that the position of the majority of states, including states of the two systems, and above all the position of the great powers, has decisive significance in the process of creating generally recognized norms of international law. Such is the actual situation. Legally, however, the wills of different states are of equal significance in the process of creating a norm of international law. This legal equality is of great importance. It follows from this that the majority of states in international relations can not create norms binding upon other states and do not have the right to attempt to impose given norms on other states. This proposition is especially important for contemporary international law, which regulates relations of states belonging to different and even opposed social systems.

---

of the Asian-African States Toward Certain Problems of International Law," *International and Comparative Law Quarterly*, XV (1966), 64-67; H. Bokor-Szegó, "The New States and International Law," *Questions of International Law* (Budapest: Hungarian Lawyers' Association, 1968), pp. 7-35; M. Sahovic, "Influence des états nouveaux sur la conception du droit international," *Annuaire français de droit international*, XII (1966), 34-35.

112. Quadri, *Diritto internazionale publico*, p. 28.

113. Quadri, "Le fondement du caractère obligatoire du droit international public," *Recueil des cours*, LXXX (1952), 625.

Basic Processes of Forming Norms of International Law

The will of states, reflected in their recognition of a customary norm of international law, is determinative. Force of circumstances compels individual states in the majority of instances to consider as binding those norms which the overwhelming majority of states already have recognized, including the states of the two systems and the great powers. But this actual situation never should be confused with the legal situation.

As regards newly emergent states, legally they have the right not to recognize a particular customary norm of general international law. If, however, a new state enters without reservations into official relations with other countries, this signifies that it accepts the specific complex of principles and norms of prevailing international law as being the basic principles of relations among states.

In practice, in all instances when it is necessary to ascertain the existence of a particular generally-recognized norm of international law, the normal procedure is to investigate whether there is a "general practice" and, if such a practice exists, whether it has been recognized as a legal norm and by how many states.

In establishing whether a state has recognized a particular rule as a norm of international law, the issue of the "silence" of a state presents significant difficulties. As I. Brownlie correctly points out, "silence may signify either tacit consent or the absence of interest in the particular matter."[114]

Assuredly, not every silence can be regarded as consent. Particularly in those instances when the respective forming of a customary norm does not affect a state's interests at the given time, its silence can not be considered to be tacit recognition of this norm. But in those instances when an emerging rule affects the interests of a particular state, the absence of objections after a sufficient time can, as a rule, be regarded as tacit recognition of this norm.

Recognition of a particular rule as an international norm by a large number of states may be a basis for presupposing that this norm has been generally recognized, but only as a presupposition, and not a final conclusion.[115]

Undoubtedly it is not always possible and perhaps even impossible in the majority of instances to determine with mathematical precision that a particular customary norm of international law has been recognized by all

114. I. Brownlie, *Principles of Public International Law*, 2d ed. (Oxford: Clarendon Press, 1973), p. 7.

115. Strupp, for example, believes that if a customary norm is applied by a significant number of states "here already is a normal presumption, a *presumptio juris* which, however, can be rebutted, a presumption in favor of the validity of this norm for all states." Strupp, "Règles générales du droit de la paix," pp. 310-311.

states without exception. However, a similar situation is created in social phenomena rather frequently, and the difficulties which may arise in the process of similar calculations never have been regarded as undermining the rule itself.

As regards the instances when a state objects in general to a customary norm of international law in the course of formation or to its application, the general view is that this customary norm can not be applied to the state. This necessarily arises out of the consensual basis of a customary norm. In its judgment in the Anglo-Norwegian dispute the International Court recognized, for example, that the ten-mile rule for the aperture of bays could not be applied to Norway, in particular because Norway always had objected to this rule.[116]

The misgivings expressed by writers who criticize the concept of tacit agreement, that acceptance of this viewpoint would lead in practice to the necessity of proving in each individual instance whether a given state had recognized the corresponding customary norm or not, are greatly exaggerated. In the overwhelming majority of instances in disputes between states which relate to this question, the issue is not whether a particular state has recognized a specific customary norm of general international law, but rather a matter of the content of this norm and of its application in a concrete situation.[117]

There have been instances, however, when a dispute involved precisely whether a norm recognized by a majority of states was binding upon other states who had not recognized this norm. The question of the three-mile breadth of territorial waters may serve as an example. As is well-known, at the 1958 and 1960 Geneva Conferences on the Law of the Sea the western states, relying upon the bourgeois doctrine adduced above, attempted to maintain that the three-mile limit of territorial waters had existed for a long time, and had been recognized as a norm of international law by the majority of states, and therefore is a norm of general international law binding upon all states. These claims of the western powers, however, did not obtain even two-thirds of the votes at the said conferences, the socialist states and a significant number of Asian and African states opposing the assertions of the western powers. Two conclusions follow from this. First, the three-mile rule is not a norm of general international law. Second, and more generally, an international

116. International Court of Justice, Reports of Judgments, Advisory Opinions and Orders, *Fisheries Case (United Kingdom v. Norway), Judgment of December 18, 1951* (Leiden: A. W. Sijthoff, 1952), p. 131; A. Verdross, *Die Quellen des universellen Völkerrechts* (Freiberg: Rombach, 1973), p. 103.

117. See, for example, Waldock, "General Course on Public International Law," p. 52.

legal norm recognized by a majority of states is not recognized by states as being binding upon all other states.

The doctrine that customary norms of international law recognized as such by a significant number of states are binding upon all states not only has no basis in contemporary international law but also conceals a very great danger. This doctrine in essence justifies the attempts of a specific group of states to impose upon new states, socialist or newly emergent states of Asia and Africa, for example, certain customary norms which never have been accepted by the new states and which may be partially or wholly unacceptable to them. Of course, this tendency on the part of the large imperialist powers to dictate norms of international law to other states in contemporary conditions is doomed to failure, but at the same time such attempts undoubtedly may lead to serious international complications.

Many bourgeois specialists in international affairs who reject the concept of "tacit agreement" at the same time adhere to the view that "recognition," "acceptance," or "consent" to consider a particular rule as legally binding is a decisive element in the process of creating a customary norm of international law.

Thus Basdevant, in considering the concept of agreement with regard to customary norms of international law to be unfounded, writes that custom "is the result of precedents which indicate recognition of such a rule as law (*opinio juris*)."[118] In another place Basdevant points out that customary norms "born spontaneously, from the exigencies of international life, acquire a positive character, as a result of which they become recognized by those who are in a position to ensure their application in international life."[119]

Professor C. de Visscher writes in several nebulous passages: " . . . In international relations a customary norm forms when a practice is, through simultaneous applications, sufficiently stabilized so that in it can be perceived an expression of an equilibrium of only a temporary stabilization of existing interests, and in consequence thereof an element of order legally accepted by the majority of states."[120]

In rejecting the concept of tacit agreement, these writers at the same time speak of *opinio juris* as a necessary element of a customary norm of international law. In Professor Basdevant's view, *opinio juris* signifies that "a corresponding rule has been recognized as a legal norm."[121] Professor C. de Visscher writes: "From the assimilation of custom to tacit

118. Basdevant, "Règles générales du droit de la paix," p. 513.
119. *Ibid.*, p. 316.
120. Visscher, "Coutume et traité en droit international public," p. 356.
121. Basdevant, "Règles générales du droit de la paix," p. 513.

convention, which in our judgment is quite fictitious, must be distinguished the requirement of *opinio juris sive necessitatis*, regarded here as reflecting the attitude of power in relation to a given practice."[122]

It must be noted that this understanding of *opinio juris* has virtually the same significance as the concept of recognition of a particular rule as a norm of international law and leads, consequently, to the concept of tacit agreement.

Frequently, however, the term *opinio juris* has a completely different meaning. Professor Kunz, for example, defines *opinio juris* as follows: "The practice must have been applied in the conviction that it is legally binding."[123] At the same time, Kunz is obliged to acknowledge the difficulties to which this concept of *opinio juris* leads. On one hand, he says, it is asserted that practice plus *opinio juris* creates a customary norm of international law, but, on the other hand, for such a norm to be formed states must act in the conviction that they are acting in conformity with a legal duty. However, insofar as a customary norm of international law still has not been formed, this conviction has no legal basis in and of itself. Kunz adds in this connection: "Hence, the very coming into existence of such a norm would presuppose that the states acted in legal error."[124]

In reality, the term *"opinio juris,"* understood in this sense, signifies that states must act in the conviction that the respective norm of international law already exists, and it follows from this that such a norm can not appear in consequence of state practice but must be assumed to exist irrespective of such practice. This reasoning inevitably leads to the conclusion that a customary norm as postulated by the said concept of *opinio juris* is not a customary norm at all, growing out of the international practice of states, but rather represents a certain norm of "natural law."

122. Visscher, *Théories et réalites en droit international public*, p. 188; see also Morelli, *Nozioni di diritto internazionale*, pp. 25-29; Arechaga, *Curso de derecho internacional publico*, I, 56-70; Sereni, *Diritto internazionale*, I, 123-128. M. Virally says that a customary norm is "based on consent." See Sørenson, ed., *Manual of Public International Law*, p. 135.

123. Kunz, "The Nature of Customary International Law," p. 667; see also L. Kopelmanas, "Custom as a Means of the Creation of International Law," *British Year Book of International Law*, XVIII (1937), 129. G. Scelle, in accordance with his general conception, sees the criteria of obligatoriness in the conformity of a customary rule to "the general welfare and social goals." He says: "Custom is born as the result of the recurrence of identical conduct, individual or collective. It is affirmed by the conviction . . . that such conduct conforms to the general welfare and social goals." G. Scelle, *Manuel de droit international public* (Paris: Editions Domat-Montchrestien, 1948), p. 10.

124. Kunz, "The Nature of Customary International Law," p. 667; see also Quadri, *Diritto internazionale publico*, p. 94; Gianni, *La coutume en droit international*, p. 157.

The difficulties arise in connection with the nondialectical approaches to the question of "recognizing practice as a norm of law" or to *opinio juris*. The creation of a customary norm of international law is a process; the elements of a legal norm build up gradually.

Opinio juris signifies that a state regards a particular customary rule as a norm of international law, as a rule legally binding on the international plane. This is an expression of the will of a state, in its way a proposal to other states. When other states also express their will in the same direction, a tacit agreement is formed with regard to recognizing a customary rule as an international legal norm.

From what has been said it follows that a customary norm of international law is the result of agreement, that is, of the concordance of the wills of states. Professor C. Chaumont rightly emphasized in his lecture at the Hague Academy that with regard to customary norms "one can not escape the logic of agreement."[125]

Modification or abolition of a customary norm of international law may be accomplished by treaty or by custom. In either case a new agreement among states is formed. Modification by custom consists of a modification of "general practice," which is accompanied by recognition as an international norm.[126] Such recognition is implied in those instances when a new practice which departs from a prevailing norm of international law is not objected to by other states.[127]

C. Treaty and Custom in Contemporary International Law

(1) The dominant role of the treaty in the development of international law. Proportionately, treaty norms presently occupy the principal place in international law as a result of the large growth in the number of international agreements.

An international treaty possesses specific features which make it a highly suitable and important means of creating norms of international law in our day. It is an agreement of states clearly expressed. This fact is

125. C. Chaumont, "Cours général de droit international public," *Recueil des cours*, CXXIX (1970), 440.

126. Professor Verdross, proceeding from the concept of law-consciousness as the basis of international law, writes: " ... A norm of international law can not be abolished by means of recurrent practice and the general diffusion of the violation which has occurred unless some new legal conception is reflected therein." Verdross, *Mezhdunarodnoe pravo*, p. 156; also see Morelli, *Nozioni di diritto internazionale*, pp. 25-26.

127. See D. B. Levin, *Diplomaticheskii immunitet* (Moscow: izd-vo AN SSSR, 1949), p. 153.

of great significance for ascertaining the existence and content of a particular norm of international law.

Moreover, in the contemporary period of rapid change in all spheres of international life the treaty is an especially suitable means of concretizing, developing, modifying, or creating new norms of international law.[128]

It is doubtful whether one can agree with G. Fitzmaurice, who asserts that international custom both now and in the future will be the basis for the development of international law. From his point of view general international law is solely customary law; treaties create only local norms. He writes: "Norms created by treaties can, as *lex specialis*, in principle only influence norms concerning the subject of the treaty but not law in general."[129]

The predominant role of the international treaty in the development of international law is a comparatively new phenomenon. It is true that even now custom still plays an important role in international law. A significant portion of the norms and principles consolidated in international treaties continue to remain, to a certain extent, customary principles and norms. Among these are, for example, the principle of respect for state sovereignty, noninterference in internal affairs, nonaggression, and equality. These principles have been fixed in the United Nations Charter. But above all they remain basically customary principles of international law for states who are not members of the United Nations. We say "basically" because some of those states have obligations under local treaties to observe the principles of the United Nations Charter. Moreover, the provisions of the Charter which fix the said principles also may not exhaust the content of these principles as customary principles of international law. It is doubtful, for example, whether the provisions of the Charter relating to equality of states fully embody the content of this principle as it exists in contemporary international law.

The treaty form also is used in connection with the further development of entire branches of international law. On the basis of a draft prepared by the International Law Commission, the 1958 Geneva Conference worked out four conventions relating to basic questions of the international law of the sea which entered into force between September 1962 and March 1966.

A second important branch of international customary law—ambassa-

128. For greater detail, see Lukashuk, *Istochniki mezhdunarodnogo prava*, pp. 47-49.

129. G. Fitzmaurice, *The Future of Public International Law and of the International Legal System in the Circumstances of Today* (Geneva: Institut de droit international, 1973), p. 9; H. W. A. Thirlway, *International Customary Law and Codification* (Leiden: A. W. Sijthoff, 1972), p. 146.

dorial law—also has been subjected to being formulated in a treaty. At the 1961 Vienna Conference, a Convention on Diplomatic Relations was adopted which entered into force in April 1964.

At the 1963 Vienna Conference, a Convention on Consular Relations was adopted which entered into force in March 1967. Since the draft of this Convention prepared by the International Law Commission deteriorated significantly at the conference, many countries (including the Soviet Union) have abstained from signing it.

As a result of the International Law Commission's long and difficult work a draft convention embracing a major branch of international law—the law of treaties—was prepared. On the basis of this draft the 1968-1969 Vienna Conference adopted the Convention on the Law of Treaties.

The norms of these conventions, to the extent they have entered into force for individual states, replace or will replace customary norms of international law in relations among their parties.

However, this does not preclude customary norms of international law continuing to be operative even among parties to the convention if for some reason individual questions remain unregulated by these conventions.

At the suggestion of the Swiss delegation at the Vienna Conference, this obvious proposition was stated in the preamble of the Convention on Diplomatic Relations of April 18, 1961, where it says that "norms of international customary law will continue to regulate questions not expressly provided for by the provisions of the present Convention." Analogous provisions are contained in the preambles of the 1963 Convention on Consular Relations and the 1969 Convention on the Law of Treaties.

Moreover, new customary norms of international law may be formed in the future in these branches.

As regards the predominant role of the international treaty in creating norms of international law in areas which up to now have not been affected or have been slightly affected by international legal regulation, this is obvious. It suffices to mention a number of the more important international treaties which have appeared in recent years: the 1963 Moscow treaty on the prohibition of nuclear testing in three spheres; the 1967 treaty on the principles of activities of states in exploring and exploiting outer space, including the moon; the 1968 treaty on the nonproliferation of nuclear weapons; the 1965 convention on the elimination of all forms of racial discrimination adopted by the United Nations General Assembly; and the two covenants on human rights adopted by the United Nations General Assembly in 1966.

The Process of Forming Norms of International Law

Taking these circumstances into account, the Soviet doctrine of international law, while by no means denying the important role of custom, regards the international treaty as the basic source of international law.[130]

The predominant role of the international treaty in the development of contemporary international law also is emphasized in the international legal literature of other socialist countries.[131]

Bourgeois international legal doctrine still basically adheres to the old concept of the predominant role of custom. With the aid of this concept, capitalist states frequently attempt to uphold old, in the majority of cases customary, norms of international law advantageous to them which were created by these states when the capitalist system was dominant in the world.

An ever greater number of international lawyers in the bourgeois countries, however, are moving away from this concept, realizing that it is hopelessly obsolete and does not reflect contemporary international reality. Thus, C. de Visscher, pointing out that in the modern era of rapid changes there is no "degree of passivity," which was important for the formation of custom, believes that the international treaty now plays the principal role in the development of international law, "leaving only a subordinate role to custom."[132]

Professor W. Friedmann writes: "It is obvious that, in the fast-moving articulate and complex international society of today, the international treaty increasingly replaces custom as the principal source of international law."[133]

130. See, for example, Durdenevskii and Krylov, eds., *Mezhdunarodnoe pravo*, p. 20; Korovin, *Mezhdunarodnoe pravo*, p. 16; F. I. Kozhevnikov, *Sovetskoe gosudarstvo i mezhdunarodnoe pravo* (Moscow: Iurizdat, 1948), p. 220; V. I. Lisovskii, *Mezhdunarodnoe pravo* (Kiev: izd-vo Kievskogo universiteta, 1955), p. 28; Tunkin, *Osnovy sovremennogo mezhdunarodnogo prava*, p. 12; Shurshalov, *Osnovnye voprosy teorii mezhdunarodnogo dogovora*, p. 8; Minasian, *Istochniki sovremennogo mezhdunarodnogo prava*, p. 47; Lukin, *Istochniki sovremennogo mezhdunarodnogo prava*, p. 56; Talalaev, *Iuridicheskaia priroda mezhdunarodnogo dogovora*, pp. 164ff; Kozhevnikov, ed., *Kurs mezhdunarodnogo prava*, p. 40; Lukashuk, *Istochniki mezhdunarodnogo prava*, pp. 42ff; Chkhikvadze and others, eds., *Kurs mezhdunarodnogo prava*, I, 170; L. A. Modzhorian and N. T. Blatova, eds., *Mezhdunarodnoe pravo* (Moscow: Iuridicheskaia literatura, 1970), p. 57.

131. See, for example, V. Outrata, *Mezinárodní právo veřejné* (Prague: Orbis, 1960), p. 26; Avramov, *Medunarodno javno pravo*, 2d ed. (1973), p. 36; V. Pěchota, *Mnohostranné mezinárodní smlouvy a přístup k nim* (Prague: Nakladatelstvi Ceskoslovenske akademie ved, 1965), p. 7; Nahlik, *Wstep do nauki prawa miedzynarodowego*, p. 170; G. Haraszti, *Some Fundamental Problems of the Law of Treaties* (Budapest: Akademiai kiado, 1973), p. 7.

132. Visscher, "Coutume et traité en droit international public," p. 359.

133. Friedmann, *The Changing Structure of International Law*, pp. 123-124.

The new edition of Kelsen's *Principles of International Law* also refers to the diminishing role of custom in comparison with the treaty. In an addition to the paragraph on custom it is pointed out that there is presently occurring an "erosion, if not the disappearance, of the conditions, which have favored the development of law through custom . . . "[134]

(2) The international treaty and general international law. Since treaty and customary norms of international law are the result of agreement between states, their operative sphere is defined by the participation of states in a clearly expressed (international treaty) or tacit (custom) agreement.

The concept that an international treaty is not a source of general international law still is significantly widespread in bourgeois international legal literature. The proponents of this concept assert that general international law is exclusively customary law. "General international law," D. Anzilotti wrote, "is exclusively customary law."[135]

H. Kelsen points out: "General . . . international law is customary law valid for all states belonging to the international community. (Customary law is law created by the habitual practice of the states.) Particular international law is valid for some states only and comprises, for the most part, norms created by treaties valid only for the contracting parties."[136]

Kunz is of the same mind. He asserts that " . . . general international law is created only by custom," and "treaty-created norms always constitute particular international law only . . . "[137]

This concept has been well-known for a long time. Even Vattel wrote: "Since it is obvious that a treaty binds only the contracting parties, the conventional law of nations is not universal, but special law."[138]

O'Connell, proceeding from the concept that international law is only general international law, writes that "traditionally international law is customary law . . . "[139] He generally does not regard international treaties as sources of international law. "It is quite incorrect," he writes, "to

134. Kelsen, *Principles of International Law*, p. 452.

135. D. Anzilotti, *Kurs mezhdunarodnogo prava*, trans. from 4th ed. by A. Sakketti and E. M. Fabrikova, ed. D. B. Levin (Moscow: izd-vo IL, 1961), p. 97.

136. Kelsen, *Principles of International Law*, p. 17.

137. Kunz, "General International Law and the Law of International Organization," *American Journal of International Law*, XLVII (1953), 457.

138. E. de Vattel, *Pravo narodov*, ed. V. N. Durdenevskii (Moscow: Gosiurizdat, 1960), p. 33.

139. O'Connell, *International Law*, I, 4.

speak of treaties as 'sources' of international law. They are no more than contracts between the parties . . . "[140]

The concept that general international law is exclusively customary law was correct during Vattel's time and even in the nineteenth century. Now, however, this concept is obsolete and does not reflect contemporary international reality.

The existence of a large number of multilateral international treaties in which all or nearly all states participate, as well as important activity in the codification of international law, create a situation whereby international treaties are becoming a means of directly creating, modifying, and developing norms of general international law.[141] It is true that in the majority of instances this takes place with some assistance of custom (see Section 3 of this chapter).

This already is being noticed also by many authoritative bourgeois specialists in international affairs. In the latest edition of Oppenheim's *International Law*, Professor Lauterpacht wrote: "*Universal* international law is created when all or practically all the members of the *Family* of *Nations* are parties to these treaties . . . many law-making treaties have been concluded which contain *general* International Law because the majority of States, including the leading Powers, are parties to them . . . "[142]

"International customary law," writes Verdross, "is the oldest source of general international law. Only recently, in connection with the growing codification of international law, has it been relegated somewhat to the second plane."[143]

General treaties now play a special role in the development of general international law. These are treaties relating to questions of interest to all states and having the purpose of creating norms binding all states—that is, norms of general international law. The question of such treaties was raised in the International Law Commission, which in 1962 included in its draft articles on the law of treaties the following definition of a general international treaty: " 'General multilateral treaty' means a multilateral treaty which concerns general norms of international law or deals with matters of general interest to the States as a whole."[144]

140. *Ibid.*, p. 22.
141. See G. I. Tunkin, "40 let sosushchestvovaniia i mezhdunarodnoe pravo," *Sovetskii ezhegodnik mezhdunarodnogo prava 1958* (Moscow: izd-vo AN SSSR, 1959), p. 19.
142. Oppenheim, *International Law*, I, 28; see also Dahm, *Völkerrecht*, I, 21.
143. Verdross, *Völkerrecht*, pp. 137-138.
144. United Nations, *Yearbook of the International Law Commission 1962*, II, 161.

The question of general international treaties is linked closely to the question of the participation of all states in such treaties. It would be an obvious contradiction to work out a treaty for the purpose of creating norms binding upon all states and at the same time to include therein a provision closing this treaty to certain states. As a French professor, E. Giraud, has wholly correctly pointed out, general international treaties "are open treaties in the sense that all states of the world in principle may become parties."[145] The right of any state to participate in general international treaties derives from basic principles of international law and, in particular, from principles of respect for sovereignty and equality of states. It follows from these principles that, on one hand, states are free to select their partners in concluding an international treaty and, on the other, all states have the right to participate in general international treaties since they are intended to regulate relations of interest to all states.

In conformity therewith, a Soviet jurist introduced the following proposal in the International Law Commission: "In the case of a general multilateral treaty, every State may become a party to the treaty."[146]

In the comments of competent authorities of the USSR upon the draft articles prepared by the International Law Commission it was pointed out: " . . . in codifying the law of treaties, it is necessary to proceed from the assumption that general international agreements should be open to participation by all States. This is required by the principle of the equality of States. Moreover, as such treaties usually regulate matters of interest to each and every State and are intended to establish or develop universally recognized principles and rules of contemporary international law which are binding on all States, to deny certain States the possibility of becoming parties to such treaties is contrary to their very spirit and purpose and is harmful to international co-operation."[147]

It is well-known that capitalist states, in violation of fundamental principles of contemporary international law, persistently strive to insert formulas in general international treaties limiting the circle of parties to such treaties to United Nations members, to members of the United Nations specialized agencies and the Statute of the International Court, as well as to states specially invited to participate by the United Nations General Assembly. This formula presently precludes the possibility of

145. Giraud, "Modification et terminaison des traités collectifs," p. 17.

146. United Nations, *Yearbook of the International Law Commission 1965*, I, 117.

147. Reports of the International Law Commission on the second part of its seventeenth session 3-28 January 1966 and on its eighteenth session 4 May-19 July 1966. GAOR (XXI), Supp. No. 9 (1966), p. 288. Doc. No. A/6309/Rev. 1.

some socialist states participating in such treaties: the German Democratic Republic, the Korean People's Democratic Republic, and the Democratic Republic of Vietnam.[148]

From the very beginning, western jurists in the International Law Commission opposed the inclusion of provisions on general international treaties in the draft articles. As already has been pointed out, however, during the first discussion of the draft article in 1962 the Commission inserted a definition of a "general multilateral treaty," as well as a provision on participation in such treaties which provided: "In the case of a general multilateral treaty, every State may become a party to the treaty unless it is otherwise provided by the terms of the treaty itself or by the established rules of an international organization."[149]

This formulation was a compromise and inadequate, but it nonetheless embodied the principle of universal participation in general treaties.

In their comments upon the Commission's draft, the governments of the United States and England expressed disagreement with the principle set forth in this article.[150]

When the Commission discussed this provision a second time, agreement was not reached on these questions, and this was noted in the Commission's report.[151] As a result thereof, the final draft articles did not contain either provisions relating to general multilateral treaties or articles on the participation of states in multilateral treaties in general.

The question of general international treaties was raised anew at the Vienna Conference on the Law of Treaties. The delegations of Hungary, the Congo (Democratic Republic), the United Arab Republic, the United Republic of Tanzania, Poland, Rumania, the Ukrainian Soviet Socialist Republic, and Czechoslovakia introduced the following amendment to draft Article 2 (definition of terms): " 'General multilateral treaty' means a multilateral treaty which is connected with questions of general interest to the international community of states."[152] At the same time, the delegations of Hungary, India, Mongolia, the United Arab Republic, Rumania, Syria, the Ukrainian SSR, Ceylon, Yugoslavia, Algeria, and Mali

148. For greater detail, see G. Schirmer, *Universalität völkerrechtlicher Vertrage und internationaler Organisationen* (Berlin: Staatsverlag der DDR, 1966).

149. United Nations, *Yearbook of the International Law Commission 1962*, II, 167-168.

150. See *Law of Treaties: Comments by Governments on parts I and II of the draft articles on the law of treaties drawn up by the Commission at its fourteenth and fifteenth sessions*, pp. 163, 151. Doc. No. A/CN.4/175, February 23, 1965.

151. See United Nations, *Yearbook of the International Law Commission 1966*, II, 189, 200.

152. United Nations Conference on the Law of Treaties, Doc. No. A/CONF.39/C.1/L.19/Rev. 1, March 29, 1968.

introduced a proposal to add to the draft convention the following article: "All states possess the right to participate in general multilateral treaties in accordance with the principle of sovereign equality."[153]

Under the pressure of the western powers, however, these amendments were not accepted by the conference. Thus, the problem of general multilateral treaties remained unresolved in the conference on the law of treaties.

At the same time, the Vienna Conference adopted a Declaration in which the conviction was expressed that "multilateral treaties which deal with the codification and progressive development of international law, or the object and purpose of which are of interest to the international community as a whole, should be open to universal participation."[154]

The concept of a general international treaty was by no means a revival of the notion of the "law-making treaty," as M. Virally suggests.[155] It reflected the extraordinarily revitalized role of a specific category of international multilateral treaties in the creation of norms of general international law. Despite a certain similarity to the concept of the "law-making" treaty, the concept of a general international treaty has a different content. The question was not of the role of the treaty in creating international legal norms in general, but of its role in creating norms of general international law.

Analyzing the situation in contemporary international law, one can define the following basic features of the general international treaty: (1) it aims to create or modify norms of general international law; (2) questions created by a general international treaty touch upon the interests of all states; (3) all states without exception have the right to participate in a general international treaty.

The inclusion in the Vienna Convention on the Law of Treaties of corresponding provisions relating to general international treaties would have furthered the progressive development of international law.

Multilateral treaties with a limited number of participants, as well as bilateral treaties, also influence the development of general international law. They sometimes lead to the conclusion of general international treaties, an example being the 1963 Vienna convention on consular questions, on which bilateral consular conventions exerted great influence. Norms of such treaties may obtain general recognition by treaty or custom and become norms of general international law.

153. *Ibid.*, Doc. No. A/CONF.39/C.1/L.74, April 1, 1968.

154. *Ibid.*, Doc. No. A/CONF.39/26, May 23, 1969.

155. See M. Virally, "Sur la classification des traités," *Communicazioni e studi*, XIII (1969), 20.

(3) The interaction of treaty and custom. International treaty and international custom are the two methods of creating norms of general international law. The essence of these methods lies in agreement between states as regards recognition of a specific rule as a norm of international law. The binding legal force of conventional and customary norms of international law is identical, as the practice of states testifies. The United Nations Charter speaks of respect "for the obligations arising from treaties and other sources of international law" (Preamble).

In principle it is possible to change a customary norm by means of treaty and a treaty norm by means of custom.[156] This is completely applicable, however, only in those instances when the question concerns one and the same group of states-parties both in the first case (when a treaty norm replaces or modifies a customary norm) and in the second (when a customary norm replaces or modifies a treaty norm). Here, in essence, arise new agreements, clearly or tacitly expressed, which supersede the previous agreements relating to recognition of the respective norms as norms of international law.

But when the group of parties to the agreement (express or tacit) is not identical, modification of a customary norm by way of treaty and of a treaty norm by means of custom is not precluded, as will be demonstrated below, unless the modified or superseded norm is of an imperative character.

Instances of modifying customary norms of international law by means of treaty are quite frequent, especially at present with the broad scope of work relating to the codification of international law. As the experience of the International Law Commission shows, the codification of "old" branches of international law inevitably involves not only the supplementation of new norms, but also the clarification and modification of prevailing customary norms of international law.[157]

In the beginning a new treaty norm usually embraces a narrower group of states than the old customary norm. Expansion of the sphere of the recognition and operation of a new norm frequently takes place by means of both treaty and custom, in consequence of which it may be a treaty norm for some states and a customary norm for others which have

156. See T. Perassi, "Teoria dommatica delle fonti di norme giuridiche in diritto internazionale," *Rivista di diritto internazionale*, XI (1917), 303; Guggenheim, *Traité de droit international public*, I, 113; Rousseau, *Principes généraux du droit international public*, I, 859; Rousseau, *Droit international public* (Paris: Sirey, 1970), I, para. 283.

157. R. Ago, "La codification du droit international et les problèmes de sa réalisation," *Mélanges Guggenheim*, pp. 93-131.

recognized it by means of custom.[158] It is as though they were mixed customary-treaty norms.

With the increased number of general international treaties, the question of extending the effect of provisions of these treaties to states who are not parties thereto and thereby transforming them into norms of general international law takes on material importance. An analysis of data on the course of ratifications of general international treaties shows that after a particular general international treaty has obtained the ratification of an overwhelming majority of states, the ratification process slows down. Taking into consideration future state practice with respect to specific treaties of this kind, in certain instances there may be sufficient grounds to presume the acceptance of norms of a particular treaty by states not parties thereto, of which we have spoken previously (see Chapter 4(B)).

The International Law Commission provided for this possibility in Article 34 of the final draft on the law of treaties, which stated: "Nothing in Articles 30 to 33 precludes a rule set forth in a treaty from becoming binding upon a third state as a customary rule of international law."[159] At the Vienna Conference, the words "recognized as such" were added to this formulation (Article 38).

It is necessary to bear in mind, however, that in this case the question is not the binding character of a treaty upon states not parties thereto, but whether a treaty norm is binding upon them not as a treaty but as a customary norm. Therefore, Professor Ulloa's assertion that treaties to which nearly all states are parties also are binding upon states who are not parties to such treaties is incorrect. The author actually has in mind the case when a state which is not party to a treaty has recognized a treaty norm as a customary norm of international law.[160]

The 1928 Pact of Paris, which established the principle of the prohibition of aggressive war, is an example of a customary norm being replaced by means of treaty. In the relations among the parties to the treaty this new principle superseded an old norm which had approved "the right of a state to resort to war" and gradually acquired, through treaty and custom, the character of a generally recognized principle of international law.

158. See G. Fitzmaurice, "Report on the Law of Treaties," in United Nations, *Yearbook of the International Law Commission 1960*, II, 72-107; Waldock, "Third Report on the Law of Treaties," *ibid., 1964*, II, 27; Verdross, *Völkerrecht*, p. 145; Virally, "The Sources of International Law," p. 129.

159. United Nations, *Yearbook of the International Law Commission 1966*, II, 182.

160. See Ulloa, *Derecho internacional publico*, I, 52.

The principle of the prohibition of aggressive war underwent further development in the United Nations Charter, which goes farther than the Pact of Paris in providing for the prohibition of the use or threat of force against the territorial integrity or political independence of any state. The new content of this principle has been recognized, but again partly by treaty and partly by custom.

As another example, one could cite the numerous local agreements concerning the regulation of fishing on the high seas which provide certain restrictions upon the freedom of their parties to fish and hunt on the high seas.

There is every basis to assert that at present, primarily as a result of the conclusion of these numerous local agreements concerning the regulation of fishing, a new principle of international law is being formed, the principle of conserving the living resources of the high seas, which is modifying the prevailing principle of the freedom to fish and hunt.

Instances of modifying a treaty norm by means of custom are less common, since treaties as a rule provide a procedure for amendment or denunciation. Legally, however, such changes are possible with the general consent of all parties to the treaty. More often in such instances the question is one of the development, supplementation, or interpretation of treaty norms.

The question of modification of a treaty by subsequent practice was raised in the Third Report of the International Law Commission's rapporteur, H. Waldock.[161] Waldock cited two judicial precedents in this connection. The first was the Judgment of the International Court of June 15, 1962, concerning the dispute between Cambodia and Thailand over the boundary in the area of the Preah Vihear Temple, in which the Court concluded that since both parties actually had recognized a boundary line other than that stipulated in the treaty over a long period of time, the result of this practice was a modification of the treaty.[162]

Thus, the International Court regarded the practice of Cambodia and Thailand in the question of fulfilling a boundary treaty, a practice which diverged from the treaty provisions, as being evidence of a supplemental tacit agreement modifying certain provisions of the treaty.

The second case cited in Waldock's report was the arbitral award of December 22, 1963 (R. Ago (President), P. Reuter, and H. P. de Vries) in the dispute between the United States and France over the interpretation of a 1946 agreement on air transport services between these countries.

161. United Nations, *Yearbook of the International Law Commission 1964*, II, 198.

162. International Court of Justice, Reports of Judgments, Advisory Opinions and Orders, *Case Concerning the Temple of Preah Vihear (Cambodia v. Thailand), Merits, Judgment of 15 June 1962* (Leiden: A. W. Sijthoff, 1962), p. 33.

It is indicated clearly in the award that a specific practice of the parties was considered by the arbiters as evidence of a "tacitly concluded agreement," which is an "independent agreement supplementing the agreement of March 27, 1946, and reflecting the same general principles.[163]

As a result of the discussion of this question, the International Law Commission included in the draft articles on the law of treaties Article 38 as follows: "A treaty may be modified by subsequent practice in the application of the treaty establishing the agreement of the parties to modify its provisions."[164]

Bourgeois international legal doctrine usually considers this problem to be a question of interpreting an international treaty, which is completely untrue. It is possible to interpret only that which is in the treaty.[165] Moreover, some bourgeois writers even attempt to pass the "Uniting for Peace" resolution of the United Nations General Assembly of November 3, 1950, as treaty interpretation,[166] although it is generally recognized that the resolution was in sharp contradiction with the provisions of the United Nations Charter.[167]

Having included in its draft an article concerning modification of a treaty by subsequent practice, the Commission made an attempt, although not wholly successfully, to formulate a norm which arises logically from the character of customary and treaty norms and which, evidently, already is being formed as a customary norm of international law. The adoption of a treaty norm on this question undoubtedly would facilitate the elimination of disputes which arise frequently in corresponding instances.

The Commission was far from thinking that any practice might modify the provisions of a treaty. The Commission's draft contains two essential elements. Practice must testify to an agreement of the parties to modify a provision of the treaty. As the Commission points out in the commentary

163. "Sentence arbitrale du 22 decembre 1963," *Revue générale de droit international public*, XXXVI (1965), 258.

164. United Nations, *Yearbook of the International Law Commission, 1966*, II, 236.

165. "The task of interpreting an international treaty," wrote Pereterskii, "is to make out the will of the parties, that is, the content of the rules established by them in the treaty which define their rights and duties and the purpose for which the given treaty was concluded." I. S. Pereterskii, *Tolkovanie mezhdunarodnykh dogovorov* (Moscow: Gosiurizdat, 1959), p. 22.

166. Professor L. Goodrich maintains that this resolution was a "liberal interpretation" of the United Nations Charter. L. Goodrich, *The United Nations* (New York: Thomas Y. Crowell Co., 1959), p. 168.

167. For greater detail, see G. I. Tunkin, "The Legal Nature of the United Nations," *Recueil des cours*, CXIX (1966), 1-68.

to this article, "in formulating the rule in this way the Commission intended to indicate that the subsequent practice, even if every party might not itself have actively participated in the practice, must be such as to establish the agreement of the parties as a whole to the modification in question."[168]

Consequently, the first condition is that only such practice as shows an agreement of the parties may introduce a change in a treaty[169]—that is, the concordance of their wills relating to such changes. Individual digressions from treaty provisions, even though they have taken place with the common consent of the parties, but do not testify to their intention to change a treaty provision, do not modify the treaty.

The second condition is that an agreement testified to by such practice must embrace all (or almost all) parties to the treaty. This question was the subject of lively discussion in the Commission. It was recognized that, in principle, such agreement must embrace "all" parties to the treaty. For practical considerations, however, the word "all" was not inserted in the article so as not to carry its content to an extreme, when even the objection of a single state (for example, of one hundred or more parties to the treaty) could block such an agreement.

The Commission's proposal on this question objectively was aimed against attempts to pass as treaty modification (or an interpretation modifying the treaty) a practice which does not testify to an agreement relating to modification of a treaty provision, as well as the practice of a majority but not all (or almost all) parties.

At the same time, the discussion of this question in the Commission showed how little it had been studied, in particular that very little is known about state practice with regard to this question. The formulation of the article proposed by the Commission was imperfect. It is doubtful that there are grounds for considering that there exists a customary norm of international law in conformity with which any treaty provisions may be modified by means of custom, or that such a norm is advisable *de lege feranda*. Such an extreme would be dangerous for the stability of international treaties.

These dangers, reinforced by the imperfections of the formulation proposed by the Commission, led to this question being generally

168. United Nations, *Yearbook of the International Law Commission 1966*, II, 236.

169. See Oriol Casanovas la Rosa, "La Modificacion de los Acuerdos Internacionales por la Practica Posterior," *Revista Española de derecho internacional*, XXI (1968), 328-345. Professor Cahier suggests, on the contrary, that international judicial and arbitral practice on this question, "although theoretically proceeding from the wills of states, in fact does not take it into account." P. Cahier, "Le comportement des états comme source de droits et d'obligations," *Mélanges Guggenheim*, p. 265.

excluded from the draft convention at the Vienna Conference on the Law of Treaties, which can only be regretted.

D. The Principles of Jus Cogens

With the International Law Commission's raising the question of the invalidity of international treaties which contravene imperative principles of international law (principles of *jus cogens*), the question of the character of these principles acquired great contemporary interest.[170]

The essence of the question lies in ascertaining whether there are in contemporary general international law imperative principles and norms, the operation of which states may not suspend by agreement in their mutual relations.

For followers of the natural law school, as well as for proponents of contemporary natural law concepts, this question is easily resolved: natural law exists independently of the will of states and is binding upon them; states must follow the prescriptions of this law. Grotius declares that natural law is so immutable that even God himself can not change it.[171]

Vattel wrote, having in mind natural law or, as he called it, "the necessary law of nature": "As this law is immutable and imposes necessary and inevitable duties, nations may not introduce any changes in these by their own agreements and may not exempt themselves therefrom by a unilateral renunciation nor mutually exempt each other.

It is this principle, in being guided by which one may distinguish lawful agreements and treaties from unlawful, and reasonable and good customs from unjust or proper censure."[172]

We find that the majority of nineteenth century writers were of the same viewpoint. Bluntschli wrote: "Treaties whose content violates generally-recognized human laws or imperative norms of international law are invalid."[173] F. Martens, adhering to Bluntschli's view, pointed out

170. For a bibliography on this question, see Professor E. Suy's report "The Concept of Jus Cogens in International Public Law" which he submitted to a conference at Lagonissi, Greece, in 1966. Carnegie Endowment for International Peace, *The Concept of Jus Cogens in International Law* (Geneva: Carnegie Endowment, 1967), pp. 17-77.

171. H. Grotius, *O prave voiny i mira*, trans. A. L. Sakketti, ed. S. B. Krylov (Moscow: Gosiurizdat, 1956), p. 1, chaps. 1, 5, 10.

172. Vattel, *Pravo narodov*, p. 27.

173. J. C. Bluntschli, *Das moderne Völkerrecht der civilisirten Staten*, 2d ed. (Nördlingen: Verlag der C. H. Beck' schen Buchhandlung, 1872), p. 236.

that an international treaty is not binding if it restricts or destroys the basic rights of states.[174]

Proponents of normativist concepts favor the view that international law does not contain imperative norms (*jus cogens*), and states may establish any international legal norms in their mutual relations by way of treaties.

The principal representative of the "pure" theory of law, Kelsen, declares that the "... content of the treaty must not conflict with a norm of general international law which has the character of *jus cogens*, and not that of *jus dispositivum.*"[175] However, in considering the question of whether norms of general international law have the character of *jus cogens*, Kelsen says that a clear answer can never be found in the traditional theory of international law. Some writers, he continues, maintain that there exists complete, or almost complete, freedom to conclude treaties; others, to the contrary, adhere to the view that treaties which are at variance with universally-recognized principles of international law are null and void. To this he makes a characteristic addition: "But they do not and can not precisely designate the norms of general international law which have the character of *jus cogens*, that is to say, the application of which can not be excluded by a treaty." At the same time, he is forced to acknowledge that a treaty by which two or more states release one another from the obligations imposed upon them by the norm of general international law prohibiting occupation of part of the open sea very likely would be declared null and void by an international tribunal competent to deal with the case.[176]

Thus, Kelsen does not give a clear answer to the question being raised, but he favors the view that all norms of general international law are of a dispositive character and that imperative norms, which can not contravene the norms of a treaty concluded by two states or a group, are only of a local character. This point of view has been expressed more concretely in the new edition of *Principles of International Law.*

This viewpoint was set forth by Guggenheim more resolutely. He wrote: "Norms of international public law are not of an imperative character. Consequently, in conformity with international law, a treaty

174. See F. F. Martens, *Sovremennoe mezhdunarodnoe pravo tsivilizovannykh narodov*, 3d ed. (St. Petersburg: Tipo. A. Benke, 1895), I, 406; see also A. N. Stoianov, *Ocherki istorii i dogmatiki mezhdunarodnogo prava* (Kharkov: Universitetskaia tipo., 1875), p. 494.

175. Kelsen, *Principles of International Law* (New York: Holt, Rinehart & Winston, 1952), pp. 322-323; the paragraph cited is absent in the new edition. See *Principles of International Law* (1967), p. 460.

176. Kelsen, *Principles of International Law* (1967), p. 483.

may have any content without any limitation whatever ... "[177] In the second edition of this treatise, however, Guggenheim expresses his opposition to the existence of the principles of *jus cogens* in contemporary international law much more cautiously. He writes: "Although there are no logical grounds not to assume the existence of principles of *jus cogens*, there are certain difficulties in assuming their existence within the limits of the actual procedure for creating international law. The principal difficulty springs from the fact that contemporary international law does not contain general rules which automatically invalidate ... conventional norms that contravene them."[178]

The arguments of opponents of *jus cogens* can be reduced to the fact that such principles are possible only in a well-organized and effective legal system, and since international law is not such a system, the existence of principles of general international law having the character of *jus cogens* is impossible. This argument is set forth especially clearly by Professor G. Schwarzenberger. "Unlike municipal law," he writes, "international customary law (in Schwarzenberger's view general international law is customary law) lacks rules of *jus cogens* or international public policy, that is, rules which, by consent, individual subjects of international law may not modify. In fact, *jus cogens*, as distinct from *jus dispositivum*, presupposes the existence of an effective *de jure* order, which has at its disposal legislative and judicial machinery, able to formulate rules of public policy and, in the last resort, can rely on overwhelming physical force."[179]

An Italian professor, A. Sereni, decisively rejects the existence of imperative principles in international law.[180] At the same time, just as many other Italian authors,[181] Sereni speaks of the existence of "constitutional principles which reflect the specific constitutional features of the international community and order," but which do not coincide with "principles of international law."[182] G. Morelli admits the existence of

177. P. Guggenheim, *Traité de droit international public* (Geneva: Librairie de l'Université, 1953), I, 57.

178. Guggenheim, *Traité de droit international public*, 2d ed., I, 128.

179. G. Schwarzenberger, *A Manual of International Law*, 5th ed. (London: Stevens & Sons, 1967), pp. 29-30; Schwarzenberger, "International Jus Cogens," *Texas Law Review*, XLIII (1965), 455-478. J. Nisot rejects the concept of *jus cogens* because it supposedly does not define "what these principles are." J. Nisot, "Le concept du *jus cogens* envisagé par rapport au droit international public," *Revue belge de droit international*, IV (1968), 7.

180. Sereni, *Diritto internazionale*, I, 166-170.

181. See, for example, S. Romano, *Corso di diritto internazionale*, 4th ed. (Padova: CEDAM, 1939), p. 31; R. Monaco, *Manuale di diritto internazionale publico* (Torino: UTET, 1960), pp. 42-46.

182. Sereni, *Diritto internazionale*, I, 112-113.

imperative norms in international law but interprets them completely differently. In Morelli's view, a treaty which contravenes an imperative norm of international law is not invalid; the treaty "is valid between the parties, but unlawful with regard to other addressees of an imperative norm."[183] But this still is tantamount to a denial of imperative norms, since a specific feature of an imperative norm is that it does not permit a digression from such a norm by agreement between two or several states, and an agreement contravening an imperative norm is invalid.

According to the concept most prevalent in contemporary bourgeois international legal literature, there are, as a rule, no imperative norms in contemporary international law, and therefore treaties concluded by states may digress from generally-recognized norms. Nonetheless, it admits that general international law contains some norms of an imperative character which may not be contravened by treaties.

As regards the character of imperative norms, the majority of bourgeois writers carry categories of municipal law over to international law, suggesting that imperative principles are principles of "public order" which do not depend upon the will and consent of states.

Professor Verdross wrote: "In principle, a state freely concludes treaties with other states on any questions; however, such agreements must remain within the limits of general international law."[184] Speaking of instances of the invalidity of an international treaty, Verdross points out: "This occurs, however, only when an international treaty violates a compulsory norm of international law. But in view of the fact that general international law, as a rule, is dispositive law (*jus dispositivum*), comparatively few instances exist of a violation of general international law by an international treaty."[185]

It should be noted that in the fourth and fifth editions of this work Verdross lays great stress upon imperative norms of international law. The reminder that general international law, as a rule, is dispositive law is omitted here and instead the following is said: "In addition, however, there are norms which may not be modified by states even as regards their mutual relations."[186]

In his report submitted to the International Law Commission Professor

183. G. Morelli, "A proposito di norme internazionali cogenti," *Rivista di diritto internazionale*, LI (1968), 116.

184. Verdross, *Mezhdunarodnoe pravo*, p. 185.

185. *Ibid.*, p. 186.

186. Verdross, *Völkerrecht*, 4th ed. (Vienna: Springer Verlag, 1959), p. 79; *ibid.*, 5th ed., (1964), p. 130. See also Verdross, "Jus Dispositivum and Jus Cogens in International Law," *American Journal of International Law*, LX (1966), 55-63.

H. Lauterpacht proposed the adoption of an article providing for the invalidity of a treaty or its individual provisions "if its performance involves an act which is illegal under international law . . . "[187]

In the commentary to this draft article he pointed out that the question is one of "the inconsistency with such overriding principles of international law which may be regarded as constituting . . . international public policy."[188] In so doing, Lauterpacht, just as the majority of bourgeois writers, identified these principles to a significant extent with moral principles.[189]

In the Third Report to the International Law Commission, G. Fitzmaurice expresses approximately the same point of view. He writes: "It is essential to the validity of a treaty that it should be in conformity with or not contravene, or that its execution should not involve an infraction of, those principles and rules of international law which are in the nature of *jus cogens*."[190]

Lord McNair suggests that imperative principles of international law exist, but that such principles are peculiar to any legal system. "It is difficult to imagine any society," he writes, "whether of individuals or of States, whose law sets no limit whatever to freedom of contract."[191]

Professor Dahm believes that imperative principles exist in international law, although they also are an exception.[192]

Professor U. Scheuner, of the University of Bonn, suggests that imperative principles of international law exist and that these are "norms of international law creating obligations upon States independent of their agreement."[193]

Professor C. Rousseau very cautiously acknowledges the existence of imperative principles, pointing out that the principle of public policy "is almost nonexistent" in international law.[194]

187. United Nations, *Yearbook of the International Law Commission 1953*, II, 154.

188. *Ibid.*, p. 155.

189. *Ibid.*

190. *Ibid., 1958*, II, 26.

191. A. McNair, *The Law of Treaties* (Oxford: Clarendon Press, 1961), pp. 213-214; see also G. Geamanu, " 'Jus Cogens' en droit international contemporain," *Revue roumaine d'études internationales*, nos. 1-2 (1967), p. 90; K. Marek, "Contribution à l'etude du *jus cogens* en droit international," *Mélanges Guggenheim*, p. 456.

192. G. Dahm, *Völkerrecht*, I, 6.

193. U. Scheuner, "Conflict of Treaty Provisions with a Peremptory Norm of General International Law and Its Consequences," *Zeitschrift für auslandisches öffentliches Recht und Völkerrecht*, XXVII (1967), 531.

194. Rousseau, *Principes généraux du droit international public*, I, 340-341.

Professor P. Reuter also does not deny the existence of imperative principles in international law but rather favors the view that there is only a "trend" toward forming them.[195]

Professor R. Quadri suggests that "there are no obstacles to speaking of the existence of international public policy in international law; that is, the aggregate of imperative norms (*jus cogens*) which annuls any norm in contravention thereof, either customary or conventional."[196] Quadri says that the force of such imperative norms "is nothing other than the power of the international social organism, whose will is the highest instance."[197]

"In any event," writes a Uruguayan professor, E. Jimenez de Arechaga, "the international law prevailing at the present time rests upon '*jus cogens*'; that is, upon specific principles and norms from which the parties to a treaty may not digress in their discretion."[198]

The discussion of this question in the International Law Commission commenced in 1963. The Commission's rapporteur, Professor H. Waldock, following the example of the previous rapporteurs (Lauterpacht and Fitzmaurice), proposed the inclusion of a draft article providing for the invalidity of treaties which contravene principles of *jus cogens*.[199]

The rapporteur's proposal to include the said article met with the unanimous approval of Commission members. "The most surprising feature of the Commission's debates is the unanimity with which members of the Commission approved the idea of *jus cogens*," writes E. Suy, a Belgian professor.[200]

This article was discussed a second time after receiving the comments of governments and the discussion of the Commission's Draft in the Sixth Committee of the United Nations General Assembly. In the Commission's final draft the article on imperative principles (Article 50) was formulated as follows: "A treaty is void if it conflicts with a peremptory norm of general international law, from which no derogation is permitted and which can be modified only by a subsequent norm of general international law having the same character."[201]

As regards the nature of imperative principles, of course, the views of

195. P. Reuter, "Principes de droit international public," *Recueil des cours*, CIII (1961), 467.

196. R. Quadri, "Cours general de droit international public," *Recueil des cours*, CXIII (1964), 335.

197. *Ibid.*

198. Arechaga, *Curso de derecho internacional publico*, I, 120.

199. United Nations, *Yearbook of the International Law Commission 1966*, II, 52.

200. Carnegie Endowment for International Peace, *Concept of Jus Cogens in International Law*, p. 50.

201. United Nations, *Yearbook of the International Law Commission 1966*, II, 247.

the members of the Commission were different. Naturally, the Commission also did not set itself the task of working out a unified conception of the nature of these principles. As the Hungarian delegate, E. Ustor, correctly noted in the Sixth Committee at the Eighteenth Session of the United Nations General Assembly, " . . . although the members of the Commission disagreed on the origin of the peremptory rules of international law, they had nevertheless agreed to recognise their existence, and their ideological differences had not prevented them from reaching a solution that met the needs of practice."[202]

The Commission refrained from attempts to work out a list of imperative principles, pointing out that this question did not relate to the law of treaties. The author of the present work pointed out in the Commission that unequal treaties undoubtedly fall within the effect of the article prepared by the Commission.[203]

In the course of discussing the draft articles on the law of treaties in the Sixth Committee of the General Assembly in 1963, 1966, and 1967, the article on imperative principles of international law received wide support, especially from delegates of socialist and developing countries. This also applies to the comments of governments upon the Commission's draft.

It became clearer, however, both from the comments of governments and from the remarks of delegates in the Sixth Committee that the United States, England, and France, as well as a number of other countries linked to them by military alliances (in particular, Canada, Belgium, Turkey) were opposing this article under various pretexts (chiefly, the pretext of the ambiguity of the article or the absence of compulsory international jurisdiction to apply it). In its comments on the Commission's draft in 1965, the United States government recommended that the Commission "reconsider the provisions of that article and all aspects of the manner in which it might be applied, particularly the question as to who will decide when the facts justify application of the rule."[204]

This was said even more decisively in a Note of the Permanent Representative of the United States to the United Nations of October 2, 1967: "If such careful and meticulous delineation of existing peremptory norms is not carried out, article 50 might have a most disastrous affect upon international co-operation and harmony because it could radically weaken the treaty structure upon which that harmony and co-operation depends so heavily."[205]

202. Sixth Committee, United Nations General Assembly (XX), *Official Records*, p. 40.

203. United Nations, *Yearbook of the International Law Commission 1963*, I, 69.

204. Law of Treaties: Comments by Governments, p. 186. Doc. No. A/CN.4/175, February 23, 1965.

205. Doc. No. A/6827/Add. 2. (XX).

The English representative in the Sixth Committee of the United Nations General Assembly, Darwin, declared in 1967 that "... the concept of *jus cogens* was still so little developed that it still was not ripe for inclusion in the codification of the law of treaties."[206]

The same tendencies manifested themselves at the Vienna Conference on the Law of Treaties. The delegations of the socialist states and of the majority of Afro-Asian states resolutely supported the article relating to imperative principles of international law. The representative of Mali, Maiga, declared in his speech at the Conference on May 7, 1968, that norms of *jus cogens* are the cornerstone of the progressive development of contemporary international law. They are, he pointed out, essential to the stability of international relations and one of the most effective instruments for ensuring peaceful coexistence of states with different economic and social systems.[207]

The delegations of the principal capitalist powers and of states linked with them attempted to prevent the adoption of this article. The United States delegation proposed to replace the text of the article submitted by the International Law Commission with the following: "A treaty is void if, at the time of its conclusion, it conflicts with a peremptory rule of general international law which is recognized in common by the national and regional legal systems of the world and from which no derogation is permitted."[208]

With the obvious purpose of confusing the issue, the English delegation at the Vienna Conference proposed to define which rules are peremptory,[209] and the English representative, Vallat, declared that the delegation of Great Britain would probably vote against the convention as a whole if the article on imperative norms were left in the convention.[210]

The United States amendment had a strong flavor of the nineteenth century German concept which represented international law as external state law. The Cuban representative, Alvares Tabio, noted quite justly with regard to this question that the United States's proposal would allow a state, by invoking its domestic legislation, to thwart any imperative

206. Sixth Committee, United Nations General Assembly (XXII), *Official Records*, p. 55 (October 11, 1967).

207. United Nations Conference on the Law of Treaties, *Official Records, Vienna, First Session, 1968-1969* (New York: United Nations, 1969), p. 327. Doc. No. A/CONF.39/C.I/SR.56.

208. *Ibid., Documents of the Conference* (New York: United Nations, 1971), p. 174. Doc. No. A/CONF.39/C.I/L.302.

209. *Ibid.*, p. 174. Doc. No. A/CONF.39/C.I/L.312.

210. *Ibid., Official Records*, p. 330. Doc. No. A/CONF.39/C.I/SR.57.

norm of international law.[211] Professor C. de Visscher called this article "the most significant innovation of the Vienna Convention."[212]

Despite the negative position of the said countries and a number of others, the article on the invalidity of treaties contravening an imperative norm of international law was adopted by the Vienna Conference on the Law of Treaties by eighty-seven votes, with eight opposed and twelve abstentions, without material changes. "A treaty is void," says Article 53, "if at the moment of conclusion it contravenes an imperative norm of general international law. Under the present Convention, an imperative norm of general international law is a norm accepted and recognized by the international community of states as a whole as a norm, the departure from which is inadmissible and which may be modified only by a subsequent norm of general international law of the same character."

The position has been taken in Soviet international legal doctrine that an international treaty must conform to the basic principles of international law.[213] However, comparatively recently the problem has been worked out theoretically by Soviet scholars.[214]

V. M. Shurshalov attempts a theoretical analysis of this question in his work *Osnovnye voprosy teorii mezhdunarodnogo dogovora*. The author upholds the generally recognized thesis that only treaties whose provisions conform to basic principles of international law have legal force and makes a number of correct observations, particularly on the question of the effectiveness of international treaties and their role in the develop-

211. *Ibid.*, p. 297. Doc. No. A/CONF.39/C.I/SR.52; see also the statement of the Tanzanian representative, Bishota, of May 7, 1968. *Ibid.*, p. 322. Doc. No. A/CONF. 39/C.I/SR.56.

212. C. de Visscher, "Stages in the Codification of International Law," in W. Friedmann, L. Henkin, and O. Lissitzyn, eds., *Transnational Law in a Changing Society: Essays in Honor of Philip C. Jessup* (New York: Columbia University Press, 1972), p. 29.

213. See, for example, Korovin, ed., *Mezhdunarodnoe pravo*, p. 16; Tunkin, *Osnovy sovremennogo mezhdunarodnogo prava*, p. 12; Kozhevnikov, ed., *Mezhdunarodnoe pravo*, pp. 242-243; Minasian, *Istochniki sovremennogo mezhdunarodnogo prava*, p. 48; Lukin, *Istochniki mezhdunarodnogo prava*, p. 75; Bobrov, *Sovremennoe mezhdunarodnoe pravo*, p. 77; Talalaev, *Iuridicheskaia priroda mezhdunarodnogo dogovora*, p. 220; Lukashuk, *Istochniki mezhdunarodnogo prava*, p. 50; Chkhikvadze and others, eds., *Kurs mezhdunarodnogo prava*, I, 172-173.

214. Professor L. A. Aleksidze's report to the Twelfth Annual Meeting of the Soviet Association of International Law in January 1969 is evidence of the growing interest in this problem in Soviet international legal doctrine. See also Tunkin, "Jus Cogens in Contemporary International Law," *University of Toledo Law Review* (1971), 107-118.

ment of international law.[215] One can not agree, however, with his opinions on the co-relation of the international treaty and of generally recognized principles of international law.

In our view, Shurshalov's views are based upon a confusion of the laws of societal development with juridical laws, with principles of international law. This leads him to regard the actual laws of societal development as the criterion of the legal validity of an international treaty. These laws of societal development are considered to be juridical principles with which the norms of a treaty are to be compared. If the treaty norms conform to such laws of societal development, they are deemed by the author to be valid; if they contradict them, to be invalid.[216]

The development of international law, just as other categories of the superstructure, ultimately is determined by the laws of societal development. Those principles and norms of international law, including those established by treaty, which conform to the laws of societal development and as a consequence are progressive, may be expected to be consolidated in international law. Principles and norms which are in contradiction to the laws of societal development and which inhibit the progressive development of society inevitably are swept away and cast aside.

The question can be raised, of course, as to the co-relation of the legal validity of a treaty and its conformity to the laws of societal development, on one hand, and the legal invalidity of a treaty and its nonconformity to the laws of societal development, on the other. There undoubtedly is a definite link here, since in the final analysis the laws of societal development define the general features of the development of international law. It is, however, incorrect to assert that the juridical lawfulness or validity of an international treaty is determined by its conformity to the laws of societal development, or the legal invalidity of an international treaty by the fact that it is in contradiction to these laws.

The validity of a treaty is determined on the basis of legal criteria provided for by international law. If a local treaty contravenes generally-recognized principles of international law of an imperative character, it is void in law.

The content of generally-recognized principles of international law also is determined in the final analysis by the general laws of societal development. These laws, however, are not themselves principles of international law or a part thereof. Identifying the laws of societal development (we are not concerned here with the meaning of the laws) with juridical norms, as

215. See Shurshalov, *Osnovnye voprosy teorii mezhdunarodnogo dogovora*, pp. 231-244.
216. *Ibid.*, pp. 237-239.

is well-known, is peculiar to the solidarists (see Chapter 6).

The conformity or nonconformity of a particular norm of international law to the laws of societal development defines its true effectiveness or efficacy. But the legal validity of a norm and its efficacy or effectiveness are not one and the same thing, although it would be incorrect to assert that the inefficacy or ineffectiveness of a norm can not influence its legal validity. The legal validity of a norm, however, can by virtue of a number of circumstances be made ineffective or less effective, since with a change of situation the degree of effectiveness of the norm may change.

V. M. Shurshalov in essence repeats the error of F. Martens, who wrote: "On this basis it is possible to make it a rule that the degree to which international treaties are binding or are to be executed is to be determined by the extent to which they conform to the truly reasonable requirements of states in their mutual relations."[217]

The general conclusion is that the existence of imperative principles and norms in contemporary international law is almost generally recognized.

The basic reason for the formation of such principles and norms is the growing internationalization of various aspects of the life of society, especially of economic life, and the expansion and intensification of international ties. As a result thereof, the number of questions whose free regulation on a local multilateral or bilateral basis may harm the interests of other states is increasing. The growth of the forces of socialism and progress, their increasing influence, and the increase in this connection of the importance of moral principles in international relations also promote the creation of imperative principles and norms of international law. Therefore, the quantity of imperative principles and norms in contemporary international law is growing.

To imperative principles should be relegated essentially all fundamental generally-recognized principles of contemporary international law, although in this connection the problem arises of the incomplete imperative nature of certain of them. Could, for example, states establish by a bilateral agreement that they will not be bound in their mutual relations by the principle of nonaggression? Obviously, there can be only one answer to this question—a negative one. Peace is indivisible, and an armed attack by one state upon another, irrespective of whether large or small states are concerned, is a breach of the general peace, in whose maintenance all states are concerned.

The question of the legal nature of imperative principles of international law is a complex one. As regards the methods of their creation, they do not differ in this respect from other principles of international law.

217. Martens, *Sovremennoe mezhdunarodnoe pravo*, 3d ed., I, 392.

Norms of general international law, including imperative principles, are created by the agreement of states. One must agree with McNair that imperative principles are "rules which have been accepted, either expressly by treaty or tacitly by custom . . . "[218]

Among the principles and norms of general international law created by agreement of states are those to which special importance is attached by these agreements.[219] This special importance is that individual states in their mutual relations and on the basis of agreement can not deviate therefrom or act otherwise than these principles and norms prescribe.

Of course, such norms have a special binding force.[220] But at the same time the question does not reduce itself to binding force in general. All norms of international law are binding upon the respective subjects of international law. Their violation entails international legal responsibility. But in the majority of cases, and therein is one of the distinctive features of international law, states may, by concluding local agreements, establish that they will apply in their mutual relations norms other than the norms of general international law pertaining to this question. Such deviation is inadmissible with regard to imperative principles and norms. This relates both to treaty and to customary norms.

Bourgeois doctrine usually considers principles of *jus cogens* to be principles of natural law. From the point of view of writers who adhere to this opinion, the recognition of principles of *jus cogens* in the Vienna Convention on the Law of Treaties signified a return to natural law. Thus, Professor A. Verdross writes: "The merit of the International Law Commission and the Vienna Convention of the Law of Treaties of May 23, 1969, based on its labors lies in the fact that they helped *jus cogens* again to carry the day in international law."[221]

If principles of *jus cogens* are created, just as other norms of international law, by the agreement of states, then they are completely distinct from the principles of *ordre public* propagated by natural law doctrine which are not dependent upon the wills of states. Therefore the special problem of the binding nature of principles of *jus cogens* upon new states

---

218. McNair, *The Law of Treaties*, p. 215. M. Virally notes that the sources of imperative principles are the same as the sources of other norms of international law. M. Virally, "Réflexions sur le 'jus cogens,' " *Annuaire français de droit international*, XII (1966), 16.

219. See L. Aleksidze, "Problema *jus cogens* v sovremennom mezhdunarodnom prave," *Sovetskii ezhegodnik mezhdunarodnogo prava 1969* (Moscow: izd-vo Nauka, 1970), p. 142; Geamanu, " 'Jus Cogens' en droit international contemporain," p. 94.

220. As Professor M. Yasseen, the Iraqi representative at the Vienna Conference on the Law of Treaties, stated: "it could be said that some rules of international law were more binding than others . . . " United Nations Conference on the Law of Treaties, *Official Records*, p. 296.

221. A. Verdross, *Die Quellen des universellen Völkerrechts*, p. 26.

does not arise distinct from the problem of the binding nature of other principles and norms of general international law upon them.

As already has been pointed out (Chapter 4(B)(2)), legally a new state has the right not to recognize particular norms of general international law. However, as already has been noted, if a new state enters without reservations into official relations with other states, this means that it accepts the particular complex of principles and norms of prevailing international law which are the basic principles of relations between states, the principles of *jus cogens* also appertaining thereto.

The actual situation now is such that the basic principles of contemporary general international law, reflecting the concordant wills of socialist, capitalist, and developing states, corresponds generally to their interests. Therefore it is doubtful whether a new state would have sufficient grounds for a negative attitude toward prevailing principles of *jus cogens*. One must add that nonacceptance by a new state, especially a small state, of particular basic principles is a risky and disadvantageous matter for it, since a position does not promote the development of its relations with other states.

Therefore, recent practice knows no cases when a new state, in entering into relations with other states, has made a reservation relating to nonacceptance of particular basic principles of general international law. This practice, however, does not mean that the right of a new state arising out of the principles of sovereignty and equality of states to not recognize particular principles and norms of general international law has ceased to exist. The general legal position on which this right is based has great importance in the process of creating norms of contemporary international law (see Chapter 4 (B)(2)).[222]

Imperative principles obviously are not immutable. As all other principles and norms of general international law, they may be modified by the agreement of states, by means of treaty or custom. In this way certain existing principles and norms of international law may acquire the character of imperative norms; new imperative principles and norms may be formed from the moment they come into existence. Certain moral norms may become imperative norms or existing imperative norms may, while remaining norms of international law, also become generally-accepted moral norms simultaneously.[223]

222. For a critique of the conception of the unconditionally binding nature of general international law on new states, see Chapter 4(B)(2). It also seems to us that H. Bokor-Szegó's conclusion that principles of *jus cogens* are binding upon new states because they express the interests of all states is unfounded. See H. Bokor-Szegó, *New States and International Law* (Budapest: Akademiai kiado, 1970), p. 70.

223. For greater detail on moral norms in relations between peoples see A. F. Shishkin and K. A. Shvarstman, *XX vek i moral'nye tsennosti chelovechestva* (Moscow: izd-vo Mysl', 1968), pp. 224-270.

The Nuremberg principles relating to crimes against humanity, for example, which in our view are included among imperative principles, represent to a certain extent all three of the aforesaid instances. The norms relating to war crimes originated long ago, but comparatively recently they have acquired an imperative character. The norms regarding crimes against peace are relatively new imperative norms. The norms relating to crimes against humanity were until recently to some extent moral norms which now are imperative norms of international law.

Since a treaty may be a means of establishing or modifying generally-recognized principles and norms or, that is to say, principles and norms of general international law, this problem does not arise with regard to general treaties in which all or almost all states participate, including, consequently, states of the two systems, among them the great powers. Such treaties may modify or abolish principles and norms of general international law, including imperative norms.

The problem of the co-relation of treaty norms and of generally recognized norms of international law arises, therefore, only with regard to local treaty norms; that is, norms of bilateral and of multilateral treaties to which a limited number of states are parties. This problem also arises equally with regard to local customary norms of international law.

The existence of imperative norms by no means inhibits the progressive development of international law; they do not obstruct the creation of new norms which go further than old norms in the direction of ensuring peace and friendly relations among states.

Chapter 5 *Subsidiary Processes of Forming Norms of International Law*

Treaty and custom are the two methods of forming and changing norms of general international law, the two direct means of establishing its norms. These means, as we have seen, sometimes are parallel, sometimes cross, sometimes merge. The completion of any of them signifies the completion of the process of forming a norm of international law, as a result of which a new norm emerges or a previously existing norm changes.

It can be said that general agreement exists with regard to recognizing treaty and custom as a means or method of forming principles and norms of general international law. But are there other methods of creating norms of international law? Very different opinions are expressed with regard to this matter not only in bourgeois but also in Soviet legal literature.

Confusion results to a significant extent from the fact that the term "sources," even when used in a so-called formal sense (a very unfortunate expression), is, as H. Kelsen points out, highly ambiguous.[1] The category of sources usually includes not just the process of forming norms of international law and its results, but also the various factors influencing the process.

In order to gain an understanding of the complex process of norm-formation, one must separate from it everything that does not enter into the process yet still influences it. That is to say, one must separate the process of forming agreement relating to recognizing a particular rule as a norm of international law from the numerous phenomena which influence the course of this process and its content.

1. H. Kelsen, *Principles of International Law* (New York: Rinehart & Co., 1952), p. 304.

The Process of Forming Norms of International Law

Norm-formation in international law is not limited to treaty and custom; several other processes enter into it. These processes do not lead directly to the formation of a norm of general international law, that is, do not lead to completion of the making of a norm, but represent specific stages in making, developing, changing, and abrogating norms of international law—that is to say, stages in the forming of agreement of states with regard to these questions.[2]

A. Resolutions of the United Nations General Assembly

International organizations (intergovernmental) are created by states on the basis of treaties which define the structure of the given organization, the jurisdiction of its organs, the effect of resolutions of these organs, and so forth.

Of course, the decisions of any international organization may have a certain legal force just for members of this organization. The numerous interpretations of Article 2(6) as supposedly establishing legal obligations for states which are not members of the United Nations have no basis thereunder.

Paragraph 6 says the Organization shall ensure that nonmember states act in accordance with the principles of the United Nations so far as may be necessary for the maintenance of international peace and security. As A. Verdross correctly remarks, the provision of the Charter does not establish "direct obligations for third states."[3] It establishes a norm which the Organization and its members must follow.

As regards the resolutions of international organizations, the resolutions of the United Nations General Assembly are of greatest interest in this respect. They are mentioned most frequently in legal literature as sources of international law.

The view repeatedly has been expressed in Soviet international legal literature that resolutions of international organizations are a source of international law. S. B. Krylov wrote that "sufficient attention is not always devoted to this source of international law, whereas the role and significance of this source are great."[4] In developing this thought, he went on to point out that resolutions such as the resolutions of the Assembly of

2. See G. I. Tunkin, "Sorok let sosushchestvovaniia i mezhdunarodnoe pravo," *Sovetskii ezhegodnik mezhdunarodnogo prava 1958* (Moscow: izd-vo AN SSSR, 1959), p. 20.

3. A. Verdross, *Mezhdunarodnoe pravo*, trans. from 3d ed. by F. A. Kublitskii and R. L. Naryshkina, ed. G. I. Tunkin (Moscow: izd-vo IL, 1959), p. 529.

4. V. N. Durdenevskii and S. B. Krylov, eds., *Mezhdunarodnoe pravo* (Moscow: Iurizdat, 1947), p. 24.

Subsidiary Processes of Forming Norms of International Law

the League of Nations, as well as its organs, "were a source of international law for League members, on condition of their being recognized and applied in practice."[5] "The activity of the United Nations, its General Assembly, and other organs, above all the Security Council," Krylov continued, "may lead to a number of resolutions of these organs being an important source of international law on the aforesaid conditions."[6]

E. A. Korovin wrote in 1957: "Resolutions of international organs and national organizations, if they have obtained international recognition, may be regarded to a certain extent as a source of international law."[7]

There is in these definitions the correct idea that resolutions of international organizations do not in themselves create norms of international law. To say, however, that resolutions of international organizations are sources of international law if they have been recognized by a state in no way defines the place of these resolutions in the process of forming norms of international law.

F. I. Kozhevnikov expresses a rather different point of view: "Resolutions of the General Assembly as a general rule only have the character of a recommendation. One may consider resolutions of this United Nations organ which are adopted unanimously as going beyond the limits of simple recommendations and as acquiring the significance of legal force."[8] However, the author puts forward no arguments in support of this thesis. Moreover, the United Nations Charter does not distinguish between General Assembly resolutions adopted unanimously and resolutions adopted by a majority vote as defined by the Charter. Although, as will be shown below, unanimity in adopting General Assembly resolutions has a certain significance, it by no means follows that this in and of itself changes the character of the resolution.

N. M. Minasian suggests that all United Nations General Assembly resolutions which do not contravene the Charter or the basic principles of international law and have been adopted unanimously or by a two-thirds vote, including representation of the three groups of states, are binding on all members of the United Nations,[9] since "the concordant will of states has been expressed therein, only not by signing them (this form has been fixed for treaties), but by voting for them."[10]

5. *Ibid.*
6. *Ibid.*, p. 25.
7. F. I. Kozhevnikov, *Mezhdunarodnoe pravo* (Moscow: Gosiurizdat, 1957), p. 9.
8. Kozhevnikov, "Obshchepriznannye prinstipy i normy mezhdunarodnogo prava," *Sovetskoe gosudarstvo i pravo*, no. 12 (1959), p. 17. Kozhevnikov later repudiated this view. See *Kurs mezhdunarodnogo prava*, 2d ed. (Moscow: izd-vo IMO, 1966), p. 41.
9. N. M. Minasian, *Pravo mirnogo sosushchestvovaniia* (Rostov: izd-vo Rostovskogo universiteta, 1966), p. 325.
10. *Ibid.*, p. 234.

The Process of Forming Norms of International Law

It is true that when a United Nations General Assembly resolution is adopted, since each delegation acts in the name of its state, the concordance of the wills of the states which voted for the resolution is present. It does not follow therefrom, however, that a norm of international law results from such concordance. The former arises only when there is a concordance of the wills of states relating to recognition of a particular rule as a norm of international law.

In this case the question is one of the concordance of the wills of states within the framework of an international organization, and the results of such concordance are defined by the charter of this organization. In voting for any resolution relating, for example, to general principles of cooperation in the cause of maintaining international peace and security, a state bears in mind that a greater significance may not be attached to its vote than that which is defined by the United Nations Charter.

G. I. Morozov also broadly interprets the provisions of the United Nations Charter relating to General Assembly resolutions. He writes: "If Assembly resolutions fully conform both to the concrete provisions and to the general principles of the Charter, if they were adopted by all members of the United Nations, are there grounds for any doubting their legal nature as sources of law? From our point of view, a negative answer should be given to this question. In ratifying the Charter, member states of the United Nations recognized it as binding on themselves; they recognized thereby the binding nature of the resolutions of its organs adopted in strict conformity with the procedure provided by the Charter and the principles proclaimed therein."[1] [1]

There is a contradiction here between the first and last theses. The purport of the first thesis is that Assembly resolutions are binding within the framework provided by the United Nations Charter. And this is correct. The purport of the last thesis is that since the Charter is binding upon member states, all resolutions adopted in conformity with the procedure established by the Charter and corresponding to the principles of the Charter are binding. The Charter provisions relating to the legal force of the resolutions of individual organs are lost sight of here. The jurisdiction of the organs is defined not only by the principles and purposes of the Organization, but above all by the specific Charter provisions concerning such jurisdiction (see Chapter 14).

In G. P. Zadorozhnyi's view, it is absurd not to regard United Nations General Assembly resolutions as sources of international law since, in his

11. G. I. Morozov, *Organizatsiia Ob"edinennykh Natsii* (Moscow: izd-vo IMO, 1962), pp. 217-218.

words, "at any international conference a lesser number of states would be sufficient to create a new norm of international law."[12] This argument is, however, completely unfounded, since international conferences do not create norms of international law but can be only stages in the process of creating such norms.

We note in passing that confusion on the question of United Nations General Assembly resolutions frequently is aggravated by stating the question incorrectly: are General Assembly resolutions sources of international law or not? In answering the question stated in this way, the position of the author of the present work, for example, sometimes is characterized as not recognizing General Assembly resolutions as sources of international law.[13] Whereas, in our view, General Assembly resolutions, being, as a rule, recommendations, may enter into the process of forming norms of international law.[14]

As will be shown below, the basic orientation of Soviet international legal doctrine on this question proceeds from the position that General Assembly resolutions are recommendations, except those which under the Charter have a binding character.

In bourgeois international legal doctrine there is a concept, which, it is true, is not widespread, that ascribes to United Nations General Assembly resolutions legal qualities they do not have. Thus, the American Commission to Study the Organization of Peace, under the chairmanship of C. M. Eichelberger, expresses the view that to a certain extent the General Assembly approximates a legislative organ. "Resolutions such as those described," says the Seventeenth Report of the Commission, "when adopted almost unanimously, are likely to be observed. If so, they are eventually recognized as binding upon the Members."[15] Further on, the report contains a highly significant reservation: "Despite its growing authority, there is a gap·between the General Assembly as at present constituted and a full-fledged legislative body."[16]

Professor P. Reuter suggests that resolutions of international organizations are "unilateral acts" and that such acts "possess to a varying but

12. G. P. Zadorozhnyi, *Mirnoe sosushchestvovanie i mezhdunarodnoe pravo* (Moscow: izd-vo Mezhdunarodnye otnosheniia, 1964), pp. 326-327.

13. See, for example, S. A. Malinin, "O kriteriiakh pravomernosti rezoliutsii General'noi Assamblei OON," *Pravovedenie*, no. 2 (1965), p. 114.

14. G. I. Tunkin, *Voprosy teorii mezhdunarodnogo prava* (Moscow: izd-vo IMO, 1962), pp. 130-136.

15. *New Dimensions for the United Nations: The Problems of the Next Decade. Seventeenth Report of the Commission to Study the Organization of Peace* (New York: Oceana Publications Inc., 1966), p. 22.

16. *Ibid.*

never an insignificant degree the character of authority (*d'autorité*) over governments and states, and sometimes over specific individuals."[17]

Some western authors believe that United Nations General Assembly resolutions are not "nonbinding" and at the present time are obliterating the distinction between such resolutions and international treaties from the standpoint of their legally binding nature. Professor E. Schwelb, of Yale University, writes: "In any case, after the 1960 Declaration [the Declaration on Granting Independence to Colonial Countries and Peoples—*G.T.*] became a fact, there are international documents which, although not concluded or ratified as treaties, are not 'nonbinding.' One can say that they comprise a third category."[18] Thereupon the author asserts that the difference between treaties and resolutions of international organizations is being obliterated.[19]

Professor R. Falk, of Princeton University, in speaking about United Nations General Assembly resolutions, is of the following opinion: "The main point is that the traditional dichotomy between what is obligatory and what is permissive is crumbling and that therefore international lawyers need a more adequate . . . theory of legal obligation . . . "[20]

Basically, however, western international legal doctrine adheres to the view that United Nations General Assembly resolutions are recommendations except for those, of course, which under the Charter have a binding character.

"It should be noted above all," A. Verdross writes, "that each organ can adopt lawful decisions only within the constraints of its power. Therefore, if the General Assembly on the basis of the United Nations Charter may direct only recommendations to states, such resolutions may be neither binding nor quasi-binding."[21]

"Whatever political or moral force such recommendations of the General Assembly may claim, they are not legally binding," writes G. Schwarzenberger.[22]

Professor M. Virally, whose previously expressed views on this question

17. P. Reuter, "Principes de droit international public," *Recueil des cours*, CIII (1963), 578.

18. E. Schwelb, "Neue Etappen der Fortentwicklung des Völkerrechts durch die Vereinten Nationen," *Archiv des Völkerrechts*, XIII (1966), 25-26.

19. *Ibid.*, p. 44.

20. R. A. Falk, "New Approaches to the Study of International Law," *American Journal of International Law*, LXI (1967), 487.

21. A. Verdross, "Kann die Generalversammlung der Vereinten Nationen das Völkerrecht weiterbilden," *Zeitschrift für ausländisches öffentliches Recht und Völkerrecht*, XXVI (1966), 693.

22. G. Schwarzenberger, *A Manual of International Law*, 5th ed. (London: Stevens & Sons, Ltd., 1967), p. 289.

were less definite,[23] now says the following: "Resolutions of the General Assembly incorporating declarations of . . . principles are not in themselves creative of new rules of international law . . . The General Assembly has no general legislative power."[24]

Some western jurists hold the view that the legal force of a General Assembly resolution depends upon the intention of the states who voted for this resolution. Thus, an American jurist, F. Sloan, in acknowledging that as a rule General Assembly resolutions do not create legal obligations, says that if a state which voted for a resolution intended to bind itself legally, the resolution in this case imposes legal obligations on it.[25] An English professor, D. Johnson, adheres to the same view.[26]

On this same plane an English jurist, F. Vallat, says that "Delegations acting without special authority from their governments are limited by the provisions of the Charter. They cannot bind their governments except so far as the Charter allows. If by their votes or their speeches they purport to bind their governments, they do so not by virtue of their position as delegates to the General Assembly but by virtue of some extraneous authority from their governments."[27]

However, in voting for a resolution in the General Assembly states act within the framework of the Charter, and irrespective of their intention, a resolution may have only that force which is provided by the Charter.[28]

23. M. Virally, "La valeur juridique des récommendations des organisations internationales," *Annuaire français de droit international*, II (1956), 87-88.

24. M. Sørenson, ed., *Manual of Public International Law* (New York: St. Martin's Press, 1968), p. 162; see also A. J. P. Tammes, "Decisions of International Organs as a Source of International Law," *Recueil des cours*, XCIV (1958), 338-339; A. Malintoppi, *Le raccomandazioni internazionali* (Milan: Dott. A. Giuffre, 1958), pp. 359-360; M. Sørenson, "Principes de droit international public," *Recueil des cours*, CI (1960), 100; D. P. O'Connell, *International Law* (London: Stevens & Sons, Ltd., 1965), I, 27; A. Sereni, *Diritto internazionale* (Milan: Dott. A. Giuffre, 1960), II(2), p. 1044; I. Brownlie, *Principles of Public International Law* (Oxford: Oxford University Press, 1965), p. 535; S. Bastid, *Droit International Public: Le droit des organisations internationales* (Paris, n.p., n.d.), p. 304; Lino di Qual, *Les éffets des resolutions des Nations Unies* (Paris: Pichon et Durand Auzias, 1967); G. Castaneda, *Legal Effects of United Nations Resolutions* (New York: Columbia University Press, 1969); C. Rousseau, *Droit international public* (Paris: Editions Sirey, 1970), I, 438-441.

25. See F. B. Sloan, "The Binding Force of a 'Recommendation' of the General Assembly of the United Nations," *British Year Book of International Law*, XXV (1948), 22, 31.

26. See D. H. N. Johnson, "The Effect of Resolutions of the General Assembly of the United Nations," *ibid.*, XXXII (1955-1956), 121.

27. F. A. Vallat, "The Competence of the United Nations General Assembly," *Recueil des cours*, XCVII (1957), 230.

28. See Verdross, "Kann die Generalversammlung der Vereinten Nationen das Völkerrecht weiterbilden," p. 693.

Recognition by states of a General Assembly resolution having the character of a recommendation as being binding is a special act not connected with voting on the resolution and goes beyond the limits of the Charter.[29]

In the opinion of Professor Lauterpacht, a former member of the International Court, United Nations General Assembly resolutions are in the nature of recommendations, and " . . . although on proper occasions they provide a legal authorization for Members determined to act upon them individually or collectively, they do not create a legal obligation to comply with them."[30]

The legal force of the resolutions of a particular international organization is defined by the particular acts on the basis of which this international organization exists and operates.

In this connection it is necessary to distinguish two aspects of the jurisdiction of an international organization and its organs: a thematic competence defining the questions subject to the jurisdiction of the organization, and a jurisdictional competence defining the legal force of acts of the organization relating to individual questions which fall within its thematic competence.

Further, one should never identify the legally binding nature of General Assembly resolutions or the resolutions of other international organizations with their lawfulness. Establishing the lawfulness of a resolution, that is, its conformity to the requirements of the charter of an international organization, is only to establish its juridical validity. After this, it is still necessary to ascertain whether a lawful resolution is legally binding or is a recommendation.[31]

One can not concur, for example, with the Nigerian professor T. O. Elias, who regards all United Nations General Assembly resolutions on questions enumerated in Article 18(2) of the United Nations Charter as legally binding on states.[32] Among the important questions mentioned in

29. See S. Bastid, "Observations sur une 'étap' dans le développement progressif et la codification des principes du droit international," *Recueil d'études de droit international en hommage à Paul Guggenheim* (Geneva: Imp. de la Tribune de Geneve, 1968), p. 145.

30. International Court of Justice, Reports of Judgments, Advisory Opinions and Orders, *Nottebohm Case (Liechtenstein v. Guatemala), Second Phase, April 6, 1955* (Leiden: Sijthoff, 1955), p. 115.

31. S. A. Malinin, in particular, has identified the lawfulness with the legally binding nature of a United Nations General Assembly resolution. See S. A. Malinin, *Pravovye voprosy razoruzheniia* (Leningrad: izd-vo LGU, 1966), pp. 134-138.

32. T. O. Elias, "Modern Sources of International Law," in W. Friedmann, L. Henkin, and O. Lissitzyn, eds., *Transnational Law in a Changing Society: Essays in Honor of Philip C. Jessup* (New York: Columbia University Press, 1972), p. 46.

Article 18(2) are both questions regarding which the General Assembly may take binding decisions and those regarding which it may only adopt recommendations. The text of Article 18(2) says within this category of questions are "recommendations in respect of the maintenance of international peace and security," which are just recommendations. But eight questions are enumerated in this point with regard to which the General Assembly adopts binding resolutions (for example, elections of permanent members of the Security Council, admission of new members, and so forth). One must bear in mind that not every binding directive is a norm of law.

Under the United Nations Charter, the General Assembly, just as other United Nations organs except the Security Council—which raises a special question—adopts binding resolutions only with regard to a narrow circle of matters, primarily organizational and financial.

Thus, the General Assembly adopts its own rules of procedure (Article 21 of the Charter), establishes the procedure of appointing and discharging the staff of the United Nations (Article 101(1)), approves the budget of the Organization and the apportionment of expenses among members in conformity with Article 17 of the Charter, admits states as members of the United Nations upon the recommendation of the Security Council (Article 4), and has the right to adopt a resolution suspending the rights of a United Nations member (Article 5) or expelling it from the Organization (Article 6). The General Assembly approves trusteeship agreements (Articles 16, 79, 85), agreements between the United Nations and specialized agencies (Article 63), and so forth. Lawful General Assembly resolutions concerning a broader circle of questions regulating the "internal law" of the United Nations have the same significance.[33]

With regard, however, to basic questions of its activity which concern relations of states with the United Nations or of states *inter se*, the General Assembly, as provided by Article 10 of the Charter, only makes recommendations.

The difference between recommendations and legally binding resolutions consists in the fact that the first is a suggestion to states whereas the second imposes legal obligations on states. In the case of a recommendation, the state itself determines its attitude thereto, whereas a binding resolution leaves no choice to the state.

Soviet international legal doctrine basically adheres to the view of

33. For greater detail see Malinin, "O kriteriiakh pravomernosti rezoliutsii General'-noi Assamblei OON," pp. 115-116; F. Durante, *L'Ordinamento interno delle Nazioni Unite* (Milan: Dott. A. Giuffre Editore, 1964); D. I. Fel'dman and M. V. Ianovskii, *General'noi Assambleia OON* (Kazan: izd-vo Kazanskogo universiteta, 1968), pp. 31-78.

which we have spoken, that United Nations General Assembly resolutions are of a recommendatory character.[34]

An analogous point of view predominates in the literature of other socialist countries.[35]

The practice of states leaves no doubt that they regard General Assembly resolutions which contain rules for the conduct of other states as recommendations. Actually, in those instances when states desired to attach a binding character to norms formulated in such resolutions, a resolution on working out a draft international treaty on the basis of the respective resolution (or declaration) was adopted. As examples, one may cite the Universal Declaration of Human Rights, on the basis of which the covenants on human rights were worked out, the Declaration on the Elimination of All Forms of Racial Discrimination, and the Declaration of Legal Principles Governing the Activities of States in the Exploration and Use of Outer Space, on the basis of which a convention and treaty respectively were worked out.

The viewpoint of the government of the USSR on this question was set forth in the "Memorandum of the Government of the USSR on the Procedure of Financing the Operations of the Emergency United Nations

34. See G. I. Tunkin, *Osnovy sovremennogo mezhdunarodnogo prava* (Moscow: Tipo. Vysshei partiinoi shkoly pri TsK KPSS, 1956), p. 13; D. B. Levin, *Osnovnye problemy sovremennogo mezhdunarodnogo prava* (Moscow: Gosiurizdat, 1958), p. 103; P. I. Lukin, *Istochniki mezhdunarodnogo prava* (Moscow: izd-vo Akademii nauk SSSR, 1960), p. 110; A. N. Talalaev, *Iuridicheskaia priroda mezhdunarodnogo dogovora* (Moscow: izd-vo IMO, 1963), p. 143; Kozhevnikov, ed., *Kurs mezhdunarodnogo prava*, p. 41; I. I. Lukashuk, *Istochniki mezhdunarodnogo prava* (Kiev: Laboratoriia pechati KGU, 1966), pp. 81-94; V. M. Chkhikvadze and others, eds., *Kurs mezhdunarodnogo prava v shesti tomakh* (Moscow: izd-vo Nauka, 1967), I, 194; Fel'dman and Ianovskii, *General'noi assambleia OON*, pp. 77-78; G. K. Efimov, *General'naia Assambleia OON* (Moscow: izd-vo Mezhdunarodnye otnosheniia, 1969), p. 86.

35. See, for example, M. Bartos, "Odluke medunarodnikh tela u sistemu pravnikh izvora," *Medunarodni problemy*, V, no. 4 (1953), pp. 12-27; P. Radoinov, "Pravnata sila na aktovete na Obshchoto S"branie na OON," *Izvestiia na Instituta za pravni nauki*, XIV, no. 2 (1964), p. 79; M. Lachs, "Le rôle des organisations internationales dans la formation du droit international," *Mélanges offerts à Henri Rolin: Problèmes de droit des gens* (Paris: Editions A. Pedone, 1964), pp. 165-166; V. Pěchota, *Mnohostranné mezinárodni smlouvy a přistup k nim* (Prague: Nakladatelstvi Ceskoslovenske akademii ved, 1965), p. 16; H. Bokor-Szegó, "The International Legal Content of the Right of Self-Determination as Reflected by the Disintegration of the Colonial System," in Hungarian International Law Association, *Questions of International Law* (Budapest: Hungarian Association of International Law, 1966), p. 17; S. Nahlik, *Wstep do nauki prawa miedzynarodwego* (Warsaw: Panstwowe wyd-wo naukowe, 1967), p. 417; A. Basak, *Decisions of the United Nations Organs in the Judgments and Opinions of the International Court of Justice* (Wroclaw: Wroclawskiego Towarzystwa Naukowe, 1969), pp. 74-102.

Forces in the Middle East and the United Nations Operations in the Congo" sent to the International Court on March 15, 1962. This Memorandum states: ". . . U. N. General Assembly resolutions, as is provided for in Article 10 of the Charter, have the character of recommendations and are not binding upon states. Member states of the United Nations themselves define their attitude toward such resolutions. All measures which arise out of General Assembly resolutions also bear only a recommendatory character and cannot create legal obligations for member states of the Organization."[36]

It is necessary, however, to say a special word about those United Nations General Assembly resolutions which themselves represent an interpretation of the United Nations Charter. Although the Charter contains no special provisions on this score, the report of Committee 2 of Commission IV of the San Francisco Conference, which has been referred to previously, says that if an interpretation of the Charter given by a particular United Nations organ is generally acceptable, it acquires binding force.[37] This rule is followed in United Nations practice. One can, therefore, regard a General Assembly resolution relating to the interpretation of a particular provision of the United Nations Charter and adopted by the votes of all United Nations members as binding.

But as I. I. Lukashuk has justly remarked, and according to the said report of Committee 2, "an interpretation of the Charter acquires binding force not because it is contained in a resolution, but in consequence of the fact that it is generally recognized."[38]

A. Verdross says that he can not agree with my view because "any authentic interpretation of a legal norm may proceed only from the authority which created it, or from a superior authority, or perhaps as a result of a procedure which has been determined by these authorities. We find such a procedure for the present case in Articles 108 and 109 of the United Nations Charter."[39]

In reality, the interpretation of a particular provision of the United Nations Charter becomes binding only when it has been recognized by all or almost all United Nations members, including the permanent members of the Security Council. Its legally binding nature is determined by such recognition, which may be expressed by various means, particularly by

36. For the text of the Memorandum, see *Mezhdunarodnaia zhizn'*, no. 5 (1962), p. 158.

37. United Nations, *Documents of the United Nations Conference on International Organization* (London and New York: United Nations Information Organizations, 1945), XIII, 710.

38. Lukashuk, *Istochniki mezhdunarodnogo prava*, p. 92.

39. Verdross, "Kann die Generalversammlung der Vereinten Nationen das Völkerrecht weiterbilden," p. 695.

custom. Voting for a resolution which gives an interpretation of the Charter is one method of such recognition, and a resolution adopted unanimously is testimony to universal recognition of the respective interpretation.

As regards the Security Council, it may take decisions binding upon members of the United Nations. Article 25 of the Charter provides: "The Members of the United Nations agree to accept and carry out the decisions of the Security Council in accordance with the present Charter." These decisions, however, are by their nature executive resolutions which do not have the purpose of creating general norms of conduct.

At the same time, resolutions of international organizations, above all resolutions of the General Assembly and Security Council adopted in conformity with the provisions of the United Nations Charter, may enter into the process of norm-formation and play a definite role in forming new principles and norms of international law and in affirming, strengthening, developing, and interpreting existing principles and norms.

Above all, resolutions of the General Assembly and Security Council for which states of both existing social systems have cast a vote, including the great powers, possess great moral and political authority. The President of the International Court, M. Lachs, undoubtedly is correct in saying that United Nations General Assembly resolutions " . . . have become a significant factor in the . . . development and codification of international law."[40] Many General Assembly recommendations are more effective than binding resolutions. This is necessary to take into consideration, but it does not dispose of the question of the legal force of General Assembly resolutions and their role in the development of international law.

Resolutions of the Security Council adopted in conformity with the Charter may in a number of instances create a specific practice or contribute to the formation of an international practice that can crystallize into a rule of conduct and therefore be a definite stage in the process of forming a customary norm of international law. Practice does not, however, always lead to the formation of a rule of conduct, and a rule of conduct, if it is formed, does not necessarily become a legal norm. The importance of Security Council decisions goes beyond the limits of the Charter and relates to the formation of customary norms of international law. But it nonetheless is very real.

Resolutions of the General Assembly influence the development of international law by two means: within the framework of the Charter and in the process of creating norms of international law by way of custom.

40. M. Lachs, *The Law of Outer Space* (Leiden: A. W. Sijthoff, 1972), p. 138.

The General Assembly, as well as the respective agencies of other international organizations, frequently approve the texts of international treaties.

Resolutions of international organizations adopting the texts of agreements enter into the process of concluding them. But a resolution of an international organization confirming the text of a treaty does not complete the process of forming a norm of international law and does not as such lead directly to the emergence of such a norm.

As regards the recommendatory resolutions adopted by the General Assembly, within the framework of the Charter such resolutions are recommendations and, as already pointed out, do not impose legal obligations on members.

But resolutions of the General Assembly and, to a lesser degree, the resolutions of other organizations play a specific role in the process of forming norms of international law by way of custom.[41] Recommendatory resolutions of international organizations, above all resolutions of the General Assembly adopted in conformity with the Charter and for which votes have been cast by states of the two systems (this is very important, since the question is the formation of norms of general international law), play an important role in the very process of forming customary norms of international law.

Specific rules, norms for the conduct of states, are formulated in General Assembly resolutions. They still are not norms of international law, but in the future they can become such by the same means as customary norms of international law are formed.

As already has been pointed out, however, the fact that a norm of any act later becomes a norm of international law is, in and of itself, not sufficient to consider this act as entering into the process of forming a norm of international law. There are more than a few norms of international law which were formulated for the first time, for example, in acts of national legislation, but this alone is no basis for including national legislative acts in the process of international norm-formation. The process of becoming a norm of international law begins only from the moment when the norm begins to be created as a norm of international law; that is, when the process acquires an interstate character.

It is obvious in this instance that the process of forming a rule of conduct which already has been fixed in a resolution of an international

41. See R. Higgins, *The Development of International Law Through the Political Organs of the United Nations* (London: Oxford University Press, 1963), pp. 2-7; K. Wolfke, "Practice of International Organizations and Customary International Law," *Polish Yearbook of International Law 1966/1967*, I (1968), 183-194.

organization has an international character. What place do recommendatory resolutions of international organizations occupy in the process of forming customary norms of international law?

Usage as a stage in the formation of a customary norm of international law reflects the practice of states, which frequently is absent in resolutions of the United Nations General Assembly or another international organ. Consequently, in this respect usage stands, as a rule, farther ahead in the process of norm-formation than a resolution of an international organization. At the same time, the concordance of the wills of states which takes place in a General Assembly resolution, even though it does not go beyond the limits of a recommendation, expresses the wish of states that members of the organization act in conformity with the norms of the resolution. This element places a resolution farther ahead than usage in the process of forming customary norms of international law.

The subsequent development depends above all upon the extent to which a norm contained in a resolution conforms to the laws of societal development, to the real co-relation of forces. The results of voting are an indicator here. Therefore, resolutions of the United Nations General Assembly adopted unanimously or by the majority stipulated in the Charter, including states of the two systems, may signify the birth and formation of those new principles and norms of international law which are proclaimed in such resolutions. One may regard as such resolutions, for example, the resolutions of the General Assembly on the question of the regulation and reduction of armaments, beginning with the resolution of December 14, 1946 (41/I), on general and complete disarmament, beginning with the resolution of November 20, 1959 (1378/XIV), on the prohibition of war propaganda of November 3, 1947 (110/II), on recognizing Africa as a nuclear-free zone of November 24, 1961 (1652/XVI),[42] on the strict observance of the prohibition of the threat or use of force in international relations and the right of peoples to self-determination of November 30, 1966 (2160/XXI), and a number of others.[43]

Similar resolutions may be stages in the process of creating customary norms of international law—stages, however, which do not complete the process of norm-formation and therefore do not lead directly to the emergence of a norm of international law. As is common in the process of forming customary norms of international law, their further development

42. For greater detail, see O. V. Bogdanov, *Vseobshchee i polnoe razoruzhenie* (Moscow: izd-vo Mezhdunarodnye otnosheniia, 1964); Malinin, *Pravovye osnovy razoruzheniia.*

43. For greater detail, see Fel'dman and Ianovskii, *General'naia assambleia OON,* pp. 80-191.

may slow down temporarily or forever. In the latter case, the process will not be completed and will not lead to the formation of a norm of international law. But it can continue and be completed by states recognizing rules established in General Assembly resolutions as norms of international law.

Resolutions of the United Nations General Assembly also frequently are means of declaring or interpreting prevailing principles and norms of international law.

When a resolution of the General Assembly or of another international organ is in the nature of declaring the existence of a particular norm of international law, it has, naturally, a declarative character. But in international law, where frequently there are disputes over whether a particular norm of international law exists or not, the significance of such resolutions, if states of different social systems have voted for them, can not give rise to doubt. This also is true of resolutions interpreting prevailing principles and norms. Although under the United Nations Charter these and other resolutions are in the nature of recommendations, on a broader plane there is every reason to anticipate that the declaration of the existence of a norm or its interpretation contained in such resolutions will be accepted in practice and be confirmed as legally binding by means of custom.

The voting of states for a General Assembly resolution which represents a declaration or interpretation of prevailing principles and norms of international law is an affirmation of the previously existing agreement that was embodied in the prevailing principles and norms, as to which there is a question in a specific case.

Moreover, for a number of states, voting for such a General Assembly resolution may be the first instance of their expressing recognition of the respective principles and norms as norms of international law or recognition of the interpretation of the principles and norms set forth in the resolution.

As an example of a General Assembly resolution which contains a declaration or interpretation of prevailing principles and norms of international law, one may mention the General Assembly Resolution (95/I) of December 11, 1946, on the principles of international law recognized by the charters and judgments of the Nuremberg and Tokyo tribunals, which says that the General Assembly "affirms the principles of international law recognized by the Charter of the Nuremberg Tribunal and sanctioned by the judgment of that Tribunal."

Also included in this category are the basic provisions of the Declaration on Granting Independence to Colonial Countries and Peoples (Resolution 1514/XV), resolution 1653/XVI of November 24, 1961, which says that "the use of nuclear or thermonuclear weapons contravenes norms of international law and the laws of humanity," the Declaration on Principles of International Law Relating to Friendly Relations and Cooperation Among States in Accordance with the Charter of the United Nations (Resolution 2625(XXV) of October 24, 1970), and a number of other resolutions of the General Assembly.

It is necessary to bear in mind in this connection that the question of whether a specific resolution or certain provisions of a resolution are a declaration or interpretation of prevailing principles and norms of international law must be decided not on the basis of philological formulations, which might be accidental, but on the basis of the true meaning of the resolution. The resolution must testify to the expression of recognition (primarily or secondarily) by the states which voted for it of the provisions set forth in the resolution as norms of international law.

It must be emphasized that in these instances the binding force of the provisions contained in the resolution is based not on the resolution itself, which can not have a greater force than is provided for by the United Nations Charter, but on the agreement of the states who voted for the resolution, which is characteristic of the process of creating and modifying norms of international law by means of custom.

The fact that as a rule the General Assembly can adopt only recommendations dealing with the most important issues of United Nations activities is one of the important manifestations of the legal nature of the United Nations (see Chapter 15).

B. Recommendations of Specialized International Organizations

The legal nature of recommendations of specialized agencies whose constitutions provide for the adoption of such recommendations addressed to member states is of considerable interest.

The provisions of constitutions of the specialized agencies on this question are not identical. Thus, for example, the constitutions of the International Civil Aviation Organization and of the World Meteorological Organization speak of standards and recommended practice, which in essence means regulations in the first case and recommendations in the second.

The question of recommendations has been formulated most precisely in the constitutions of the International Labor Organization and UNESCO. The Constitution of the International Labor Organization says that a recommendation adopted by the General Conference of the ILO "will be communicated to all Members for their consideration with a view to effect being given to it by national legislation or otherwise" (Article 19

Subsidiary Processes of Forming Norms of International Law

(6)). The UNESCO Rules of Procedure provide that in recommendations the "General Conference formulates principles and norms for the international regulation of any particular question and invites Member States to take whatever legislative or other steps may be required—in conformity with the constitutional practice of each State and the nature of the question under consideration—to apply the principles and norms aforesaid within their respective territories."[44]

Member states are not legally bound to fulfill recommendations. But the constitutions of a number of specialized agencies provide that if a recommendation is adopted, the member states, irrespective of their attitude toward the given recommendation, shall be bound to undertake the specific actions. Thus, according to the Constitution of the International Labor Organization, each member of the Organization is obliged within twelve or, in an extreme case, eighteen months, to submit this recommendation to the respective competent authorities for the purpose of taking decisions pursuant thereto and to notify the Director-General of the ILO about this decision. At the same time, member states are obliged, according to the Constitution of the ILO, periodically to notify the Director-General of the ILO with regard to the state of their legislation and practice concerning matters touched upon in the recommendation (Article 19(6), pars. b,c,d). The submission by member states of information concerning measures which they have taken to effectuate recommendations approved by the General Conference also is provided for by the Constitution of UNESCO (Article VIII, as well as Articles XV and XVI of the Rules of Procedure relating to recommendations and conventions).

The legal nature of recommendations of international organizations has given rise to more than a few disputes. Thus, Professor M. Virally, although he points out that "from a strict legal viewpoint its addressee . . . is not bound to apply it and even is not bound to keep its existence in mind,"[45] nevertheless suggests that if a state executes a recommendation adopted by an international organization, it fulfills its obligations and, in the event of nonfulfillment, it is "guilty" before the organization.[46]

In the view of Professor P. Vellas, of Toulouse University, the

44. The Rules of Procedure concerning recommendations made by the General Conference to member states and to the adoption of international conventions by the General Conference were confirmed by the General Conference at its fifth session, and amended at the seventh session. *Sbornik pravil po sozyvu i provedeniiu konferentsii* (New York: UNESCO, 1964).

45. Virally, "La valeur juridique des récommendations des organisations internationales," pp. 83-84.

46. *Ibid.*, pp. 87-88.

recommendations of specialized agencies "possess a considerable socio-juridical power of applicability."[47]

The legal adviser of UNESCO, H. Saba, speaks of "nonratified norms," by which he means recommendations,[48] clearly underestimating the difference existing between conventions and recommendations adopted by international organizations.

It is important above all, in our view, not to confuse the actual effectiveness of recommendations of international organizations with their legally binding nature. Not only legal norms may be effective. The effectiveness of a norm as such does not make it legal. Moral norms in a number of instances are more effective than certain legal norms, but they continue to remain moral norms.

The assertion that the legal force of recommendations of such international organizations as the International Labor Organization, UNESCO, and certain others consists in the fact that in consequence of their adoption states are bound to perform certain actions also is incorrect. The respective obligations are fixed in the articles of the constitutions of these organizations, and these articles begin to operate when a specific legal fact takes place: the adoption by an international organization of a particular recommendation. The duty to submit a recommendation for the consideration of competent agencies, to communicate the results of this consideration to the international organization, to submit information on matters touched upon in the recommendation, has been provided for by the constitutions of these international organizations. It is true that a recommendation adopted in such organizations defines the extent of the information to be submitted by all member states. In prescribing a specific form of state action, however, the norms of a recommendation are not legally binding upon them. Each state decides for itself whether to act in accordance with the recommendation.

Moreover, in contrast to regulations, recommendations—to which we refer here—do not have the purpose of creating international obligations of states. If a state has adopted a regulation, it is bound to it as an international treaty. If a state effectuates the norms of a recommendation, it does not by virtue thereof become bound by international obligations.

Such is the situation existing at the present time as regards specialized agencies of the United Nations. But another legal significance for recommendations of a particular international organization also is wholly

47. P. Vellas, *Droit international public; institutions internationales* (Paris: Librairie générale de droit et jurisprudence, 1967), p. 214. ["... d'une force d'applicabilité socio-juridique considérable"]

48. H. Saba, "L'Activité quasi-législative des institutions spécialisées des Nations Unies," *Recueil des cours*, CXI (1964), 660.

possible. Thus, for example, in the Council for Mutual Economic Assistance recommendations adopted by the Council become, after their approval by interested states, distinctive international agreements. As E. Ustor indicates precisely: " . . . a recommendation of the CMEA is by its very nature not binding. But it undoubtedly acquires binding force through the specific consent of the member States."[49] Here, as appears from the Charter of CMEA, recommendations adopted by the Council have the purpose to create as a result of their approval international obligations for members of the organization.[50]

The legal significance of recommendations of a particular international organization therefore is determined by the Charter of this organization or, to express it more precisely, by the law of this organization.

The real effectiveness of the norms of recommendations, that is, the degree of their influence on the conduct of states, is another question. The more a recommendation of an international organization is responsive to the pressing requirements of the cooperation of states in a given sphere, the higher its effectiveness. One must concur with Professor Vellas that recommendations of international organizations relating to cooperation in economic, scientific, and technical domains have, in a number of instances, very great effectiveness.[51]

The role of normative recommendations of specialized international organizations undoubtedly is growing in international relations. Therefore, ascertaining their legal nature and true role is of both theoretical and practical importance.

C. Decisions of the International Court and of International Arbitration Tribunals

There are two opposing points of view in bourgeois legal literature on the significance of decisions of international courts and arbitral tribunals as sources of international law.

One viewpoint, expressed most frequently in "common law" countries, exaggerates the role of judgments of the International Court. Thus, Lauterpacht, in a detailed work, *The Development of International Law by the International Court*, whose second edition appeared in 1958, writes

49. E. Ustor, "Decision-Making in the Council for Mutual Economic Assistance," *Recueil des cours*, CXXXIV (1971), 219.

50. P. A. Tokareva, ed., *Mnogostoronee ekonomicheskoe sotrudnichestvo sotsialisticheskikh gosudarstv; sbornik dokumentov*, 2d ed. (Moscow: Iuridicheskaia literatura, 1972), pp. 123-124, reproducing Articles 2(4)(a) and 4(1) of the CMEA Charter.

51. Vellas, *Droit international public; institutions internationales*, p. 214.

the following with regard to decisions of the International Court: "They state what the law is. Their decisions are evidence of the existing rule of law. That does not mean that they do not in fact constitute a source of international law. For the distinction between the evidence and the source of many a rule of law is more speculative and less rigid than is commonly supposed . . . insofar as they show what are the rules of international law they are largely identical with it."[52]

In noting that there is no legislative body in international relations, G. Fitzmaurice, an English jurist who was a member of the International Court, writes: "The international community is therefore peculiarly dependent on its international tribunals for the development and clarification of the law, and for lending to it an authority more substantial and less precarious than can be drawn from the often divergent or uncertain practices of States, or even from the opinions of individual publicists, whatever their repute."[53]

Another English jurist, C. W. Jenks, declares in a summary discussion in which he draws an analogy with the development of the English judicial system: "International law now has its supreme Court and that supreme Court is approaching with judicial statesmanship the task of giving a new vitality to the law."[54] And further, in developing Lauterpacht's idea, Jenks says that "in respect of a widening range of questions the Court is progressively substituting judicial precedent for formless and debatable custom."[55]

On the same plane, an Australian jurist, O'Connell, asserts that "As the judge in the common law system plays a fundamental role in the formulation of general principles, in their application and modification by reference to contingent circumstances, in extension by analogy and deduction from accepted hypothesis, so does the judge in the system of international law."[56]

This concept finds no support in the provisions of the Statute of the International Court. Article 38 of the Statute says that the Court shall be obliged to decide disputes submitted to it on the basis of international

52. H. Lauterpacht, *The Development of International Law by the International Court*, 2d ed. (London: Stevens & Sons, Ltd., 1958), p. 21.

53. G. Fitzmaurice, "Hersch Lauterpacht: The Scholar as Judge," *British Year Book of International Law*, XXXVII (1961), 14.

54. C. W. Jenks, *The Common Law of Mankind* (London: Stevens & Sons, Ltd., 1958), p. 181.

55. *Ibid.*, p. 180. For greater detail, see C. W. Jenks, *The Prospect of International Adjudication* (London: Stevens & Sons, Ltd., 1964).

56. O'Connell, *International Law*, I, p. 28; an Israeli jurist trained in England, S. Rosenne, says that the International Court has become a "powerful instrument for the progress" of international law. See S. Rosenne, *The Law and Practice of the International Court* (Leiden: A. W. Sijthoff, 1965), II, 607.

law. With regard to the specific sources to be applied by the Court, Article 38(1)(d) says that the Court shall apply "subject to the provisions of Article 59, judicial decisions and the teachings of the most highly qualified publicists of the various nations, as subsidiary means for the determination of rules of law." Article 59 of the Statute provides: "The decision of the Court has no binding force except between the parties and in respect of that particular case."

It by no means follows that decisions of the Court "are evidence of the existence of a rule of law." This concept, arising out of Anglo-American "common law" doctrine, is inapplicable to international law. To ascribe such a role to the International Court is to go beyond the provisions of its Statute.

Lauterpacht asserts that judgments of the Court also are international law. He equates them, therefore, to international treaties and customs enumerated in Article 38(1)(a) and (b) of the Statute. But if the Statute says that the Court shall apply international treaties and international custom as part of international law by which it must be guided, the Statute says otherwise with respect to judicial decisions. They may be used only as one of the subsidiary means for determining the existence or absence of a particular norm of international law. It also must be noted that the Statute places judicial decisions on the same level as doctrine.

Lauterpacht goes further, asserting that the Court may regard its decisions as an expression of international law notwithstanding the provisions of the Statute. "They are not binding *upon States*. Neither are they binding upon the Court. However, no written provisions can prevent them from showing authoritatively what international law is, and no written rule can prevent the Court from regarding them as as such."[5][7]

If the Court regarded its decisions as an embodiment of international law and consequently as binding upon states, this would expressly contravene its Statute. But the International Court, as any other international organ, was created on the basis of agreement: the United Nations Charter and the Statute of the Court. The powers and functions of an international organ, particularly of the International Court, are defined by its Statute, and the Court can not pretend that greater significance is attached to its decisions than has been established by the Statute of the Court.

There is no basis for presupposing that the Statute of the International Court has been changed by customary means on the basis of the general agreement of United Nations members, and even Lauterpacht himself does not say this.

57. Lauterpacht, *The Development of International Law by the International Court*, p. 22.

The Process of Forming Norms of International Law

Another point of view expressed in bourgeois literature with regard to judicial decisions is that they are not sources of international law. Thus, Professor A. Verdross, in combining judicial decisions and doctrine, says: "Judicial decisions therefore can never be guided exclusively by an individual prior decision or by doctrine. It can use a prior decision and doctrine in order to ascertain whether a norm of international law is not sufficiently clear. Therefore, judicial practice and doctrine are not independent sources of international law; they are only subsidiary sources of law which serve to help understand doubtful provisions of law."[58]

Citing Article 59 of the Statute of the International Court, H. Kelsen writes that a "decision of the Court can not have the character of a precedent."[59]

In Oppenheim's treatise *International Law* edited by Lauterpacht we read: "In the absence of anything approaching the common law doctrine of judicial precedent, decisions of international tribunals are not a direct source of law in international adjudications."[60]

"Decisions of international courts or tribunals," writes G. Schwarzenberger, "do not have the effect of precedents in the technical sense of English law ... such authority as international decisions may claim is purely persuasive."[61]

The majority of Soviet writers adhere to the view that decisions of the International Court and international arbitral tribunals are not a means of creating or modifying its norms,[62] but are subsidiary sources.

Article 38 of the Statute of the International Court provides that the Court, in considering cases submitted to it by states, shall act "in accordance with international law." It is not empowered to make changes in prevailing international law, but should be guided by it. The Statute expressly rejects the concept of "judicial precedent," establishing in

58. Verdross, *Mezhdunarodnoe pravo*, pp. 164-165.

59. Kelsen, *Principles of International Law*, p. 394.

60. L. Oppenheim, *International Law*, ed. H. Lauterpacht, 8th ed. (London: Longmans, 1955), I, 31.

61. Schwarzenberger, *A Manual of International Law*, p. 255; Waldock expresses a view close to this. See H. Waldock, "General Course on Public International Law," *Recueil des cours*, CVI (1962), 91. Brownlie remarks that "the Court applies law and does not make it." Brownlie, *Principles of Public International Law*, p. 17.

62. See, for example, E. A. Korovin, ed., *Mezhdunarodnoe pravo* (Moscow: Gosiurizdat, 1951), pp. 17-18; Kozhevnikov, ed., *Mezhdunarodnoe pravo*, p. 9; Levin, *Osnovnye problemy sovremennogo mezhdunarodnogo prava*, pp. 101-102; G. P. Kaliuzhnaia and D. B. Levin, *Mezhdunarodnoe pravo* (Moscow: Gosiurizdat, 1960), p. 32; Kozhevnikov, ed., *Kurs mezhdunarodnogo prava*, pp. 41-42; Lukashuk, *Istochniki mezhdunarodnogo prava*, pp. 95-96; Chkhikvadze and others, eds., *Kurs mezhdunarodnogo prava v shesti tomakh*, I, 195; L. A. Modzhorian and N. T. Blatova, eds., *Mezhdunarodnoe pravo* (Moscow: Iuridicheskaia literatura, 1970), p. 60.

Subsidiary Processes of Forming Norms of International Law

Article 59 that "the decision of the Court has no binding force except between the parties and in respect of that particular case." With this reservation, the International Court can use its decisions "as subsidiary means for the determination of rules of law." Consequently, according to the Statute of the International Court, its decisions are not part of the process of creating or modifying norms of international law.

What role do decisions of the International Court have on the broader plane of forming norms of international law? The International Court does not consist of representatives of states. It is composed of persons elected by representatives of states (respectively, in the Security Council and General Assembly of the United Nations), but who act as "independent judges" (Article 2 of the Statute). Decisions of the Court reflect the opinion of the members of the Court, who are specialists in international law. This brings decisions of the Court closer to doctrine, and not without reason does the Statute of the Court speak of judicial decisions and teachings of international law simultaneously.

But the International Court is at the same time one of the principal organs of the United Nations, fulfilling its judicial functions in conformity with the United Nations Charter and its own Statute. It considers cases submitted to it by states and whose parties are states. Decisions of the Court are binding upon the parties to the case, and the United Nations Charter provides that the parties shall be bound to comply with such decisions (Article 94).

These specific features are the basis for considering that decisions of the International Court enter into the process of norm-formation as part of international practice in that they relate to the declaration of the existence of norms of international law or their interpretation. This practice, it is true, can not be placed on the same level with state practice, since the International Court is not composed of representatives of states.

Inasmuch as this is so, what has been said previously with regard to the formation and modification of norms of international law by way of custom is applicable to decisions of the International Court. As part of international practice, decisions of the International Court can lead to completion of the process of norm-formation by their being recognized by states and being consolidated in international law. Of course, only those decisions of the International Court for which judges representing the different social and legal systems have voted and which frequently are cited in the practice of relations among states actually have a chance of being consolidated.[63]

63. In its decision of December 18, 1951, in the Anglo-Norwegian fisheries dispute the International Court expressed the view that the so-called ten-mile rule upheld by England—that the waters of bays and gulfs may be considered to be internal waters of

Regrettably, however, if one takes the practice of the International Court as a whole, we find more than a few decisions that do not correspond to prevailing international law, decisions in which a one-sided interpretation of the latter is reflected.[64]

The considerations set forth above also relate basically to decisions of international arbitral tribunals created by agreement between two or more states to consider interstate disputes. However, in carrying less weight for wholly understandable reasons than decisions of the International Court, the decisions of international arbitral tribunals stand, in comparison with the former, closer to international legal doctrine.

D. National Legislation and Decisions of National Judicial Instances

National legislative acts, as well as decisions of national courts, can be, first and foremost, one of the means of establishing norms of international law. Their role is defined by the fact that norms of international law are created by means of agreement among states. National legislation and decisions of national courts can in a number of instances be regarded as expressing recognition by a specific state of a particular rule as a norm of international law.

National courts are state organs and, as Lauterpacht correctly points out, "their decisions within any particular State, when endowed with sufficient uniformity and authority, may be regarded as expressing the *opinio juris* of that State."[65]

It is necessary, however, to be more precise. Judicial decisions, although on questions concerning international relations, can all the same have significance only within the limits of the national law of a given state. In order to have significance for international norm-formation, such a

---

a coastal state only if the breadth of the aperture of such bays and gulfs does not exceed ten miles—is not a principle of international law. This position was consolidated in the 1958 Convention on the Territorial Sea and Contiguous Zone, which provided that the waters of bays and gulfs, the breadth of whose aperture does not exceed twenty-four miles, shall be considered internal waters of the coastal state. Thus, the 1958 Convention establishes not a ten-mile, but a twenty-four mile rule.

64. For example, the decision relating to the recognition of consular jurisdiction in the Franco-American case on the rights of American nationals in Morocco, and others. S. B. Krylov, *Mezhdunarodnyi sud* (Moscow: Gosiurizdat, 1958). One also should mention in this connection the 1962 advisory opinion in the case of certain expenses of the United Nations and the 1966 judgment in the Southwest Africa case. See M. Iuranov, "Otkaz v pravosudii (Reshenie Mezhdunarodnogo Suda po delu o Iugo-Zapadnoi Afriki)," *Sovetskoe gosudarstvo i pravo*, no. 5 (1957), pp. 45-54.

65. Lauterpacht, *The Development of International Law by the International Court*, p. 20.

Subsidiary Processes of Forming Norms of International Law

decision must express, just as the legislative act of a state, the acceptance or recognition of a particular rule as a norm of international law.[66]

The role of national legislation and of decisions of national courts is not limited to the fact that they have significance for establishing the existence of principles and norms of international law. The said acts can, for example, contain proposals to other states, an expression of readiness on the part of a given state to recognize a particular rule as a norm of international law on condition that other states will agree to act in an analogous manner. In this respect, the Decree on Peace of November 8, 1917, is especially characteristic, wherein the Soviet state advanced a whole series of international legal principles, first and foremost the principle of the prohibition of aggressive war, the principle of the criminality of such war, the principle of self-determination of nations, and others. This was not just the formulation of the policy of a socialist state, but also a proposal to all other states to recognize these principles as principles of international law.[67]

The actions of a state in the person of its legislative or judicial organs can, as already has been pointed out, also signify recognition on the part of a state of a norm being formed or already prevailing as a norm of international law as regards the state concerned.

Therefore, in both the first and second instance the actions of a state can be part of the process of forming a customary norm of international law.

66. K. Strupp speaks of the need for a decision to express *opinio juris gentium*. K. Strupp, "Règles générales du droit de la paix," *Recueil des cours*, XLVII (1934), 307-308.

67. For greater detail see N. V. Mironov, *Sovetskoe zakonodatel'stvo i mezhdunarodnoe pravo* (Moscow: izd-vo Mezhdunarodnye otnosheniia, 1968).

Chapter 6 *Doctrine and the Opinions of Social Organizations*

A. International Legal Doctrine

In the nineteenth and even at the beginning of the twentieth century, many jurists regarded international law as, to a significant extent, "doctrinal" law, the law of "scholars." They ascribed to the science of international law not just the role of declaror, but also the role of creator, of its norms. J. C. Bluntschli, for example, called treatises of international law the "surrogate of legislation in which private persons who know the law expound and systematize prevailing legal norms."[1]

There is no doubt that doctrine previously played a significantly larger role as a source of international law than at the present time.

The opinions of authoritative specialists on international law of various countries are now one means of establishing the existence or absence of a particular norm of international law, as well as of interpreting them.

Article 38 of the Statute of the International Court provides that in deciding cases the Court may apply "the teachings of the most qualified publicists of the various nations, as a subsidiary means for the determination of the rules of law."

Taking into account the significant difficulties which frequently arise in establishing the existence or interpreting norms of international law (especially with regard to customary norms), the science of international law often renders important service in this area.

At the same time, there is no doubt that as state practice becomes more accessible as a result of the publication of various kinds of diplomatic and other state documents, as well as of decisions of international organiza-

1. J. C. Bluntschli, *Das moderne Völkerrecht der civilisirten Staten*, 2d ed. (Nordlingen: Verlag der C. H. Beck'schen Buchhandlung, 1872), p. 7.

[186]

Doctrine and the Opinions of Social Organizations

tions and international courts, the role of doctrine as a means of establishing the existence of norms of international law and of interpreting them is tending to diminish.[2]

The scientific investigations of international lawyers are not part of the process of international law-making, although they exert some influence upon it. There is virtually complete agreement in Soviet legal literature on this question. The overwhelming majority of bourgeois international lawyers also adhere at present to the view that international legal doctrine is not a method of creating norms of law, but plays only that subsidiary role defined in Article 38 of the Statute of the International Court.[3]

It is characteristic that even the International Court, as H. Waldock notes, never has cited international legal doctrine in its judgments, although, as he correctly suggests, this does not mean that doctrine exerts no influence upon these judgments.[4]

If it is of a progressive character, the science of international law may have a material impact upon the development of international law. In uncovering the laws of societal development, in noticing and supporting new trends or progressive new principles and norms which may not be completely formulated, in waging a struggle against everything obsolete which impedes social progress, and in unmasking reactionary forces clinging to obsolete principles and norms that inhibit the progressive development of international law, science may contribute significantly to its development.

B. Opinions and Resolutions of Social and Scientific Organizations

At the present time there are a significant number of international and national social and scientific organizations which either are specially concerned with questions of international law or from time to time express views on such questions. These organizations are highly diverse both by their character and their social significance. Among them are congresses of advocates of peace representing hundreds of millions of people, and also organizations such as the World Federation of Trade

2. L. Oppenheim, *International Law*, ed. H. Lauterpacht, 8th ed. (London: Longmans, 1955), I, 33.

3. For example, see A. Verdross, *Mezhdunarodnoe pravo*, trans. from 3d ed. by F. A. Kublitskii and R. L. Naryshkina, ed. G. I. Tunkin (Moscow: izd-vo IL, 1959), p. 165; Oppenheim, *International Law*, I, 33. An Italian professor, R. Ago, essentially ascribes a law-creating role to (legal) science. See R. Ago, "Positive Law and International Law," *American Journal of International Law*, LI (1957), 691-733.

4. See H. Waldock, "General Course on Public International Law," *Recueil des cours*, CVI (1962), 95-96.

Unions, a very broad mass organization. On the other hand, there are such legal organizations as the International Association of Democratic Jurists (IADJ), a broad organization of jurists, the Institute of International Law, whose membership under the existing statute may not exceed 130 persons, international legal specialists from various countries, and the International Law Association, numbering several thousand persons, far from always international legal specialists. There also are a large number of national organizations for questions of international law.

From the standpoint of the process of international norm-formation, these organizations all have in common the fact that they are not agencies reflecting the will of states. Their views and resolutions therefore do not enter into the process of international norm-formation.

But these organizations are so diverse that their impact upon the process of creating international legal norms also is highly diverse.

Draft conventions, resolutions, and so forth prepared by special legal organizations (as, for example, the Institute of International Law, the International Law Association, and others) occupy the same place with regard to the process of norm-formation in general as does international legal doctrine.

The resolutions of mass international organizations which express the opinion of broad circles of the public have another significance. While perhaps not always formulating a particular provision of international law with sufficient precision, they express the aspirations of peoples which governments may only consider. If in socialist states, where governments listen to the voice of the people and express its will, such organizations and their views help state agencies in formulating the corresponding international legal position of the state, then in capitalist states they are a means of public opinion pressuring the government. Of the mass international organizations one should especially single out the movement of the advocates of peace. This movement, taking as its basic task the struggle for the maintenance and strengthening of peace, devotes great attention to international law as a means of struggle for peace. In their resolutions and appeals, organs of the movement of advocates of peace, expressing the will of hundreds of millions of vanguard people, raise vital questions of contemporary international relations and international law, as, for example, the problem of disarmament, prohibition of war propaganda, definition of aggression, and others.[5]

5. On this question see M. I. Lazarev, *Kongress narodov v zashchitu mira i osnovnye printsipy mezhdunarodnogo prava* (Moscow: Gosiurizdat, 1953); N. Ul'ianova, "Mizhnarodnopravoe znacheniia dokumentiv vsevitn'ogo rukhu prikhil'nikov miru," *Radians'ke pravo*, no. 3 (1959), pp. 21-27; V. M. Chkhikvadze, *Bor'ba za mir—neodolimoe dvizhenie sovremennosti* (Moscow: izd-vo Mysl', 1969).

Doctrine and the Opinions of Social Organizations

In our time the opportunities for the popular masses to involve themselves actively in deciding international questions have grown immeasurably. "Peoples are more actively taking the decision of questions of peace and war into their own hands."[6] The international working class, the most consistent fighter against imperialist wars, is the organizing force of the all-people's struggle for peace. Naturally, under these conditions the influence of working class organizations and of broad people's organizations of the struggle for peace upon the development of international law is increasing more and more.

6. *Programma Kommunisticheskoi partii Sovetskogo Soiuza* (Moscow: Politizdat, 1964), p. 58.

Chapter 7 *The Problem of "General Principles of Law"*

The problem of "general principles of law" was and still is the subject of lively discussion chiefly in connection with Article 38(1)(c) of the Statute of the Permanent Court of International Justice and, at present, the Statute of the International Court.

This problem has occupied a very large place in international legal literature, primarily in consequence of the endeavors of the followers of new natural law concepts, who have attempted to find support for their own theoretical constructions in the Statute of the Permanent Court of International Justice.

Some representatives of the "law of precedent" see a tendency in this provision of the Statute of the International Court to enlarge the role of the international court and an attribution of functions thereto which resemble the law-making functions of courts in "common law" countries.[1]

Other bourgeois authors, believing that "general principles of law" do not have a significant place in international law, point out that the Permanent Court of International Justice not once has referred in its decisions to the corresponding paragraph of its own Statute which speaks of "general principles of law."[2]

The majority of bourgeois authors, citing the *travaux préparatoires* of the Commission of Jurists for Drafting the Statute of the Permanent

1. Lauterpacht said that Article 38(1)(c) of the Statute is an important landmark in the history of international law. See L. Oppenheim, *International Law*, ed. H. Lauterpacht, 8th ed. (London: Longmans, 1955), I, 30.

2. J. Basdevant, "Règles générales du droit de la paix," *Recueil des cours*, LVIII (1936), 503; C. Rousseau, *Principes généraux du droit international public* (Paris: Editions A. Pedone, 1944), I, 897-898; Rousseau, "Principes de droit international public," *Recueil des cours*, XCIII (1958), 485.

Court of International Justice of the League of Nations, adhere to the view that Article 38 of the Statute of the International Court of the United Nations has in mind principles of national legal systems common to all "civilized states."

As regards the character of these principles and their place in international law, there are greatly differing opinions in bourgeois international legal literature.

In D. Anzilotti's view, the "general principles of law" mentioned in Article 38 of the Statute of the Permanent Court of International Justice and now in Article 38 of the Statute of the International Court are, first and foremost, general principles of international law, and then the principles recognized in the legislation of all countries. As principles of national legal systems, they are not part of international law. However, says Anzilotti, such principles may be used by an international court as material for the creation of a norm of international law.[3]

Another Italian writer, G. Morelli, believes that Article 38 of the Statute of the International Court does not speak about principles of international law. He goes on to add: "The question is the criteria which should guide the Court in rendering a decision in the event it declares that neither a customary nor conventional rule exists that is applicable to the instance being considered."[4] In this event, according to Morelli, the decision of the Court is to be based on nonlegal principles. A norm of international law is created not by general principles, but by judges on the basis of general principles extracted from national legal systems.

According to Anzilotti and Morelli, therefore, Article 38 of the Statute of the Permanent Court of International Justice and of the Statute of the International Court has empowered the Court to create norms of international law from the principles of national legal systems. Such an interpretation can and could have been defended previously on the basis of the text of Article 38 of the Statute of the Permanent Court of International Justice, although it would not have conformed to the general spirit of the Statute, but at the present time, since as a result of the International Court it indicates precisely that the Court settles disputes "in accordance with international law," this interpretation clearly has become incorrect. The Court does not create international law; it applies it.

Proponents of the "pure" theory of law are partial to the view that

3. D. Anzilotti, *Corso di diritto internazionale*, 3d ed. (Rome: Athenaeum, 1928), pp. 106-107.

4. G. Morelli, "Cours général de droit international public," *Recueil des cours*, LXXXIX (1956), 470-471; Morelli, *Nozioni di diritto internazionale*, 3d ed. (Padova: CEDAM, 1951), p. 44.

"general principles of law" are not an independent source of international law.

The leading representative of this theory, Professor H. Kelsen, doubts the possibility that principles " . . . common to the legal orders of the civilized nations . . . " exist, pointing to the ideological differences existing among states. Digressing to the doctrine of "gaps" in international law, he points out that any international dispute can be settled on the basis of treaty or customary international law. Consequently, the reference to "general principles of law" is superfluous. He also supports this conclusion by citing Article 38 of the Statute, pursuant to which the Court must decide cases "in accordance with international law." "Hence it might be argued," he says, "that 'the general principles of law' are applicable only if they are part of international law, and this means part of the law referred to in clauses (a) and (b) of Article 38. Then, clause (c) is superfluous."[5]

At the present time, two viewpoints on the question of the character of "general principles of law" are most prevalent in bourgeois international legal literature: the moderate normativistic and the natural law.

As representatives of the first point of view, one can take a Swiss professor, P. Guggenheim, who, it seems to us, is moving away more and more from the "pure theory of law," and a French professor, C. Rousseau.

Professor Guggenheim writes with regard to Article 38 of the Statute of the International Court: "The most important international law code of procedures, therefore, admits the existence of a third group of norms as a base for judicial decisions. As we already have pointed out, in considering the question of gaps there is no technical necessity for such an expansion of the legislative procedure. Since gaps do not exist in international law, founded upon customary and conventional law, any dispute submitted to the jurisdiction of an international court can be settled. There is no place therefore, for a *non liquet.* "[6]

The inclusion in the Statute of a reference to "general principles of law," that is, principles applied *in foro domestico*, says Guggenheim, arose out of the desire to fill gaps and, for this purpose, to enlarge the rights of the Court.[7]

There is no doubt, continues Guggenheim, that all general principles of law whose application is expressly provided for in agreements on arbitration and judicial settlement enter into conventional law. But even in those

5. H. Kelsen, *Principles of International Law*, ed. R. W. Tucker, 2d ed. (New York: Holt, Rinehart & Winston, 1967), p. 540.
6. P. Guggenheim, *Traité de droit international public*, 2d ed. (Geneva: Librairie de l'Université, 1967), I, 292.
7. *Ibid.*, pp. 295-296.

instances when this was not so, certain international arbitrators at their own initiative applied general principles of law from the domain of national private or public law. The validity of these principles in such cases can be proved within the body of customary law. "Therefore," the author concludes, "general principles of law are based either on conventional or customary law."[8]

In the opinion of Guggenheim, who cites international judicial and arbitral practice in this connection, not all general principles of law which are part of the various legal systems are included in international law. "Only a very insignificant number of such principles have been incorporated into the international legal order."[9]

C. Rousseau writes: "By means of custom and treaty, states themselves define the extent of their rights and duties. But they also may be limited by the fact that they recognize by general consent that specific legal principles which already exist in other spheres of law will be applied in their mutual relations."[10] In international judicial and arbitral decisions, Rousseau says, general principles of law means the "principles which are common to the legal systems of the various civilized states."[11]

Citing, just as other bourgeois writers, the *travaux préparatoires* relating to the drawing up of the Statute of the Permanent Court of International Justice, he adheres to Phillimore's view that general principles of law are those principles "accepted by all nations *in foro domestico*," and to La Pradelle's view that these are the "principles on which national law is based."[12]

Rousseau suggests that in Article 38 of the Statute of the Permanent Court of International Justice the question was one of the "principles common to the domestic legal order and the international legal order," "of the law in general (*du droit sans épithète*), embracing both international and domestic law."[13] An analysis of international judicial and arbitral decisions, Rousseau says, leads to the conclusion that "general

8. *Ibid.*, p. 298.

9. *Ibid.* In his work *General Principles of Law as Applied by International Courts and Tribunals*, B. Cheng, in maintaining that " . . . the essence of general principles of law is the fact of their being common to all legal systems," is obliged to acknowledge that "international custom or customary international law, understood in a broad sense, may include all that is unwritten in international law, *i.e.*, both custom and general principles of law." B. Cheng, *General Principles of Law as Applied by International Courts and Tribunals* (London: Stevens & Sons, Ltd., 1953), pp. xv, 23.

10. C. Rousseau, *Principes généraux du droit international public*, I, 890; Rousseau, *Droit international public* (Paris: Sirey, 1970), I, 371-375.

11. *Ibid.*

12. *Ibid.*, p. 892.

13. *Ibid.*, p. 901.

principles of law are a specific and distinct source of international law."[14] Any other conclusion, in Rousseau's opinion, would lead to the view that the reference in the Statute to general principles of law is superfluous.[15]

Rousseau suggests that "general principles of law" include not only principles common to the various national legal systems, but also general principles of international law which "do not coincide either with conventional or with customary rules."[16]

In the opinion of Verdross, who is a representative of the modern natural law orientation, "general principles of law" are those similar provisions which underlie the legal systems "of civilized peoples." They are a reflection of natural law—not principles of natural law directly, but those principles which have already been reflected positively in the prevailing legal systems of states.[17]

Verdross believes that "general principles of law" rest upon a general legal consciousness. One must distinguish them from general principles of international law in "the narrow sense," since "general principles of law" are not reflected in either treaties or custom.[18] International law, he says, "is not exhausted by treaty or customary international law; general principles of law should be added to them."[19]

Verdross maintains that "general principles of law" are the basis of all international law. At the same time, they form a constituent part thereof and are applied in those instances when positive international law does not contain principles and norms applicable to a particular case.[20]

It is Verdross's view that Article 38 of the Statute of the International Court has in view "not all legal norms of the various states which happen to coincide, but only those principles of law which rest upon common legal ideas and which can be carried over into interstate relations."[21] The author admits the possibility of deciding disputes between states on the basis not only of conventional and customary norms, but also of solely "general principles of law."[22]

14. *Ibid.*, p. 913.

15. *Ibid.*, p. 925.

16. *Ibid.*, p. 914.

17. A. Verdross, *Mezhdunarodnoe pravo*, trans. from 3d ed. by F. A. Kublitskii and R. L. Naryshkina, ed. G. I. Tunkin (Moscow: izd-vo IL, 1959), p. 45; Verdross, *Völkerrecht*, 5th ed. (Vienna: Springer Verlag, 1964), pp. 23-24.

18. *Ibid.*, respectively, pp. 160, 147.

19. *Ibid.*, respectively, pp. 164, 151.

20. *Ibid.*, respectively, pp. 43-44, 22.

21. Verdross, *Völkerrecht*, p. 148. In this edition the position is given differently from that which was translated into Russian.

22. Verdross, *Mezhdunarodnoe pravo*, pp. 163-164; Verdross, *Völkerrecht*, p. 150; see also Verdross, "Les principes généraux de droit dans le système des sources de droit international public," *Recueil d'études de droit international en hommage à Paul*

Another representative of the modern natural law orientation, Le Fur, asserts that although "general principles of law" are not directly principles of natural law, the number of which is very limited, they arise directly from natural, or objective, law. Both general principles and natural law have as their initial basis the concept of justice and morality, which is common and, one can say, natural for man. In order to become "general principles of law," principles of natural law must find their positive expression in the national law of the "civilized states."[23]

The majority of Soviet writers are of the opinion that Article 38(1)(c) of the Statute of the International Court does not have in view a special source of international law, a special form of creating norms of international law. "General principles of law" can only be principles of international law.

V. M. Koretskii suggests that "general principles of law" are "general (or fundamental) principles of *international* law."[24] In developing this idea, Academician Koretskii goes on to say: "Article 38 of the Statute of the International Court (which also contains a reference to 'the general principles of law recognized by civilized nations') just begins with a statement of the duty of the Court 'to decide in accordance with international law such disputes as are submitted to it.' Consequently, the Court is bound to apply principles of international law, but by no means principles of domestic law of individual states."[25]

Professor V. N. Durdenevskii also believes that "general principles of law" are "by their very nature the most fundamental provisions of international customary law."[26] He includes the five well-known

Guggenheim (Geneva: Imp. de la Tribune de Geneve, 1968), pp. 521-530;A. Blondel, "Les principes généraux de droit devant la Cour Permanente de Justice Internationale et la Cour Internationale de Justice," *ibid.*, pp. 201-236; A. Favre, "Les principes généraux du droit, fonds commun du droit des gens," *ibid.*, pp. 366-390.

23. L. Le Fur, "La coutume et les principes généraux du droit comme sources du droit international public," *Recueil d'études sur les sources du droit en l'honneur de François Geny* (Paris: Librairie du Recueil Sirey, 1935), III, 368; Le Fur, "Règles générales du droit de la paix," *Recueil des cours*, LIV (1935), 205.

24. V. M. Koretskii, *"Obshchie prinstipy prava" v mezhdunarodnom prave* (Kiev: izd-vo Akademii nauk Ukrainskoi SSR, 1957), p. 45.

25. *Ibid.*, pp. 45-46.

26. V. N. Durdenevskii, "Piat'printsipov," *Mezhdunarodnaia zhizn'*, no. 3 (1955), p. 45; see also Durdenevskii and S. B. Krylov, eds., *Mezhdunarodnoe pravo* (Moscow: Iurizdat, 1947), pp. 26-27; E. A. Korovin, ed., *Mezhdunarodnoe pravo* (Moscow: Gosiurizdat, 1951), p. 17; G. I. Tunkin, *Osnovy sovremennogo mezhdunarodnogo prava* (Moscow: Tipo. Vysshei partiinoi shkoly pri TsK KPSS, 1956), p. 4; F. I. Kozhevnikov, ed., *Mezhdunarodnoe pravo* (Moscow: Gosiurizdat, 1957), p. 8; N. M. Minasian, *Sushchnost' sovremennogo mezhdunarodnogo prava* (Rostov-na-Donu: izd-vo Rostovskogo universiteta, 1962), p. 177; this problem unaccountably was passed over in V. M. Chkhikvadze and others, eds., *Kurs mezhdunarodnogo prava v shesti tomakh* (Moscow: izd-vo Nauka, 1967), I.

principles of peaceful coexistence and certain other principles of international law among them.

This question is treated somewhat differently by Professor D. B. Levin. While not characterizing "general principles of law" as a whole, he points out that the "fundamental principles of international law occupy an important place among them," after which he limits himself to an analysis of these "fundamental principles."

In Levin's view, the fundamental principles of international law are, on one hand, the "normative ideas underlying the entire system of international law." As an example of such normative ideas he cites the "principles of sovereignty and equality of states," and "the principles of freedom of the seas or the inviolability of diplomatic representatives."[27]

We note at once that the provisions cited by Levin as examples of "normative ideas" are principles of international law, that is, the most general norms from which arise, however, specific rights and duties of states. These, consequently, are not ideas, but legal norms.

"On the other hand," says Levin, "fundamental principles of international law are one of the forms of reflecting and consolidating international law, organically linked with the specific peculiarities of the latter, and above all with the fact that norms of international law are established by way of the concordance of the wills of states on the basis of general principles, written or unwritten, which they have previously recognized. In this sense fundamental principles of international law are one of the sources of international law."[28]

The author does not show, and it is doubtful in general whether one could demonstrate, that if the basic peculiarity of international law is that its norms are created by the concordance of the wills of states, the "fundamental principles of international law" can be regarded as an independent source of international law side by side with treaty and custom. He himself speaks of fundamental principles as "general principles which they (states) have previously recognized," that is, consequently, of principles which entered into international law either by custom or by treaty.

P. I. Lukin suggests that "general principles of law are those principles consolidated in the legislation of all member states of the United Nations or in the legislation of the majority of the most important states in each one of the basic legal systems of the world."[29] But at the same time he

27. See D. B. Levin, *Osnovnye problemy sovremennogo mezhdunarodnogo prava* (Moscow: Iurizdat, 1958), p. 100.

28. *Ibid.*, pp. 100-101.

29. P. I. Lukin, *Istochniki mezhdunarodnogo prava* (Moscow: izd-vo AN SSSR, 1960), p. 100.

says that as a result of the difference of socioeconomic systems, it is impossible in the majority of cases to establish such general principles.[30]

M. Bartos, a Yugoslav professor, suggests that "general principles of law" in international law are by their origin the "general principles and general institutions of law recognized by civilized nations,"[31] having, as one can suppose from the author's conception, a normative character. Bartos, however, emphasizes that as soon as such principles have entered into international law, they break off from municipal law and "in the future fully share the fate of the system of international law."[32]

In the opinion of a Hungarian student of this question, G. Herczegh, Article 38(1)(c) of the Statute of the International Court does not point to a special source of international law, but grants to the Court the power when deciding concrete cases to have recourse, if there are gaps in international law, to principles of municipal law which are common to the legal systems of all members of the international community.[33]

In speaking of "general principles of law," one must point above all to the fact that the enormous bourgeois literature on this question was and is based primarily upon Article 38 of the Statute of the Permanent Court of International Justice and on the materials of the Committee of Jurists of the League of Nations for the preparation of this Statute.

Meanwhile, the Statute of the International Court of the United Nations is a new international agreement. This agreement was created in different conditions than the Statute of the Permanent Court of International Justice, and one should not attach to the provisions of the Statute of the International Court that significance which the Committee of Jurists attached in 1920 to the analogous provisions of the Statute of the Permanent Court of International Justice.

The meaning which was placed in this point by the drafters of the Statute of the Permanent Court of International Justice is only of historical importance for an understanding of the corresponding provision of the Statute of the International Court. Evidently the drafters, representing different types of bourgeois law, had in mind expanding the possibilities for the Court in deciding cases by granting it the right to refer to principles common to the national legal systems of bourgeois states. However, this is not important in interpreting Article 38(1)(c) of the

30. *Ibid.*

31. M. Bartos, "Transformation des principes généraux en règles positives du droit international," in V. Ibler, ed., *Mélanges offerts à Juraj Andrassy* (The Hague: Martinus Nijhoff, 1968), p. 1.

32. *Ibid.*, p. 2.

33. G. Herczegh, *General Principles of Law and the International Legal Order* (Budapest: Akademiai kiado, 1969), pp. 97-98.

Statute of the International Court, but rather that which the states represented at the San Francisco Conference, where this Statute was adopted and signed, had in mind. A sufficient reference point for this is the fact that a very important provision was inserted into Article 38 of the Statute of the International Court, that the Court "is to decide in accordance with international law such disputes as are submitted to it . . ."[34]

There is no doubt that this is of material importance in interpreting Article 38(1)(c) of the Statute of the International Court. Above all, the unfoundedness of the concept that "general principles of law" are principles of national legal systems "common to all civilized states" becomes obvious.

One can not but note that there have been and are attempts to use this concept, irrespective of the wish or desire of the scholars and jurists who support it, against the socialist states and the new Asian and African states. The basic legal principles of the leading capitalist powers as, for example, the doctrine of "acquired rights," adequate compensation for nationalized property of aliens, and others usually are included among the "general principles of law," and they are proclaimed to be common to "civilized peoples." Here is manifested the desire to use "general principles of law" in order to proclaim principles of the bourgeois legal system to be binding upon all.[35] Such efforts are juridically unjustified and politically harmful, for they can lead only to an aggravation of relations among states.[36]

The attempts to justify the inclusion of the said "principles" among the "general principles of law recognized by civilized peoples" by references to judicial and arbitral decisions are scientifically unfounded. First and foremost, the judicial and arbitral practice which bourgeois writers cite is the practice of a specific group of bourgeois states. It is not "general" in

34. See S. B. Krylov, *Istoriia sozdaniia OON*, ed. G. I. Tunkin (Moscow: izd-vo IMO, 1960), p. 228.

35. See Koretskii, *"Obshchie printsipy prava" v mezhdunarodnom prave.*

36. It is very doubtful that Abi-Saab's view reflected the true situation. He writes with regard to general principles of law: "This source of international law is very important from the point of view of the newly independent states. It is through it that they hope their legal systems will contribute to the development of international law." G. M. Abi-Saab, "The Newly Independent States and the Rules of International Law: An Outline," *Howard Law Journal*, VIII (1962), 109. The experience of the International Law Commission, of the Sixth Committee of the General Assembly, and of international conferences in our view shows that the new states attach primary importance in this respect to the international treaty. See R. Ago, "La codification du droit international et les problèmes de sa realisation," *Mélanges Guggenheim*, p. 100.

The Problem of "General Principles of Law"

the sense that this must be understood at the present time, and it has not been recognized as a legal norm by states of the two systems.

The viewpoint of the majority of Soviet international lawyers, as noted above, correctly emphasizes, in counterbalance to the predominant bourgeois doctrine, that the existence of similar principles in national legal systems, even though of all states, does not signify that they therefore have effect in international law; any provision, in order to be applied in international law, must enter by treaty or customary means. But as regards equating "general principles of law" with general principles of international law, this seems to us to be unjustified.

It is no accident that Article 38(1)(c) of the Statute of the International Court—and the Statute is a virtually universal international treaty—speaks not of "general principles of international law" but of "general principles of law." Professor C. Rousseau is right in stating that the question is one of the principles of law in general, of the principles common not only to national legal systems but also to international law as a special system of law.

But the question arises whether in contemporary conditions of the existence of states not only with different but also with opposed socioeconomic systems there can exist normative principles common to socialist law and to bourgeois law. One must say very definitely that normative principles which would be common to the two opposed systems of law, socialist and bourgeois, do not exist. The principles of these legal systems, even in those instances when externally they appear to be identical, are fundamentally distinct by virtue of their class nature, role in society, and purposes. Since a norm of law is not a "pure" rule of conduct deprived of social content, the externally (or technically) similar principles or norms of the said legal systems of this kind are different, and not identical, norms.

This does not mean that the norms of the opposed types of law have nothing in common. The content of a norm of law is formed from a rule of conduct and a purpose, which naturally always has a social and not a technical character. A legal norm is not simply a rule of conduct; it always is purposeful. In addition, to characterize the essence of a legal norm one must take into account the social consequences of its operation. Norms of socialist and bourgeois law are fundamentally distinct by virtue of their content and essence. But rules of conduct as part of the content of the corresponding norms of socialist and bourgeois law very frequently are identical.

This generally has a certain significance for the formation of norms of international law. The existence of externally identical principles and norms in different systems of national law frequently leads to the emergence of corresponding principles and norms of international law. It is possible, for example, to mention such principles of international law as the principle of state sovereignty, the principle of state sovereignty over territorial waters, many norms of the covenants of human rights, especially the covenant on civil and political rights, and so forth.

The principles of national legal systems exert great influence upon the development of international law, but they can not be principles of the latter. The juridical and social nature of norms of national legal systems and norms of international law are different. The principles and norms of a national legal system reflect the will of the ruling class of a given state (in the USSR, the will of the whole people), whereas the class content of norms of international law is different; norms of international law can not reflect the will of the ruling class of a single state. Norms of national law can be changed by a state at its discretion, so that principles which are "common" to various national legal systems today can cease to be such tomorrow. And, finally, the principles of a national legal system are binding only within the limits of that system, since a state can not promulgate international norms which are legally binding upon other states.

The normative principles of national legal systems can be material for the creation of corresponding principles of international law. But the principles of international law which have arisen in this way and which externally are frequently very similar to principles of national law are in fact, as pointed out above, otherwise; their content and essence are changed.

The conclusion is, therefore, that there can not exist normative legal principles which would be common to socialist and bourgeois law, nor normative legal principles which would be common to contemporary international law and to national systems of law.

There are, however, general legal concepts, logical rules, modes of legal technique, which are used in interpreting and applying law in general, both international and national, irrespective of the social essence of the law. This kind of "principle" is not normative and does not establish rights and duties, but it is necessary for an understanding of the co-relation of norms of law and their social content. Among such rules are, for example: *lex specialis derogat generali, lex posterior derogat priori, nemo plus juris transferre potest quam ipse habet*, and others.

Although this kind of provision is legal, it is not in essence a norm of law. Therefore it is doubtful whether there are scholarly and practical grounds for C. W. Jenks's appeal "to develop from the common elements in these legal systems, all of which are still in process of evolution, a universal legal order . . . "[37] or H. Waldock's thesis that "general principles of law" are the "common law of the international community."[38]

The next question is: how do the said non-normative provisions common to existing national legal systems enter into international use:

(1) are they a "reservoir" from which the International Court or other international instances can draw upon when necessary;[39]

(2) or does Article 38(1)(c) of the Statute of the International Court mean that the provisions common to different national legal systems become applicable in international law only by virtue of that fact;[40]

(3) or do such principles common to different national systems of law, although non-normative before being applied in international law, enter into it through the usual processes of forming norms of international law; treaty or custom?[41]

If the International Court at its discretion could draw from national legal systems the principles which in the opinion of the respective writers are normative, it would possess law-creating functions. But, as has been shown above, the Court does not possess such powers.

The second point of view also can not be deemed to be justified. If one presumes that Article 38(1)(c) of the Statute of the International Court means the inclusion in the system of international law of all principles common to the various national legal systems, it should be borne in mind that the respective writers have normative principles in mind and consider as common all those which contain identical rules of conduct—which clearly does not correspond to reality. Numerous principles of national legal systems which from the viewpoint of these authors should be regarded as common are not applied in international law at all (for example, electing members of legislative organs, the right of individuals to resort to a court, and so on). If not all principles which in the view of these authors are common to national legal systems are to be applied in international law, then the question arises: who selects which to apply and which not? The point of view being considered does not answer this question.

Even if one takes the non-normative provisions to which we have referred that are common to the various national legal systems, far from

37. See C. W. Jenks, *The Common Law of Mankind* (London: Stevens & Sons Ltd., 1958), p. 169.

38. See H. Waldock, "General Course on Public International Law," *Recueil des cours*, CVI (1962), 54.

39. *Ibid.*, p. 56; S. Nahlik, *Wstep do nauki prawa miedzynarodwego* (Warsaw: Panstwowe wyd-wo naukowe, 1967), p. 382.

40. See Rousseau, *Principes généraux du droit international public*, I, 890.

41. See Guggenheim, *Traité de droit international public*, I, 298; M. Genovski, *Osnovi na mezhdunarodnoto pravo*, 2d ed. (Sofia: Nauka i izkustvo, 1966), p. 26.

all can be applied in international law. Thus, for example, such a general provision as *nemo judex in sua causa* is not applicable in international law since there is no compulsory international jurisdiction here.

"General principles of law" are those principles not only common to national systems of law but also simultaneously peculiar to international law. The statement that a given principle is common to national legal systems does not make this principle a "general principle of law," that is, of law in general. It is still necessary to prove that this principle also is peculiar to that special system of law which is called international law. Only if there is an affirmative response to this question can such a principle be considered "common" to any law, a "general principle of law."

But how can a particular provision, even a non-normative one which has significance for the application of a norm, "become applicable" in international law? Obviously only by its being recognized by states as "applicable in international law," or, that is to say, through an international treaty or international custom.[42]

In interpreting the respective provision of the Statute of the International Court, attention is usually called to its first part, "general principles of law," and insufficient attention is devoted to the second part, "recognized by civilized nations." To be applicable in international law, the corresponding "general principles of law" must be recognized by states as "being applicable in international law," which, as pointed out previously, occurs either by international treaty or by international custom.

Consequently, in our view, "general principles of law" are those non-normative provisions common to national legal systems and to international law which, however, have significance for applying norms of prevailing law; they usually are formed in national law (but nothing prevents them from being formed in international law as well) and enter into international law through treaty or custom.

This interpretation means that Article 38(1)(c) of the Statute of the International Court has in view not a special "source" of international law, but specific juridical provisions, here called principles, which are non-normative.

Therefore, two means of forming, developing, and modifying norms of general international law exist: treaty and custom. There also are subsidiary processes (resolutions of international organizations, international courts, and arbitral tribunals; national legislation; and decisions of munici-

42. See M. Diez de Velasco, *Instituciones de derecho internacional publico* (Madrid: Tecnos, 1973), p. 138.

pal judicial instances) which are specific stages in the process of forming norms but which do not lead to its completion.

At the same time, another means of creating international legal norms has emerged in contemporary international law. We have in mind the binding resolutions of international organizations. In this case international legal norms are created by their being adopted by a majority of members of an international organization, which has a certain external similarity to municipal legislation. Such international legal norms, however, are created on the basis of the agreement of states, that is, on the basis of the charter of the international organization. Moreover, although such resolutions are binding upon all member states of the organization, also including the states which voted against their adoption, a member state of an international organization legally can avoid the application of any such resolution to it by withdrawing from the organization.

Part III *The Legal Nature and Essence of Contemporary General International Law*

Chapter 8 *The Legal Nature of Agreement as the Mode of Creating Norms of International Law*

A. The Bourgeois Doctrine of "Agreement"

Principles and norms of international law are created, modified, and liquidated as a result of agreement between states. This agreement is embodied either in the form of an international treaty or of an international custom.

The doctrine that only agreement of states can create binding norms of international law has its own history, which must be dwelt upon briefly in order to show what the theory we set forth has in common with the bourgeois concept of agreement and how it is distinctive from it.

Hugo Grotius and a number of writers of the eighteenth and nineteenth centuries who followed him believed that the so-called positive international law, in which they included both conventional and customary law, is created, in contrast to natural law, by the general consent of states.[1]

According to Grotius, all law, including international law, is partially natural law and partially law created by will (*jus voluntarium*). Natural law is "the dictate of right reason." Instituted law, or law created by will, has will as its source; it may be instituted by the will of God or by the general consent of peoples.[2]

The latter law also received the appellation "positive" law from subsequent writers. Vattel already distinguishes natural or "necessary" law from "positive" law established by the general consent of peoples.[3]

1. See H. Grotius, *O prave voiny i mira*, trans. A. L. Sakketti, ed. V. N. Durdenevskii (Moscow: Gosiurizdat, 1959), Book 1.

2. *Ibid.*, Book 1, chap. 1, XI, 2; XIII, XIX, 1; XV, 1.

3. See E. de Vattel, *Pravo narodov*, ed. V. N. Durdenevskii (Moscow: Gosiurizdat, 1960), pp. 27, 34; R. J. Phillimore, *Commentaries on International Law*, 3d ed. (London: Butterworths, 1879), p. 38; F. F. Martens, *Sovremennoe mezhdunarodnoe pravo tsivilizovannykh narodov* (St. Petersburg: Knizhnyi sklad E. Gart'e, 1882), I, 11.

The ideas of bourgeois revolutions resounded in the natural law conceptions of that time; they were directed against feudal law, which did not correspond to the dictates of "right reason." They advanced "reasonable" principles which, although progressive in comparison with the feudal orders, were in reality only principles of a new exploitative society.

With the completion of the bourgeois struggle against feudalism, its revolutionary ardor dried up, natural law theory was rejected as having performed its service, and the positivist orientation, called upon to be the basis of bourgeois reality, became predominant in bourgeois legal science.

The concept that agreement between states is the legal basis of all international law was widely disseminated in the domain of theory during the second half of the nineteenth and the beginning of the twentieth centuries. This doctrine proceeded from the fact that since sovereign states are entering into international relations, under these conditions the sole mode of creating norms binding upon subjects of law is agreements between them.[4]

The bourgeois doctrine of agreement as a means of creating norms of international law correctly reflects one aspect of reality—namely, that agreement between states is the sole mode of creating principles and norms of international law. But the doctrine being considered did not correctly analyze the process of forming a norm, its essence, and frequently limited itself to a purely dogmatic approach, declining in general to undertake an investigation of this question.

In transferring categories of municipal law into international law, Triepel proceeds in his widely known work *Völkerrecht und Landesrecht* from the premise that in international law only a higher will which stands above the wills of individual states can create norms binding upon a state. This will is formed as a result of agreement between states. Agreement creates a "common will" (*Gemeinwille*), which is the result of the fusion of identical wills of various states. In Triepel's view, the common will stands higher than the will of an individual state, is a supranational will, and as such serves as a source of legal norms binding upon states.[5]

4. See H. Triepel, *Völkerrecht und Landesrecht* (Leipzig: Verlag von C. H. Hirschfeld, 1899), pp. 32, 75, 83ff.; D. Anzilotti, *Corso di diritto internazionale*, 3d ed. (Rome: Athanaeum, 1928), I, 43, 63ff; T. Perassi, "Teoria dommatica delle fonti di norme giuridiche in diritto internazionale," *Rivista di diritto internazionale*, XI (1917), 220; L. Oppenheim, *International Law*, 4th ed. (London: Longmans, Green, 1928), pp. 18-19; K. Strupp, "Les règles générales du droit de la paix," *Recueil des cours*, XLVII (1934), 307.

5. Triepel, *Völkerrecht und Landesrecht*, p. 32; Triepel, having worked out the concept of a common will in detail, which he regards as higher than the wills of states with respect to those participating in the creation of the "common will," was not the initiator of this notion. It is already completely evident in Grotius. Among the writers who preceded Triepel one also can mention A. W. Heffter, who thirty years before

Consequently, according to Triepel, the legal nature of agreement as a means of creating norms of international law consists in the fact that identical wills of states are fused into a "common will," which is a higher will.

Of the writers of recent decades who adhere to this point of view, one could mention Séfériades, who wrote in 1936: "In our view, international law as a whole has as its basis not the individual sovereign will of a state (Jellinek), even with an unsustainable qualification relating to self-limitation, but the wills of states as coinciding wills which, once unified, can not be separated . . . This union of wills forms a higher will . . . "[6]

In Anzilotti's opinion, agreement is an expression of a united will (*concorde volontà*). This will creates a norm of international law. Anzilotti's "united will," just as Triepel's, is the result of the fusion of the wills of individual states. But, as Anzilotti himself pointed out, he, in contradistinction to Triepel, seeks the source of norms not in some "higher will" standing above the will of individual states, but in a "basic norm" which obliges states to fulfill international agreements.[7]

Thus, if Triepel, in attempting to bring international law within the characteristics of national law, considered a norm of international law to be a product of a higher will with regard to states, then Anzilotti treats an agreement which creates norms of international law differently. The "general will" reflected in an agreement is used by Anzilotti essentially only as a characteristic of agreement and not as a basis for the emergence of a norm of international law. A norm of international law emerges because there exists a "basic norm" binding a state to fulfill international agreements—*pacta sunt servanda*. Anzilotti's theory, in contrast to Triepel's, emphasized the coordinate character of international law.

Another Italian international lawyer, T. Perassi, rejects both the concept of a "higher will" and the concept of a "common will." These theories, he says, would be admissible if it were possible to represent agreement as a juridical act which, although the result of a coincidence of the wills of individual states, relates to a specific subject, in contrast to states. Since, however, this is impossible, one can not accept the view linked with the concept of a higher collective will that norms of international law are "commands."[8]

Triepel wrote: " . . . prevailing law is created for independent states only through a common will (*consensu*) . . . " A. W. Heffter, *Das europäische Völkerrecht der Gegenwart auf den bisherigen Grundlagen*, 5th ed. (Berlin: Verlag von E. H. Schroeder, 1867), p. 4.

6. S. Séfériades, "Aperçu sur la coutume juridique internationale et notamment sur son fondement," *Revue générale de droit international public*, X (1936), 145; H. Heller, *Die Souveranität* (Berlin: Walter de Gruyter & Co., 1927), pp. 122-124.

7. Anzilotti, *Corso di diritto internazionale*, pp. 43, 63, 64ff.

8. Perassi, "Teoria dommatica delle fonti," pp. 291-292.

Perassi closes his investigation with the assertion that in international law agreement is a "source of legal norms." He refuses to go farther, even to merely investigate the legal nature of agreement. Norms of international law, says Perassi, are created by agreement between states, but why an agreement creates a norm of law this jurist is unable to say; the question exceeds the bounds of legal research, which he understands to be purely dogmatic research.[9]

Agreement itself is characterized by Perassi as the result or embodiment of the coincidence of wills. "Agreement," he says, "is an act having international relevance; the coincidence of the wills of two or more states is essential to agreement."[10]

Proponents of natural law concepts which have been widely propagated during the last half-century (see Chapter 9) acknowledge agreement as a means of creating norms of international law only for treaty norms. But treaty law in their view rests upon natural law, which does not depend upon the will and agreement of states.

The principal objective role of contemporary international legal concepts of natural law consists of undermining the consensual basis of international law and thereby creating greater possibilities for an international legal justification of the imperialist policy of *diktat*, coercion, and military adventurism.

One also encounters at the present time proponents of the concept of agreement as the sole means of creating norms of international law, but they are not numerous.[11]

9. *Ibid.*, pp. 201ff.

10. *Ibid.*, p. 290. Giuliani also opposes interpreting the "collective will" as a "superior will." A superior will, he says, "presupposes the material and social supremacy of the organism or organisms to which this will appertains. But this does not give agreement." The "collective will of a state" simply means the "agreement of wills" (*accordo di volontà*). See M. Giuliano, *La comunita internazionale e il diritto* (Padova: CEDAM, 1950), p. 81.

11. K. Strupp wrote: "If states are equal and if a supreme authority does not exist to dictate laws to them, nor a power of majority rule, one only can come to a single conclusion: there is no international law without coincident wills, without a treaty." Strupp, "Règles générales du droit de la paix," p. 301. C. Hyde says: "The basis of the law, that is to say, what has given to some principles of general applicability the quality or character of law, has been the acquiescence of the several independent States which were to be governed thereby." C. C. Hyde, *Mezhdunarodnoe pravo*, trans. from 2d rev. ed. by I. S. Shokhor, ed. V. N. Durdenevskii (Moscow: izd-vo IL, 1950), I, 59. C. Rousseau writes that in international law "the agreement of states is the sole means of creating legal norms. Here the elaboration of any legal rule depends upon the agreement of the subjects whose relations this rule is intended to regulate." C. Rousseau, *Droit international public* (Paris: Recueil Sirey, 1953), p. 11; see also M. J. Sierra, *Tratado de derecho internacional publico*, 2d ed. (Mexico: [Editorial Porrua], 1955), p. 24; A. Ulloa, *Derecho internacional publico*, 4th ed. (Madrid: Ediciones

B. *Agreement as the Result and the Embodiment of the Concordance of the Wills of States*

The bourgeois theory of agreement contained a rational core—namely, the proposition that agreement between states is the sole mode of creating norms of international law. It was based upon the special character of the subjects whose relationships are regulated by international law.

This theory was closely linked with the ideas of bourgeois liberalism inherent in the premonopolistic stage of the development of capitalism. It was derived from the principle of equality of states, inspired in the majority of instances by the idea of the "rule of law" in international relations, which, of course, was understood only as relations among "civilized" states.

Being characterized by a formalistic dogmatic approach to the question, however, the bourgeois concept of agreement has not uncovered the essence of agreement as a mode of creating norms of international law, has passed over those processes of struggle and cooperation which take place in creating norms of international law, and has not shown the social essence of international law.

Marxist-Leninist theory permits one to penetrate deeper into the content of norm-formation processes in international law and, not restricting itself to an analysis of phenomena which are occurring, reveals the essence of these processes and therefore offers a new concept of agreement as a mode of creating norms of contemporary international law.

As already has been pointed out, the bourgeois theory usually regards agreement between states as the result of the "coincidence of the wills" of these states, which gives a "common will." This interpretation of agreement is unfounded.

We note first of all that the wills of states are treated by bourgeois science as the wills of certain abstract "communities" divorced from their class content.

Marxist-Leninist theory exposes the class character of the will of a state as it enters into international relations. The character of this will is determined by the nature of the state: in capitalist countries, it is the will of the ruling class in the state concerned; in the Soviet state, which has been transformed in the contemporary era into a state of the whole people, it is the will of the entire people.

The unfoundedness of the bourgeois theory of agreement becomes

---

iberoamericanas, 1957), I, 51-52; L. M. Moreno Quintana, *Tratado de derecho internacional* (Buenos Aires: Editorial Sudamericana, 1963), I, 71.

especially obvious under contemporary conditions, with the existence of states of two opposed social systems.

What is the legal nature of the agreement of states creating a norm of international law?

Let us examine what happens in the process of forming agreement between states during the creation of a norm of general international law. This can be followed most easily in the example of concluding a treaty. At international conferences for the conclusion of general international treaties, there always exist more or less significant differences between the basic international legal positions of those states participating in the conference. In the course of the conference, at sessions, during unofficial meetings of delegates, and frequently even outside the conference place (through normal diplomatic channels or special meetings between representatives of states), the concordance of the wills of states takes place, usually by means of mutual concessions.

During the work of the conference, each delegation or group of delegations strives to have its or their joint international legal position reflected as much as possible in the draft treaties which must be adopted by the conference. The result fixed in the text of the treaty as a rule differs to a greater or lesser degree from that which each state taking part in the negotiations to conclude the treaty had proposed.

The concordance of the wills of states in the process of creating norms of international law is the struggle and cooperation of states. In this struggle, a state itself seeks allies first among states whose international legal position is close to the international legal position of the state or group of states concerned.

At the same time, any international conference to work out norms of international law, if the states participating in it have been inspired by the aspiration to reach a decision on the questions raised, includes the cooperation of states. This cooperation naturally takes place not only among states whose international legal positions coincide or are close, but also to some extent among all participants in the conference.

Of course, the degree of such cooperation between various states is far from identical. Without cooperation, however, as a rule one can not create a norm of international law whose general recognition can be relied upon. By means of mutual concessions states attempt to come to an agreed decision acceptable to the participants. This process in the majority of instances is exceedingly difficult and slow, but quite necessary.

Attempts to resolve this kind of question by voting without sufficient efforts to bring the wills of states into concordance usually only harm the cause. Apart from that, such attempts lead to an aggravation of relations among states, and they practically never promote the development of international law. A norm created by such means that is unacceptable to a significant number of states has little effect and, in addition, its adoption terminates, at least temporarily, the searches for a more perfect norm acceptable to the overwhelming majority of states.

The process of creating a customary norm of international law is rather more complex. The essence of this process, however, also consists in the concordance of the wills of states relating to the recognition of a particular rule as a norm of international law (see Chapter 6).

The concordance of the wills of states in the process of creating a norm of international law affects both rules of conduct and its recognition as a legal norm. These are two aspects of the process of norm-formation which frequently are not coincidental or chronological. Confusing them, as we shall show below, can lead to material mistakes.

As a rule, the concordance of the wills of states relating to a rule of conduct takes place first—by means of either treaty or custom—in forming norms of international law. In the creation of treaty norms, this occurs by means of negotiations, in discussions at international conferences, and in international organizations, and is completed by adopting the text as final. This completes the concordance of the wills of states relating to the content of the treaty norm of international law,[12] but it does not finish the process of its coming into being. It is true, states act in this case as though the rule of conduct fixed in the text of the treaty will become a norm of international law in the future. But the concordance of the wills of states relating to the content of a treaty norm still does not make it binding upon states.

The second aspect is the concordance of the wills of states relating to recognition of a rule of conduct as a norm of international law. Completion of this process may or may not coincide with the first. Thus, for example, when a treaty enters into force from the moment it is signed and the signing of the treaty is not preceded by initialing, the two aspects of the process coincide chronologically.

When the treaty is subject to ratification, these two aspects of the process do not coincide. The acts completing the concordance of the wills of states relating to the content of the respective norms in this case will be the initialing or signature, and the acts completing the concordance of the wills of states relating to recognizing the respective rules as norms of international law, by the exchange of instruments of ratification or their transfer to the depositary.

The provisions of a treaty also may contain other conditions for the process of creating norms of this treaty to be completed. In multilateral

12. The institute of reservations to multilateral treaties is an exception to the general rule.

international treaties this is most commonly a specific number of ratifications needed for the treaty to enter into force.

The two aspects of the process of norm-formation appear, as a rule, even more distinctly in the formation of customary norms of international law. The first part of the process of forming a customary norm of international law as a rule leads only to the formation of a usage. The rule of conduct already has emerged, its content has been defined, and states take this rule into account in their actions. Therefore, the concordance of the wills of the states as regards the content of the norm already exists.

But, as already has been pointed out, in order to complete the process of forming a customary norm of international law, the usage must be recognized by states as a norm of international law. The recognition by states of a usage as a norm of international law is an expression of the wills of states. If a number of states or many states, or all states, recognize a particular usage as a norm of international law, this means the concordance of the wills of these states has occurred with regard to such recognition, and the process of creating a customary international legal norm has been completed.

The process of bringing the wills of states into concordance with regard to the content of a rule of conduct does not always lead to this rule being recognized as a norm of international law. The process may stop at the first stage, and in this event the respective rule does not become an international legal norm. Such, for example, are norms of a treaty which has not entered into force.

Those resolutions of the United Nations General Assembly which are not binding also may serve as an example of the concordance of the wills of states regarding the content of a rule of conduct without a concordance of wills regarding recognition of this rule as a norm of international law.

Thus, not every concordance of the wills of states leads to the formation of a norm of international law, that is, to an agreement concerning recognition of the respective rule as a norm of international law.

One must mention in this connection the logical error which some opponents of the concordance of wills theory make. They assert, for example, that the theory of the concordance of wills is of no use because there are unlawful treaties which embody the concordance of wills of the respective states but do not give a norm of international law.

In logic, this error is called a paralogism. In the present case, this error emerges as follows: a norm of international law is the result and expression of the concordance of the wills of states; a treaty is the result of the concordance of the wills of states; therefore, it is a norm of international law. But if every norm of international law is the result and expression of a concordance of wills, then not every concordance of wills gives a norm of international law.

It already has been indicated that the concordance of the wills of states may not lead to the formation of a norm of international law because it does not include the concordance of such wills regarding the recognition of the corresponding rule as a norm of international law.

Even when, however, there are both elements, to wit, the concordance of the wills of states regarding the content of the respective rule and the concordance of the wills of states regarding its recognition as a legal norm, the process may not lead to the formation of a norm of international law. This occurs when, for example, a treaty, according to international law, is void.

Of course, this instance also is covered by the aforecited proposition that a norm of international law is the result and expression of the concordance of the wills of states, but not any concordance of the wills of states leads to the formation of a norm of international law.

For agreement and, therefore, for the formation of a norm of international law it is not mandatory that the wills of the states participating in the agreement be identical and fused into a single will.

If we take as an example the creation of norms of contemporary general international law, the wills of different and even opposed class natures (socialist and capitalist states), manifesting the purposes which the various states set, collide here in the process of norm-creation.

At the same time, these wills have something in common. V. I. Lenin pointed out that a "will is sometimes unified in one respect and nonunified in another."[13] In this case, the wills of socialist and capitalist states hold in common the fact that they are directed at the same time toward the creation of a specific international legal norm; they are concordant both with regard to the content and to the recognition of a specific rule as a norm of international law, that it comprises an agreement giving a norm of law.

Despite the absence of identity in the wills of states which take part in an agreement relating to the creation of a norm of general international law, and despite the fact that they are not fused into one, the agreement takes place and a norm of international law emerges. Therefore, neither identity of wills nor their fusion is an essential feature of agreement as a means of creating norms of international law.

The identity and fusion of the wills of states participating in the

13. V. I. Lenin, "Dve taktiki sotsial-demokratii v demokraticheskoi revoliutsii," *Polnoe sobranie sochinenii*, 5th ed. (Moscow: Gospolitizdat, 1960), XI, 73. [First published at Geneva, July 1905.]

creation of norms of international law is not precluded, but it is not an essential element of the agreement embodied in a legal norm.

The concordance of the wills of states includes the interconditionality of wills, reflected in the fact that the consent of a state to recognize a particular norm as a norm of international law is given on condition of analogous consent by another or other states.[14]

Thus, agreement as a mode of creating norms of international law is the result and expression of the concordance of the wills of states.[15]

C. The International Legal Positions of States and Concordant Wills Reflected in Norms of International Law

The international legal position of a state includes the general attitude of a state toward international law, its progressive development, and the observance of principles and norms; its notion of the character of international law; its role in society; the principles and norms for whose introduction into international law a state struggles; its understanding of the principles and norms of prevailing international law; and so forth. To put it briefly, the international legal position of a state includes its viewpoint with regard to all questions of international law expressed not only in its statements, but above all in its real conduct, in its actions.

14. See D. B. Levin's review of G. I. Tunkin, *Voprosy teorii mezhdunarodnogo prava* (Moscow: izd-vo IMO, 1962), in *Sovetskii ezhegodnik mezhdunarodnogo prava 1963* (Moscow: izd-vo Nauka, 1964), pp. 552-553; G. Schirmer, *Universalität völkerrechtlicher Verträge und internationaler Organisationen* (Berlin: Staatsverlag der DDR, 1966), p. 83.

15. In speaking of the distinction between the Soviet concept of the concordance of wills and the old bourgeois concept of agreement, Professor Suzanne Bastid remarks that according to the new concept, the wills do not merge into one but are directed toward attaining a single goal, and that the "wills have been interconditioned." See S. Bastid, *Grands problèmes politiques contemporains* (Paris, n.p. 1961), pp. 249-250. Professor P. Ziccardi notes that "it is not accurate to regard this doctrine of sources [that is, the said Soviet concept—G.T.] as strictly voluntaristic in the usual meaning of this word. [Reviewing the French translation of Tunkin's *Voprosy teorii mezhdunarodnogo prava*], *Communicazione e studi*, XII (1966), 922. Professor C. Chaumont, in adhering to this concept as a whole, points out that "agreement does not imply that the content of wills is identical." C. Chaumont, "Cours general de droit international public," *Recueil des cours*, CXXIX (1970), 379. However, the majority of bourgeois jurists, in approaching this question formalistically, mistakenly believe the Soviet concept to be a simple revival of the old notion of agreement. See, for example, A. Verdross, *Völkerrecht*, 5th ed. (Vienna: Springer Verlag, 1965), p. 138; R. Quadri, *Diritto internazionale publico*, 4th ed. (Palermo: G. Priulla Editore, 1963), p. 94; Quadri, "Cours générale de droit international public," *Recueil des cours*, CXIII (1964), 322-323.

Of course, in the creation of particular norms of international law that part of the international legal position of a state which relates directly to the particular question is of greatest importance.

In the process of creating norms of general international law, treaty or customary, the international legal positions of various states collide, and the process of bringing these positions into concordance occurs—the concordance of the wills of states, which may lead to the creation of an international legal norm.

What happens to the international legal position of a state in this process, and what is the co-relation between the concordant will of a state reflected in a norm and its international legal position?

The international legal position of a state can be subjected to change in the course of creating a norm of international law. Frequently at an international conference, where the positions of other states become well-known, the delegation of the respective state comes to the conclusion that the initially contemplated international legal position of that state must be changed with regard to a particular question.

Of course, when an international legal position of a state is initially formed, it takes into account the known or presumed international legal positions of other states, as well as the peripetia of the impending struggle. But an international legal struggle is formulated by people who can not take into account all circumstances, who make mistakes in evaluating them, who proceed on the basis of incorrect assumptions about the course of the conference, and so forth. If there later appear new circumstances or if new appraisals of facts arise, this may lead to a change in the international legal position of a state with regard to particular questions of international law.

Under these conditions, the concessions made by this state in the search for a compromise acceptable to all can be the result of a change in the international legal positions of this state.

But concessions in the process of creating a norm of international law also can occur without changing the international legal position of a state. A state may reach a compromise on particular questions but, as before, consider that it would be better to do otherwise and to uphold those principles and norms which it previously favored.

Even the adoption of a compromise proposal as a norm of international law binding upon the state concerned does not prevent this state from continuing to favor the adoption of another norm which, from its viewpoint, is more advisable and necessary.

An example is the 1963 Moscow Treaty on the prohibition of nuclear testing in three spheres. The Soviet Union, which before the conclusion of this treaty favored the complete prohibition of all nuclear tests, came to adopt the compromise proposal to prohibit nuclear tests in the atmosphere, in outer space, and under water, supposing that this treaty would serve the cause of peace. Participation in the Moscow Treaty, however, does not prevent the Soviet Union nor any other party to this treaty from continuing to achieve the prohibition of all nuclear tests and the conclusion of an appropriate agreement for this purpose.

Thus, the concordant wills of states reflected in a norm of international law do not always and even as a rule do not fully reflect the international legal position of the respective states.

Moreover, one must bear in mind that the concordance of the wills of socialist and capitalist states in the process of creating norms of international law does not affect the world-outlook principles of their international legal positions, since socialist and bourgeois ideologies are incompatible.

D. The Unfoundedness of the Concept of the "Fundamental Norm"

The bourgeois doctrine of agreement, having correctly established that agreement between states is the sole means of creating norms of international law, has gone in a vicious circle as a result of a dogmatic approach to the question. If agreement is the sole means of creating norms of international law, say bourgeois jurists, the binding force of its norms rests upon the international legal principle or norm *pacta sunt servanda*. But on what is the legal force of this principle based? If one says that it is based on agreement, a new question arises: on what is the legal force of that agreement based? This juridical construction did not answer the question and went on *ad infinitum*.

They began to search for a way out in a certain hypothetical "fundamental norm" as the base point from which international law, and even law in general, came. The "fundamental norm" was regarded as a postulate, unavoidable for any legal system, a hypothetical norm beyond which legal research can not go.

D. Anzilotti, who was the first to extensively work out the bourgeois concept of agreement as the single mode of creating norms of international law in *Corso di diritto internazionale*, first published in 1912, writes: "Any legal system consists of norms whose binding force originates in a fundamental norm and to which, directly or indirectly, all norms of this system are reduced." The fundamental norm defines, therefore, what norms comprise the particular legal system and reduces them to a unity. The international order is characterized by the fact that the principle *pacta sunt servanda* is not based, as is the case in municipal law,

Agreement as the Mode of Creating Norms of International Law

upon a higher norm; it is itself the higher norm. The norm that "states must respect the treaties contracted by them" is, thus, a formal criterion which distinguishes the norms of which we are speaking from other norms and which reduces them to a unified system; all norms, and only the norms, which come down to the said principle as a necessary and exclusive source of their binding force relate to the category of norms of which we are speaking. These norms constitute international law or, that is to say, "the legal order of the community of states."[16]

Since, says Anzilotti, sovereign states act in the international community, the norms of law prevailing among states only can be the result of agreement among equals.[17]

The principle *pacta sunt servanda* as a "fundamental norm" has no juridical basis, in Anzilotti's view, although this does not preclude its basis from an ethical, political, or other viewpoint. "This principle," Anzilotti says, "precisely because it is a fundamental norm of which we are speaking, is not subject to further proof from the viewpoint of the norms themselves. It must be regarded as an objective absolute value, or, that is to say, as a primary and unprovable hypothesis which necessarily comes down to this, just as any other order known to mankind. This does not mean that the said principle can not be based upon other viewpoints. It only means that any basis which can be given from another point of view (ethical, political, and so forth), has no relationship with that science which limits itself to the study of the said norms."[18]

T. Perassi develops the same view. Believing that a jurist should not go beyond the limits of "juridical dogmatic," Perassi says that any legal norm presupposes another norm on which the legal significance of the first norm is based. In the final analysis at least one norm concerning the "process of norm-formation" must exist. This is the ultimate point beyond which one can not go without leaving the bounds of international law. This "fundamental norm," Perassi says, should be regarded as a norm of international law, a juridical norm.[19] The "fundamental norm" of international law, in Perassi's view, is the norm by virtue of which agreement represents a "source of legal norms" in international law. This is a postulate which is necessary in order to create a juridical theory. At the same time, it is a logical conclusion from the principle according to which for juridical dogmatic "the legal order is a postulate."[20]

16. D. Anzilotti, *Corso di diritto internazionale*, 4th ed. (Padova: CEDAM, 1955), I, 44-45.

17. *Ibid.*, p. 46.

18. *Ibid.*, pp. 43-44.

19. Perassi, "Teoria dommatica delle fonti," pp. 197-198.

20. *Ibid.*, p. 201.

H. Kelsen, who rejects the concept of agreement, also comes to a "basic norm" as the norm defining the mode of creating norms of international law. According to Kelsen, norms of law are such because " . . . their validity is derivable from a higher, that is, a more general norm, as the particular is derivable from the general," or because these norms are created through "acts" by those individuals who have been authorized by a higher norm to create norms.[21] In any case, for Kelsen "the basis of the binding nature of norms can only be a norm."[22]

Beginning with the "lowest norm of international law," Kelsen comes to the conclusion that the basic norm is the principle *pacta sunt servanda.* This is a norm of general international law created by custom. Conventional law, Kelsen says, rests upon customary law. The norm *pacta sunt servanda* is not, therefore, the ultimate "basic norm," since this could only be a norm which is the basis of the binding nature of custom as the foundation of all international law. "The basic norm of international law," Kelsen says, "therefore, must be a norm which countenances custom as a norm-creating fact, and might be formulated as follows: The states ought to behave as they have customarily behaved."[23] This norm, in Kelsen's opinion, is a "presumed or hypothetical norm."[24]

Kelsen stresses the formal character of the basic norm in his concept. "The basic norm of a positivist pure theory of law is not a norm of justice," he says.[25]

P. Guggenheim adheres very closely to Kelsen's view: "Any legal order," he says, "consists of a system of rules which derive their authority from a fundamental norm to which they all are reduced, directly or indirectly. The fundamental norm defines which norms comprise the given legal order and brings them into unity. Thus, the fundamental norm is the common source of all the rules of international public law."[26]

In the second edition of his *Traité de droit international public,* however, Guggenheim relegates the "fundamental norm" to a much more

21. H. Kelsen, *Principles of International Law*, ed. R. W. Tucker, 2d ed. (New York: Holt, Rinehart & Winston, 1967), pp. 557-558.

22. Kelsen, *Das Problem der Souveranität und die Theorie des Völkerrechts,* 2d ed. (Tübingen: Verlag von J. C. B. Mohr, 1928), p. 105.

23. Kelsen, *Principles of International Law,* p. 564.

24. Kelsen, "Théorie du droit international public," *Recueil des cours,* LXXXIV (1953), 129; see also G. Morelli, *Nozioni di diritto internazionale,* 3d ed. (Padova: CEDAM, 1951), pp. 7-11, 28-29.

25. Kelsen, "Vom Geltungsgrund des Rechts," F. A. Frhr. v. d. Heydte and others, eds., *Völkerrecht und Rechtliches Weltbild; Festschrift für A. Verdross* (Vienna: Springer Verlag, 1960), p. 165.

26. P. Guggenheim, *Traité de droit international public* (Geneva: Librairie de l'Université, 1953), I, 6.

modest role. "Of course," he says, "the fundamental norm is of interest only on a scientific plane, and that is limited."[27] In explaining this, he writes: "There is no doubt that rules of a higher order, conventional and . . . customary, can not be conceived of without some other norm which gives them validity. This fundamental rule is not established by the customary mode of creating norms of law and can not be called a legal norm or a rule of positive law."[28] This, in Guggenheim's view, is a "presumed norm, a hypothesis, which permits us to regard the legal order as a system of prevailing norms, the point of departure for recognizing the validity of legal rules which in fact are applied . . . "[29]

In an attempt to combine the normativist concept of a fundamental norm with "natural law" concepts, a West German international lawyer, G. Dahm, asserted that two fundamental norms exist. First and foremost, in his view, the principle *pacta sunt servanda*, which "is not a logical requirement, but a requirement of reason," is a fundamental norm.[30] In believing that the said norm is the fundamental norm of treaty law, he presupposes a second norm for customary law. The latter he formulates as follows: "Law is that corresponding to the will, values, and law-consciousness of the international community and that in general is observed as a norm of practical conduct."[31] The author believes that yet a "third group of rules" should be added to the two fundamental norms of international law—to wit, "rules of international constitutional law."[32] Dahm's entire eclectical construction remains, however, completely unproved and illogical.

The concept of a "fundamental norm" proceeds from a notion of law in general and of international law in particular as a self-contained, exclusive system of legal norms. This is reflected most clearly in the "pure theory of law" of Kelsen and his followers, which is characterized by a complete separation of law from reality.

Proceeding from Kant's philosophical system and delimiting the sphere of "ought" (*sollen*) and the sphere of "reality" (*sein*), Kelsen relegates law to the sphere of the ought, completely divorcing it from other social phenomena. According to Kelsen, norms of law are judgments about what ought to be in contrast to what is. In applying Kantian "pure forms of thought," Kelsen comes to "pure" norms of law which are not dependent upon reality. The domain of law, according to Kelsen, is an exclusive

27. *Ibid.*, 2d ed. (1967), I, 38.
28. *Ibid.*, p. 37.
29. *Ibid.*
30. G. Dahm, *Völkerrecht* (Stuttgart: W. Kohlhammer Verlag, 1958), I, 12.
31. *Ibid.*, p. 13.
32. *Ibid.*

system, divorced from reality. In this domain there exists only a pure legal imperative. Kelsen thereby avoids an investigation of the social content of law in the sphere of empty, nonexistent, "pure" legal norms.

The followers of contemporary natural law and sociological theories criticize the "pure theory of law" chiefly for its being divorced from reality.

C. de Visscher, for example, says that "of all contemporary doctrines, Professor Hans Kelsen's neo-positivism is the doctrine which is most deliberately ana most completely isolated from social reality."[33] "The pure theory of law," de Visscher says, is a reflection of a certain contemporary tendency which "on the pretext of the requirements of science or unity of method arbitrarily limits the content of law and narrows or distorts legal reality."[34]

A. Verdross, in criticizing the theory which regards international law and law in general as an exclusive world, says that "instead of investigating from the beginning whether positive law is itself an exclusive order, it is simply asserted, purely dogmatically, that it is such an order."[35]

In criticizing positivism, R. Ago, an Italian professor, declares that any theory of international law which reduces international law to "positive law," "in contrast to any forms of abstract, ideal law or law created by thought," goes in a vicious circle. Positivism believes that all norms of law are created by authority. "Now," R. Ago says, "the 'competence' of the authority creating law has no sense if it is not a legal competence established by law; if, in turn, law can only be the product of the law-making activity of a 'competent' authority, there is clearly a vicious circle from which legal positivism cannot escape."[36]

But a critique of normativism from the position of contemporary natural law and sociological orientations does not and can not reveal its basic flaws.

Contemporary normativism, which represents a combination of positivism and neo-Kantianism, is one of the varieties of reactionary bourgeois legal doctrine attempting to mask the exploitative essence of bourgeois

33. C. de Visscher, *Théorie et réalites en droit international public*, 2d ed. (Paris: Editions A. Pedone, 1955), p. 90.

34. *Ibid.*, p. 91.

35. A. Verdross, *Mezhdunarodnoe pravo*, trans. F. A. Kublitskii and R. L. Naryshkina, ed. G. I. Tunkin (Moscow: izd-vo IL, 1959), p. 42; see also J. Stone, "Problems Confronting Sociological Inquiries Concerning International Law," *Recueil des cours*, LXXXIX (1956), 89.

36. R. Ago, "Positive Law and International Law," *American Journal of International Law*, LI (1957), 702.

Agreement as the Mode of Creating Norms of International Law

state and law by carrying formalism to an extreme and being divorced from reality.[37]

The attempt to represent law as an exclusive system, divorced from reality, and to seek an explanation of law in law itself is wholly unfounded. The universal relationship of phenomena is itself a law in nature and society. International law has not been partitioned off from other social phenomena by an impassable barrier. The futility of attempts to find an explanation of law in general and international law in particular in law itself is demonstrated by the concept of the "fundamental norm." The attempt to base the binding force of norms of international law or, that is to say, the attempt to explain law as a social phenomenon without going beyond the domain of law, also has proved to be impossible. The "fundamental norm" tears apart the Kelsenian "legal sphere," goes beyond the limits of law, and undermines the basic positions of normativism.

The doctrine of the "fundamental norm" is purely a logical construction which does not correspond to reality. This concept is not in a position to explain the historical development of international law and the real co-relation of the norms of international law itself, as well as of international law and other social phenomena.

If the "fundamental norm" is regarded as a *conditio sine qua non*, one can agree that contemporary international law can not be conceived without the norm *pacta sunt servanda*. But there also are other important norms of international law without which it is unthinkable—for example, the principle of state sovereignty. Contemporary international law is inconceivable without this principle.

Of course, the significance of various principles and norms of international law is not the same. There are principles and norms which have paramount importance for ensuring peace and developing friendly relations among states. Other principles and norms, of lesser significance, regulate relations between states on less important questions. There are fundamental principles without which contemporary international law is inconceivable.

But if it is correct that the existence of contemporary international law is impossible without a particular principle, this still does not mean that this principle is a "fundamental norm" in the sense that all international law rests upon it and proceeds therefrom. Such also is the position with the norm *pacta sunt servanda*.

37. See D. B. Levin, *O sovremennykh burzhuaznykh teoriiakh mezhdunarodnogo prava* (Moscow: Tipo. MGEI, 1959), p. 12.

The Legal Nature and Essence of International Law

Norms of international law are created as a result of agreement of states. But this does not mean that international law is based on the principle *pacta sunt servanda* as some "fundamental" or primary norm. In reality, the development of international law has not proceeded at all from such a "fundamental norm." As regards the principle *pacta sunt servanda*, this principle developed as a customary norm together with other norms of international law. It is closely linked with such principles of international law as the principle of respect for state sovereignty, the principle of equality, and others. These principles, together with other basic principles of contemporary international law, are interconnected and interconditional. They are a reflection and a juridical consolidation of the fact that sovereign states act in international relations, and this ultimately is determined by the degree of the development of productive forces and the productive relationships corresponding thereto.

Chapter 9 *The Character and Essence of Contemporary General International Law*

The problem of the essence of contemporary international law is of great interest both on a theoretical and practical political plane. Revealing the essence of contemporary international law, and consequently its role in international relations and the societal laws of its development, on the basis of the tenets of Marxist-Leninist theory is of paramount importance in the struggle of the forces of peace and socialism for the progressive development of international law and the enhancement of its role in international relations as a means of ensuring international peace, in the struggle against colonialism and neocolonialism, and in the development of peaceful coexistence among states and peoples. In the domain of theory, working out the complex problem of the essence of contemporary international law is the basis of an effective struggle against reactionary bourgeois concepts of international law.

A. Bourgeois Science on the Social Nature of International Law

Bourgeois legal science denies the class character of the law of capitalist society and conceals its exploitative essence. It seeks the social content of law in categories which it characterizes as common to all nations, to all mankind. The same picture is to be observed, naturally, in the bourgeois theory of international law.[1]

The positivists, including proponents of the theory of agreement as the sole mode of creating a norm of international law (Triepel, Anzilotti,

1. On bourgeois concepts of international law see D. I. Baratashvili, *Amerikanskie teorii mezhdunarodnogo prava* (Moscow: Gosiurizdat, 1956); D. B. Levin, *O sovremennykh burzhuaznykh teoriiakh mezhdunarodnogo prava* (Moscow: Tipo. MGEI, 1959).

Perassi, and others), have refused to investigate the social nature of norms of international law, saying that this is not a matter for legal science.

During the period of imperialism, positivism in bourgeois legal science is degenerating into pure normativism. Thus, normativism in the form of Kelsen's "pure theory of law" is characterized by the complete separation of law from other social phenomena. According to Kelsen, as already has been pointed out, the sphere of law is exclusive, divorced from the true reality of the system. By this means, Kelsen avoids investigating the social content of law in the sphere of nonexistent, "pure" legal norms.

At the same time, there has been a definite digression from positivism in the bourgeois theory of law and a rebirth of natural law concepts during the period of imperialism, especially during the general crisis of capitalism after the Great October Socialist Revolution.

The representatives of contemporary natural law theories seek the social content of international law in the "idea of law," "justice," "reason," the "idea of order," "conscience," and so forth.[2]

In the opinion of Professor A. Verdross, who proceeds from Hegelian philosophy, the essence of law consists in the "idea of law" or, that is to say, in the idea of a "world order." The purpose of any legal order is the prohibition of the use of force. This is a basic "general value." Its normative expression is the "idea of law," the essence of which lies in the idea of "world order." Citing Aristotle and Thomas Aquinas, Verdross says that the idea of law in its subsequent development is transformed into the idea of "moral society," since the prohibition of the use of force is insufficient to secure lasting peace. For this it is also necessary that the fundamental rights of all members of the community be secured; otherwise people will be forced to resist tyranny. Herein also lies the "essence of the idea of international law."[3]

The link between the "idea of law" and the natural law of Verdross is ambiguous. The "idea of law" is embodied first of all in natural law, which is conceived as a law corresponding to the moral nature of man as he exists in the real world. Some features of human nature remain constant, whereas others change. Therefore, one can not work out an immutable and complete system of natural law.[4]

"Positive" law, in Verdross's view, is based on a higher legal order, which is natural law. Norms of "positive" law operate only within the limits of the prescriptions of natural law, within the limits defined by the

2. On contemporary concepts of natural law see G. P. Zhukov, *Kritika estestvenno-pravovykh teorii mezhdunarodnogo prava* (Moscow: Gosiurizdat, 1961).

3. See A. Verdross, *Mezhdunarodnoe pravo*, trans. from 3d ed. by F. A. Kublitskii and R. L. Naryshkina, ed. G. I. Tunkin (Moscow: izd-vo IL, 1959), p. 35.

4. *Ibid.*, p. 40.

"idea of law."[5] E. Sauer, a West German professor, also sees the essence of law in the "idea of law," which he identifies with "justice."[6]

It is wholly obvious that the "idea of law," as representing "order" or "world order" in general, does not correspond to reality.

Another representative of contemporary natural law theories, L. LeFur, sees the basis and social content of international law in "justice." He says that natural law, which in his view and that of a number of other bourgeois jurists is the basis of international law and a constituent part thereof, "has as its ultimate basis the idea of justice and morality which is common and, one can say, natural to all people."[7]

R. Redslob maintains that international law consists of "ideal and positive law," wherein "ideal law" stands higher than "positive law." "Ideal law" is established by "human conscience" and defines the "highest values." It springs from the internal conviction of the subject of a duty and is a "categorical imperative."[8]

B. Smyrniadis sees the basis of international law in "international morality, insofar as it is responsive to the conscience of the civilized world."[9]

M. Sibert, a French professor, draws from "human reason" the principles of "theoretical, rational, natural law" which, in his view, are the basis of all international law.[10]

A West German jurist, E. Kaufmann, believes that "objective reason" should be recognized as the single true "source" from which law springs.[11]

One frequently encounters the echoes of medieval theories of the divine character of international law which proclaim the will of God or a substance created by God to be the content of "natural" law. A Spanish

5. *Ibid.*, p. 37.

6. E. Sauer, *Grundlehre des Völkerrechts*, 3d rev. ed. (Köln-Berlin: Carl Heymanns Verlag, 1955), p. 2.

7. L. LeFur, "La coutume et les principes généraux du droit comme sources du droit international public," *Recueil d'études sur les sources du droit en l'honneur de François Geny* (Paris: Librairie du Recueil Sirey, 1935), III, 368; LeFur, "Règles générales du droit de la paix," *Recueil des cours*, LIV (1935), 205.

8. R. Redslob, *Traité de droit des gens* (Paris: Librairie du Recueil Sirey, 1950), pp. 62-63.

9. B. Smyrniadis, "Positivisme et morale internationale en droit des gens," *Revue générale de droit international public*, XXVI (1955), 116. See also R. Laun, "Naturrecht und Völkerrecht," *Jahrbuch für internationales Recht*, IV (1954), 32. Laun expressly identifies "natural law" with morality.

10. M. Sibert, *Traité du droit international public* (Paris: Librairie Dalloz, 1951), I, 9.

11. E. Kaufmann, "Règles générales du droit de la paix," *Recueil des cours*, LIV (1935), 319.

The Legal Nature and Essence of International Law

jurist, J. S. de Erice y O'Shea, states that "law comes to us from God."[1][2] An Italian jurist, G. del Vecchio, says that the "idea of justice" which lies at the base of law in general, including international law, "consecrates the dignity of the human being in that there is therein an absolute, thanks to the divine imprint . . ."[1][3] Verdross says that the "unity of the legal consciousness of mankind commanded by the Creator" lies at the basis of law.[1][4]

In essence the natural law theory inevitably leads to religion in one form or another. Believing that natural law does not depend upon the wills of people, is not created by people, the proponents of these theories take the path which leads to a religious explanation of the origin and content of law. They either end in ultimate logical conclusions which refer expressly to God as the ultimate Creator of law or they do not reach the end but stop halfway, which all the same leads to religion.[1][5]

Bourgeois scholars usually explain the rebirth of natural law theories as a reaction to normativism, especially the normativism of the "Vienna school" carried to an extreme, which, they say, has proved to be completely inadequate for an explanation of international legal phenomena.[1][6]

There is no doubt that the exposure of the defects of normativism and its scientific unfoundedness was one reason for the departure of bourgeois science from normativist positivism. But the principal reason, of course, is not this. There were serious social reasons which first and foremost also explain the digression of bourgeois jurists from positivism and the rebirth of natural law theories. Capitalism has turned into a stage of imperialism, which, as V. I. Lenin has pointed out, is characterized by an aspiration for domination, and not for freedom, a sharp aggravation of all the contradictions of capitalism. With the victory of the Great October Revolution there commenced the period of the general crisis of capitalism. The

12. J. S. de Erice y O'Shea, *Derecho diplomatico* (Madrid: Instituto de Estudios Politicos, 1954), I, 18-19.

13. G. del Vecchio, *Il diritto internazionale e il problema della pace* (Rome: Editrice Studium, 1956), p. 26.

14. Verdross, *Mezhdunarodnoe pravo*, p. 46.

15. A Swiss professor, R. L. Bindschelder, correctly points out that "natural law" can in any case only be a law established by the will of a superhuman authority. See R. L. Bindschelder, "Zum Problem der Grundnorm," in F. A. Frhr. v. d. Heydte and others, eds., *Völkerrecht und rechtliches Weltbild: Festschrift für A. Verdross* (Vienna: Springer Verlag, 1960), p. 164. See also Kelsen, "Die Grundlage der Naturrechtslehre," *Osterreichische Zeitschrift für öffentliches Recht*, XIII (1963), 35-37.

16. See, for example, C. de Visscher, *Théories et réalites en droit international public*, 2d ed. (Paris: Editions A. Pedone, 1955), p. 90; G. Dahm, *Völkerrecht* (Stuttgart: W. Kohlhammer Verlag, 1958), I, 11.

breaking away of a number of European and Asian states from the capitalism system, the creation of the mighty world system of socialism, is convincing evidence of the correctness of the conclusions of the Marxist-Leninist theory concerning the inevitable demise of capitalism and its replacement by a higher social system. After the October Revolution, the breakup of the colonial system of imperialism, now living out its last days, commenced.

Seeing the threat to its domination, the imperialistic bourgeoisie are striving to repudiate the legality which they have created, including also in the domain of international relations, are striving to grasp hold of any kind of desperate attempts to preserve their own dominance. The references to general, abstract categories of "natural law" are appearing under these conditions. As Professor G. Schwarzenberger correctly remarks, the primary role of the natural law theory is to "justify action that by positive law is illegal . . . "[17] Is it not because, in particular, the natural law doctrine possesses, according to the apt expression of one of its proponents, Professor H. van Panhuys, an "obstinate vitality"?[18]

If during the period of bourgeois revolutions natural law theories were part of the ideology of the bourgeoisie who fought against feudalism and played a progressive role, then under contemporary conditions the reactionary bourgeoisie refers to "natural law."

In proclaiming "natural law" to be the basis of "positive" law and part of international law in general, bourgeois jurists, willingly or not, give imperialism the opportunity to cite in justification of its aggressive actions abstract, admittedly different, interpretations of "natural law" principles derived from the "nature of man," from the idea of justice, and so forth. It is characteristic that in our time aggressive circles more often prefer to resort to references to "justice" which correspond to the interests of monopolies, and not to generally-recognized principles and norms of international law.

In comparing the natural law theories with normativism on a theoretical plane, it is necessary to point out that if the divorcing of law from other social phenomena is characteristic of normativism, then confusing them is peculiar to natural law theories. One or the other leads to a distortion of the essence of law in general and of international law in particular.

However, the attempts of various bourgeois sociological schools (solidarism, realism, personalism, and such) to overcome the excesses of normativism and natural law theories and to find a median point have not

17. G. Schwarzenberger, *The Inductive Approach to International Law* (London: Stevens & Sons, 1965), p. 186.

18. H. van Panhuys, "In Search of an International Law of Emergency," *Netherlands Yearbook of International Law*, III (1972), 150.

been crowned with success either. The problem rests in the final analysis upon recognizing the class character of law, which bourgeois science can not accept. In rejecting normativism, therefore, bourgeois sociological concepts of international law are forced in one way or another to resort to natural law theories. As D. B. Levin correctly says, "a natural law tinge is peculiar to some extent to virtually all bourgeois sociological theories of international law."[19]

Solidarism, for example, seeks the basis of law in general and of international law in particular in "social solidarity." One of the founders of solidarism, L. Duguit, despite the reality of bourgeois society, declares "social solidarity" to be the basic principle of social life. Solidarity, in Duguit's view, is supposedly a natural law of human society arising out of the nature of man. Law is an embodiment of social solidarity. "Man lives in society," says Duguit, "and can live only in society; society exists only thanks to the solidarity which links the individuals that comprise it. Consequently, the rule of conduct is made binding by the very force of things for man in society, which can be formulated as follows: to do nothing that would cause damage to social solidarity in one of its two forms, and to do everything that can be done to effectuate and develop mechanical and organic social solidarity. All objective law is summarized in this formula, and a positive law, to be lawful, must be a reflection, development, or application in practice of this principle."[20]

G. Scelle, developing this concept in the sphere of international legal theory, believes "social solidarity" to be the basis and essence of any law.[21]

In declaring "social solidarity" to be the basis of law, the solidarists further confuse the laws of societal development (as they understand them, of course) with law and thus come to the position of natural law theory.

In an inquiry into the question of the formal sources of international law, published in 1937, one of the proponents of solidarism, the French professor Scelle, maintained that the laws of societal development are "objective law" (*droit objectif*), law in the juridical sense. According to

19. Levin, *O sovremennykh burzhuaznykh teoriiakh mezhdunarodnogo prava*, p. 26.

20. L. Duguit, *Konstitutsionnoe pravo, obshchaia teoriia gosudarstva*, trans. A. Iashchenko, V. Krasnokutskii, and B. Syromiatnikov, Preface to Russian translation by P. Novogorodtsev and the author (Moscow: Tipo. t-va I. D. Sytin, 1908), p. 18.

21. G. Scelle, "Essai sur les sources formelles du droit international," *Recueil d'études sur les sources du droit en l'honneur de François Geny*, III, pp. 400-401. Professor G. Perrin, of the University of Lausanne, speaks of "international solidarity." See G. Perrin, "Le fondement et les limites du droit des gens," *Schweizerisches Jahrbuch für internationales Recht*, XII (1955), 43.

Scelle, this objective law comprises the basis of law. He wrote: "The validity of positive law is based upon its conformity to the "laws of causality" of the existence of society. This primary legal basis we call objective law because it can not contain any subjective element, for it still has not been perceived, interpreted, or desired by human intelligence. On the contrary, once human intervention begins, it does not limit itself to perceiving and interpreting; it evaluates; it attempts to direct and to use the source of law for itself, as a result of which a subjective element is introduced. To the element of necessity is added the element of will; to the element of causality, finality; and, doubtless, to the discovery, error. All positive law is to some extent a distortion of objective law and therefore is imagined to be an imperfect juridical product. It may even happen that a source will be so distorted by the subjectivity of its interpreters that it will cease to be law and become nonlaw; positive law may be antijuridical."[22]

However, in the *Cours de droit international public* which appeared in 1948, Professor Scelle expresses himself less definitely and more cautiously on this question. Already he does not maintain that the laws of causality are laws in the juridical sense; he says that a material source of law is the "legal potential" of society which corresponds to "social necessity." Norms of law arise from this material source. International law, he asserts, can be explained only in proceeding from the social factors of international life, which themselves are the result of the "laws of causality."[23]

The laws of societal development, that is first and foremost the laws of the development of the economic structure of society, exist independently of the will and desire of people. People can come to know these laws, to use them in their own interests to the extent this is possible, but they can not abolish them. The laws of societal development are reflected in the principles and norms of international law, but they themselves are not legal norms.

The inability of bourgeois legal science to expose the essence of law in general and of international law in particular is determined by its class character, by the limits of the world outlook of the ruling class. As we have seen, bourgeois legal science either refuses to investigate the social nature of law in general or does not seek it where it in fact exists. It is not in a position to escape from the vicious circle because of its class character. To expose the class nature of bourgeois law would mean that bourgeois science would oppose this law—that is, would cease to be bourgeois science.

22. Scelle, "Essai sur les sources formelles du droit international," p. 401.
23. Scelle, *Manuel de droit international public* (Paris: Editions Domat-Montchretien, 1948), p. 9.

B. The Societal Laws of the Development of International Law

(1) The laws of societal development and international law. Marxist-Leninist theory, as a genuinely scientific theory, allows us to analyze the complex system of interconnections of social phenomena, to separate major links from minor, primary from secondary, to establish the dependence of the partial laws of development of individual social phenomena from the general laws of development of human society. "In extending and developing philosophical materialism," Lenin wrote, "Marx completed and enlarged its cognition of nature to a cognition of *human society*. Marx's *historical materialism* was the greatest triumph of scientific thought. The chaos and arbitrariness which had ruled until then in the views of history and politics were strikingly changed by the integral and harmonious scientific theory showing how there develops from one structure of social life, in consequence of the growth of productive forces, another higher structure—for example, from serfdom grows capitalism."[2][4]

Applied to international law, historical materialism makes it possible to ascertain its place in the system of social phenomena, to establish the dependence of its development on the basic laws of the development of human society, and to reveal the specific developmental laws of international law.

International law, just as law in general, is a category of the superstructure. Therefore, the general law of the development of human society having the closest relationship to international law is the law of the dependence of the social superstructure on the base; that is, the economic structure of society.

In formulating this law, Marx wrote in the preface to *A Critique of Political Economy*: "In the social production of their life, people enter into specific, necessary relationships irrespective of their will, production relationships which correspond to the specific degree of development of their material productive forces. The aggregate of these productive relationships comprises the economic structure of society, the real base on which the legal and political superstructure rises and to which the specific forms of social consciousness correspond. The means of production of material life condition the social, political, and spiritual processes of life in general. The consciousness of people does not determine their being, but, on the contrary, their social being determines their consciousness. At a certain stage of their development, the material productive forces come into contradiction with the existing productive relationships, or—this is

24. V. I. Lenin, "Tri istochnika i tri sostavnykh chastei marksizma," *Polnoe sobranie sochinenii*, 5th ed. (Moscow: Gospolitizdat, 1961), XXIII, 44. [First published in *Prosveshchenie*, no. 3 (1913).]

merely a legal expression of the latter—with the relationships of ownership within which they had developed up to then. From the forms of development of productive forces these relationships are transformed into their fetters. Then comes an epoch of social revolution. With a change of economic base, there occurs more or less quickly an upheaval in the entire enormous superstructure."[2 5]

State and law, as part of the superstructure, change with a modification of the base, and the state and law correspond to each socioeconomic formation. How does this law of the dependence of the superstructure on the base operate with regard to international law? In contemporary conditions there exist two fundamental bases: the capitalist and the new socialist base coming to replace it. And at the same time there exists a general international law common to the socialist and capitalist states.

The critics of Marxist-Leninist international legal theory attempt to assert in this connection that Marxism is in no position to explain the existence of contemporary general international law and that supposedly the application of Marxist theory to international law leads to the conclusion that two international laws exist.

Thus E. McWhinney, a Canadian professor, writes: "Since law is, in Marxist terms, a product of the market-place and each economic system thus gets the body of law appropriate to its state of economic development, how may two economic systems—capitalism and communism—yield identical bodies of international legal doctrine? Or, putting it in more traditional Marxist language, if international law, like national law, belongs to the superstructure and is determined uniquely by the base of production relationships, how can radically different (Capitalist and Communist) economic bases yield the same superstructure of international law?"[2 6]

25. K. Marx and F. Engels, "K kritike politicheskoi ekonomii," *Sochineniia*, 2d ed. (Moscow: Gospolitizdat, 1959), XIII, 6-7.

26. E. McWhinney, *"Peaceful Coexistence" and Soviet-Western International Law* (Leiden: A. W. Sijthoff, 1964), p. 46; see also J. B. Quigley, Jr., "The New Soviet Approach to International Law," *The Harvard International Law Club Journal*, VII (1965), 8; H. Kelsen, *The Communist Theory of Law* (New York: Frederick A. Praeger, 1955), p. 148; W. Friedmann, *The Changing Structure of International Law* (New York: Columbia University Press, 1964), p. 327; B. Ramundo, *The Soviet (Socialist) Theory of International Law* (Washington, D.C.: George Washington University, 1964), p. 57; the review of the French edition of my book *Voprosy teorii mezhdunarodnogo prava* by I. Lapenna in *International and Comparative Law Quarterly*, XIV (1965), 1427-1428; B. Dutoit, *Coexistence et droit international à la lumière de la doctrine Soviétique* (Paris: Editions A. Pedone, 1966), pp. 75, 164; J. L. Hildebrand, *Soviet International Law* (Cleveland: Western Reserve Distributors, 1969), p. 67.

The trouble with these critics of the Marxist-Leninist theory of international law lies in the fact that, just as the many other critics of Marxism who existed before them, they attempt to represent Marxist-Leninist theory as a form of vulgar materialism. Their assertion that Marxist-Leninist theory supposedly considers any phenomenon of the superstructure as directly determined by the economic system of society, as representing a simple reflection of economic relations, is nothing other than the fruit of their own imagination.

What Engels said nearly eighty years ago on the subject of distortion of Marxism is wholly applicable to these critics. In a letter to J. Bloch of September 21-22, 1890, Engels wrote: ". . . According to the materialist conception of history, the *ultimately* determining element in history is the production and reproduction of real life. More than this neither Marx nor I have ever asserted. Hence if somebody twists this into saying that the economic element is the *only* determining one, he transforms that proposition into a meaningless, abstract, senseless phrase. The economic situation is the basis, but the various elements of the superstructure—political forms of the class struggle and its results, to wit: constitutions established by the victorious class after a successful battle, and so forth, juridical forms, and even the reflexes of all these actual struggles in the brains of the participants, political, juristic, and philosophical theories, religious views and their further development into systems of dogma—also exercise their influence upon the course of the historical struggles and in many cases preponderate in determining their *form*. There is an interaction of all these elements in which, amid all the endless host of accidents . . . the economic movement finally asserts itself as necessary. Otherwise the application of the theory to any period of history would be easier than the solution of a simple equation of the first degree."[27]

The view has been expressed in Soviet international legal literature that two groups of international legal principles and norms exist which correspond to the two socioeconomic systems, but as we pointed out in 1956, this view was never shared by the majority of Soviet international lawyers.[28]

In fact, only Marxist-Leninist theory allows us to explain scientifically both the existence of contemporary general international law and its social nature. The Marxist-Leninist theory of international law, in revealing the mechanism of its development on the basis of the general tenets of historical materialism, shows why, despite the existence of two dia-

27. K. Marx and F. Engels, *Izbrannye proizvedeniia v dvukh tomakh* (Moscow: Gospolitizdat, 1948), II, 467-468.
28. See G. I. Tunkin, "Mirnoe sosushchestvovanie i mezhdunarodnoe pravo," *Sovetskoe gosudarstvo i pravo*, no. 7 (1956), p. 5.

metrically opposed bases, general international law exists and why these bases influence it.

The emergence of a new social system and the existence of two opposed social systems does not mean that they are isolated from one another. The intensity of international economic as well as of other ties is increasing with the growth of the productive forces of human society and with the development on this basis of a world division of labor. The division of the world into two opposed social systems, the formation of two world markets, has not stopped this objective world process, although it has introduced much that is new into it (see Chapter 13).

This general societal law is the major objective premise of the peaceful coexistence of states with a diametrically opposed social system and of general international law. At the same time, it is necessary to emphasize that the very possibility of peaceful coexistence of the socialist and capitalist states immediately conditions the possibility of the existence of general international law,[29] since the basic contradiction of contemporary international relations lies in the relations between states of the two systems.

In proving that at the basis of societal development lies the development of its productive forces, which at each stage of their development correspond to a specific economic structure of society, and in showing how in connection with the development of productive forces the international division of labor develops and international economic and other international ties expand, and that in contemporary society these ties acquire legal forms, Marxist-Leninist theory creates a firm basis for international legal theory.

The concept of the concordance of wills of states (or agreement) as a mode of creating norms of contemporary international law, widely accepted in the Soviet science of international law, helps to reveal on the basis of the general tenets of the Marxist-Leninist theory of law the specific mechanism of the influence of the economic structure of society upon the development of international law—that is, the mechanism of the influence of the two bases upon contemporary international law.

As already has been pointed out, norms of contemporary international law are created and changed on the basis of agreement between states. This agreement embraces the concordant wills of states relating to the content of a particular rule of conduct and to its being recognized as a norm of international law.

Marxist-Leninist theory reveals the class content of the will of a state, showing that this will in a society with antagonistic classes is the will of

29. Tunkin, *Osnovy sovremennogo mezhdunarodnogo prava* (Moscow: Tipo. Vysshei partiinoi shkoly pri TsK KPSS, 1956), p. 7.

The Legal Nature and Essence of International Law

the economically and politically ruling class in the particular society, and under socialism the will of the entire people led by the working class.[30]

The content of the will of a state—that is, its international legal position—is formed under the influence of the entire aggregate of the conditions of the existence of the ruling class in a state, and under socialism, of the entire people. The economic structure of society is the primary base which defines in the final analysis the international legal position of a state in its primary features.

In reality, the economic structure determines the class nature of a state, the fundamental principles of its internal and foreign policy, the major features of its national law, and all other parts of the superstructure. This general societal law is the main societal law. But this does not mean that it is possible to "directly infer" the international legal position of a particular state from the economic structure of society.

Forming an international legal position, that is, the content of the will of a state, is a complex process in which the economic structure of society and its societal laws exert a determinative influence. Various parts of the superstructure, however, also exert influence upon the formation of the international legal position of a state: ideology, national law, international legal doctrine, and so forth. One can not reduce to a basic societal law nor "infer" the will of a state or the will of its ruling class in each individual instance from the economic structure of society without taking other influences into account. At the same time, it is possible to gain an understanding of this process only by proceeding from the societal laws of the co-relation of base and superstructure.

The economic structure of human society in our days is characterized by the existence of two opposed world economic systems whose development occurs pursuant to directly opposed laws. Moreover, there are developing countries whose economic system is characterized by a complex intertwining of elements of different socioeconomic entities. All these bases exert, ultimately through the wills of states, a determining influence on the development of international law.

At the same time, international economic relations, which are a basis category and whose influence on international law is a basis influence,

30. On class will and state will in connection with the creation of norms of law see D. A. Kerimov, *Svoboda, pravo i zakonnost' v sotsialisticheskom obshchestve* (Moscow: Gosiurizdat, 1960); P. S. Romashkin and others, eds., *Teoriia gosudarstva i prava* (Moscow: izd-vo AN SSSR, 1962); *Obshchaia teoriia sovetskogo prava* (Moscow: Iurizdat, 1966); A. I. Denisov, ed., *Teoriia gosudarstva i prava* (Moscow: MGU, 1967); V. M. Chkhikvadze, *Gosudarstvo, demokratiia, zakonnost'* (Moscow: Iurizdat, 1967); N. G. Aleksandrov, ed., *Teoriia gosudarstva i prava* (Moscow: Iurizdat, 1968); A. F. Shebanov, *Forma sovetskogo prava* (Moscow: Iurizdat, 1968); R. L. Bobrov, *Osnovnye problemy teorii mezhdunarodnogo prava* (Moscow: izd-vo Mezhdunarodnye otnosheniia, 1968).

exert influence on international law. The view has been repeatedly expressed in Soviet international legal literature that international economic relations are the basis of international law. According to this view, international economic relations, as a secondary (basis), are determined by the fundamental bases but are themselves the basis of international law. This construction implies that the influence of the fundamental bases is effectuated only through international economic relations. An analysis of practice shows, however, that despite the growing weight of international economic relations in the life of society and in international relations, the decisive basis influence in forming the international legal position of states is the direct influence of the fundamental bases and the categories of the superstructure resting on these bases. Nonetheless, the role of the influence of international economic relations is growing in the overall amount of basis influences on international law.

Thus, the influence of the economic structure of society and its societal laws affects the process of creating norms of international law through the will of a state, since the content of this will basically is determined by the economic conditions of the existence of the ruling class in a given state. The economic structure of society exerts a decisive influence in the process of creating norms of international law upon the wills of states not only through "direct action" but also through other categories of the superstructure, whose operation in general can not go beyond the limits determined by the economic structure of society.

(2) The unfoundedness of the bourgeois concept of ubi societas ibi jus. The denial of the class character of law leads bourgeois science to the maxim "where there is society, there is law" (ubi societas ibi jus). Law and society, say bourgeois jurists, are indivisible. Human society is impossible without law. Law is represented as an ahistorical category, independent of the social system and peculiar to any human society.

Thus, G. Fitzmaurice, an English jurist and member of the International Court, writes: "The view that seems to be closest both to the realities of the matter and to the historical facts is the "social" view, or in other words the idea embodied in the maxim ubi societas ibi jus. This maxim is more than a statement of mere fact . . . It is not simply that where society is found, law is found, but that it must be so found—that law is a necessary condition of the existence of society as such—which is to say a necessary condition of any systematized form of inter-relationships."[31]

The maxim ubi societas ibi jus, which for a century has been accepted by bourgeois and even prebourgeois legal science as an axiom, is un-

31. G. Fitzmaurice, "The General Principles of International Law Considered from the Standpoint of the Rule of Law," Recueil des cours, XCII (1957), 38.

founded. Marxist-Leninist theory has shown that there was a time when human society knew neither a state nor law, although there were specific rules of conduct then. The development of productive forces led to the emergence of private ownership of the means of production. The possibility of appropriating another's labor, of the exploitation of man by man, was created. Private ownership of the means of production was the basis for the development of inequality among the various groups of human society, the division of society into classes. The state arose as the organ of the economically dominant class in society, as the organ strengthening and consolidating its domination. Together with the state, law emerged, which was distinguished from the rules of conduct which had existed in the prestate society primarily by the fact that it reflected the will not of all society but only of the ruling class and that it was directed at maintaining and developing the social orders favorable and advantageous to this ruling class. Fulfillment of these new norms, legal norms, by members of society was ensured when necessary through coercion applied by agencies of the state.

When there was no law in general, there could be no international law. Since law emerged as a result of the division of society into classes and of the rise of the state, in the beginning it was national law. In the course of time, international law regulating relations among states began to be formed. The same basic reasons which led to the formation of national law also gave rise to the emergence of international law.

International law, just as national law, inheres in a class society. But class society, as has been proved by the basic tenets of Marxism, represents merely a certain stage in the development of human society, which also had existed where there were no classes. This society was characterized by a low level of the development of productive forces. A high development of the productive forces of society also inevitably leads to the disappearance of classes, of the state, and of law. "The development of socialist statehood," says the Program of the CPSU, "gradually leads to its transformation into social *communist self-government*, in which the Soviets, trade, cooperative, and other mass organizations of the working people are united."[3 2] Mankind is approaching a new organization of society which will not have law, and therefore, not international law. This, of course, does not mean that the society of the future will have no rules of conduct. A highly-organized human society, as communist society will be, inevitably presupposes the existence of rules of conduct. "Communist society will be a highly-organized commonwealth of laboring people. There will be formed uniform generally-recognized rules of

32. *Programma Kommunisticheskoi partii Sovetskogo Soiuza* (Moscow: Politizdat, 1964), p. 109.

communist communal life, whose observance will become an internal need and habit of all people."[3][3]

Bourgeois science errs in accepting any rules of conduct, including rules of conduct in tribal society, as norms of law. The maxim "where there is society, there are rules of conduct" would be correct, but the maxim "where there is society, there is law" (*ubi societas ibi jus*) is incorrect. The rules of conduct which will exist in communist society will by their nature be different from norms of law.

The maxim "where there is society, there is law" is closely linked with the widespread thesis in bourgeois legal science that law is a reflection of "community": community of interests, community of ideology, and so forth. As confirmation of this thesis, many bourgeois scholars point out that the existence of law in general and of international law in particular would be impossible without a specific community among people. Of course, the existence of human society, and therefore of law, is inconceivable without a specific community among people. But it does not follow from this that the community is the reason for the emergence of law or is reflected in law. History shows exactly the opposite: in preclass society, where this community was more significant, there was no law, and law appears only with the emergence of class contradictions, with the disturbance of the tribal community.

(3) International law and international organization. The notion of law as a nonclass system of norms common to all mankind leads bourgeois science to the conclusion in the domain of international legal theory that international law is developing along the same path as national law and is now at an elementary stage of development which national law has long since undergone. They therefore call international law a "primitive" law which, however, is developing in the same direction as national law has developed, to wit, in the direction of centralization. Some, but far from all bourgeois jurists, go further, believing that international law will become a "real" law only with the creation of a world state or an approximation of a world state (see Chapter 14).

D. Anzilotti has said that norms of international law possess the character which norms of social groups had during the period preceding the emergence of state organization, and that in comparison with municipal law, international law is "incomplete and imperfect."[3][4] It is true that Anzilotti pointed out in this connection that norms of international law could not be otherwise and that the emergence of a world

33. *Ibid.*, pp. 109-110.

34. D. Anzilotti, *Corso di diritto internazionale*, 4th ed. (Padova: CEDAM, 1955), I, 47.

federation "would actually mean the end of international law, which would be superseded by the internal public law of the new state."

In Kelsen's view, the basic difference between national and international law lies in the fact that the first is a centralized and the second is a decentralized and therefore primitive legal system.[35] Kelsen maintains that so long as the sovereignty of states is recognized, international law can not leave this "primitive condition." He calls for the liquidation of state sovereignty and the creation of a "world state" which would ensure the "development and application of international law."[36]

In developing the same concept of the uniform path of development of international and national law, Professor J. Kunz says that the "private wars" of the Middle Ages were eliminated by means of centralization. The same course must be followed in international relations. The progressive development of international law can not be brought about merely by treaties. "This can only be brought about," Kunz says, "by political action, changing the actual sociological conditions on which the present international community is based . . . A more advanced international law must be based on the full recognition by states of the primacy of international law and on enforceable sanctions both for the maintenance of peace and security and for the enforcement of international law in general by organs of the international community."[37]

Lauterpacht gives a very thorough exposition of this concept in one of its extreme variants in Oppenheim's *International Law*. He writes: "The historic idea of a 'general international organisation,' an idea prominent in the legal and political thought of the past three centuries, connotes an association of States of potentially universal character for the ultimate fulfillment of purposes which, in relation to individuals organised in political society, are realised by the State. The achievement of these purposes, which are outlined below, is as essential to the Law of Nations as it is to the internal law of the State. Failing their accomplishment, or an attempt at their accomplishment, International Law must be deemed to dwell in the realm of a twilight existence in which its very claim to be considered as a system of law is precarious and controversial. To that extent, which is fundamental in its scope and nature, the cause of International Law is identical with that of a general political organisation

35. H. Kelsen, *Principles of International Law*, ed. R. W. Tucker, 2d ed. (New York: Holt, Rinehart & Winston, 1967), p. 20.

36. *Ibid.*, pp. 189-190; Kelsen, *Das Problem der souveranität und die Theorie des Völkerrechts*, 2d ed. (Tübingen: Verlag von J. C. B. Mohr, 1928), p. 320.

37. J. Kunz, "Sanctions in International Law," *American Journal of International Law*, LIV (1960), 347.

of mankind as distinguished from organs of international administration and co-operation for particular purposes. For it is only under the shelter of and through such general organisation endowed with overriding and coercive power for creating, ascertaining, and enforcing the law that International Law can overcome its present imperfections. For this reason it is proper that the constitution of international society—such as was embodied in the Covenant of the League of Nations and is now embodied in the Charter of the United Nations—should be studied by reference to its approximation to these essential objects of any political society under the rule of law."[38]

An American professor, P. Jessup, asserts still more categorically that international law can be transformed into real law only if a world government is created. Jessup writes: "Until the world achieves some form of international government in which a collective will takes precedence over the individual will of the sovereign state, the ultimate function of law, which is the elimination of force for the solution of human conflicts, will not be fulfilled."[39]

One should dwell first and foremost upon the general societal laws of the development of international and municipal law. There is no doubt that such societal laws exist. Among them, for example, is the societal law reflecting the fact that at a certain stage of the development of human society there was neither municipal nor international law and that in the future, at a very high stage of the development of human society, there also will not be such.

The existence of certain general societal laws of the development of international and municipal law, however, does not mean that international law does not have its own specific societal laws of development. Attempts to approach international law with the yardstick of national law are scientifically unfounded, since the specific nature of the phenomenon being investigated is not taken into account. International law is a distinctive law.

The basic peculiarities of international law arise from the fact that it regulates first and foremost, and primarily, the relations between sovereign states. In taking exception to the argumentation of proponents of a "world state," some specialists on international law in the West, not without justification, point out that the creation of a "world state" would

38. L. Oppenheim, *Mezhdunarodnoe pravo*, trans. from 6th ed., ed. S. B. Krylov (Moscow: izd-vo IL, 1948), I(1), p. 340.
39. P. Jessup, *A Modern Law of Nations* (New York: Macmillan Company, 1968), p. 2.

mean the elimination of international law, since in this event international law would be superseded by the municipal law of the "world state."[40]

The major peculiarities of international law as law regulating the relations between sovereign states are determined by the societal laws of historical development. The existence of sovereign states at the present time is not dependent upon the will or desire of individual persons. It is not that governments do not wish to part with sovereign authority, as the proponents of eliminating state sovereignty (Kelsen, Scelle, and others) so frequently lament. The existence of sovereign states is conditioned by the historical societal laws of our epoch.

As regards the link between the development of international law and the development of international organization, there is no doubt that during the period after the First and especially after the Second World War, one observes a tendency to expand the role of international organizations both in developing international law and in ensuring the observance of its norms.[41]

International organizations now play an important role in creating norms of international law and ensuring supervision over their observance, and strongly influence the conduct of states for the purpose of having them observe norms of international law. There is every reason to suppose that this role of international organizations will grow in the future.

But there are no reasons to believe that international organizations can be transformed into the likeness of a state authority and fulfill the same or similar functions in creating and ensuring the observance of norms of international law which agencies of state authority fulfill with regard to national law (see Chapter 15).

A world state represents a serious danger to international law. From the concept that only the creation of a world state can make international law a "real" law, it is only one step to completely denying the validity of contemporary international law and recognizing as hopeless all attempts

40. See, for example, Anzilotti, *Corso di diritto internazionale*, I, 47; H. Drost, *Grundlagen des Völkerrechts* (Munich-Leipzig: Verlag von Duncker & Hamblot, 1936), p. 2; H. A. Smith, *The Crisis in the Law of Nations* (London: Stevens & Sons, 1947), p. 22; G. Sperduti, "Osservazioni sulle basi sociali dell'ordinamento internazionale," *Rivista di diritto internazionale*, XXXVIII (1955), 3-16; Verdross, *Mezhdunarodnoe pravo*, pp. 24-25.

41. See Chapters 4 and 5. Professor Bourquin is correct in noting this new fact, although he somewhat exaggerates its significance. He writes: "Whereas the functioning of international law previously was based on the actions of states, it now rests to a significant extent on international organizations such as the United Nations and the numerous specialized agencies grouped around it." M. Bourquin, "L'Humanisation du droit des gens," *La téchnique et les principes du droit public: études en l'honneur de G. Scelle* (Paris: Librairie générale de droit et jurisprudence, 1950), I, 48.

to enlarge its role in ensuring peace and averting war. In reality, if one believes that enhancing the effectiveness of international law is inseparably linked with the creation of a world state, which under contemporary conditions is impossible, the future prospects for the development of international law would be very inauspicious.

In fact, however, this is not so at all. Enhancing the role of international law in international relations occurs not by moving toward a world state and eliminating state sovereignty, but as a result of developing and strengthening the basic principles and norms of prevailing international law, introducing new principles and norms therein aimed at the development of international cooperation and ensuring the peaceful coexistence of states on the basis of equality, respect for sovereignty, and noninterference in internal affairs.

Since the existence of sovereign states is a historic societal law of our epoch, only agreement between these sovereign states is and can be the basic legally binding nature of norms of international law. Agreement of states on the basis of equality as a mode of creating norms of international law continues to remain the characterstic feature of the development of international law in our epoch.

In comparison, moreover, with the preceding period, this situation is being consolidated and is developing. If previously the great imperialist powers frequently declared to be generally recognized norms those norms which they themselves had established, and imposed these norms upon the weaker states, at the present time any attempts of imperialist states to impose norms advantageous to them as norms of international law not only are unlawful but are doomed to failure beforehand.

C. Modification of the Character and Essence of General International Law During the Past Half-Century

The question of evaluating the changes which have taken place in international law since the Great October Socialist Revolution is not just of theoretical interest. It arises, in particular, during the discussion in the United Nations of the most important questions of the progressive development of international law and its codification, wherein the international legal positions of the states of the two systems are in conflict.

(1) Fundamental changes in general international law since the Great October Socialist Revolution. Under the influence of the growing might of the forces of socialism, of the national liberation movement, and of all the

forces of democracy and progress, international law has undergone material changes since the Great October Socialist Revolution. The attempt of German fascism and Japanese imperialism to destroy international law and to replace it with delirious ideas of the dominance of a superior race brought forth the unity of all progressive forces. This general democratic upsurge not only led to the rout of fascism, militarily and in the realm of ideas, but also ensured a significant development of international law, reflected above all in the United Nations Charter.

The fundamental principles of international law, that central part which has the greatest significance from the viewpoint of ensuring international peace, the independence of peoples, and the development of international cooperation and which first and foremost determines the fact of international law (see Chapter 3), have changed fundamentally during the past half-century.

The changes which have occurred in international law naturally have affected all of its branches and institutes, the changes in individual branches of international law being above all the consequence of the change in the fundamental principles. Thus, in the domain of responsibility, whose importance in the general system of international law is difficult to underestimate, there has been an extension of international legal responsibility for war and its consequences (see Chapters 17 and 18).

Together with this there arose a new important institute of international law: responsibility of individuals for crimes against humanity, as they have been defined in the Statute and Judgment of the International Military Tribunal in Nuremberg.

Significant changes have taken place in the law of treaties. Contemporary international law declares void international treaties imposed upon a state through the unlawful use of force or those which contravene principles of international law having the character of *jus cogens* and recognizes a special status for treaties concluded with regard to an aggressor state.[42]

In the domain of sources of international law, the international treaty has become the principal source. Resolutions of international organizations, and especially of the United Nations, are playing larger and larger roles in the process of forming norms of international law.

In the domain of subjects of international law, new entities have emerged which are different from states, the traditional subjects of international law. These are international organizations, as well as nations fighting for their independence. International organizations possess a limited status as subjects of international law, but they are playing an ever greater role in international relations.

42. See Articles 52, 53, and 75 of the 1969 Vienna Convention on the Law of Treaties.

In ambassadorial law there has been a trend toward expanding the group of persons who enjoy diplomatic immunity and privileges. Thus, according to the 1961 Vienna Convention on Diplomatic Relations, together with diplomats, the basic diplomatic privileges are accorded to administrative and technical personnel of diplomatic representations and, to a certain extent, also to service personnel.[43]

Material changes also have taken place or are occurring in the law of neutrality. In recent years many states, especially new states of Asia and Africa, adhere to a policy of neutrality. The international legal formulation of this policy, in consequence whereof international obligations arise for the respective state, is taking place, as L. A. Modzhorian correctly points out, through unilateral declarations of a state wishing to adhere to a policy of neutrality, tacitly or expressly recognized by the remaining states and through bilateral or multilateral agreements.[44] The content of the status of a permanently neutral state has changed in connection with the change of the international situation and of international law. Neutrality in time of war has acquired primary importance in general. These new phenomena in the domain of neutrality mark a significant change in this branch of international law.[45]

The intensification and deepening of international ties, determined first and foremost by the development of productive forces and the international division of labor, has led to the emergence of new areas of international legal regulation.

The origin of a branch of international law which might be called the law of international security has enormous, but to a significant extent still potential, importance. Included within it are, first and foremost, international legal questions of disarmament, the prohibition of the testing of nuclear weapons, the creation of nuclear-free zones, the nonproliferation of nuclear weapons, collective security, and others.

A new branch of international law is developing which by analogy with sea and air law is called space law.[46]

The growth of the number and the expansion of the jurisdiction of international organizations has led to the emergence of a branch of international law which usually is called the law of international organiza-

43. Article 37, Vienna Convention on the Law of Treaties. V. K. Sobakin, comp., *Sovremennoe mezhdunarodnoe pravo; sbornik dokumentov* (Moscow: izd-vo Mezhdunarodnye otnosheniia, 1964), pp. 310-311.
44. L. A. Modzhorian, *Osnovnye prava i obiazannosti gosudarstv* (Moscow: Iurizdat, 1965), p. 42.
45. For greater detail see B. V. Ganiushkin, *Neitralitet i neprisoedinenie* (Moscow: izd-vo Mezhdunarodnye otnosheniia, 1965); O. I. Tiunov, *Neitralitet v mezhdunarodnom prave* (Perm': Permskii gosudarstvennyi universitet, 1968).
46. See G. P. Zhukov, *Kosmicheskoe pravo* (Moscow: izd-vo Mezhdunarodnye otnosheniia, 1966).

tions. This law partially relates to general international law and partially is the law of individual international organizations.

Norms of international public law affecting commercial and other economic relations among states are developing rapidly, and thus international economic law is being formed.

A branch of international law known by the name "international labor law," whose norms define the rights and duties of states in the domain of regulating labor conditions, has developed significantly. This branch of international law is embodied chiefly in conventions of the International Labor Organization.[47]

The profound changes which have occurred in international law since the Great October Socialist Revolution, above all under the influence of the changes which it wrought in the world and the ideas it advanced, lead to the conclusion that the question is not one of partial changes, but of those which are changing materially the entire character and essence of international law.

International law before the Great October Socialist Revolution, which we call the old international law, was essentially the law of the strong; it recognized and legally consolidated the domination of force in international relations.[48] This has emerged most clearly in such principles, for example, as the "right of a state to wage war," the "right of the victor," and others. If a state were sufficiently strong and could count upon victory, it always had the legal possibility of using the "right to wage war" and to resort to war in order to satisfy its actual or imaginary claims against another state. Moreover, victory in war allowed the victor to exceed the limits of the claims previously submitted.[49] International law sanctioned that which was obtained by force.

Contemporary international law prohibits resort to war, prohibits the use or threat of force against the territorial integrity and political independence of any state or by any means incompatible with the purposes of the United Nations. States are obliged to settle their disputes only by peaceful means.

Thus, the new international law prohibits aggressive war, is an instrument of the struggle for peace. Already the emergence of the principle of

47. See S. A. Ivanov, *Problemy mezhdunarodnogo regulirovaniia truda* (Moscow: izd-vo Nauka, 1964); I. Szaszy, *International Labour Law* (Budapest: Akademiai kiado, 1968).

48. Professor E. Pashukanis was correct in speaking with regard to this international law that "with its help they divide the loot." See E. B. Pashukanis, *Ocherki po mezhdunarodnomu pravu* (Moscow: izd-vo Sovetskoe zakonodatel'stvo, 1935), p. 9.

49. See Chapters 17 and 18.

nonaggression has modified the character of international law to a significant extent.[50] In its subsequent development international law swung its face still more toward peace.

The old international law recognized two equal conditions of relations between states: a state of peace and a state of war. A significantly greater place was given to questions of war than to questions of peaceful relations.[51] Of the numerous international conventions concluded in the second half of the nineteenth and beginning of the twentieth century, the overwhelming majority treat the law of war. Thus, of fourteen documents (thirteen conventions and one declaration) signed at the Second Hague Peace Conference in 1907, only two concerned peaceful relations between states. All the other documents were devoted to the law of war.

At the present time, the unleashing of war is the most flagrant violation of international law, entailing not only the grave responsibility of the aggressor state but also the personal criminal responsibility of the persons guilty of the war. A state of war has ceased to be a "normal" state of relations between states in international law; it is the result of the gravest violation of international law.

More and more attention is being devoted to questions of regulating and strengthening peaceful relations between states. In contrast to what was previously, the majority of international conventions concluded since the Second World War are devoted to peaceful relations between states.

Under contemporary international law, war is not a duel, a contest between equal parties. The parties are not in an identical legal situation: one party, the aggressor, has committed the gravest breach of law, having unleashed a war, and is waging the war in violation of international law; and the other party is waging the war in self-defense, that is, on the basis of international law.

Elimination of the "right of a state to wage war" and the emergence in international law of the principle of nonaggression has led to the liquida-

50. An American professor, C. Eagleton, in stressing the significance of the principle of the prohibition of aggressive war in international law, drew exceedingly far-reaching and incorrect conclusions. He wrote: "To deny to a state the right to make war is a change of fundamental character from which many consequences flow. The law of war and the law of neutrality would disappear—if they already have not disappeared. The means for peaceable settlement of disputes would have to be strengthened so that a community of decision would replace the right now claimed by each state to judge its own disputes. Thus the very foundations of international law are being changed." C. Eagleton, "Ferment or Revolution?" *American Journal of International Law*, L (1956), 920.

51. In Grotius's celebrated work *On the Law of War and Peace* published in 1625 the "law of war," as is well-known, is given priority.

tion of the "right of the victor" and the institute of conquest and to the expansion of the principles of state responsibility for war and its consequences (see Chapter 18).

The old international law contained norms and institutes which were an instrument of the colonial enslavement of peoples and which consecrated and juridically strengthened the colonial regime and other forms of the dependence and exploitation of peoples. The right to acquire "no man's" territory (the rights of the indigenous populace of underdeveloped countries not being taken into account), the right of conquest, spheres of influence, institutes of colonial law, the regime of the protectorate, and others related to this category of norms and institutes of international law. These norms and institutes existed side by side with democratic principles and norms of the old international law while being in sharp contradiction with them.

Despite its imperfections, especially in the struggle against various forms of neocolonialism, contemporary international law as a whole is anticolonial. With the recognition of the principle of self-determination of nations as a generally accepted principle of international law, the latter has turned against the colonial system. From a means of enslaving peoples, it has become an instrument of struggle for the liberation of peoples of colonies and dependent countries. Colonialism contravenes the very bases of contemporary international law.

The idea of the equality of all peoples, irrespective of race, language, religion, and so forth, is being consolidated more and more in international law.

The idea of the equality of the two systems together with the equality of states irrespective of their social system is winning recognition. The realization that any attempts to decide international questions on a plane unacceptable to the socialist countries are futile and harmful to the cause of peace and that agreement between states of the two systems is the sole means of deciding such questions is forcing its way more and more into international organizations and international conferences.[52]

The old international law was primarily a law of the so-called "civilized" or "Christian" states. The enormous continent of Africa and an important part of Asia had not entered into international relations, being the object of colonial oppression and exploitation. "Only the Christian states and their colonies belong to the sphere of international relations," wrote Professor M. Kapustin, of Moscow University.[53] "The spatial effect

52. See R. L. Bobrov, "Printsip ravnopraviia dvukh sistem v sovremennom mezhdunarodnom prave," *Sovetskoe gosudarstvo i pravo*, no. 11 (1960), pp. 42-50.

53. M. Kapustin, *Obozrenie predmetov mezhdunarodnogo prava* (Moscow: Universitetskaia tipo., 1856), II, 41.

of international law," said Professor F. Martens, of Petersburg University, "is limited just to those peoples who recognize the basic principles of European culture and are worthy of the name of educated peoples."[54]

In consequence of the breakup of the colonial system of imperialism, there has been an expansion of the spatial sphere of the effect of international law. On this basis, international law more and more is becoming a universal law.

Contemporary international law precludes discrimination against states on the basis of such criteria as being "civilized" or "uncivilized," "Christian" or "non-Christian." The reference to "civilized" nations encountered in the Statute of the International Court now seems to be an obvious anachronism.

The essence of contemporary general international law also has changed. The expression "general" in this case is of material significance, since taken as a whole contemporary international law has no single class essence. One must distinguish in this respect between general international law and local international legal norms, whose essence in many instances differs from the essence of general international law.

The Marxist-Leninist theory of law considers the essence of law (as regards national law) to be the "general will of a particular class expressed therein."[55] This proposition is generally recognized in Soviet legal science.

Norms of international law are created not by one state, but by states; they reflect the concordant wills of states. The co-relation of the wills of states which participate in creating norms of international law with the wills of peoples depends upon the character of each individual state. The will of a capitalist state always is the will of its ruling class, determining, of course, the entire aggregate conditions of the existence of this class, including the struggle of the working class and all the working people. The will of the Soviet state of the whole people is the will of the entire Soviet people led by the working class; in contrast, in the international arena to the will of the ruling classes of capitalist states, it is the will of the toiling classes. The Soviet state of the whole people "continues the cause of the dictatorship of the proletariat: the construction of communism, and together with the other socialist states wages a class struggle against imperialism in the international arena."[56]

In the process of creating norms of international law, the wills of

54. F. F. Martens, *Sovremennoe mezhdunarodnoe pravo tsivilizovannykh narodov*, 2d ed. (St. Petersburg: Tipo. Ministerstva putei soobshcheniia, 1887), p. 180.

55. Chkhikvadze, *Gosudarstvo, demokratiia, zakonnost'*, p. 293.

56. "Tezisy TsK KPSS '50 let Velikoi Oktiabr'skoi sotsialisticheskoi revoliutsii,' " *Pravda*, June 25, 1967, p. 4.

various states, above all the wills of states whose class essence is opposed, come into conflict. The process of creating norms of international law is the process of the struggle and cooperation of states, and naturally, being the result of this process, norms of international law themselves bear its imprint.

The creation of norms of international law takes place in specific juridical forms peculiar to contemporary international law, through the concordance of the wills of states as sovereign and equal subjects completed by an agreement fixing the content of a norm and recognizing it as a norm of international law. In this process the wills of states juridically are of equal importance. As Professor L. A. Aleksidze has noted correctly, one can not speak on the juridical plane about whose will has prevailed in the process of creating a norm of international law, since the question is one of agreement of sovereign states on the basis of equality.[57]

As already has been pointed out, however, the actual influence of different states and groups of states in the process of creating norms of international law is far from identical. Contemporary international law is developing under the ever growing influence of the socialist and other peace-loving states; the legal principles upheld by these states are being introduced into international law more and more.

The content and essence of norms of general international law, being the result of the norm-formation process, depend not only upon the actual situation (for example, the co-relation of forces at a conference, the influence of public opinion, the skill of diplomats, and so forth) but also upon the legal aspect of this process. The co-relation of forces upon a specific question of international law, of course, is of primary importance. But despite the preponderance of forces of a particular group of states, a norm of international law can not be created by the dictate of this group of states; it emerges only in consequence of agreement of states on the basis of equality.

The existence of states belonging to two opposed social systems creates specific limits for agreements between them. And since only those international legal norms which embrace the agreement of all states are norms of contemporary general international law, the norms of general international law, therefore, may not exceed the said limits.

This means that norms of contemporary general international law can not be socialist, since agreement on this basis between socialist and capitalist states is impossible. Socialist international legal norms can be created only in relations between socialist states. On the other hand,

57. L. A. Aleksidze, "O klassovoi prirode sovremennogo mezhdunarodnogo prava," *Sovetskoe gosudarstvo i pravo*, no. 6 (1967), pp. 56-58.

norms of contemporary general international law can not be an embodiment of an imperialistic policy, since agreement between socialist and
capitalist states also is impossible on this basis.

The principles and norms of contemporary general international law as
a whole are of a general democratic character, since agreement between
socialist and capitalist states is possible only on this basis.[58] The notion of
being generally democratic, however, is a very broad concept. The degree
of the democratic nature of specific norms of international law is
determined by the influence which has been exerted on the creation and
development of such norms by the forces which favor the progressive
development of international law and the forces which impede such
progress.

The social consequences which regulate the influence of this system of
law upon the corresponding social relationships have important significance for the characteristic features of the content and essence of
international law. A. A. Piontkovskii undoubtedly is right that one can
not consider norms of law while ignoring legal relationships, although one
can not agree with his thesis that the regulating influence of norms of law
always is realized through legal relationships.[59]

The regulating influence of contemporary general international law is
such because it was formed and is developing further under the decisive
influence of the socialist states, the developing countries, and the other
forces of peace and socialism, and as a whole is aimed at ensuring peace
and peaceful coexistence, at the freedom and independence of peoples,
against colonialism in all of its manifestations, and at the development of
peaceful international cooperation in the interests of all peoples. Contemporary international law promotes the progress of human society, and
this progress inevitably is linked to socialism, leads to socialism, and
facilitates the struggle for socialism.

Contemporary general international law can be defined as the aggregate
of norms which are created by agreement between states of different
social systems, reflect the concordant wills of states and have a generally
democratic character, regulate relations between them in the process of
struggle and cooperation in the direction of ensuring peace and peaceful
coexistence and freedom and independence of peoples, and are secured,
when necessary, by coercion effectuated by states individually or collectively.

58. See Tunkin, *Osnovy sovremennogo mezhdunarodnogo prava*, p. 8.
59. See A. A. Piontkovskii, "O nekotorykh voprosakh sovetskoi pravovoi nauke na
sovremennom etape," *Sovetskoe gosudarstvo i pravo*, no. 2 (1964), p. 42; see also
S. N. Bratus', "Soderzhanie i forma prava," *Uchenye zapiski vsesoiuznogo nauchno-
issledovatel'skogo instituta Sovetskogo zakonodatel'stva*, XIV (1968), 38.

The Legal Nature and Essence of International Law

The changes which have taken place in international law in the post-October period give reason to speak of a new[60] contemporary international law which can be called briefly the law of peaceful coexistence and self-determination of peoples.

Some bourgeois international lawyers attempt to represent the concept of the *new international law* advanced by Soviet jurists as an appeal to cast aside existing international law and to replace it with another,[61] or assert that one could recognize contemporary international law as new only if all or the majority of its principles and norms differed fundamentally from the principles and norms of the international law which previously existed.[62] Both assertions are completely unfounded.

First, the concept of a new international law in no way calls for a repudiation of prevailing international law. Just to the contrary. According to this concept, international law has undergone such progressive substantive changes that prevailing international law should be classified as new. And since from the viewpoint of this concept this new international law basically is responsive to the requirements of contemporary international relations, the principal task is to ensure the strict observance by states of prevailing international law.

On the other hand, this concept in no way diminishes the significance of the further progressive development of international law. If contemporary international law already is not a "traditional" or "classical" international law, if it has already become an important means of ensuring peace, the independence of peoples, and the development of equal international cooperation, this naturally does not signify that such means do not need further improvement. In noting the new progressive phenomena in international law and in showing how social forces have ensured this progress, this concept facilitates finding the paths and methods for the further progressive development of international law.

Recognition of contemporary international law as new does not mean, further, that it thereby is treated as having nothing in common with the old international law. The new international law has emerged as a result of the gradual accumulation of quantitative changes which have been turned into qualitative.

It would, of course, be a simplification to believe that the new international law emerged after the Great October Socialist Revolution as

60. See R. L. Bobrov, "Velikaia Oktiabr'skaia sotsialisticheskaia revoliutsiia i mezhdunarodnoe pravo," *Pravovedenie*, no. 1 (1957), p. 87.

61. See, for example, F. Vallat, "International Law—A Forward Look," *Yearbook of World Affairs*, XVIII (1964), 248.

62. See, for example, the speech of the United States representative, F. Plimpton, in the Sixth Committee of the United Nations General Assembly. Doc. No. A/C.6/SR. 722 (XVI), December 1, 1961.

a *deus ex machina*, that the October Revolution liquidated the old international law and created a new one. The question is not one of national but of international law, whose norms are created on the basis of agreement between states. The new revolutionary international legal ideas and principles advanced by one or several states can not, consequently, change existing international law at once.

The changes which led to the transformation of the old international law into a qualitatively new one were the result of a prolonged and persistent struggle of the Soviet state, of other socialist countries, and of the new states which have emerged on the ruins of the colonial system, a result of the struggle of all progressive forces. The October Revolution was the beginning of the formative period of the new international law, and not its completion. It put forth the international legal ideas and principles which exerted and continue to exert a decisive influence upon the development of international law.

Classifying contemporary international law as new does not mean that one thereby recognizes only that which is new and casts aside everything that is old in international law. Some principles and norms of the old international law actually have been liquidated and replaced by new progressive principles and norms. Other principles and norms have remained, but have undergone more or less substantive changes. Several important principles and norms relating to new domains of international legal regulation have emerged. The general character and essence of international law has changed.

The emergence of a qualitatively new international law is a negation of the old quality. But every dialectical negation is a moment of development; there is not only a destruction of the old, but a retention in the new of the positive content of the former level of development.

As already has been pointed out, despite the significant changes in international law that have taken place since the Great October Socialist Revolution which were reflected not only in a change of its principles and norms but also in a qualitative change of the social consequences of its operation and its essence, contemporary international law needs to be further improved. This improvement of international law can be ensured only by the resolute struggle of the forces of socialism and progress against the forces of reaction and war.

The struggle goes on for the further progressive development of international law and for the enhancement of its effectiveness in order to make it a more efficacious means of ensuring peace and the development of friendly relations between states, of freedom and the independence of peoples.

There are many fields of international law in which one can expect further progressive development in the immediate future. Codification of the law of treaties has been carried out. A convention on the law of treaties was adopted at the 1968-1969 Vienna Conference which, as a whole, is a significant step forward in developing this most important branch of international law. The prerequisites have matured for settling a number of new urgent problems of the international law of the sea, particularly problems relating to the conservation of marine resources, exploitation of the wealth of the seabed, the regime of the high seas, and so forth.

The branch of international law relating to the protection of human rights is developing. An important event in this domain is the adoption by the United Nations General Assembly on December 21, 1965, of an international convention on the elimination of all forms of racial discrimination, and on December 16, 1966, of the covenants on human rights.

There are possibilities for the progressive development of a number of other branches and institutes of international law: international labor law, the law of international trade, state succession, responsibility, and air law.

With regard to questions of international law relating directly to the maintenance of international peace and ensuring the independence of peoples, that is, the fundamental questions of international law, the struggle of the two orientations in international politics is so intense that movement forward is proceeding very slowly. In this domain, however, one can note such positive phenomena as the 1963 Moscow treaty on the prohibition of nuclear tests in three spheres; the treaty on the principles of the activity of states in exploring and exploiting outer space, including the moon and other celestial objects, signed in 1967; and the treaty on the nonproliferation of nuclear weapons, signed in 1968.

As already pointed out, the raising of the question of the codification and progressive development of the basic principles of contemporary international law by the socialist and some developing countries in the United Nations has itself aroused the embittered resistance of the imperialist powers. These principles comprise the most important part of international law, and with them come the concerns of states in the major questions of foreign policy. The basic principles of contemporary international law are aimed at ensuring peace, peaceful coexistence, and the independence of peoples, and therefore the imperialist powers impede in every possible way the work concerning their further development. Despite the fact that definite positive work has been done since the adoption of the decision to work out these principles by the General Assembly in 1961, serious pressure is required on the part of all peace-loving forces to compel the imperialist forces to go forward on this question.

A serious struggle is in prospect for the further development of anticolonial provisions of international law applicable to the new situation created as a result of the breakup of the colonial system. Norms directed against methods of neocolonialism are contained in various branches of international law (basic principles, law of treaties, law of international trade, and so forth). The further development of these kinds of principles and norms will be promoted by ensuring the economic and political independence of the developing countries and their economic and social progress.

It follows from what has been said above that the struggle for the observance of the principles and norms of international law acquires special significance under contemporary conditions.

The perfecting of specific international mechanisms (international organizations, various means for the peaceful settlement of international disputes, and others), distinct from municipal mechanisms and created by taking into account the complex character of the contemporary international situation, can be an important factor for increasing the effectiveness of international law.

The decisive prerequisite for the efficacy of international law, however, is the growth of the might, organization, and activeness of all forces of the world, state and social. In the contemporary epoch, when " ... the world socialist system, the forces struggling against imperialism and for a socialist reconstruction of society, determine the main trend of the historical development,"[63] there are sufficient reasons for counting upon a serious enlargement of the role of international law in international relations.

(2) The position of bourgeois practice and doctrine on the question of changes in international law. The concept that international law has undergone a fundamental transformation was characteristic of the international legal position of the imperialist powers immediately after the end of the Second World War. Interpreting this transformation in their own way, they maintained that international law, if it had not already, then was close to rejecting the sovereignty of states, to recognizing individuals as subjects of international law, to transforming an international organization into some likeness of a superstate, and to sanctioning broad interference in the internal affairs of states. They calculated that it would

63. *Materialy XXIII s"ezda KPSS* (Moscow: Politizdat, 1966), p. 183.

be advantageous to them to direct the development of international law in this way and, with the aid of the United Nations, to use it in the struggle against the socialist countries and the national liberation movements in the colonies.

Reality, however, cruelly deceived their expectations. The formation of the world socialist system and the rapid growth of its influence in international affairs, the disintegration of the colonial system, and the emergence of dozens of new states which, as a rule, favor peace, the growth of the international revolutionary movement of the working class, and the unfolding of the people's struggle for peace frustrated the plans of the imperialists. Their predominant position in the United Nations was undermined. The development of international law did not proceed along the path of liquidating state sovereignty and of expanding the possibilities for interference in the internal affairs of other states, as the imperialist powers supposed, but instead along the path of strengthening the principles of respect for sovereignty and noninterference in internal affairs and other important principles of international law—the introduction into international law of new progressive principles directed against aggression and colonialism and toward the strengthening of peaceful coexistence of states.

Under these conditions, the imperialist states are reconsidering, or rather already have reconsidered, their attitude toward the progressive development of international law and the evaluation of the results of its development. In striving to impede the progressive development of international law, in attempting to drag it backward, they are beginning to deny the existence of substantive changes in international law during the past decades. The old international law seems to them to be significantly more suitable for the policy "from a position of strength" than the new international law, which is aimed at strengthening peaceful coexistence.

This new orientation has been manifested very precisely, in particular, in the position of the delegations of the United States and its allies during the discussion of the question of the future work of the United Nations in the field of the codification and progressive development of international law at the Sixteenth Session of the United Nations General Assembly, as well as in many other instances (law of treaties, convention on the elimination of all forms of racial discrimination, questions of sovereignty over natural resources, and so forth). In objecting to the evaluation of the results of the development of international law since the Great October Socialist Revolution given in a speech of the Soviet Representative in the Sixth Committee of the United Nations General Assembly, the American delegate actually developed the thesis that material changes have not taken place in international law during this period and that international law remains basically as it was fifty years ago.

The delegations of the Soviet Union and other socialist countries, as well as the majority of delegations of the nonsocialist countries which are not members of aggressive military blocs of the western powers, proceeded from the fact that important changes have taken place and are taking place in international law which should be reflected and formulated in undertaking the codification of the principles of peaceful coexistence, that is, the basic principles of international law. The imperialist powers and the participants in their aggressive blocs, relying upon the thesis advanced by the United States delegate, attempted to prevent the adoption of a draft resolution proposed by a number of socialist and neutral countries on the codification of the basic principles of peaceful coexistence. Seeing, however, that this proposal had the support of the overwhelming majority of delegations, and feeling the weakness and unpopularity of their position, the western powers were obliged to vote for the resolution, which provides that the General Assembly at its Seventeenth Session will consider the principles of international law concerning the development of friendly relations and cooperation among states.[64]

The predominant bourgeois doctrine of international law reflects the said policy trends of the imperialist powers. It is characterized by the nonrecognition of a number of new important principles and norms which have emerged in international law during the past half-century and a denial of a material change in international law as a whole. The tendency to regard law as the sum of technical norms, the denial of the class character of law, recognition of the evolution and the denial of the revolutionary changes, and a view of the history of law in general and of international law in particular as a single stream of development of juridical thought lead bourgeois international lawyers to recognize only more or less significant but not fundamental changes in general international law.

It is true that some bourgeois jurists believe material changes have occurred in international law and even speak of a "new international law." Naturally none of them, however, links these changes with the new epoch in the history of human society opened by the Great October Socialist Revolution. At the same time, they frequently attach exaggerated importance to secondary phenomena and frequently see material changes where such changes have not actually occurred.

64. G.A. Res. 1686 (XVI), December 18, 1961.

A. Alvarez, the well-known Chilean international lawyer, for example, remarks in his book *Le droit international nouveau* that international law "has undergone, since the middle of the nineteenth century and especially since 1939, changes which affected not merely details but also, and especially, its substantive elements, its structure, so that at the present time it is essentially different from classical international law."[65]

The cause of change in international law Alvarez sees in the change of the living conditions of peoples, in the emergence of a "new social regime"—a "regime of interdependence."[66] The old international law, says Alvarez, rested upon an individualistic regime, when the individual was regarded as something divorced from social life. Now the individual is considered to be a part of society, that is, part of a higher organization. Society has its own personal interests; it gives birth to "general interest." Law, both national and international, must be based upon this new regime, and states must have not only those rights and duties which arise from their expression of will but also those which arise from the general interest.[67]

"The *regime of social interdependence* gives birth to a new conception of international law, a *law of social interdependence.*" This "new international law," Alvarez continues, "strives not only to delimit the rights of states . . . , but also, and especially, to harmonize them, taking into account the general interest."[68]

Alvarez correctly notes the intensification of the interdependence of states caused by the expansion and deepening of international ties and the growing influence of these processes upon international law. But the development of international ties he considers one-sidedly, without taking into account the real moving forces and contradictions. He therefore pays attention only to one facet of the influence of these ties on international law, without noting that there is reflected in international law not just the growing interdependence of states but also the inevitable struggle between them, the struggle between the socialist and capitalist states, the struggle of the new states against imperialism, and the struggle of the forces of peace and socialism as a whole against the forces of reaction.

An English jurist, C. W. Jenks, appeals for the creation of a new international law, a "common law of mankind" from the common elements of national legal systems. "We must seek to develop," he writes, "from the common elements in these legal systems [having in mind the

65. A. Alvarez, *Le droit international nouveau dans ses rapports avec la vie actuelle des peuples* (Paris: Librairie Pedone, 1959), p. 409.

66. *Ibid.*, p. 313.

67. *Ibid.*, p. 314.

68. *Ibid.*, p. 606.

basic national legal systems of the modern day—*G.T.*], . . . which are still in process of evolution, a universal legal order which gives reasonable expression to our sense of right and justice."[69] As has been shown above, however, norms of international law are created differently than Jenks suggests. Jenks speaks at the same time of the profound changes that have occurred in international law during the past half-century. "The developments in the substance of the law of nations which have occurred in the first half of the twentieth century," Jenks writes, "have so transformed the character and content of the international legal system that it can no longer be satisfactorily presented within the framework of the classical exposition of international law."[70]

The basic nature of these changes, in Jenks's view, consists in the fact that they have become a "common law of mankind" in an early phase of its development. One can agree with far from all of the specific estimations of the changes which have occurred in international law as given by Jenks. In our view, for example, the assertion that contemporary international law grants rights and entrusts duties directly to individuals, together with states and other subjects of international law, is untrue.[71] But one must note his interesting descriptions of the role of international law in the modern world and his numerous proposals with a view to further improving international law.[72]

Professor W. Friedmann, of Columbia University, suggests that "many profound changes that have affected . . . international law to such an extent that it is today something very different even from what it was a generation ago."[73] The primary difference between contemporary international law and "traditional," in Friedmann's view, lies in the fact that a new important part, which he calls "co-operative international law," has emerged. The "traditional" part of contemporary international law is predicated on the conflict of national interests, whereas "co-operative international law" requires a community of these interests.[74]

While noting correctly some new phenomena in international law, in particular the expansion of its operative sphere in connection with the emergence of new states, the emergence of new branches of international

69.C. W. Jenks, *The Common Law of Mankind* (London: Stevens & Sons, 1958), p. 169.

70. *Ibid.*, p. 7.

71. *Ibid.*, p. 8.

72. Jenks, *Law in the World Community* (London: Longmans, 1967); Jenks, *A New World of Law?* (London: Longmans, 1969).

73. Friedmann, *The Changing Structure of International Law*, p. vi; Friedmann, "General Course in Public International Law," *Recueil des cours*, CXXVII (1969), 91-95.

74. *Ibid.*, p. 367.

law, of principles obliging states to cooperate with each other in the interests of peace, and so forth, Friedmann, however, passes over the most important change in international law. He does not note the emergence of such important principles as the principle of the prohibition of the use of force, the principle of self-determination of peoples and nations, the principle of peaceful coexistence, the criminality of aggressive war, and responsibility of individuals for crimes against humanity.

One must agree with Friedmann when he speaks of the increasing importance in comtemporary international law of the principles and norms regulating the cooperation of states in various fields. However, the division of international law into two parts, which he suggests, one of which would be based upon a conflict of interests, and the second, upon their community, originates in an incorrect understanding of peaceful coexistence in the West, which relates to the "cold war" period, as supposedly excluding cooperation among states. As has been demonstrated previously, peaceful coexistence includes cooperation among states. Struggle and cooperation between states in international relations and in international law, reflecting the contradiction and community of interests, exist simultaneously and mutually penetrate each other; struggle does not preclude cooperation, and cooperation permeates struggle. Therefore, the division of international law into the "law of coexistence" and "law of cooperation" proposed by Friedmann is artificial.

An American professor, Q. Wright, also speaks of the "new international law." But he limits himself to noting the emergence in international law of such new important provisions as the prohibition of aggressive war; the principle of self-determination of peoples; the principle of respect for human rights; the legal personality of international organizations.[75]

E. Giraud, a French professor, writes that there is a "radical difference" between international law as it was before the League of Nations and contemporary international law.[76] He notes in this connection only one basic change, to wit, the emergence of the principle of the prohibition of the use of force, which "represents enormous progress on the path to creating a true international legal order."[77]

L. Henkin, an American professor, also speaks very convincingly of the enormous significance of the principle of the prohibition of the use of force in international relations: "After hundreds of years," he writes,

75. Q. Wright, *The Role of International Law in the Elimination of War* (Manchester: Manchester University Press, 1961), pp. 27-29; see also C. Fenwick, "International Law: The Old and the New," *American Journal of International Law*, LX (1960), 477-483.

76. E. Giraud, "L'intérdiction du recours à la force," *Revue générale de droit international public*, XXXIV (1963), 501-544.

77. *Ibid.*, p. 511.

"nations finally agreed on a legal principle against national force in order to add the influence of law as a further deterrent to war. It would be tragic if nations allowed force to descend again to the level of national political interest as each nation saw that interest."[78]

For bourgeois international legal doctrine as a whole, however, the nonrecognition of many substantive changes and of the fundamental difference of contemporary international law from that previously existing is characteristic.

The followers of "political realism" have primacy of place in this respect. Thus, Professor H. Morgenthau, in refusing to see any substantive changes in international law, suggests that it is primitive and resembles the law which prevails in some preliterate societies, for example, the Australian aborigines or the Yurok tribe of northern California.[79] The French sociologist, R. Aron, writes that no progress has occurred in international law.[80] R. Laun, a West German professor, maintains that international law always has been recognized and is now recognized as a "right to dominate" based upon the so-called "law of the strongest."[81] Professor G. Schwarzenberger, of the University of London, the major representative of "political realism" in western European international legal doctrine, although in his work *The Inductive Approach to International Law* he takes some steps toward recognizing material changes in international law,[82] basically retains his previous position which he formulates as follows: "In the spheres that from the point of view of power, matter most, organised post-1945 world society distinguishes itself primarily from pre-1914 international society by its wider use of two-level politics or power politics in disguise."[83] Schwarzenberger does not deny the emergence of many new important principles in international law, such as, for example, the principle of the prohibition of aggressive war, the principle of the prohibition of the use of force in international relations, and so forth, but he unjustifiably suggests that these new principles and norms are not universal, that they are not binding upon all states, and

78. L. Henkin, "International Law and the Behavior of Nations," *Recueil des cours*, CXIV (1965), 276.

79. H. Morgenthau, *Politics Among Nations*, 3d ed. (New York: Alfred A. Knopf, 1960), p. 278.

80. R. Aron, *Paix et guerre entre les nations*, 3d rev. ed. (Paris: Calmann-Levy, 1962), p. 717.

81. R. Laun, "Le droit des peuples à disposer d'eux-mêmes," *Annuaire des Anciens Auditeurs de l'Académie de droit international de la Haye*, XXVIII (1958), 99.

82. Schwarzenberger, *The Inductive Approach to International Law*, p. 185; Schwarzenberger, *International Law and Order* (London: Stevens & Sons, 1971), p. 19.

83. Schwarzenberger, *The Inductive Approach to International Law*, p. 188.

therefore they have not changed general international law, although they have narrowed the sphere of its actual application.

The majority of other bourgeois international lawyers also tend to deny, although less clearly so, the fundamental changes in international law. Thus, in the opinion of the well-known Belgian professor, C. de Visscher, the major change in international law lies in the fact that the United Nations Charter attaches great importance to respect for human rights, which, in his view, are the basis of the "international order."[84] But at the same time, de Visscher notes that the "human rights so frequently mentioned in the United Nations Charter, have a place there which is at once eminent and ill-defined."[85] De Visscher does not attach great importance to the emergence in international law of such an important principle as the principle of the prohibition of the use of force,[86] and he decisively rejects the existence of the principle of self-determination of peoples.[87]

The well-known English international lawyer, G. Fitzmaurice, entitled one paragraph of his interesting report submitted to the jubilee session of the Institute of International Law at Rome in 1973 as follows: "Traditional International Law Continues to Remain the Basis for the Future."[88] The author acknowledges the existence in international law of such important principles as nonuse of force, the invalidity of international treaties imposed by force, the prohibition of crimes against humanity, the invalidity of treaties contrary to *jus cogens*, the principle of respect for human rights, and the principle of cooperation,[89] but he does not consider them to be "new" principles, suggesting that this denotes only the triumph of "natural law" principles over a positivist approach. As a whole, Fitzmaurice's concept comes down to the fact that modern international law is still good enough, but only because "traditional international law" in its natural law interpretation continues to remain its basis.

The most authoritative bourgeois treatises which have appeared in recent years, the authors of which are proponents of various orientations in bourgeois international legal doctrine, go in the same direction. In them, as has been previously mentioned in part, we sometimes find a general denial of any basic changes in international law, more frequently a

84. Visscher, *Théories et réalites en droit international public*, pp. 158-162.

85. *Ibid.*, p. 162.

86. *Ibid.*, p. 359.

87. *Ibid.*, p. 166.

88. G. Fitzmaurice, *The Future of Public International Law and of the International Legal System in the Circumstances of Today* (Geneva: Institut de droit international, 1973), para. 19.

89. *Ibid.*, paras. 109-112.

recognition of only some of them, but never do we see an evaluation of contemporary international law as a qualitatively new international law.

Thus, Professor A. Verdross regards the principle of self-determination of peoples as one of the important principles of contemporary international law,[90] and he notes the importance of the principle of the prohibition of aggressive war, although he suggests that reprisals with the use of armed force are permitted by general international law.[91] The emergence of a new international law, however, he sees in the "law of an organized international society," which in general Verdross considers to be different from contemporary general international law.[92]

P. Reuter, a French professor, sees the primary change in international law in the emergence of certain features of international society based upon a community of interests. From the viewpoint of the structure of international society, the basic element, in Reuter's view, lies in the development of international organization, in consequence of which "the latter has been transformed from an unorganized international society into a partially organized one."[93] In emphasizing, however, that the organization of international society is of an "exceedingly superficial character," Reuter comes to the conclusion that in general, despite certain changes, the fundamentals of international law as a whole remain as before.[94]

There is nothing in the treatise of the Italian professor, R. Quadri, about new principles of international law. Quadri denies the existence of the principle of the prohibition of the use of force in contemporary international law. Believing that the principles of the United Nations Charter are provisions of a "special legal order," he maintains that "the right of a state to wage war" is a norm of general international law at the present time.[95]

In his "General Course on Public International Law," an English professor, H. Waldock, while recognizing that significant changes have taken place in international law, among which he includes the prohibition of aggressive war, a partial prohibition of the use of force in general, as well as the international responsibility of individuals for crimes against

90. Verdross, *Völkerrecht*, 5th ed. (Vienna: Springer Verlag, 1964), p. 576.

91. *Ibid.*, p. 426.

92. *Ibid.*, p. 661.

93. P. Reuter, "Principes de droit international public," *Recueil des cours*, CIII (1961), 457.

94. *Ibid.*, pp. 457-458.

95. R. Quadri, *Diritto internazionale publico*, 4th ed. (Palermo: G. Priulla Editore, 1963), p. 23; see also R. Monaco, *Manuale di diritto internazionale publico* (Torino: UTET, 1960), pp. 414-425; A. Sereni, *Diritto internazionale* (Milan: Dott. A. Giuffre, 1956), I, 68.

humanity,[96] at the same time passes over the other important new principles of international law in silence.

We find virtually a complete denial of substantive changes in international law in the three-volume treatise of the Argentine professor, L. M. Moreno Quintana. He speaks, for example, of the 1928 Pact of Paris, in which the parties renounced resort to war for the settlement of international disputes, but he does not mention at all the fact that this international treaty was an important landmark in formulating the very important generally recognized principle of international law prohibiting aggressive war. Moreno Quintana only notes pessimistically that the "absence of sanctions for those who violate this pact deprived the document of any effectiveness." He denies the existence in contemporary international law of norms providing for the criminal responsibility of individuals for crimes against humanity, calling the Nuremberg and Tokyo trials of the major war criminals precedents "deserving regret."[97]

A Peruvian professor, A. Ulloa, although he notes the importance of the United Nations Charter and other international treaties for the progressive development of international law in his two-volume treatise on international law,[98] believes at the same time that its basic principles have not changed. "The basic principles of international law," he says, "survived the war."[99] Ulloa in essence denies the existence of the principle of the prohibition of the use of force in contemporary international law.[100] He recognizes the existence of the principle of self-determination of peoples and emphasizes its significance, but he sees nothing new in comparison with the "principle of nationality."[101]

A West German professor, F. Berber, recognizes that the prohibition of the use of force in relations between states is not an actual generally recognized norm of international law.[102] He emphasizes that the emergence of the principle of aggressive war as a result of the conclusion of the Briand-Kellogg Pact was a genuine "revolution" in international law.[103]

96. H. Waldock, "General Course on Public International Law," *Recueil des cours*, CVI (1962), 230, 236-237.

97. L. M. Moreno Quintana, *Tratado de derecho internacional* (Buenos Aires: Editorial sudamericana, 1963), II, 401.

98. A. Ulloa, *Derecho internacional publico*, 4th ed. (Madrid: Ediciones iberoamericanas, 1957), I, 82.

99. *Ibid.*, p. 79.

100. *Ibid.*, pp. 283-284.

101. *Ibid.*, pp. 130-152.

102. F. Berber, *Lehrbuch des Völkerrechts* (Munich-Berlin: C. H. Beck'sche Verlagsbuchhandlung, 1962), II, 38.

103. *Ibid.*, p. 36.

At the same time, Berber resolutely refuses to recognize the existence in international law of the responsibility of individuals for crimes against peace and, to a certain extent, for crimes against humanity. He maintains that the Nuremberg International Military Tribunal could judge the Nazi leaders only for war crimes and partially for crimes against humanity, but he denies the legality of the provisions of the Statute and the Judgment of the Tribunal with respect to crimes against peace.[104] This type of crime, Berber declares, "international law did not know before 1945 and does not know at the present time."[105] Berber goes farther, asserting that if the principle of responsibility for crimes against peace had become a norm of general international law, then "this was not a step forward in international law" and "was not a constructive contribution to the cause of averting war" supposedly because the rulers of every belligerent state would play to win the war in order to avoid being put in the dock, and this would only lead to a prolongation of wars.[106]

Berber denies the existence in contemporary international law of the principle of the self-determination of peoples, as well as the emergence of other new important principles.[107]

The general conclusion is that, despite the existence of certain progressive tendencies, bourgeois international legal science as a whole has lagged behind the development of events and does not reflect many substantive changes which have taken place and are taking place in international law during recent decades, not to mention the fact that it does not notice the profound transformation of the general character and essence of international law.

D. The Question of an "Intermediate Status" Between War and Peace

The numerous conflicts created by imperialists in various parts of the globe (the Anglo-French-Israeli aggression against Egypt in 1956, the American aggression in Vietnam which already has lasted several years, Israeli aggression against the Arab states, and so forth), as well as the tense state of international relations conditioned by the policy "from a position of strength," the arms race, and the creation of military blocs and military bases directed against the socialist and other peaceloving states, have served as the basis for proposals to reform contemporary international law

104. *Ibid.*, pp. 254-257.
105. *Ibid.*, p. 257.
106. *Ibid.*, pp. 262-263.
107. *Ibid.*, I, 75ff.

by introducing into it a third, so-called "intermediate status" between peace and war.

Professor P. Jessup, having set forth the concept of an "intermediate status" in greatest detail, defines its basic features as follows:[108]

(a) Hostility and strain exist in relations among states. Recalling the practice of the Turkish Empire prior to the middle of the eighteenth century not to make treaties of peace with Christian states, but only armistices because the Koran forbade peace treaties with infidels, Jessup suggests this practice is one of the elements of the "intermediate status";

(b) The issues between the parties are so fundamental and deep-rooted that no solution of a single question could terminate them;

(c) At the same time, the parties have no intention or, at least, decision to resort to war in order to solve the disputed questions.

Jessup proposes to legitimize this state, inserting it between "peace" and "war." He says in this connection that international law should not be divorced from reality and that it should be brought into conformity with the real international situation.

First, what status does it have under prevailing international law? The answer to this question must be definite and categorical: contemporary international law knows no "intermediate status."

International tension is not a normal state from the standpoint of international law. The "cold war" policy which caused this condition contravenes international law and is linked to serious violations of it. This policy creates no juridical status whatever that could be sanctioned by contemporary international law.[109]

Somewhat distinct from the concept of an "intermediate status" but close to it is the concept of a "status mixtus." Proponents of this concept maintain that there is no precise delimitation between peace and war and that an "intermediate" or "mixed" status exists which is characterized by the fact that one observes the use of armed force by some states against others side by side with peaceful relations.

An English professor, G. Schwarzenberger, wrote during the Second World War that international practice supposedly created legal norms which related neither to the law of peace nor the law of war, but represent a *status mixtus*. "The doctrine of war as a status and objective phenomenon," he says, "breaks down over the reality of the *status mixtus*. This status is not separated from those of peace and war by any objective

---

108. P. Jessup, "Should International Law Recognize an Intermediate Status between Peace and War," *American Journal of International Law*, XLVIII (1954), 100-102.

109. Professor Verdross says that it is impossible to prove the existence of special legal norms corresponding to "cold war." See Verdross, *Mezhdunarodnoe pravo*, pp. 111-112.

tests. States contend by power in peace and war. In the state of peace, they are limited to the use of economic and political power. In the *status mixtus*, they supplement these forms of power by the use of military power. In the state of war, they use all available forms of power. It betrays an over-estimation of the difference between political and economic power as compared with military power, to imagine that, within a system of power politics, there is any qualitative difference between the states of peace and war."[110]

In his review of the French edition of *Voprosy teorii mezhdunarodnogo prava*,[111] Professor Schwarzenberger insists that in his 1943 article and at the present time he had and has in view the "lack of any objective distinction between states of peace and war in an *unorganized* international society, *i.e.*, primarily under international customary law," and that the situation has changed "in contemporary international law under the Charter of the United Nations . . . "[112]

One can only welcome this remark of Professor Schwarzenberger. If, however, his position on this question were to be wholly clear, one must bear in mind that according to Schwarzenberger's theory, two international laws exist at the present time: general, or universal, international law, which is customary law, and the law of the United Nations, which is not general international law. It is true that in his recent works Schwarzenberger calls the principles of the United Nations Charter "near-universal" law.[113]

But general international law continues to exist side by side with the principles of the United Nations Charter according to Schwarzenberger's theory, and all the changes which have occurred in international law during the past fifty years have not affected it; the "right of a state to wage war," the "right of the victor," "de bellatio," and so forth, exist in it as formerly.[114]

It is true that since Schwarzenberger recognizes that principles of the United Nations Charter have become virtually universal, then according to his conception the operative sphere of these old norms is very limited.

An Argentine professor, L. M. Quintana, in identifying himself with Schwarzenberger's concept as regards the "status mixtus," suggests for his

---

110. Schwarzenberger, "Jus pacis ac belli?" *American Journal of International Law*, XXXVII (1943), 474.

111. Tunkin, *Droit international public: problèmes théoriques* (Paris: Editions A. Pedone, 1965).

112. *Yearbook of World Affairs*, XX (1966), 293.

113. See Schwarzenberger, *The Inductive Approach to International Law*, p. 112.

114. Schwarzenberger, *International Law as Applied by International Courts and Tribunals: The Law of Armed Conflict* (London: Stevens & Sons, 1968), II, 54, 63.

part that it should be called a neutral state (*estado neutro*) in which "there is neither war nor peace" (*no hay ni guerra ni paz*).[115]

Schwarzenberger's assertion that there is no precise boundary between peace and war under international law could find some basis in international law before the Great October Socialist Revolution, which recognized the "right of a state to wage war." The old international law permitted not only war, but also armed reprisals and the so-called pacific blockade, which were not regarded as war.

Even after the prohibition of aggressive war pursuant to the 1928 Pact, there remained the loophole of justifying war by pretending it was something else, to which the imperialist powers frequently also resorted. It is well-known that the colonizers preferred to call the wars they waged for the purpose of enslaving colonial peoples "police actions," "reprisals," "armed conflict," and so forth, and thereby to show that such actions do not fall within the effect of the Pact of Paris.

The situation changes with the adoption of the United Nations Charter, which prohibits not only aggressive war, but also the use or threat of force against the territorial integrity and political independence of any state or by any other means inconsistent with the purposes of the United Nations. As already has been pointed out, these norms at the present time are norms of general international law. The use of force contravening the provisions of the United Nations Charter is not only a violation of the Charter, but also of general international law.

One must agree with Professor Lachs, who writes: "International law does not know nor recognize any intermediate status between war and peace. The precise delimitation of these two institutes was recognized long ago, when war still was a legal means of settling international conflicts. The emergence of this dividing line is justified even more at the present time, when aggressive war has been prohibited, when this line must represent the border between law and no law. The obliteration of this border not only is without legal justification, but it plays into the hands of those for whom the prohibition of an annexationist war is politically disadvantageous."[116]

There is still the third variant of the theory of the "intermediate status" advanced by an American professor, M. S. McDougal. McDougal believes that there exists in international law not one "intermediate status," but a countless number of such states. "Between the polar extremes, that is, between the lowest and the highest level of coercion," he says, "there

115. L. M. Moreno Quintana, "El Tercer Estado del derecho internacional," *Bibliotheca Grotiana* (Munich, 1954), II, 39.

116. M. Lachs, *Zhenevskie soglasheniia 1954 goda ob Indo-Kitae* (Moscow: izd-vo IL, 1955), p. 180.

exist not one intermediate stage, but a countless number of stages, and in using the concept 'war' and 'peace' and other concepts the decision-maker has not two or three, but a large number of positions to which he may refer."[117]

It is correct, of course, that norms of international law juridically tolerate various concrete situations within certain limits. As any legal norms, they presuppose a certain possibility of freedom of action within the limits of these norms. But the diversity of concrete relations between states by no means signifies that every such specific legal state is reflected in general international law as some special status.

McDougal's assertion that there are a countless number of intermediate stages between peace and war among which there is no precise boundary does not correspond to contemporary international law.

We now regard the suggestion of an "intermediate status" *de lege feranda*. It follows from the aforecited statements of Jessup that he only is suggesting that an "intermediate status" be established, and he does not maintain that it is provided for by prevailing international law.

International law, of course, can not be divorced from reality, but this in no way means that it must juridically legitimize any practice of particular states in international relations. That is why it is important to explain toward what practice the proposal of an "intermediate status" is oriented, perhaps, besides, irrespective of the subjective wishes and intentions of the authors and advocates of this proposal.

The proposal to introduce an "intermediate status" into international law is aimed essentially at legitimizing the tension in international relations, the distrust among states which has existed since the Second World War, and to legitimize the policy "from a position of strength," the state of "cold war," and even (in its extreme variants) armed aggression.

It is possible that some proponents of the "intermediate status" sincerely believe in the advisability of introducing this new juridical state into international law because it is much better than war. But the state of international tension is fraught with events which could lead to war. "In addition to the moral necessity of peace," stated the Prime Minister of India, Nehru, at the 1960 session of the United Nations General Assembly, "every practical consideration also leads us to this conclusion because, as everyone knows, one must make a choice now, in our atomic age, between the complete destruction and perishing of civilization, on one hand, or some form of peaceful coexistence between countries, on the other. There is no middle path."[118]

117. M. S. McDougal, "Peace and War: Factual Continuum with Multiple Legal Consequences," *American Journal of International Law*, XLIX (1955), 67.

118. "Za mirnoe sotrudnichestvo vsekh stran," *Pravda*, October 6, 1960, p. 3.

The initiators and organizers of the "cold war" themselves have pointed to the danger. The former United States Secretary of State, John Foster Dulles, said: "There is today what is called a "cold" war. There is a struggle going on which is worldwide in scope. The danger constantly exists that that struggle could break from the so-called cold war into a hot war."[119]

The sanctioning of an "intermediate status" by international law would mean a step backward in the development of international law. It would be essentially substituting a state of "cold war," a state which also would legalize many instances of armed aggression, for peaceful coexistence.

The proposal to introduce an "intermediate status" does not correspond to the societal laws of the development of contemporary international law. Under the influence of the growing forces of peace and progress, international law has a tendency to move forward, and not backward; it is becoming a more and more improved and effective means of developing and strengthening peaceful coexistence.

119. J. F. Dulles, "Tasks and Responsibilities of the Foreign Service," *Department of State Bulletin*, XXXIV (1956), 588.

Part IV *International Law, Foreign Policy, and Diplomacy*

The co-relationship of international law, foreign policy, and diplomacy has three aspects: the influence of foreign policy upon the development of international law; the converse influence of international law upon the foreign policy of a state; and the use of international law by states as a support for foreign policy.

Chapter 10 *The Influence of Foreign Policy and Diplomacy Upon the Development of International Law*

Norms of international law are created in the process of relations among states as a result of a clearly expressed or tacit agreement among them. In this process each state defends specific principles and has its own international legal position, which may coincide with or be different from the positions of other states. The position of a state on questions of international law is a part of its foreign policy position. Norms of international law regulate relations between states and affect the interests of a state, so it is natural that the international legal position of each state is derived from those principles upon which the foreign policy of the particular state is based in general and pursues the same goals as the foreign policy as a whole.

In the process of creating new or of changing prevailing norms of international law, each state strives to have the principles of its foreign policy reflected and secured as fully as possible in norms of international law. That is to say, each state strives to have its position reflected as fully as possible in norms of international law which are in the course of being elaborated.

Although not the only means, diplomacy is the most important means of effectuating foreign policy. It may be defined as activity (including the content, modes, and methods of the activity of general and special state agencies of foreign relations) of heads of states, of governments, of departments of foreign affairs, of special delegations and missions, and of diplomatic representations appertaining to the effectuation by peaceful means of the purposes and tasks of the foreign policy of a state.[1]

One would not err in saying that diplomacy plays the primary role in the process of creating norms of international law. This proposition

1. See D. B. Levin, *Diplomatiia* (Moscow: Sotsekgiz, 1962), pp. 14-15.

applies to the formation of international legal norms by either conventional or customary means.

The process of forming norms of international law by means of treaty, irrespective of what questions a specific treaty touches upon, is essentially and on the whole a diplomatic process. It commences with negotiations between states, discussions at conferences and in organs of international organizations, and so forth. In the broadest sense of the word, all of this is negotiation, although in each instance the form may be different. This initial stage of the process of concluding an international treaty is the most important and decisive. The content and form of agreements between states are formed precisely at this stage; that is to say, a concordance of the wills of states occurs with regard to the normative content of the treaty.

Negotiations concerning the conclusion of an international treaty, as well as those appertaining to other questions, in whatever form they are conducted, themselves represent the diplomatic process. They occupy such a large place in diplomacy that the latter frequently is defined narrowly as "the art of conducting negotiations and concluding treaties between states."[2]

W. Garden wrote in his voluminous treatise on diplomacy that: "Diplomacy in the broadest sense of the word is the science or the art of negotiations."[3] "Diplomacy," says C. Calvo, "is the science concerning the relations which exist between various states . . . " or "simply the art of negotiations."[4] In his well-known book *Diplomacy*, H. Nicholson takes as the point of departure for his investigation of questions of diplomacy the definition given in the *Oxford Dictionary of the English Language*, which says: "Diplomacy—the conduct of international relations by means of negotiations; a method with whose aid these relations are regulated and conducted by ambassadors and envoys; the work or art of a diplomat."[5]

The positions of different states, their wills, are brought into concordance, usually by means of mutual concessions, precisely during the course of negotiations concerning the conclusion of an international treaty and in the process of diplomatic activity connected with such negotiations. These concordant wills are reflected in the norms of the international treaty.

2. *Bol'shaia Sovetskaia Entsiklopediia*, 2d ed. (Moscow: Gos. nauchnoe izd-vo "Bol'shaia sovetskaia entsiklopediia," 1949-1958), XIV, 405.

3. [W. Garden], *Traité complet de diplomatie, ou théorie générale des relations exterieures des puissances de l'Europe* (Paris: Librairie de Treuthel et Wurtz, 1833), I, 1-2.

4. C. Calvo, *Dictionnaire de droit international public et privé* (Berlin: Imp. G. Bernstein, 1885), I, 250.

5. H. Nicholson, *Diplomatiia* (Moscow: OGIZ Gospolitizdat, 1941), p. 20.

The subsequent stages of the process of concluding an international treaty (signature, ratification, exchange or deposit of instruments of ratification, and others) also are linked to a significant degree with diplomatic activity.

Customary norms of international law grow out of the practice of relations between states and of the foreign policy actions of states. Since diplomacy occupies the primary place in the foreign policy activity of a state, it is natural that customary norms of international law are formed to a significant extent in the process of diplomatic activity.

The role of foreign policy and diplomacy is even more significant in the final stage of the process of creating a customary norm of international law. Recognition by states of existing practice as a norm of international law occurs, as a rule, by means of conclusive actions and, consequently, first and foremost of foreign policy, especially diplomatic, actions.

At the same time, it must be noted that diplomacy is not the only means of the foreign policy of states. At present, the framework of relations between states has been expanded significantly in comparison with the nineteenth and beginning of the twentieth century. These relations embrace such new domains as scientific and technical cooperation, cooperation in industry and social security, cultural cooperation, and so forth.[6] At the same time, if the domain of foreign policy and the domain of diplomacy previously coincided during peace time, foreign policy now includes many questions which go beyond the bounds of diplomacy.

The extent to which the foreign policy and diplomacy of a specific state influence the development of international law depends upon a number of circumstances.

Norms of international law formed in the process of the struggle and cooperation of states are the result of a clash of different foreign policy aspirations, of the clash and the concordance of the wills of different states. Sovereign states are involved in the process of forming norms. The wills of states which clash during the creation of norms of international law juridically are of equal significance. But, of course, the actual influence of such wills is not identical.

The actual situation is such that in international relations in general and in the creation of norms of international law in particular the great powers play a special role. On the juridical plane, the principles of respect for state sovereignty and of the equality of states, which are an important means of defending the independence of weak states from the encroachments of strong powers, ensure at the same time a special role for the great powers in the process of creating norms of international law.

6. For greater detail, see Levin, *Diplomatiia*, p. 26ff.

International Law, Foreign Policy, and Diplomacy

A new international legal norm may not, by virtue of the sovereign equality of states, be imposed upon any one state. Consequently, it also may not be imposed upon a great power. Therefore norms which are not recognized by the great powers, or even some of the great powers, would not bind them. This means that the operative domain of such norms would be so limited that one could not say such norms had real importance. This circumstance has special significance in those instances when one speaks of norms relating directly to the maintenance of international peace and security, since the real means of ensuring peace and, at the same time, the instruments of war, are first and foremost in the hands of the great powers. Therefore, practice frequently takes the course of a preliminary agreement on questions among the great powers, since the absence of agreement among them renders useless, and sometimes even harmful, the adoption of decisions concerning international problems of a general order.

The influence of a state's foreign policy and diplomacy upon the development of international law depends primarily upon the character of foreign policy and diplomacy and the character of international legal principles which this state adduces and advocates.

The general line of the development of international law is determined by the laws of societal development. A state which advances international legal principles not corresponding to these laws of societal development and, consequently, to a general line of international legal development which is inconsistent with the expectations of peoples, can not be expected to exert substantial influence upon the development of international law.

The intrinsic weakness of the foreign policy and diplomacy of imperialist states in the process of developing international law springs from the fact that, in representing a social system which is becoming obsolete, they set themselves against the progressive development of international law and attempt to drag international law backward. "For imperialist states," says the Program of the CPSU, "diplomacy was and remains an instrument for imposing their will upon other peoples and an instrument for the preparation of wars."[7]

In carrying out the policy "from a position of strength," imperialist powers, for example, attempt to prove that the use of force by one state against another is admissible under contemporary international law at least "to protect the life and property of its citizens,"[8] or under other

7. *Programma Kommunisticheskoi partii Sovetskogo Soiuza* (Moscow: Politizdat, 1964), p. 56.

8. Thus, for example, the United States government referred to the need to "protect the lives of American citizens" in order to justify armed intervention in the

pretexts. The purpose is to justify the acts of aggression which are committed systematically by imperialist states even after the adoption of the United Nations Charter. However, there exists in contemporary international law a generally-recognized principle which prohibits the use of force and even the threat of force by a state against the territorial integrity and political inviolability of another state or by any means incompatible with the purposes of the United Nations. Undoubtedly, such efforts to justify aggression and to drag international law backward are doomed to failure.

Other examples of such reactionary tendencies are the support for colonialism by proponents of the policy "from a position of strength," the attempts to deny the principle of self-determination of peoples as a principle of contemporary international law, as well as efforts to transform this principle into an empty shell. But life condemns to failure the foreign policy and diplomacy of states which support such tendencies. Despite their vain attempts, the principle of self-determination of peoples is being strengthened and implemented.

The policy "from a position of strength" also has sustained a defeat in many other areas of international law. Thus, at the First Conference on the Law of the Sea in 1958 proponents of this policy failed in their efforts to impose a three-mile breadth of territorial waters on other states as a norm of international law. At the Second Conference on the Law of the Sea in 1960, even though the United States used every means of pressure to their fullest upon the small states, the proponents of the policy "from a position of strength" again failed to effectuate their proposal, this time for a six-mile breadth of territorial waters.

The policy of imposing norms of international law with the aid of economic and political pressure, threats, and bribery—an integral part of the policy "from a position of strength"—suffered one failure after another.

As the influence of the policy "from a position of strength" upon the development of international law weakened, the influence of the foreign policy of states of the socialist camp at the same time increased. The foreign policy and diplomacy of socialist states is armed with the theory of Marxism-Leninism and a knowledge of the laws of societal development. Proceeding on the basis of a new and higher social system replacing capitalism, they adduce and defend progressive international legal principles which correspond to the laws of societal development and which are aimed at ensuring peace and friendly cooperation between states and the free development of peoples.

Dominican Republic in 1965. See R.-J. Dupuy, "Les États Unis, l'O.E.A. et l'O.N.U. a Saint-Domingue," *Annuaire français de droit international*, XI (1965), 75-76.

The most important element of the influence of the foreign policy and diplomacy of the Soviet state, and later of the other socialist countries, upon the development of international law was and is the support of their international legal positions by the working class and by the broad popular masses of other countries. This is the result of the internationalization of the foreign policy of a socialist state, which is reflected in the fact that, objectively, its basic state interests, excluding any elements of the exploitation of other peoples, are in harmony with the fundamental interests of the peoples of other countries.

That is why the foreign policy and diplomacy of the Soviet Union and the other socialist countries were a basic factor in those progressive changes which have occurred in international law during the period of the coexistence of states of two opposed social systems, and their influence upon the development of international law continues to grow steadily. "The foreign policy of the socialist state," says the Program of the CPSU, "at the basis of which lie the principles of peace, equality, self-determination of peoples, respect for the independence and sovereignty of all countries, as well as the honorable, humane methods of socialist diplomacy, are exerting a growing influence upon the world situation."[9]

The independent states of Asia, Africa, and Latin America, in supporting the principles of peaceful coexistence in their foreign policy, are exerting an ever greater influence upon the development of international law. The international legal position of these states and the socialist countries regarding basic questions of international law in the majority of instances either coincide or are very close.

The development of contemporary international law is taking place under the ever growing influence of the foreign policy and diplomacy of states of the socialist camp and of other states standing on the platform of peaceful coexistence.

9. *Programma Kommunisticheskoi partii Sovetskogo Soiuza*, p. 56.

Chapter 11 *The Influence of International Law on Foreign Policy and Diplomacy*

International law, just as national law, influences the social relationships which it regulates. This authority is exercised by means of normative influence upon the conduct of subjects of international law.

The principles and norms of international law determine the rights and duties of states and of other subjects of international law. Hence, there are two types of links among foreign policy, diplomacy, and international law: (a) as concerns the obligations of states, international law acts as a limitation with regard to foreign policy and diplomacy; (b) as concerns rights, it, on the contrary, acts as a means of or support for foreign policy and diplomacy.[1]

It must be mentioned, however, that this contrast is not absolute. There is an element of limitation not only in a legal duty, but also in a subjective right, since every right is a limited right.

The general character of the influence of international law on relations between states and, consequently, on the foreign policy of individual states and their diplomacy, is determined by the character of a given specific international law which, as any law, may promote or impede the progressive development of society. Of course, law, including international law, can not stop the process of societal development, and if law sharply contravenes the laws of societal development, it inevitably yields to these objective laws. Then new norms come to replace the obsolete norms.

Contemporary international law is the law of peaceful coexistence and of the free development of peoples. The character of the influence of

1. Professor M. Virally expressed this proposition vividly in the following words: "Depending upon what it is used for [law—G.T.], a subject of law sees the system of law either as directed against it or as being at its service." M. Virally, "Le phénomene juridique," *Revue du droit public et de la science politique en France et à l'etranger*, LXXXII (1966), 11.

contemporary international law on the international relations, foreign policy, and diplomacy of states for the purpose of ensuring the peaceful coexistence and freedom of peoples is also determined by this.

How effective is the influence of international law on the foreign policy and diplomacy of states?

We already have considered the theory that contemporary international law is "ineffectual" and "primitive," and "true" international law will be possible only if a world state, or something closely approximating this, is created (see Chapter 9). An exaggeration of the role of compulsory jurisdiction, which frequently is portrayed as a panacea for all international ills, in particular has been linked with this conception.[2]

The possibility of applying state coercion in order to ensure the observance of norms is one of the important distinctive features of law, including international law. It is common knowledge, however, that coercion in international law, by virtue of the peculiarities of this law, is less effective than coercion in national law. But it should be borne in mind that the real influence of a legal norm on the conduct of subjects of law is not determined only by the possibility of coercion.

The influence of international law on the foreign policy of states also depends to a significant degree upon the moral authority of norms of international law, this being determined primarily by the extent to which such norms correspond to the innermost desires of the peoples to ensure peace.

In general, the effectiveness of the influence of contemporary international law on the foreign policy of states is determined by the co-relation of the forces of peace and war in the international arena. Since international law as a whole aims to ensure peace and peaceful coexistence, the forces which are supporting peace are, at the same time, the forces supporting international law. Therefore, the effectiveness of the influence of international law upon the conduct of subjects of law depends primarily upon the might and the activeness of all the forces of peace.

In this respect it is very important to have definite criteria which would show the real attitude of a state toward international law in order to have a more accurate idea of the positions of states on this question. The co-relation between the principles of a state's foreign policy and the principles of contemporary international law is such a criterion.

The foreign policy of a state is connected closely with its domestic policy, as though it were a continuation thereof. The general foreign policy line of a state is determined primarily by the bases of its social

2. See G. I. Tunkin, *Ideologicheskaia bor'ba i mezhdunarodnoe pravo* (Moscow: izd-vo Mezhdunarodnye otnosheniia, 1967), pp. 158-166.

system, of the class nature of the state. "The nature of a socialist system," writes Academician V. M. Khvostov, "is the opposite of the nature of capitalism. Hence the contrast of the foreign policy of socialism with the policy of imperialism; hence, also the struggle of the two lines in international politics which has been waged in the world arena already for half a century."[3] At the same time, a state formulates its foreign policy by taking into account the changing domestic and international situation.

From the viewpoint of foreign policy, all states of the world may be broken down at the present time into three groups: (1) socialist states; (2) states which are participants in the military blocs of the western powers; (3) new states which arose from the ruins of the colonial system. What is the co-relation of the principles of foreign policy of states from each group with the principles of contemporary international law?

Contemporary general international law aims at ensuring the peaceful coexistence of all states, primarily the states of two opposed social systems, and at ensuring the free development of peoples.

The struggle for the peaceful coexistence of states with different social systems and the struggle for the freedom and independence of peoples are immutable characteristics of the foreign policy of the Soviet state as a genuinely socialist foreign policy. The same applies to the foreign policy of other states of the socialist commonwealth.

"The Communist and Workers' parties participating in the present meeting," says the 1957 Declaration of the Meeting of Representatives of Communist and Workers' Parties of the Socialist Countries, "declare that the Leninist principle of peaceful coexistence of the two systems, having been developed further in contemporary conditions in the decisions of the Twentieth Congress of the CPSU, is a firm basis of the foreign policy of the socialist countries and a dependable basis for peace and friendship between peoples."[4] "The countries of socialism," said the 1960 Statement of the Meeting of Representatives of Communist and Workers' Parties, "are sincere and faithful friends of peoples who are struggling to be liberated or who already have been liberated from the imperialist yoke and oppression."[5]

The Twenty-fourth Congress of the Communist Party of the Soviet Union again confirmed the immutability of these two important orientations of Soviet foreign policy. In its resolution on the report of the

3. V. Khvostov, "Sovetskaia vneshniaia politika i ee vozdeistvie na khod istorii," *Kommunist*, no. 10 (1967), p. 81.

4. *Dokumenty Soveshchaniia predstavitelei kommunisticheskikh i rabochikh partii* (Moscow: Gospolitizdat, 1957), p. 10.

5. *Dokumenty Soveshchaniia predstavitelei kommunisticheskikh i rabochikh partii* (Moscow: Gospolitizdat, 1960), p. 38.

Central Committee of the CPSU, the Congress charged the Central Committee "henceforth consistently to implement the principle of peaceful coexistence, to expand mutually advantageous links with capitalist countries." The Congress noted that the "CPSU is unfailingly loyal to the Leninist principle of solidarity with peoples struggling for national and social liberation. Just as before, the fighters against the remaining colonial regimes can count upon the full support of our side."[6]

In accordance with the policy of peaceful coexistence that they are pursuing, socialist states consistently favor observance of the principles and norms of international law. This policy has been affirmed in numerous bilateral and multilateral documents, in practical proposals which the socialist states have made in international organizations and at conferences, and in all of the international actions of these states.

Thus, there are no contradictions between the principles of foreign policy of the socialist states and contemporary international law. The tendency to violate international law is not, therefore, characteristic of the foreign policy of socialist states. On the contrary, states of the socialist commonwealth act as a basic bulwark of contemporary international law.

The new states which have emerged as a result of the liberation of colonies are confronted with enormous problems of developing their economy, of raising the living standard and culture of their peoples, and of strengthening their political and economic independence. Therefore, those new states which are in a position to pursue an independent foreign policy orient it toward peaceful coexistence, the struggle against colonialism and neocolonialism, and the development of equal, mutually advantageous international economic and cultural relations.

Consequently, there also is in this case no contradiction between the foreign policy orientation of states and the principles of contemporary international law. Of course, we have in mind prevailing international law and not the law of the past or the so-called "classical" international law against which certain representatives of the developing countries aim their arrows, mistakenly accepting, under the influence of western international legal doctrine, this "classical" international law for prevailing international law.

The policy pursued at the present time by a group of countries which includes the imperialist powers and their allies in aggressive military blocs is known as the policy "from a position of strength." This policy relies upon force, upon armed force; the arms race, the organization of aggressive military blocs and military bases, war propaganda, and the maintenance of international tension are an integral part of it. Being

6. *Materialy XXIV s"ezda KPSS* (Moscow: Politizdat, 1971), pp. 194, 196.

screened by preposterous references to a military threat on the part of the Soviet Union, it in fact expressly reflects the interests of the largest monopolies which make a fortune on the arms race and are prepared to use armed force in order to maintain their domination both within their own states and in other countries.

Reliance upon the use and threat of force as an instrument of foreign policy contravenes the fundamental principles of contemporary international law. Therefore, the policy "from a position of strength" and "cold war" diplomacy contain a constant tendency to violate international law and the desire to move international law to the side.[7]

As the most recent examples of the manifestation of this tendency, one may cite the aggression of England, France, and Israel against Egypt in 1956, the United States's intervention in Lebanon and Jordan in 1958, Belgian aggression in the Congo, United States's intervention against Cuba in 1961, interference of the United States in the internal affairs of Laos, armed intervention of the United States in the Dominican Republic in 1965, Israeli aggression against the Arab states in 1967, and especially the war of the United States against the Vietnamese people.

The contradiction between the foreign policy of imperialist states and international law reflects the contradictions between the aggressive essence of imperialism and the limited possibilities of effectuating imperialist plans.[8] This contradiction between the policy of imperialist states and international law now is being crystallized in the course of forming norms of international law. In contemporary conditions, when the international legal principles adduced in the process of the forming of norms by states that support the policy of peaceful coexistence enjoy the powerful support of peoples, imperialist states frequently conceal their true objectives and, in a number of instances regarding the acceptance of new democratic provisions of international law, go beyond that which corresponds to the real principles of their foreign policy. In so doing imperialist governments usually believe that they will manage to get around these norms and to distort their intent by way of interpretation, and so forth.

7. Hans J. Morgenthau writes: " . . . rarely has history witnessed a more relentless drive toward expansion, more oblivious of risks, and more ruthless in brushing obstacles aside than that of the United States. The Westward expansion of the U.S. would have been impossible without the violation of the treaties guaranteeing the Indians their land. And thus, those treaties had to be broken . . . When . . . economic, military or political pressure was not sufficient, we did not hesitate to go to war." H. J. Morgenthau, reviewing D. Perkins, *The American Approach to Foreign Policy*, in *The New Republic*, May 19, 1952, p. 20.

8. See A. Sovetov, "Osobennosti sovremennogo mezhdunarodnogo razvitiia," *Mezhdunarodnaia zhizn'*, no. 11 (1960), p. 16.

The so-called realist orientation in the theory of diplomacy and international law is a reflection of the policy "from a position of strength" and "cold war" and of attempts theoretically to justify it which, however, unwittingly reveal the contradiction between this policy and international law. This orientation has been broadly propagated enough in the United States, and its echoes also are noticeable in certain other countries.

The essence of the "realist" orientation consists of the following: international relations are relations of power. Events occurring in international relations are "power processes." An aspiration to dominate is a characteristic feature of international relations. The realist approach to foreign policy means that one must achieve one's objectives in foreign policy by any means, without taking into account principles of law and morality.

One of the most zealous proponents of this conception is an American professor, Hans Morgenthau, who in criticizing the "legalistic approach" to problems of international politics actually calls upon diplomacy to put international law aside and to be guided in its actions only by the co-relation of power.

The societal laws of the development of international relations Morgenthau attributes to human nature. "Political realism," he writes, "believes that politics, like society in general, is governed by objective laws that have their roots in human nature."[9] "International politics," says Morgenthau, "like all politics, is a struggle for power."[10] "The aspiration for power," he continues, "being the distinguishing element of international politics, as of all politics, international politics is of necessity power politics."[11]

The aspiration to dominate which supposedly arises out of human nature is declared to be a societal law of international relations since it is a peculiarity, Morgenthau maintains, of any human association. "The tendency to dominate," Morgenthau writes, "in particular, is an element of all human associations, from the family through fraternal and professional associations and local political organizations, to the state."[12]

Although Morgenthau defines "power" in sufficiently vague terms as "man's control over the minds and actions of other men,"[13] in fact the idea that the armed strength of states is the power which must be taken

9. Hans J. Morgenthau, *Politics Among Nations*, 3d ed. (New York: Alfred A. Knopf, 1960), p. 4.
10. *Ibid.*, p. 27.
11. *Ibid.*, p. 31.
12. *Ibid.*, p. 34.
13. *Ibid.*, p. 29.

into account in international relations runs throughout the author's entire discussion.

In asserting that international law is a primitive law resembling the law that exists in certain preliterate societies, such as the Australian aborigines and the Yurok of northern California, Morgenthau comes to deny the regulatory role of international law.[14]

In Morgenthau's view, the task of diplomacy is fourfold. Diplomacy must (1) determine its objectives in the light of the power actually and potentially available for the pursuit of these objectives; (2) assess the objectives of other states and the power actually and potentially available for the pursuit of these objectives; (3) determine to what extent these different objectives are compatible with each other; (4) employ the means suited to the pursuit of its objectives.[15] What means may diplomacy employ? "The means at the disposal of diplomacy," says Morgenthau, "are three: persuasion, compromise and threat of force."[16]

Thus, according to Morgenthau, diplomacy must take only power into account; international law has no place in his theory. We also note that the "threat of force," which Morgenthau regards as one of the means of diplomacy, is prohibited by contemporary international law (Article 2(4), United Nations Charter).

Reality notwithstanding, Morgenthau maintains that diplomacy suffers defeat supposedly because it attaches too great a significance to the legal aspect of international events. "The old diplomacy has failed," he writes, "it is true, but so has the new one. The new diplomacy has failed and was bound to fail, for its legalistic tools have no access to political problems to be solved."[17]

The former Minister of External Affairs and then Prime Minister of Canada, Lester Pearson, advocates an analogous theory in his book *Diplomacy in the Nuclear Age.* In glorifying power politics, he does not leave a place for international law in international relations or in diplomacy. He appeals for the "collection and use of force" as a backing for diplomacy.[18] Pearson maintains that in the nuclear age "our immediate and temporary protection from these grim consequences of our own genius requires the possession of overwhelming, destructive power."[19] At

14. *Ibid.*, p. 278. See also Morgenthau, *In Defense of the National Interest* (New York: Alfred A. Knopf, 1951), p. 136.

15. Morgenthau, *Politics Among Nations*, pp. 539-540.

16. *Ibid.*, p. 541.

17. Morgenthau, *Politics in the Twentieth Century* (Chicago: University of Chicago Press, 1962), I, 358.

18. L. B. Pearson, *Diplomacy in the Nuclear Age* (Cambridge, Mass.: Harvard University Press, 1959), pp. 63-65.

19. *Ibid.*

the same time, Pearson is compelled to recognize that this concept operates in a vicious circle, because an attempt to obtain overwhelming supremacy in armaments gives birth to an arms race, and the ending can not be a happy one.[20]

The eminent propagandist of the "policy of strength," George Kennan, the former United States ambassador to the USSR, in criticizing a "legalistic" and "moralistic" approach to international problems, lays bare completely the contradiction between this policy and international law. He asserts that international law not only is ill-suited as a means of regulating international problems, but that even attempts to use it for such purposes are harmful; he calls international law a "legal straitjacket," while recognizing that it inhibits effectuation of the "policy of strength." "The national state pattern," he says, "is not, should not be, . . . a . . . static thing. By nature, it is an unstable phenomenon in a constant state of change and flux. History has shown that the will and the capacity of individual peoples to contribute to their world environment is constantly changing. It is only logical that the organizational forms (and what else are such things as borders and governments?) should change with them. The function of a system of international relationships is not to inhibit this process of change by imposing a legal straitjacket upon it but rather to facilitate it; to ease its transitions, to temper the asperities to which it often leads, to isolate and moderate the conflicts to which it gives rise, and to see that these conflicts do not assume forms too unsettling for international life in general. But this is a task of diplomacy, in the most old-fashioned sense of the term. For this, law is too abstract, too inflexible, too hard to adjust to the demands of the unpredictable and the unexpected."[21]

And thus the slogan: international law is unsuitable as a means of regulating international problems; it even impedes their regulation. Hail diplomacy without international law![22]

20. *Ibid.*, p. 65.

21. G. F. Kennan, *American Diplomacy 1900-1950* (Chicago: University of Chicago Press, 1951), p. 98.

22. Some American international lawyers point out that a disregard for international law in United States foreign policy and diplomacy resulted in particular from the fact that international law was excluded from the list of subjects in which persons entering the American diplomatic service are examined, as well as excluded from the curricula of law schools and replaced by a course in "international relations." J. Kunz, "The Swing of the Pendulum: From Overestimation to Underestimation of International Law," *American Journal of International Law*, XLIV (1950), 139; C. T. Oliver, "Historical Development of International Law," *Recueil des cours*, LXXXVIII (1955), 424. On the "realist" orientation see also D. B. Levin, "Ob osnovnykh napravleniiakh sovremennoi burzhauznoi nauki mezhdunarodnogo prava," *Sovetskii ezhegodnik*

Influence of International Law on Foreign Policy and Diplomacy

The majority of American international lawyers nonetheless do not accept the theory of the "realists." They also, however, do not oppose these concepts with any serious criticism. Some limit themselves to complaints against the diminished role of international law;[23] others make serious concessions to the theory of the "realists," sometimes sliding down to their position to a significant degree;[24] still others, McDougal for example, in polemicizing with the "realists" reach essentially the same conclusions by other means or come very close to the theory of the "realist" orientation.[25]

Representatives of the "pure" theory of law, Professors H. Kelsen and J. Kunz, have opposed the "realist" orientation somewhat more resolutely. In speaking of the so-called "political approach" to international law, Kelsen is completely correct in saying: "This view is in my opinion nothing but an attempt to justify the nonapplication of the existing law in case its application is in conflict with some interest, or rather, with what the respective writer considers to be the interest of his state."[26]

In criticizing "neorealism," Professor J. Kunz, points out that it actually leads "to a denial of international law." "In reaching such conclusions," he says, "the so-called neorealism becomes completely unrealistic, and should be combatted very energetically."[27]

In another of his works, Kunz expresses an interesting view linking nihilistic concepts of the "realists" with the crisis of the capitalist system, or, as he prefers to express it, the crisis of "Western Christian culture." He writes: "Under the modern 'realistic' conception, international law as such is denied; it is held by preachers of a 'national self-interest' that in international relations 'legal questions largely are irrelevant.' This attitude must lead to a lower and lower respect for the rule of the law. This attitude is itself the outcome of the deep-seated crisis of our Western

mezhdunarodnogo prava 1959 (Moscow: izd-vo AN SSSR, 1960), pp. 88-119; Levin, *O sovremennykh burzhuaznykh teoriiakh mezhdunarodnogo prava* (Moscow: Tipo. MEGI, 1959).

23. See, for example, Oliver, "Historical Development of International Law," pp. 424-427.

24. Thus, for example, Professor P. Potter, in appealing for an enhanced role of international law in international relations, at the same time leans toward the "realist school" in justifying "ultra and extraordinary actions." See P. Potter, "The Need for a Return to International Law," *American Journal of International Law*, XLV (1951), 540; Potter, "Legal Aspects of the Situation in Korea," *ibid.*, XLIV (1950), 712.

25. See, for example, P. Jessup, *The Use of International Law* (Ann Arbor: University of Michigan Law School, 1959), pp. 9-10ff.

26. H. Kelsen, *Principles of International Law*, ed. R. W. Tucker, 2d ed. (New York: Holt, Rinehart & Winston, Inc., 1967), p. x.

27. J. Kunz, "La crise et les transformations du droit des gens," *Recueil des cours*, LXXXVIII (1955), 38.

Christian culture, which is now struggling for its very survival. Of that total crisis, the crisis of international law is only one facet."[2][8]

The criticism of international law by "realists" is scientifically unfounded and rather reminds one of the seeking out of plausible pretexts to get rid of international law and untie the hands of power politics.

Indeed, the "realists" criticism of the "legalistic approach" to international problems actually is in no way directed against a legalistic approach, but only against a formal, normativist approach. As has already been said, in legal science normativism is characterized by the isolation of law from that basis on which it arises and develops, from the economic system of society, from its class structure and policy. In the normativists' conception, norms of law in general and norms of international law in particular are "pure," are technical rules of conduct devoid of social content. The unfoundedness of normativism has been proved by life; it has been subjected to sharp criticism both in socialist and in capitalist countries. In addition, the application of law in general and of international law in particular requires a knowledge not only of law, but also of the actual circumstances of the case. Law regulates exceedingly complex relationships, and naturally the application of a legal norm as a general rule to a concrete social relationship can not be simply a mechanical process. The practice of applying national law, and also of international law, is convincing evidence of this.

A legal approach and a formal approach to questions are not one and the same thing. Proponents of the "realistic" orientation attempt to pass a formal, normativist approach to law and to its application as a legal approach in general and, in refuting normativism, assert that they thereby are proving the unfoundedness of a "legal approach" to international problems. But normativism has already fallen without the participation of the "realists." As regards the present reasonable legal approach to international problems, the arrows of the "realists" are going wide of the mark.

Is international law useful as a means of regulating relations among states or, as the "realists" maintain, does it only obstruct the regulation of international problems? Let us raise the question more concretely. Do those limitations or, expressing it juridically, those obligations which the following principles of international law impose upon states benefit the cause of peace and the development of international cooperation: the prohibition of the use of force in international relations; the obligation to resolve all international disputes only by peaceful means; respect for state sovereignty; equality of states, noninterference in the internal affairs of

28. Kunz, "The United Nations and the Rule of Law," *American Journal of International Law*, XLVI (1952), 504.

Influence of International Law on Foreign Policy and Diplomacy

other states; self-determination of peoples; conscientious fulfillment of international obligations; and the guarantee of basic human rights? Or the obligations derived from such norms of international law as state sovereignty over its territorial waters, immunity of the premises of a diplomatic representation, inviolability of the person of a diplomat, and so forth? The answer to this question has been given by life itself. The practice of international relations shows that ignoring international law, that is, ignoring those limitations which international law places upon foreign policy and diplomacy, is peculiar to states which adhere to the policy "from a position of strength," leads to an aggravation of the international situation, and is fraught with military conflicts.

Moreover, viewing international law as a purely "static factor" is far from corresponding to reality. International law, just as national law, not only strengthens existing relations, but also is an important means of modifying them and of creating new relations between states. In the words of C. W. Jenks, who has done much to expose the creative role of international law, "law becomes a means of doing things by cooperative action."[29]

The Declaration on Principles of International Law adopted unanimously by the United Nations General Assembly on October 24, 1970, emphasizes that "the conscientious observance of the principles of international law affecting friendly relations and cooperation between states, and the conscientious performance by states of obligations undertaken in accordance with the Charter, have the greatest importance for the maintenance of international peace and security and for the attainment of other purposes of the United Nations" and that the "enormous political, economic, and social changes and scientific progress which have occurred in the world since the adoption of the United Nations Charter attach growing importance to these principles and the need for their more effective application in the activity of states where they have not been realized."

The basic thesis of the "realistic" orientation, consisting in the fact that the societal law of contemporary international relations is a struggle for domination, for the domination of one state over another, of one people over another (bellum omnium contra omnes), is false and unscientific. Power decides the outcome of this struggle; the destiny of the weak is subordination to the stronger; it is a societal law that the strong subdue and, consequently, exploit the weaker.

Hence hysterical appeals to strengthen the means for subduing and enslaving other peoples and, above all, to build up the military potential, primarily the nuclear potential, of the Atlantic bloc and other aggressive

29. C. W. Jenks, *A New World of Law?* (London: Longmans, 1969), p. 127.

military alliances. It is not difficult to note that the concept of the "realists" reproduces the basic features of the foreign policy of the imperialist states.

The theoretical unfoundedness of the "realist" orientation is determined first and foremost by the fact that certain societal laws of international relations claimed by them to be universal are in fact only societal laws of imperialism. The aspiration to dominate and subject other peoples is in no way peculiar to the foreign policy of the socialist countries. It also is not peculiar to the policy of neutralist states. The argumentation of the "realists" that the aspiration to dominate is a characteristic feature of foreign policy in general is intended to whitewash the policy "from a position of strength" and to slander the foreign policy of the states of the socialist system. The societal laws of the capitalist system are claimed by "realists" to be the societal laws of the development of international relations in general, while the capitalist system not only has ceased to be the only system in the world but also is no longer the most influential system. A new, higher social system, the system of socialism, transformed into the decisive factor of world development, is being developed and strengthened side by side with the capitalist system.

"Political realism" emasculates social content from international politics, attempting to represent international relations as a game of some abstract forces which have no class content. Morgenthau speaks in this connection about "perennial forces" that have shaped the past and will determine the future of human society.[30]

This philosophical premise is used by proponents of "political realism" to resort to such a political sleight-of-hand as identifying the policy of the Soviet Union with the policy of Tsarist Russia. Thus, Professor F. M. Schumann writes: "During the time of the tsars, the world mission of Russia and its world pretensions were represented by the Orthodox Church, and later by pan-slavism, just as now, under the Soviets, they are represented by 'international communism.' "[31] The same notion is voiced in G. Kennan's article "Peaceful Coexistence: A Western View."[32]

This attempt of the "realists" to operate with abstract and perennial categories such as "power processes" and "perennial forces" as categories devoid of social content is wholly unfounded. Abstract forces which are distinguished from one another only by quantitative indicators do not

30. Morgenthau, *Politics Among Nations*, p. 10; see also Morgenthau, *A New Foreign Policy for the United States* (New York: Frederick A. Praeger, Inc., 1969), p. 120.

31. F. M. Schumann, *The Cold War: Retrospect and Prospect* (Baton Rouge: Louisiana State University Press, 1962), p. 11.

32. G. F. Kennan, "Peaceful Coexistence: A Western View," *Foreign Affairs*, XXXVIII (1960), 178-180.

operate in international relations. States are the primary actors in the international arena: socialist and capitalist states, and new states which have arisen in consequence of the liberation of the colonies. If one limits oneself to a comparison only of socialist and capitalist states, then their class nature is opposed, and the foreign policies which they pursue are fundamentally distinguished one from the other by their social content.[33] This, of course, does not mean that there can be nothing in common between these two policies; both socialist and, in a number of instances, bourgeois foreign policy can, for example, be a policy of peaceful coexistence, that is, be directed toward ensuring peace and developing cooperation among states for these purposes.

The "realistic" orientation, in pretending to the role of the most modern doctrine, in fact is a captive of the obsolete concepts of the German school of *Machtpolitik* of the second half of the nineteenth century. In preaching the dominance of power in international relations, it does not take into account the enormous changes in the international situation which have occurred during the period of the coexistence of the two systems.

The downfall of the policy "from a position of strength" is the best evidence of the unfoundedness and the unrealistic nature of the concepts of the "realists" concerning the co-relation of foreign policy and international law in our day.

International law is a system of legal norms which are subject to observance by states. It consequently must be a guiding principle for diplomacy. There can not be peaceful coexistence without observance of the norms of international law.

In our epoch of unprecedented technological progress, which has opened up to mankind enormous inexhaustible reserves of energy and at the same time has led to the creation of weapons whose destructive force exceeds man's imagination, in the epoch of the beginning of space navigation, the observance of norms of international law by states is becoming a necessity dictated by the common interests of all mankind. Violations of international law can lead to the catastrophic consequences of a world nuclear war, which would affect all persons and all states.

The need to struggle for the observance of the principles and norms of international law by states is entering more and more into the consciousness of peoples, especially those peoples which have endured all of the burdens, deprivations, and sufferings brought down upon them by the

33. A French professor, R. Bosc, correctly points out in criticizing Morgenthau's conception that Morgenthau evidently believes "states are interchangeable or their reactions to events are identical; he distinguishes only between strong and weak states." R. Bosc, *Sociologie de la paix* (Paris: SPSES, 1965), p. 23. [" . . . il ne connait que des États forts et des États faibles"]

Second World War, those who experienced the horrors of nazism. It is no wonder that "political realism" does not find any wide propagation in Europe, but prospers primarily in the United States, on whose cities and villages not one bomb fell during the Second World War and whose land was not trampled by the filthy boots of fascist "supermen."

The need to enhance the role of international law in international relations was emphasized in United Nations General Assembly Resolution 1505 (XV) of December 12, 1960, concerning future work in the field of the codification and progressive development of international law. This resolution points out that " . . . conditions prevailing in the world today give increased importance to the role of international law—and its strict and undeviating observance by all governments—in strengthening international peace, developing friendly and co-operative relations among the nations, settling disputes by peaceful means and advancing economic and social progress throughout the world."

The General Assembly Resolution 1686 (XVI) of December 18, 1961, on the same question notes the " . . . important role of codification and progressive development of international law with a view to making international law a more effective means of furthering the purposes and principles set forth in Articles 1 and 2 of the Charter of the United Nations."

With the growth of the forces of peace, which are coming out for the undeviating observance of principles and norms of international law, the influence of international law on the foreign policy and diplomacy of states is increasing. The task is for the unified forces of the mighty socialist camp, the peace-loving nonsocialist states, the international working class, and all forces upholding the cause of peace, to ensure the observance of the principles and norms of international law, above all its fundamental principles, and not to permit a world war.

Chapter 12 *International Law as a Support for Foreign Policy*

As already has been pointed out, in defining the legal duties of states international law fixes specific limits for their foreign policies and diplomacy. On the other hand, in fixing the rights of states, it opens the possibility of states using international law in the interests of their foreign policy and diplomacy. The preceding chapter was devoted primarily to the first aspect; the present chapter, to the second.

The fact that states strive to rely upon international law in effectuating their foreign policy and diplomacy can not be doubted. The foreign policy documents of various states are replete with references to international law in general and to individual principles and norms.

International law is not only a legal, but also an important political and moral factor. The foreign policy action of a state which rests upon international law acquires by virtue thereof not just legal, but also political and moral advantages.

An analysis of the question of the possibility of states using international law for the purpose of achieving the goals of their foreign policy must begin with the process of forming norms of international law, which are created in the course of the struggle and cooperation of states as a result of agreement between them. As already has been pointed out, each state participating in the process of creating, developing, and modifying norms of international law very naturally seeks to have its international legal position, as a part of its foreign policy program as a whole, be reflected as fully as possible in the working out of norms of international law. That is to say, each state seeks to have the legal principles which it upholds recognized by other states as norms of international law.

Thus, the very process of creating norms of international law is being used by states for the purpose of achieving certain goals of their foreign policy.

We shall now consider the possibility of using prevailing international law as an instrument of the foreign policy of states.

International law defines the rights and duties of states. It is natural that in its foreign policy and diplomacy every country has the possibility in specific instances of relying upon international law, of upholding its rights, and of demanding the fulfillment of obligations by other states.

This, of course, does not mean that international law can be an instrument of any policy. Norms of international law can be used as an instrument of the foreign policy of individual states only within the limits defined by the content of these norms, that is, the content of the agreement between states in consequence of which a particular norm of international law has emerged, developed, or been modified.[1]

As a whole, contemporary international law is directed at ensuring the peaceful coexistence of states, at developing cooperation between them in the interests of peace.

Of the two basic orientations in foreign policy which presently exist—the policy "from a position of strength" and the policy of peaceful coexistence—only the latter corresponds to the general character of international law.

The policy "from a position of strength" and the arms race connected therewith, the knocking together of aggressive military blocs leading not to peace but to war, contravene international law. And if references to international law frequently are encountered in practice for the purpose of justifying the policy "from a position of strength," it should not follow from this, of course, that contemporary international law can be used in support of such a policy. Such efforts as, for example, the attempts to justify the aggression of England, France, and Israel against Egypt, or the aggression of Belgium against the Congo, or the aggression of the United States in Vietnam, have no basis whatever in international law.

International law can be a support only for that foreign policy whose principles conform to international law. In this case, a state may rely upon international law. The policy of peaceful coexistence and of the liberation of peoples from the colonial yoke is such a policy. In conformity with the nature of contemporary international law, it is an instrument in the hands of peace-loving states and peoples in the struggle for strengthening peace and averting a new war, for the freedom and independence of peoples.

Thus, international law is, on one hand, a system of norms binding upon states and regulating the conduct of states; and on the other, within

1. See G. I. Tunkin, *Osnovy sovremennogo mezhdunarodnogo prava* (Moscow: Tipo. Vysshei partiinoi shkoly pri TsK KPSS, 1956), p. 8.

defined limits a support (or, in a specific sense, an instrument) of the policy of such states. These are two aspects of one and the same phenomenon.

The existence of the aforesaid two contradictory aspects of international law usually confuses many bourgeois jurists. Corbett's book, *Law in Diplomacy*, which appeared in 1959, can serve as one example of how unresolved the problem of the co-relation of international law and foreign policy is for some of them. Corbett blames Soviet science for the fact that it does not consider it necessary to reconcile the concepts of law as an instrument of policy and law as a system of norms regulating relations among states. If, says Corbett, international law is the aggregate of norms regulating relations among states, then it consequently in some measure controls the conduct of governments. "But," Corbett continues, " . . . international law, if it is to regulate, must operate as a limitation upon, rather than a tool of, national aims and practice. If it is an objective regulating device, it cannot at the same time be subservient to the passing purposes of governments."[2]

The fact is, however, that the dual role of international law as a "regulator" and as a "support" or "instrument of policy" of the subjects of law reflects reality. It, as already has been pointed out, is determined by the content of norms of international law which, just as norms of national law, influence the conduct of subjects of law by defining their rights and duties.

If international law is a support or instrument of foreign policy, this does not mean that a state may take international law into its own hands and, as a sculptor from clay, fashion from it that which is necessary. Norms of international law are the result of agreement between states, and an individual state can not change them at its discretion.

One can not, therefore, concur with Professor D. B. Levin's view that "in applying norms of international law, diplomacy fills them with concrete political content, according to which the purport and the entire significance of such norms may be changed . . . It has happened more than once that some of these provisions and norms of international law have served directly opposite purposes. The most progressive principles and institutes of international law can in the hands of reactionary diplomacy be transformed into an instrument of a reactionary policy."[3]

2. P. Corbett, *Law in Diplomacy* (Princeton: Princeton University Press, 1959), p. 101.

3. D. B. Levin, *Diplomaticheskii immunitet* (Moscow: izd-vo AN SSSR, 1949), p. xiii; the same thought, in a less specific form, is in E. A. Korovin, ed., *Mezhdunarodnoe pravo* (Moscow: Iurizdat, 1951), p. 12. This question, in our view, is treated more correctly but also not completely accurately in D. B. Levin's article "K voprosu o

D. B. Levin's view can be based only on one of the following presuppositions: (a) norms of international law are technical rules which have no social content; (b) although norms of international law have their own content, a state may take just the form from such norms and pour new content therein. Neither the first nor the second presupposition can be accepted.

Norms of international law are not empty forms to which every state may bring a particular content. As any legal norm, a norm of international law has its own form and content. The latter is determined by the content of that agreement in consequence of which this norm exists (see Chapter 9).

An individual state can not introduce new content into a norm of international law. Changing the content of a norm of law is to change the norm, which is not possible as a result of the unilateral actions of a state, but by virtue of agreement among states. No single *power* can change a norm of international law in a unilateral manner.

The concept that a state may take from norms of international law only their form was expressed by E. B. Pashukanis in his day. In his exceedingly contradictory argumentation Pashukanis in fact asserted that the Soviet state "applied a number of forms" of international law and that there was only an external resemblance between the institutes of international law applied by the Soviet state and the institutes applied by bourgeois states. In Pashukanis's view, general international law exists side by side with this.[4]

Form without content, however, is not a norm. A state can not take only the form of an international legal norm, place new content therein, and assert that this is a norm of international law. Such a norm would be some sort of new norm but, naturally, not an international legal norm, since one state can not create norms of international law.

If one admits that every state can introduce changes into norms of international law by its unilateral actions the latter, as an objective system of norms regulating relations among states, disappears, and an external law of individual states emerges in its place.

Norms of international law have their own content which, of course, can be changed in the course of international relations by treaty or custom. Such change always occurs in consequence of agreement between

sootnoshenii diplomatii i mezhdunarodnogo prava v svete printsipa mirnogo sosushchestvovaniia," *Sovetskii ezhegodnik mezhdunarodnogo prava 1960* (Moscow: izd-vo AN SSSR, 1961), p. 113; Levin, *Diplomatiia* (Moscow: Sotsekgiz, 1962), pp. 151-152.

4. See E. B. Pashukanis, *Ocherki po mezhdunarodnomu pravu* (Moscow: izd-vo Sovetskoe zakonodatel'stvo, 1935), pp. 16-17.

states, in the process of whose formation the unilateral actions of states, as already pointed out, play a role.

Even though states may use international law as a support for foreign policy, this does not mean that international law is merged with policy. Mixing international law with policy inevitably leads to a denial of the normative character of international law, that is to say, to a denial of international law, which becomes buried in policy and vanishes as law.

Professor McDougal's concept of the policy approach to international law is an example of this kind of mixing or blending of foreign policy and international law.

Although Professor McDougal also criticizes Kennan, Morgenthau, and Schwarzenberger for exaggerating the importance of "naked force" in international relations, he comes—it is true, by other paths—to essentially the same conclusions with regard to the role of international law as do the authors whom he criticizes. If Kennan and Morgenthau rather openly and unceremoniously cast international law aside and call upon diplomacy not to take it into consideration, McDougal, while not denying the importance of international law in so many words and sometimes also stressing it, in fact drowns international law in policy. In consequence thereof, international law in McDougal's concept is devoid of independent significance as a means of regulating international relations; it disappears into policy and, moreover, is transformed into a means of justifying policies which violate international law.[5]

Just as Kennan and Morgenthau, McDougal criticizes a "legalistic approach" to international problems. To him, international relations also represent first and foremost "power processes."[6] "World power processes," or, to express it in everyday language, international relations are, in McDougal's view, "processes of coercion." McDougal speaks of the "complex process of coercion in the contemporary world arena," of the "great variety and differing intensities of the events in the coercion process."[7]

McDougal declares to be unfounded the view that international law is a system of legal rules regulating the relations among states. This notion of international law leads, McDougal asserts, "too many people to make sharp and unreal distinctions between law and policy . . . " Too often it is

---

5. M. S. McDougal, "International Law, Power and Policy: A Contemporary Conception," *Recueil des cours*, LXXXII (1953), 137-259.

6. *Ibid.*, p. 171.

7. M.S. McDougal and F. Feliciano, *Law and Minimum World Public Order* (New Haven: Yale University Press, 1961), p. 7.

assumed that "technical rules which are to constitute international law" can resolve the question of what ought to be done.[8]

The author's scornful gesture toward "technical rules" (although, of course, norms of international law are not technical rules) should be noted; it brings McDougal very close to Kennan.

McDougal concentrates his attention on so-called "decision-making," by which he means the process of formulating and effectuating foreign policy.

What is the role of international law in this process? Does McDougal believe that in making a decision one must take international law into account, observe the norms of international law? Not at all.

McDougal maintains that the application of "common rules" of international law requires a "policy choice."[9] Consequently, in the author's view, it is not necessary to take into account and observe norms of international law in making policy decisions, but on the contrary, one must begin by "choosing a policy." The author bases the necessity of this preliminary "policy choice" on the fact that in applying a norm of international law there may be varying opinions as to what ought to be done.[10]

As regards international law, it is by no means clear what role the author assigns to it in the "policy choice." Since the "policy choice" precedes the application of the norm of international law, this "choice" obviously is made independently of the existing norms.

McDougal asserts that the process of "decision-making" is a process in which norms of international law are created, interpreted, and reinterpreted.[11] But the "decision-making" process consists of unilateral actions of states. Consequently, according to McDougal, every state creates international law in the process of "decision-making." The author does not say this expressly, but this conclusion inevitably springs to mind. Not without reason does McDougal maintain that in his concept the dispute as to whether the "decision-maker" applies international law or national law is futile.[12]

In any event, for McDougal the role of international law consists not in defining the limits of possible or proper conduct of states. "The realistic function of those rules [that is, norms of international law—G.T.]

8. McDougal, "International Law, Power and Policy," p. 144; see also O. J. Lissitzyn, *International Law Today and Tomorrow* (New York: Oceana Publications, 1965), pp. 39-40; M. A. Kaplan and N. B. de Katzenbach, *The Political Foundations of International Law* (New York: John A. Wiley & Sons, 1961), p. 231.

9. McDougal, "International Law, Power and Policy," p. 155.

10. *Ibid.*, pp. 152-153.

11. *Ibid.*, pp. 182-183.

12. *Ibid.*, p. 184.

considered as a whole," writes McDougal, "is, accordingly, not mechanically to dictate . . . decision but to guide the attention of decision-makers to significant . . . factors in typical . . . contexts of decision, to serve as summary indices to relevant crystallized community expectations, and, hence, to permit creative and adaptive, instead of arbitrary and irrational, decisions."[13]

McDougal is right that international law, just as national law, in the majority of instances does not and can not determine specific foreign policy actions of states. These actions are determined by numerous factors, including international law (see Chapter 8). But international law is a very specific, though not determinative, factor. The specific feature of this determinant of foreign policy consists in the fact that international law, while not determining specific decisions of states, fixes the limits of possible or proper decisions by establishing the rights and duties of states.

McDougal denies precisely this. To him, law does not limit a state in effectuating its foreign policy and diplomacy, but only serves it; the limits of propriety disappear, and the limits of possible conduct are expanded to any limits necessary to effectuate the policy.

Professor R. Fisher, of Harvard University, is completely correct in writing as follows: "Seeking a realistic analysis of the decision process, McDougal finds that the deciders are not actually bound by rules and prescriptions but rather have them at their disposal. Decision-makers, he discovers, come out any way they want to and how they will want to depends upon their biases and policy objectives. McDougal welcomes this fact with open arms."[14]

But McDougal does not stop here; he goes farther. He imperceptibly leaves international law to the side and crosses over to a purely subjective "postulating the base values of international law . . . " He proclaims nine such "values" (respect for human dignity, free access to "wealth processes," and so forth).[15] These precepts postulated by the author are declared to be the bases of an "international law of human dignity." The said "base values" should, in McDougal's view, be the criteria for evaluating the foreign policy of states and the guiding principles of this policy.[16] "Decisions," that is to say, the policy of states, should

13. McDougal and Feliciano, *Law and Minimum World Public Order*, p. 57.

14. R. Fisher, "Law and Policy in International Decisions," *Science*, CXXXV (1962), 659.

15. In his passing and far from complete critique of McDougal's conception, an Australian professor, J. Stone, is correct in pointing to the purely subjective character of these "base values." See J. Stone, "Problems Confronting Sociological Enquiries Concerning International Law," *Recueil des cours*, LXXXIX (1956), 73.

16. McDougal, "International Law, Power and Policy," p. 190.

correspond to these "values," and not to norms of prevailing international law.[17]

McDougal does not prove and does not even attempt to prove that the "values" which he has proposed are generally-recognized principles of international law. However, even if the question were one of such principles, one could not concur with the assertion that states must be guided only by these extremely broad general principles, not taking into account the concrete norms of international law. International law as an objectively existing system of norms disapppears.

It is necessary to stress that McDougal's concept gives rise to objections on our part not for raising the question of the values of international law. Such values exist. It is natural that one must seek them in international law itself; they are embodied above all in its basic principles. One can and must also raise the question of the values of international law *de lege ferenda*, having in mind the possibility of bringing it closer to general human values.

Objections in this respect arise from the fact that the values proclaimed by McDougal are actually taken from outside international law and are announced as guidance for the actions of states. Among the values put forward by Professor McDougal are both general human values such as, for example, respect for human dignity, and values peculiar to the capitalist system but not to the socialist system, such as, for example, free access of individuals to the "wealth processes."

Thus, in McDougal's concept international law on one hand merges with "decision-making" processes, that is, with policy, and on the other hand it moves aside, inasmuch as in decision-making states are supposed to be guided not by international law based on the agreement of states but by unilaterally proclaimed "base values."

One must agree with Professor S. V. Anderson, of the University of California, who characterizes the essence of McDougal's concept as follows: "Law is policy. Policy is human dignity. Human dignity is fostered in the long run by the success of American foreign policy. Therefore, law is the handmaiden of the national interest of the United States. (Other countries will substitute their own national policy in place of the American.) It is clear that such 'law' does not regulate behavior: it does not restrain, but liberates. Law becomes merely an increment to power."[18]

It is no wonder that McDougal and his supporters attempt to justify

17. *Ibid.*, p. 183.
18. S. V. Anderson, "A Critique of Professor Myres S. McDougal's Doctrine of Interpretation by Major Purposes," *American Journal of International Law*, LVII (1963), 382.

with references to "international law" any violations of this law by the United States, particularly the American intervention in the Dominican Republic in 1965 and especially the aggressive war of the United States in Vietnam.[19]

J. N. Moore, for example, in his article in the *American Journal of International Law*, invokes the spirit of McDougal's concept in searching for a justification of American aggression in Vietnam not in the "black-letter rules" of international law. He writes: "Lawfulness of assistance to either faction [that is, to the South Vietnamese authorities—*G.T.*] must be determined in reference to genuine self-determination and the requirements of minimum world public order, not in blind reliance on black-letter rules . . . "[20]

Professor W. Friedmann, of Columbia University, with complete justification, says sarcastically with regard to such argumentation that "in the absence of third-party determination, 'minimum world public order' means, Humpty-Dumpty-like, what the policy-maker wants it to mean, a catch-all phrase to justify whatever action the writer wishes to justify."[21]

Professor R. A. Falk, of Princeton University, who identifies himself with the basic positions of McDougal's concept although he also criticizes him on many questions, says in justification of McDougal's concept, having in mind foreign policy decision-makers: "Rational actors use every means at their disposal, including law, to maximize their values."[22] However, he also is forced to disassociate himself from McDougal on the question of states using international law as an instrument of their policy. "McDougal, in my judgment," he writes, "confirms the auto-interpretive role [of law—*G.T.*] of national elites so as to virtually nullify the distinction I deem crucial between the impartial application of law and its adversary use."[23]

Were McDougal to have limited himself to the assertion that states use international law as an objectively existing system of legal norms in order to achieve the goals of their foreign policy, then, as was said previously, there would be no dispute. But in McDougal's concept the state, first of all, can, in being guided by "overriding values," pay no attention to

19. See J. N. Moore and J. L. Underwood, in collaboration with M. S. McDougal, *The Lawfulness of United States Assistance to the Republic of Vietnam* (May 1966), mimeo.

20. J. N. Moore, "The Lawfulness of Military Assistance to the Republic of Viet-Nam," *American Journal of International Law*, LXI (1967), 31.

21. W. Friedmann, "Law and Politics in the Vietnamese War: A Comment," *ibid.*, LXI (1967), 783.

22. R. A. Falk, *Legal Order in a Violent World* (Princeton: Princeton University Press, 1968), p. 87.

23. *Ibid.*, p. 7.

international law, but if it wishes to use it, then to interpret it in such a way as is suitable for the achievement of its goals.

From a political point of view, McDougal's concept objectively is directed toward clearing international law out of the way, clearing a path for the policy whose effectuation this law impedes, that is to say, for an aggressive policy.

McDougal's concept is based on the positions of "political realism" which, as we already have pointed out, calls to mind the basic features of German concepts of *Machtpolitik* of the second half of the nineteenth century. In its basic legal orientation, this concept also is not new. Its roots stretch out from German concepts of external state law which, in turn, were closely linked with the said theories of *Machtpolitik*.

McDougal's concept, the core of which consists in the fact that international law is fused with policy, is scientifically unfounded.

International law, just as national law, while closely linked with policy, does not merge into it. Its principles and norms are created in the process of relations between states under the influence of their foreign policy as a result of agreement. As soon as it has been crystallized in the political cauldron of relations among states, a norm of international law becomes a special category, a legal category. It takes on an independent existence, and, although it can never be divorced from policy, nevertheless, without losing political significance, it becomes a special social phenomenon distinct from policy.

Part V *The Legal Nature of Contemporary General International Organizations*

Chapter 13 *The Laws of Societal Development and International Organizations*

One of the characteristic features of contemporary international relations is the rapid development of and increase in the role of interstate organizations. We can not consider all of these organizations though, as will be pointed out below, but while we so limit ourselves we are fully aware at the same time of the large and ever growing role of the so-called nongovernmental international organizations. Obviously, however, the nature and functions of these organizations have a special character, and they must be the subject of an independent investigation.[1]

International organizations have become a permanent and very important phenomenon of international life. Contemporary international (intergovernmental, interstate) organizations are created by states through the conclusion of international treaties. They are specific entities in the fabric of international relations which, though elevated above them structurally, are intertwined in these relations and constitute a distinctive part thereof. International organizations are not situated above international relations, but are within the system of these relations. Relationships between states permeate international organizations, which represent a specific form of such relations.

The increase in the number and the expansion of the functions of international organizations are changing the structure of international relations. International organizations are drawing to themselves a significant number of questions of a direct bilateral or multilateral character which previously were dealt with in relations between states. Relations between states relating to questions falling within the jurisdiction of the

---

1. On this question, see G. I. Morozov, *Mezhdunarodnye organizatsii* (Moscow: izd-vo Mysl', 1969); A. S. Beliakov, ed., *Mezhdunarodnye nepravitel'stvennye organizatsii; spravochnik* (Moscow: izd-vo Nauka, 1967).

[305]

respective international organization are handled by this organization. That is to say, in these instances an international organization is as though it were standing among states, and the links among states pass in such instances through the more or less complex mechanism of this international organization.

The development of international organizations has meant the development of new methods of resolving international problems and an increase in the importance of these new methods in comparison with traditional methods. These new methods are highly diverse and are characterized in general by the application of the various mechanisms of international organizations.

In connection with the growth of the role of international organizations in contemporary international relations, the question of their legal nature, by which we mean their most important international legal features, acquires great theoretical and practical importance.

Moreover, the study of the legal nature of international organizations presents significant difficulties because, on one hand, international organizations, as already has been pointed out, are a specific form of relations among states and, on the other hand, enter into international relations as individual entities. Professor M. Virally correctly notes in his extensive study devoted to the United Nations: "Great difficulties and confusion in studying the world organization are created by the fact that the internal sphere and external environment are intertwined. The world organization appears to us as both a social structure within which all states of the world already have taken or should take places. At the same time, this organization is an autonomous entity in the world international community."[2]

International organizations are an institution of modern human society. The basic features of this institution, therefore, including its legal nature, are determined by the laws of societal development.

At the present time there exist two opposed social systems in the world: socialist and capitalist. "The development of the world socialist system and the world capitalist system occurs in accordance with directly opposed laws."[3] Consequently, side by side with the general laws of societal development there also operate specific laws of development peculiar to each of the two opposed social systems. In addition, there exist specific societal laws for the development of countries which have come to be called "developing," although one must bear in mind that they do not represent a single group in terms of the direction of their social

2. M. Virally, *L'Organisation mondiale* (Paris: Colin, 1972), p. 30.
3. *Programma Kommunisticheskoi partii Sovetskogo Soiuza* (Moscow: Politizdat, 1964), p. 22.

Laws of Societal Development and International Organizations

development, but can be broken down into two categories: countries developing along a capitalist path, and countries developing along a noncapitalist path.

The legal nature of general international organizations in which states of opposed social systems take part is determined in the final analysis by both the general laws of societal development and by the clash of specific laws peculiar to each of the existing social systems. Moreover, the legal nature of international organizations in which states of only one social system take part are formed under the decisive influence of the laws peculiar to that system and the general laws of societal development.

It is exceedingly important, therefore, for a correct scientific analysis of the legal nature of international organizations to distinguish international organizations whose membership in its social aspect is different.

Moreover, many bourgeois international lawyers analyze the legal nature and the long-term development of international organizations on the basis of composite data relating both to general and to western European international organizations.[4]

Of course the comparison of local international organizations *inter se*, as well as their comparison with general international organizations, is not only possible but is also necessary in the course of scientific research. The objection is not to the comparison, but to the mixing; for example, the inclusion of features peculiar to some local international organizations whose members are of the same social composition or ascribing to general international organizations trends of development peculiar to such local organizations.

Under contemporary conditions one must bear in mind at least the following basic categories of international organizations: general international organizations, in which states of different social systems take part, and local international organizations, among which are organizations in which states of different social systems take part, organizations of socialist states, organizations of developing countries, and organizations of capitalist states.

In the present work we limit ourselves to considering the legal nature of general international organizations.

In our view, those general laws of societal development peculiar to several socioeconomic formations, such as the internationalization of

4. See, for example, I. Detter, *Law Making by International Organizations* (Stockholm: P. A. Norstedt & Söners Forlag, 1965), pp. 319-329; D. W. Bowett, *The Law of International Institutions* (London: Stevens & Sons, 1964), pp. 273ff; this confusion also occurs in the works of K. Skubiszewski, a Polish jurist. See K. Skubiszewski, "A New Source of the Law of Nations: Resolutions of International Organizations," *Recueil d'Études de droit international en hommage à Paul Guggenheim* (Geneva: Imp. de la Tribune de la Geneve, 1968), pp. 508-520.

economic, political, scientific, and cultural life, as well as the existence of sovereign states, exert a formative influence upon the legal nature of contemporary general international organizations. The clash of the developmental laws of the two opposed socioeconomic systems, concretely reflected in the clash of the foreign policies of socialist and capitalist states in international organizations, has special significance for the character of contemporary international organizations. The law of decolonization materially influences the character of contemporary international organizations. As a result of the breakup of the colonial system and the emergence in international organizations of a large number of new states formed in consequence of the liberation of the colonies, the co-relation of forces in international organizations has materially changed, and this can not but affect their further development.

A. The Internationalization of Economic Life and International Organizations

The development of the productive forces of human society is accompanied by a deepening and an expansion of the international division of labor which, in its turn, is an important condition and indicator of the development of productive forces.[5]

The international division of labor, which is specialization and cooperation on an international scale, embraces an ever wider sphere of human activity—first and foremost, production and consumption, science and technology, and economic life in general. This division of labor assumes the appearance of economic, scientific, technical, and other ties between states in various spheres of human activity.

The process of the internationalization of economic life first acquires significant depth and a tendency to become world-wide under conditions of capitalism. "The bourgeoisie," said Marx and Engels in the *Manifesto of the Communist Party*, "have made the production and consumption in all countries cosmopolitan by exploiting the world market . . . In place of the old local and national seclusion and self-sufficiency, we have intercourse in every direction, universal interdependence of nations. As in material, so also in intellectual production."[6] And sixty years later, in 1913, Lenin wrote: "Developing capitalism knows two historical tendencies on the

5. For greater details see E. T. Usenko, *Formy regulirovaniia sotsialisticheskogo mezhdunarodnogo razdeleniia truda* (Moscow: izd-vo Mezhdunarodnye otnosheniia, 1965), pp. 9-40.

6. K. Marx and F. Engels, "Manifest kommunisticheskoi partii," *Sochineniia*, 2d ed. (Moscow: Gospolitizdat, 1955), IV, 427-428.

national question. The first: the awakening of national life and national movements, the struggle against any national oppression, the creation of national states. Second: the development and quickening of any relations among nations, the breaking of national partitions, the creation of an international unity of capital, of economic life in general, of politics, of science, and so forth.

"Both tendencies are the essence of the world law of capitalism. The first predominates at the beginning of its development; the second characterizes mature capitalism moving toward its transformation into a socialist society."[7]

The emergence of the first socialist state in the world and then of the world system of socialism, the division of the world into two opposed social systems, the struggle between these systems in the course of which the leading system—the socialist—supplants the other already obsolete system, have not stopped the world process of the internationalization of economic life, as well as the internationalization of other aspects of societal life. There is not and could not be a force which could eliminate world economic relations, and the attempts of the imperialists to cut the Soviet state out of this system inevitably were doomed to failure. "There is a force greater," said V. I. Lenin, "than the desire, will, or decision of any of the hostile governments or classes; this force is general world economic relations, which compel them to enter upon the path of intercourse with us."[8]

The two social systems are not and can not be isolated from each other in the domain of economics or politics, nor in other spheres. At the present time, two world markets, socialist and capitalist, developing according to their own special laws, have been formed on the basis of the two social systems. But a world division of labor and a world market exists and is developing together therewith.[9]

The productive forces of human society at the present time exist first and foremost as the productive forces of individual states. Therefore, links among these national complexes of productive forces take the form of international links, that is, links going beyond the bounds of states.[10]

International economic relations are productive, secondary economic

7. V. I. Lenin, "Kriticheskie zametki po natsional'nomu voprosu," *Polnoe sobranie sochinenii*, 5th ed. (Moscow: Gospolitizdat, 1961), XXIV, 124.

8. Lenin, "O vnutrennei i vneshnei politike respubliki: otchet VTsIK i SNK 23 dekabria [1921]," *Polnoe sobranie sochinenii*, XLIV, 304-305.

9. For greater detail, see M. V. Senin, *Razvitie mezhdunarodnykh ekonomicheskikh sviaszei* (Moscow: izd-vo Mysl', 1968), pp. 48-49.

10. For greater detail see Usenko, *Formy regulirovaniia sotsialisticheskogo mezhdunarodnogo razdeleniia truda*; see also R. L. Bobrov, *Sovremennoe mezhdunarodnoe pravo* (Leningrad: izd-vo LGU, 1962), p. 54.

relations,[11] and the state complexes of productive forces and the productive relations existing in each state which correspond thereto are primary with regard to international economic relations.

It is natural, therefore, that the character and essence of international economic links at the present time are not of the same kind; they are determined basically by the character and essence of the social systems of the states among which such links occur. Consequently, in speaking of the internationalization of economic life and the development of international economic relations on a world scale, one should bear in mind the contradictions among the various elements of this system.

International economic relations serve as an important developmental base for other international relationships: political, cultural, and others. If international economic relations are a base category, then these other international relationships are of a superstructure character. But it would be incorrect to regard these latter as a superstructure only above international economic relations, as Professor R. L. Bobrov has correctly noted.[12]

Since international economic relations are, as already has been pointed out, secondary, their influence upon other international relations is a secondary influence with regard to the base. In addition, it is not the sole influence relating to the base. International relations of a superstructure character do not experience the influence of the economic system of various states only through international economic relations. The economic system of individual states influences the foreign policy of these states (and therefore international relations of a superstructure character) both directly and through national categories of the superstructure. Through these two channels, the fundamental base complexes, that is, the economic systems of individual states, influence international relations of a superstructure character, as well as contemporary international organizations and international law.

The intensification of the internationalization of economic and other aspects of life, reflected in the intensification of international economic, scientific, technical, and other ties, inevitably leads to an increasing number of questions which can not be resolved successfully on a bilateral or narrowly regional basis, but require the participation of all or a significant number of states. This is reflected in particular in the increased number of multilateral treaties in which a large quantity of states participate.

Another aspect of the development of economic and other international ties is the complexity of the questions which arise in the course of

11. See Marx and Engels, *Sochineniia*, XII, p. 735.
12. Bobrov, *Sovremennoe mezhdunarodnoe pravo*, pp. 16-17.

Laws of Societal Development and International Organizations

effectuating such ties and the emergence of the need to create permanent international mechanisms which concern themselves with such questions. This leads to the creation of international organizations as organs of state cooperation for the purpose of settling the said questions.

Such organizations arise primarily in those areas of international relations where they are engendered by the requirements of economic, scientific, and technical ties. These were, for example, the International Telegraphic Union, founded in 1865, the General Postal Union, created in 1875, and so forth.

The functions of these international organizations at first were very limited. A significant growth in the number of participants in international organizations, however, and the need to ensure the operative resolution of questions leads to an expansion of the rights and powers of international organs in settling such questions, of course within the bounds defined in each individual instance by the statute of the organization. The expansion of the jurisdiction of international organizations takes place, therefore, both along the line of expanding the circle of questions over which it has jurisdiction and along the line of expanding the powers of the international organs in settling these questions.

With the intensification and complication of international ties, the number of international organizations also grows. Together with international organizations in the sphere of economic, scientific, and technical cooperation, international organizations in the domain of culture, education, and even international organizations for questions of peace and security are emerging.

Thus, the intensification of the internationalization of economic and other areas of contemporary social life leads to the creation of international organizations in various domains of international ties, to an expansion of their functions and powers, and to an increase of their role in international relations generally. However, both the character of internationalization itself and the other laws of societal development, acting in another direction, define the perimeters of this process.

B. Coexistence of the Two Opposed Social Systems and International Organizations

The most important law of societal development of our epoch is the existence of two opposed social systems developing according to different laws, and the struggle between them, in which a new social system is superseding the old system.

General international organizations are created and function on the basis of agreement between states of different social systems, and therefore what has been said earlier about the link between international law and peaceful coexistence also is applicable to the co-relation of international organizations and peaceful coexistence. General international organizations can develop only on the basis of peaceful relations, relations of peaceful coexistence between states with different social systems. The events of the Second World War graphically confirmed that war destroys general international organizations, undermining the only basis on which they can exist and develop. At the same time, the postwar period has shown no less convincingly that the development of international relations along the line of peaceful coexistence promotes the development and activity of general organizations, especially the United Nations, and the atmosphere of "cold war" retards their development and reduces the effectiveness of their activity.

The struggle of the two opposed systems in contemporary general international organizations generally manifests itself as the struggle of two foreign policy orientations opposed by virtue of their class essence: the foreign policy of socialist states and the foreign policy of the imperialist powers and their allies. The policy of the socialist states in international organizations is first and foremost a policy of peaceful coexistence. On this plane it is shared by many developing and even capitalist countries. The policy of the imperialist states and their allies generally is characterized by a rejection of peaceful coexistence and by aggressive aspirations against the socialist states. Under these conditions, only a struggle of states, and on a broader plane, of all forces favoring peaceful coexistence, ensures as a whole the position that contemporary general international organizations are organs of peaceful coexistence.

This is reflected first and foremost in the charters of general international organizations. These charters define as the basic purpose of the respective general international organizations either the maintenance of peace and struggle against the threat of war (the United Nations) or assistance in achieving this purpose (the specialized international organizations).

The United Nations Charter proclaims that the United Nations has as its purpose "to maintain international peace and security and for this purpose to take effective collective measures to prevent and eliminate a threat to the peace and to suppress all acts of aggression or other breaches of the peace, and to promote through peaceful means, in conformity with the principles of justice and international law, the reconciliation or settlement of international disputes or situations which might lead to a breach of the peace" (Article 1).

Article 1 of the Constitution of UNESCO says: "The purpose of the

Organization is to contribute to peace and security by promoting collaboration among the nations through education, science and culture in order to further universal respect for justice, for the rule of law and for the human rights and fundamental freedoms which are affirmed for the peoples of the world, without distinction of race, sex, language or religion, by the Charter of the United Nations."

The Constitution of the International Labor Organization, as amended after the Second World War, says that the activity of the organization should promote the "securing of the permanent peace" (Preamble).

A second aspect of peaceful coexistence is the development of international cooperation in economic, political, cultural, and other spheres, which under contemporary conditions is a very important condition for maintaining international peace. Thus, for example, considerable attention is given to the development of international cooperation in various domains of the activity of the United Nations, whose basic task is to maintain international peace and security.

The development of cooperation between states in the respective special fields is the principal task of international organizations for specialized questions.

It already has been pointed out that struggle and cooperation in the international arena mutually permeate each other. But the co-relation between them in various international organizations is not the same. The fact is that contradictions between states, and especially between states of different social systems, affect various domains of international cooperation to varying degrees.

The closer the questions of the respective international organization to the peculiarities of the social and state system and bases of foreign policy of states of the two systems, the sharper is this struggle. The questions of disarmament, of the eradication of colonialism, of the elimination of racial discrimination, and of human rights, and so forth, may serve as examples.

In fields which do not directly affect the peculiarities of the economic system, the possibilities for states of different social systems are broader, and the struggle between them less acute. Examples of such organizations are the Universal Postal Union, International Telecommunications Union, World Meteorological Organization, Intergovernmental Maritime Consultative Organization, World Health Organization, and so forth.

Virtually the entire range of existing international contradictions are reflected in the United Nations as a universal international organization of a political character. In comparison with other international organizations, the tension of political struggle here is significantly higher.

The thesis that struggle and cooperation of states occurs in contempo-

The Legal Nature of International Organizations

rary general international organizations, not just of states of different social systems but also of states in general, is merely a statement of fact. Appeals to make contemporary general international organizations only organs of cooperation, and reproaches directed to Soviet and other scholars who speak of struggle, can not serve the cause of peace and the development of international cooperation. In distorting the real situation in international organizations, such appeals disorient the forces of progress. The real situation is that only the struggle of progressive forces in contemporary general international organizations can ensure and, to the extent of their growing might, is ensuring that the activity of such international organizations actually makes a contribution to the cause of peace and the development of international cooperation.

The presence in the membership of contemporary general international organizations of states of the two opposed social systems and the struggle between them affects the operative sphere and the jurisdiction of international organizations in two contrary directions.

The sphere of activity of international organizations, which are created on the basis of agreement between states and operate on the basis of understandings between them, includes only questions upon which agreement between states is possible. Therefore, questions of the peculiarities of a social system and questions of ideology, upon which agreement is impossible, are outside the sphere of activity of contemporary general international organizations. This objective law of societal development limits the sphere of activity and the jurisdiction of contemporary general international organizations.

The United Nations is an example. The principal task of the United Nations is the maintenance of international peace and security. The basic causes of wars are found in the nature of the capitalist social system. As V. I. Lenin has pointed out, "war is not a contradiction with the fundamentals of private ownership, but a direct and inevitable development of these fundamentals."[13] The United Nations, however, does not and can not assume as its task the liquidation of these basic causes of wars, since these are questions of a social system that lie outside the jurisdiction of the United Nations. But in addition to these basic causes of international wars, there are numerous direct causes of international conflicts and wars, and the sphere of activity of the United Nations is limited in questions of the maintenance of international peace and security to precisely this domain.

In fields which are closely linked with the peculiarities of the economic system of states of the two systems, the creation of general international

13. Lenin, "O lozunge soedinennykh shtatov evropy," *Polnoe sobranie sochinenii,* XXVI, p. 353.

organizations is much more difficult. Among such organizations are, for example, the International Bank for Reconstruction and Development, created in 1945, the International Monetary Fund, formed in the same year, the International Finance Corporation, organized in 1957—in which the USSR does not participate. Of course, it is of no little significance here that the imperialist powers, and above all the United States, from the very beginning transformed these organizations into an instrument for effectuating their own policy.[14]

Together with the limited function which we have considered, the law of societal development also operates in the direction of expanding the sphere of activity and the jurisdiction of international organizations. The policy of the socialist states in international organizations, supported by many nonsocialist countries, contemplates that international organizations are genuine organs of peace and international cooperation on the basis of equality and independence of peoples. The socialist states are struggling against attempts of imperialist powers to transform international organizations into an instrument of aggression and imperialist policy. Therefore, the growth of the influence of the socialist states in international organizations promotes the normalization and expansion of the activity of international organizations.

To illustrate this situation it suffices to list a number of important problems with which contemporary international organizations have engaged themselves as a result of the efforts of the socialist countries and other progressive forces: problems of peaceful coexistence, the liquidation of colonialism, disarmament, economic assistance to less developed countries, the elimination of racial discrimination, the codification of international law, human rights, and so forth.

C. The Breakup of the Colonial System and International Organizations

One of the most important laws of societal development in our day is the breakup of the colonial system.[15] The colonial system could not exist for long in the new epoch opened by the Great October Socialist Revolution, in an epoch of a general upsurge in the struggle against the exploitation of man by man, since colonialism is the most detestable manifestation of such exploitation.

14. G. I. Morozov and others, eds., *Spetsializirovannye uchrezhdeniia OON v sovremennom mire* (Moscow: izd-vo Nauka, 1967), pp. 196-277; K. Ia. Chizhov, *Mezhdunarodnye valiutno-finansovye organizatsii kapitalizma* (Moscow: izd-vo Finansy, 1968), pp. 14-15.

15. See *Programma Kommunisticheskoi partii Sovetskogo Soiuza*, p. 5.

The Legal Nature of International Organizations

The influence of this law of societal development upon international organizations can be divided into two stages: the first stage precedes the formation of independent states as a result of the national liberation struggle; the second follows the formation of a significant number of such states. During the first stage of struggle for the liberation of colonies, of all the forces which waged this struggle only the socialist states participated directly in the process of the creation and of the activity of international organizations. During the second stage, a greater and greater number of the new states which emerged in consequence of the liberation of the colonies aligned themselves with the socialist states. This substantially changed the situation, since the national liberation movement had the opportunity to exert a more direct influence in international organizations through these states.

And here the laws of societal development were transformed into life through the struggle of progressive forces against the forces of reaction. This struggle was especially sharp during the creation and in the course of the activity of the United Nations, which inevitably had to place the problem of decolonization on the agenda.

The struggle of progressive forces against the forces of reaction was intertwined with interimperialist contradictions and struggle. During the Second World War, this struggle was especially acute between the United States and England. The imperialist circles of England, fearing that the upsurge of the national liberation movement and the growth of the international influence of the Soviet Union could lead to England's losing her colonies, strove so that the future international organization would be at least a factor holding in check the struggle of colonial peoples for their independence. Meanwhile, American monopolies reckoned that as a result of the breakup of the English and French colonial empires they would manage to establish their own dominance in the former English and French colonies and thus expand their sphere of exploitation. The United States, therefore, favored proposals aimed at undermining the colonial domination of England and France but at the same time would guarantee against an "excessive" scope of the national liberation struggle of the colonial peoples, which in this case inevitably would be transformed into a struggle against any colonizers.

Precisely this aspiration underlay the proposals on the colonial question advanced by the United States. The draft declaration on the colonial question which was submitted by United States Secretary of State, Cordell Hull, at the Moscow Tripartite Conference of Ministers of Foreign Affairs on September 24, 1943, said that the United Nations must be responsible for the future of the colonial countries and must prepare these countries so that "they might become qualified for independent national status." It was pointed out in the draft declaration that every country having a "political tie with colonial peoples" should "progressively grant self-government to colonial peoples . . . in the light of the various stages and preparedness for independence," should "fix at the earliest practicable moments the dates when each colonial people shall be accorded the status of full independence within a system of general security." It was proposed to create an "international trusteeship organization" consisting of the representatives of the United Nations which would operate through regional commissions composed of representatives of countries "having substantial interests in the respective areas."[16]

This proposal of the United States met with the resolute opposition of Great Britain. In March 1943, when the said draft declaration was sent by Hull to English Foreign Secretary, Anthony Eden, during a visit of the latter to Washington, the English treated it more than coldly. Thereafter, the Americans persistently sought the consent of the English to publish the declaration of the colonial question, but the latter no less persistently avoided a discussion of this declaration, which was aimed at the Achilles heel of the British Empire.[17]

At the San Francisco Conference, however, where the Soviet Union strove so that the new international organization, in contrast to the League of Nations, would be an organ promoting the liberation of colonies and not impeding the self-determination of peoples, the United States to a significant extent actually united itself with England and the other colonial powers against the Soviet proposals. As a result thereof, the provisions of the United Nations Charter on the system of trusteeship and on non-self-governing territories were of a somewhat contradictory character, although no doubt remained that the question was one of ultimately granting to all peoples the possibility of exercising their right to self-determination and that the Organization and its members must "develop friendly relations among nations on the basis of the principle of equality and the self-determination of peoples" (Article 1).

The development of the national liberation movement broke the resistance of the colonial powers, who had attempted to use certain "overly cautious" provisions of the United Nations Charter with respect to decolonization for their own purposes. Under the influence of events and in consequence of the increased weight of the anticolonial forces,

16. S. B. Krylov, *Istoriia sozdaniia OON*, ed. G. I. Tunkin (Moscow: izd-vo IMO, 1960), pp. 21-23.

17. See C. Hull, *The Memoirs of Cordell Hull* (New York: Macmillan Co., 1948), II, 1234-1238.

anticolonial tunes echoed more loudly in the resolutions of the United Nations, although the imperialist states impede the realization of these resolutions to a significant degree.[18]

At the present time, about half of the members of general international organizations are from states formed as a result of the breakup of the colonial system. These basically are economically less-developed countries with small populations. The struggle for economic and cultural development, for strengthening political and economic independence against the attempts of imperialists to take advantage of the economic weakness of these states in order to impose new forms of subordination and exploitation (neocolonialism), are the most important problems of these states. The new states, naturally, bring their needs to international organizations. They demand with complete justification that the international organizations, and above all the United Nations, devote more attention to the problems affecting that portion of mankind which up to now had not entered directly into the international arena.

At the same time, the new states manifest great concern about general questions of the maintenance of international peace and security, not only because atomic war threatens existing human civilization in general, but also because international peace and the development of international cooperation are the best basis for their internal development and facilitate their struggle to strengthen political and economic independence.

General international organizations are becoming more universal not only in form, but also in substance. The attainment of complete universality is obstructed by the policy of certain imperialist powers who, on the one hand, persistently do not admit some socialist states to general

18. For greater detail on the colonial question in the United Nations, see Krylov, *Istoriia sozdaniia OON*; D. I. Baratashvili, *Za svoboda i nezavisimost' narodov* (Moscow: izd-vo IMO, 1960); Baratashvili, *Novye gosudarstva Azii i Afriki i mezhdunarodnoe pravo* (Moscow: izd-vo Nauka, 1968); L. A. Modzhorian, "Raspad kolonial'noi sistemy imperializma i Organizatsiia Ob"edinennykh Natsii," *Sovetskii ezhegodnik mezhdunarodnogo prava 1960* (Moscow: izd-vo AN SSSR, 1961), pp. 121-140; Modzhorian, *Kolonializma vchera i segodnia* (Moscow: izd-vo Mezhdunarodnye otnosheniia, 1967); G. I. Morozov, *Organizatsiia Ob"edinennykh Natsii* (Moscow: izd-vo IMO, 1962), pp. 426-491; L. V. Speranskaia, *Printsip samoopredeleniia v mezhdunarodnom prave* (Moscow: Gosiurizdat, 1961); R. A. Tuzmukhamedov, *Natsional'nyi suverenitet* (Moscow: izd-vo IMO, 1963); Tuzmukhamedov, "OON i likvidatsiia kolonializma," *Sovetskii ezhegodnik mezhdunarodnogo prava 1964-1965*, pp. 48-57; N. V. Chernogolovkin, *Krushenie kolonializma i mezhdunarodnoe pravo* (Moscow: Gosiurizdat, 1963); S. Krasil'shchikova, *OON i natsional'no-osvobitel'noe dvizhenie* (Moscow: izd-vo IMO, 1964); G. B. Starushenko, *Natsiia i gosudarstvo v osvobozhdaiushchikhsia stranakh* (Moscow: izd-vo Mezhdunarodnye otnosheniia, 1967); L. Antonowicz, *Likwidacja kolonializmu za stanoviska prawa miedzynarodowego* (Warsaw: Panstwowe wyd-wo naukowe, 1964); R. Arzinger, *Das Selbstbestimmungsrecht im allgemeinen Völkerrecht* (Berlin: Staatsverlag der DDR, 1966).

international organizations, and on the other, prevent the realization of the right to self-determination by peoples of the remaining colonies (for example, South-West Africa, Angola, and others).

The emergence in international organizations of a large number of new states exerts a salutary influence upon their activity. This leads first and foremost to the fact that the problems of the activity of many international organizations now are being subjected to material changes. Questions of economic and cultural development of the new states, problems of health in these countries, and so forth occupy a larger place in the work of international organizations.

The co-relation of forces in international organizations has changed materially. Thus, for example, if previously in the General Assembly of the United Nations the imperialist powers had a firm majority of two-thirds of the votes and could pass any resolution advantageous to them, now the situation is different. This majority is no more, although now the imperialist powers still frequently manage, using various forms of pressure on small states, to pass resolutions clearly contrary to the United Nations Charter (for example, on leaving American armed forces in South Korea, on the representation of China, and so forth). At the same time, in the majority of instances relating to the most important questions the imperialist powers find themselves in a minority (for example, the 1960 Declaration of Granting Independence to Colonial Countries and Peoples and the 1961 General Assembly resolution on banning the use of nuclear weapons). This situation frequently leads to the imperialist powers sometimes being compelled, in order to avoid being placed in a politically disadvantageous position, to vote for resolutions against which they resolutely struggled. Of course, they have in mind in this connection to obstruct the effectuation of these resolutions in the future. The General Assembly resolution adopted at the beginning of 1961 on the question "Consideration of the Principles of International Law Concerning Friendly Relations and Cooperation of States in Accordance with the United Nations Charter," for which the imperialist powers voted but whose implementation they have stubbornly prevented, is an example.

D. The Existence of Sovereign States and International Organizations

One of the most important laws of the development of mankind in our epoch which has direct relation to international organizations is the existence of sovereign states.

This law of societal development can be felt in all international organizations. Its basic manifestation is the principle of sovereign equality of the member states, which is itself the guiding principle of the structure and activity of contemporary general international organizations.

The sovereignty of member states of an international organization is reflected first and foremost in the fact that contemporary general international organizations are created and operate on the basis of charters which are international treaties concluded by sovereign states.

It is true that there are certain new phenomena in this field. The inevitable expansion of the functions of international organizations leads to numerous subsidiary organs being created with them which in a number of instances operate to a certain extent as autonomous international organizations although subordinated to the international organizations which created them (for example, the regional economic commissions of the United Nations for Europe, Asia and the Far East, Latin America, and Africa).

The most significant innovation is the creation of an Organization for Industrial Development. The decision to create this organization was adopted by the United Nations General Assembly in Resolution 2089 (XX) of December 20, 1965. The Twenty-first Session of the General Assembly confirmed the Charter of this organization.[19] According to these resolutions, the United Nations Organization for Industrial Development, "established as an organ of the General Assembly, shall function as an autonomous organization within the United Nations, . . . "[20] Resolution 2152 (XXI) determines that the principal organs of the Organization will be the Industrial Development Board, consisting of forty-five members, elected by the General Assembly from the members of the United Nations, members of specialized agencies, and members of the International Atomic Energy Agency.

It is pointed out in this resolution that decisions of the board will be taken by a simple majority of those present and voting (point 9). It further determines that the expenses for administrative and research activities will be included in the regular budget of the United Nations, and operational expenses will be met from other sources (points 20, 21, and 22 of the resolution).

Despite these peculiarities of the creation of the United Nations Organization for Industrial Development, it would be incorrect in this instance not to note the treaty basis of this organization. It is an international organization of a secondary order, an organ of an already existing international organization created by an international treaty. It is one of the subsidiary organs of the General Assembly, whose creation is provided for by Article 22 of the United Nations Charter. The funda-

19. G.A. Res. 2152 (XXI), November 17, 1966.
20. *Ibid.*

Laws of Societal Development and International Organizations

mental legal basis of such an international organization, even if it is called "autonomous," is the treaty by which the primary international organization was created, in this case, the United Nations Charter.

In reality, the existence of such a subsidiary organization depends completely upon the existence of this basic international treaty and the international organization which has given birth to the said subsidiary organization.

An important manifestation of the sovereignty of member states is the general proposition that any amendment of the charter of an international organization can not become binding upon a member state of this organization without its consent (see Chapter 15).

The principle of sovereignty is further manifested in the fact that the organs of general international organizations endowed with the right to adopt decisions consist of the representatives of the member states acting in accordance with the instructions of their governments. This is a very important feature of contemporary international organizations.

The fact that resolutions of general international organizations, with certain exceptions, have the character of recommendations and are not legally binding upon members of the organization also is a manifestation of the principle of sovereignty (see Chapter 5).

Finally, in all general international organizations, member states have the right to withdraw from the organization (see Chapter 15).

Chapter 14 *The Basic Features of the Legal Nature of General International Organizations. The Charter as the Basis of an Organization's Activity*

A. Charters of International Organizations: Treaties or Constitutions?

The question of the legal nature of charters of international organizations is undoubtedly of great theoretical and practical interest. Is a charter of an international organization an international treaty *sui generis* or is it a constitution of an international organization, similar to the constitution of a state?

According to constitutional theory, charters of contemporary international organizations, and above all of the United Nations, are constitutions or are basically constitutions and only partially international treaties, and therefore the provisions of the law of treaties are nonapplicable or virtually nonapplicable to them. The basic idea of this theory, which is oriented toward American and English constitutional practice, is that the charters of international organizations as constitutions are "flexible" documents from whose provisions one may digress in practice, and this digression will not be a violation, but a modification of these charters.

"And as formal amendments of an international constitutional document, such as the U.N. Charter," writes an American professor, W. Friedmann, "are almost impossible to achieve, the adjustment generally proceeds by the consolidation of practices or by *de facto* revisions. Thus a whole body of parliamentary law has been developed in the United Nations, a formalised interplay between the various named organs of the United Nations, and the Committees set up by them. The text of the Charter would, for example, entirely fail to account for the *de facto* shift in the relative competences of the Security Council and the General Assembly ... The Uniting for Peace Resolution of 1950 can be regarded as an indirect amendment of the Charter, transferring certain functions from the Security Council to the Assembly without the complex process of amendment provided by the Charter itself . . . "[1] In drawing a parallel between the United Nations Charter and the United States Constitution, the author writes further: "National constitutions, notably that of the United States, have also been greatly moulded by the interplay of social change, legal practices, and legal interpretations."[2]

E. Jimenez de Arechaga, a Uruguyan professor who entitled his book *Derecho constitucional de las Naciones Unidas*, characterizes as follows the constitutional theory as it concerns the United Nations Charter. Attempting at the outset to justify the legality of Resolution 377(V) of November 3, 1950, "Uniting for Peace," with references to the provisions of the United Nations Charter, and then in fact recognizing that such a justification is impossible, he writes: "This constitutional development shows that the Charter is an international document which is not static and which has demonstrated that it possesses to a high degree the quality of a constitution in adapting itself to unexpected changes and new circumstances. It is possible to assert that few national constitutions have undergone in the process of their application such important and rapid changes as has the United Nations Charter . . . "[3]

There is no doubt whatever that the constitutional theory is worked out and propagandized strenuously in the West because it is aimed at justifying the numerous violations of the charters of general international organizations, and above all of the United Nations, which did and do occur under the pressure of the imperialist powers. Herein is the political significance of this theory.

The legal argumentation in justification of this theory is worked out most thoroughly in S. Rosenne's article "Is the Constitution of an International Organization an International Treaty?"[4]

Professor Rosenne asserts that the application of the law of treaties to the charters of international organizations reveals a whole series of basic departures from the general law of treaties.[5] These departures he sees in the following issues: admission to an organization in comparison with accession to a treaty;[6] reservations to an instrument in those instances

1. W. Friedmann, *The Changing Structure of International Law* (New York: Columbia University Press, 1964), p. 153.
2. *Ibid.*, p. 154.
3. E. Jimenez de Arechaga, *Derecho constitucional de las Naciones Unidas* (Madrid: Escuela de funcionarios internacionales, 1958), p. 204.
4. S. Rosenne, "Is the Constitution of an International Organization an International Treaty?" *Communicazioni e studi*, XII (1966), 21-89.
5. *Ibid.*, p. 50.
6. *Ibid.*, p. 55.

when the instrument contains no provisions regarding reservations;[7] suspension of membership in an international organization, expulsion from an organization, withdrawal from it;[8] amendment of charters;[9] interpretation of charters.[10]

The author then draws, though cautious in form, very far-reaching conclusions. In essence Rosenne maintains that although by their origin the charters of international organizations are international treaties, as regards their operation they are basically not treated as treaties. "The question," he writes, "whether the constitution of an international organization is itself an international treaty does not permit of an unqualified answer. The reply will depend on the circumstances in which the question is raised. There is no room for doubt that the process by which a State forms its will to be a member of an international organization on its internal plane, by which it expresses that will on the international plane, both come within the normal scope of law of treaties, domestic and international as the case may be."[11]

But with regard to the operation of the charter of an international organization, Rosenne says the following: "The fact that so many cardinal aspects relating to the very essence of the legal relationships created by membership in an international organization and participation in its constituent instrument are in practice governed by principles and rules fundamentally different from those applicable to the corresponding aspects of participation in multilateral treaties must raise serious doubts as to whether the constituent instruments of international organizations are of the same *genus*, in international law, as multilateral treaties."[12]

The author dwells in special detail on interpreting the United Nations Charter, showing that the International Court in "appropriate instances" has applied methods of interpreting the Charter which are characteristic of national constitutions and not of international treaties.[13] But one immediately notes that Rosenne does not even make an attempt to prove in this connection that such practice conforms to international law and is not a violation thereof. The emphasis upon the problem of interpretation is completely understandable since even the "Uniting for Peace" resolution and the practice based thereon in the majority of instances are

7. *Ibid.*, pp. 58-64.
8. *Ibid.*, p. 64.
9. *Ibid.* pp. 64-65.
10. *Ibid.*, pp. 67-80.
11. *Ibid.*, p. 86.
12. *Ibid.*, p. 66.
13. *Ibid.*, pp. 70, 79.

claimed by western authors to be based upon an interpretation of the United Nations Charter.[14]

Upon closer examination of the arguments advanced by Professor Rosenne in justification of the conclusion concerning the nonapplicability or the basic nonapplicability of the law of treaties to the charters of international organizations, there are insufficient grounds for such a conclusion.

The charters of international organizations are international treaties having certain peculiarities, treaties *sui generis*. The statute of an international organization, in contrast to the usual multilateral international treaty, creates a permanent international entity which functions on its basis. It defines not only the rights and duties of states-parties to the treaty, but also the purposes and tasks of the organization, being an international organism distinct from states, the functions and jurisdiction of organs of the organization, the mutual relations between the organization and the member-states, and so forth. In other words, the statute of an international organization is a more complex phenomenon than the ordinary multilateral treaty.

It is natural, therefore, that the conclusion, and especially the operation of an international treaty such as the charter of an international organization, has certain peculiarities. However, all the basic provisions of the law of treaties are applicable to the charters of international organizations, in a number of instances with insignificant changes. In particular, the following provisions of the law of treaties are applicable to them: the conclusion and entry into force of multilateral treaties, except for certain provisions relating to reservations; the invalidity of treaties; the amendment and interpretation of treaties; the operation of international treaties; and above all the basic principle of this section of the law of treaties— *pacta sunt servanda*; the significance of treaties for third states; and so forth. It is necessary to remark once again that the application of individual norms of the law of treaties relating to the said sections may reveal the need to adapt some of them. The International Law Commission therefore acted correctly in having included in the final draft of the law of treaties Article 4, which says: "The application of the present articles to treaties which are constituent instruments of an international organization or are adopted within an international organization shall be subject to any relevant rules of the organization."[15]

14. See L. Goodrich, *The United Nations* (New York: Thomas Y. Crowell Co., 1958), p. 168; Arechaga, *Derecho constitucional de las Naciones Unidas*, pp. 204-205.
15. United Nations, *Yearbook of the International Law Commission 1966* (New York: United Nations, 1967), II, 191.

In doing so, the Commission by no means proceeded from those considerations ascribed to it by Professor Rosenne, who welcomes the first paragraph of this article as supposedly signifying recognition in principle of the inapplicability of the law of treaties to the charters of international organizations.[16] The text of the article itself testifies to the contrary. The article speaks, first, of treaties "which are constituent instruments of international organizations," that is, the Commission believes such charters to be international treaties. Second, the article said "the application of the present articles to treaties which are constituent instruments of international organizations . . . ," that is, the Commission proceeded from the fact that as a whole the draft articles are applicable to the charters of international organizations, with the exception, of course, of those instances when an international organization has its own rules regarding a given concrete question.

At the Vienna Conference on the Law of Treaties, the text of the article relating to this question was changed somewhat. Article 5 of the Convention on the law of international treaties adopted by the conference is even more precise than the Commission's text in saying that the provisions of the Convention as a whole shall apply to the constituent instruments of international organizations. This article provides: "The present Convention shall apply to any treaty which is an establishing act of an international organization without prejudice to the respective rules of this organization."

Thus, the charters of international organizations are a special category of international treaties. The attempt to ascribe certain features of state constitutions to the charters of international organizations has no justification, since international organizations are qualitatively different from states.

The aspiration to convert similar conceptions into reality is a great danger for any general international organization, of which the experience of the United Nations is especially clear evidence. Professor C. de Visscher is absolutely right when he says in this connection: "The dynamism of an organization must be adapted to the treaty bases of the regulations in order to avoid serious political crises."[17]

B. The Jurisdiction of International Organizations

The numerous violations of the United Nations Charter which have taken place under the influence of imperialist states have led to the

16. Rosenne, "Is the Constitution of an International Organization an International Treaty?" p. 87.

17. C. de Visscher, *Les effectivités du droit international public* (Paris: Editions A. Pedone, 1967), p. 78.

emergence of various legal constructions having the purpose to justify these violations. Since these violations of the Charter were connected primarily with a violation of the jurisdiction of the United Nations in general and the distribution of such jurisdiction among the organs of the United Nations, these constructions have endeavored to prove the possibility of freely manipulating this jurisdiction.

Among such constructions are the theory of "inherent jurisdiction" and the theory of "implied powers" of international organizations.

(1) The concept of "inherent jurisdiction." The content of the concept of "inherent jurisdiction" (*compétence inhérente*) of international organizations amounts in its general features to the following. The practice of the United Nations and other international organizations, say the proponents of this concept, shows that their activity goes beyond the limits provided by their charters. From this the conclusion is drawn that a generally recognized norm of international law exists to the effect that international organizations have "inherent jurisdiction," meaning that any international organization can undertake activities necessary to achieve its purposes irrespective of the specific provisions of the organization's charter.

The concept of "inherent jurisdiction" of international organizations was reflected in particular in the opinion of the International Court of July 20, 1962, on the question of certain expenses of the United Nations. The opinion of the Court says that "when the Organization takes action which warrants the assertion that it was appropriate for the fulfillment of one of the stated purposes of the United Nations, the presumption is that such action is not *ultra vires* the Organization."[18]

F. Seyersted, a Norwegian jurist who is a staunch advocate of the concept of "inherent jurisdiction," defines it as follows: "The legal capacity of intergovernmental organizations to perform 'sovereign' and international acts is, like that of States, not confined to what can be positively deduced from their constitutions, but comprises all acts which are not *precluded* by their constitutions and which do not impose new obligations upon parties who are not subject to their jurisdiction. If the constitution does not define the matters with which the Organization can deal, as is the case of the Nordic Council, then it can deal with any matter. And if the constitution does not preclude certain types of acts or *exhaustively* enumerate the acts which the Organization may perform, as very few constitutions do, then it can perform any type of acts. And so it

18. International Court of Justice, Reports of Judgments, Advisory Opinions and Orders, *Certain Expenses of the United Nations, Advisory Opinion of July 20, 1962* (Leiden: Sijthoff, 1962), p. 168.

The Legal Nature of International Organizations

can if there is no constitution. This principle of inherent capacities reflects more adequately the position as it is in practice."[19]

In application to the specific question of creating United Nations armed forces, the same author reasons as follows: " . . . it is submitted that the United Nations has the legal competence to establish military forces even in the absence of specific authority therefor in the Charter . . . This is an inherent capacity of the organization . . . The capacity is well within the scope of the first purpose of the United Nations, which is stated in Article 11 of the Charter . . . "[20]

In stating correctly that the practice of contemporary international organizations often goes beyond the provisions of their charters, the proponents of this concept draw unjustified legal conclusions therefrom.

Can one draw from the fact of the existence of the practice of going beyond the limits of the provisions of charters of international organizations the conclusion that a generally recognized norm of international law exists with regard to the "inherent jurisdiction" of international organizations? How could such a norm arise?

As already has been said, a customary norm of international law arises from international practice in consequence of the recurrent actions of states. Practice in and of itself, however, is not yet a norm of international law. The process of forming a customary norm of international law is completed only with the recognition by states of a customary rule as a norm of international law.

Proponents of "inherent jurisdiction" make a logical generalization from individual facts and declare it to be a norm of international law. But the norm logically inferred, even if the conclusion itself is sufficiently justified, still is not a norm of law. In order to become a norm of international law, this logically inferred norm must be recognized by states as a legal norm. In this case, such recognition by states of the said norm does not exist, and not a single proponent of "inherent jurisdiction" attempts to show the contrary. It is obvious that member states of various international organizations agree in individual instances, albeit tacitly, to a respective international organization performing particular actions not expressly provided for by its charter. States do this not by virtue of legal duty, which would arise for them from the said norm if it existed, but by virtue of a free expression of will.

Thus, norms of general international law relating to "inherent jurisdiction" of international organizations do not exist.

19. F. Seyersted, "International Personality of Intergovernmental Organizations," *Indian Journal of International Law*, IV (1964), 55.

20. Seyersted, "Can the United Nations Establish Military Forces and Perform Other Acts Without Specific Basis in the Charter?" *Österreichische Zeitschrift für öffentliches Recht*, XII (1962), 214.

This concept also does not find a basis in the charters of general international organizations. There are no general international organizations whose charters would empower the international organizations to use any means to achieve the purposes stipulated in their charters. Nor are there such provisions even in the charters of west European organizations which have specific features of supranationality.

Contemporary general international organizations are created by states, and only states may define the character of each organization created by them, the purposes it will strive to accomplish, and the means which they place at the disposal of this organization. All this is done by concluding an international treaty—the charter of the organization.

C. M. Chaumont, a French professor, properly emphasizes that "the creator states of an organization conclude an agreement not only regarding the nature of its purposes, but also regarding the means for accomplishing these purposes."[21]

Meanwhile, it follows from the concept of "inherent jurisdiction" that an international organization created by treaty between states is immediately separated from its base.

Since the charters of international organizations are international treaties, the concept of "inherent jurisdiction" contravenes the basic principle of the law of treaties—*pacta sunt servanda*. It follows from this principle that states should fulfill their obligations in good faith according to the charter of the international organization, that more should not be required of member states than is provided by the charter, and that member states have the right to require that the organization act in conformity with its charter.

The concept of "inherent jurisdiction" contravenes the principles of interpreting international treaties. Article 31(1) of the 1969 Vienna Convention on the Law of Treaties establishes: "A treaty must be interpreted in good faith in conformity with the ordinary meaning of the provisions in the context of the treaty and in light of the subject and purpose of the treaty."[22]

Meanwhile, the concept of "inherent jurisdiction" ascribes a certain

21. C. M. Chaumont, "La Signification du principe de specialité des organisations internationales," *Mélanges offerts à Henri Rolin; Problèmes de droit des gens* (Paris: Editions A. Pedone, 1964), p. 59.

22. It was pointed out in a Letter of the French Government to the International Court on February 15, 1962: "Member States of the United Nations, whether original members or not, have subscribed to the obligations of the Charter, but nothing more. The Charter is a treaty, by which states have limited their jurisdiction only to the extent that they have consented." International Court of Justice, Pleadings, Oral Arguments, Documents, *Certain Expenses of the United Nations (Article 17, Paragraph 2, of the Charter). Advisory Opinion of 20 July 1962* (Leiden: A. W. Sijthoff, 1962), p. 133.

magical force wrested from the context of the treaty to the purposes of the treaty, transforming them into something independent and essentially superseding the entire treaty. As the Soviet member of the Court, Academician V. Koretskii, correctly noted, such a presumption with respect to the purposes of a treaty would signify a return to the long condemned maxim "the ends justify the means."[2 3]

Finally, the concept of "inherent jurisdiction" contravenes the legal nature of contemporary international organizations. One must cite in this connection the words of the Polish member of the Court, at that time the President of the Court, Winiarski, contained in his dissenting opinion regarding the Advisory Opinion of the International Court on certain expenses of the United Nations. "The Charter," declared Winiarski, "has set forth the purposes of the United Nations in very wide, and for that reason too indefinite terms. But—apart from the resources, including the financial resources of the Organization, it does not follow, far from it, that the Organization is entitled to seek to achieve those purposes by no matter what means. The fact that an organ of the United Nations is seeking to achieve one of those purposes does not suffice to render its action lawful. The Charter, a multilateral treaty which was the result of prolonged and laborious negotiations, carefully created organs and determined their competence and means of action.

"The intention of those who drafted it was clearly to abandon the possibility of useful action rather than to sacrifice the balance of carefully established fields of competence, as can be seen, for example, in the case of the voting in the Security Council. It is only by such procedures, which were clearly defined, that the United Nations can seek to achieve its purposes. It may be that the United Nations is sometimes not in a position to undertake action which would be useful for the maintenance of international peace and security or for one or another of the purposes indicated in Article 1 of the Charter, but that is the way in which the Organization was conceived and brought into being."[2 4]

The nonconformity of the jurisdiction of the United Nations to the purposes proclaimed in its Charter is by no means the result of the lack of foresight of the founders of this international organization, but, as already pointed out (see Chapter 13), a manifestation of the nature of contemporary international organizations.

The concept of inherent jurisdiction, supposedly guided exclusively or basically by the purposes proclaimed in the charter of an international organization, fundamentally contravenes the legal nature of contemporary general international organizations as interstate formations of peaceful coexistence.

23. International Court of Justice, *Certain Expenses of the United Nations*, p. 268.
24. *Ibid.*, p. 230.

(2) The concept of "implied powers." The concept of "implied powers" (*compétence implicite*), of international organizations frequently is interpreted so broadly that it closely approximates the concept of "inherent jurisdiction."

In the Advisory Opinion of the International Court in the case concerning reparation for injuries suffered in the service of the United Nations this concept was formulated as follows: "Under international law, that the Organization must be deemed to have those powers which, though not expressly provided in the Charter, are conferred upon it by necessary implication as being essential to the performance of its duties."[25] The Court referred in this connection to the Advisory Opinion of the League of Nations Permanent Court of International Justice of July 23, 1926.[26]

In justifying this position, the International Court referred to the presumption of the conformity of jurisdiction to the purposes and functions of an organization, that is to say, to the "principles of effectiveness," coming close to the concept of "implied jurisdiction." "It must be acknowledged," the Court maintains in this Advisory Opinion, "that its members, by entrusting certain functions to it, with the attendant duties and responsibilities, have clothed it with the competence required to enable those functions to be effectively discharged."[27] The Court added that the "rights and duties of an entity such as the Organization [the United Nations—G.T.] must depend upon its purposes and functions as specified or implied in its constituent documents and developed in practice."[28]

The concept of "implied powers" was applied by the western powers to justify General Assembly resolution 377(V), "Uniting for Peace."

This resolution maintains, first, that it should be implied that if an organ has not undertaken necessary actions provided for by the United Nations Charter, another organ may assume the fulfillment of these duties. "... Failure of the Security Council to discharge its responsibilities on behalf of all the Member States ... does not relieve Member States of their obligations or the United Nations of its responsibility under the Charter to maintain international peace and security."

The conclusion is drawn from this that another organ, to wit, the General Assembly, can assume, in the event the Security Council fails to act, the adoption of appropriate measures, including the "use of armed

25. International Court of Justice, Reports of Judgments, Advisory Opinions and Orders, *Reparation for Injuries Suffered in the Service of the United Nations, Advisory Opinion of April 11, 1949* (Leiden: A. W. Sijthoff, 1949), p. 182.

26. *Ibid.*, pp. 182-183.

27. *Ibid.*, p. 179.

28. *Ibid.*, p. 180.

forces when necessary, to maintain or restore international peace and security."[29] The conclusion concerning the "implied power" of the General Assembly was formulated as follows in the resolution: " ... discharge by the General Assembly of its responsibilities in this respect calls for possibilities of observation which would ascertain the facts and expose aggressors; for the existence of armed forces which could be used collectively; and for the possibility of timely recommendation by the General Assembly to Members of the United Nations for collective action which, to be effective, should be prompt."

The concept of the "implied powers" of international organizations and their organs as set forth in the above advisory opinion of the International Court of 1949 and in the illegal United Nations General Assembly resolution 377(V) lay at the basis of bourgeois doctrine on this question. In its turn, this doctrine resorts to the concept of "implied powers" generally to justify the "Uniting for Peace" resolution and the actions undertaken on the basis of this resolution.

Thus, Professor L. Goodrich maintains on this plane that the General Assembly "has at least a 'residual responsibility' of its own."[30] Professor de Arechaga also speaks of the "residual functions" (*la reserva de funciones*) of the General Assembly of the United Nations.[31] "Taking effective collective measures to suppress aggression," he writes, "is within the limits of the Charter, one may say, in the center of the Charter. It obviously follows from this that the General Assembly can discuss and recommend the taking of effective collective measures to suppress aggression."[32]

D. W. Bowett, an English professor, in devoting an extensive monograph to the question of United Nations armed forces, raises the question: "Is it necessary at all to locate specifically in the Charter provisions the constitutional authority of United Nations Forces? In other words, cannot a more general argument for their legality be relied upon?"[33] And of course the author answers this question affirmatively, resorting to the concepts of "inherent" and "implied" jurisdiction as they have been formulated in the advisory opinions of the International Court in question.[34]

In formulating a broad concept of "implied powers," bourgeois jurists in fact maintain that there exists a norm of international law according to

29. G.A. Res. 377(V), November 3, 1950.
30. Goodrich, *The United Nations*, p. 177.
31. Arechaga, *Derecho constitucional de las Naciones Unidas*, p. 197.
32. *Ibid.*, p. 198.
33. D. W. Bowett, *United Nations Forces* (London: Stevens & Sons, 1964), p. 307.
34. *Ibid.*, pp. 307-311.

which one should imply that member states of an international organization have granted it that jurisdiction which is necessary to effectuate the
purposes and functions of the organization. Bowett defines "implied
powers" as those powers "which may reasonably be deduced from the
purposes and functions of the organisation in question."[35]

Professor B. Rouyer-Hameray, of the University of Strasbourg, writes:
"One should suppose that the authors of an agreement or treaty intended
to create norms which in practice could operate. It is necessary, therefore,
to presume an intention to create everything necessary for their effective
operation: if states have created an international organization, they
intended to create everything necessary for it to function . . . "[36]

A. Sereni, an Italian professor, in declaring that the question of
"implied powers" is one of interpreting the charter of an international
organization, actually comes to assert that there is a generally obligatory
norm of international law regarding "implied powers." "The determination of the implied powers of international organizations," wrote Sereni,
"is, therefore, the result of interpretation, although also an extension, of
the constitution of the organization, and not a process of creating new
norms . . . "[37]

In this connection, however, Sereni places in such interpretation a
content which transforms it into the creating of new norms even in
violation of the organization's charter. "With the exception of provisions
contained in the constitution," he says, "any organization has the implied
power to interpret the constitution for the purpose of determining its own
jurisdiction as regards its purposes and functions and therefore to establish
the extent of its own jurisdiction."[38] The author even admits, although
by way of exception, that such a determination of the jurisdiction of the
organization also can be exercised by an organ not entrusted by the
Charter with the functions regarding which a question may arise in a
concrete instance.[39]

Of course, in practice it is impossible to provide clauses for all possible
instances of future activity in the charters of international organizations,
especially in the charter of an organization such as the United Nations,
whose functions are exceedingly broad and diverse. Therefore, in working
out the charters the parties inevitably presuppose that a number of
questions of the activity of an international organization, not of course

35. Bowett, *The Law of International Institutions* (London: Stevens & Sons, 1964),
p. 275.

36. B. Rouyer-Hameray, *Les competences implicites des organisations internationales* (Paris: R. Pichon et R. Durand-Auzias, 1962), pp. 80-81.

37. A. Sereni, *Diritto internazionale* (Milan: Dott. A. Giuffre, 1960), II, 980.

38. *Ibid.*, p. 985.

39. *Ibid.*

the major questions, remain to be decided on the basis of the charter provisions in the process of the functioning of the organization. On this level, one may speak of "implied powers."

"Implied powers" is not a norm of general international law. What has been said before about the absence in international law of norms concerning "inherent jurisdiction" also relates generally to the "implied powers" of international organizations. The 1949 opinion of the International Court and the majority of bourgeois jurists go farther than what corresponds to contemporary international law. On this plane, the view of the American member of the International Court, G. Hackworth, expressed in his dissenting opinion in this case, deserves attention, although one can not completely agree with it. Warning of the danger of a broad interpretation of "necessary implication," Hackworth declared: "There can be no gainsaying the fact that the Organization is one of delegated and enumerated powers. It is to be presumed that such powers as the Member States desired to confer upon it are stated either in the Charter or in complementary agreements concluded by them. Powers not expressed cannot freely be implied. Implied powers flow from a grant of expressed powers, and are limited to those that are 'necessary' to the exercise of powers expressly granted."[40]

Professor Chaumont defines the "implied powers" (*pouvoirs implicites*) of an international organization as follows: "By implied powers are understood those powers which, while not textually provided for by the creators of the organization, have been recognized or accepted by member states within a certain period of the life of the organization as auxiliary or subordinate means to accomplish the permanent ends for which the organization was founded."[41]

Here, however, the question is actually one of the creating of new, subordinate, and more precise norms through additional agreements among the members.[42]

Thus, "implied powers" of international organizations can occur. The question of the existence and extent of such jurisdiction in each individual

40. International Court of Justice, *Reparation for Injuries Suffered in the Service of the United Nations*, p. 198.

41. Chaumont, "La signification du principe de specialité des organisations internationales," p. 59.

42. On this plane, P. Reuter believes the adoption by international organizations of "executive regulations by which organs of an international organization clarify obligations defined in the charters without broadening them" is a manifestation of "implied powers." As an example he mentions the United Nations General Assembly resolution establishing rules for registering international treaties at the United Nations. P. Reuter, *Institutions internationales*, 4th ed. (Paris: Presses Universitaires de France, 1963), p. 215.

instance is a question of interpreting the charter of the respective international organization with those additions and changes which might have been formed in the course of its activity on the basis of agreement of the members of the given organization.

The general rules of interpreting international treaties, with those possible changes which may exist within the framework of the respective international organization, apply to interpreting the charters of international organizations. This has been recognized repeatedly by the International Court, and the practice of the international organizations themselves; and international legal doctrine proceeds from this. Thus, in the 1962 advisory opinion on the question of certain expenses of the United Nations, the International Court again confirmed the proposition, although in its conclusions it actually moves far away from it. The Court pointed out: "On the previous occasions when the Court has had to interpret the Charter of the United Nations, it has followed the principles and rules applicable in general to the interpretation of treaties, since it has recognized that the Charter is a multilateral treaty, albeit a treaty having certain special characteristics."[43]

The interpretation of an international treaty is the establishment of the result of the concordance of the wills of states as it was expressed in the treaty. Interpretation of a treaty includes also an elucidation of the concordance of wills with regard to what was implied but was not precisely expressed in the treaty text and the accompanying documents. If certain changes and additions have been made in the treaty in the course of applying it, then naturally the interpretation of a treaty at a particular moment will also embrace the concordance of the wills of the parties to the treaty which has occurred in connection with such additions and changes.

One should above all reject the concept of interpretation which attaches exaggerated significance to the purposes and functions proclaimed in the charter of an international organization at the expense of diminishing the significance of the specific provisions of the charter.

For that reason, without treating in detail the problems of interpreting international treaties, it is necessary to point out that implied powers can not be sought in the charter of every international organization. As A. D. McNair justly points out, "many treaties contain express conditions, and in some treaties conditions are implied."[44] But the author, not without justification, warns against an enthusiasm for "implying." "Conditions," he says, "should be implied only with great circumspection; for if they are

43. International Court of Justice, *Certain Expenses of the United Nations*, p. 157.
44. A. D. McNair, *The Law of Treaties* (Oxford: Clarendon Press, 1961), p. 436.

implied too readily, they become a serious threat to the sanctity of a treaty."[4][5]

The "implied power" of an international organization in reality exists when in order to exercise the jurisdiction clearly granted to the organization as a whole or its organ (but not generally to effectuate the purposes and functions of the organization) it is necessary to resort to actions which not only do not contravene the charter of the organization but also are customary in international practice.

Thus, for example, if the charter of an organization provides for the organization's rendering assistance to states in a specific field but is silent about the possibility of the organization's concluding agreements with the respective states, one can suppose with assurance that the conclusion of such agreements is an "implied power" of this organization. The conclusion of such agreements not only is necessary to effectuate a specific jurisdiction of the organization, but is at the present time a normal means of formalizing such relations between states and international organizations.

C. Amendment of the Charters of International Organizations

The most important features characterizing the legal nature of contemporary general international organizations and their charters is the fact that no amendments to these charters become binding upon member states without their consent.

In this sphere there are a number of new phenomena. The previous requirement of the unanimity of members of the organization has passed away; it no longer is applied either at the stage of adopting amendments to charters of international organizations nor at the stage of their entry into force. According to the charters of the majority of contemporary general international organizations, amendments to charters are adopted by two-thirds of the votes of the organization or special conferences where all members of the organization are represented. Amendments usually enter into force after their ratification or adoption by two-thirds of the members of the organization; in some organizations this majority must include specific members of the organization: in the United Nations, all permanent members of the Security Council; in the International Labor Organization, five of the ten members of the Council included in the category of basic industrial powers.

An amendment to the charter of an international organization ratified or adopted by the requisite majority of members of the organization

45. *Ibid.*

usually, but not always, enters into force for all members of the organization (United Nations, International Labor Organization, World Health Organization). Sometimes this rule is applied only with respect to less significant important amendments to a charter, whereas the more important amendments enter into force after their adoption by two-thirds of the member states and only for those states which have accepted these amendments (World Meteorological Organization).

The constitutions of UNESCO and of the Food and Agricultural Organization (although the latter, as already pointed out, is not essentially a general international organization) go the farthest on this level. Article 13(1) of the UNESCO Constitution reads: "Proposals for amendments to this Constitution shall become effective upon receiving the approval of the General Conference by a two-thirds majority; provided, however, that those amendments which involve fundamental alterations in the aims of the Organization or new obligations for the Member States shall require subsequent acceptance on the part of two-thirds of the Member States before they come into force." Amendments to the Food and Agricultural Organization Constitution are adopted by the Conference by two-thirds of the states voting on condition that the majority of those who voted for the amendment constitute more than half of the members of the organization. An amendment not involving new obligations for members of the FAO enters into force immediately, unless otherwise provided in the conference resolution adopting the amendment (Article 19).

Thus, in both UNESCO and the FAO some amendments to the constitution of the organization enter into force after their adoption by an organ of the organization without subsequent ratification or approval by member states.

It would be incorrect to deprecate the importance of these new phenomena in the question of amending the charters of international organizations. But at the same time one can not lose sight of the fact that all these changes leave the basic process of amending the charters of international organizations unaffected—the concordance of the wills of states. Any amendment to the charter of a general international organization can not become binding upon member states of the organization without its consent, explicitly or tacitly expressed. This also is applicable to those instances when, according to the charter of an international organization, amendments to the charter which have been adopted or for which two-thirds of the members of the organization have expressed themselves enter into force for all members of this organization.

If a state does not consider it possible to adopt a charter amendment which is entering into force, it has according to the provisions prevailing in contemporary general international organizations either the right to withdraw from the organization (the United Nations and the majority of specialized agencies) or is considered automatically to have left the organization (the International Civil Aviation Organization and the Intergovernmental Maritime Consultative Organization). In some specialized agencies of the United Nations (ICAO, IMCO), continuation of membership in the organization for states who have not ratified an amendment which has entered into force is allowed with respect to specific amendments, that is to say, a different legal regime for member states is permitted.[46]

The question of the possibility of amending the charters of international organizations by subsequent practice, that is, by means of custom, is much more complex. In order to ignore or first and foremost to justify the violations of the United Nations Charter which have taken place under the pressure of western powers, many bourgeois international lawyers frequently speak of the practice of the United Nations and other international organizations as something which must be followed in the future as well, almost forgetting about the charters of these organizations. In analyzing this practice, they mix together lawful acts with actions which are a violation of the charters, and they come to the more or less identical conclusion that the practice of an international organization can modify its charter. The view of L. Goodrich, of Columbia University, relating to the practice of the United Nations is characteristic. "In actual practice," writes Goodrich, "the structure of power and influence in the United Nations has been quite different from what was initially envisaged. The Charter itself has not been amended. The composition, functions, and powers of organs have remained the same on paper. But in the course of the day-to-day interpretation and application of these provisions, a quite different system of power relationships has emerged from that which was anticipated at the time the Charter was approved in San Francisco."[47]

We have spoken previously (see Chapter 4, Section C) about the possibility of amending an international treaty through custom being applicable in principle also to the charters of international organizations. In admitting the possibility of the amendment and development of a treaty through custom, however, one must be cautious, since the question is one of the subsequent agreement of the parties not clearly expressed changing a clearly expressed agreement which has been embodied in the treaty. To establish the existence of an agreement not clearly expressed, naturally, is more difficult. In addition, an agreement not clearly ex-

46. For greater detail, see R. Zacklin, *The Amendment of the Constitutive Instruments of the United Nations and Specialized Agencies* (Leiden: A. W. Sijthoff, 1968), pp. 161-166; E. Yemin, *Legislative Powers in the United Nations and Specialized Agencies* (Leiden: A. W. Sijthoff, 1969).
47. Goodrich, *The United Nations*, p. 115.

pressed in this case is an exception with regard to the provisions concerning amendment of the treaty which are fixed in the treaty itself.

Special caution must be shown in appraising the practice of international organizations. The fact is that the question here is one of a permanently functioning entity where there may occur, as the experience of the United Nations illustrates, recurrent practice which was simply a violation of the United Nations Charter and in no way an amendment thereof.

From that which was said in Chapter 4, Section C, below, about treaties in general being applicable to the charters of international organizations, it follows that the amendment through custom of certain provisions of the charter of an international organization which are not basic is possible in those instances when: (a) a practice has been formed in a given international organization with which all members of this organization have agreed; (b) this practice is evidence of an agreement of members of the organization to amend the respective provisions of its charter.

The basic element is that the charter of an international organization, being an international treaty, can be amended only by states-parties to this treaty, and not by the international organization itself, created by the treaty. The subsequent practice of an international organization is at the same time the practice of states, since the actions of an international organization are basically determined by the actions of member states of this organization. If such practice is evidence of the existence among participants in the organization of an agreement concerning the making of certain amendments to the previously constituted agreement of these states expressed in the charter of the organization, then, as already has been pointed out, such agreement achieved through custom may not change the basic provisions of the treaty, that is, in the present case the charter of the international organization.

What has been said seems to us to reflect existing practice, which also testifies to the fact that this does not relate to the provisions of charters affecting the bases of a particular international organization.

The practice of the United Nations Security Council on the question of the abstention of permanent members of the Council is a clear example of the modification of the charter provisions of an international organization by subsequent practice which corresponds to the said requirements. As is well-known, according to Article 27(3) of the United Nations Charter, decisions of the Security Council concerning all questions of a nonprocedural character are considered adopted when nine members of the Council (previously seven) have cast their votes for them, including the concurring votes of all its permanent members. This point does not provide for cases when the permanent members abstain from voting on nonprocedural questions.

In practice the Security Council, as a result of the clearly expressed or tacit consent of the members of the Council, has established the rule that the abstention of a permanent member of the Security Council during a vote is not regarded as a negative vote and does not prevent the adoption of the decision.

Logically, this rule proceeds from the fact that every permanent member of the Security Council has the opportunity to determine its attitude toward the resolution being discussed and to vote for it, if it supports it, or to abstain, if it does not support its adoption but nevertheless has no objections to its being adopted, or to vote against if it objects to the given decision.

This rule, formed in the practice of applying Article 27 of the United Nations Charter, introduces some change into this article. Tacitly adopted by the members of the United Nations, it has been completely consolidated in the practice of the Security Council's work.

On the other hand, General Assembly Resolution 377(V) of November 3, 1950 (the so-called "Uniting for Peace" resolution), as it does not correspond to the aforesaid requirements, is a violation of the Charter and not a modification thereof. This resolution has the purpose of amending the basic provisions of the Charter (the principle of the unanimity of the permanent members of the Security Council, the co-relation of the jurisdiction of the General Assembly and the Security Council, and so forth), and many states resolutely opposed it, including one permanent member of the Security Council. Meanwhile, even the provisions of the Charter relating to amendment of the Charter provide that no change of the Charter may occur without the consent of all the permanent members of the Security Council.

One can not concur with J. Castenada, a Mexican jurist, who, while proceeding from theoretical propositions that on the whole are correct, permits inaccuracies in stating the facts and in consequence thereof comes to the unjustified conclusion that all members of the United Nations, supposedly including the Soviet Union, agreed with the "Uniting for Peace" resolution, as a result whereof this resolution modified the United Nations Charter. Castenada writes: "The thesis which will be here sustained is that the Uniting-for-Peace resolution could not, by itself, have the legal consequences of altering the collective security system of the Charter, but that it was the starting point, as well as the nucleus of a rule shaped during the subsequent years, through the conscious and repeated acquiescence to it, either tacit or stated, of all groups of United Nations Members; and that by virtue of this rule, the legal situation prevailing at present as regards the collective security system of the United Nations is different in an appreciable degree and in several aspects, from the original Charter's system."[48]

The argumentation adduced by the author in evidence of this thesis amounts to the following: The "Uniting for Peace" resolution was approved by the General Assembly with the votes of all members of the United Nations except the socialist states. On the other hand, on the question of intervention in Egypt, the socialist states voted for a number of resolutions adopted by the General Assembly. Only Israel voted against the key resolution in the General Assembly. As the states which voted against or abstained on the resolutions regarding the invasion of Egypt had previously voted in favor of the "Uniting for Peace" resolution, it can be said that after the Suez crisis not a single member of the United Nations was left who at one time or another had not approved the "Uniting for Peace" resolution and, therefore, had not accepted juridically its necessary implications.[49]

The author, however, lost sight of exceedingly important facts: the Soviet Union voted in 1956 only for those General Assembly resolutions which contained appeals to the belligerents to reach a cease-fire agreement, recommendations to all United Nations members to refrain from deliveries of arms to the area of military activities [Resolution 997(E-1)], appeals to Israel, England, and France to withdraw their forces from Egyptian territory [Resolution 1002(E-1)], and so forth. In abstaining from the resolutions concerning the creating of emergency armed forces and their functioning [Resolutions 998, 1000(E-1)], since the state being subjected to aggression considered the creating of such forces useful, the Soviet Union set forth its position on this question precisely. The Representative of the Soviet Union, V. Kuznetsov, stated at the 567th Session of the First Emergency Session of the General Assembly on November 7, 1956, the following: "As regards the creation and stationing on Egyptian territory of an international police force, the Soviet delegation is obliged to point out that this Force is being created in violation of the United Nations Charter.

"The General Assembly resolution on the basis of which it is now proposed to form this Force is inconsistent with the Charter. Chapter VII

48. J. Castenada, "Certain Legal Consequences of the Suez Crisis," *Revue Egyptienne de droit international*, XIX (1963), 3.

49. *Ibid.*, p. 9; see also I. Detter, *Law Making by International Organizations* (Stockholm: P. A. Nordstedt & Söners Forlag, 1965), p. 39. In a review of this book H. Blix says Detter's comments that during the 1956 Suez Crisis the Soviet Union supposedly agreed that Resolution 377(V) "does not correspond to reality." H. Blix, "The Beginnings of International Legislation," *Cooperation and Conflict*, I (1966), 109.

of the Charter empowers the Security Council, the Security Council only, and not the General Assembly, to set up an international armed force and to take such action as it may deem necessary, including the use of such a force, to maintain or restore international peace and security."

The position of the Soviet state, therefore, was expressed sufficiently clearly: the Soviet Union expressly declared that the creation and use of armed forces on the basis of a General Assembly resolution is a violation of the United Nations Charter.

The Soviet Union repeatedly opposed and protested against other measures contravening the Charter, in particular measures concerning the operation of the armed forces and their financing.[50]

The interpretation which R. Zacklin gives of the proposal of the Soviet government made in June 1967 to convene an emergency session of the General Assembly also is untrue.[51] The Soviet government declared in this proposal that it considers it essential that the General Assembly, in accordance with Article 11 of the United Nations Charter, consider the situation which has arisen and adopt a decision designed to bring about the liquidation of the consequences of aggression and the immediate withdrawal of Israeli forces behind the armistice lines.[52]

There is no basis whatever for interpreting this declaration as evidence of the Soviet Union's having recognized Resolution 377(V), as Zacklin claims. There is no reference to this resolution in the declaration of the Soviet government, and the proposal to convene a special session of the General Assembly could be based on Article 20 of the United Nations Charter. In any case, there is nothing in this statement, or in other statements of the Soviet government, giving grounds to interpret them as agreement with the basic provisions of Resolution 377(V) that United

50. See in particular the Memorandum of the USSR Government to the International Court on the Procedure of Financing the Operations of the United Nations Emergency Force in the Middle East and the United Nations Operations in the Congo, in International Court of Justice, Pleadings, Oral Arguments, Documents, *Certain Expenses of the United Nations*, pp. 270-274; the Memorandum of the Government of the USSR Regarding Certain Measures to Strengthen the Effectiveness of the United Nations in the Safeguarding of International Peace and Security, Doc. No. S/5811, July 10, 1964; the Memorandum of the Ministry of Foreign Affairs of the USSR on the Question of the Financial Situation of the United Nations, Doc. No. A/5729, September 11, 1964; the Memorandum of the Government of the USSR of March 16, 1967, relating to "U.N. Operations for the Maintenance of International Peace and Security," *Izvestia*, April 6, 1967, p. 1.

51. Zacklin, *The Amendment of the Constitutive Instruments of the United Nations*, p. 188.

52. Doc. No. A/6717. [Request for the summoning of an emergency special session of the General Assembly: letter dated 13 June 1967 from the Representative of the USSR to the Secretary-General.]

Nations armed forces may be created on the basis of a resolution of the United Nations General Assembly.

In a Memorandum of March 16, 1967, the Soviet government once again confirmed its position on the question of the creation and use of United Nations armed forces. "At the same time," the Memorandum says, "the Soviet government considers it necessary to emphasize once again that any attempts to revise the provisions of the Charter concerning the use of armed forces in the name of the United Nations or the conditions of financing such operations will encounter a negative attitude on the part of the Soviet Union."[53]

Consequently, the thesis that Resolution 377(V) and the practice based on it have introduced changes into the Charter of the United Nations is unjustified. This resolution has left a dark stain on the history of the United Nations as a flagrant violation of the basic principles of this organization.

One must agree with Professor M. Seara Vazquez of Mexico that the "Uniting for Peace" resolution was an "attempt against the very concept of the Organization," violated the basic provisions of the United Nations Charter, and therefore is void *ab initio*.[54]

53. *Izvestia*, April 6, 1967, p. 1.
54. M. Seara Vazquez, "Las reformas a la Carta de las Naciones Unidas," *Estudios de Derecho Internacional Homenaje a D. Antonio de Luna* (Madrid: Instituto Francisco de Vitoria, 1968), p. 442.

Chapter 15 *The Basic Features of the Legal Nature of Contemporary General International Organizations (continued)*

A. The Interstate Character of General International Organizations

The objective process of the internationalization of production and of other aspects of the life of contemporary society is leading, as already has been pointed out, to an expansion of the functions and powers of international organizations. At the same time, laws of societal development, such as the existence of sovereign states and the coexistence and struggle of the two opposed social systems, lead to the fact that both the process of internationalization itself and the expansion of the functions and powers of international organizations are occurring in interstate forms.

Contemporary general international organizations as interstate entities are characterized in general by the following features: they are created by states through the conclusion of international treaties and operate on the basis of such treaties (see Chapter 14); states remain sovereign and equal both within and without an international organization; the mechanism of an international organization is brought into operation by states; member states have the right to withdraw from the organization; the basic resolutions of international organizations are of a recommendatory nature (see Chapter 5).

(1) The principle of the equality of states in international organizations. We already have said that by virtue of the laws of societal development contemporary general international organizations are so structured that the member states of such organizations continue to remain sovereign entities (see Chapter 13).

The question of the application of the principle of equality of states

[344]

within contemporary international organizations is, theoretically and practically, more complex. In approaching the question formally, some bourgeois jurists come to maintain the "sovereign equality" in general is not compatible with the nature of contemporary international organizations. The principle of equality, they assert, supposedly requires the adoption of resolutions only on the basis of unanimity, whereas unanimity is not now applied in international organizations. Thus, Professor G. Scelle, citing Article 2(1) of the United Nations Charter, which says that the organization is based on the principle of the sovereign equality of all its members, wrote that "philosophically this is impossible, false, and hypocritical."[1] An international organization, Scelle wrote further, is "incompatible with the system of the unanimity limited even to the five great powers because the principle of 'equal sovereignty' implied that a state is bound only by those norms of law which have been signed and ratified by its government."[2]

The application of the principle of equality of states within international organizations, naturally, has its own peculiarities in comparison with general international law. In order to effectuate the purposes and tasks of a respective international organization, its principles, particularly the principle of equality of members, must be so formulated as to best promote the effectuation of the organization's tasks. Therefore, as Professor C. A. Colliard points out, the principle of equality of states "adjusts itself" to the purposes and tasks of the organization.[3] But at the same time it remains one of the most important principles of the structure and activity of contemporary general international organizations.

The principle of equality signifies above all the equal right of all states to participate in general international organizations since such organizations take up questions of interest to all states and their activity affects the rights and interests of all states.[4]

In general international organizations each member state has an equal right to raise questions and put forward proposals for discussion in the organization. Every member has an equal right, in accordance with the organization's charter, to be represented in organs of the organization and to take part in the discussion of issues. In taking decisions, each state has one vote. This is the situation in the United Nations. Of thirteen

1. G. Scelle, "Préalable à l'intégration d'une société internationale universelle," *Mélanges Séfériades* (Athens: Imp. de Ange Ath. Klissiounis, 1961), I, 8.
2. *Ibid.*, p. 9.
3. See C. A. Colliard, "Quelques réflexions sur la structure et le fonctionnement des organisations internationales," *Mélanges offerts à Henri Rolin: Problèmes de droit des gens* (Paris: Editions A. Pedone, 1964), p. 68.
4. See G. Schirmer, *Universalität völkerrechtliche Verträger und internationaler Organisation* (Berlin: Staatsverlag der DDR, 1966).

specialized agencies of the United Nations, to which one should add the International Atomic Energy Agency, which is linked to the United Nations by an agreement on cooperation, only three apply the system of weighted voting: the International Bank for Reconstruction and Development, the International Monetary Fund, and the International Finance Corporation.[5] These international organizations, however, are not actually general international organizations since the socialist states do not participate in them.

Practical necessity has led to the establishment in all general international organizations of a more or less uniform structure: a plenary organ (assembly, congress) in which all states are represented; a particular organ (council) consisting of representatives of a limited number of members of the organization, and a secretariat. Frequently, a specific number of places in the council of the organizations are allocated to the more important states within the operative sphere of the organization (Intergovernmental Maritime Consultative Organization, International Labor Organization, International Atomic Energy Agency) or through other means ensure the permanent representation of such states in the council (for example, International Civil Aviation Organization). The permanent members of the United Nations Security Council are expressly enumerated in the United Nations Charter.

In the United Nations there also exists the principle of unanimity of the great powers in the Security Council, engendered for exceedingly important reasons: the diverse role of states in international relations, especially in the maintenance of international peace and security; the existence of two opposed social systems and the necessity of guarantees against the United Nations being transformed into an instrument of states of one social system; the need to ensure the effectiveness of decisions of the organization on the maintenance of international peace and security, and so forth.

5. See K. Ia. Chizhov, *Mezhdunarodnye valiutno-finansovye organizatsii kapitalizma* (Moscow: izd-vo Finansy, 1968). The author very aptly remarks in particular: "The organizers of the International Monetary Fund understood that all member countries would lay a claim to take part in the administration of this institution. At the same time, they clearly were aware that an organ created from equal representatives of all countries would be difficult to use in their own interests. Therefore, the principle of equality was not laid down as the basis of the organization of the IMF, but the recognition of the economic inequality of states, pursuant to which the status of members of the international organization is determined by their economic power. As a result, the organizational form of a stock-company was deemed most responsive to the requirements submitted by the imperialist states to the International Monetary Fund, since it ensured the predominance of the United States and a small group of other imperialist countries in this international agency" (pp. 15-16).

From the viewpoint of the principle of equality of states, the principle of the unanimity of the great powers in the Security Council is subjected to the most serious attacks. Many writers maintain that this principle establishes the hegemony of the great powers and is incompatible with the principle of the equality of states. Comparing the "right of veto" with the principle of sovereign equality of all members of the United Nations proclaimed in Article 1 of the United Nations Charter, H. Kelsen maintains that "there is an open contradiction between the political ideology of the United Nations and its legal constitution."[6]

A. Ulloa, a Peruvian professor, states that the Charter is a "step backward" as regards the principle of equality of states.[7] He says, in particular, that the institute of permanent members and the principle of unanimity of the great powers in the Security Council "eliminate the proclaimed principle of international equality."[8]

An Indian author calls the formula of Article 2(1) of the Charter an "empty phrase."[9] "The special privileges of the Great Powers in the Security Council and otherwise," the author writes, "make nonsense of the principle."[10]

To that which has been said about the importance of the principle of unanimity of the great powers in the Security Council as a guarantee against the United Nations being transformed into an instrument of states of one social system, it should be added here that precisely this principle prevents in a specific international situation the hegemony of certain great powers in the Security Council and, consequently, in the United Nations, and is a guarantee of the realization of the principle of equality of member states of the United Nations.[11] In reality, if this principle did not exist, the Security Council could easily be transformed into a dangerous weapon in the hands of the imperialist powers and be used not only against the socialist states, but also, and even most likely, against the weak states of Asia, Africa, and Latin America.

The principle of the sovereign equality of states frequently is referred to in order to justify the claim of the supremacy of the General Assembly in comparison with the Security Council. This idea is one cornerstone of a

6. H. Kelsen, *The Law of the United Nations* (London: Stevens & Sons, 1951), p. 277.

7. A. Ulloa, *Derecho internacional publico*, 4th ed. (Madrid: Ediciones iberoamericanas, 1957), II, 457.

8. *Ibid.*, p. 458.

9. R. Anand, "Sovereign Equality of States in the United Nations," *Indian Journal of International Law*, VII (1967), 200.

10. *Ibid.*

11. See G. I. Tunkin, "The Legal Nature of the United Nations," *Recueil des cours*, CXIX (1966), 1-68.

draft amendment of the United Nations Charter set forth in the book of two American writers, Grenville Clark and Louis B. Sohn, which is so widely publicized in the United States and other countries.[12]

Of course, the United Nations General Assembly, where all members of the Organization are represented, where every member has one vote, and decisions are taken by a majority vote (on important questions by a two-thirds majority), is closer in structure to an international conference than other organs of the United Nations. Therefore the principle of the sovereign equality of states is manifested more directly here. On this plane it was pointed out in an explanatory memorandum of forty-nine Asian and African states on the question of the composition of the General Committee that the General Assembly is the body "reflecting the principle of sovereign equality of all Member States."[13] As already has been said, however, it would be untrue to regard the said principle as not operative in other organs of the United Nations, although there, as an analysis of the provisions of the Charter shows, it adapts itself to the conditions of the activity of contemporary international organizations in general and to the specific peculiarities of the United Nations dictated by the contemporary international situation.

The supremacy of the General Assembly in comparison with the Security Council may seem more advantageous to small states, which have a majority of votes in the General Assembly. Here, however, a consideration of a legal principle divorced from reality, that is, from the real consequence of its operation in a concrete situation, leads to the incorrect conclusion that the supremacy of the General Assembly would strengthen the international organization and would be useful for the small states.[14] As Professor M. Virally correctly notes, the idea of "international democracy" and the taking of decisions by a majority of votes of states is a "deceptive" idea.[15]

In reality, if the jurisdiction to take decisions on questions of the maintenance of international peace and security requiring action (Article 11), were transferred from the Security Council to the General Assembly, a completely new situation would arise which would represent a danger above all for the small powers. The imperialist powers would have broad

12. See G. Clark and L. Sohn, *World Peace Through World Law*, 3d ed. (Cambridge, Mass.: Harvard University Press, 1966), pp. 35-49. Also see Commission to Study the Organization of Peace, *New Dimensions for the United Nations* (New York: Oceana Publications, 1966).

13. Doc. No. A/5519 (XVIII), September 17, 1963.

14. See, for example, Ulloa, *Derecho internacional publico*, II, pp. 457-464; Anand, "Sovereign Equality of States in the United Nations."

15. M. Virally, *L'O.N.U. d'hier à demain* (Paris: Editions du Sueil, 1961), pp. 114-115.

opportunities to use the various combinations, to apply the old "divide and conquer" policy, from which small countries have suffered so much in the past.

(2) The right to withdraw from an international organization. The right of member states to withdraw from an international organization is a *conditio sine qua non* of the interstate character of the organization, although the right to withdraw also may exist in associations of states having a state character (Article 17, Constitution of the USSR).

The right to withdraw exists in all general international organizations irrespective of whether it is specified in the charter of an international organization. Naturally, it is exercised in conformity with the provisions of the respective international organization's charter or supplemental agreements of the organization's members.[16]

The constitutions of all specialized agencies of the United Nations, except for the World Health Organization, the Charter of the International Atomic Energy Agency, as well as the charters of the majority, if not all, of the other specialized general international organizations contain provisions on the right of withdrawal from the organization. However, the absence in the charter of an international organization of a reference to the right of withdrawal from the organization can not, of course, be interpreted as the absence of such a right. In his monograph, *Termination of Membership of International Organizations*, an Indian jurist, N. Singh, comes to the correct conclusion that if the charter of an international organization is silent about the right to withdraw from the organization, such a right is presupposed since "anything which is not conceded in favour of the international organisation is retained by the member-State, which by virtue of its sovereignty must be vested with the residuary jurisdiction."[17]

The right of withdrawal also exists in the United Nations, although the Charter is silent about it. However, the San Francisco Conference approved a report of Committee I/2, which spoke of the right of

16. On the question of the right to withdraw from an international organization see in particular S. B. Krylov, *Istoriia sozdaniia OON*, ed. G. I. Tunkin (Moscow: izd-vo IMO, 1960), pp. 115-118; E. A. Shibaeva, *Spetsializirovannye uchrezhdeniia OON* (Moscow: izd-vo Mezhdunarodnye otnosheniia, 1966), pp. 61-63; L. Goodrich and E. Hambro, *The Charter of the United Nations*, 2d ed. (London: Stevens & Sons, 1949), p. 144; N. Singh, *Termination of Membership in International Organizations* (London: Stevens & Sons, 1958), pp. 23-26, 80-98; N. Feinberg, "Unilateral Withdrawal from an International Organization," *British Year Book of International Law*, XXXIX (1963), 215-218; F. Dehousse, "Le droit de retrait aux Nations Unies," *Revue belge de droit international*, I (1965), 30-48.

17. Singh, *Termination of Membership in International Organizations*, pp. 80-81.

withdrawal from the Organization "for good and sufficient reasons."[18] The Representative of the USSR, A. Gromyko, stated in this connection at a plenary session of the Conference that the right to withdraw from the Organization "is a reflection of state sovereignty."[19] The United States delegate, in turn, pointed out that "in an organization of sovereign states it was clear that all members would possess the faculty of withdrawal."[20] Kelsen's view, that the right to withdraw from the United Nations does not exist since it was not specified in the United Nations Charter, is based on a narrow formalistic approach and has no basis in international law.[21] One also can hardly agree with the view of M. Scerni, an Italian professor, who suggests that the right of withdrawal from the United Nations exists only for instances of amending the Charter, and in all other "exceptional instances" there is only a right "to refuse to some degree to cooperate in the organization."[22]

When in 1965 Indonesia declared its withdrawal from the United Nations, the question of the right to withdraw could not arise in general and, as Professor G. Schwarzenberger correctly pointed out, the question could only be whether the utterances were sufficient grounds for such withdrawal.[23]

However, in this sole instance in United Nations practice, the question did not receive precise legal treatment. The Statement of the Government of Indonesia in 1965 said that "Indonesia has decided at this stage and under present circumstances to withdraw from the United Nations." However, the telegram of the ambassador of Indonesia to the United States to the Secretary General of the United Nations of September 19, 1966, said that the Indonesian government "has decided to resume full cooperation with the United Nations and to resume participation in its activities starting with the twenty-first session of the General Assembly."[24]

The return of Indonesia to the United Nations occurred as an admission without the procedure which obviously would have been necessary had Indonesia withdrawn from the United Nations in 1965.

18. United Nations, *Documents of the United Nations Conference on International Organization, San Francisco, 1945* (London and New York: United Nations Information Organizations, 1945), VII, 577.

19. *Ibid.*, p. 264. [The Statement was in fact made by the Ukrainian delegate.]

20. *Ibid.*, p. 265.

21. See Kelsen, *The Law of the United Nations*, pp. 124-129.

22. M. Scerni, "Aspetti giuridici del ritiro dalle Nazioni Unite," *La Comunita Internazionale*, XX (1965), 239.

23. G. Schwarzenberger, "Indonesia and the U.N.," *The Times*, January 11, 1965, p. 9, col. 5.

24. *United Nations Juridical Yearbook 1966* (New York: United Nations, 1968), pp. 222-223.

B. International Organizations as Organs of Peaceful Coexistence

In Chapter 13 we concluded that contemporary general international organizations are organs of peaceful coexistence. How do the general character and purposes of international organizations concretely reflect this in the legal norms defining the composition, structure, and activity of international organizations?

First, the principle of nondiscrimination on the basis of socioeconomic systems, arising out of the principle of equality of states, is characteristic of contemporary general international organizations. And in fact the charters of general international organizations do not contain membership limitations tied to the socioeconomic system of states. According to the United Nations Charter, "admission to membership of the Organization is open to all peaceloving states . . . " (Article 4). This general requirement, arising out of the basic principles of contemporary international law and the purposes of the United Nations, did not contemplate and never has been interpreted as having in view the socioeconomic system of a state. The attempts of western powers not to admit certain socialist states into the United Nations using various far-fetched pretexts, but in fact because they were socialist states, were a flagrant violation of the Charter.

A second important principle relating to this aspect of the legal nature of general international organizations is the principle of the distinctive equality of the different social systems. The principle of equality of states is not sufficiently observed in the structure of the organs and in the activity generally of contemporary general international organizations; it is still necessary to take into account that member states belong to different socioeconomic systems. A quantitative approach on the basis of the equality of states is, therefore, inadequate. The question is one that under contemporary conditions is exceedingly important for the activity of any general international organization so that states representing the various social systems take part in working out and deciding various questions of the organization's activity on the basis of equality.

This proposition is only beginning to force its way through, but a few examples where it has been applied to a greater degree than others show its fruitfulness. The clearest examples of the application (though incomplete) of this principle within the United Nations system are the composition of the Committee on the Peaceful Use of Outer Space and the Committee on Disarmament. Six socialist, six capitalist, and eight developing countries comprise the Committee on Disarmament, and eight socialist, nine western, and eleven developing countries, the Committee on Outer Space. Contemporary general international organizations can function successfully only on the basis of coordination between the states of different social systems and of taking into account the interests of these groups of states. In this respect the principle of equality of different social systems represented in general international organizations has important significance, and there is every reason to expect that it will be more widely introduced into these organizations.

A third juridical aspect of the legal nature of general international organizations as organs of peaceful coexistence is the guarantees against the use of an international organization by states affiliated with one socioeconomic system against states belonging to another socioeconomic system.

The Soviet side pointed to the importance of this problem in 1925, in connection with the question of the possibility of the Soviet Union's entering the League of Nations. In a Soviet press communique concerning the statement of the People's Commissar of Foreign Affairs of the USSR, G. V. Chicherin, to the German journalist Stein on October 17, 1925, it was said: "The Soviet government can not subordinate its actions and decisions arising out of the fundamental principles of the Soviet system to the resolutions of a majority of those states which are constructed on completely different bases."[2][5]

Bourgeois international legal doctrine is silent on this problem. In considering the questions of the functions, jurisdiction, and effectiveness of international organizations, bourgeois international lawyers usually ignore the class nature of member states of international organizations, trends in their policy, the struggle which takes place, though to an unequal extent, in various international organizations, the real co-relation of forces, and so forth. In this instance, as in many others, the formalistic approach is a convenient means for avoiding problems and masking the essence of social phenomena.

This danger is especially great with respect to an international organization such as the United Nations. Reality is such that in contemporary general international organizations the socialist states are for the time being an insignificant minority in relation to the total number of member states. The leading capitalist states strive to use general international organizations and, above all, the United Nations against the socialist countries, as well as in the interests of their colonialist or neocolonialist policy. The danger of transforming general international organizations under these conditions into an instrument of capitalist states is very real. The change in the co-relation of forces in the United Nations, as well as in other general international organizations in connection with the entry of a large number of new states which have emerged in consequence of the

25. Ministerstvo inostrannykh del SSSR, *Dokumenty vneshnei politiki SSSR* (Moscow: Gospolitizdat, 1957–), VIII, 633.

liberation of the colonies reduces somewhat, but by no means completely removes, this danger.

How to avoid this problem was a cardinal issue when the United Nations was created, although nothing was said expressly about it. As the well-known commentator on the United Nations Charter, Professor L. Goodrich, is forced to acknowledge, at the time when the United Nations was created, the western powers expected that the West would predominate in it as it had predominated in the League of Nations.[26]

Naturally, the question was one primarily of the Security Council, which under the Charter was endowed with special responsibility in the fundamental and very crucial area of activity of the international organization, in the cause of maintaining international peace and security.

It is well-known how difficult it was to find a satisfactory resolution of this question. It was necessary to ensure the possibility of rapid and effective actions based on the principle of the sovereign equality of states and at the same time to take into account their unequal role in international relations. But above all the principal task was to ensure that the organization was not transformed into an instrument of states of one social system.

The two possible extreme solutions were unacceptable. The principle of unanimity of all members of the Council, which had existed in the League of Nations, would have the same parallel effect which it had within the framework of the League of Nations. The taking of decisions by majority vote (simple or qualified) contravened the said principal requirement.[27]

At the suggestion of the American President, Franklin Roosevelt, the principle of unanimity of the permanent members of the Security Council was finally adopted at the Yalta Conference of the three great powers.[28] According to Article 27 of the Charter, all decisions of the Security Council, with the exception of procedural questions, are considered adopted when the votes of seven (at present, nine) members of the Council, including the concurring votes of all permanent members of the Council, have been cast in favor.

Thus, the Yalta formula provided for the adoption of Security Council decisions by a majority vote; however, this majority must include the concurrent votes of the permanent members of the Council. The Statement of the delegations of the four host governments at the San Francisco

26. See L. Goodrich, *The United Nations* (New York: Thomas Y. Crowell Co., 1959), p. 41.

27. See Tunkin, "The Legal Nature of the United Nations."

28. For greater detail, see N. A. Ushakov, *Printsip edinoglasiia velikikh derzhav v Sovete Bezopasnosti OON* (Moscow: izd-vo Mezhdunarodnye otnosheniia, 1965), pp. 58-60.

Conference of June 7, 1945, pointed out that the proposed formula for adopting measures in the Security Council by a majority of seven members makes the activity of the Council less liable to obstruction than it was in the League of Nations, whose rules provided for complete unanimity.[29] The "Yalta formula" took into account the special role of the great powers in international relations. The aforesaid Statement of the host powers at the San Francisco Conference said with regard to this question: "In view of the basic responsibility of the permanent members, one can not expect them under present conditions existing in the world to assume obligations to act in such serious matters as the maintenance of international peace and security in conformity with a decision with which they did not agree. Therefore, for the adoption of decisions by the Security Council by a majority vote to be possible, the sole practical method will be to provide for the unanimity of the permanent members plus the concurrent votes of at least two non-permanent members with respect to non-procedural decisions."[30]

This Statement, therefore, emphasized wholly correctly, particularly on the basis of the experience of the Second World War, the special role of the great powers in questions of peace and war.

It was very important, however, that nowhere was this said. The Yalta formula precluded the possibility of transforming the Security Council, and consequently, the entire United Nations into an instrument of states of one social system. The Yalta formula embraced the principle of peaceful coexistence of states of different social systems. In reality, of the five permanent members of the Security Council, one state, the USSR, was a state of another, a socialist, social system. Decisions of the Security Council, therefore, could be taken only on the basis of the agreement of states of the two opposed social systems.

On this plane, Professor M. Lachs is certainly correct in noting: "The principle of unanimity, which was born towards the end of the war, has today grown in importance and has acquired a new meaning. In a concrete historical situation, it not only reflects the equality of states, but it also stands against any discriminatory practices by one of the dominating political systems in the world today against the other. It means that no important decision can be taken without the agreement and support of the Socialist states. This new equality of the political systems is probably the most important feature of international relations today."[31]

29. Cited according to V. N. Durdenevskii and S. B. Krylov, comps., *Organizatsiia Ob"edinennykh Natsii; sbornik dokumentov* (Moscow: Gosiurizdat, 1956), p. 30.

30. *Ibid.*

31. M. Lachs, "The United Nations and Peaceful Co-Existence," *Polish Perspectives*, III, no. 4 (1960), p. 9.

The thesis is widely publicized in the West that the adoption of the Yalta formula was a mistake, as a result of which the Soviet veto in the Security Council would not allow the United Nations to fulfill its duties regarding the maintenance of peace and security.[32] An objective analysis of the operation of the unanimity rule of the great powers shows, however, that the veto of the Soviet Union was a reliable means against the use of the United Nations as an instrument by states of one social system against states of another social system. Thus, in 1946, in connection with the Security Council's consideration of the request of Syria and Lebanon concerning the withdrawal of English and French forces from the territory of these states, the Soviet Union, in supporting this just request, vetoed a draft English and French resolution which actually sanctioned a further stay of foreign forces in Syria and Lebanon. In 1961 the Soviet Union prevented by its veto the adoption of a resolution by the Security Council aimed at supporting colonialist claims of Portugal against India to Goa, Daman, and Diu. The Soviet Union was obliged to use its veto dozens of times against discriminatory proposals of western powers which had the purpose of admitting to the United Nations states whom they chose and of not admitting other such equal states only because they were socialist states.

It is true that the veto sometimes has been used also by colonial powers in their colonialist interests. One can mention as an example France's vote in 1947 against a proposal of the Soviet Union to create a commission to observe the implementation of a Security Council resolution regarding the Indonesian question, England's veto in 1963 of the draft resolution of Ghana, Morocco, and the Philippines which called upon the English government not to transfer authority to the white minority in southern Rhodesia, and others. But most frequently of all the imperialist powers, above all the United States, simply have no need to use the veto. They have succeeded in voting down proposals objectionable to them, having the requisite majority of votes in the Security Council. "One of the more persistent myths surrounding the United Nations," writes J. G. Stoessinger, an American professor, "concerns the use of the veto power by the Soviet Union and the United States. It is an established fact that by late 1965 the Soviet Union had vetoed 103 Security Council resolutions, whereas the United States had yet to cast its first veto. Hence, it is said that the Soviet Union's frequent use of the veto has hampered ... the United Nations by preventing it from acting, while the United States has exercised remarkable self-discipline by never using the veto at all."[33] The

32. See, for example, Goodrich, *The United Nations*, pp. 164-176.
33. J. G. Stoessinger, *The United Nations and the Superpowers* (New York: Random House, 1965), p. 3.

author goes on: "To say that the United States has never used the veto power is literally correct, but highly misleading in a broader sense. The implication would be that one superpower had . . . put national interest above international considerations while the other had . . . subordinated national interests in order to further international co-operation. The fact of the matter is that the United States has not used the veto because it has been able to protect and promote its national interest in other ways. By obtaining majority votes against resolutions it opposes the United States has never been forced to cast a veto. The key to this American 'hidden veto' is, of course, the composition of the Security Council. It is a fact that a majority of the members of the Council have regularly been military allies of the United States."[3][4]

There are dozens of instances of the use of the "hidden veto" by the imperialist powers. It was used, for example, in 1946 against a proposal of the Ukrainian SSR concerning the withdrawal of English forces from Greece, in the same year against a Ukrainian proposal concerning the actions of English forces in Indonesia, in 1950 against a proposal of the USSR concerning the withdrawal of American forces from the island of Taiwan and the cessation of aggressive actions of the United States against the People's Republic of China, against a Soviet proposal concerning the cessation of American-Anglo intervention in Lebanon and Jordan in 1958, and in many other instances.

The Yalta formula, of course, is not ideal. As we have seen, the veto sometimes may be used for reactionary purposes. Nevertheless, the principle of unanimity of the great powers in the Security Council belongs among the fundamental principles of the United Nations, reflecting one of the principal laws of our epoch. The violations of this principle in the practice of the United Nations under the influence of the policy of imperialist powers (especially Resolution 377(V) of November 3, 1950, and the United Nations practice based thereon), therefore, frequently has led to a situation highly dangerous for the cause of peace and for the United Nations itself.

In other general international organizations, to wit, in international organizations for specialized questions, there does not exist an institute similar to the principle of the unanimity of the great powers in the Security Council. As has been pointed out, for a number of reasons there is usually not the bitter struggle in these organizations that takes place in the United Nations. The absence of the said institute in these organizations, however, leads in certain questions, as for example, the admission of members to these organizations, to the capitalist states pursuing a policy of discrimination with respect to certain socialist states. Thus, the German

34. *Ibid.*, pp. 13-14.

Democratic Republic, the Korean People's Democratic Republic, and the Democratic Republic of Vietnam persistently are not admitted by the western powers to the United Nations specialized agencies, although the Federal Republic of Germany, South Korea, and South Vietnam are members of these international organizations.

As is clear from the above, the guarantees of which we are speaking still have not been properly developed in general international organizations. Moreover, the need for them up to now has not been adequately realized nor has it been acceptable to speak of this directly. Meanwhile, the future development of general international organizations and the enlargement of their role in ensuring peace and the development of international cooperation, in our view, is linked to a significant extent with the working out and realization of these guarantees.

C. The International Legal Personality of International Organizations

The emergence among the large number of intergovernmental international organizations of those which possess international legal personality was a result of the increased role of international organizations in international life. International organizations grew out of international conferences and, as P. Reuter notes correctly, at first were only a continuation of these conferences.[35]

The proposition that international organizations can be, and many are, subjects of international law is, at present, essentially generally recognized, and disputes with regard to this question can be regarded as the legacy of history.[36] In Soviet international legal literature only a few writers continue to adhere to the view, which was predominant in Soviet literature until the mid-1950s, that international organizations are not subjects of international law. Thus, Professor V. Shurshalov maintains in a recently published book, *Mezhdunarodnye pravootnosheniia*, that international organizations are not subjects of international law but are subjects of international legal relations.[37]

In every legal system there may be various subjects of law. In

35. P. Reuter, *Institutions internationales*, 4th ed. (Paris: Presses Universitaires de France, 1963), p. 188.

36. On disputes in Soviet international legal literature see Shibaeva, *Pravovoi status mezhpravitel'stvennykh organizatsii* (Moscow: izd-vo Iuridicheskaia literatura, 1972), pp. 83-88; L. Valki, "The Juristic Personality and Treaty-Making Power of International Organizations," *Questions of International Law* (Budapest: Hungarian International Law Association, 1968), pp. 285-308.

37. V. M. Shurshalov, *Mezhdunarodnye pravootnosheniia* (Moscow: izd-vo Mezhdunarodnye otnosheniia, 1971), pp. 58-76.

international law, together with the traditional and still primary subjects of international law, new subjects—international organizations—have emerged. International organizations are an institute of contemporary society, distinct from a state, but it would be incorrect to assert on this basis that they can not be subjects of international law just as it would be incorrect, in acknowledging that international organizations are subjects of law, to equate them to states. International organizations are distinct from the state as a type of subject of international law. Extensive international practice already is evidence of this.

Many international organizations have specific international rights and duties, may by their actions acquire rights and assume legal duties, and bear international legal responsibility for their actions. In conformity with their charters, international organizations are in specific international legal relationships with the member states of these organizations; they conclude international treaties with states and with other international organizations; representations of states frequently are attached to international organizations; sometimes international organizations have representations in states; international organizations exchange representatives between themselves; international organizations and their officials enjoy privileges and immunities on the basis of international law; they bear international legal responsibility in the event unlawful actions are committed; and so forth. That is to say, many international organizations possess international legal personality.

On the other hand, the treaties concluded by international organizations between themselves and with states are distinct from treaties between states; missions of international organizations and missions to international organizations by their functions and in the overwhelming majority of instances by their legal status are different from diplomatic representations;[38] the international legal responsibility of international organizations is far from identical to state responsibility; and so forth.

One must, therefore, concur with the view of the International Court, which in its advisory opinion of April 11, 1949, on the question of

38. The functions of permanent missions of states to international organizations sometimes can be more important than the functions of some diplomatic representations, but by their very nature they differ significantly from the functions of the latter. Therefore, the trend toward identifying somewhat the functions of permanent missions with the functions of diplomatic representations which has crept into the commentary to Article 7 of the "Draft Articles on Representatives of States to International Organizations" adopted by the International Law Commission at its Twentieth Session in 1968 seems unjustified. See the "Report of the International Law Commission on the Work of its Twentieth Session," in United Nations, *Yearbook of the International Law Commission 1968* (New York: United Nations, 1968), II, 200.

reparation for injuries suffered in the service of the United Nations came to the conclusion that: (1) the United Nations is a subject of international law; (2) this does not mean that the United Nations is recognized as a state, which it certainly is not, or that the legal personality of the United Nations is the same as the legal personality of a state.[39]

(1) The legal basis and extent of the legal personality of international organizations. The question of the legal basis of international organizations as subjects of international law has important theoretical and practical significance. The problem lies first of all in whether the international legal personality of international organizations and its scope are determined by general international law or whether the legal personality of each international organization is based on its charter.

Under contemporary international law, each state is a subject of international law. States as subjects of international law are equal *inter se*, that is to say, all states have the same amount of international legal personality.

The concept of "inherent legal personality" of international organizations has received some publicity in bourgeois international legal doctrine recently, especially since the advisory opinion of the International Court of July 20, 1962, on the question of certain expenses of the United Nations. According to this concept, international organizations are subjects of international law on the basis of general international law just as are states, and legal personality inheres in every international organization to the same extent that it inheres in states. The charter of an international organization, under this theory, has significance only in that it may serve the legal personality peculiar to any international organization in conformity with the purposes of the organization.[40]

In support of this view one may point to the fact that international organizations very frequently perform legal actions not provided for by their charters. The conclusion is drawn from this that the legal personality of international organizations is not based on their charters, but directly on norms of general international law.

This view as regards the legal personality of international organizations

39. International Court of Justice, Reports of Judgments, Advisory Opinions and Orders, *Reparation for Injuries Suffered in the Service of the United Nations*, Advisory Opinion of April 11, 1949 (Leyden: A. W. Sythoff, 1949), p. 179.

40. See, for example, F. Seyersted, "International Personality of Intergovernmental Organizations," *Indian Journal of International Law*, IV (1964), 19, 26-27, 48; a more cautious formulation is H. Chiu, *The Capacity of International Organizations to Conclude Treaties, and the Special Legal Aspects of the Treaties so Concluded* (The Hague: Martinus Nijhoff, 1966), p. 21; and even more cautiously in Reuter, *Institutions internationales*, p. 218.

based on treaty was precisely expressed in the draft articles on the "application of norms of international law to treaties concluded by international organizations submitted in 1972 by Professor R.-J. Dupuy to the Institute of International Law. The respective article of this draft states: "Any international organization may conclude treaties when carrying out its functions or in order to realize its purposes unless the Charter of this organization provides otherwise."[41]

The majority of members of the Institute committee on this question favored the Dupuy proposal (Briggs, Pescatore, Seyersted, Verosta). A number of committee members opposed this article, finding it too broad (Lachs, Reuter, Salmon). Professor P. Reuter pointed out in his remarks that "charters may be supplemented by customary means, so reference to the purposes, tasks, and functions of the organization is insufficient."[42]

In Dupuy's final report submitted to the Institute in 1973, the said article was formulated as follows: "Any international organization may conclude agreements in carrying out its competence or realizing its purposes unless the legal status of this organization provides otherwise."[43]

What has been said previously (see Chapter 14) relating to the unfoundedness of the theory of "inherent jurisdiction" is wholly applicable also to the concept of "inherent legal personality." International reality is such that far from all intergovernmental international organizations are subjects of international law, and the scope of legal personality of those organizations which possess it is very different. The concept of "inherent legal personality," like the concept of "inherent jurisdiction," is in contradiction to the fundamental principles of contemporary international law, in conformity with which the charter of an international organization is the juridical basis of its existence and activity.

The viewpoint of A. Sereni comes to almost the same conclusions as does the concept of "inherent legal personality," although he does not maintain that all international organizations possess legal personality. Sereni, citing Anzilotti, proceeds from the proposition that only the international legal order, that is, general international law, can attach to a particular entity the status of a subject of international law. Since, in Sereni's view, a treaty can not create norms of general international law, it is not in a position to create a subject of international law. In general, he

41. R.-J. Dupuy, *L'Application des règles du droit international général des traités aux accords conclus par les Organisations internationales; rapport provisoire* (Geneva: Institut de droit international, 1972), p. 101.

42. Dupuy, *Rapport définitif* (Geneva: Institute de droit international, 1973), p. 43.

43. *Ibid.*, p. 27.

says, an international treaty can not create an international organization. Its emergence is of a factual nature; an international organization exists from the moment it begins to function through its organs. It acquires international legal personality if the functions of its organs may create rights and duties for it under international law. And if an international organization possesses legal personality, this legal personality is equal to the legal personality of all other subjects of international law with which the organization does business.[44] This is purely a speculative construction which, as is obvious from the preceding, is in sharp disaccord with reality.

Norms defining the legal status of international organizations do not exist in contemporary general international law. The fact that international organizations conclude agreements with states in all instances when a question arises of the legal status of the organization, its organs, officials, and so forth, is testimony, in particular, to this. If general international law defined the legal status of international organizations, such agreements would be unnecessary, and if they still were concluded, they undoubtedly would contain references to the respective norms of general international law. At the same time, general international law does not contain norms preventing the allotment of the legal personality to international organizations. The legal personality of an international organization is based on its charter, which also defines the scope of this legal personality.[45]

The frequently cited advisory opinion of the International Court of April 11, 1949, also proceeds in general from this position. It says in this opinion that in order to answer the question of whether the United

44. A. Sereni, *Diritto internazionale* (Milan: Dott. A. Giuffre, 1960), II(2), pp. 837-852.

45. See G. I. Tunkin, *Osnovy sovremennogo mezhdunarodnogo prava* (Moscow: Tipo. Vysshei partiinoi shkoly pri TsK KPSS, 1956), pp. 17-18; R. L. Bobrov, "O pravovoi prirode Organizatsii Ob"edinennykh Natsii," *Sovetskii ezhegodnik mezhdunarodnogo prava 1959* (Moscow: izd-vo AN SSSR, 1960), pp. 229-240; G. I. Morozov, *Organizatsiia Ob"edinennykh Natsii* (Moscow: izd-vo IMO, 1962), pp. 196-202; A. N. Talalaev, *Iuridicheskaia priroda mezhdunarodnogo dogovora* (Moscow: izd-vo IMO, 1963), p. 27; S. A. Malinin, "O pravosub"ektnosti mezhdunarodnykh organizatsii," *Vestnik leningradskogo gosudarstvennogo universiteta*, no. 17 (1965), p. 114; I. I. Lukashuk, *Storony v mezhdunarodnykh dogovorakh* (Moscow: Iurizdat, 1966), pp. 124-125; Shibaeva, *Spetsializirovannye uchrezhdeniia OON*, p. 24; V. M. Chkhikvadze and others, eds., *Kurs mezhdunarodnogo prava v shesti tomakh* (Moscow: izd-vo Nauka, 1967—), I, 160. In the literature of other socialist countries see in particular, C. Berezowski, *Prawo miedzynarodowe publiczne* (Warsaw: Panstwowe wyd-wo naukowe, 1966), I, 168; P. A. Steiniger, ed., *Völkerrecht* (Berlin, n.p., 1966), pp. 112-113; M. Genovski, *Osnovi na mezhdunarodnoto pravo*, 2d ed. (Sofia: Nauka i izkustvo, 1966), p. 109; Valki, "The Juristic Personality and Treaty-Making Power of International Organizations," p. 299.

Nations has such a nature as involves the capacity to bring international claims, "the Court must first enquire whether the Charter has given the Organization such a position that it possesses, in regard to its Members, rights which it is entitled to ask them to respect. In other words, does the Organization possess international personality?"[4][6]

The International Law Commission also proceeded from the same position. As a result of the discussion of the question of the capacity to conclude international treaties in 1962, the International Law Commission inserted in draft Article 3 a paragraph of the following content: "In the case of international organizations, capacity to conclude treaties depends on the constitution of the organization concerned."[4][7]

In discussing the first report in 1963 of the special rapporteur on relations between states and intergovernmental organizations, El-Erian, an Egyptian jurist, almost all members of the International Law Commission who treated the question of the legal personality of international organizations (Tunkin, Yasseen, Ago, Verdross, Gros) expressed the view that there were no norms in general international law defining the legal status of international organizations and that in each concrete instance this position is defined by the charters of these organizations.[4][8] Professor Verdross, in particular, noted: " . . . States were at the origin of international law, whereas international organizations were creations of States; their existence rested on agreements concluded between States, and their legal status depended on the content of those agreements."[4][9]

The view that contemporary international law does not contain norms defining the legal status of international organizations and, therefore, the legal personality of international organizations is based upon its charter, is, it seems to us, predominant in western international legal literature.[5][0]

The special rapporteur of the International Law Commission for treaties with the participation of international organizations, Professor P. Reuter, laid this correct position at the base of his investigation. In his second report submitted in 1973 to the Commission Professor Reuter

46. International Court of Justice, *Reparation for Injuries Suffered in the Service of the United Nations*, p. 178.

47. United Nations, *Yearbook of the International Law Commission 1962*, II, 164.

48. *Ibid., 1963*, I, 299-305.

49. *Ibid.*, p. 304.

50. See in particular Kelsen, *The Law of the United Nations*, pp. 329-330; L. Gross, "Expenses of the United Nations for Peace-Keeping Operations," *International Organization*, XVII (1963), 9-10; P. Pescatore, "Les relations extérieures des communautés européenes," *Recueil des cours*, CIII (1961), 27-28; D. W. Bowett, *The Law of International Institutions* (London: Stevens & Sons, 1963), pp. 273, 296; H. Mosler, "Réflexions sur la personnalité juridique en droit international public," *Mélanges Rolin*, pp. 243-246.

points out that "the legal capacity of an international organization depends on the special constitutive act and its corresponding law and not on any norms of general international law."[51]

In its documents the International Law Commission usually employed the formula "international organizations may possess legal capacity." Thus, the report of the Commission on the work of the first part of the Seventeenth Session says that the Commission "recognized that international organizations may possess a certain capacity to enter into international agreements and that these agreements fall within the scope of the law of treaties."[52] The Commission thereby emphasized that a particular international organization may or may not be a subject of international law.

And so the legal personality of an international organization is defined by its charter. But what does this mean? H. Kelsen expressed the view that "if the constituent treaty does not contain a provision conferring expressly upon the community international juridical personality, that is to say, unrestricted legal capacity under international law, the community has only those special capacities as conferred upon it by particular provisions."[53] It is completely obvious that such a limited normativist approach does not arise out of the basic provisions of contemporary international law and does not explain the existing practice, which is not disputed by states.

In defining the legal personality of an international organization, attention must be given to possible changes in certain nonbasic provisions of its charter which may have occurred in the course of the organization's activity with the general consent of its members (see Chapter 14). Thus, for example, if the charter of the organization in general contains no provisions concerning the concluding of international treaties, the organization nonetheless may conclude such treaties with the general consent of the members of the organization. If the practice of concluding treaties by this organization is stabilized and does not raise objections, it will be evidence of the agreement of the organization's members to introduce such an addition to the charter (see Chapter 14).

Finally, on the basis of and in conformity with the provisions of a charter of an international organization a certain expansion of the scope of the legal personality of an organization is possible through the adoption

51. Second Report on the Question of Treaties Concluded Between States and International Organizations or Among Two or More International Organizations, Doc. No. A/CN.4/271, May 15, 1973, para. 41.

52. United Nations, *Yearbook of the International Law Commission 1965*, II, p. 158.

53. Kelsen, *The Law of the United Nations*, pp. 329-330.

of decisions by its respective organs if such decisions reflect the agreement of all members of the organization. Thus, for example, the United Nations Charter empowers the organization to conclude international treaties on specific questions. In practice, however, treaties also are concluded with regard to many other questions on the basis of decisions of the respective United Nations organs. And if such practice does not contravene the Charter nor give rise to objections on the part of the members, it may be regarded as evidence of a supplemental agreement resting upon the respective provisions of the Charter.

(2) The legal personality of international organizations and third states. Under contemporary international law the legal personality of states is a legal personality *erga omnes.* It does not require recognition by other states.

The status of international organizations is different, since their legal personality is based upon their charters. The charter of an international organization as an international treaty is binding only upon its members and, therefore, the legal personality of an international organization is binding only upon the members of this organization. For states who are not members of the organization its charter is *res inter alios acta.*[54]

Any state, of course, can recognize the legal personality of an international organization of which it is not a member. Such recognition may relate to the legal personality of the given organization in general or only to individual elements (for example, the privileges and immunities of all or only some officials of the organization). The respective obligations for such a state with respect to the given organization, of course, arise not from the charter of this organization but from a special agreement (clearly or tacitly expressed).

The participation of all states in a particular international organization possessing international legal personality or the recognition of the legal personality of such an organization not only by its members but also by all other states makes such an international organization a generally-recognized subject of international law, a subject *erga omnes.* The United Nations and the majority of the specialized agencies are such subjects or approximate thereto.[55]

The theory is widely publicized in bourgeois international legal doctrine that the participation of a majority of states in an international organiza-

54. See C. M. Chaumont, "La signification du principe de specialité des organisations internationales," *Mélanges Rolin*, p. 62; Mosler, "Réflexions sur la personnalité juridique en droit international public," p. 250; G. Schwarzenberger, *A Manual of International Law*, 5th ed. (London: Stevens & Sons, 1967), p. 80.
55. See Tunkin, *Osnovy sovremennogo mezhdunarodnogo prava*, p. 19.

tion makes this organization a subject of international law *erga omnes*. In confirmation of this view the advisory opinion of the International Court of April 11, 1949, on reparation for injuries suffered in the service of the United Nations is usually cited: " . . . fifty States, representing the vast majority of the members of the international community, had the power in conformity with international law, to bring into being an entity possessing objective international personality, and not merely personality recognized by them alone . . . "[56]

This theory, just as the concept which proclaims customary norms of international law recognized by a majority of states are binding upon all states, has no basis in contemporary international law (see Chapter 4).

Still further in this direction is the view that all international organizations possess international legal personality which is legal personality *erga omnes*.[57]

A more moderate view on this question is that the number of members of an international organization is of no significance, and any lawfully created international organization possessing international legal personality is a subject of international law *erga omnes*.[58]

As evidence of this view, Sørenson refers to the practice of some local international organizations of concluding agreements with nonmember states or with other international organizations. But this practice rather disproves Sørenson's thesis. Is it not true that the conclusion by such organizations of respective agreements with nonmember states also expands the operative sphere of their legal personality? Evidently conscious of the weakness of this argument, Sørenson says very cautiously that "undoubtedly an international custom is being formed that no third state may contest the legal personality of an international organization established in conformity with the principles of international law for a legal purpose."[59]

In reality, one could speak of the objective legal personality of international organizations only if according to general international law all international organizations respectively established by international legal criteria *ipso facto* were subjects of international law *erga omnes*, as happens with regard to states. But as already has been said, such norms do not exist in contemporary international law.

56. International Court of Justice, *Reparation for Injuries Suffered in the Service of the United Nations*, p. 185.

57. See, for example, Seyersted, "International Personality of Intergovernmental Organizations," pp. 60, 68.

58. See, for example, M. Sørenson, "Principes de droit international public," *Recueil des cours*, CI (1960), 138-139; Sereni, *Diritto internazionale*, II(2), pp. 843-846.

59. Sørenson, "Principes de droit international public," p. 139.

Chapter 16 *The Problem of a World State and Prospects for the Development of International Organizations*

A. Bourgeois Concepts of a World State

Bourgeois philosophers, politicians, and jurists maintain that the existence of sovereign states is a source of wars and that to make wars impossible it is necessary to create a world state, without affecting, of course, the basic principles of the capitalist system. This abstract scheme, divorced from reality, is advanced persistently in bourgeois international legal literature as the most progressive trend of contemporary political and legal thought, and its opponents are portrayed as reactionaries who have failed to keep pace with life.

At the present time, the concept of the world state has two basic orientations. The first approaches the problem of creating a world state on a logical basis, planning *de lege feranda*. Here is your design of an ideal arrangement which can save you from wars, say proponents of this orientation; take it or leave it.

"Before the atomic bomb," writes R. Hutchins, "we could accept the plan of a world state or reject it ... Our slogan must be: a world government is necessary; therefore it is possible."[1]

Proponents of the second orientation maintain that rapid scientific and technical progress and the expansion of international ties, especially in economics and science, gradually are creating the base for a world state. The task is to reconstruct existing international organizations, beginning with economic and scientific, in conformity with this new situation, transforming them into supranational organizations.

1. R. Hutchins, "Constitutional Foundations for World Order," in S. H. Mendlovitz, ed., *Legal and Political Problems of World Order* (New York: Fund for Education Concerning World Peace Through World Law, 1962), p. 67.

The first orientation is abstract and formalistic. Existing international organizations, assert the proponents of this approach, are imperfect; they do not guarantee against the outbreak of wars. States wage war, and therefore to exclude wars it is necessary to create a supranational organization which could suppress an attempt by any state to take up arms. But to do this it is necessary that states renounce their sovereignty. If they could be persuaded to renounce their sovereignty and to agree to the creation of a world state, everything would be all right. "The notion of the sovereignty of individual states," wrote H. Kelsen soon after the First World War, "up to now, correctly or incorrectly, has stood in the path of any measures having the purpose to transform the international legal order into an effective organization . . . "[2]

Professor P. C. Jessup, a [former] member of the United Nations International Court from the United States, wrote in 1948 that the sole means of ensuring peace is the creation of an "international government." "There must be organs, empowered to lay down rules (a legislature); there must be judicial organs to interpret and apply those rules (a judiciary); and there must be organs with power to compel compliance with the rules (a police force)."[3]

A resolute opponent of state sovereignty, the French professor G. Scelle, in favoring the creation of a world federation, wrote: "If the proposed plan turns out to be inadmissable and the so-called external sovereignty must remain the patrimony of hundreds of states, themselves defining the extent of their discretionary authority, it is better to say together with the poet: 'Lose all hope; we henceforth shall remain at the threshhold of hell.' "[4]

Seeing the cause of wars in state sovereignty just as many other bourgeois jurists, an English professor, G. Schwarzenberger, comes to the conclusion that the appearance of the atomic bomb urgently dictates the renunciation of state sovereignty. He writes: "To hold that power politics and war are inevitable consequences of the organization of international society on the basis of sovereign States and empires, which, being sovereign, insist on their freedom of armaments, tends to become a commonplace." Evidently, however, the advent of the atom bomb was necessary to induce statesmen to make declarations such as "every succeeding discovery makes greater nonsense of old-time conceptions of

2. H. Kelsen, *Das Problem der Souveranität und die Theorie der Völkerrechts*, 2d ed. (Tübingen: Verlag von J. C. B. Mohr, 1928), p. 320.

3. P. C. Jessup, *A Modern Law of Nations* (New York: Macmillan Company, 1948), pp. 2-3.

4. G. Scelle, "Préalable à l'integration d'une société internationale universelle," *Mélanges Séfériades* (Athens: Imp. de Ange Ath. Klissiounis, 1961), p. 12.

sovereignty."[5] Schwarzenberger concludes that the sole answer to the threat of world destruction is the creation of a world federation.[6]

Since the Second World War there have appeared and still appear in capitalist countries, as mushrooms after a rain, various more or less detailed plans for creating a world government or world federation, most frequently by restructuring the existing United Nations Organization.

At the present time, for example, a plan for reforming the United Nations worked out by the American professors Grenville Clark and Louis B. Sohn is being publicized widely. Their book, *World Peace Through World Law*, was issued in the United States in 1966 in a third edition and has been translated into many foreign languages. One must give the authors their due for having invested enormous labor in this work, which contains a draft of a revised United Nations Charter with detailed commentary, as well as plans for disarmament, plans for creating a United Nations military force, suggested changes in the Statute of the United Nations International Court, and other proposals.

At the basis of the entire plan lies, in the words of the authors themselves, "the adoption on a world-wide basis of the measures and institutions which the experience of centuries has shown to be essential for the maintenance of law and order, namely, clearly stated laws against violence, courts to interpret and apply that law and police to enforce it."[7]

According to the revised draft of the United Nations Charter proposed by Clark and Sohn, the United Nations would be transformed into the likeness of a world state having its own legislative, executive, and judicial organs, as well as military force.

The supreme organ of the United Nations would be a General Assembly, consisting of representatives elected during a specific transitional period by national legislative organs, and thereafter directly by the people.[8] The number of delegates from each state would depend, although not expressly, upon the size of its population. The delegates would not be respresentatives of states. The authors suggest a sample apportionment of representation of various states in the General Assembly which would ensure a firm majority to the western powers and their

5. G. Schwarzenberger, *The Frontiers of International Law* (London: Stevens & Sons, Ltd., 1962), p. 312.

6. *Ibid.*, p. 313.

7. G. Clark and L. B. Sohn, *World Peace Through World Law*, 3d ed. (Cambridge, Mass.: Harvard University Press, 1966), pp. xv-xvi; see also *The United Nations: The Next Twenty-Five Years* (New York: Commission to Study the Organization of Peace, 1969).

8. Clark and Sohn, *World Peace Through World Law*, pp. 20-25.

allies.[9] Decisions of the General Assembly would be adopted by a simple majority of votes.[10]

The General Assembly would enact laws on questions relegated to the jurisdiction of the Organization, adopt measures to implement them, create military forces, bring states and individual persons to responsibility for violating laws, and so forth. The laws enacted by the General Assembly would be binding not only upon member states of the Organization, but also directly upon individuals.[11]

The existing Security Council would be transformed into an Executive Council elected by the General Assembly and would be an organ subordinate to it. And here, in contrast to the present situation, Council members would not be representatives of governments, but would act in a "personal capacity." The principle of the permanent Council members is not provided.[12] The General Assembly, and not the Council, would adopt measures in the event of a threat to the peace, breach of the peace, or act of aggression. Only when the General Assembly is not in session and the circumstances require that measures be taken immediately would the Executive Council take "provisional" measures, but a session of the General Assembly would have to be convened immediately, to which the Council reported its actions and which decided what measures should be taken.[13]

The General Assembly would establish the procedure for creating a permanent military force of the new Organization. It would be comprised not of national contingents, but of volunteers from the various countries.[14] This military force would be stationed at various points of the globe "in order to facilitate prompt action."[15]

Finally, the plan proposed by Clark and Sohn provides for the establishment of the compulsory jurisdiction of the International Court.[16]

The proposal of the World Association of World Federalists approved at a conference of this Association held in Japan in 1963 may serve as another example of plans to create a world state.[17]

9. *Ibid.*, pp. 28-29.
10. *Ibid.*, p. 53 (Article 17).
11. *Ibid.*, pp. 34-39 (Articles 10 and 11).
12. *Ibid.*, pp. 66-83 (Articles 23-27).
13. *Ibid.*, pp. 111-113 (Article 39).
14. *Ibid.*, p. 321.
15. *Ibid.*, p. 325.
16. *Ibid.*, p. 337.
17. For the text of the plan see the *Japanese Annual of International Law*, VIII (1964), 37-43.

The so-called Tokyo Declaration and Proposals of the Association of Federalists declare that under contemporary conditions "man must choose between world law and world war."[18] "The United Nations," these documents go on to state, "should be transformed into a world federation with universal membership and with limited but adequate powers . . ." According to the draft, the world federation would promulgate laws and have a world inspectorate, police forces, and a court with compulsory jurisdiction.[19]

Professor K. S. Tabata of Kyoto University, whose article accompanies the publication of the said documents in the *Japanese Annual of International Law*, explains that the plan prefers to speak of a "world federation" and not a "world state," since the creation of a supranational organization "founded on the present national state system" is envisaged. However, he continues, this plan provides for a significant limitation of state sovereignty.[20]

According to this plan, the United Nations General Assembly would be transformed into a "world parliament." Representation in the parliament would be based on size of population and "other relevant factors."[21] A "world executive council," replacing the United Nations Security Council, would consist of persons elected by the General Assembly, and they would not be representatives of the governments of the member states. The Council would be subordinate to the General Assembly and act according to its instructions. A "federal world force" would be created in order to take measures to implement "provisions of the Charter, the laws enacted thereunder, and the decisions of the International Court of Justice and other organs of the U.N."[22] A unified citizenship would be established; each citizen of a member state simultaneously would be a citizen of the world federation. The Charter and laws enacted thereunder would extend directly to citizens.[23]

The other orientation which, borrowing certain theses of historical materialism, regards the creation of a world state as an inevitable consequence of scientific and technological development and the expansion of international ties is now much more influential than the dogmatic orientation.

This second orientation found powerful support and authoritative

18. *Ibid.*, p. 37.
19. *Ibid.*, pp. 37-41.
20. K. S. Tabata, "World Federation: The Eleventh World Conference of the World Association of World Federalists, Tokyo, 1963," *ibid.*, p. 31.
21. *Ibid.*, p. 40.
22. *Ibid.*, pp. 39-40.
23. *Ibid.*, p. 41.

expression in the Encyclical of Pope John XXIII, *Pacem in Terris*, promulgated in 1963. "The progress of science and technology," says the Encyclical, "has . . . influenced men to work together and live as one family."[24] The bonds among people and nations have increased sharply. "At the same time the interdependence of national economies has grown deeper, . . . so that they become, as it were, integral parts of the one world economy" (p. vi).

The social progress, order, and security of one state necessarily are connected with the progress of other states. Under such circumstances, each individual state, if it were isolated from other states, would not be in a position to provide for its own development.

In paying verbal tribute to traditional Catholic natural law doctrine, based on the nature of man created by God, the Encyclical in fact acknowledges the decisive significance of the contemporary development of the productive forces of society. In noting that the development of science and technology and of economic and other ties among states leads to the creation of problems which can not be solved successfully either by individual states or by old methods of diplomacy—the conclusion of treaties—the Encyclical points out: "It can be said, therefore, that at this historical moment the present system of organization and the way its principle of authority operates on a world basis no longer correspond to the objective requirements of the universal common good . . . " (p. vi).

The conclusion which the Encyclical draws in this connection is that: "Today the universal common good poses problems of world-wide dimensions, which cannot be tackled or solved except by the efforts of public authorities endowed with wideness of powers, structures, and means of the same proportions: that is, of public authorities which are in a position to operate in an effective manner on a world-wide basis . . . such a form of public authority must be established" (p. vi).

This orientation builds its conclusions, therefore, on the fact of the development of economic, scientific, technical, cultural, and other international ties.

Thus, while proceeding from several different basic positions, these two orientations come to the single conclusion of the need to create a world state. Proponents of this concept allege that the sole means of increasing the effectiveness of the United Nations, as well as of other international organizations, in the cause of securing peace and developing cooperation lies in the direction of a world state. They also appeal for all efforts to be directed to this end.

24. *Die Furche*, XIX, no. 17 (1963), Special Supplement: Enzyklika "Pacem in Terris," p. vi.

B. Marxism and the Problem of a World State

Bourgeois conceptions of a world state are theoretically unfounded and politically harmful. The claims by proponents of a world state that their concepts are the most progressive have no basis whatever.

These conceptions have been subjected to well-known criticism by a number of bourgeois writers, who call attention first and foremost to the fact that such concepts ignore reality and are impracticable.

An American professor, W. Friedmann, says, for example, with regard to the Clark-Sohn plan that it "ignores the basic social factors of international society." "The only observations directed to the practicability of the proposals," writes Friedmann, "are those made by Mr. Clark in the introduction. They base the practicability of the proposals primarily on the overwhelming destructive force of the new weapons, on a moral reluctance of the average American to engage in mass destruction inherent in nuclear war, and on a world-wide desire to lift the burden of competitive armaments. While these are unquestionably factors to be considered, no serious student of international politics and society regards them as the *only* relevant factors."[25]

Professor Q. Wright says that at present "it seems unlikely that the United Nations can develop into anything deserving the name of world federation . . . "[26]

Professor M. Virally comes to the following conclusion: "It would thus be completely mistaken to regard the United Nations system as a 'step' on the path to the hypothetical golden age of a 'world state.' "[27]

Other bourgeois writers also point to the danger of plans to transform the United Nations into a world state.

Thus, for example, Professor M. Bourquin, in summing up the results of a number of investigations devoted to the positions of various states with regard to the United Nations, has remarked that the majority of these works conclude that under present conditions a fundamental restructuring of the United Nations is impossible and that this path is fraught with dangers for the international organization. "In planning for a significant enlargement of the powers of the United Nations," writes Bourquin, "it is too often forgotten that these powers would not be granted to an homogeneous entity whose concern would be only for the general interests of the international community, but would be in the hands of an

25. W. Friedmann, *The Changing Structure of International Law* (New York: Columbia University Press, 1964), p. 276.

26. Q. Wright, *The Role of International Law in the Elimination of War* (Manchester: Manchester University Press, 1961), pp. 54-55.

27. M. Virally, *L'Organisation mondiale* (Paris: Colin, 1972), p. 22.

association of states, each of which would act primarily on the basis of national motives, and would attempt to use those resources which this association makes available to it in the interests of their own policy.

"Legally, the authority of the organization itself would grow, and, therefore, the authority of the community which this organization represents. But this would merely be a fiction, since the powers of the organization are to be exercised by a majority; both this majority and above all the Powers around which it is formed would benefit from the advantages connected with these changes. In our world, so deeply divided, this would mean transferring a very dangerous weapon into their hands, which could lead to the ruin of the organization instead of strengthening it."[28]

Professor C. de Visscher also points to this danger, declaring that a world federation "could be transformed into instruments of the antagonisms that divide the peoples."[29]

And Professor A. Verdross, not without justification, remarks: "Can one truly believe that a minority will agree to subordinate itself to a majority when such different civilizations and economic systems exist in the world? Central authority can function only when a minimum homogeneity exists among the members of society. Otherwise, a state always is threatened with being destroyed by civil war."[30]

The criticism of the concept of a world state by bourgeois international lawyers, however, does not uncover the fundamental reasons of its unfoundedness, which lie in the fact that these are in contradiction to the laws of societal development of our day.

In reality, the first of these orientations in the bourgeois concept of a world state ignores these laws in general, approaching the question with formalistic logic. The second orientation bases its conclusions upon the internationalization of economic life and the development of economic, scientific, technical, cultural, and other ties among states. This is, of course, the most important developmental law of contemporary society, which greatly influences the development of international organizations. But it is not the only law influencing the character of contemporary international organizations (see Chapter 13).

Marxism-Leninism approaches the problem of a world state from the viewpoint of the interaction of the laws of societal development. As has

28. M. Bourquin, *L'État souverain et l'Organisation internationale* (New York: Manhattan Publishing Company, 1959), p. 32.

29. C. de Visscher, *Théories et réalités en droit international public*, 2d ed. (Paris: Editions A. Pedone, 1955), p. 450.

30. A. Verdross, "Le problème d'une autorité politique mondiale," *Comprendre*, no. 28 (1965), p. 17.

been shown previously (see Chapter 13), these laws do not operate in a single direction with regard to the character of contemporary international organizations.

It is necessary to point out that the view, widely held in the West, that the Soviet Union and Soviet jurists oppose a world state, oppose an effective international organization, while western countries and western jurists favor a world state in principle and therefore an effective international organization, is completely unjustified.

Marxism-Leninism links the possibility of a world association of nations first and foremost with the liquidation of capitalism as the last exploitative socioeconomic formation and with the creation of a socialist society. "The purpose of socialism," wrote V. I. Lenin, "is not only to eliminate the splintering of mankind into petty states and any isolation of nations; is not only the rapprochement of nations, but also their amalgamation."[31] But in order to create the conditions for this, more than just the liquidation of private ownership and the creation of a socialist state is needed. Lenin pointed out that national and state differences among peoples and countries will last "for a very, very long time even after realization of the dictatorship of the proletariat on a world-wide scale."[32]

Even on the domestic plane in a number of instances socialism inherits from capitalism such deep roots of national discord and economic, political, and cultural inequality that a considerable time is required to liquidate them. In international relations, naturally, the matter is far more complex. Each state represents both a political and an economic unit. With the various historical strata of contradictions between states and between nationalities are associated a number of economic, political, cultural, and other problems.

Within the framework of the world socialist system, however, these differences and contradictions gradually are being overcome on the basis of a new socialist social structure and Marxist-Leninist ideology. Various forms of state unions of socialist states are possible on the path to a classless, stateless communist society. The creation of a world federation or another form of uniting free states and nations is conceivable, therefore, only on the path of liquidating private ownership, exploitation, class and national contradictions, on the path of constructing socialism and communism. "A United States of the World (and not of Europe)," wrote V. I. Lenin, "is that state form of union and freedom of nations which we link with socialism, as the complete victory of communism does

31. V. I. Lenin, "Sotsialisticheskaia revoliutsiia i pravo natsii na samoopredeleniia," *Polnoe sobranie sochinenii*, 5th ed. (Moscow: Gospolitizdat, 1962), XXVII, 256.
32. Lenin, "Detskaia bolezn' levizny v kommunizme," *ibid.*, CLI, 77. [First published in June 1920.]

not lead to the final disappearance of any state, including a democratic state."[33]

The theoretical unfoundedness of bourgeois concepts and plans to create a world state is determined by the basic unfoundedness of bourgeois methodology, which is characterized by the divorcing of the superstructure from the base. A state is regarded as something that can be reconstructed as a cardinal form at the will of politicians and jurists irrespective of the economic structure of society. The causes of war, whose liquidation is the *leitmotif* of all plans for a world state, bourgeois scholars misrepresent as state sovereignty, whereas the very existence of sovereign states is a natural consequence of the economic structure of society, and both sovereignty and the state will disappear only when this structure is changed.

The deep roots of wars are found in the economic system and in the specific class structure of society which it determines. Moreover, bourgeois concepts of a world state originate, and by their class nature can not but originate, from the possibility of creating a world state and liquidating wars without affecting the economic system of capitalism.

In stressing the basic distinction between Marxism and bourgeois pacifism on the question of the causes of wars, V. I. Lenin wrote: "Socialists always have condemned wars among peoples as a barbaric and brutal affair. But our attitude toward war differs in principle from that of bourgeois pacifists (proponents and advocates of peace) and anarchists. At the outset we distinguish ourselves by the fact that we understand the inevitable connection of wars with the class struggle within a country; we understand the impossibility of eliminating wars without eliminating classes and creating socialism."[34]

As has already been pointed out above, contemporary international organizations by their very nature can not take as their purpose the struggle against these basic causes of wars, but they can do much in the struggle against the causes of the order "produced" from the basic causes.

Under contemporary conditions, the plans to create a world state not only are utopian, but reactionary. Attempts to implement them even partially would bring great harm to the cause of developing and strengthening the United Nations and other international organizations as instruments of peace, since they are directed against the very bases of contemporary international organizations, defined by the laws of societal development.

The plans for a world state conceal the reactionary character of

33. Lenin, "O lozunge soedinennykh shtatov evropy," *ibid.*, XXVI, 354.
34. Lenin, "Sotsializm i voina (Otnoshenie RSDRP k voine)," *ibid.*, XXVI, 311. [First published at Geneva in August 1915.]

imperialism, creating the illusion of a peaceful, progressive imperialism. In criticizing Kautsky's reactionary theory of "ultra-imperialism," V. I. Lenin pointed out that it suggests to workers "that imperialism is not bad, that it is close to inter- (or ultra-) imperialism, and is capable of ensuring a permanent peace."[35]

Irrespective of the aspirations of their authors, bourgeois concepts of a world state objectively reflect the policy of imperialist monopolies which, having stretched their tentacles to many countries, would strengthen their position as world exploiters with the aid of any form of world government.

In belittling the significance of state sovereignty and calling for its liquidation, bourgeois concepts of a world state disarm peoples ideologically and facilitate interference by imperialist powers in the internal affairs of weaker states for the purpose of suppressing liberation movements, for the purpose of the economic and political enslavement of peoples.[36]

The plans to create a world state are linked in imperialist ideology with the struggle against social revolutions and the national liberation movement. As Jessup correctly points out, a world state "will enact law and will take steps to suppress armed rebellion against its authority . . . The right of resistance would not be recognized . . . The law of a world state would therefore deny the right of revolution."[37] "The international community," Jessup continues, "would have to take cognizance of and remedy situations within states which are provocative of rebellion. It would have to be prepared, as the federal government of the United States is prepared, to render armed assistance to any of its members whose local forces are inadequate to preserve domestic peace and tranquillity."[38]

Bourgeois concepts of a world state objectively mislead peoples both on the internal and international planes. On the internal plane, they parry the blow from the capitalist system, alleging that the roots of wars are not linked with the social system of an exploitative society. On the international plane, they are oriented in essence at undermining the basic principles of contemporary international organizations, as well as at diverting attention from the urgent problems of perfecting international

35. Lenin, "Imperializm, kak vysshaia stadiia imperializma (populiarnyi ocherk)," *ibid.*, XXVII, 416.

36. See A. I. Denisov, "Imperialisticheskaia ideia 'vsemirnogo pravitel' stva' i 'evropeiskoi federatsii' i ee reaktsionnaia rol'," *Vestnik moskovskogo universiteta; seriia obshchestvennykh nauk*, no. 7 (1949), pp. 97-112; D. B. Levin, *O sovremennykh burzhuaznykh teoriiakh mezhdunarodnogo prava* (Moscow: Tipo. MGEI, 1959), pp. 54-58.

37. Jessup, *Modern Law of Nations*, p. 185.

38. *Ibid.*, p. 186.

organizations as instruments of ensuring peace and developing international cooperation. As a French professor, E. Giraud, has properly pointed out, " . . . in proposing today to realize the impossible, they impede useful efforts and in no way further the progress of mankind."[39]

The interstate character of contemporary international organizations is dictated by the objective developmental laws of our epoch. And from the viewpoint of the interests of strengthening international peace and security, international organizations of the interstate type are the best form of international organization for our days.

C. Ways of Strengthening the United Nations

The question of ways to develop the United Nations is of particular significance because of the importance of the Organization itself and because the trend toward departing from the basic provisions of the Charter under the slogan of strengthening it has been manifested in the United Nations with special strength.

It follows from what has been said previously that the question of strengthening international organizations, and especially the United Nations, as instruments of peace and of the development of international cooperation must be approached by taking into account the laws of societal development which define the basic features of contemporary international organizations. Taking account of these laws means not only that any innovations having the purpose of improving the United Nations should not be divorced from the realities of today, but also, above all, that they should conform to the laws of societal development in our epoch— that is to say, should reflect the basic, protracted, profound processes of international relations and not be the product of a temporary co-relation of forces similar to the "Uniting for Peace" Resolution 377(V).

An analysis of the juridical nature of the United Nations as laid down in its Charter shows that as a whole it reflects the laws of societal development in our epoch. According to the Charter, the United Nations is an interstate organization of the peaceful coexistence of states of different social systems which should function on the basis of the agreement of such states. "The Organization is based on the principle of the sovereign equality of all its Members" (Article 2(1)). The principle of peaceful coexistence "to practice tolerance and live together in peace with one another as good neighbours" (Preamble) runs throughout the entire Charter. The Charter strengthens the inadmissibility of the Organization's

39. E. Giraud, "La révision de la Charte des Nations Unies," *Recueil des cours*, XC (1956), 326.

interfering "in matters which are essentially within the domestic jurisdiction of any state (Article 2(7)), which excludes questions of the socioeconomic system of states from the operative sphere of the United Nations. The Charter contains guarantees against transforming the Organization into the instrument of states of a single social system. The basic purposes of the Organization are to maintain international peace and security and to develop cooperation in various spheres. Only the provisions of the Charter relating to decolonization, which as a whole were a step forward but as a result of the opposition of imperialist powers inadequately reflected the corresponding law of societal development, were overtaken by the course of events.

If the Charter provisions fundamentally correspond to the laws of societal development of our epoch, then a basic condition for increasing the effectiveness of the United Nations as an instrument of peace is to purify its practice of those violations of the Charter which sometimes are presented, without any grounds, as a new constitution of the United Nations.

In its Memorandum of July 10, 1964, "Regarding Certain Measures to Strengthen the Effectiveness of the United Nations in the Safeguarding of International Peace and Security," the Soviet government justly pointed out: "The United Nations Charter contains the essential principles for peaceful and good-neighbourly relations among States. Therefore, to enhance the effectiveness of the United Nations in keeping the peace means first of all putting an end to violations of the Charter, permanently ridding the Organization of all remnants of the 'cold war' period, creating within the United Nations a situation favourable to the cooperation of all States as equals."[40]

Not breaking the fundamental principles of the Charter, not attempting to transform the United Nations into the likeness of a world state, which could lead only to the disintegration of the United Nations, but strengthening the fundamentals of the Charter by strictly observing the Charter's provisions—this is the only means of increasing the effectiveness of the United Nations as an instrument of peace and international cooperation.

In this respect, restoring the relationship between the General Assembly and the Security Council provided by the Charter and refraining from attempts to circumvent the unanimity principle of permanent members of the Security Council have special significance.

The General Assembly Resolution of November 3, 1950, well-known under the name "Uniting for Peace," was the clearest manifestation of the policy of the United States and its allies, which had the purpose of transferring the center of gravity in deciding basic questions of maintain-

40. Doc. No. S/5811 (XIX), July 10, 1964, p. 3.

ing peace and security from the Security Council to the General Assembly in order to use the then existing favorable co-relation of forces in the United Nations organ to ensure their complete domination in the Organization. Since 1956, with the changed situation in the General Assembly in connection with the admission of a large number of new members, the United States had attempted already, as Professor Stoessinger correctly points out,[41] to give the greatest possible power to the Secretary-General who at the time faithfully and loyally served the western powers.

A change of situation in the Secretariat and the General Assembly undoubtedly was an important if not decisive factor in changing United States policy with respect to the Security Council. Since the Soviet Union always insisted that the Security Council fulfill its duties in conformity with the Charter, this change led to the Security Council beginning to work again and, as some observers remark, under these conditions "the problem of the veto in practice does not arise."[42]

These reassuring symptoms show that a return to the Charter provisions on the general question of maintaining peace and security, despite the pessimistic appraisals of certain writers,[43] is by no means impossible.

Giving the United Nations a truly universal character is of the greatest significance for strengthening the Charter. The fact, for example, that the western powers have made the representation of the Chinese People's Republic impossible in the United Nations already has caused enormous harm to the United Nations and the cause of peace.

The requirement that the Charter be strictly observed relates to a number of those provisions which arise out of the fundamental principles of this organization. This is not only a requirement of international law, but also a requirement of political wisdom and international morality. The United Nations, just as other international organizations, was created by an international treaty, a Charter in which the member states determined that the Organization would act in conformity with the provisions of the Charter. The cardinal principle of international law, *pacta sunt servanda*, is fully applicable to the United Nations Charter. Respect for this principle is a fundamental principle of international legality.

The aforesaid does not mean that work should not be done to perfect existing mechanisms of the United Nations. However, here it is very important to eliminate as soon as possible such remnants of the "cold

41. J. G. Stoessinger, *The United Nations and the Superpowers* (New York: Random House, 1965), pp. 170-171.

42. R.-J. Dupuy, "Des nations unanimes et désunies," *Comprendre*, nos. 31-32 (1968), p. 34.

43. See, for example, M. Virally, *L'O.N.U. d'hier à demain* (Paris: Editions de Seuil, 1961), p. 67.

war" as the intersession committee, the collective measures committee, the United Nations Commission for Korea, and others.

In evaluating the existing United Nations system, it should not be forgotten that the United Nations is not a self-sufficient organization; the activity of the Organization depends upon the policy of member states and especially the policy of the great powers. Of course, the United Nations exerts influence upon the policy of states. It is necessary, however, to proceed from the real situation and the nature of the United Nations; the influence of the policies of states upon United Nations actions is primary and decisive.

Therefore, the principal factor in increasing the effectiveness of the United Nations as an instrument of peace and international cooperation is the forces which could exert pressure upon the ruling classes and the governments of states whose policy does not correspond to the interests of peace and consequently the requirements of the United Nations Charter. There are such forces in modern society; these are the forces of peace.

One could say that all this is not a full guarantee against an outbreak of war. This is certainly true. The many wars that have occurred since the Second World War, particularly the aggressive war of the United States in Vietnam which has aroused the deep indignation of world society, are evidence of this. But to reveal existing guarantees of peace, imperfect but real, is much better than to build castles in the sky, which are destroyed at their first confrontation with reality and which make the forces of peace disorganized and unprepared for that great struggle against the forces of aggression which they must wage constantly and with more energy and organization.[44]

44. See G. I. Tunkin, "Une organisation internationale universelle: illusions et réalité," *Comprendre*, nos. 31-32 (1968), pp. 69-79.

Part VI *The General Character and Forms of State Responsibility Under International Law*

The historic changes that have taken place in international law since the Great October Socialist Revolution have necessarily also affected that branch of international law relating to state responsibility. We must dwell on these changes, for they still are far from adequately treated and worked out in international legal doctrine.

The sanction as an " . . . indication of those measures of state coercion which are applied to those violating a prohibition or those failing to execute the command of a norm of law" is inherent in norms of international law as legal norms.[1] Of course, in international law both the sanctions themselves and their realization have many peculiarities in comparison with sanctions in national law.

Responsibility in international law, in any event responsibility in a broad sense, embraces both the problem of sanctions and the question of their realization.[2] That is to say, international legal responsibility is the legal consequences of violating norms of international law.

We are not concerned here with the question of the obligation to compensate for damage caused by lawful actions. This duty sometimes is provided for by international law.[3] In these cases one also frequently speaks of responsibility (liability for risk), although the legal nature of this kind of obligation to compensate damage is different from the nature of responsibility for a breach of law.

1. A. I. Denisov, ed., *Teoriia gosudarstva i prava* (Moscow: izd-vo Moskovskogo universiteta, 1967), p. 291.

2. As applied to national law, O. E. Leist believes that " . . . responsibility is the application and realization of a sanction in the event of a breach of law." O. E. Leist, *Sanktsii v sovetskom prave* (Moscow: Gosiurizdat, 1962), p. 85.

3. C. W. Jenks, "Liability for Ultra-Hazardous Activities in International Law," *Recueil des cours*, CXVII (1966), 105-200.

The legal consequences of violating norms of international law take many forms and may affect not only the offending state, but also the injured state, other states, and international organizations. Such consequences may, for example, depending upon the character of the breach, include the duty of the offending state to compensate for the damage caused; the right of the injured state to apply enforcement measures permitted by international law against the offending state; the right of other states to render assistance to the injured state; and perhaps the duty of an international organization to undertake certain actions against the offending state.[4]

The subjects of international legal responsibility are the subjects of international law; consequently, they are above all, and primarily, states. At the same time, responsibility of an international organization is not, precluded, for example, in the event that it fails to fulfill a treaty which it has concluded with a state or with another international organization. In isolated instances there occurs responsibility of physical persons. Thus, the principle of individual responsibility (side by side with state responsibility) for crimes against peace, war crimes, and crimes against humanity is recognized in contemporary international law.[5]

In the present work we are not concerned with the responsibility of international organizations and physical persons, limiting ourselves only to state responsibility.

State responsibility may arise either as a result of an unlawful action of a state (for example, violations by state authorities of the immunity of a foreign diplomatic representative) or as a result of an unlawful failure to act, that is, the failure of a state to take measures which it must effectuate in order to fulfill its obligations under international law (for example, legislative measures necessary to fulfill an international treaty to which the said state is a party).

Since the actions of a state in practice are expressed in the actions of its agencies, the international legal responsibility of a state arises out of the actions of its agencies (state administration, legislative, and judicial).

In intending, as already has been indicated, to dwell primarily upon certain new phenomena in the field of international legal state responsibility, we leave to one side the "traditional" disputes over state responsibility for actions of its agencies and officials exceeding the limits of their

4. In this sense see R. Ago, "Second Report on State Responsibility," United Nations, *Yearbook of the International Law Commission 1972* (New York: United Nations, 1972), II, 177-197.

5. See the charters and judgments of the Nuremberg and Tokyo international military tribunals and the United Nations General Assembly resolution of December 11, 1946, confirming the principles of international law recognized by the Charter of the Nuremberg tribunal.

authority (*ultra vires*), for actions of superior and inferior agencies, in questions of fault, in denial of justice, and other such areas.

International legal state responsibility arises in the event it violates its obligations under international law. One should point in this connection to one very widespread but mistaken view that the causing of damage by one state to the interests of another necessarily entails international legal responsibility. Causing damage is not necessarily a violation of international law and consequently does not necessarily entail international legal state responsibility.[6] A state's action may be wholly lawful and all the same cause damage to the interests of another state, especially if such interests are understood broadly.

Since treaty and customary norms have identical binding force, state responsibility arises in the event of a violation of either customary or treaty norms of international law.[7] What difference can there be in the question of responsibility when in one case a state has violated a particular customary principle or customary norm of international law, and in another case, a principle or norm fixed in an international treaty? Take, for example, the case of a violation of the principle of freedom of the high seas. As long as the 1958 Geneva Convention on the High Seas had not entered into force, this principle was a generally recognized customary principle of international law; after the Geneva Convention had entered into force, this principle, in the form in which it was fixed in this Convention, became a treaty norm for its parties. Of course, there are no grounds for believing that responsibility for a violation of this principle changed once it had become a treaty |norm] for the respective states. A violation of either a customary or a treaty norm of international law is an international delict.[8]

These legal consequences which ensue for a state as a result of its violation of international law are the content of international legal responsibility.

6. This proposition can be regarded as generally recognized. See, for example, D. Anzilotti, *Corso di diritto internazionale*, 4th ed. (Padova: CEDAM, 1955), I, 404; A. Ulloa, *Derecho internacional publico*, 4th ed. (Madrid: Ediciones iberoamericanas, 1957), II, 251-252; A. Verdross, *Mezhdunarodnoe pravo*, trans. F. A. Kublitskii and R. L. Naryshkina, ed. G. I. Tunkin (Moscow: izd-vo IL, 1959), p. 353; P. Guggenheim, *Traité de droit international public* (Geneva: Librairie de l'Université, 1954), II, 2.

7. P. Fauchille, *Traité de droit international public* (Paris: Rousseau & Cie., 1922), I (Part 1), p. 517.

8. One can not, therefore, agree with the authors of the textbook *Mezhdunarodnoe pravo* published in 1947, who distinguish between responsibility for a delict and responsibility for a violation of an international treaty (p. 148).

Chapter 17 *The Character of State Responsibility Under International Law Before the Great October Socialist Revolution*

Under the old international law state responsibility included the obligation of an offending state to compensate damage caused, as well as the application of enforcement measures, including measures utilizing armed force.

Under the influence of civilist concepts in the science of international law, the view was widespread that state responsibility amounted to the duty to compensate damage caused. According to this concept, the failure of a state to fulfill its obligations under international law entailed a new obligation: the obligation to compensate damage (financial and moral) caused to another state.

This concept was worked out in detail in the second half of the nineteenth and in the beginning of the twentieth century.

A. Heffter, in noting that international law does not know "crime" in the form in which it exists in national law, believed at the same time that the concept of "breach of law" does exist in international law. "Each such breach of law," he said, "obliges the one acting unlawfully to give satisfaction to the one who has suffered damage, since always when an arbitrary action results in a wrong (*Ungleichheit*), this violation must be eliminated; this is the law of justice (*Gerechtigkeit*)."[9]

F. F. Martens, crediting Heffter with creating the concept that international legal obligations originate from delicts, points out that "Heffter's theory on this question suffers only from the defect that it mixes together civil law with international."[10]

9. A. Heffter, *Das europäische Völkerrecht der Gegenwart auf den bisherigen Grundlagen*, ed. F. H. Geffcken, 8th ed. (Berlin: Verlag H. W. Muller, 1888), p. 220.

10. F. F. Martens, *Sovremennoe mezhdunarodnoe pravo tsivilizovannykh narodov*, 3d ed. (St. Petersburg: Tipo. A. Benke, 1895), I, 429.

At the same time, Martens expresses essentially the same idea as Heffter. "A crime," says Martens, "gives the victim a right to compensation for financial damage and moral injury caused to him. Although one does not speak in international relations of crimes committed by a people, nevertheless it is possible here to violate a right establishing, just as in private relations, the obligation of the guilty party to make financial compensation, to restore property, or to give moral satisfaction to the injured state."[11]

In his monograph *Völkerrecht und Landesrecht*, H. Triepel devotes comparatively little attention to general questions of state responsibility, considering primarily the more specific problems of state responsibility for the actions of its agencies, of individuals located on the state's territory, and so forth. However, he also works out these questions on the basis of the said concept.[12]

We find a considerably expanded and better founded elaboration of this concept in Anzilotti's special monograph devoted to the problem of state responsibility in international law, published in 1902. "State responsibility," says Anzilotti, "is in the nature of reparation, and not of satisfaction; consequently, the right of the injured state is limited by the requirement of compensating damage and of possible guarantees for the future, but it can not acquire the character of punishing the guilty state."[13] In developing this notion, Anzilotti goes on to point out that "a juridical relationship which arises between states as a result of the violation of a right, and which reflects responsibility, has the essential features of a liability relationship."[14] In his treatise on international law Anzilotti says: "As a result of an unlawful action, that is, speaking generally, as a result of a breach of an international obligation, there emerges a new juridical relationship between the state to which the said unlawful action is imputed and the state in respect of which this obligation was not fulfilled; the first is bound to effectuate compensation, and the second may demand such compensation. This constitutes the sole consequence which international norms, being an expression of the mutual promises of states, can link with the breach of law . . ."[15]

The distinction between civil and criminal responsibility, Anzilotti goes on to point out, and between compensation of damage and punishment, which exists in national law, is completely unknown in international law, which also reflects in this respect a stage of social development long since

11. *Ibid.*

12. H. Triepel, *Völkerrecht und Landesrecht* (Leipzig: Verlag von C. H. Hirschfeld, 1899), p. 323.

13. D. Anzilotti, *Teoria generale della responsibilita dello stato nel diritto internazionale* (Florence: F. Lumachi Libraio-Editore, 1902), p. 96.

14. *Ibid.*, p. 97.

15. Anzilotti, *Corso di diritto internazionale*, I, 385-386.

passed by national law. "It was characteristic of an earlier stage in the development of law that compensation of damage was at the same time a punishment, which consisted of compensating the harm caused."[16]

In the last edition of his treatise on international law, however, published posthumously, Anzilotti withdraws somewhat from his earlier point of view. Previously, Anzilotti had denied the "satisfaction" character of responsibility and had maintained that it bears only the character of "reparation." Now, although he says that responsibility in international law remains generally "within the framework of civil responsibility," he recognizes two forms of responsibility: satisfaction and reparation. Responsibility is expressed as satisfaction when nonfinancial damage has been caused, although, he says, there are instances when satisfaction, arising out of the infliction of nonfinancial damage, is expressed in the payment of a specific amount of money. By reparations Anzilotti means responsibility which arose in consequence of the infliction of financial damage and which is expressed either in restitution or in compensation of the harm.[17]

This concept was, in fact, also predominant in bourgeois international legal literature during the period of the League of Nations. It is true that the working out of the problem of state responsibility at that time was limited almost exclusively to the problem of state responsibility for damage caused on its territory to the person or property of aliens. The emphasis, therefore, was laid upon compensation of damage.

Fauchille, for example, formulated this point of view as follows: "When state responsibility occurs, the question is one of reparations, that is, of restoring the previously existing situation, of compensation for damage caused to interests, or of satisfaction, which is expressed in a disavowal or removal of an official from a post, initiating the prosecution of the guilty person, public declarations, apologies made by way of diplomacy, and so forth."[18]

In a monograph on the responsibility of states in international law, C. Eagleton has asserted that the failure of a state to meet obligations under international law "imposes upon the guilty state the further obligation to make reparation for the injury caused ... "[19] "Responsibility," says Eagleton, "is simply the principle which establishes an obligation to make good any violation of international law producing injury, committed by the respondent state."[20]

16. *Ibid.*, p. 386.
17. *Ibid.*, pp. 425-427.
18. Fauchille, *Le droit international public*, I (Part 1), p. 535.
19. C. Eagleton, *The Responsibility of States in International Law* (New York: New York University Press, 1928), p. 3.
20. *Ibid.*, p. 22.

C. de Visscher defined state responsibility thus: "International responsibility is a basic idea which amounts to the duty of a state to eliminate the consequences of an unlawful act . . . "[21]

The concept that state responsibility is expressed in an obligation to compensate financial and moral damage caused by an unlawful act also runs throughout the various draft codifications of norms of international law relating to state responsibility for damage caused on its territory to the person or property of aliens.

Thus, in the "Bases for Discussion" drawn up by the preparatory committee of the Conference for the Codification of International Law in 1929, state responsibility is defined as follows: "Responsibility involves for the State concerned an obligation to make good the damage suffered insofar as it results from failure to comply with the international obligation. It may also, according to the circumstances, and when this consequence follows from the general principles of international law, involve the obligation to afford satisfaction to the State which has been injured in the person of its national, in the shape of an apology (given with the appropriate solemnity) and (in proper cases) the punishment of the guilty persons."[22]

An analogous formulation was given in a resolution of the Institute of International Law, adopted in 1927, on the international responsibility of states for damage caused on their territory to the person or property of aliens.[23]

The Harvard draft gave the following definition of state responsibility: "A state is responsible, as the term is used in this convention, when it has a duty to make reparation to another state for the injury sustained by the latter state as a consequence of an injury to its national."[24]

The said concept also was reflected in the judgments of the Permanent Court of International Justice. Thus, the Court's decision of July 26, 1927, in the dispute between Germany and Poland over "the Chorzow factory," said: "It is a principle of international law that the breach of an engagement involves an obligation to make reparation in an adequate form. Reparation therefore is the indispensable complement of a failure to apply a convention and there is no necessity for this to be stated in the convention itself."[25]

21. C. de Visscher, "Le déni de justice en droit international," *Recueil des cours*, LII (1935), 421; see also E. M. Borchard, *The Diplomatic Protection of Citizens Abroad* (New York: Banks Law Publishing Co., 1928), p. 178.

22. United Nations, *Yearbook of the International Law Commission 1956*, II, 255.

23. H. Wehberg, *Tableau général des résolutions de l'institut de droit international* (Basel: Editions juridiques et sociologiques, 1957), p. 139.

24. Harvard Law School, "Research in International Law," *American Journal of International Law Supplement*, XXIII (1929), 140.

25. Permanent Court of International Justice, Collection of Judgments, Series A,

The said concept artificially narrowed state responsibility, reducing it to the obligation of an offending state to compensate the damage caused. Furthermore, it was not logically coordinated: if a violation of an international obligation gave rise to a new obligation, the obligation to compensate the damage caused, then a violation of the latter should, according to this concept, give rise to a further new obligation, and *ad infinitum.*[2][6]

In fact, the proponents of this theory also have proceeded on the basis of the possibility of applying enforcement measures to the offending state. Much attention has been devoted in international legal literature to questions of intervention, reprisals, and, finally, to war as a reaction to a violation of international law. Actually, the said concept amounted to the obligation to compensate harm as though it were the first stage of effectuating responsibility. If the offending state did not fulfill this obligation, enforcement measures could be taken against it.

We find this interpretation, for example, in F. Liszt. He says that a guilty state should first restore, insofar as this is possible, the previously existing situation and pay monetary compensation. In serious cases, in addition to financial compensation, satisfaction is required which consists of an expression of condolences, a salute to the flag of the injured state, and so forth. If the threat of a recurrence of the illegal actions exists, it is possible to take security measures which might be expressed in particular in a pledge of part of the state's territory. If the offending state refuses to grant financial compensation or satisfaction, coercion is admissible. First, the question must be one of using arbitration or measures of self-help of a nonmilitary nature, and as a last resort, the injured state may resort to war.[2][7]

According to another concept, the international law of that time provided a number of consequences for a delict, beginning with the

No. 8, *Case Concerning the Factory at Chorzow* (Leyden: A.W. Sijthoff, 1927), p. 21.

26. Guggenheim, *Traité de droit international public*, II, 64.

27. F. Liszt, *Das Völkerrecht*, 11th ed. (Berlin: J. Springer, 1918), p. 182. In a number of doctoral dissertations defended not so long ago at the University of Geneva, the authors maintain that responsibility under international law amounts to the obligation to compensate damage caused and that only the failure to fulfill this obligation can entail sanctions. P. A. Bissonnete, for example, writes: "Since the injured state is obliged to demand compensation of damage before resorting to sanctions, one can conclude that the consequence in general international law of a breach of law is reparation." P. A. Bissonnete, *La satisfaction comme mode de réparation en droit international* (Annemasse: imp., 1952), p. 12. See also P. A. Zannas, *La responsabilité internationale des États pour les actes de négligence* (Montreaux: Gauguin & Laubscher, 1952), p. 22; A. Suat Bilge, *La responsabilité internationale des États et son application en metiére d'actes législatifs* (Istanbul, 1950), pp. 15, 36.

obligation to compensate the damage caused and ending with the use of armed force. This view was held, for example, by J. C. Bluntschli, who wrote: "In international law, the strength of the legal order also is ensured by the fact that new law emerges out of a breach of law. The illegality committed is transformed into a right of the victim to demand from the offender, in accordance with the circumstances, restoration of the previously existing situation, compensation of damage, satisfaction, retribution, or punishment. When a breach of law consists only of the failure to fulfill an obligation assumed, without injuring the prestige of the state and without breach of the peace, it can be equated to a civil breach of law, which gives the injured person the right to initiate a civil suit for the purpose of restoring the previously existing legal situation (for example, the return of property, payment of a debt, or compensation of damage). In such instances international law also is satisfied only by elimination of the illegality and restoration of the right."[28]

If damage has been caused to the honor and dignity of a state, in Bluntschli's view the injured power has the right to demand appropriate satisfaction. Such satisfaction goes somewhat beyond simply restoring the situation as it existed. Depending on the circumstances, it may be expressed in punishment of the guilty persons, and so forth. If necessary, enforcement measures are applied to obtain satisfaction.

When a breach of law takes the form of an intrusion into the legal sphere of another state, the latter, says Bluntschli, has the right not only to secure elimination of the breach of law, restoration of the previous situation, as well as compensation of damage, but also satisfaction, a penalty, and sometimes, depending upon the circumstances, other guarantees against the renewal of unlawful actions. If there has been a breach of the peace, the injured state also has the right to punish the offender. The provision of the criminal law that juridical persons can not be subjected to criminal punishment does not apply in international law. "A state which permits a breach of the peace may thereby create a danger to its own existence, and a war to which it has given rise may lead to its destruction. This is punishment under international law, and world history is evidence of its reality."[29]

This point of view, which might be called the concept of the "proportionate reaction to a violation of international law," as well as the theory that a violation of international law entails the obligation to compensate damage caused, and that only in the event this obligation is not fulfilled can sanctions be applied to the offending state, have given to a certain degree a distorted idea of international legal reality of that time.

28. J. C. Bluntschli, *Das moderne Völkerrecht der civilisirten Staten*, 2d ed. (Nördlingen: C. H. Beck, 1872), p. 259.

29. *Ibid.*, p. 260.

Even if one believes that under the old international law a state could lawfully resort to war only in the event its rights were violated (the "just war" doctrine), international law all the same did not oblige a state first to submit a claim concerning compensation of damage and to appeal to arms only in the event of a refusal to satisfy this claim. The Hague conventions of 1899 and 1907 do not contain such provisions.

As regards the "proportionate reaction" to a violation of international law, this principle could have been considered operative only with respect to compensation of damage and to reprisals; it did not, however, extend to war. If again one proceeds from the concept of "just war," under the old international law a state could resort to war in defense of any right which, in its opinion, had been violated.[30]

The Hague conventions of 1899 and 1907 do not contain any legal norms which would limit the right of a state to resort to war irrespective of the seriousness of the breach of law. It is true that the conventions of 1899 and 1907 concerning peaceful settlement of disputes distinguish between "serious disagreements or disputes" and international disputes "involving neither honor nor vital interests." In the first instance, the possibility of the recourse to arms is expressly mentioned in the conventions. Article 2 of these conventions says: "In case of serious disagreement or dispute, before an appeal to arms, the Contracting Powers agree to have recourse, as far as circumstances allow, to the good offices or mediation of one or more friendly powers." In the second instance, the possibility of recourse to arms is not mentioned. Article 9 of the conventions says: "In disputes of an international nature involving neither honor nor vital interests, and arising from a difference of opinion on points of fact, the Contracting Powers deem it expedient and desirable that the parties who have not been able to come to an agreement by means of diplomacy, should, as far as circumstances allow, institute an International Commission of Inquiry, to facilitate a solution of these disputes by elucidating the facts by means of an impartial and conscientious investigation."[31]

In dividing conflicts between states into the two said categories, the conventions of 1899 and 1907 on the peaceful settlement of international disputes (the provisions of both conventions on this question are identical) contain no provisions as to the grounds upon which a state could resort to war.

30. *De lege feranda*, Bluntschli suggested certain limitations of the right of a state to resort to war. Article 520 of the Code of International Law which he compiled provided: "A lawful *causus belli* justifies war only when restoration of the violated right and appropriate satisfaction and compensation are impossible to obtain without difficulty through peaceful means." *Ibid.*, p. 291.

31. L. A. Modzhorian and V. K. Sobakin, comps., *Mezhdunarodnoe pravo v izbrannykh dokumentakh*, ed. V. N. Durdenevskii (Moscow: izd-vo IMO, 1957), II, 248-249.

For a war to be considered "just," it was required only that military actions were commenced with an advance and unambiguous warning, which must have taken the form of either a reasoned declaration of war or an ultimatum with a conditional declaration of war.[32] However, the nonfulfillment of even this requirement did not entail in practice any juridical consequences.

War was considered by many authors as one of the international legal methods of settling disputes among states, although, as is shown farther on, this was by no means so. The fact that they called war an "extreme measure" had no juridical but only practical significance, since naturally if a state could secure satisfaction of its claims without using force it would be common sense for it to prefer not to appeal to arms. "In any event," wrote Martens, "not arbitration but war remains up to the present time the usual means of deciding international disputes."[33] Another well-known Russian international lawyer, N. Korkunov, wrote: "A state which avoids the voluntary execution of duties falling upon it can be compelled to do so by military actions undertaken against it."[34]

We have mentioned the "just war" doctrine, according to which a state could resort to war only in defense of a violated right. To a certain extent, however, this doctrine idealized the actual situation in the old international law. The Hague conventions of 1899 and 1907, which may be considered to be codifications of the international law then prevailing in this domain, did not contain provisions that one state could resort to war against another only in the event its rights were violated. The actual situation was such that, although a state which had unleased a war attempted, as a rule, to cite in justification of its actions any real or imagined claims resting on international law, states, especially strong ones, did not want to assume an obligation under which one could resort to war only on the basis of claims which could be justified legally. It is not surprising, therefore, that the majority of international lawyers of that time, taking the actual situation into account, rejected the "just war" doctrine.[35]

Bluntschli, who was a proponent of the "just war" doctrine, pointed out that war in reality was a factual state of affairs, but in the interests of peace, he said, it is important as far as possible to regard it as a lawful measure of self-help, that is, as a measure undertaken in defense of a violated right.[36]

32. See the 1907 Convention on the Opening of Military Actions, *ibid.*, III, 40.

33. Martens, *Sovremennoe mezhdunarodnoe pravo*, I, 13.

34. N. Korkunov, *Mezhdunarodnoe pravo* (St. Petersburg: Tipo. Morskogo ministerstva, 1886), p. 4.

35. H. Kelsen, *Principles of International Law*, ed. R. W. Tucker, 2d ed. (New York: Holt, Rinehart & Winston, 1967), p. 33.

36. Bluntschli, *Das moderne Völkerrecht*, p. 287.

State Responsibility Before the October Socialist Revolution

In the old international law, at least in those instances when it was undertaken in defense of a violated right, war outwardly was represented as an enforcement measure with respect to the offending state. On this basis, some writers considered war to be a sanction. Korkunov wrote, for example, that in international law coercion "not only is not impossible, but even, on the contrary, nowhere does it take on such vast dimensions as in international life, appearing here in the terrible form of war."[3 7]

One can name Kelsen and Guggenheim among the contemporary authors who adhere to the view that war was a sanction under the old international law. Moreover, they also believe that this position has been retained in contemporary international law. "If reprisals and war," Kelsen wrote, "—typical measures of self-help—are not considered as legal sanctions because a minimum of centralization is considered to be an essential element of the law, the social order we call general international law cannot be regarded as law in the true sense of the term."[3 8]

In P. Guggenheim's view, war is a "measure of legal protection," "a sanction" of international law.[3 9]

We already have spoken of the unfounded assertions of Kelsen and Guggenheim that war is admissible under contemporary international law. The question which interests us now is war in connection with the problem of sanctions in international law. In this respect one also can not agree with Kelsen and Guggenheim.

First of all, even if regarded only as a reaction to a violation of international law, war under the old international law was not dependent in any way upon the seriousness of the breach of law, which is an essential constituent element of a sanction. As already has been pointed out, a state could resort to war in the event of any violation of international law which affected its rights.

The consequences of war had absolutely no connection with responsibility for the breach of law committed. With the outbreak of war, a special international law—the law of war—came into effect. Absolutely nothing remained of the relations which arose in consequence of the breach of law that led to war. According to the law of war, the parties were in an equal legal position. The former offender ceased to exist. The legal consequences of war also had no connection whatever with the initial breach of law.

The legal consequences of war did not depend upon whether a state began the war in defense of a violated right or without any legal grounds, as, for example, to seize parcels of land from a neighboring state, but were determined by the results of the armed contest between the belligerents.

37. Korkunov, *Mezhdunarodnoe pravo*, p. 4.
38. Kelsen, *Principles of International Law*, p. 31.
39. Guggenheim, *Traité de droit international public*, II, 93.

International law sanctioned that which was gained by force. This was the "right of the victor."

This situation again testifies to the fact that the "just war" doctrine had no foundation in the old international law. The justness or unjustness of a war meant nothing, either for the conduct of the war or for its consequences.

Under the old international law, war created a new legal situation characterized by the unlimited right of the victor, that is to say, by the right of the victor limited only by his physical possibilities to force the defeated side to fulfill the demands submitted to it. These demands juridically did not depend upon whether they were submitted by the state which had unleashed the war or the state upon whom the attack was committed.

Also, they need not have been in accordance with the claims put forward before the war. Moreover, they could be submitted by the party which before the war had not put forward any claims at all against the defeated state.

The said claims had a special legal basis, the right of the victor, which thus was an inevitable corollary of the admissibility of war as a method of settling international disputes. Professor Lauterpacht, even in 1952, maintained that "international law sets no limits—other than that determined by compelling considerations of humanity—to the discretion of the victor . . . "[40]

This means that, contrary to the generally accepted view, war was regarded under the old international law not just as a legal method of settling disputes.

If this had been so, the victor could pretend to lay claim only to the satisfaction of claims which had led to the war, that is to say, could pretend to lay claim only to the settlement to his advantage of the dispute which actually had existed.

Thus, with its external resemblance to an enforcement measure, war was not a sanction under the old international law. It was a factual state of affairs whose origin virtually was unregulated by international law, but to which international law linked specific juridical consequences.

What has been said also means, and this was an important feature of the old international law, that the principles of international legal state responsibility in essence were not extended to war and its consequences.

International law contained certain principles of state responsibility relating to violations of the laws and customs of war. Thus, the Fourth Hague Convention of 1907 established that the belligerent party which

40. L. Oppenheim, *International Law*, ed. H. Lauterpacht, 7th ed. (London: Longmans, 1952), II, 603.

violates the laws and customs of war "shall, if the case demands, be liable to pay compensation. It shall be responsible for all acts committed by persons forming part of its armed forces."[41] There was the well-known institute of military reprisals; however, the principles of responsibility did not extend as a whole to war and its consequences.

International law, having recognized the "right to wage war," did not contain principles and norms under which the unleashing of wars would be appraised as aggression. As regards the consequences of war, international law recognized the "right of the victor." Naturally, therefore, the question of responsibility for war did not arise, and the juridical consequences of war were not linked with the circumstances which had led to war.

41. Article 3 of the 1907 Convention on the Laws and Customs of Land Warfare, Modzhorian and Sobakin, comps., *Mezhdunarodnoe pravo v izbrannykh dokumentakh*, III, 42.

Chapter 18 *State Responsibility Under Contemporary International Law*

A. The Concept of the International Legal Criminal Responsibility of a State

In attempting to comprehend the changes which have occurred in the domain of international legal state responsibility, some bourgeois jurists have come to the conclusion that a new type of state responsibility—criminal responsibility—has emerged in international law. The proponents of this concept have maintained that if at an earlier stage of the development of international law state responsibility was restricted to the duty to compensate damage caused, then contemporary international law goes further, providing for the criminal responsibility of a state as a subject of international law.

The concept of the criminal responsibility of a state has been propagated to a certain extent in bourgeois international legal literature since the First and, especially, the Second World Wars. Proponents of this concept fell into two categories: some adhere to the view that only a state can be the subject of international criminal responsibility, and individual persons can bear criminal responsibility only under national law (Bustamante, Donnedieu de Vabres); others believed that both a state and individuals could be subjects of criminal responsibility under international law (Pella, Saldana, Levy).[1]

One of the most active propagandists of the criminal responsibility of states, a Rumanian professor, V. V. Pella, maintained in his works, particularly in *La criminalité collective des États et le droit pénal de l'avenir* published in 1925,[2] that criminal responsibility of a state already

---

1. For greater detail, see D. B. Levin, "Problema otvetstvennosti v nauke mezhdunarodnogo prava," *Izvestiia akademii nauk SSSR; otdelenie ekonomiki i prava*, no. 2 (1946), pp. 99-115.

State Responsibility Under Contemporary International Law

exists in international law and that full recognition of this new type of responsibility would have great significance in increasing the effectiveness of international law.

Proceeding from the premise that international law should develop along the same path as national law, Pella believed that criminal responsibility of a state must inevitably emerge in international law and that the domain of its application would expand. He maintained that a "state has its own will and, consequently, is capable of committing crimes . . . "[3]

"We should like to affirm as forcefully as possible," Pella wrote after the Second World War, "that *if* criminal law is to be called upon to protect international peace and civilization, one should not exclude the principle of criminal responsibility of a state therefrom."[4]

In his work *La guerre-crime et les criminels de guerre*, published in 1946, Pella appended "A Plan for an International Criminal Code" which he had prepared before the Second World War. Proposals for an international criminal code had been worked out by the author for the International Criminal Law Association, the Inter-Parliamentary Union, and the International Law Association. These proposals were discussed in committees of the said organizations, and thus the final "Plan for an International Criminal Code" reflects not only Pella's point of view but to a certain extent also the point of view of a number of other proponents of the concept of international criminal responsibility of a state.

The following classification of the crimes of states is given in the "Plan for an International Criminal Code":

(1) War crimes, reflected in the commission by a state first of one of the following actions: (a) declaration of war upon another state; (b) intrusion of armed forces upon the territory of another state, with or without a declaration of war; (c) attack by land, naval, or air forces, with or without a declaration of war, upon the territory, vessels, or aircraft of another state; (d) sea blockade of coasts or ports of another state; (e) support of armed bands which, having been formed on its territory, intrude into the territory of another state, or a refusal, despite the demand of the state being subjected to the intrusion, to take on its own territory all measures in its power to deprive the said bands of any assistance or protection.[5]

2. V. V. Pella, *La criminalité collective des états et le droit pénal de l'avenir* (Bucharest: Imp. de l'état, 1925).

3. Pella, "La repression des crimes contre la personalité de l'état," *Recueil des cours*, XXXIII (1930), 821-822.

4. Pella, *La guerre-crime et les criminels de guerre* (Geneva: Revue de droit international de sciences diplomatiques et politiques, 1946), p. 58.

5. The author refers in this connection to the text of the definition of aggression worked out by the Committee on Security Questions of the General Commission of the 1933 Conference on Disarmament on the basis of the Soviet draft definition of aggression.

(2) Production, sale, or use of prohibited means of waging war, and other violations of the laws and customs of war.

(3) Creation and training of armed forces exceeding the prescribed contingents.

(4) Extermination, enslavement, or persecution, in time of peace or war, of specific groups of the population for reasons of race, politics, or religion.

(5) Failure to take measures to prevent crimes against the independence and territorial integrity of another state which have been prepared on the territory of the state concerned.

(6) Admittance or the rendering of aid to persons and organizations which are preparing on the territory of the state crimes against the interests of another state, particularly an attempt against the life and liberty of the head of a foreign state, members of the government, and so forth.

(7) Interference in an internal political struggle in another state.

(8) Indefinite threats to use force against another state.

(9) Conducting maneuvers or mobilization for the purpose of a military demonstration.

(10) Violation of the immunity of foreign diplomatic representatives.

(11) Counterfeiting of money and any other disloyal actions committed by one state for the purpose of causing injury to another, or against whose commission the state does not take the necessary measures.

(12) Any other actions which may violate normal international relations.[6]

Pella includes as criminal sanctions which should be applied to a state: diplomatic sanctions (warning, breaking off of diplomatic relations, recalling the exequatur from consuls, and so forth); legal sanctions (sequestration of the property of a state's nationals, and others); economic sanctions (economic blockade or boycott, embargo, and others); other sanctions (censure, penalty, deprivation for a certain time of representation in international organizations, deprivation of a mandate to administer a trust territory, complete or partial occupation of the territory of a state, deprivation of independence).[7]

In addition, the "Plan for an International Criminal Code" provides for security measures that might be undertaken with respect to a state which has committed a crime, namely: destruction of strategic railways and fortifications; prohibiting military production; confiscation of armaments; limitation of the size of armed forces; complete disarmament; the formation of demilitarized zones on the territory of the state and the

6. Pella, *La guerre-crime et les criminels de guerre*, pp. 148-150.
7. *Ibid.*, pp. 153-154.

establishment of control over them; distribution of military units at various points of a state's territory for the purposes of control.[8]

Pella proposed to create within the framework of the United Nations International Court a special criminal chamber to consider cases concerning the crimes of states.[9]

The draft code prepared by Pella has gone no further.

H. Lauterpacht, who also is a proponent of international criminal responsibility of a state, writes: "The comprehensive notion of an international delinquency ranges from ordinary breaches of treaty obligations, involving no more than pecuniary compensation, to violations of International Law amounting to a criminal act in the generally accepted meaning of the term."[10]

In Lauterpacht's view, the state and the persons acting on its behalf bear criminal responsibility for such violations of international law as by reason of their gravity, ruthlessness, and contempt for human life place them in the category of criminal acts as this is understood in the law of "civilized countries."[11] Lauterpacht includes as such crimes the wholesale massacre of aliens resident within a state's territory and the preparation and launching of an aggressive war. Lauterpacht suggests that universal recognition of the principles of international law relating to the punishment of war criminals is new evidence of the existence of the criminal responsibility of a state, since war criminals bear punishment for actions which they commit, as a rule, on behalf of agencies of the state.[12]

The theory of the unity of the paths of development of international and national law, according to which the development of law represents a unified process wherein national law and international law are only at different stages, is a basic concept of the criminal responsibility of a state (see Chapter 9).

Proponents of the concept of the criminal responsibility of a state are prepared to acknowledge that until recently international law was unaware of the criminal responsibility of a state, but they explain this by the fact that international law supposedly was in a primitive state. They maintain, however, that recently international law has moved far forward, as a result whereof, by analogy with national law, the criminal responsibility of a state has emerged.

8. *Ibid.*, p. 155.

9. *Ibid.*, p. 129.

10. L. Oppenheim, *International Law*, ed. H. Lauterpacht, 8th ed. (London: Longmans, 1955), I, 339.

11. *Ibid.*, p. 355.

12. *Ibid.*, p. 356; H. Donnedieu de Vabres, "Le procès de Nuremberg devant les principes modernes du droit penal international," *Recueil des cours*, LXX (1947), 562.

It is characteristic that objections to the concept of criminal responsibility of a state in bourgeois literature were based, as a rule, on this same theory of the unity of the paths of the development of law. Thus, Anzilotti writes in *Teoria generale della responsabilita dello stato nel diritto internazionale* that in a sense compensation for damage in international law replaces punishment, but the analogy is not significant. In the early stages of the development of law, Anzilotti continues, punishment (*poena*) is not distinguished from compensation for losses because punishment "had a private, and not a public character"; punishment was compensation, and vice versa. The theory that punishment is distinct from compensation for damage was formulated at a time when a state found itself in a position to assume the function of defending an objective right, "consequently, at a stage of development which international law still has not reached and possibly will never reach."[13] In his treatise on international law Anzilotti again says that the difference between civil and criminal responsibility is unknown to international law because the latter is at an earlier stage of development than national law.[14]

J. Basdevant's objections to the concept of the criminal responsibility of a state follow along the same line. In his preface to J. Dumas's book, *De la responsabilité internationale des États*, in which the author adheres to the concept of the international legal criminal responsibility of a state, Basdevant says with regard to the views of the book's author: "There is no doubt that these views, in comparison with existing law, are in advance of their time."[15]

Consequently, for both Anzilotti and Basdevant, there is no criminal responsibility in international law not because this law is of a special kind, but because it is at a lower stage of development in comparison with national law.

Other critics of the concept of criminal responsibility of a state proceed from the fact that criminal responsibility is inapplicable to corporations. Thus, even R. Phillimore wrote in his *Commentaries Upon International Law*: "To speak of inflicting punishment upon a State is to mistake both the principles of criminal jurisprudence and the nature of the legal personality of a corporation. Criminal law is concerned with a natural person; a being of thought, feeling, and will. A legal person is not, strictly speaking, a being of these attributes, though, through the mediums of representation and of government, the will of certain individuals is

13. D. Anzilotti, *Teoria generale della responsabilita dello stato nel diritto internazionale* (Florence: F. Lumachi Libraro-Editore, 1902), pp. 96-97.

14. Anzilotti, *Corso di diritto internazionale*, 4th ed. (Padova: CEDAM, 1955), I, 386.

15. J. Dumas, *De la responsabilité des États* (Paris: Recueil Sirey, 1930), p. xi.

considered as the will of the corporation; but only for certain purposes. There must be *individual* will to found the jurisdiction of criminal law. Will by *representation* can not found that jurisdiction."[16]

In a two-volume monograph, *The Crime of State*, Professor P. N. Drost develops a concept fairly close to the views of Phillimore just quoted. Drost suggests that "acts of state" may be crimes of state under international law. But "crimes of state," according to Drost, are not "governmental crimes." A state can not be a criminal.[17]

Proceeding from the concept which regards the state as a fiction, Drost rejects the concept of criminal responsibility of a state under international law. ". . . the state as such," he says, "can not act or do anything at all. It can not defend its crimes for exactly the very same reason that it can not commit crime."[18]

At the same time, Drost recognizes a state's financial responsibility for an international delinquency. In his view, state responsibility is limited to "civil liability."[19]

As regards criminal responsibility for "crimes of state" under international law, it falls upon individual persons. In this connection Drost believes that if it is impossible to imagine a "criminal state," then a "criminal government" is impossible. "A criminal state," he writes, "is juridically speaking a nonsense; the criminal government, on the contrary, a juristic reality and challenge of the first order . . . The punishability of the state is both a legal and a practical impossibility. Governments could and should be punished, if the international legal order were to provide the implementation of criminal justice."[20] However, even in the event of the criminality of a government under international law, in Drost's opinion the crimes always remain "individual crimes," and physical persons bear criminal responsibility for them.[21]

In lectures at the Hague Academy of International Law in 1927 on the topic "Crimes et délits contre la sureté des États étrangers," Professor M. Bourquin conceded that international law possibly is moving toward a "revival" of the idea of criminal responsibility of a state. At the same time, he believed that the concept of a "crime of state" was still far from having achieved the "necessary technical definiteness" in prevailing law.[22]

16. R. Phillimore, *Commentaries Upon International Law*, 3d ed. (London: Butterworths, 1879), I, 5.

17. P. N. Drost, *The Crime of State* (Leiden: A. W. Sijthoff, 1959), I, 283-292.

18. *Ibid.*, p. 293. [Drost is quoting a remark of Justice R. Jackson at the Nuremberg Trial.]

19. *Ibid.*, p. 294.

20. *Ibid.*, p. 304.

21. *Ibid.*, p. 305.

22. M. Bourquin, "Crimes et délits contre la sureté des États étrangers," *Recueil des cours*, XVI (1927), 124.

One also must note that the concept of the criminal responsibility of a state in international law was developed primarily by criminologists, who have been more inclined to transfer national law into international law than are specialists in international law, amongst whom this concept has found and finds comparatively few advocates.[23]

The concept of the international criminal responsibility of a state did not obtain support in the International Law Commission, which discussed this question in connection with the problem of state responsibility for damage caused on its territory to the person and property of aliens. The Commission's rapporteur on this question, G. Amador, touched upon the question of criminal responsibility only with respect to physical persons in the draft articles contained in his first report.[24] In the commentary to this report, however, the rapporteur actually favored the criminal responsibility of a state.[25]

Almost all members of the Commission who expressed themselves on the question of the criminal responsibility of a state were agreed that such responsibility is unknown to contemporary international law and that the Commission should not put forward a detailed proposal (François, Amador, Krylov, Fitzmaurice, Žourek).[26]

A correct understanding of the changes which have taken place in the area of international legal state responsibility can not be achieved by mechanically transferring the categories of national law into international law. Obviously, it is necessary, taking into account the peculiarities of international law, to establish the basic features of the new phenomena in international law and not to attempt to squeeze them into the Procrustean bed of national law categories.

The correct view already has been expressed in Soviet literature that the concept of criminal responsibility of a state is wholly unfounded, although the argumentation advanced against this concept is not sufficiently full and precise.

The late correspondent-member of the Academy of Sciences of the USSR, A. N. Trainin, who made a significant contribution to working out the question of the responsibility of war criminals, decisively rejected the concept of the criminal responsibility of a state in international law. In noting that as a subject of international law a state may be a subject of

23. A. N. Trainin was completely correct in noting this. See A. N. Trainin, *Zashchita mira i bor'ba s prestupleniiami protiv chelovechestva* (Moscow: izd-vo AN SSSR, 1956), p. 38.

24. United Nations, *Yearbook of the International Law Commission 1956* (New York: United Nations, 1957), II, 220.

25. *Ibid.*, p. 183.

26. *Ibid.*, I, 239-241.

international legal responsibility, that sanctions may be applied to a state, Trainin pointed out that these sanctions are not criminal law sanctions. "Criminal sanctions, and this is a generally recognized position, are determined by agencies of criminal justice," wrote Trainin.[27] However, he said, there was no organ of criminal justice in the League of Nations system and none exists now in the United Nations system.

On the plane of substantive criminal law, Trainin went on to say, the concept of the international criminal responsibility of a state also is unfounded. Criminal responsibility rests upon guilt, in the form of fault or negligence; the concepts and institutes of imputability, the stages of committing a crime, complicity, and punishment play a very essential role in criminal justice. Without such concepts and institutes criminal law and criminal responsibility are inconceivable. However, all the said institutes and concepts can not be applied to a state. Therefore, concluded Trainin, in the domain of substantive law, as in the domain of procedure, attempts to regard the sanctions applicable to a state as criminal sanctions prove to be "in profound incongruity with the basic principles of criminal justice."[28]

There is no exact indication that the concepts of guilt and complicity are inapplicable to a state as a subject of international law, although the international legal concept of guilt can not be identified with the concept of guilt in national legal systems. On the same basis, Trainin's argumentation against the concept of criminal responsibility of a state is completely correct. It proceeds from the fact that the criminal sanction as a category of national law is not applicable as a sanction of international law with respect to a state which is a specific subject of this distinctive legal system.

Proponents of the concept of criminal responsibility of a state suggest that if in international law there are sanctions which fall outside the limits of civil law responsibility in national law, these are criminal sanctions. But this conclusion is the result of transferring concepts of national law into international law without taking into account the specific features of the latter. If certain international legal sanctions fall outside the limits of civil law responsibility, this still does not mean that such sanctions are necessarily criminal sanctions.

The list of criminal sanctions for states cited by Pella in his "Plan for an International Criminal Code" shows clearly enough how artificial it is to equate these categories of state responsibility to criminal punishments under national law.

The noncomparability of international legal sanctions in respect of a state with criminal sanctions results from the incomparability of a state

27. Trainin, *Zashchita mira i bor'ba s prestupleniiami protiv chelovechestva*, p. 41.
28. *Ibid.*, pp. 41-42.

and individuals. International law, whose subjects are above all politically sovereign entities—states—has its own types of sanctions and means of effectuating them.

We find no mention whatever of the criminal responsibility of a state in the documents relating to the surrender of Germany and Japan, in the Statutes of the Nuremberg and Tokyo International Military Tribunals, nor in the peace treaties of 1947. Meanwhile, where, if not in these documents, should criminal responsibility for the gravest delinquencies committed by aggressors be mentioned if criminal responsibility of a state were in mind at all?

When aggressive war and certain other violations of international law are called crimes, one only wishes to emphasize thereby, with regard to the state, the especially dangerous character of the delinquency. On this plane, as Professor R. Ago has noted correctly, the question becomes purely terminological.[29] As regards physical persons, the specific executors of such actions, in contemporary international law the question is one in reality of an international crime and of the criminal responsibility arising therefrom.[30]

B. Some New Aspects of State Responsibility

(1) Prohibition of the use of force and state responsibility. As already has been pointed out, the principle of international legal state responsibility in the old international law essentially did not extend to war or its consequences in general.

The emergence of the principle of the prohibition of aggressive war, later transformed into the principle of the prohibition of the use or threat of force in international relations, signified a revolution in international law generally and also introduced fundamental changes into the institute of international legal state responsibility.

The elimination of the "right of a state to go to war" led to the disappearance of the "right of the victor" which arose directly out of the unlimited right of a state to resort to force. Eliminating the "right of the

29. See R. Ago, "Second Report on State Responsibility," in United Nations, *Yearbook of the International Law Commission 1971,* II, p. 184.

30. See Trainin, *Zashchita mira i bor'ba s prestupleniiami protiv chelovechestva;* M. Iu. Raginskii and S. Ia. Rozenblit, *Mezhdunarodnyi protsess glavnykh iaponskikh voennykh prestupnikov* (Moscow: izd-vo AN SSSR, 1950); P. S. Romashkin, *Voennye prestupleniia imperializma* (Moscow: Gosiurizdat, 1953); Romashkin, *Prestupleniia protiv mira i chelovechestva* (Moscow: izd-vo Nauka, 1967); A. I. Poltorak, *Niurnbergskii protsess* (Moscow: izd-vo Nauka, 1966); N. S. Alekseev, *Otvetstvennost' natsistskikh prestupnikov* (Moscow: izd-vo Mezhdunarodnye otnosheniia, 1968).

victor" in turn meant the elimination to such institutes of international law as "conquest" and "indemnities."

The institute of conquest, which was based directly on the "right of the victor," was clear evidence of the fact that war under the old international law represented a means not only of settling international disputes but also of changing a legal situation. According to the old international law, the victorious state had the right to annex the part of the defeated state's territory which it occupied, and if the enemy were completely defeated, to seize all its territory, the defeated state being regarded as subjugated.

As regards the seizure of the occupied part of the defeated state's territory in those instances when the enemy had not been completely defeated, even though the view was widespread in international legal doctrine that such acquisition is legally justified in a peace treaty,[31] in reality the basis of annexing the territory was the "right of the victor." Only the victor, irrespective of the causes and character of the war, had the right to appropriate the enemy territory he had occupied during the war. The extent to which he succeeded in realizing this right depended upon the co-relation of forces.

F. F. Martens wrote with regard to conquest as a method of acquiring territory: "This most ancient method of acquisition remains up to the present the most frequently applied."[32]

"According to the correct point of view," says Oppenheim in his treatise on international law, "occupied territory may be annexed by a belligerent on the grounds that his enemy, having ceased military operations, has given up every right he had over this territory."[33]

A second form of the institute of conquest was "subjugation," which was reflected in the elimination of the armed forces of a state, the occupation of its entire territory, and its annexation by the victorious state.

The well-known Swiss specialist on international affairs, Max Huber, wrote: "A subject of international law has the individual right, arising from international society, to annihilate other such subjects fully or partially; it thereupon acquires that in which their material existence is expressed, that is to say, it acquires their state territory."[34]

31. See, for example, F. von Liszt, *Mezhdunarodnoe pravo*, trans. from 2d ed. by M. Mebel', ed. V. E. Grabar (Iur'ev: izd. M. A. Polonskaia , 1902), pp. 313-325.

32. F. F. Martens, *Sovremennoe mezhdunarodnoe pravo tsivilizovannykh narodov*, 2d ed. (St. Petersburg: Tipo. Ministerstva putei soobshcheniia, 1887), I, 353.

33. Oppenheim, *Mezhdunarodnoe pravo*, trans. from 6th ed. by A. A. Santalov and V. I. Shiganskii, ed. S. A. Golunskii (Moscow: izd-vo IL, 1950), II(2), p. 137.

34. M. Huber, *Die Staatensuccession* (Leipzig: Verlag von Duncker & Humblot, 1898), p. 20.

In Fauchille's treatise on international law, we read: "The complete defeat of one belligerent state by another (*debellatio*) puts an end to the war by eliminating the political existence of one of the adversaries. The state disappears, dies away as a legal entity."[35]

"Subjugation," and the "right of the victor" on which it was based, are regarded by some bourgeois writers as institutes of prevailing international law, which does not correspond to reality at all and objectively is a manifestation of reactionary trends in bourgeois international legal doctrine.

Kelsen, for example, writes: "The territory of a conquered state may be annexed by a victorious state with the intention of incorporating it permanently or with the intention of disposing of it sooner or later, for instance, by ceding it to a third state or by establishing a new state on it. Whatever the intention of the conqueror may be, the annexed territory legally becomes its own territory, even if the war waged by the victor against the vanquished was an illegal war and the annexation of the vanquished state an international delict."[36]

C. C. Hyde says in his treatise on international law: "It may be in fact possible for a belligerent to occupy the entire domain of its enemy, and after having overcome all resistance, to destroy its life as a State and to appropriate its territory as the fruits of victory."[37]

Professor C. Rousseau, of the University of Paris, also believes that a state may, by the total defeat of the adversary, annex its territory."[38]

In Oppenheim's well-known English treatise on international law, revised by Lauterpacht, it says: "Although complete conquest, accompanied by destruction of the enemy's armed forces, actually puts an end to armed combat, and thus to the war, nevertheless the final ending does not come yet, since everything depends on what kind of decision the victor takes concerning the fate of the defeated state. If the victor wishes to restore to his post the captured or exiled head of the defeated state, he ends the war with the conclusion of the ensuing peace treaty. But if the victor wishes to take possession of the whole conquered territory, he annexes it and this formally ends the war by subjugation."[39]

Many statesmen of the western powers still are trying to rely upon the

35. P. Fauchille, *Traité de droit international public* (Paris: Rousseau & Cie., 1921), II, 1030.

36. H. Kelsen, *Principles of International Law*, ed. R. W. Tucker, 2d ed. (New York: Holt, Rinehart & Winston, 1967), pp. 313-314.

37. C. C. Hyde, *Mezhdunarodnoe pravo, ego ponimanie i primenenie soedinennymi shtatami ameriki*, ed. B. A. Dranov (Moscow: izd-vo IL, 1954), VI, 386.

38. See C. Rousseau, *Droit international public* (Paris: Recueil Sirey, 1953), p. 250; Rousseau, *Droit international public*, 4th ed. (Paris: Dalloz, 1968), pp. 152-153.

39. Oppenheim, *Mezhdunarodnoe pravo*, II(2), p. 139.

specter of the "right of conquest." Thus, the United States Department of State, in a memorandum on the Berlin question of December 20, 1958, maintained that the rights of the western powers to occupy German territory " . . . derive from the total defeat of the Third Reich and the subsequent assumption of supreme authority in Germany."[40]

The well-known American pundit, Walter Lippman, in criticizing this position of the Department of State, wrote: "For some strange reason we have decided to maintain that our rights in Berlin are based on the right of conquest. I would not say that this is the kind of reason that ought to be cited by the defenders of civilization." Lippman called the "right of conquest" a "primitive, stupid, and detestable principle."[41]

The elimination of the "institute of conquest" went hand in hand with the emergence and strengthening of the principles of the prohibition of aggressive war in international law.

Being a resolute opponent of reactionary institutes of international law from the first days of its existence, the Soviet state has opposed annexations and indemnities. The Decree on Peace adopted by the Second All-Russian Congress of Soviets on November 8, 1917, said: "The Workers' and Peasants' Government, which was created by the Revolution of October 24-25 and which rests upon the Soviets of Workers', Soldiers', and Peasants' Deputies, proposes to all belligerent peoples and their governments to begin negotiations immediately for a just, democratic peace.

"The just or democratic peace for which the overwhelming majority of the workers and toiling classes, exhausted, worn out, and tormented by the war, yearn is the peace that the Russian workers and peasants have demanded definitely and steadfastly since the overthrow of the tsarist monarchy; such a peace the Government considers to be an immediate peace without annexations (that is, without seizing foreign lands, without forcibly annexing foreign peoples) and without indemnities."[42]

In the League of Nations period, the small states, fearful for the fate of their territories, repeatedly introduced proposals concerning the nonrecognition of forcible seizures of territory. A number of documents adopted at inter-American conferences after the First World War also contain provisions relating to nonrecognition of conquest as a method of acquiring territory.[43]

40. "Legal Aspects of the Berlin Situation," *The Department of State Bulletin*, XL (1959), 9.

41. *Pravda*, April 11, 1959, p. 2.

42. Ministerstvo inostrannykh del SSSR, *Dokumenty vneshnei politiki SSSR* (Moscow: Gospolitizdat, 1957–), I, 11-12.

43. H. Wehberg, *Krieg und Eroberung im Wandel des Völkerrechts* (Frankfurt and Berlin: Alfred Metzner Verlag, 1953), pp. 90-97.

One must agree with Professor H. Wehberg, who says: "It is necessary to emphasize as strongly as possible that the classical theory of acquisition of territory by subjugation (*debellatio*) assumed, with regard to annexation, the admissibility of war. As long as war was considered a lawful means of settling disputes, it was completely logical that international law provided for the possibility of acquiring foreign territory by means of war. This was the time when in the final analysis the law of force was operative and the weak were at the mercy of the arbitrariness of the strong."[44]

With the emergence in international law of the principle of the prohibition of aggressive war, and later of the principle of the prohibition of the use of force in international relations, the "right of conquest" fell to the ground, since it had rested upon recognition of the state's right to wage war, upon recognition of war as a means of settling international disputes.

A second basic consequence of the "right of the victor" was the institute of indemnities.

In an exploitative society, war was a means of enriching the ruling classes. Complete pillage or destruction of property on the adversary's territory occupied by forces of the victor was a common practice in antiquity and in the Middle Ages. Grotius cited Livy's statement that: "when everything is placed under the command of the one who has the advantage in war, then any appropriation of property and the discretionary imposition of penalties depend upon the arbitrary action of the conqueror."[45] And Grotius himself considered this rule to be a prevailing norm of international law. He wrote: "For, as the things which had belonged to individuals, do, by the laws of war, become the property of those who conquer them, so also the property of the general body becomes the property of the victors, if these so choose." He cited Xenophon in this connection: "There is an ancient law among men that when an enemy town is taken the property and money come into the possession of the victor."[46]

Indemnities have been in especially wide use since the end of the eighteenth century, having replaced to a significant extent the unorganized plundering of the population by the victorious country with organized plundering.

The institute of indemnities was founded upon the "right of the victor." A characteristic feature of indemnities was the fact that the

44. *Ibid.*, p. 102. [" . . . dass die klassische Theorie über den Gebietserwerb im Wege der *debellatio* bzw. der Annexion . . . "]

45. H. Grotius, *O prave voiny i mira*, trans. A. Sakketti, ed. V. N. Durdenevskii (Moscow: Gosiurizdat, 1956), p. 671.

46. *Ibid.*, p. 640.

victor, irrespective of who began the war and how it was waged, had the right to compel the defeated state to pay it a sum whose amount usually was fixed by the peace treaty. The victor, and he only, irrespective of the circumstances of the origin of the war, had the right to demand payment of indemnities from the defeated state.

Although indemnities usually were called "indemnification of war costs," which might include the expenses of the victorious state in waging the war and the damage caused to it and to its nationals as a result of the war, in fact it was tribute imposed by the victor upon the vanquished; the amount of such tribute was determined solely by the co-relation of their strength.

"The principle of an indemnity for war costs," wrote Fauchille, "imposed by the victor upon the vanquished, is admissible and understandable when the indemnity includes the expenses of the victor in carrying out military actions and the damage inflicted in consequence of the adversary's resistance. But in the nineteenth century indemnity of war costs in practice became for the victor a means of enrichment at the expense of another, a means of satisfying an insatiable greed for enrichment."[47]

It should be noted that the practice condemned by Fauchille is characteristic not only of the nineteenth century; it was dominant both in the feudal period and in slave-owning society.

As already has been pointed out, the Soviet state proposed in the Decree on Peace to renounce indemnities in concluding a peace treaty which would have put an end to the First World War.[48] There is no doubt that the Soviet state's opposition to indemnities as an institute of international law, in which the basis of international plunder and robbery clearly was reflected, the consistent policy of the Soviet state directed against the old international-legal concepts, and the growth of the democratic movement in all countries and the increase in its influence dealt a decisive blow to the institute of indemnities.

In the Versailles Treaty the allies already had refrained from using the term "war costs" and spoke only of "reparations." Under the Versailles Treaty, Germany acknowledged responsibility for all losses and damage incurred by the Entente and its nations in consequence of the war unleashed upon them by Germany and its allies (Article 231). Germany was obliged to compensate all damage caused to the civilian population of the Allied and Associated Powers (Article 232).

In the documents relating to the termination of the Second World War, in the working out of which the Soviet Union took an active part, there is,

47. Fauchille, *Traité de droit international public*, II, 1041.
48. *Dokumenty vneshnei politiki SSSR*, I, 12.

of course, no allusion whatever to indemnities. The question is one of reparations as one form of responsibility for the unleashing and waging of an aggressive war by Germany, Japan, and their allies.

The communique of the Crimea Conference of the leaders of the three allied powers—the Soviet Union, United States of America, and Great Britain—of February 4-11, 1945, pointed out: "We have considered the question of the damage caused by Germany to the Allied Nations in this war and recognized it as just that Germany be obliged to make compensation for this damage in kind to the greatest extent possible."[49]

It was pointed out in the decisions of the 1945 Berlin Conference of the three powers that "in accordance with the Crimea decision that Germany be compelled to compensate to the greatest extent possible for the loss and suffering that she has caused the United Nations and for which the German people can not escape responsibility, the following agreement on reparations was reached . . . "[50] Here, therefore, is emphasized the link between Germany's responsibility for aggressive war and its duty to compensate for the damage caused by this war.

The Protocol concerning the talks among the heads of the three governments at the Crimea Conference said with regard to the question of reparations in kind from Germany: "Germany must pay in kind for the losses caused by her to the Allied nations in the course of the war." It was further pointed out in this Protocol that the removal of equipment, machine tools, vessels, and so forth as reparations from Germany "should be carried out chiefly for the purpose of destroying the war potential of Germany."[51] Compensation for material damage is linked in this document with measures of a preventive character directed against a renewal of an aggressive policy on the part of Germany.

The 1947 peace treaties, in pointing out that Germany's former allies bear "their share of the responsibility for this war," establish that these states must compensate the appropriate allied powers for losses caused by "military actions and occupation" of territories of those states, it being stipulated that compensation of these losses be made not in full but in part.

Thus, as a result of the expansion of the principles of state responsibility for war and the elimination of the "right of the victor," the institute of indemnities was replaced by reparations.

The institute of reparations which superseded the institute of indemnities differs fundamentally from the latter. If indemnities were based upon

49. Ministerstvo inostrannykh del SSSR, *Sbornik deistvuiushchikh dogovorov, soglashenii i konventsii, zakliuchennykh SSSR s inostrannymi gosudarstvami* (Moscow: Gosiurizdat, 1925–), XI, 69.
50. *Ibid.*, p. 114.
51. *Ibid.*, p. 81.

the "right of the victor," then the institute of reparations is based, as is correctly pointed out in Soviet literature,[52] upon the principle of international legal state responsibility. This means that the institute of reparations, just as the principle of responsibility for aggressive war in general, is directed at the maintenance of international peace.

The emergence in international law of the principle of the prohibition of aggressive war and of the principle of the prohibition of the use of force in international relations (the principle of nonaggression) signified the end of the "right of the victor." Victory in and of itself can not give rights to either side.

In contrast to the old international law, the aggressor at the present time is not simply a party to an armed conflict; the aggressor is a lawbreaker; his actions, representing from the very beginning the gravest criminal violation of international law, can not create any rights whatsoever for him. Being a breach of the law which entails state responsibility, the actions of the aggressor remain such irrespective of the outcome of the armed conflict.

War on the part of states opposing the aggression or enforcement measures undertaken by the United Nations against the aggressor by decision of the Security Council are a lawful use of force. States acting against the aggressor have specific rights which, however, do not arise from the fact of victory.[53] Indeed, if such rights arose from the fact of victory, as they did under the old international law, the victorious side would have them irrespective of which side committed the aggression and unleashed the war.

The major distinctive feature of the new international law in the field of state responsibility is responsibility for aggression. Such responsibility is derived from the principle of the prohibition of the use of force in international relations. Aggression is the gravest breach of the law, for its consequences at the present time could be the greatest calamity for all mankind. Hence the gravity of responsibility for such a breach of the law.

The application of the principle of international legal responsibility to war and its consequences was reflected and strengthened in international treaties and agreements relating to the Second World War.

The Declaration concerning the defeat of Germany and the assumption by the allies of supreme authority with respect to that country says that Germany bears responsibility for the war.[54] It is emphasized in the Potsdam Agreements that the "German people have begun to atone for

52. See V. V. Evgen'ev, *Mezhdunarodnopravovoe regulirovanie reparatsii posle vtoroi mirovoi voiny* (Moscow: Gosiurizdat, 1950), p. 65.

53. See G. I. Tunkin, "Berlinskii vopros v svete mezhdunarodnogo prava," *Mezhdunarodnaia zhizn'*, no. 2 (1959), p. 48.

54. *Sbornik deistvuiushchikh dogovorov*, XI, 84.

the terrible crimes committed under the leadership of those whom in the hour of their success, they openly approved and blindly obeyed." In those same Potsdam Agreements it says further that the "German people can not escape responsibility" for the loss and suffering which Germany caused to the United Nations.[55]

The principles of responsibility for aggressive war also were reflected in the 1947 Peace Treaties. It says in the Peace Treaty with Italy: "Whereas Italy under the Fascist regime became a party to the Tripartite Pact with Germany and Japan, undertook a war of aggression and thereby provoked a state of war with all the Allied and Associated Powers and with other United Nations, and bears her share of responsibility for the war . . . "[56]

The peace treaties with Finland, Rumania, Bulgaria, and Hungary also say that, having become allies of Hitlerite Germany and having participated on her side in the war, these countries bear their "share of responsibility for this war."[57]

A clear expression of the application of the principle of responsibility with respect to Germany and Japan is the documents of the Nuremberg and Tokyo international military tribunals, which affirmed that aggressive war is the gravest criminal violation of international law that entails the international responsibility of the state and the criminal responsibility of physical persons who are guilty of committing crimes against peace, war crimes, and crimes against humanity.

Thus, instead of the "right of the victor," contemporary international law provides state responsibility for aggression. This means that the legal consequences of war are not determined by the outcome of the armed conflict, not by who is victorious. The Charter of the Organization of American States of April 30, 1948, correctly points out that "victory does not give rights."[58]

The legal consequences of an armed conflict are determined first of all by the fact of which state committed the aggression and, consequently, must bear responsibility for this gravest breach of law. Additional responsibility can be added to this for violating the laws and customs of war, as occurred with regard to Hitlerite Germany and Japan.

If, however, contemporary international law prohibits states from resorting to war in international relations and war is not a means of

55. *Ibid.*, pp. 109, 114.

56. Preamble of the 1947 Peace Treaty with Italy, *ibid.*, XIII, 88-89.

57. Preamble of the 1947 Peace Treaty with Finland, Rumania, Bulgaria, and Hungary, *ibid.*, XIII, 26, 54, 203, 235.

58. Article 5. L. A. Modzhorian and V. K. Sobakin, comps., *Mezhdunarodnoe pravo v izbrannykh dokumentakh*, ed. V. N. Durdenevskii (Moscow: izd-vo IMO, 1957), II, 202.

acquiring state territory, this does not mean that sanctions can not be applied to the aggressor in the form of taking away part of its territory. An aggressor state going unpunished corresponds least of all to contemporary international law, which provides severe responsibility for a breach of the peace.

We must dwell upon incorrect interpretations of this question.

Professor H. Wehberg, for example, writes: " . . . The use of force in and of itself can not destroy the right of another, at least not such a far-reaching right as the right to territory. The unlawful use of force, as such, can not destroy an existing right. Not to accept this position is to acknowledge that might stands above right."[59]

There is, however, a material contradiction in this argument. First, Professor Wehberg says that the use of force in and of itself can not destroy an existing right, and this is true. Second, he speaks of the unlawful use of force, but also makes the reservation that the use of force as such can not destroy a right. In this case the reservation not only is unnecessary, but is incorrect, since the unlawful use of force not only can not as such destroy a right but also is the gravest breach of the law. One can not place on the same level a just use of force, that is, a use of force permitted by international law, and an unjust use of force, that is, a use of force in violation of international law. This vagueness, as we shall see later, leads Professor Wehberg to some wholly incorrect conclusions.

He has not avoided the confusion which often arose when this question was discussed between the First and Second World Wars. The fact is that, strange as it may seem at first glance, the oft-encountered maxim "any change of state territory carried out with the aid of force is contrary to international law" is imprecise and essentially untrue.

The aggressor and the victim of aggression do not have equal status under contemporary international law, which is developing in the direction of applying ever more severe measures against an aggressor, since at the present time aggression threatens mankind with incalculable casualties. Professor Wehberg is mistaken when he places an aggressor and the other states which have opposed him on the same level; in doing so he in essence pays tribute to the obsolete concepts which he himself so resolutely opposes.

Here is what Professor Wehberg says: "The proposition that the unlawful use of force in and of itself can not eliminate a foreign right must also operate to the advantage of those states which waged an

59. Wehberg, *Krieg und Eroberung im Wandel des Völkerrechts*, pp. 102-103. [" . . . dem Wege der Gewalt allein ein anderes Recht nicht zerstort werden, am wenigsten ein so weittrangendes Recht wie das der Kompetenz über ein Territorium."]

aggressive war and which suffered defeat from the states against whom the attack was committed. It is true that a state subjected to an attack has the right of self-defense, but only to repulse the attack. Self-defense does not permit, however, the use of armed force which goes beyond repulsing the attack. A state subjected to an attack can only defend itself and also take measures to obtain compensation for damage."[60]

A West German professor, W. Schätzel, expresses himself in the same vein. Calling any increment of territory an annexation, the author attempts to substantiate the proposition that no territorial changes whatever are admissible in consequence of war. "The question of the admissibility of annexation as a result of war," says Schätzel, "comes down to the question of the admissibility of war."[61] Confusing the distinction between an aggressive and a defensive war, the author in fact attempts to limit the international legal responsibility of the aggressor, asserting that responsibility for aggression can not lead to territorial changes.

There are both correct and incorrect propositions in the arguments. The "right of the victor" is rejected, and this is completely correct. But at the same time the responsibility of the aggressor also is rejected. It turns out that no measures whatever can be taken with regard to the aggressor except measures for the purpose of compensating the damage caused.

However, the responsibility of the aggressor state under contemporary international law is not restricted to compensation for damage caused. It also includes those measures with regard to an aggressor which may be expressed, in particular, by taking away part of its territory for the purpose of preventing aggression in the future.

The allies in the anti-Hitlerite coalition proceeded from these very propositions with respect to the aggressor states in the Second World War.

The taking of certain territories from Germany and Japan in consequence of the Second World War differs fundamentally from the previous seizures of territory which took place on the basis of the "right of the victor." The actions of the allies with regard to Germany and Japan were based above all on the principle of international legal state responsibility for the aggression which it committed. The juridical classification of the taking of certain territories from Germany and Japan which was done in connection with the Second World War, in those instances when this taking went beyond the limits of compensating the respective states for territories previously seized from them by Germany and Japan, is completely different from the seizure of territory on the basis of the

60. *Ibid.*, pp. 103-104.
61. W. Schätzel, "Die Annexion im Völkerrecht," *Archiv des Völkerrechts*, II (1950), 2.

"right of the victor." Here is found the application and confirmation of a new progressive principle directed toward the maintenance of international peace—the principle of responsibility for aggression.

(2) Subjects of legal relations in instances of international legal state responsibility. The violation of international law by a state gives rise to specific legal relationships. Who are the participants in such legal relationships, or, in other words, for whom do international competences and duties arise in consequence of breaches of the law?

Under contemporary conditions, this question acquires especially important significance, particularly with regard to breaches of the law which endanger peace.

According to the old international law, in the event of a breach of international law, legal relationships arose only between the offending state and the state whose subjective right was violated in consequence of the unlawful actions of the first state. Proceeding from the fact that international law regulates relations among sovereign entities, Anzilotti pointed out that no one state can consider itself a judge when a violation of international law is committed by another state unless its own rights are affected by this breach of the law. "States," he wrote, "have neither the right nor the duty to suppress violations of international law as such, but only the right to react against those violations which are aimed directly against them . . . "[62] In the latter instance the injured state may, however, take action against the offender not for the purpose of compelling him to respect the violated international law, but only in order to realize its own illegally violated right.[63]

Anzilotti, it is true, recognized the interest that all states have in the observance of norms of international law and the possibility of collective actions against the offending state, but not on legal grounds.

This concept even now is adhered to mechanically by the majority of bourgeois international lawyers.

"According to the generally accepted doctrine," writes Rousseau, "international responsibility is always a relationship between one state and another state." In explaining this proposition, he says that international responsibility "presupposes that one state complains of damage caused to it and demands compensation."[64]

Professor Verdross also points out that the legal relationships arising in connection with international legal responsibility are legal relationships

62. Anzilotti, *Teoria generale della responsibilita dello stato*, p. 88.
63. *Ibid.*, pp. 88-89.
64. Rousseau, *Droit international public* (1953), p. 357; G. Schwarzenberger, *International Law and Order* (London: Stevens & Sons, 1971), p. 35.

between the offending state and the state which directly suffered damage in consequence of this breach of the law. "International legal responsibility," he says, "arises in principle *only* with regard to *those states* which are the immediate victims of unlawful international actions. Accordingly, in the event of the violation of a norm of customary law or of a multilateral treaty, in principle only those states may act which have suffered damage from the breach of international law. The existence in other states of purely idealistic interests in preserving the international legal order is insufficient motive for submitting demands."[65] At the same time, Verdross admits the possibility of coming to the support of an injured state. But, he adds, "in this event independent action does not take place, but only support of the state which has suffered from the breach of the law."[66]

This theory also was reflected in the decisions of the Permanent Court of International Justice, particularly in its decision in the case of the *Phosphates in Morrocco.*[67]

According to another theory, in the event of more serious violations of international law, any state, even though it has not suffered direct damage from the breach of the law, has the right to take measures against the offending state.

Thus, Heffter believed that there are those violations of international law which affect all states equally and which give them all the right to take measures against the offender. Heffter includes among the said breaches of law, in particular: the organized striving for world domination or for domination over territory belonging to all nations (as, for example, the high seas), violation of the rights of diplomatic representatives, refusal to satisfy claims which have been widely recognized, and others.[68] Bluntschli[69] and L. Kamarovskii[70] have expressed analogous opinions.

The danger of this concept consisted not so much in the fact that it provided the possibility of collective state actions in the event of violations of international law, as in the fact that the occasions for such actions were chosen arbitrarily and were justified by references to those

65. A. Verdross, *Mezhdunarodnoe pravo*, trans. F. A. Kublitskii and R. L. Naryshkina, ed. G. I. Tunkin (Moscow: izd-vo IL, 1959), pp. 355-356.

66. *Ibid.*, p. 357.

67. Permanent Court of International Justice, Series A/B, Judgments, Orders and Advisory Opinions, *Phosphates in Morocco* (Leiden: A. W. Sijthoff, 1938), p. 28.

68. A. Heffter, *Das europäische Völkerrecht der Gegenwart auf den bisherigen Grundlagen*, 8th ed. (Berlin: Verlag H. W. Muller, 1888), pp. 224-225.

69. See J. C. Bluntschli, *Das moderne Völkerrecht der civilisirten Staten*, 2d ed. (Nördlingen: C. H. Beck, 1872), pp. 264-265.

70. See L. A. Kamarovskii, *O mezhdunarodnom sude* (Moscow: Tipo. T. Malinskii, 1881), p. 7.

State Responsibility Under Contemporary International Law

norms of international law which in reality did not exist. This theory, therefore, frequently was used to justify collective interventions (for example, interventions of the Holy Alliance).

This theory, which in fact was an exceedingly free or, more precisely, arbitrary interpretation of international law of that time, had comparatively few supporters. According to the then predominant theory, the general interest of a state was insufficient grounds for submitting any claims whatever to the offending state.

The rule that only the injured state has the right to submit claims against a delinquent state or to undertake enforcement measures against it permitted by international law remains valid even at the present time for a significant number of breaches of international law affecting only relations between two states: that which violated international law and that which suffered directly therefrom.

Contemporary international law, however, does not stop at this. Very important new elements, which still have not been reflected in science, have emerged.

Thus, according to the old international law, war between two states was regarded as a matter concerning only them. Juridically, every state had the right to resort to war in order to effectuate its claims; consequently, it waged war on the basis of this right. Other states against whom no armed actions were directed had no right to object.

These provisions of international law were explained in the final analysis by the character of international relations existing then, and above all by the character of economic ties among states. War between two states could not affect or only slightly affected other states by virtue of the insufficiently broad international ties.

In this respect the situation has changed materially and continues to change. The intensification of international ties has led to the fact that any war to a greater or lesser extent directly affects the interests and even the rights of all states. An enormous danger has appeared of any armed conflict between states developing even into a world war which, with the existence of modern types of weapons, promises incalculable suffering and sacrifice for peoples. Peace has become virtually indivisible. "If four centuries ago there was every reason to recognize that peace is indivisible," said the Minister of Foreign Affairs of the USSR, A. A. Gromyko, in a Statement, "then it is many times more correct in our day with the modern means of waging war, when only minutes are required to overcome the distance between the most remote countries of the world."[71]

71. Statement of the Minister of Foreign Affairs of the USSR, A. Gromyko, on the Occasion of the Speech of Secretary of State C. Herter, *Pravda*, August 31, 1959, p. 2.

These changes in the international situation have been reflected in international law. Such principles of international law have emerged as the principle of nonaggression and the prohibition of the use of force in international relations and the still more far-reaching principle of peaceful coexistence.

A breach of the peace, or a threat to breach the peace, now affects not only the interests, but also the rights, of all states. From the aforesaid principle of international law arises the subjective right of a state to peace.

The maintenance of international peace in our time is the concern of all states.[72] Under contemporary international law every state has not only the right but to a certain extent also the duty to take measures within the limits permitted by international law for the purpose of ensuring international peace and security and, therefore, to demand that other states have observed the norms of international law relating to the securing of peace.

On these provisions of international law in particular are based the numerous statements of the Soviet Union against the policy of individual states aimed at knocking together aggressive blocs, against the entry therein of a particular state, against creating foreign military bases or launching sites for missiles on their territories, and against other actions leading to an aggravation of the international situation or directly creating a threat to the peace, to say nothing of actions which already are a breach of the peace or acts of aggression.

A Note sent in December 1957 by the Soviet government to the governments of member states of the United Nations said: "The Soviet government proceeds from the fact that in contemporary conditions every government bears responsibility not only for the fate of the people of its own country but also to a certain extent for the fate of world peace, and therefore can not be indifferent to the aggravation of the international situation which has occurred. If, unfortunately for mankind, the world plunges into a new war, no state can feel secure. In this event the conflagration of a nuclear and missile war undoubtedly would bring to all peoples incalculable misfortune whose consequences would be experienced by many generations of people."[73]

In their replies to these ideas of the Soviet Union many states attempted to assert that such notions supposedly are an interference in internal affairs, since every state can freely enter into agreement with other states and carry out any military measures on its territory insofar as it is not bound by special agreements.

72. See, for example, H. Rolin, "Verso un concetto di ordine publico realmente internazionale," *Communicazioni e studi*, X (1960), 72.
73. *Pravda*, December 13, 1957, p. 3.

State Responsibility Under Contemporary International Law

The reference to internal affairs in this case, however, is completely unfounded. The concept of "internal affairs" is not a territorial concept, and in no way signifies that any measures undertaken by a state on its territory relate to its "internal affairs." There is still less basis for classifying as "internal affairs" aggressive military agreements concluded by a state with other states. The actions of a state affecting international peace and security do not at the present time relate exclusively to the domestic jurisdiction of a state.

The right of a state which is not an immediate victim of damage as a result of a breach of the law to take specific measures in the event of such a breach does not arise only in connection with breaches of the law which affect or might affect the maintenance of international peace and security. It arises, for example, in the case of a violation of the principle of self-determination of peoples, the Nuremberg principles, the principles of freedom of the seas, of the principle of conserving living resources of the sea, and so forth.

The said position was reflected in the judgment of the International Court in the dispute between Belgium and Spain regarding the Barcelona Traction Company of February 5, 1970. The Court pointed out in this judgment that a " . . . distinction should be drawn between the obligations of a State towards the international community as a whole and those arising *vis à vis* another State . . . By their very nature the former are the concern of all States. In view of the importance of the rights involved, all States can be held to have a legal interest in their protection; they are obligations *erga omnes*.

"Such obligations derive, for example, in contemporary international law, from the outlawing of acts of aggression, and of genocide, as also from the principles and rules concerning the basic rights of the human person . . . "[74]

Thus, in the aspect which we are examining, a peculiarity of the legal relationships arising under contemporary international law as a result of a violation of international law is, first and foremost, the fact that the subjects of these legal relationships can be not only the delinquent state and the state which has suffered directly, but in a number of instances other states as well.

A second peculiarity of the said legal relationships is that international organizations also can be party to them. In a number of instances international organizations, in conformity with the provisions of their

74. International Court of Justice, Reports of Judgments, Advisory Opinions and Orders, *Case Concerning the Barcelona Traction, Light and Power Company, Limited* (New Application: 1962) (Belgium v. Spain). Second Phase. Judgment of 5 February 1970 (Leiden: A. W. Sijthoff, 1970), p. 32.

charters, not only have the right but also are obliged to take a particular measure in the event of a violation of international law. Thus, in the event of aggression legal relations arise not only between the victim state of the aggression and the aggressor state, but also among all other states and the aggressors (the right to use force against an aggressor by way of collective self-defense) and among the United Nations and other states. The United Nations is obliged to take measures against an aggressor; states waging a struggle against an aggressor must notify the Security Council immediately of the measures they are taking, and so forth.

(3) Types and forms of state responsibility in contemporary international law. We intend to touch upon basically two questions here: the nature of sanctions in contemporary international law and the methods of effectuating them.

According to the theory predominant in bourgeois international legal doctrine before the First World War and frequently even at the present time (see above), sanctions are alien to international law, which knows no authority standing above states, and state responsibility is reflected only when an obligation arises to compensate damage caused. This theory did not even reflect the true situation in the old international law, since, as already pointed out, the failure of a delinquent state to perform the obligation to compensate damage caused gave to the injured state the right to apply enforcement measures with regard to that state.

The character of sanctions in contemporary international law is materially different from sanctions in the old international law. This is linked above all with the emergence of new international delicts and the division, which has been established in international law, of all international delicts into two categories: especially dangerous violations of international law which in international documents and literature frequently are called international crimes; and other violations of international law.

In Soviet legal literature the notion of the need to distinguish "between simple violations of international law and international crimes undermining its very foundations and most important principles" already has been expressed.[75]

In his work *Otvetstvennost' gosudarstv v sovremennom mezhdunarodnom prave*, D. B. Levin, making this generally correct notion more precise, writes: "In contemporary international law, insofar as the question is one of an international delict, there is being formed side by side with the previous concept of a breach of international law a new concept of an international crime, or crime against humanity, designating that conduct

75. Levin, "Problema otvetstvennosti v nauke mezhdunarodnogo prava," p. 105.

of a state which undermines the foundations of the international community."[76]

In our view, the division of international breaches of law into delicts and crimes already has taken shape in international law, but there is no doubt that the category of international crimes is tending to expand. This is the result of the struggle of the forces of peace and progress, reflected in the fact that international law is becoming ever more irreconcilable toward actions infringing the foundations of the peaceful coexistence of states, the freedom and independence of peoples, "the dignity and worth of the human person" (Preamble, United Nations Charter).

The category of international crimes[77] includes first and foremost crimes against peace, war crimes, and crimes against humanity as they have been defined in the charters and judgments of the Nuremberg and Tokyo international military tribunals. The United Nations Charter, General Assembly resolutions, and other state practice strengthen these provisions.[78]

Also included in this category of international delicts are the practice of colonialism, the refusal to grant independence to colonial peoples, and racial discrimination, insofar as they already have not been covered by the international crimes just enumerated. Recognition of these actions as not only international delicts but also as especially dangerous delicts, that is, international crimes, has been reflected in United Nations General Assembly resolutions, in the Convention on the elimination of all forms of racial discrimination, in the covenants on human rights, and in many other international documents, as well as in the day-to-day practice of states.[79]

It is not our task to establish a more precise listing of violations of international law which enter into this category. We only have attempted

76. D. B. Levin, *Otvetstvennost' gosudarstv v sovremennom mezhdunarodnom prave* (Moscow: izd-vo Mezhdunarodnye otnosheniia, 1966), p. 22.

77. The use of criminal law terminology presents certain well-known inconveniences, but there still is no other appropriate terminology. In any event, the use of such terminology in international law does not necessarily mean, despite the opinion of some authors, and in this case does not signify, "the renaissance of a criminal law concept as regards state responsibility." Č. Čepelka, *Conséquences juridiques du délit en droit international contemporain* (Prague: Universita Karlova, 1965), p. 63.

78. On this question, see Trainin, *Zashchita mira i bor' ba s prestupleniiami protiv chelovechestva*; Romashkin, *Prestupleniia protiv mira i chelovechestva*; Poltorak, *Niurnbergskii protsess*; Levin, *Otvetstvennost' gosudarstv v sovremennom mezhdunarodnom prave*, pp. 22-29.

79. See Romashkin, *Prestupleniia protiv mira i chelovechestva*, pp. 321-350; D. I. Baratashvili, *Novye gosudarstva Azii i Afriki i mezhdunarodnoe pravo* (Moscow: izd-vo Nauka, 1968), pp. 113-181; Levin, *Otvetstvennost' gosudarstv v sovremennom mezhdunarodnom prave*, p. 21.

to show that this category of especially dangerous violations of international law, named international crimes, exists in contemporary international law.

Comparatively few changes have occurred in the sphere of sanctions in the case of ordinary violations of international law. State responsibility remains reparational in character. Sanctions come down to compensation for the damage, being accompanied by possible enforcement measures if the delinquent state does not fulfill this duty. The legal relationships arising in consequence of the delict are limited as a rule to the injured state and the delinquent state. International organizations also frequently participate at the present time in such legal relationships within the operative spheres of international organizations.

As regards sanctions relating to the international crimes of a state, phenomena new in principle have emerged. And even the international delicts of this category are a new phenomenon in international law. In this case, sanctions are not limited to compensation for damage, but also include measures having the character of preventive punishment. It must be emphasized again in this connection that the question is one of an international legal category, as distinct from a category of national law.[80]

The measures provided for by the Potsdam agreement concerning Germany are an example of such sanctions. These measures, as is obvious, did not amount to compensation for damage. They included the occupation of the entire territory of Germany, the assumption of supreme power

80. The attempt of a Czechoslovak author, Č. Čepelka, to disprove this proposition and to cram the situation existing in contemporary international law into the procrustean bed of the old "reparational theory" clearly failed. Čepelka maintains that the traditional doctrine of "compulsory reparations also is a suitable theoretical base for contemporary international law." He asserts that under contemporary international law an obligation arises first for the aggressor state to effectuate restitution and to compensate the injury committed as a result of its violation of international law, but he also permits in supplementation thereof satisfaction, which in his view also is the only obligation of the aggressor state. Among the forms of satisfaction, he says, "the obligation to give guarantees for the future against the recurrence of the delict which is in question" has special significance.

Čepelka, therefore, reduces the sanctions with regard to an aggressor state to the "obligations" of the aggressor state. As is clear from the propositions he develops, the effectuation of such sanctions necessarily presupposes the conducting of negotiations and the conclusion of an agreement with the aggressor state. Either thesis is obsolete and does not correspond to contemporary international law. Under contemporary international law the question is one in the case above all of the right of the United Nations or of the states fighting against aggression to impose sanctions on the aggressor state. The sanctions themselves are not limited to "obligations" of the aggressor state, but also include direct measures of coercion which can be imposed on the aggressor even without negotiations, and not just as a result of its failure to fulfill "reparational obligations" or "obligations to grant satisfaction." See Čepelka, *Conséquences juridiques du délit en droit international contemporain*, pp. 62, 73.

by the allies, and in general the effectuation of measures having the purpose above all: (1) to eradicate German militarism and Nazism and to guarantee that Germany never again threatened her neighbors or the maintenance of peace; to prevent with this purpose any fascist or militarist activity and propaganda; to encourage the development of democracy in Germany; (2) to eliminate excessive concentration in the German economy, cartels, syndicates, trusts, and other monopolistic combinations which enabled fascism to come to power and the preparation and effectuation of Hitlerite aggression.

It is doubtful whether one can agree with Professor Ago, who maintains that the demand for reparation should precede the application of a sanction. "What seems to emerge clearly from the practice of States," Ago writes, "is the existence of an order of priority between the two possible consequences of an internationally wrongful act in the sense that the claim for reparation must . . . precede the application of the sanction, even where recourse to a sanction would be permissible in principle. By offering adequate reparation—that is to say, by eliminating the consequences of its wrongful conduct as far as possible—the guilty State should normally be able to avoid the sanction."[81]

As already has been pointed out, a similar conception in the nineteenth century reflected, though not fully, the situation which existed in international law of that time. Contemporary international law, where all international breaches of law are divided into ordinary breaches of law and international crimes, provides for the possibility of the simultaneous application with regard to the offending state of both reparations and of measures in the nature of preventive punishment.

To some, albeit inadequate, extent Professor Ago recognizes this situation, when he says: "Of course, this principle does not preclude recognition of the fact that there may be exceptional cases in which the faculty of reacting against an internationally wrongful act by applying a sanction must necessarily be immediately exercisable and can not be made conditional on a prior attempt to obtain reparations which, *a priori*, has no real prospect of success."[82]

The application of sanctions against a delinquent state in the event of a threat to the peace, breach of the peace, or act of aggression relates, first and foremost, to the jurisdiction of the United Nations. One can say the same about sanctions regarding international delicts relating to this category such as the refusal to grant independence to colonial peoples, the practice of colonialism, racial discrimination, and so forth, since all these

81. Ago, "Second Report on State Responsibility," p. 183; also Ago, "Third Report on State Responsibility," Doc. No. A/CN.4/246, para. 38 (March 5, 1971).
82. Ago, "Third Report," para. 21.

delicts are regarded as a violation of the principles of the United Nations Charter which create or might create a threat to international peace.

Individual states, of course, also have the right to react against this kind of violation of international law. Means of pressure on the offender which might be applied by individual states outside the limits of the United Nations are rather numerous, but they differ materially from the means applied by the United Nations.

The United Nations Charter does not limit the right of the Organization to take measures with or without the use of armed force either in the event of a threat to the peace or in the event that a breach of the peace or act of aggression already has been committed. Meanwhile, in the absence of an armed attack, individual states only can take measures of pressure which are not connected with the use of armed force against other states. Only in the event of an armed attack can a state use armed force against the attacking state, but in this event the question already is not one of sanctions but one of using the right of self-defense.

The aforesaid classification of international state responsibility has been based upon the degree of danger of the international delicts. It is not arbitrary, but reflects the actual situation existing in international law.

A classification of state responsibility based on the nature of sanctions also has a certain significance.

The view has been expressed in Soviet literature that on this plane state responsibility under international law may be political, material, or moral.[83]

It seems to us that one can not speak of moral responsibility as a special type of responsibility for the following reasons. First, the expression "moral responsibility" can be understood as responsibility that is not legal, but arises from a violation of rules of international morality. For that reason it is in fact more correct to speak in this case of political responsibility, since the so-called moral satisfaction contemplated is political action.

The expression "political responsibility" also is not very apt since it too has a nuance of nonlegal responsibility.

There is also no doubt that all types of the responsibility of a state as a political entity have to a certain extent a political character. Nonetheless, one can hardly object to isolating financial responsibility as an independent type of responsibility. At the same time, there are forms of responsibility not linked to financial compensation. It is more correct to treat all these forms of nonmaterial responsibility as political responsibility.

83. See F. I. Kozhevnikov, ed., *Mezhdunarodnoe pravo* (Moscow: Gosiurizdat, 1957), p. 126; Trainin, *Zashchita mira i bor'ba s prestupleniiami protiv chelovechestva*, p. 43.

In this case we will have two types of responsibility—political and financial. All forms of state responsibility except financial responsibility, from so-called moral satisfaction to the various measures connected with limiting a state's sovereignty, and so forth, will be treated as political responsibility.

And finally, the question arises of whether the duty of a delinquent state to bear these sanctions corresponds to the right of a state or international organization to apply the sanctions.

In the opinion of R. Ago, an Italian professor, the question in this case is not one of the subjective right to which the obligation of the state that has committed the delict to bear the sanction corresponds. Here one has in view the legal capacity to effectuate the sanction or, that is to say, the capacity granted by the right "to cause damage to another in the form of a sanction, to commit an action or omission which in another instance is prohibited, but which becomes legal precisely and exclusively as a sanction."[84]

This viewpoint, in our opinion, does not take into account the specific nature of international law sufficiently. Norms of international law, including norms relating to sanctions, are created on the basis of agreement between states which are subjects of this system of law. In principle there is no authority in international law standing above states and capable of effectuating sanctions. Sanctions in international law are applied by states individually or collectively or by an international organization on the basis of its charter, that is, an international treaty.

Therefore, in international law and in the case of effectuating sanctions, states or an international organization exercise rights which correspond to the duties of the delinquent states to subordinate themselves to these sanctions.

If a state against whom sanctions were being undertaken had no duty to subordinate itself to them, it could regard the measures applied against it as actions with regard to which it had no legal obligations whatever and against which, therefore, it could lawfully act.

However, the action of a state which has committed a breach of law against sanctions applied to it would be a new breach of law. This is especially obvious in the example of the United Nations applying sanctions. The offending state can not oppose the application of sanctions undertaken on the basis of a legally adopted decision of the Security Council. If, for example, enforcement measures were undertaken against any state pursuant to such a Security Council decision, the said offending state would be bound to submit to them.

84. Ago, "Le délit international," *Recueil des cours*, LXVIII (1938), 429-430.

Part VII *International Law in Relations Between the Countries of the World System of Socialism*

The relations among countries of the world system of socialism, whose economic basis is comprised of socialist relations of production, represent a new, higher type of international relations. The socialist commonwealth is a social, economic, and political commonwealth of free sovereign peoples who are united by the close bonds of international socialist solidarity and by the unity of common interests and purposes.[1] "The world system of socialism," says the Program of the CPSU, "*is a new type of economic and political relations between countries.* Socialist countries have an economic basis of the same type—social ownership of the means of production; a state system of the same type—the authority of the people headed by the working class; a single ideology—Marxism-Leninism; common interests in defending revolutionary achievements and national independence from infringements of the imperialist camp; a single great objective—communism. This socioeconomic and political community creates the objective basis for lasting and friendly interstate relations in the socialist camp."[2]

The liquidation of private ownership of the instruments and means of production and the formation of socialist relations of production create the prerequisites for developing friendship between nations and states. "One of the greatest achievements of the world socialist system," says the 1960 Statement of the Meeting of Representatives of Communist and Workers' Parties, "consists of confirming in practice the Marxist-Leninist position that with the collapse of class antagonisms, the antagonism of nations collapses. In contrast to the laws of the capitalist system, in which

1. See *Programmnye dokumenty bor'by za mir, demokratii i sotsializm* (Moscow: Gospolitizdat, 1961), p. 51.
2. *Programma Kommunisticheskoi partii Sovetskogo Soiuza* (Moscow: Gospolitizdat, 1964), pp. 20-21.

there are inherent antagonistic contradictions among classes, nations, and states leading to military clashes, there are in the nature of the socialist system no objective reasons for contradictions and conflicts between states and their constituent peoples, and its development leads to the ever greater unity of states and nations and to a strengthening of all forms of cooperation between them."[3]

An even greater rapprochement between socialist countries is occurring in all areas of relations, which at the same time continue to remain interstate relations between sovereign and equal socialist states. "Complete equality, mutual respect for independence and sovereignty, and fraternal mutual assistance and cooperation are characteristic features of relations between the countries of the socialist commonwealth. In the socialist camp or in the world commonwealth of socialist countries—these are one and the same—no one has nor can have any special rights and privileges whatsoever."[4]

Economic ties are being strengthened within the framework of the world economic system of socialism, which is developing on the basis of the economic laws of socialism and which in itself represents the aggregate of the national economies of sovereign, independent states. The international socialist division of labor is developing. The Twenty-third Special Session of the Council of Mutual Economic Assistance, which took place in Moscow on April 23-26, 1969, with the leaders of communist and workers' parties and of governments of member countries of the Council of Mutual Economic Assistance participating, emphasized that the commonwealth of socialist states "must rest upon the system of a firm and stable international socialist division of labor which ensures the close interaction of the national economies of the member countries of CMEA."[5]

In contrast, the international capitalist division of labor, which reflects the exploitative relations of the weak by the strong, is formed spontaneously in the struggle of monopolies and countries, intensifies the unequal standard of economic development, and leads to the formation of the deformed, unbalanced economic structure of less-developed countries, the international socialist division of labor is carried out in accordance with a plan which takes into consideration the interests of individual states and of the socialist commonwealth as a whole, combining international specialization with the composite economic development of the individual countries.[6]

3. *Programmnye dokumenty za mir*, p. 52.
4. *Programma Kommunisticheskoi partii Sovetskogo Soiuza*, p. 21.
5. "Kommiunike o XXIII spetsial'noi sessii Soveta Ekonomicheskoi Vzaimopomoshchi," *Pravda*, April 27, 1969, p. 1.
6. See the "Basic Principles of the International Socialist Division of Labor"

Relations Between Countries of the World System of Socialism

Economic cooperation between countries of socialism is carried out in various forms: coordination of national economic plans; specialization and cooperation in production; foreign trade; the granting of credits by countries more highly developed economically to less developed countries; the delivery of complete sets of equipment for manufacturing and other enterprises; the sending of assistance in assembling and starting such enterprises; cooperation in the training of personnel; scientific and technical cooperation, including the transfer of technical documentation free of charge; the exchange of specialists for the purpose of becoming acquainted with scientific and technological achievements and with production experience; and so forth. The development of relations among socialist states manifested the possibility and necessity of the transition to a new, higher stage of cooperation among them, to socialist economic integration. Socialist integration is the objective, planned, regulated process of optimizing and bringing together national economic complexes. The objective of such integration is the achievement of a higher level of international socialist division of labor and a more rational utilization of productive, scientific, and technical resources in the interests of each country and of the socialist commonwealth as a whole.

The Complex Program for the Further Deepening and Improvement of Cooperation and of the Development of Socialist Economic Integration of the Member Countries of the Council of Mutual Economic Assistance, adopted by the Twenty-fifth Session of CMEA in July 1971 and approved by all CMEA members, lays down a broad plan of measures for the effectuation of socialist economic integration.

International organizations of socialist countries, in whose activity the socialist principles of international relations are manifested clearly, are playing a growing role in the development of economic, scientific, and technical ties between states of the world socialist system. First and foremost among these are the Council of Mutual Economic Assistance, created in 1949, the International Bank for Economic Cooperation, founded in 1964, the International Investment Bank, which commenced operations in January 1971, and a number of more specialized organizations.[7]

approved by the Meeting of Representatives of Communist and Workers' Parties of Member Countries of CMEA in June 1962. P. A. Tokareva and others, comps., *Mnogostoronnee ekonomichsekoe sotrudnichestvo sotsialisticheskikh gosudarstv; sbornik dokumentov* (Moscow: izd-vo Iurid. lit., 1967), pp. 23-39.

7. The Organization for the Cooperation of Socialist Countries in Tele- and Postal Communications, the Central Despatch Administration for the Combined Grid Systems, the Common Pool of Freight Cars, the Organization for Cooperation in the Ball-Bearing Industry, the Organization for Cooperation in Ferrous Metallurgy, the Joint Institute of Nuclear Research, and others. On this question see V. I. Morozov, *Sovet ekonomicheskoi vzaimopomoshchi—soiuz ravnykh* (Moscow: izd-vo

Cultural ties between socialist states have been greatly developed. All countries of the socialist camp are bound together by agreements on cultural cooperation aimed at developing relations in various spheres of culture. Cultural ties among socialist countries, including ties in the fields of literature, theater, libraries, sport, and so forth, expand from year to year. Founded upon a profound respect for the distinctive features and traditions of each national culture, such cooperation enriches the spiritual life of the socialist nations and promotes their future cultural progress.

Socialist states carry out close cooperation in the field of foreign policy and defense measures for the purposes of defending the gains of socialism from possible feeble imperialist swoops and of struggling for international peace. The strengthening and improvement of the mechanism of the Warsaw Treaty Organization is underway.

The close fraternal cooperation of socialist states in all spheres of relations is an important factor in the successes of individual socialist countries and of the entire socialist camp as a whole.

The new international relations being established among socialist states are characterized not only by the especially close cooperation of such states in the political, economic, cultural, and other spheres of interstate relations but also by the new quality of these relations. A specific feature of the new type of international relations which distinguishes it from other historical types of international relations is the fact that these are relations permeated with socialist internationalism—relations of fraternal friendship, cooperation, and mutual assistance for the purposes of achieving the greatest successes in the construction of socialism in individual countries and of strengthening the socialist commonwealth as a whole. "After the victory of the socialist revolution," states the document *The Tasks of the Struggle Against Imperialism in the Contemporary Stage and the Unity of the Activities of Communist and Workers' Parties and of All Antiimperialist Forces*, adopted June 17, 1969, by the international Meeting of Communist and Workers' Parties, "in many countries the construction of socialism, carried out on the basis of general laws of societal development, develops in various forms which take into account specific historical conditions and distinctive national features. The successful development of this process presupposes the strict observance of the principles of proletarian internationalism, of mutual assistance and support, of equality, of sovereignty, and of noninterference in the internal affairs of one another."

Mezhdunarodnye otnosheniia, 1964); V. Karpich, *Bank sodruzhestva ravnykh*, ed. K. A. Larionov (Moscow: izd-vo Mezhdunarodnye otnosheniia, 1966); P. A. Tokareva, "Stanovlenie sistemy mezhdunarodnykh organizatsii sotsialisticheskikh gosudarstv," *Sovetskoe gosudarstvo i pravo*, no. 10 (1967), pp. 64-72; Tokareva and others, comps., *Mnogostoronnee ekonomicheskoe sotrudnichestvo sotsialisticheskikh gosudarstv.*

Chapter 19 *Socialist International Legal Principles and Norms*

The fundamental principles of the new type of international relations go back to those propositions which were created by Marxist-Leninist theory and by the practice of the workers' movement as principles of the international workers' movement and of the relations of nations and peoples, for whose realization the communist and workers' parties have struggled (see Chapter 1).

With the victory of the proletarian revolution in Russia and the formation of the first socialist state in the world, these principles are becoming principles of state policy which the power of the proletariat has taken into its own hands. The creation of the Union of Soviet Socialist Republics as an equal union of free nations was an implementation of the principles of proletarian internationalism. The grandiose successes of the Soviet multinational state, as a firm step toward communism, and the strengthening of fraternal friendship between socialist nations are the greatest examples of the validity of the principles of proletarian internationalism.

The principles of proletarian internationalism also are reflected in the foreign policy of the first socialist state in the world; they were and are the foundation of this policy. The foreign policy of the Soviet Union has corresponded and does correspond fully to the requirements of proletarian internationalism. This policy, and now the foreign policy of other countries of the socialist camp as well, has been and is responsive not only to the interests of the peoples of these countries but also to the interests of the proletariat of all countries and to the interests of the peoples of all countries.

The formation of the world socialist system signified a new stage in the development of the principles of proletarian internationalism. So long as only one socialist state existed, the said principles could not become principles of international relations because it is necessary that at least several states be guided by them in their foreign relations. Some experience in applying the said principles was gained in relations among the Soviet republics prior to the formation of the Union of Soviet Socialist Republics and in relations between the Soviet Union and the Mongolian People's Republic.

As a consequence of the formation of the world socialist system, the principles of proletarian internationalism are becoming the guiding principles of the new type of international relations.[8]

With the development of relations among socialist states, the principles of proletarian internationalism as moral and political principles of qualitatively new state relations gradually also are becoming international legal principles in relations between states of the world system of socialism. That is to say, a legal dimension has been added to the moral and political aspect of these principles; legal obligations, to the moral and political obligations.

The principles of proletarian internationalism have become international legal principles of relations between countries of the socialist system by way of custom and, partially, by treaty. These principles, which have been applied in the practice of relations between socialist countries,

8. On the principles of proletarian internationalism see G. I. Tunkin, "Sotsialisticheskii internatsionalizm i mezhdunarodnoe pravo," *Novoe vremia*, no. 51 (1957), pp. 10-11; E. A. Korovin, "Proletarskii internatsionalizm v mezhdunarodnoi praktike," *Mezhdunarodnaia zhizn'*, no. 2 (1958), pp. 29-39; Sh. Sanakoev, "Proletarskii internatsionalizm—osnova vzaimootnosheniia stran sotsializma," *ibid.*, no. 7 (1958), pp. 30-43; Tunkin, "Novye tip mezhdunarodnykh otnoshenii i mezhdunarodnoe pravo," *Sovetskoe gosudarstvo i pravo*, no. 1 (1959), pp. 81-94; Korovin, "Proletarskii internatsionalizm i mezhdunarodnoe pravo," *Sovetskii ezhegodnik mezhdunarodnogo prava 1958* (Moscow: izd-vo AN SSSR, 1959), pp. 50-69; Korovin, *Osnovnye problemy sovremennykh mezhdunarodnykh otnoshenii* (Moscow: izd-vo Sotsekgiz, 1959), pp. 57-85; W. Hänisch and G. Herder, "Der proletarische Internationalismus, das Grundprinzip in den Beziehungen zwischen den sozialistischen Staaten," *Staat und Recht*, VIII (1959), 789-807; E. T. Usenko, "Osnovnye mezhdunarodno-pravovye printsipy sotrudnichestva sotsialisticheskikh gosudarstv," *Sovetskoe gosudarstvo i pravo*, no. 3 (1961), pp. 16-29; Usenko, *Formy regulirovaniia sotsialisticheskogo mezhdunarodnogo razdeleniia truda* (Moscow: izd-vo Mezhdunarodnye otnosheniia, 1965), pp. 80-121; H. Wünsche, "Die Bedeutung des sozialistischen Internationalismus für die Restigung der Souveränität der sozialistischen Staaten und die Organisierung ihrer brüderlichen Zusammenarbeit," H. Wünsche, ed., *Rechtsbeziehungen der sozialistischen Länder* (Berlin: Staatsverlag der DDR, 1966), pp. 11-44; Sh. Sanakoev, *Mirovaia sistema sotsializma* (Moscow: izd-vo Mezhdunarodnye otnosheniia, 1968), pp. 72-101; Usenko, "Mezhdunarodnoe pravo vo vzaimootnosheniiakh sotsialisticheskikh gosudarstv," *Sovetskii ezhegodnik mezhdunarodnogo prava 1966-1967* (Moscow: izd-vo Nauka, 1968), pp. 30-46; Tunkin, "V. I. Lenin i printsipy otnoshenii mezhdu sotsialisticheskimi gosudarstvami," *ibid. 1969*, pp. 16-29; Tokareva, "Pravovye osnovy Soveta Ekonomicheskoi Vzaimopomoshchi," *ibid.*, pp. 69-82.

have been recognized by all states of the world system of socialism as international legal principles. This finds confirmation, in particular, in the numerous treaties and declarations signed between socialist states, in the joint documents of the communist and workers' parties of these countries, and in national party and state documents. It is emphasized in the said declarations and statements that relations between countries of the socialist camp are built upon the basis of Marxist-Leninist principles of proletarian internationalism. Thus, the Joint Soviet-Polish Statement of July 22, 1959, in connection with the arrival of the party-governmental delegation of the Soviet Union in Poland says: "Friendship between the peoples of both countries, founded upon a profound community of ideology, upon the Leninist principles of proletarian internationalism, is being strengthened and is developing even more."[9]

The Communique of June 19, 1959, concerning the arrival in the Soviet Union of a party-governmental delegation of the German Democratic Republic for a visit of friendship notes that the indestructible alliance of both states is based upon the "noble principles of proletarian internationalism." The Representatives of the CPSU and SEPG declare that "They consider it the duty of both parties also to strengthen further the fighting unity of the socialist countries and the fraternal solidarity of the communist and workers' parties on the basis of the Marxist-Leninist doctrine and the principles of proletarian internationalism."[10]

In the Joint Statement of April 9, 1958, on the results of negotiations between the party-governmental delegations of the Soviet Union and the Hungarian People's Republic it is stated that Hungarian-Soviet relations are built "upon the basis of fraternal mutual assistance and the great principles of proletarian internationalism."[11]

It is emphasized in the Treaty on Friendship, Cooperation, and Mutual Assistance of September 7, 1967, between the USSR and the Hungarian People's Republic that friendship, fraternal mutual assistance, and all-round close cooperation between the USSR and the HPR is based upon "the firm principles of socialist internationalism."[12] There are analogous provisions in the most recent treaties of the USSR concerning friendship, cooperation, and mutual assistance with other socialist countries.

"The principles of Marxism-Leninism, the principles of proletarian internationalism," says the 1957 Declaration of the Meeting of Representatives of Communist and Workers' Parties of the Socialist Countries, "verified by experience comprise the basis of mutual relations of countries

9. *Izvestia*, July 23, 1959, p. 1.
10. *Ibid.*, June 21, 1959, p. 1.
11. *Ibid.*, April 10, 1958, p. 1.
12. *Vedomosti verkhovnogo soveta SSSR* (1967), no. 49, item 642.

of the world socialist system and of all communist and workers' parties."[13]

"The strict observance of the principles of Marxism-Leninism and of socialist internationalism," states the 1960 Statement of the Meeting of Representatives of Communist and Workers' Parties, "is an indestructible law of mutual relations between socialist countries."[14]

The principles of socialist internationalism and the other international legal principles and norms being formed on their basis in relations among countries of the world socialist system are qualitatively new socialist principles which correspond to the new socialist type of international relations.

The principle of socialist internationalism enters into the system of international legal principles of socialist internationalism first and foremost as the most general, predominant, and characteristic principle of the new type of international relations. "Socialist countries," says the 1957 Declaration of the Meeting of Representatives of Communist and Workers' Parties of the Socialist Countries," build their mutual relations upon the principles of complete equality, of respect for territorial integrity, state independence, and sovereignty, and of noninterference in one another's internal affairs. These are the most important principles; however, they do not exhaust the entire essence of relations among socialist countries. Fraternal mutual assistance is an integral part of their mutual relations. The principle of socialist internationalism finds its true manifestation in such mutual assistance."[15]

As an aspect of interstate relations, the principle of socialist internationalism is the result of applying the principle of proletarian internationalism to relations between states of the socialist type. Proletarian internationalism has signified and does signify above all the unity of the proletariat of various countries in the class struggle against capital for a socialist reconstruction of society. Therefore, the principle of socialist internationalism as a principle of relations among socialist states signifies above all the unity of the socialist states in that class struggle between socialism and capitalism which takes place in the international arena in specific forms and which comprises the basic content of contemporary international relations. An important part of this struggle is the joint defense of the socialist system from any attempts of forces of the old world to destroy or subvert any socialist state of this system.

The principle of socialist internationalism is given concrete expression in the mutual relations of countries of the socialist commonwealth first

13. *Programmnye dokumenty bor'by za mir*, p. 10.
14. *Ibid.*, p. 51.
15. *Ibid.*, p. 10.

and foremost in the principles of fraternal friendship, close cooperation, and comradely mutual assistance.

Both the principle of socialist internationalism and the more concrete principles deriving therefrom reflect objective laws of societal development and therein is their greater strength.

The liquidation of private ownership, upon which for centuries rested the desire of one people to exploit and enslave another, creates the base for the rapprochement of the peoples of the socialist countries. "Socialism brings together peoples and countries," says the Program of the CPSU.[16]

The desire for a close union is an objective law of societal development of the world system of socialism. "The experience of the world socialist system has confirmed the necessity for the *closest union* of those countries breaking away from capitalism and a unification of their efforts in the construction of socialism and communism. A policy for the construction of socialism which is isolated and detached from the world commonwealth of socialist countries is unfounded theoretically because it is contrary to the objective laws of the development of socialist society. It is harmful economically because it leads to a squandering of social labor, a reduction in the rate of the growth of production, and the dependence of countries upon the capitalist world. It is reactionary and dangerous politically because it does not unite, but rather divides peoples before the united front of imperialist forces, nourishes bourgeois-nationalist tendencies, and ultimately could lead to the loss of socialist gains."[17]

In accordance with the international legal principles of fraternal friendship and close cooperation, each state of the socialist commonwealth has not only a moral and political but also a legal duty to strengthen friendship and close cooperation with the other countries of the world system of socialism.

The principle of comradely mutual assistance includes the right of each state of the world system of socialism to obtain assistance from other socialist countries and, at the same time, the obligation of each socialist state to render assistance to other socialist countries. This obligation of mutual assistance applies equally to the spheres of political, economic, military, and other relations.

The Soviet state, as the "oldest" socialist state whose historic fate has been the most difficult task of paving the way for a new socioeconomic formation, always precisely fulfills its duties arising from the principle of socialist internationalism. A vivid manifestation of this policy is the assistance of the Soviet Union to the Hungarian people in 1956 and the assistance, together with other socialist countries, to the people of

16. *Programma Kommunisticheskoi partii Sovetskogo Soiuza*, p. 134.
17. *Ibid.*, p. 21.

Czechoslovakia in 1968 in protecting socialist gains and, ultimately, in defending their sovereignty and independence from sudden swoops of imperialism, as well as the assistance to the Vietnamese people in their struggle against United States's aggression.

The principle of proletarian internationalism also is manifested in the foreign policy of socialist states on a wider plane, including close cooperation and mutual consultations concerning questions of the general international situation.

It must be noted that the unity of the fundamental purposes and principles of the foreign policy of socialist states is not determined simply by the common character of the social system. There is also the common character of the social system among capitalist states; however, there is not and can not be a unity of foreign policy for any prolonged period since the capitalist system is characterized not only by antagonistic contradictions between classes but also by sharp contradictions between states. The unity of purposes and principles of the foreign policy of socialist states derives from the fundamental principles of the new social and state system, from the fundamental principles of the socialist social system.

The principle of proletarian internationalism and the principles of fraternal friendship, close cooperation, and mutual assistance deriving therefrom also permeate economic and other relations among socialist states. Economic cooperation among countries of the socialist camp always includes mutual assistance. Such assistance may take the form of direct assistance without compensation (the assistance of the Soviet Union to a number of socialist countries after the World War in rehabilitating their national economy, assistance on the part of socialist countries to the Korean People's Democratic Republic in rehabilitating its war-destroyed economy, assistance to the Democratic Republic of Vietnam, and so forth), the granting of credits on favorable terms, the rendering of assistance by the countries more developed economically to less developed countries in exploiting industry, agriculture, and so forth.

In economic relations among capitalist states the greatest advantage is derived, as a rule, by the stronger. A country developing economically attempts to hold back the economic development of a weaker country to a low level in order to enjoy advantages in the future which its higher industrial development allows.

The economic relations of the countries of socialism are characterized, on the contrary, by comradely mutual assistance. The more economically-developed countries not only do not attempt to use the economic weakness of the less developed countries in their own interests but, on the contrary, render them disinterested assistance in order to help them achieve the fastest growth of the national economy.

The principle of mutual advantage, in conformity with the requirements of proletarian internationalism, takes on a different character in the economic relations of countries of the socialist camp. Mutual advantage is not understood here in a purely commercial sense. A socialist state takes into account not only the interests of its country in its economic relations, but also the interests of the socialist camp as a whole.

In addition to that which enters into the content of the principles of fraternal friendship, close cooperation, and mutual assistance as principles derived from the broader principle—the principle of proletarian internationalism—the latter also provides that each state of the socialist camp must take into account in its activity both the national interests of its people and the common interest of the entire world system of socialism. "The Marxist-Leninist parties and the peoples of socialist states," says the Program of the CPSU, "proceed from the fact that the successes of the entire world system of socialism depend upon the contribution and effort of each country, and they therefore consider the utmost development of the productive forces of its country to be an internationalist duty."[18]

The objective laws of societal development of the world system of socialism and the principles of proletarian internationalism reflecting such laws of societal development create the possibility of the harmonious combination of the interests of the entire socialist community and of the national interests of the states which comprise it.

Other principles of socialist internationalism appear on the plane of interstate relations as principles of respect for the sovereignty of a socialist state based upon the realization by peoples of the right to self-determination, of noninterference in the internal affairs of another state which reflects respect for national peculiarities and expectations of each people, and of the complete equality of socialist states which reflects the Marxist-Leninist thesis of the equality of nations.

There are, as is well-known, principles of the same name in general international law. This does not mean, however, that one is referring to one and the same principles.

The principles of respect for state sovereignty, noninterference in internal affairs, and equality of states were advanced as general democratic principles during the period of bourgeois revolutions and over the course of time became generally-recognized principles of international law.

The proletariat and its revolutionary parties, waging a struggle for the building of a new society, support those democratic principles, are

18. *Ibid.*, pp. 22-23.

developing them further, and are struggling for their consistent application. V. I. Lenin declared that not only the demand for the self-determination of nations, "but *all* points of our maximum democratic program were
advanced *earlier*, even in the seventeenth and eighteenth centuries, by the
petty bourgeoisie."[1][9]

At the same time, as already has been pointed out, even before the
formation of the world system of socialism Marxist-Leninist theory had
worked out the fundamental principles of relations among countries of
socialism, utilizing the entire sum of the historical experience of national
and state relations, the practice of the world workers' movement, and also
the experience of the Soviet multinational state. With the formation of
the world system of socialism on this basis, the said international legal
principles which comprise the unified system of principles of socialist
internationalism also were formed.

The socialist principles of respect for state sovereignty, noninterference
in internal affairs, and equality of states and peoples differ fundamentally
from the corresponding principles of general international law; these
socialist principles have another content: the rules of conduct themselves
are changed partially as part of the content of the norms and, especially,
the special aspect of the norm changes. On the sociological plane, socialist
principles reflect the concordant wills of states of one social system
and—of special importance—of the socialist system. The social consequences of the operation of socialist international legal principles differ
completely from the consequences of the operation of norms of general
international law. The immediate reason for this is the qualitative
distinctiveness of the special aspect of socialist principles from the
principles of general international law and the difference in the social
relations which are regulated by socialist principles, on one hand, and by
principles of general international law, on the other.

As a whole these are not general democratic principles, but are
completely different socialist international legal principles which relate to
a new, higher type of international law—a socialist international law. They
aim at strengthening and developing relations of the fraternal commonwealth of socialist countries, at ensuring the construction of socialism and
communism, and at protecting the gains of socialism from the infringements of forces hostile to socialism.

The socialist character of these principles is emphasized, in particular,
in the Communique Concerning the Special Session of the Council of
Mutual Economic Assistance, held in April 1969, where they are named as
Marxist-Leninist principles. "Their mutual economic, scientific, and tech-

19. V. I. Lenin, "Sotsialisticheskaia revoliutsiia i pravo natsii na samoopredeleniia,"
Polnoe sobranie sochinenii, 5th ed. (Moscow: Gospolitizdat, 1962), XXVII, 256.

nical ties are built upon the basis of principles of interstate relations of a new type—of socialist internationalism, complete equality, respect for sovereignty and national interest, mutual advantage, and comradely mutual assistance. Historical experience has fully confirmed the living force of these Marxist-Leninist principles."[20]

The principles of socialist internationalism are interconnected and comprise a unified system whose guiding principle is the principle of socialist internationalism. This interconnection of the principles of socialist internationalism and their cosubordination to the guiding principle of socialist internationalism must be taken into account both in defining the content of the individual principles and in applying them.

In general international law the content of the principles of respect for state sovereignty, noninterference in internal affairs, and equality is restricted by granting states specific rights and by conferring duties upon them. But these principles contain no provisions that provide states with a real possibility of exercising such rights. How a state manages to take advantage of these rights is its own affair; general international law imposes no obligations upon other states in this respect.

By virtue of the laws of societal development of capitalism, the said principles of general international law are of a curtailed nature in relations between capitalist states. Thus, the principle of respect for state sovereignty in relations between capitalist states goes together with the actual dependence of small states upon large states, the economic dependence of small countries frequently leading to the sovereignty of such states being transformed into an empty form. In addition, there is always a tendency in relations between capitalist states to violate principles of international law. The history of the international relations of capitalist society, including the period since the adoption of the United Nations Charter, is full of examples of the flagrant violation of the principles of respect for state sovereignty, noninterference in internal affairs, and equality of states.

This by no means diminishes the role of principles of general international law; their observance is a necessary condition and the most important guarantee of peaceful coexistence.

In socialist international relations there is not only strict respect for the sovereignty of states, as understood in general international law, but also the provision of the real possibility of a state's exercising its sovereign rights, of defending state sovereignty. In contrast to economic relations between capitalist countries, economic cooperation of socialist states excludes the use of economic assistance to the prejudice of the sovereignty of any state. It is founded upon the combination of the interests of

20. *Pravda*, April 27, 1969, p. 1.

individual countries with the interests of the entire system and leads to the strengthening and development of the nation's economy.

The ballyhoo raised in the bourgeois press in connection with the Czechoslovak events of 1968 about the "doctrine of limited sovereignty" of socialist states supposedly advanced by the Soviet Union was only a recurrent action in the ideological struggle against the socialist countries. The position of the Soviet Union on the question of sovereignty was confirmed once again in the address of Comrade L. I. Brezhnev at the Fifth Congress of the Polish Worker's Party in November 1968. "The socialist states," declared Comrade Brezhnev, "stand for strict respect for the sovereignty of all countries. We resolutely oppose interference in the affairs of any states and violations of their sovereignty." It is well-known that the very unity of the countries of socialism on the basis of socialist internationalism, and the might of the Soviet Union as the most powerful socialist power, more than once have served and continue to be the basic guarantee of the sovereignty and even of the existence of some socialist states. Many countries whose sovereignty previously was trampled upon brazenly by imperialist states first acquired genuine independence in the fraternal family of peoples of the world socialist system. "The solidarity and close unity of the socialist countries is a true guarantee of the national independence and sovereignty of each socialist country."[2] [1]

The repeated efforts of imperialist powers to infringe upon the sovereignty of individual socialist states inevitably have broken and will be broken on the indestructible unity of the socialist camp.

Yet another feature of the principle of respect for state sovereignty in relations among countries of the socialist camp should be noted. The sovereignty of socialist states actually is popular sovereignty, popular not only in form but in substance because a socialist state serves the people and acts in its interests. Under these conditions, respect for the sovereignty of states is becoming, in content, respect for the rights of the peoples of the respective states.

The same also is characteristic of such principles of socialist internationalism as the principles of equality and of noninterference in the internal affairs of states. They go beyond the principles of general international law of the same name and are qualitatively new principles which reflect the specific features of the new type of international relations. Therefore, the principles of equality and noninterference as principles of proletarian internationalism include, for example, not only the mutual obligations not to violate each other's respective rights, but also the duty to render assistance in the enjoyment of these rights, as well as jointly defending them from the infringements of imperialists, in conformity with the principle of socialist internationalism.

21. *Programmnye dokumenty bor'by za mir*, p. 11.

With regard to relations of equality among socialist countries, the 1957 Soviet-Hungarian Declaration states: "This equality differs fundamentally from that fictitious 'equality' which exists between imperialist powers and which in reality signifies exploitation of the peoples of small states and the plundering of the wealth of these states by imperialist monopolies."[22]

The principles of socialist internationalism, as noted previously, are principles of Marxist-Leninist theory which acquired the character of international legal principles in the process of relations among socialist states. Having become such, however, they continue to retain a close tie with Marxist-Leninist theory. Reflecting the concordant wills of socialist states, where the communist and workers' parties, building their policy on the basis of Marxist-Leninist theory, are the guiding force, these principles are being developed as a result of the further elaboration of this theory and the practice of relations among the countries of socialism.

Other socialist principles and norms also are being formed together with the international legal principles of socialist internationalism, which are the basic principles of relations among states of the world system of socialism.

These principles and norms are created primarily by the conclusion of bilateral and multilateral treaties among socialist states.

In recent years the number of treaties concluded among socialist states has increased significantly, and the operative sphere of treaty norms has expanded. Together with treaties on friendship, trade, and boundaries and agreements on financial questions, there have appeared agreements on cultural cooperation, new consular conventions, conventions concerning the regulation of the nationality of persons with dual citizenship, as well as treaties on rendering legal assistance in criminal and civil cases, agreements on social security, and so forth.

Parallel with broad bilateral cooperation, the multilateral cooperation of socialist states has developed rapidly, in connection with which the number of international organizations and multilateral treaties of socialist states is increasing. Among such multilateral treaties are for example: the 1958 Agreement on Fishing in the Waters of the Danube; the 1959 Agreement on Fishing in the Black Sea; the 1959 Agreement on Cooperation in Veterinary Medicine; the 1959 Agreement on Cooperation in the Quarantine and Protection of Plants from Pests and Diseases; the 1961 Agreement on Cooperation in Technical Supervision Over Vessels and Their Classification; the 1962 Agreement on Cooperation and Mutual Assistance in Customs Questions; the 1962 Agreement on Cooperation in Marine Fishing; and the 1963 Agreement on Accounts Pertaining to Non-Trade Payments. A number of interdepartmental agreements also

22. *Deklaratsii, zaiavlenii i kommiunike Sovetskogo pravitel'stva s pravitel'stvami inostrannykh gosudarstv* (Moscow: Gospolitizdat, 1957), p. 90.

could be mentioned, as for example; the 1966 Agreement on International Passenger Service and the 1966 Agreement on International Railway Freight Service. As noted above, in many instances the development of multilateral international cooperation has led to the creation of international organizations of socialist states.[23]

The treaties among states of the socialist camp represent a new type of international treaty which reflects the specific features of the new social system, the principles of socialist international relations. With regard to treaties between the USSR and other socialist states, a resolution of the Twenty-third Congress of the CPSU states: "The system of treaty relations of the Soviet Union with other countries of socialism has been strengthened. The fraternal friendship of our peoples is embodied in these treaties."[24]

Socialist norms and institutes partly are formed anew in relations among socialist states and partly are formed as a result of the fact that new content is injected into the norms and institutes of general international law in their practical application in relations among states of the world system of socialism.

Thus, the coordination of national economic plans and the specialization and cooperation of production, having been consolidated in the Charter of CMEA and in the Fundamental Principles of the International Socialist Division of Labor adopted in June 1962 at the Meeting of Representatives of the Communist and Workers' Parties of Member Countries of the Council of Mutual Economic Assistance, are new institutes in form and content. They grew from the practice of cooperation of the countries of socialism.

On the other hand, the international legal norms regulating consular

23. For the texts of multilateral treaties among socialist states, see Tokareva and others, comps., *Mnogostoronnee ekonomicheskoe sotrudnichestvo sotsialisticheskikh gosudarstv.* With regard to treaties between socialist states in particular see L. A. Lunts, ed., *Voprosy mezhdunarodnogo chastnogo prava* (Moscow: Iurizdat, 1956); M. Boguslavskii and A. Rubanov, "Pravovoe sotrudnichestvo SSSR so stranami narodnoi demokratii," *Sovetskii ezhegodnik mezhdunarodnogo prava 1958,* pp. 254-272; Lunts, *O soglasheniiakh mezhdu evropeiskimi stranami narodnoi demokratii o vzaimnoi pomoshchi v grazhdanskikh delakh* (Moscow: Iurizdat, 1958); T. Donner, "Chekhoslovatskie dogovory o iuridicheskoi pomoshchi," *Biulleten' chekhoslovatskogo prava,* no. 1 (1958), pp. 72-81; Lunts, "Voprosy mezhdunarodnogo chastnogo prava v otnosheniiakh mezhdu stranami mirovoi sotsialisticheskoi sistemy," *Sovetskii ezhegodnik mezhdunarodnogo prava 1959,* pp. 72-82; Lunts, ed., *Problemy mezhdunarodnogo chastnogo prava* (Moscow: Iurizdat, 1960); Usenko, *Formy regulirovaniia sotsialisticheskogo mezhdunarodnogo razdeleniia truda;* Wünsche, ed., *Rechtsbeziehungen der sozialistischen Länder;* Lunts, "Conflict of Laws in International Sale: Theory and Practice of Socialist Countries," *Recueil des cours,* CXIV (1965), 5-57.

24. *Materialy XXIII s"ezda KPSS* (Moscow: Politizdat, 1966), p. 183.

and boundary relations and cooperation in legal questions and social security which have been fixed in the respective bilateral treaties between socialist states basically are analogous in form to those norms applied in the practice of other states. But in the mutual relations of the countries of the socialist commonwealth they have acquired a new content corresponding to the new quality of international relations.

Thus, for example, the following norm is contained in the Consular Treaty of April 25, 1958, between the USSR and the Federal Republic of Germany: "The consul and consular offices shall not be subject to the jurisdiction of the receiving state in respect of acts performed in their official capacity" (Article 8(1)).[25] Norms analogous in form are contained in the bilateral treaties and conventions on consular questions concluded between the USSR and socialist countries. As already has been pointed out, however, these are different legal norms. The aforesaid legal norm of the consular conventions concluded between socialist states reflects the will of states-parties to the convention which aims at developing and strengthening relations between them on the basis of the principles of socialist internationalism. Meanwhile, the respective norm of the Consular Treaty between the USSR and the FRG expresses the concordant wills of these states, aimed at improving relations between them on the basis of the principles of peaceful coexistence. The social consequences of the operation of these norms, of course, also are different.

25. G. E. Vilkov and I. P. Blishchenko, comps., *Soglasheniia SSSR po konsul'skim voprosam* (Moscow: izd-vo IMO, 1962), p. 81.

Chapter 20 *Principles and Norms of General International Law in Relations Between States of the World Socialist System*

As has been pointed out previously (see Chapter 8), the most important principles of contemporary international law are of an imperative character, and states may not establish in their bilateral or local multilateral relations norms which would contravene these fundamental principles.

There is no doubt, however, that the principles of *jus cogens* are not principles which do not allow the progressive development of international law and the creation on the basis of equality and voluntariness of local international legal norms of general international law in developing friendly relations among states and ensuring peace, that reflect a higher degree of international integration than general international law.

Moreover, being the law of peaceful coexistence of states with a different social system, contemporary general international law can not impede the creation of local international legal norms which by their social content are distinct from norms of general international law. In co-relation with general international law, the international legal principles of socialist internationalism are just such local principles.

The principles of proletarian internationalism and other socialist norms arising in relations between countries of the socialist camp are international legal principles and norms of a new, higher type of international law—a socialist international law, the basis of which is being formed in relations among states of the socialist system and which is coming to replace contemporary general international law.[1]

1. See G. I. Tunkin, "Novyi tip mezhdunarodnykh otnoshenii i mezhdunarodnoe pravo," *Sovetskoe gosudarstvo i pravo*, no. 1 (1959), p. 85; W. Hänisch and G. Herder, "Der proletarische Internationalismus das Grundprinzip in den Beziehungen zwischen den sozialistischen Staaten," *Staat und Recht*, VIII (1959), 803; E. T. Usenko, *Formy regulirovaniia sotsialisticheskogo mezhdunarodnogo razdeleniia truda* (Moscow: izd-vo Mezhdunarodnye otnosheniia, 1965), p. 121; Usenko, "Mezhdunarodnoe pravo vo

General International Law and the World Socialist

Socialist principles and norms are replacing the corresponding principles and norms of general international law in relations between countries of the world system of socialism. This does not mean, however, that principles of general international law simply are cast aside in relations between countries of the socialist commonwealth.

The emergence of the principles of socialist internationalism, of course, is a negation of an old quality, the quality of the respective principles of general international law. But, as any dialectical negation, it is a moment of development, a stage of transition to a higher quality. The new which has emerged is linked with the old, the progressive aspects of the old being retained therein in their diluted form. The progressive elements of the content of the respective principles of general international law corresponding to the new conditions are retained in the principles of socialist internationalism.

The international legal principles of socialist internationalism operate in relations between countries of the socialist commonwealth. They have, therefore, a more limited sphere of application in comparison with general international law. At the same time, the principles of socialist internationalism, reflecting the features of socialist international relations, go further than the principles of general international law in ensuring friendly relations between states.

Consequently, the presence of principles of socialist internationalism and of other socialist principles and norms in relations between countries of the world system of socialism by no means contravenes the requirements of general international law.

Another aspect of the co-relation of principles and norms of general international law and of socialist principles and norms is the co-relation in the process of their operation. In this sense socialist principles and norms are special norms, whereas the principles and norms of general international law are general norms. In conformity with the well-known proposition that a special norm takes precedence over a general norm, in those instances when there are socialist principles and norms, these principles and norms are operative; in those instances when relations between socialist countries are not covered by socialist principles and norms, the

vzaimootnosheniiakh sotsialisticheskikh gosudarstv," *Sovetskii ezhegodnik mezhdunarodnogo prava 1966/1967* (Moscow: izd-vo Nauka, 1968), pp. 30-46; Tunkin, "V. I. Lenin i printsipy otnoshenii mezhdu sotsialisticheskimi gosudarstvami," *Sovetskii ezhegodnik mezhdunarodnogo prava 1969* (Moscow: izd-vo Nauka, 1970), pp. 16-29; Usenko, "Mezhdunarodnopravovye problemy sotsialisticheskoi integratsii," *Sovetskii ezhegodnik mezhdunarodnogo prava 1970* (Moscow: izd-vo Nauka, 1972), pp. 13-25; Tunkin, "V. I. Lenin i printsipy otnoshenii mezhdu sotsialisticheskimi gosudarstvami," *Sovetskii ezhegodnik mezhdunarodnogo prava 1969* (Moscow: izd-vo Nauka, 1970), pp. 16-29.

principles and norms of general international law are operative. Thus, the principle of peaceful coexistence is replaced in relations between states of the socialist camp by the higher, more profound, and qualitatively new principle of socialist internationalism, which is a fundamental and specific principle of a new type of international relations. Such principles of socialist internationalism as the principles of respect for sovereignty, equality, and noninterference in internal affairs replace the corresponding principles of general international law in relations of the new type. The principle of nonaggression is not mentioned in the various documents concluded between socialist states, since it is overlapped in relations between socialist states by the more profound principle of socialist internationalism.

As examples of the operation of principles and norms of general international law in relations between countries of the socialist commonwealth, one may point to the norms of the 1958 Geneva Conventions on the law of the sea, the norms of the 1961 Vienna Convention on Diplomatic Relations, and others. These principles and norms must be observed by socialist countries in their mutual relations and, when necessary, references to them are made.

Since, however, the principles of socialist internationalism are being guided by principles of the new type of international relations, the interpretation and application of principles and norms of general international law in relations between countries of the world system of socialism takes place in the light of these guiding principles, infusing a "new spirit" into these principles and norms.

The theoretical unfoundedness of the concept equating principles of relations between countries of the socialist camp with principles of general international law is that it does not take into account the specific features of relations between countries of the socialist camp. But the specific feature exists, and it must, since the question is one of relations between states of a new historical type, of relations between socialist states.

To assert that relations between socialist countries should be regulated only by principles of general international law is to deny the different class character of relations between the countries of socialism, to be derailed from party principle into the morass of bourgeois normativism.

Politically analogous concepts objectively are aimed at depreciating relations between countries of the socialist camp, dissolving them in the general mass of relations between states, undermining the unity of countries of the socialist camp, weakening it in the struggle for the rapid construction of socialism and communism and in warding off all of the imperialist harassments.

The scientific Marxist-Leninist approach to the problem of relations between countries of the socialist camp requires that the specific features of these relations be taken into account, and this specific feature as regards principles of interstate relations finds its clearest manifestation in the principle of socialist internationalism.

Bibliography of Published Works of G. I. Tunkin: 1938-1973

The list of publications below was prepared especially for this edition by Professor Tunkin. The translator has reordered the list somewhat, has added items 1, 2, 8, 14, 44, 65, 91, 96, and 159, has verified or supplied pagination and other publication data for all items, and has interpolated all data concerning reviews of items 4-6, pseudonyms, and foreign translations. References are provided only for the English-language editions of *International Affairs* and *New Times*.

DISSERTATIONS

1. *Parlamentskaia reforma 1832 goda v Anglii.* Moscow, 1938. 120 pp. (Defended at the Moscow Juridical Institute, 1938; Candidate of Juridical Sciences.)

    Contents: I. English Electoral Law Before the Reform (Historical Outline); II. The Reform Movement; III. The Reform Bill.

    Abstract: Moskovskii iuridicheskii institut NKIu Soiuza SSR, *Uchenye zapiski* (Moscow: Iuridicheskoe izd-vo NKIu SSSR, 1941), III, 16-17.

2. *Koreiskii vopros posle vtoroi mirovoi voiny v svete mezhdunarodnogo prava.* Moscow, 1954. 949 pp. (Defended at the Moscow State Institute of International Relations; the degree of Doctor of Juridical Sciences was confirmed January 8, 1955.)

    Contents: I. International Agreements Concerning Korea After the Second World War and the Principle of Self-Determination of Nations; II. The Liberation of Korea by the Soviet Army, the Democratic Transformation in North Korea; III. The Occupation of South Korea by American Forces; IV. Negotiations in the Joint Soviet-American Commission for Korea; V. The Creation by American Occupation Authorities of a Separate Puppet Government in South Korea; VI. The Formation of the Korean People's Democratic Republic; VII. The Korean Question at the Third and Fourth Sessions of the United Nations General Assembly; VIII. Korea in the Plans of the Aggressive Policy of American Imperialists in Asia in Connection with the Victory of the People's Revolution in China; IX. Civil War and United States Aggression in Korea; X. Violation of the Laws and Customs of War by United States Armed Forces in Korea; XI. United States Aggression Against China; XII. The Struggle to End the War in Korea and the Peaceful Settlement of the Korea Question.

BOOKS

3. *Osnovy sovremennogo mezhdunarodnogo prava; uchebnoe posobie* (Moscow, 1956). 48 pp. (Vysshaia partiinaia shkola pri TsK KPSS) Printing 20,000 copies.
    Translated: *Hsien-tai kuo-chi-fa ti chi-pen wen-t'i* (Peking: Shih-chieh chih-shih ch'u-pan she, 1958).
    "Grundlagen der modernen Völkerrechts," in E. Menzel, ed., *Drei sowjetische Beiträge zur Völkerrechtslehre* (Hamburg: Hansischer Gildenverlag, 1969), pp. 1-57.
4. *Voprosy teorii mezhdunarodnogo prava* (Moscow: Gosiurizdat, 1962). 330 pp. Printing 3,000 copies.
    Translated: *Das Völkerrecht der Gegenwart: Theories und Praxis*, trans. Klaus Wolf, ed. Herbert Standke (Berlin: Staatsverlag der DDR, 1963). 280 pp.
    A Nemzetközi jog elméletének kérdései, trans. P. Bela, ed. M. Ferenc (Budapest: Kozgazdasagi es jogi könyvkiado, 1963). 325 pp.
    Zagadnienia teorii prawa miedzynarodowego, trans. W. Morawiecki, Preface by M. Lachs (Warsaw: Panstwowe wyd-wo naukowe, 1964). 412 pp.
    Droit international public; problèmes theoriques, Preface by M. Virally (Paris: Editions A. Pedone, 1965). 250 pp.
    al-Qānūn al-duwalt al-'āmm, translated from the French edition by Ahmed Rida, revised by E. Foda ([Cairo]: al-Haiy'at al-Misriyat al-'Ammah li'l-Kuttāb, 1972).

Reviews: *Sovetskoe gosudarstvo i pravo*, no. 5 (1963), p. 167.
(R. L. Bobrov)
Pravovedenie, no. 1 (1963), pp. 141-144. (A. N. Talalaev)
Sovetskii ezhegodnik mezhdunarodnogo prava 1963 (1965), pp. 550-553. (D. B. Levin)
American Journal of International Law, LVII (1963), 673-676. (J. N. Hazard)
Canadian Yearbook of International Law, II (1964), 335-338. (E. McWhinney)
Hastings Law Journal, XVI (1964), 138. (D. Berger)
Revista Española de Derecho Internacional, XVII (1964), 169-192. (M. Aguilar Navarro)
Staat und Recht, XIII (1964), 1451-1464.
Year Book of World Affairs, XIX (1965), 276. [G.S.]
Annuaire français de droit international, XI (1965), 1115-1118. (A. Ch. Kiss)
Archives de Philosophie de Droit, XII (1967), 384. (K. Stoyanovitch)
Communicazioni e studi, XII (1966), 921-922. (P. Ziccardi)
International and Comparative Law Quarterly, XIV (1965), 1427-1428. (I. Lapenna)
Revue générale de droit international public, XXXVI (1965), 861-863. (Ch. Rousseau)
Year Book of World Affairs, XX (1966), 292-293. [G.S.]

5. *Ideologicheskaia bor'ba i mezhdunarodnoe pravo* (Moscow: izd-vo Mezhdunarodnye otnosheniia, 1967). 176 pp. Printing 6,000 copies.
    Translated: *Ideologický boj a mezinárodní právo*, trans. M. Srnská (Prague: Statni pedagogické nakladatelství, 1968). 118 pp. Mimeographed.
    Ideorogī Toso to kokusai-hō, trans. Setsuo Iwafuchi (Kyoto: Hōritsu Bunka Sha, 1969). 215 pp.
    "Der ideologische Kampf und das Völkerrecht," in E. Menzel, ed., *Drei sowjetische Beiträge zur Völkerrechtslehre* (Hamburg: Hansischer Gildenverlag, 1969), pp. 307-461.
    Reviews: *Sovetskii ezhegodnik mezhdunarodnogo prava 1968* (1969), pp. 433-436. (L. A. Aleksidze)
    Sovetskoe gosudarstvo i pravo, no. 4 (1968), pp. 140-143. (E. T. Usenko)
    Časopis pro Mezinárodní Právo, XI (1967), 372. (J. Toman)
    American Journal of International Law, LXII (1968), 209-211. (J. N. Hazard)
6. *Teoriia mezhdunarodnogo prava* (Moscow: izd-vo Mezhdunarodnye otnosheniia, 1970). 511 pp. Printing 9,000 copies.

Translated: *Völkerrechtstheorie*, trans. H. Müller and V. Rathfelder, ed. T. Schweisfurth (Berlin: Berlin Verlag, 1972). 492 pp.

Theory of International Law, trans. with an introduction by William E. Butler (Cambridge, Mass.: Harvard University Press, 1974).

Reviews: *Sovetskoe gosudarstvo i pravo*, no. 12 (1970), pp. 144-147. (I. I. Lukashuk)

Allam-és Jogtudomanyi, XIV (1971), 101. (A. Csillag)

Časopis pro Mezinárodní právo, XV (1971), 88-91. (B. Gotz)

Pravnik, CX (1971), 606. (M. Srnská)

Staat und Recht, XIX (1970), 2019. (F. Seidel)

American Journal of International Law, LXV (1971), 416-418. (W. E. Butler)

Nederlands Juristenblad, December 1970, p. 1385.

Osteuropa Recht, XVIII (1972), 208-210. (D. Frenzke)

Comment: "Renewed Emphasis upon a Socialist International Law," *American Journal of International Law*, LXV (1971), 142-148. (J. N. Hazard)

" 'Socialist International Law' or 'Socialist Principles of International Relations,' " *American Journal of International Law*, LXV (1971), 796-800. (W. E. Butler)

"Socialist International Law Revisited," *American Journal of International Law*, LXVI (1972), 596-600. (C. Osakwe)

"Obsuzhdenie problem teorii mezhdunarodnogo prava," *Pravovedenie*, no. 6 (1970), pp. 132-134. (V. L. Iushchenko)

7. *V. I. Lenin i sovremennoe mezhdunarodnoe pravo* (Moscow: izd-vo Znanie, 1970). 63 pp. Coauthor V. F. Fedorov. Printing 53,000 copies.

8. *Comparabilité des diplômes en droit international; étude structurelle et fonctionelle* (Paris: UNESCO, 1972). 83 pp. Coauthor R.-J. Dupuy. (English language edition, 1973)

ARTICLES AND REVIEWS

1940

9. "Parlamentskaia reforma 1832 g. v Anglii," *Uchenye zapiski moskovskogo iuridicheskogo instituta* (Moscow: izd-vo NKIu SSSR, 1940), Vyp. II, 103-182.

Bibliography of Published Works of G. I. Tunkin: 1938–1973

1946

10. "Problemy gosudarstvennogo ustroistva Kitaia," *Sovetskoe gosudarstvo i pravo*, nos. 8-9 (1946), pp. 31-46. Pseud. M. Eremeev.
11. "K voprosu o Gonkonge i Koulune," *Novoe vremia*, no. 19 (1946), pp. 8-11. Pseud. M. Eremeev.
    Translated: "Hong Kong and Kowloon," *New Times*, no. 19 (1946), pp. 8-10.

1947

12. "Gosudarstvo i pravo frantsii ot burzhuaznoi revoliutsii do 1871 g.," in Vsesoiuznyi institut iuridicheskikh nauk ministerstva iustitsii SSSR, *Vseobshchaia istoriia gosudarstva i prava. Chast' III. Ot angliiskoi revoliutsii do velikoi oktiabr'skoi sotsialisticheskoi revoliutsii* (Moscow: Iuridicheskoe izd-vo Ministerstva iustitsii SSSR, 1947), pp. 57-88. Part I, section II, chapter 1.
13. "K itogam natsional'nogo sobraniia v Kitae," *Izvestiia*, February 11, 1947, pp. 3-4. Pseud. M. Eremeev.

1948

14. Responsible Ed., *Programma po mezhdunarodnomu publichnomu pravu (dlia iuridicheskikh institutov i iuridicheskikh fakul'tetov, universitetov)* (Moscow: Tipo. Moskovskogo iuridicheskogo instituta, 1948). Compiled by F. I. Kozhevnikov.
15. "O mezhdunarodnoi zashchite prav cheloveka," *Sovetskoe gosudarstvo i pravo*, no. 7 (1948), pp. 1-10. Pseud. G. Tavrov.

1950

16. "Koreiskii vopros posle vtoroi mirovoi voiny," *Sovetskoe gosudarstvo i pravo*, no. 7 (1950), pp. 27-42. Pseud. G. Tavrov.

1951

17. "Izoblichaiushchie dokumenty," *Sovetskoe gosudarstvo i pravo*, no. 8 (1951), pp. 92-95. Pseud. G. Tavrov.
    Review of *Documents and Materials Exposing the Instigators of the Civil War in Korea. Documents from the Archives of the Rhee Syngman Government* (Pyongyang: Ministry of Foreign Affairs of the Democratic People's Republic of Korea, 1950).

18. "Bezzastenchivoe narushenie mezhdunarodnykh soglashenii i norm mezhdunarodnogo prava," *Sovetskoe gosudarstvo i pravo*, no. 9 (1951), pp. 49-61.

19. "Prestupnaia voina amerikanskikh imperialistov protiv koreiskogo naroda," *Trudy instituta prava akademii nauk SSSR*, I (1951), 85-111. Pseud. G. Tavrov.

1952

20. "Dogovor podgotovki voiny," *Sovetskoe gosudarstvo i pravo*, no. 2 (1952), pp. 41-51. Pseud. G. Tavrov.

21. Ed., with introduction, *Konstitutsiia i osnovnye zakonodatel'nye akty Koreiskoi narodno-demokraticheskoi respubliki*, trans. from the Korean by Iu. N. Mazur and Han Dik Pon (Moscow: izd-vo Inostran- noi literatury, 1952), pp. 5-52. Pseud. G. Tavrov.

1953

22. "Sovetskoe opredelenie agressii v Organizatsii Ob"edinennykh Natsii," *Sovetskoe gosudarstvo i pravo*, nos. 2-3 (1953), pp. 89-101.

1954

23. "Obshcheevropeiskii dogovor i mezhdunarodnoe pravo," *Pravda*, April 10, 1954, p. 3. Pseud. G. Tavrov.

24. "Kollektivnaia bezopasnost' i gosudarstvennyi suverenitet," *Pravda*, May 8, 1954, p. 3. Pseud. G. Tavrov.

25. "Evropeiskaia bezopasnost' i Organizatsiia Ob"edinennykh Natsii," *Pravda*, May 28, 1954, p. 3. Pseud. G. Tavrov.

26. "Atlanticheskii dogovor i vozrozhdenie germanskogo imperializma," *Pravda*, September 20, 1954, p. 3. Pseud. G. Tavrov.

27. "Chto skryvaetsia za razgovorami o 'vosstanovlenii suvereniteta' Zapadnoi Germanii," *Pravda*, September 27, 1954, p. 4. Pseud. G. Tavrov.

28. "Starye plany pod novoi vyveskoi (Zapadnoevropeiskii soiuz i Evro- peiskoe Oboronitel'noe soobshchestvo)," *Pravda*, December 14, 1954, p. 3. Pseud. G. Tavrov.

1955

29. "Parizhskie soglasheniia i mezhdunarodnoe pravo," *Sovetskoe gosu- darstvo i pravo*, no. 2 (1955), pp. 13-22.

30. "Vopros o zapreshchenii atomnogo oruzhiia i mezhdunarodnoe pravo," *Pravda*, May 26, 1955, p. 3. Pseud. G. Tavrov.
31. "Zakonnye prava Kitaia v OON dolzhny byt' vosstanovleny," *Novoe vremia*, no. 28 (1955), pp. 3-5.
   Translated: "China's Lawful Rights in the United Nations," *New Times*, no. 28 (1955), pp. 3-5.
32. "Germanskaia Demokraticheskaia Respublika—polnopravnyi sub"ekt mezhdunarodnogo prava," *Izvestiia*, October 9, 1955, p. 3.
33. "Evropeiskie problemy i Parizhskie soglasheniia," *Novoe vremia*, no. 44 (1955), pp. 6-9. Pseud. G. Tavrov.
   Translated: "The Paris Agreements and European Problems," *New Times*, no. 44 (1955), pp. 6-8.
34. "V zashchitu prav cheloveka," *Izvestiia,* December 10, 1955, p. 4.

1956

35. "O nekotorykh voprosakh mezhdunarodnogo dogovora v sviazi s Varshavskim dogovorom," *Sovetskoe gosudarstvo i pravo*, no. 1 (1956), pp. 98-104.
36. "Koreiskii vopros," *Mezhdunarodnaia zhizn'*, no. 2 (1956), pp. 81-96. Pseud. G. Tavrov.
   Translated: "The Korean Question," *International Affairs*, no. 2 (1956), pp. 82-96.
37. "Za kollektivnuiu bezopasnost' v Evrope," *Mezhdunarodnaia zhizn'*, no. 3 (1956), pp. 117-121.
   Review of *Problema kollektivnoi bezopasnosti v Evrope* (Warsaw: Panstwowe wyd-wo naukowe, 1955).
   Translated: "For Collective Security in Europe," *International Affairs*, no. 3 (1956), pp. 121-126.
38. "Mirnoe sotrudnichestvo ili 'promezhutochnoe sostoianie'," *Novoe vremia*, no. 25 (1956), pp. 8-11.
   Translated: "Peaceful Cooperation or 'Intermediate Status,' " *New Times*, no. 25 (1956), pp. 8-10.
39. "Mirnoe sosushchestvovanie i mezhdunarodnoe pravo," *Sovetskoe gosudarstvo i pravo*, no. 7 (1956), pp. 3-13.
40. "Spor o Panamskom kanale," *Mezhdunarodnaia zhizn'*, no. 9 (1956), pp. 132-134. Pseud. G. Tavrov.
   Reprinted: *Izvestiia*, September 7, 1956, p. 3.
   Translated: "The Panama Canal Dispute," *International Affairs*, no. 9 (1956), pp. 134-136.
41. "Ugrozy primeneniia sily zapreshcheny mezhdunarodnym pravom," *Pravda*, September 2, 1956, p. 5.

42. "Pora vosstanovit' predstavitel'stvo Kitaia v OON," *Mezhdunarod-naia zhizn'*, no. 10 (1956), pp. 25-34.
  Translated: "Time to Restore China's Representation in the U.N.," *International Affairs*, no. 10 (1956), pp. 27-35.

43. "Vooruzhennaia agressiia protiv Egipta—grubeishee narushenie mezhdunarodnogo prava," *Sovetskoe gosudarstvo i pravo*, no. 10 (1956), pp. 10-16. Unsigned.

44. Ed., *Konstitutsiia i osnovnye zakonodatel'nye akty Federativnoi Narodnoi Respubliki Iugoslavii*, comp. A. M. Zubov and A. A. Khanov (Moscow: izd-vo Inostrannoi literatury, 1956).

1957

45. "Soužiti státu dvou soustav a mezinárodni právo," *Mezinárodni politika*, I (1957), 330-337.

46. Review of R. Quadri, *Diritto internazionale publico*, 2d ed. (Palermo: G. Priulla, 1956), in *Sovetskoe gosudarstvo i pravo*, no. 9 (1957), pp. 152-155.

47. "Nekotorye novye iavleniia v posol'skom prave," *Mezhdunarodnaia zhizn'*, no. 12 (1957), pp. 63-71.
  Translated: "Some Developments in International Law Concerning Diplomatic Privileges and Immunities," *International Affairs*, no. 12 (1957), pp. 64-71.

48. "Voprosy posol'skogo prava na IX sessii Komissii mezhdunarodnogo prava OON," *Sovetskoe gosudarstvo i pravo*, no. 12 (1957), pp. 73-83.

49. "Sotsialisticheskii internatsionalizm i mezhdunarodnoe pravo," *Novoe vremia*, no. 51 (1957), pp. 10-11.
  Translated: "Socialist Internationalism and International Law," *New Times*, no. 51 (1957), pp. 10-11.

1958

50. "Co-existence and International Law," *Recueil des cours*, XCV (1958), 1-81.

51. "Zhenevskaia konferentsiia po mezhdunarodnomu morskomu pravu," *Mezhdunarodnaia zhizn'*, no. 7 (1958), pp. 63-70.
  Translated: "The Geneva Conference on the Law of the Sea," *International Affairs*, no. 7 (1958), pp. 47-52.

52. "Deistviia SShA—vooruzhennaia agressiia," *Literatura i zhizn'*, July 20, 1958, p. 3.

53. "Amerikanskaia agressiia na Dal'nem Vostoke—gruboe narushenie mezhdunarodnogo prava," *Pravda*, September 7, 1958, p. 5.
54. Ed., with preface, A. P. Movchan, *Mezhdunarodnaia zashchita prav cheloveka* (Moscow: Gosiurizdat, 1958), pp. 3-4.
55. "Dva proekta Komissii mezhdunarodnogo prava OON," *Sovetskoe gosudarstvo i pravo*, no. 12 (1958), pp. 66-74. Coauthor V. A. Romanov.

1959

56. "Novyi tip mezhdunarodnykh otnoshenii i mezhdunarodnoe pravo," *Sovetskoe gosudarstvo i pravo*, no. 1 (1959), pp. 81-94.
   Translated: "Ein neuer Typ der internationalen Beziehungen und das Völkerrecht," *Sowjetwissenschaft*, III (1959), 709-726.
57. "Berlinskii vopros v svete mezhdunarodnogo prava," *Mezhdunarodnaia zhizn'*, no. 2 (1959), pp. 46-56.
   Translated: "The Berlin Problem and International Law," *International Affairs*, no. 2 (1959), pp. 36-43.
   "Die Berlin-Frage und das Völkerrecht," *Sowjetwissenschaft,* III (1959), 357-367.
58. "La Question de Berlin et le droit international," *Études soviétiques,* no. 133 (April 1959), pp. 21-24.
59. "XXI s"ezd KPSS i mezhdunarodnoe pravo," *Sovetskoe gosudarstvo i pravo*, no. 6 (1959), pp. 40-49.
   Translated: "Der XXI. Parteitag der KPdSU und das Völkerrecht," *Aussenwirtschaftsdienst des Betriebsrates mit Recht der europ. Gemeinschaften*, VI (1959), 438-448.
60. "Sovetskii soiuz i mezhdunarodnoe pravo," *Mezhdunarodnaia zhizn'*, no. 11 (1959), pp. 52-60.
   Translated: "The Soviet Union and International Law," *International Affairs*, no. 11 (1959), pp. 40-45.
61. "XI sessiia Komissii mezhdunarodnogo prava OON," *Sovetskoe gosudarstvo i pravo*, no. 11 (1959), pp. 69-78. Coauthor V. A. Romanov.
62. "Sorok let sosushchestvovaniia i mezhdunarodnoe pravo," *Sovetskii ezhegodnik mezhdunarodnogo prava 1958* (Moscow: izd-vo AN SSSR, 1959), pp. 15-42. English summary pp. 42-49.
   Summary: *International Affairs*, no. 3 (1958), p. 125.
   Translated: "Vierzig Jahre Koexistenz und Völkerrecht," in R. Arzinger, ed., *Gegenwartsprobleme des Völkerrecht* (Berlin: VEB Deutscher Zentralverlag, 1962), pp. 7-39.

63. "Nezadachlivye komentatory mezhdunarodnogo prava," *Izvestiia*, May 27, 1959, p. 5.

64. Ed., with introduction, A. Verdross, *Mezhdunarodnoe pravo*, trans. F. A. Kublitskii and R. L. Naryshkina (Moscow: izd-vo Inostrannoi literatury, 1959), pp. 5-18.

65. Ed., with introduction, I. S. Pereterskii, *Tolkovanie mezhdunarod-nykh dogovorov* (Moscow: Gosiurizdat, 1959), pp. 3-4. Coeditor S. B. Krylov.

1960

66. "Khoroshii primer mezhdunarodnogo sotrudnichestvo (k itogam konferentsii po Antarktike)," *Mezhdunarodnaia zhizn'*, no. 2 (1960), pp. 55-60.
    Translated: "An Example of International Cooperation," *International Affairs*, no. 2 (1960), pp. 42-45.

67. "The Role of International Law in International Relations," in F. A. Frhr. v. d. Heydte and others, eds., *Völkerrecht und rechtliches Weltbild; Festschrift für Alfred Verdross* (Vienna: Springer Verlag, 1960), pp. 293-305.

68. "Neobosnovannye pritiazaniia," *Izvestiia*, February 18, 1960, p. 3.

69. Introduction, *Sovetskii ezhegodnik mezhdunarodnogo prava 1959* (Moscow: izd-vo AN SSSR, 1960), pp. 11-15.

70. Ed., with introduction, S. B. Krylov, *Istoriia sozdaniia Organizatsii Ob"edinennykh Natsii* (Moscow: izd-vo IMO, 1960), pp. 3-9.

71. "Diplomaticheskie privilegii i immunitety," in A. A. Gromyko and others, eds., *Diplomaticheskii slovar' v trekh tomakh* (Moscow: Gospolitizdat, 1960), I, 448-454.

72. "Istochniki mezhdunarodnogo prava," *ibid.*, I, 573-576.

73. "Razoblachennaia legenda," *Pravda*, July 24, 1960, p. 5.

74. "O iuridicheskoi prirode obychnykh norm mezhdunarodnogo prava," *Voprosy mezhdunarodnogo prava* (Moscow: izd-vo IMO, 1960), Vyp. 2, pp. 3-17.

75. "Konferentsiia Assotsiatsii mezhdunarodnogo prava," *Vestnik akademii nauk SSSR*, no. 11 (1960), pp. 105-107.

76. "Za mir bez oruzhiia i nezavisimost' narodov," *Sovetskoe gosudarstvo i pravo*, no. 11 (1960), pp. 3-13. Peredovaia; unsigned.

1961

77. "Proekt kodeksa konsul'skogo prava (K itogam XII sessii Komissii mezhdunarodnogo prava OON)," *Sovetskoe gosudarstvo i pravo*, no.

1 (1961), pp. 56-66. Coauthor D. V. Bykov.
Summary: *Staat und Recht*, X (1961), 930-932.

78. Ed., with preface, C. Berezowski, *Nekotorye problemy territorial'-nogo verkhovenstva*, trans. V. L. Kon (Moscow: izd-vo Inostrannoi literatury, 1961), pp. 5-12.

79. "Venskaia konventsiia o diplomaticheskikh snosheniiakh," *Mezhdunarodnaia zhizn'*, no. 6 (1961), pp. 72-80.
     Translated: "Vienna Convention on Diplomatic Relations," *International Affairs*, no. 6 (1961), pp. 51-56.

80. "Peaceful Coexistence and International Law," *The Ceylon Law Society Journal*, VII (1961), xvi-xviii.
     Translated: *Tan San Tu Fan*, no. 1 (Vietnam, 1961).

81. "The Role of International Law in Strengthening Peace," *United Nations Review*, VIII, no. 8 (1961), pp. 18-20, 36.

82. "Diplomatie und Völkerrecht," *Osterreichische Zeitschrift für Aussenpolitik*, I (1961), 292-301.

83. "Remarks on the Juridical Nature of Customary Norms of International Law," *California Law Review*, XLIX (1961), 419-430.

84. "Mezhdunarodnopravovye aspekty zakliucheniia germanskogo mirnogo dogovora," *Sovetskoe gosudarstvo i pravo*, no. 10 (1961), pp. 179-192.
     Summary: *Staat und Recht*, XI (1962), 384-387.

85. "Mezhdunarodnye organizatsii," in A. A. Gromyko and others, eds., *Diplomaticheskii slovar' v trekh tomakh* (Moscow: Gospolitizdat, 1961), II, 279-283. Unsigned.

86. "Mezhdunarodnopravovaia otvetstvennost' gosudarstva," *ibid.*, II, 277-279. Unsigned.

87. "Mirnoe sosushchestvovanie," *ibid.*, II, 297-300. Unsigned.

88. Introduction, *Sovetskii ezhegodnik mezhdunarodnogo prava 1960* (Moscow: izd-vo AN SSSR, 1961), pp. 15-23. English summary pp. 23-27.

89. "Problema mezhdunarodnopravovoi otvetstvennosti gosudarstva v Komissii mezhdunarodnogo prava OON," *ibid.*, pp. 92-101. English summary pp. 101-104.

90. "Der rechtliche Standpunkt," *Die Sowjetunion heute*, VI (Bonn, September 10, 1961), pp. 3-4.
     Reprinted: *Sowjetunion heute*, no. 39 (Vienna, September 24, 1961).

91. Ed., *Problemy mezhdunarodnogo prava; sbornik statei iuristov-mezhdunarodnikov stran narodnoi demokratii* (Moscow: izd-vo Inostrannoi literatury, 1961).

1962

92. "XXII s"ezd KPSS i zadachi sovetskoi nauki mezhdunarodnogo prava," *Sovetskoe gosudarstvo i pravo*, no. 5 (1962), pp. 3-17.
   Translated: "The 22nd Congress of the CPSU and the Tasks of the Soviet Science of International Law," *Soviet Law and Government*, I, no. 3 (1962/63), pp. 18-28.
   Summary: *Staat und Recht*, XI (1962), 2259-2260.
93. "Vragi Kuby popiraiut mezhdunarodnoe pravo," *Pravda*, September 19, 1962, p. 5.
94. "XXII s"ezd KPSS i mezhdunarodnoe pravo," *Sovetskii ezhegodnik mezhdunarodnogo prava 1961* (Moscow: izd-vo AN SSSR, 1962), pp. 15-28. English summary pp. 28-35.
95. "La guerre froide et le droit international," *Comprendre*, XXV (1962), 25-37.
96. Ed., *Ocherki mezhdunarodnogo morskogo prava* (Moscow: Gosiurizdat, 1962). Coeditor V. M. Koretskii.

1963

97. "Alcuni nuovi problemi della responsabilita dello stato nel diritto internazionale," *Communicazioni e studi*, XI (1963), 1-49.
98. "Pravo dogovorov na XIV sessii Komissii mezhdunarodnogo prava OON," *Sovetskoe gosudarstvo i pravo*, no. 2 (1962), pp. 97-103. Coauthor B. N. Nechaev.
   Summary: *Staat und Recht*, XII (1963), 1311-1312.
99. "Coexistence of Opposites: Soviet Attitude to International Law," *The Times*, February 25, 1963, p. 14, cols. 3-4.
100. "Printsip mirnogo sosushchestvovaniia—general'naia liniia vneshnepoliticheskoi deiatel'nosti KPSS i Sovetskogo gosudarstva," *Sovetskoe gosudarstvo i pravo*, no. 7 (1963), pp. 26-37.
   Summary: *Staat und Recht*, XII (1963), 2081-2082.
101. "Granitsy gosudarstv i mirnoe sosushchestvovanie," *Izvestiia*, August 27, 1963, p. 2.
   Translated: "Staatsgrenzen und friedliche Koexistenz," *Die Sowjetunion heute*, VIII, no. 19 (1963), pp. 25-26.
102. "Pakt o nenapadenii—vazhnyi shag k razriadke," *Mezhdunarodnaia zhizn'*, no. 10 (1963), pp. 11-19.
   Translated: "Non-Aggression Pact: Important Step Towards Detente," *International Affairs*, no. 10 (1963), pp. 9-14.
   "Der Nichtangriffspakt-ein wichtiger Schritt zur Entspannung," *Sowjetwissenschaft*, VIII (1964), 1-11.

103. "International Law and Peace," in *International Law in a Changing World* (New York: Oceana Publications, Inc., 1963), pp. 72-79.

104. "Uspekh politiki mirnogo sosushchestvovaniia," *Sovetskii ezhegodnik mezhdunarodnogo prava 1962* (Moscow: izd-vo AN SSSR, 1963), pp. 17-20. English summary pp. 21-24.

1964

105. "Mezhdunarodnoe pravo i gosudarstvennye granitsy," *Izvestiia*, January 8, 1964, p. 2.

106. "Pravo dogovorov na XV sessii Komissii mezhdunarodnogo prava OON," *Sovetskoe gosudarstvo i pravo*, no. 2 (1964), pp. 84-92. Coauthor B. N. Nechaev.

107. "Le droit international de la co-existence pacifique," in *Mélanges offerts à Henri Rolin: Problèmes de droit des gens* (Paris: Editions A. Pedone, 1964), pp. 407-418.

108. "La codification des principes de co-existence pacifique," *Revue de droit contemporain*, XI, no. 1 (1964), pp. 79-89.

Translated: "Codification of the Principles of Peaceful Coexistence," *Review of Contemporary Law*, XI, no. 1 (1964), pp. 79-88.

109. "Novyi tip mezhdunarodnykh otnoshenii i mezhdunarodnoe pravo," in F. I. Kozhevnikov, ed., *Mezhdunarodnoe pravo* (Moscow: izd-vo Mezhdunarodnye otnosheniia, 1964), pp. 94-120. (Chapter 4)

1965

110. "Vopreki mezhdunarodnomu pravu," *Izvestiia*, January 29, 1965, p. 2.

111. "Voennye prestupniki i revanshisty," *Za rubezhom*, no. 12 (1965), p. 5.

112. "Akt proizvola," *Izvestiia*, February 13, 1965, p. 2.

113. "Pravo dogovorov na XVI sessii Komissii mezhdunarodnogo prava OON," *Sovetskoe gosudarstvo i pravo*, no. 3 (1965), pp. 70-77. Coauthor B. N. Nechaev.

114. "Die rechtliche Natur der UNO und der Weg zur Festigung der internationalen Organisation," *Vereinte Nationen*, XIII (1965), 121-126.

115. "Organizatsiia Ob"edinennykh Natsii: 1945-1965 gg. (Mezhdunarodnopravovye problemy)," *Sovetskoe gosudarstvo i pravo*, no. 10 (1965), pp. 58-68.

Translated: "The United Nations: 1945-1965 (Problems of International Law)," *Soviet Law and Government*, IV, no. 4 (1966), pp. 3-12.

1966

116. "The Legal Nature of the United Nations," *Recueil des cours*, CXIX (1966), 1-68.
117. "Pravo dogovorov na XVII sessii Komissii mezhdunarodnogo prava OON," *Sovetskoe gosudarstvo i pravo*, no. 4 (1966), pp. 56-62. Coauthor B. N. Nechaev.
118. "Zakonnoe pravo (GDR dolzhna byt' priniata v OON)," *Pravda*, September 15, 1966, p. 3.
119. "Der Nürnberger Prozess und das Völkerrecht," *Blätter für deutsche und internationale Politik*, XI (1966), 790-797.

1967

120. "Konferentsiia Assotsiatsii mezhdunarodnogo prava," *Sovetskoe gosudarstvo i pravo*, no. 1 (1967), pp. 139-140. Coauthor O. V. Bogdanov.
121. "Neobosnovannye deistviia," *Vodnyi transport*, January 7, 1967, p. 4. [The *Zagorsk* at Port Dal'nyi.]
122. "S tochki zreniia mezhdunarodnogo prava," *Novoe vremia*, no. 8 (1967), pp. 7-8.
    Translated: "From the Standpoint of International Law," *New Times*, no. 8 (1967), pp. 7-8.
123. "Velikaia Oktiabr'skaia sotsialisticheskaia revoliutsiia i stanovlenie novogo mezhdunarodnogo prava," *Pravovedenie*, no. 1 (1967), pp. 19-28.
124. "Ustarel li Ustav OON?" *Novoe vremia*, no. 20 (1967), pp. 10-12.
    Translated: "Is the U.N. Charter Out of Date?" *New Times*, no. 20 (1967), pp. 10-12.
125. "Novye printsipy mezhdunarodnogo prava," *Novoe vremia*, no. 35 (1967), pp. 3-5.
    Translated: "New Principles of International Law," *New Times*, no. 35 (1967), pp. 3-6.
126. "Poniatie i sushchnost' sovremennogo mezhdunarodnogo prava," in V. M. Chkhikvadze and others, eds., *Kurs mezhdunarodnogo prava v shesti tomakh* (Moscow: izd-vo Nauka, 1967), I, 9-38. Coauthor I. I. Lukashuk.

127. "Mirnoe sosushchestvovanie gosudarstv dvukh sistem i mezhdunarodnoe pravo," *ibid.*, I, 73-97. (Chapter 4)
128. "Printsip mirnogo sosushchestvovaniia," *ibid.*, II, 16-32. (Chapter 2)
129. "Bor'ba dvukh kontseptsii v mezhdunarodnom prave," *Sovetskoe gosudarstvo i pravo*, no. 11 (1967), pp. 140-149.
130. "Mezhdunarodnopravovoe znachenie Dekreta o mire," *Vestnik moskovskogo gosudarstvennogo universiteta; pravo*, no. 5 (1967), pp. 3-12.
131. "The Union of Soviet Socialist Republics," in R.-J. Dupuy, ed., *The University Teaching of Social Sciences: International Law* (Paris: UNESCO, 1967), pp. 93-98.

1968

132. "Le conflit ideologique et le droit international," in *Recueil d'Études de droit international en hommage à Paul Guggenheim* (Geneva: Imp. de la Tribune de Geneve, 1968), pp. 888-898.
133. "Sessiia Instituta mezhdunarodnogo prava," *Sovetskoe gosudarstvo i pravo*, no. 2 (1968), pp. 112-113.
134. "OON i prava cheloveka," *Novoe vremia*, no. 9 (1968), pp. 4-6.
   Translated: "The U.N. and Human Rights," *New Times*, no. 9 (1968), pp. 4-6.
135. "Agressiia protiv V'etnama i mezhdunarodnoe pravo," *Novoe vremia*, no. 33 (1968), pp. 14-15.
   Translated: "International Lawyers Discuss Vietnam," *New Times*, no. 33 (1968), pp. 14-15.
136. "Mezhdunarodno-pravovye idei Velikoi Oktiabr'skoi sotsialisticheskoi revoliutsii," *Sovetskii ezhegodnik mezhdunarodnogo prava 1966-1967* (Moscow: izd-vo Nauka, 1968), pp. 15-24. English summary pp. 25-29.
137. Review of E. T. Usenko, *Formy regulirovaniia mezhdunarodnogo sotsialisticheskogo razdeleniia truda* (Moscow: izd-vo Mezhdunarodnye otnosheniia, 1965), *ibid.*, pp. 316-317. Coauthor G. P. Kaliuzhnaia.
138. "Organisation internationale universelle: illusions et realité," *Comprendre*, nos. 31-32 (1968), pp. 69-79.
139. Review of R. Arzinger, *Das Selbstbestimmungsrecht im allgemeinen Völkerrecht der Gegenwart* (Berlin: Staatsverlag der DDR, 1966), in *Sovetskoe gosudarstvo i pravo*, no. 11 (1968), pp. 157-158.

140. "L'Agression américaine au Vietnam à la lumière du droit international," *Conference mondiale des juristes pour le Vietnam* (Brussels: Association internationale des juristes democrates, 1968), pp. 73-76.

141. "Remarks on the Normative Function of Specialized Agencies," in *Estudios de Derecho Internacional. Homenaje a D. Antonio de Luna* (Madrid: Instituto Francisco de Vitoria, 1968), pp. 282-291.

142. "The Principal Developments in International Law During the Course of the Last Half Century," *Revue egyptienne de droit international*, XXIV (1968), 1-3.

1969

143. "Menschenrechte und Völkerrecht," *Vereinte Nationen*, XVII (1969), 9-12.

144. "O material'noi otvetstvennosti kolonizatorov," *Novoe vremia*, no. 9 (1969), pp. 8-10.
  Translated: "Material Responsibility of the Colonial Powers," *New Times*, no. 9 (1969), pp. 8-10.

145. "Peaceful Coexistence and International Law," in G. I. Tunkin, ed., *Contemporary International Law* (Moscow: Progress, 1969), pp. 5-35.

146. "Pravovoe polozhenie Antarktiki," in Sovetskaia antarkticheskaia ekspeditsiia, *Atlas Antarktiki* (Leningrad: Gidrometeorologicheskoe izd-vo, 1969), II, 97-104. Coauthor A. P. Movchan.

1970

147. "Leninskii printsip mirnogo sosushchestvovaniia i ego protivniki," *Pravda*, October 9, 1970, pp. 3-4.

148. "Leninskie printsipy ravnopraviia i samoopredeleniia narodov i sovremennoe mezhdunarodnoe pravo," *Vestnik moskovskogo gosudarstvennogo universiteta; pravo*, no. 2 (1970), pp. 62-71.

149. "La coexistencia pacifica y las Naciones Unidas," *Foro Internacional*, XI (1970), 409-420.

150. "V. I. Lenin i printsipy otnoshenii mezhdu sotsialisticheskimi gosudarstvami," *Sovetskii ezhegodnik mezhdunarodnogo prava 1969* (Moscow: izd-vo Nauka, 1970), pp. 16-29. English summary pp. 29-32.

1971

151. "Dva napravleniia v mirovoi politike i mirnoe sosushchestvovanie,"

Mirovaia ekonomika i mezhdunarodnye otnosheniia, no. 2 (1971), pp. 3-13.

152. " 'General Principles of Law' in International Law," in R. Marcic and others, eds., *Internationale Festschrift für A. Verdross zum 80 Geburtstag* (Munich-Salzburg: Wilhelm Fink Verlag, 1971), pp. 525-532.

153. "Mezhdunarodnoe pravo i ideologicheskaia bor'ba," *Mezhdunarodnaia zhizn'*, no. 10 (1971), pp. 34-43.
    Translated: "International Law and Ideological Struggle," *International Affairs*, no. 11 (1971), pp. 25-31.

154. "Jus Cogens in Contemporary International Law," *University of Toledo Law Review*, nos. 1-2 (1971), pp. 107-118.

1972

155. "Vertag zwischen UdSSR und BRD," *Die Sowjetunion heute*, XVII, no. 8 (1972), p. 73.

156. "Mirnoe sosushchestvovanie i klassovaia bor'ba," *Vestnik agenstva pechati "Novosti,"* no. 59 (1972), pp. 1-6.

157. "Zadachi sovetskoi nauki mezhdunarodnogo prava v svete reshenii XXIV s"ezda KPSS," *Sovetskoe gosudarstvo i pravo*, no. 7 (1972), pp. 30-36.

158. "Zur Aufnahme der beiden deutschen Staaten in die UNO," *Vereinte Nationen*, XX (1972), 114-117.

159. "Novyi tip mezhdunarodnykh otnoshenii i mezhdunarodnoe pravo," in F. I. Kozhevnikov, ed., *Kurs mezhdunarodnogo prava*, 3d ed. (Moscow: izd-vo Mezhdunarodnaia otnosheniia, 1972), pp. 52-65. (Chapter 4)

1973

160. "Printsip neprimeneniia sily kak zakon mezhdunarodnoi zhizni," *Mezhdunarodnaia zhizn'*, no. 3 (1973), pp. 16-19.
    Translated: "The Principle of Non-Use of Force as a Law of International Life," *International Affairs*, no. 4 (1973), pp. 13-15.

161. "Sovetskaia programma mira i nekotorye problemy mezhdunarodnogo prava," *Sovetskii ezhegodnik mezhdunarodnogo prava 1971* (Moscow: izd-vo Nauka, 1973), pp. 13-25. English summary pp. 25-28.

Glossary of International Legal Terms

agressiia	aggression
anneksiia	annexation
annulirovat'	to annul
bezatomnaia zona	nuclear free zone
bezopasnost'	security
blokada	blockade
mirnaia blokada	pacific blockade
bor'ba	struggle
chaianie	expectation
deponirovanie	deposit
derzhava	Power
diplomatiia	diplomacy
dobrosovestno	in good faith
dobrye uslugi	good offices
dogovor	treaty
dogovor-sdelka	contractual treaty
dogovor-zakon	law-making treaty
dokladchik	rapporteur
doktrina	doctrine
druzhba	friendship
edinstvo v pol'zu mira	Uniting for Peace
eksterritorial'nost'	extraterritoriality
golosovanie	vote
gospodstvo	domination
gosudarstvo	State
gramota	instrument, letter
veritel'nye gramoty	credentials
ratifikatsionnye gramoty	instruments of ratification
granitsa	frontier, border, boundary
grazhdanin	citizen, national
inostranets	alien, foreigner

Glossary of International Legal Terms

internatsionalizm	internationalism
proletarskii internatsionalizm	proletarian internationalism
sotsialisticheskii internatsionalizm	socialist internationalism
interventsiia	intervention
istochnik	source
iurisdiktsiia	jurisdiction
konsul'skaia iurisdiktsiia	consular jurisdiction
iurist-mezhdunarodnik	international lawyer
kapituliatsiia	capitulation
kodifikatsiia	codification
kolonializm	colonialism
kompetentsiia	competence, jurisdiction
immanentnaia kompetentsiia	inherent jurisdiction
podrazumevaemaia kompetentsiia	implied powers
konechnye tsennosti	goal values
konferentsiia	conference
konsultativnoe zakliuchenie	advisory opinion
kontributsiia	contribution
konventsiia	convention
kosmicheskoe prostranstvo	outer space
mezhdunarodnaia organizatsiia	international organization
mezhdunarodnyi sud OON	International Court of Justice
mir	peace
mirnoe sosushchestvovanie	peaceful coexistence
mirovaia sistema sotsializma	world system of socialism
mirovoe gosudarstvo	world state, world government
mnogostoronnyi	multilateral
morskoe dno	seabed
narod	people
narushenie	violation, breach
nasilie	coercion
natsiia	nation
neitralitet	neutrality
nenapadenie	nonaggression
neprikosnovennost'	integrity
nerasprostranenie	nonproliferation
neravenstvo	inequality
nezavisimost'	independence

norma	norm, rule
norma imperativnogo kharaktera	*jus cogens*
normoustanavlivaiushchii	norm-establishing, law-making
ob"edinenie	unification
obiazannost'	duty
obiazatel'stvo	obligation
obmen notami	exchange of notes
obrazovanie norm	norm-formation
obshchepriznannyi	generally-recognized
obshchestvo	society, community
obshchie printsipy prava	general principles of law
obsledovanie	inquiry
obychai	custom
obyknovenie	usage
ogovorka	reservation
opredelenie	definition, determination
osnovnaia norma	basic norm
osvobozhdenie	liberation
otdelenie	separation
otkaz ot voiny	renunciation of war
otkrytoe more	high seas
otmena	abrogation, repeal
otnoshenie	relationship, attitude
mezhdunarodnye otnosheniia	international relations
mirnye otnosheniia	peaceful relations
otvetstvennost' gosudarstva	state responsibility
pakt	pact, covenant
parafirovanie	initialing
peregovory	negotiations
podpisanie	signature
poiavlenie	emergence
pokorenie	subjugation
pomoshch'	aid, assistance
bratskaia pomoshch'	fraternal assistance
popravka	amendment
posol	ambassador
posrednichestvo	mediation
postanovlenie	decree, resolution, provision
postoiannaia palata	Permanent Court of
mezhdunarodnogo pravosudiia	International Justice

postoiannyi chlen	permanent member
povedenie	conduct
prava cheloveka	human rights
pravitel'stvo	government
pravo	law, right
bozhestvennoe pravo	divine law
estestvennoe pravo	natural law
mezhdunarodnoe pravo	international law
obshchee pravo	common law
posol'skoe pravo	ambassadorial law
pozitivnoe pravo	positive law
pravomernaia voina	just war
pravonarushenie	breach of law
pravo na samoopredelenie	right to self-determination
na voinu	*jus ad bellum*
pravoporiadok	legal order
pravoprieemstvo	state succession
pravosposobnost'	legal capacity
pravosub"ektnost'	legal personality
prestuplenie	crime
protiv chelovechestva	crime against humanity
protiv mira	crime against peace
primenenie sily	use of force
primirenie	conciliation
priniatie reshenii	decision-making
printsip	principle
priznanie	recognition
proekt	draft
promezhutochnoe sostoianie	intermediate status
propaganda voiny	war propaganda
protivorechie	contradiction
rang	rank
rasovaia diskriminatsiia	racial discrimination
ravnopravie	equality
razoruzhenie	disarmament
razrabotka	working out, drafting
razreshenie	settlement
mirnoe razreshenie	peaceful settlement
rekomendatel'nyi	recommendatory
reparatsiia	reparation
repressalii	reprisals

Glossary of International Legal Terms

revolutsiia	revolution
samooborona	self-defense
samoopredelenie	self-determination
samopomoshch'	self-help
samoupravlenie	self-government
sanktsiia	sanction
sblizhenie	rapprochement, coming together
sila	force, power, strength
politika sily	power politics
s pozitsii sily	from a position of strength
soderzhanie	content
sodruzhestvo	commonwealth
soglashenie	agreement
soglasie	consent
soiuznik	ally
solidarnost'	solidarity
sotrudnichestvo	cooperation
soznanie	consciousness
spor	dispute
stolknovenie	conflict
storona	party, side
strana	country
sub"ekt	subject
suverenitet	sovereignty
territorial'naia voda	territorial waters
tolkovanie	interpretation
udovletvorenie	satisfaction
ugnetenie	oppression
ugroza	threat
ushcherb'	damage, injury
ustav	charter, constitution, statute, covenant
ustupka	concession
vlianie	influence
vmeshatel'stvo	interference
vneshniaia politika	foreign policy
vnutrennee delo	internal affair
vnutrigosudarstvennyi	domestic
voina	war

vol'	will
soglasovanie vol'	bringing wills into concordance
sovpadenie vol'	coincidence of wills
vozmeshchenie	compensation
vybor politiki	policy choice
vykhod	withdrawal
vynosiashchii reshenii	decision-maker
vzaimoponimanie	mutual understanding
zakhvat	annexation
zakon	law
zakonomernost' razvitiia	
obshchestva	law of societal development
zasedanie	session
plenarnoe zasedanie	plenary session
zavoevanie	gain, conquest

Table of Treaties and of United Nations General Assembly Resolutions

Numbers in brackets indicate page numbers.

International Treaties and Agreements

1899

July 23: Convention for the Pacific Settlement of International Disputes, signed at The Hague   [50, 57, 58, 391, 392]

1906

April 7: General Act of the International Conference of Algericas, signed at Algericas   [101]

1907

Aug. 18/31: Convention between Russia and England on the Affairs of Persia, Afghanistan, and Tibet, signed at St. Petersburg   [13]

Oct. 18: Convention for the Pacific Settlement of International Disputes, signed at The Hague   [50, 57, 58, 247, 391, 392]

Oct. 18: Convention Respecting the Laws and Customs of War on Land, signed at The Hague   [394, 395]

1915

Feb. 25/March 9: Agreement among Russia, Great Britain, and France on the Partition of Asiatic Turkey, concluded at Petrograd   [13]

June 20/July 3: Secret Russo-Japanese Convention Relating to Influence in China, signed at Petrograd   [12]

Table of Treaties

1918

March 3: Peace Treaty between the RSFSR and the Central Powers, signed
at Brest-Litovsk [6, 19]

1919

June 28: Treaty of Peace with Germany, signed at Versailles [409]
June 28: Covenant of the League of Nations [50, 58, 59, 75, 76, 241]
June 28: Constitution of the International Labor Organization, Part XIII
(Labor) of the Treaty of Peace, signed at Versailles [102, 176, 177,
313]

1920

Dec. 16: Statute of the Permanent Court of International Justice, protocol
of signature opened for signature at Geneva [191, 193, 197]

1921

Feb. 26: Treaty of Friendship between the RSFSR and Persia, signed at
Moscow [11–14, 19]
Feb. 28: Treaty of Friendship between the RSFSR and Afghanistan,
signed at Moscow [11, 19]
March 16: Treaty of Friendship between the RSFSR and Turkey, signed
at Moscow [11–13, 19]

1924

May 31: Agreement between China and the Soviet Union on General
Principles for the Settlement of Common Problems, signed at
Peking [14]

1925

Dec. 17: Treaty of Friendship and Neutrality between the Soviet Union
and Turkey, signed at Paris [19]

1927

Oct. 1: Treaty of Nonaggression and Neutrality between the Soviet Union
and Persia, signed at Moscow [19]

1928

Aug. 27: Treaty on Renunciation of War as an Instrument of National
Policy, signed at Paris [51, 52, 56, 59, 125, 126, 143, 144, 264, 268]
Sept. 26: General Act for the Pacific Settlement of International Disputes,
adopted at Geneva [59, 60]

Table of Treaties

1940

March 25: Treaty on Trade and Navigation between the Soviet Union and Iran, signed at Teheran   [100]

1941

Aug. 14: Atlantic Charter, released simultaneously at London and Washington   [62]

1943

Dec. 12: Treaty on Friendship, Mutual Assistance, and Postwar Cooperation between the Soviet Union and Czechoslovakia, signed at Moscow   [100]

1944

Dec. 7: Convention on International Civil Aviation, opened for signature at Chicago   [176]

1945

Feb. 11: Protocol of the Proceedings of the Crimea Conference, signed at Yalta   [410]

April 21: Treaty on Friendship, Mutual Assistance, and Postwar Cooperation between the Soviet Union and Poland, signed at Moscow   [100]

June 5: Declaration Regarding the Defeat of Germany and the Assumption of Supreme Authority with Respect to Germany by the Governments of the United States, USSR, United Kingdom, and the Provisional Government of the French Republic, signed at Berlin   [411]

June 26: Charter of the United Nations, signed at San Francisco   [38, 45, 55, 62, 64–67, 71, 73, 78, 134, 144, 145, 163, 164, 167, 168, 175, 241, 244, 263, 264, 267, 268, 277, 289, 319, 322, 324–327, 331–335, 338, 341, 343, 349, 350, 362, 364, 368, 370, 379, 380, 424]

    Preamble: [71, 80, 142, 377, 421]
    Article 1:   [31, 62, 64, 71, 72, 292, 312, 317, 330, 347]
    Article 2:   [31, 52–54, 57, 60, 96, 162, 292, 345, 347, 377, 378]
    Article 4:   [169, 351]
    Article 5:   [169]
    Article 6:   [169]
    Article 10:   [169, 171]
    Article 11:   [76, 77, 328, 342, 348]
    Article 16:   [169]
    Article 17:   [169]

Dec. 19: Agreement between the United Nations and the International Labor Organization, protocol signed at New York   [107]

1947

Feb. 3: Agreement between the United Nations and UNESCO, protocol signed at New York   [107]

Feb. 10: Peace Treaty with Bulgaria, signed at Paris   [38, 404, 410, 412]

Feb. 10: Peace Treaty with Hungary, signed at Paris   [38, 404, 410, 412]

Feb. 10: Peace Treaty with Italy, signed at Paris   [38, 404, 410, 412]

Feb. 10: Peace Treaty with Rumania, signed at Paris   [38, 404, 410, 412]

Feb. 10: Peace Treaty with Finland, signed at Paris   [38, 404, 410, 412]

Oct. 11: Convention on the World Meteorological Organization, signed at Washington   [176]

1948

Feb. 4: Treaty on Friendship, Cooperation, and Mutual Assistance between the Soviet Union and Rumania, signed at Moscow   [100]

March 18: Treaty on Friendship, Cooperation, and Mutual Assistance between the Soviet Union and Bulgaria, signed at Moscow   [100]

April 30: Charter of the Organization of American States, signed at Bogotá   [412]

Aug. 20: Agreement between the International Labor Organization and the Food and Agricultural Organization   [107]

Aug. 23: Agreement between the International Labor Organization and UNESCO   [107]

Nov. 15: Agreement between the United Nations and the Universal Postal Union, signed at Paris   [107]

Dec. 9: Convention on the Prevention and Punishment of the Crime of Genocide, opened for signature at New York   [81]

July 17/Nov. 29: Agreement between the World Health Organization and the Food and Agricultural Organization   [107]

1949

April 26: Agreement between the United Nations and the International Telecommunications Union   [107]

Aug. 12: Convention for the Amelioration of the Condition of the Wounded and Sick in Armed Forces in the Field, signed at Geneva [81]

Aug. 12: Convention for the Amelioration of the Condition of Wounded, Sick and Shipwrecked Members of Armed Forces at Sea, signed at Geneva   [81]

Aug. 12: Convention relative to the Treatment of Prisoners of War, signed at Geneva   [81]

Table of Treaties

Aug. 12: Convention relative to the Protection of Civilian Persons in Time of War, signed at Geneva [81]

1953

March 31: Convention on the Political Rights of Women, opened for signature at New York [81]

1954

July 20: Agreement between the Commander-in-Chief of the French Union Forces in Indo-China and the Commander-in-Chief of the People's Army of Vietnam on the Cessation of Hostilities in Vietnam, signed at Geneva [38]

1955

May 14: Treaty on Friendship, Cooperation, and Mutual Assistance Among Albania, Bulgaria, German Democratic Republic, Poland, Rumania, Soviet Union, and Czechoslovakia, signed at Warsaw [430]

June 14: Revised Standard Agreement on Technical Assistance between the United Nations, ILO, FAO, UNESCO, ICAO, WHO, ITU, and WMU, on one side, and Jordan, on the other, signed at Amman [107]

1956

Feb. 29: Trade Agreement between the Soviet Union and Canada, signed at Ottawa [100]

Oct. 26: Statute of the International Atomic Energy Agency, opened for signature at New York [349]

1957

Feb. 17: Agreement between the United Nations, ILO, FAO, UNESCO, ICAO, WHO, ITU, and WMU, on one side, and Saudi Arabia, on the other, signed at Jedda [108]

Feb. 20: Convention on the Nationality of Married Women, opened for signature at New York [81]

1958

Jan. 21/April 2: Basic Agreement between the World Health Organization and Ghana for the Provision of Technical Advisory Assistance, signed at Brazzaville and Accra [108]

Jan. 28: Agreement on Fishing in Waters of the Danube between the Soviet Union, Bulgaria, Rumania, and Yugoslavia, signed at Bucharest [441]

Feb. 17: Basic Agreement between the World Health Organization and

Indonesia for the Provision of Technical Advisory Assistance, signed at New Delhi   [108]

April 25: Consular Treaty between the Soviet Union and the Federal Republic of Germany, signed at Bonn   [443]

April 29: Convention on the Territorial Sea and the Contiguous Zone, signed at Geneva   [34, 97, 100, 134, 184]

April 29: Convention on the High Seas, signed at Geneva   [34, 97, 100, 134, 383]

April 29: Convention on Fishing and Conservation of the Living Resources of the High Seas, signed at Geneva   [34, 100, 134]

April 29: Convention on the Continental Shelf, signed at Geneva   [34, 97, 100, 134]

Sept. 18: Agreement on Navigation between the Soviet Union and the United Arab Republic, signed at Cairo   [100]

1959

April 24: Agreement between the International Labor Organization and the Intergovernmental Maritime Consultative Organization   [107]

May 11: Agreement between the International Atomic Energy Agency and the Soviet Union on the Making Available of Special Fissionable Materials to the Agency, signed at Vienna   [108]

July 7: Agreement between the Soviet Union, Bulgaria, and Rumania on Fishing in the Black Sea, signed at Varna   [441]

Nov. 26: Agreement on Cultural Cooperation between the Soviet Union and Guinea, signed at Moscow   [100]

Dec. 14: Charter of the Council of Mutual Economic Assistance, signed at Sofia   [179]

Dec. 14: Agreement on Cooperation in Veterinary Medicine, signed at Sofia   [441]

Dec. 14: Agreement on Cooperation in the Quarantine and Protection of Plants from Pests and Diseases, signed at Sofia   [441]

1961

April 18: Convention on Diplomatic Relations, signed at Vienna   [34, 135, 245]

Dec. 15: Agreement on Cooperation in Technical Supervision Over Vessels and Their Classification, signed at Warsaw   [441]

1962

July 5: Agreement on Cooperation and Mutual Assistance in Customs Questions, signed at Berlin   [441]

Table of Treaties

1968

July 1: Treaty on the Nonproliferation of Nuclear Weapons, opened for signature at London, Moscow, and Washington [34, 38, 79, 135, 254]

1969

May 23: Convention on the Law of Treaties, signed at Vienna [34, 91, 135, 141, 158, 244, 245, 254, 326, 329]

1970

Aug. 12: Treaty on Nonaggression between the Soviet Union and the Federal Republic of Germany, signed at Moscow [38, 72]

Nov. 18: Treaty on Bases for Normalizing Relations between Poland and the Federal Republic of Germany, signed at Warsaw [38, 72]

1971

Feb. 10: Treaty on the Prohibition of the Emplacement of Nuclear Weapons and Other Weapons of Mass Destruction on the Seabed and Ocean Floor and in the Subsoil Thereof, opened for signature at London, Moscow, and Washington [34]

Sept. 3: Quadripartite Agreement on Berlin, signed at Berlin (American Sector) [38]

Oct. 30: Principles of Cooperation between the Soviet Union and France, signed at Paris [72]

Dec. 16: Convention on the Prohibition of the Development, Production, and Stockpiling of Bacteriological, Biological, and Toxin Weapons and Their Destruction, opened for signature at London, Moscow, and Washington [34]

1972

May 29: Basic Principles of Relations between the United States and the Soviet Union, signed at Moscow [38, 73]

Dec. 21: Treaty on the Bases for Relations between the Federal Republic of Germany and the German Democratic Republic, done at Berlin [72]

United Nations General Assembly Resolutions

41(I)   Principles Governing the General Regulation and Reduction of Armaments, December 14, 1946 [76, 174]

95(I)   Affirmation of the Principles of International Law Rec-

ognized by the Charter of the Nuremberg Tribunal,
December 11, 1946 [84, 175]

Index

[485]

Index